HTML Sourcebook
Third Edition

A Complete Guide to HTML 3.2 and HTML Extensions

Ian S. Graham

WILEY COMPUTER PUBLISHING

John Wiley & Sons, Inc.
New York • Chichester • Weinheim • Brisbane • Singapore • Toronto

Executive Publisher: Katherine Schowalter
Editor: Philip Sutherland
Assistant Editor: Pam Sobotka
Managing Editor: Mark Hayden
Electronic Products, Associate Editor: Mike Green
Text Design & Composition: Benchmark Productions, Inc.

This publication is designed to provide accurate and authoritative information in regard to the subject matter covered. It is sold with the understanding that the publisher is not engaged in rendering legal, accounting, or other professional service. If legal advice or other expert assistance is required, the services of a competent professional person should be sought.

Library of Congress Cataloging-in-Publication Data:

ISBN: 0-471-17575-7
Printed in the United States of America
10 9 8 7 6 5 4 3 2 1

To my friend Mike

—Ian Graham

Contents

Preface

In 1995, in the introduction to the first edition of this book, I stated that the World Wide Web had "taken the Internet by storm." At the time I hoped this was appropriate, but felt in my heart that I was probably overstating things, if only a little. In retrospect, or course, it was a gross understatement. Over the past two years—and two editions of this book—the Web has grown far beyond everyone's expectations (well, perhaps not Marc Andreessen's!), to become one of the core new technologies of the 1990s. Thousands if not tens of thousands of companies now offer Web-based products or services, and the trickle of products available in late 1994 has grown, by late 1996, into a torrent. Purely Web-based companies such as Netscape Communications are now market-valued in the billions of dollars—and Netscape did not even exist two years ago. Other software companies such as Oracle and Microsoft are totally redesigning their product and business models, while businesses from news and entertainment to financial services, high technology, and manufacturing are adopting these new technologies as either a new way of working internally, or a new way of communicating with clients and customers. This is not the simple swell of "a storm," but a social tidal wave of epic proportions.

We are witnessing not just the birth of a new technology, but of a whole new paradigm of culture and communication. This is because the World Wide Web model makes distributing and accessing any form of digital data easy and inexpensive for anyone—company or consumer—with profound implications for business, culture, and society. Thus it is no surprise that seemingly "everyone" is now buying or downloading the latest in Web tools and is madly learning how to build pages so that they too can join this new electronic world.

The Web Model

A tool may be easy to use, but it usually requires skill and training to be used well. This is certainly true of the tools involved in preparing and distributing information via hypertext documents and Internet hypertext servers. Just as designing a book or magazine requires experience and knowledge in the tools of design and typography, preparing well-designed, useful, and reliable Web resources requires an in-depth understanding of how the tools that deliver these resources work. The intention of this book, as with the first two editions, is to help you develop this understanding. Given a basic feeling for what the Internet is—simply a tool, or courier service, for sending digital information from one place to another—there are four essential concepts that you need to understand:

1. *Uniform resource locators*, or *URLs*. These are the means by which Internet resources are addressed on the World Wide Web. If you want to specify a resource on the Internet, you specify its URL.

2. The *HyperText Markup Language*, or *HTML*. This is the markup language with which World Wide Web hypertext documents are written, and is what allows you to create hypertext links, fill-in forms, et cetera. Writing good HTML documents involves both technical issues (proper construction of the document) and design issues (ensuring the information content is clearly presented to the user).

3. The *HyperText Transfer Protocol (HTTP)* and HTTP *client-server* interactions. HTTP servers are designed specifically to distribute hypertext documents. You must know how the underlying HTTP protocol works if you are to take advantage of its powerful features.

4. *Server-side resource processing.* This lets a user with a Web browser interact with resources on an HTTP server, by providing a tunnel through the server to these resources. This can be either through the so-called *common gateway interface,* or through special modules built into the server.

The goal of this book is to explain these main concepts and to give you the tools you need to use them in developing your own high-quality World Wide Web products. The remainder of this preface looks briefly at these components and explains their basic features, and then outlines the organization of the book. A figurative summary of these different components, and the relationship between them, is found in Figure P.1.

Uniform Resource Locators

Uniform resource locators, or URLs, are a naming scheme for specifying how and where to find any Internet server resource, such as those available from Gopher, FTP, or WAIS servers. For example, the URL that references the important file *bunny_hop.zip* in the directory */pub/web/browsers* on the anonymous FTP server *ftp.banzai.net* is simply:

```
ftp://ftp.banzai.net/pub/web/browsers/bunny_hop.zip
```

World Wide Web hypertext documents use URLs to reference other hypertext resources.

The HyperText Transfer Protocol

The *HyperText Transfer Protocol,* or HTTP, is an Internet communications protocol designed expressly for the rapid distribution of hypertext documents. Like other Internet tools such as FTP, WAIS, and Gopher, HTTP is a *client-server* protocol. In the client-server model a *client* program, running on the user's machine, sends a message requesting service to a *server* program running on another machine on the Internet. The server responds to the request by sending a message back to the client. In exchanging these messages, the client and server use a well-understood *protocol.* FTP, WAIS, and Gopher are other examples of Internet client-server protocols, all of which are accessible to a World Wide Web browser. However, the HTTP protocol is designed expressly for hypertext document delivery. Almost all Web services are delivered using HTTP servers.

Figure P.1 Schematic diagram illustrating the basic components of the World Wide Web. The user's tool is the *browser*, or *user agent*: the program that can understand and display an *HTML* document. The browser can interpret *URLs* to determine where a resource is and which protocol to use to access it, and can communicate over the Internet using these protocols to access desired resources. One of the most important protocols is *HTTP*; most servers on the Web use the HTTP protocol and are called *HTTP servers*, or *Web servers*. Using a Web server's *CGI* or *common gateway interface* (or other, similar mechanisms), users can access other resources on the Web server machine, such as databases.

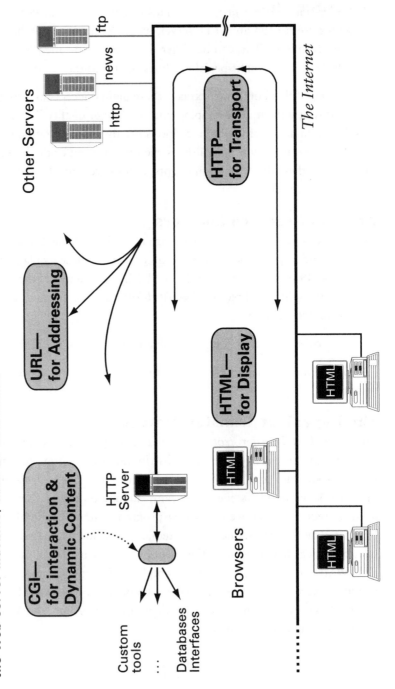

Server-Side Resource Processing

At the simplest level, HTTP servers act much like anonymous FTP, delivering up files when clients request them. However, HTTP servers support additional important features:

- The ability to return to the client not just files but also information generated by other programs running on the server.

- The ability to take data sent from the client and pass this information on to other programs on the server for further processing.

The special server-side utilities that implement these features are often called *gateway* programs, as they usually act as a gateway between the HTTP server and other local resources, such as databases. Just as an FTP server can access many files, an HTTP server can access many different gateway programs; in both cases you specify which (file or program) resource you want through a URL.

The interaction between the server and these gateway programs is governed by the *common gateway interface (CGI)* specifications. Using the CGI specifications, a programmer can easily write simple programs or scripts to process user queries, interrogate databases, make images that respond to mouse clicks, and so on.

Many servers also let you program gateway-like functionality directly into the server, for increased speed and performance.

The HyperText Markup Language

The *HyperText Markup Language*, or *HTML*, is the language used to prepare Web hypertext documents. These are the documents you distribute on the World Wide Web and are what your human clients actually see. HTML contains commands, called *elements* or *tags*, to mark text as headings, paragraphs, lists, quotations, and so on. It also has tags for including images within the documents, for including fill-in forms that accept user input, and, most important, for including hypertext links connecting the document being read to other documents or Internet resources such as WAIS databases or anonymous FTP sites. It is this last feature that allows the user to click on a string of highlighted text and access a new document, an image, or a film clip from a computer thousands of miles away. And how does the HTML document specify where this other document is? Through a URL, which is included in the HTML markup instructions and which is used by the user's browser to find the designated resource.

What resources can URLs point to? They can be other HTML documents, pictures, sound files, movie files, or even database search engines. They can be downloadable programs in Java or other languages. They can be located on the user's computer or anywhere on the Internet. They can be accessed from HTTP servers or from FTP, Gopher, WAIS, or other servers. The URL is an immensely flexible scheme, and in combination with HTML, yields an incredibly powerful package for preparing a web of hypertext documents linked to each other and to Internet resources around the world. This image of interlinked resources is in fact the vision that gave rise to the name, World Wide Web.

Overview of the Book

This book is an introduction to HTML, URLs, HTTP, and the CGI interface, and to the design and preparation of resources for delivery via the World Wide Web. It begins with the HTML language. Almost every resource that you prepare will be presented through an HTML document, so that your HTML presentation is your "face" to the world. It is crucial that you know how to write proper HTML, and that you understand the design issues involved in creating attractive, useful documents if you are to make a lasting impression on your audience and present your information clearly and concisely. It won't matter if the Internet resources you make available are the best in the world if your presentation of them is badly designed, frustratingly slow to access, or difficult to follow.

HTML is not only fundamental to the Web, it is also an obvious place to start. You can write simple HTML documents and view them with a WWW browser such as Microsoft Internet Explorer, Netscape Navigator, Mosaic, or lynx without having to worry about CGI programs, HTTP servers, and other advanced features. You can also easily include, in your documents, URLs pointing to server resources around the world, and get used to how the system works: Browsers understand HTML *hypertext anchors* and the URLs they contain and have built-in software to talk to Internet servers using the proper protocols. You can accomplish a lot just by creating a few pages of HTML.

Chapter 1 is an elementary introduction to HTML and to the design issues involved in preparing HTML documents. This nontechnical chapter combines a brief overview of HTML with some aspects of the document design process. The details of the HTML language and more sophisticated client-server issues are left to later chapters. Chapter 1 should give you a broad sense of how HTML documents work and are designed.

Design issues are very important in developing good World Wide Web presentations. HTML documents are not like text documents, nor are they like traditional hypertext presentations, since they are limited by the varied capabilities of browsers and by the speed with which documents can be transported across the Internet. Chapter 2 discusses what this means in practice, and gives guidelines for avoiding major HTML authoring mistakes. In most cases this is done using examples, with the important issues being presented in point form, so that you can easily extract the main points on first reading.

At the same time, designing an HTML document *collection* is more than just writing pages—the design of a collection is critically important, and involves issues that are not always apparent from the point of view of a single page. Chapter 3 looks in detail at the issues surrounding document collection design, and will help you through the process of designing a real document "web."

One point that is emphasized in Chapters 1, 2, and everywhere else in the book, is the importance of using correct HTML markup constructions when you create your HTML documents. Although HTML is a relatively straightforward language, there are many important rules specifying where tags can be placed. Ensuring that your documents obey these rules is the only way you can guarantee that they will be properly displayed on the many different browsers your clients may use. All too often, writers prepare documents that look wonderful on one browser but end up looking horrible, or even unviewable, on others.

Although some general rules for constructing valid HTML are included in Chapters 1 and 2, Chapter 4 and the references therein should be used as detailed guides to correct HTML. In particular, Chapter 4 presents a detailed exposition of the HTML language and of the allowed nesting of the different HTML markup instructions. Chapter 5 continues along this line, but looks at the experimental HTML features that are not yet formally part of the "standard" HTML language, or that are not yet widely supported. You should use Chapter 4 as a guide for writing universally viewable HTML documents, while Chapter 5 can be viewed as a preview of coming attractions.

Of course, HTML is only a beginning. To truly take advantage of the system, you need to understand the interaction between WWW client browsers and HTTP servers, and to be able to write server-side gateway programs that take advantage of this interaction. These topics are covered in Chapters 6 through 9. Chapter 6 describes the URL syntax in detail, while Chapter 7 delves into the specifics of the HTTP protocol used to communicate with HTTP servers, and discusses the basics of HTTP server operation. Chapter 8 then describes the details of the common gateway interface (CGI) specification for writing server-side programs that interface with an HTTP server. Chapter 9 then gives several concrete examples of real-world CGI programs, to show how the issues from Chapters 6 through 8 affect gateway program design. This chapter also contains a reference list of resources useful in developing CGI applications—many of these resources are available right over the Web, just waiting for you to go and get them.

Graphics are an important addition to any Web page, either as simple images or as clickable imagemaps. However, they must be carefully processed to make them Web-friendly: The image files must be small, in the right format, and of the right "style" for display by computer. These and other image-related issues are discussed in Chapter 10.

Chapters 4 through 10 are the technical core of this book, and will be useful reference material when you are writing HTML documents or server CGI programs.

Chapter 11 looks at auxiliary tools useful in developing and organizing HTML documents. There are tools for converting collections of e-mail letters into hypertext archives, for creating a hypertext "Table of Contents" for large collections of related HTML files, for checking for invalid links, or even for creating searchable indexes of entire collections. Almost all of these tools are available over the Internet, either from anonymous FTP sites or from HTTP servers. URLs are provided in the text to indicate the locations of these programs and of additional documentation, when available. Finally, URLs are also used to point out sites on the Web that maintain up-to-date catalogs of resources of this type. It is impossible for any book to be up-to-date when listing current technical resources, and these URLs will help you get the most recent information on these topics. Chapter 11 does not discuss HTML editors, or HTTP server or Web browser programs—there are simply too many of them, and insufficient space in the book to do these subjects justice. Instead, we provide URLs pointing to catalog sites providing up-to-date information on these topics.

Chapter 12, the final chapter in the book, is a guide to Web site development, and describes how to go about planning and implementing a site, starting from the ground floor. This chapter looks at planning issues (determining why you are building a site, defining your audience, planning the site layout, etc.), cost analysis (how to estimate the costs of different site components), and maintenance (how to maintain the site, and how to estimate the costs of this process). Finally, this chapter contains several examples of advanced HTML design that can be used to create distinctive, professional Web pages. These examples reflect the principles of HTML and Web design that were presented elsewhere in the book, and can be thought of as a "graduation collection" of page design—if these examples make sense to you, then you are well on your way to being an HTML guru.

But, to really keep up with modern site design, you must get out there and browse the Web! Reading a book in which a writer spouts off his own ideas of good and bad design is all well and good, but you, as a writer and designer of HTML documents and Web sites, will only appreciate how things look and feel by going out there and looking and feeling. The content of this book is merely a framework for appreciating what tens of thousands of creative individuals are already doing. So, go and see for yourself!

Note for the Third Edition—Book Archive Site

For those of you familiar with the first and second editions, this third edition has been both expanded and brought up-to-date. In addition, an archive of all the example documents and programs in the book, hypertext links to all the book (hypertext) references, and regular updates to the book content are available on-line at the URL:

```
http://www.utoronto.ca/webdocs/HTMLdocs/Book/Book-3ed/
```

After all, who needs a CD-ROM, when you've got the Web?

Introduction to the HyperText Markup Language

What is a text markup language? A markup language is a way of describing, using instructions embedded within a document, what the document text means, or what it is supposed to look like. For example, suppose I want to indicate that the word "albatross" should be displayed in boldface. A markup language might express this desire with commands of the form

```
[beg_bold] albatross [end_bold]
```

meaning: "turn on boldface, write the word 'albatross', and then turn off boldface." In this example, the text strings `[beg_bold]` and `[end_bold]` are part of the markup language, which here turns boldface on and off. In general, a markup language has many such codes, to allow for a rich description of the document content and desired rendering.

Every electronic text processing tool uses some kind of markup language. As a familiar example, the Reveal Codes command in WordPerfect allows you to see the actual markup commands; in this case these are sequences of unprintable characters, unlike the printable commands used in the above example. Nevertheless, the idea is the same: A markup language is just a collection of codes, embedded in the document, that explain the meaning or desired formatting for the marked text.

Physical versus Semantic Markup

There are two basic approaches for a markup language. The first is *physical markup*. In this approach, the markup tags explicitly say how the document should look, and contain commands such as: "*indent 0.5 inches, print the word 'Frozen Albatross' using an 18-point Arial font . . . "* and so on. This is ideal for printing the text, but bad if printing is not the primary goal. Suppose, for example, you want to display the document on a computer that is not capable of the requested formatting. In this case the physical formatting information is useless, and the computer has no easy way of determining a good alternative presentation of the text.

The second approach is known as *logical* or *semantic markup*. Here, the markup language defines the *functional role* of the text, and not how it looks. Thus, in the above example, the semantic markup might be

```
[beg_heading] Frozen Albatross [end_heading]
```

which simply means "*the text, 'Frozen Albatross', is a heading.*" The advantage of this approach is that you have encoded the true structural meaning of the text, and not its physical representation. It is then easy to translate this heading into the formatting commands: "*indent 0.5 inches, print the word 'Frozen Albatross' using an 18-point Arial font . . .*" should you be printing the document to paper, or into other instructions should you be presenting the document via some other medium, such as a computer display or a Braille reader. Thus, although semantic formatting is more difficult (you have to think about what each part of the document means when you add the markup instructions), it is a much more powerful and flexible way of describing text, and has become the technique of choice for modern document processing systems, including word processors such as Word and WordPerfect, which now incorporate many semantic markup features into their markup model.

What is *HyperText Markup Language*, or HTML? Despite all the hype, HTML is simply another markup language. However, unlike the others, HTML is designed specifically for marking up electronic documents for delivery over the Internet, and for presentation on a variety of possible displays. As a result, HTML is very much a semantic markup language, designed to specify the *logical* organization of a text document; there are very few physical formatting commands in HTML. In addition, HTML has important extensions that allow for *hypertext links* from one document to another, as well as other extensions that allow for user input and user interaction.

It is important to stress these design principles, because they explain the large differences between authoring with HTML and writing documents using word processors. HTML was *not* designed to be the language of a "What You See Is What You Get" (WYSIWYG) word processor such as Word or WordPerfect. Instead, HTML takes a "What You Get Is What You Meant" (WYGIWYM) approach, such that authors must construct documents with sections of text (and/or images and other embedded objects, such as Java applets) marked as *logical* entities, such as titles, paragraphs, lists, quotations, and so on. The interpretation of these marked elements is then largely left up to the browser displaying the document. This approach builds enormous flexibility into the system, and allows the same document to be displayed by browsers of very different capabilities. Consequently, there are browsers for machines ranging from fancy UNIX graphics computers to plain-text terminals such as VT-100s. In viewing the same well-designed HTML document, a graphical browser like Netscape Navigator might present major headings in a large, slanted and boldfaced font (since elegant typesetting is possible with graphics displays) and include attractive inlined graphical elements indicated by the HTML markup, while a text-only browser like lynx might just center the title, use a single font for all the text, and display text alternative descriptions to the images; and a Braille browser would present the same text information in a completely different way. However different they appear, all these presentations will reproduce the logical organization and meaning of the original text document, since this information was built in using the HTML language.

HTML is also designed to be an *extensible* language. "Extensible" simply means that new features, commands, and functionality can be added to the language, without "breaking" older documents that don't use these new features. In fact, HTML is a rapidly evolving language, with new features being added on a regular basis. This book summarizes most of the current and forthcoming commands, and provides references to other sources that will allow you to keep up with the changes.

Since HTML is constantly evolving, it is important to have a way of indicating which version of the language you are talking about. This is done through the *version number* of the HTML specification. The very first definition of HTML was called Version 1, or HTML 1.0. This quickly evolved into the next "definitive" version of HTML, known as Version 2, or HTML 2.0. *All browsers* support—at a minimum—the HTML 2.0 standard. After 2.0, the numbering scheme became somewhat confused, due to the proliferation of vendor-specific (Netscape, Microsoft, etc.) additions to the language. The most important of these additions have now been incorporated into a new HTML standard, known as HTML 3.2 (skipping over the number 3, for reasons too convoluted to explain). This standard is described in detail in Chapter 4.

As mentioned, HTML is not a stationary target, and there is much effort underway to add new features and improve old ones. Chapter 5 discusses many of these up-and-coming changes, which largely fall under the categories of internationalization, embedded objects, and stylesheets. HTML authors should be aware that if they use some of the advanced features discussed in Chapter 5, there will be many people who cannot properly read the document content.

Overview of the HyperText Markup Language

So what does an HTML document look like? A simple example is shown in Figure 1.1. As you can see, this looks just like a plain text document. In fact, that is exactly what it is—an HTML document contains only the printable characters that you ordinarily type. Consequently, you can prepare an HTML document using a simple text editor, such as the NotePad editor on a Windows PC, TeachText on the Macintosh, or vi on a UNIX workstation. You don't need a special HTML editor to create HTML documents.

Markup Elements and Tags

The things that make an HTML document special are the HTML markup *tags*. These are sections of text enclosed by a less-than and greater-than sign (`<...>`), and are the markup instructions that explain what each part of the document means. For example, the tag `<H1>` indicates the *start* of a level 1 heading, while the `</H1>` tag marks the *end* of a heading of level 1. Thus, the text string

```
<H1>This is a Heading</H1>
```

marks the string "This is a Heading" as a level 1 heading (there are six possible heading levels, from **H1** to **H6**). Note how a forward slash inside the tag indicates an end tag.

TIP: Tag Names Are Case-Insensitive   The names inside the tags are *case-insensitive*, so that `<h1>` is equivalent to `<H1>`, and `<STRONG>` is equivalent to `<StROng>`. Capitalization is recommended to make the tags stand out.

An HTML document is described as being composed of *elements*. For example, the string

```
<h1>This is a Heading</H1>
```

is an **H1** element, consisting of an **H1** start tag, the enclosed text, and an **H1** end tag. You will also often see an **H1** element referred to as the *container* of a heading, since the start and stop tags *contain* the text that makes up the heading.

Some elements, instead of being containers, are *empty*. This simply means they do not affect a block of text and thus do not use an end tag. An example is the **BR** element in Figure 1.1, in the line:

```
some kind of <STRONG> exciting <BR> fact</STRONG>
```

The tag `<BR>` forces a line break at the location of the tag, just after the word "exciting" (see Figures 1.2 and 1.3). The **BR** element does not affect any enclosed text (a line break does not "contain" anything) so an end tag is not required.

Element Attributes

Sometimes, an element takes *attributes* that define properties or special information about the element. Attributes are much like variables, and are usually assigned *values* that define these special properties. For example, the element

```
<H1 ALIGN="center">This is a Heading</H1>
```

takes an **ALIGN** attribute, which states that, where possible, the heading should be centered on the display. Note that attributes always appear in the start tag of an element.

Another example, used to include an image within an HTML document, is found in the **IMG** element. An **IMG** element appears via the tag:

```
<IMG SRC="filename.gif">
```

The **SRC** attribute specifies the name of the image file to be included in the document (actually a uniform resource locator [URL] "pointing" to the image file—URLs are discussed in Chapter 2 and, in detail, Chapter 6). The attribute name, like the element name, is case-insensitive. Thus the above line could equally well be written as either of:

```
<iMg src="filename.gif">
<iMg SrC="filename.gif">
```

However, the value *assigned* to an **SRC** attribute is *case-sensitive*; case-sensitivity can be preserved by enclosing the string in quotation marks. As you may have noticed, the **IMG** element is empty (like the **BR** element), since it merely inserts an image and does not affect a block of text.

HTML Is a Structured Language

HTML is a *structured* language, which means that there are rules for where elements can and cannot go. These rules are present to enforce an overall *logical structure* upon the document. For example, a heading element like `<H1>...</H1>` can contain text, text marked for emphasis, line breaks, inline images, and hypertext anchors (discussed in Example 2)—but it cannot contain any other HTML element. As a result, the markup

```
<H1><H2>...text ... </H2></H1>
```

is invalid. Obviously, it does not make sense for a heading to "contain" another heading, and the HTML language rules reflect this reality.

In addition, elements can *never overlap*—this means that tag placement like

```
<EM> <H2> EM and H2 overlap—this is illegal </EM> </H2>
```

is illegal. There are many such structural rules; they are given in detail in Chapters 4 and 5. This chapter and Chapter 2 illustrate the most obvious cases.

Summary

1. HTML documents are divided into *elements*. Elements are usually marked by *start* and *end tags*, and take the form `<NAME>.. some text ..</NAME>`, where the enclosed text is the content of the element. Some elements do not affect a block of text, and are hence called "empty" elements. Empty elements do not require end tags.

2. Some elements can take *attributes*. An attribute appears within the start tag and defines properties of the element. For example, heading elements can take the **ALIGN** attribute to specify how the heading should be aligned on the display (e.g., `<H1 ALIGN="center"> text .. </H1>` to center-align a heading).

3. Elements names and attribute names are *case-insensitive*. Thus, `<NAME ATTRIBUTE="string">`, `<NamE ATtRiButE="string">`, and `<name attribute="string">` are equivalent. However, the attribute value (here the string `string`) may be *case-sensitive*. If you suspect the value is case-sensitive, you should enclose it inside double quotation marks (`"..."`).

4. The placement of elements in a document must obey the HTML nesting rules, which specify where elements can and cannot appear. For example, a heading element, such as **H1**, cannot contain a list or another heading, but can contain a hypertext anchor. In addition, elements *cannot overlap*. Details of the nesting rules for HTML elements are provided in Chapters 4 and 5.

Example 1: A Simple HTML Document

We could go on explaining HTML, but it is easier to get a feel for the language, and for HTML documents, by looking at some examples; the details of the language are found in Chapter 4 if you are in a rush. Figure 1.1 shows a simple but complete HTML document, and is designed to illustrate the overall document structure and some of the simpler markup elements. This document was created using the UNIX vi editor and was saved in a file named *ex1.html*. The *.html* filename extension is important, as WWW browsers and HTTP servers understand files with this suffix to be HTML documents, as opposed to "plain" text documents, such as e-mail letters or program listings. On PCs running Windows 3.1 or DOS (yes—some people still use DOS), the extension is *.htm*, since four-letter extensions are not possible. More will be said later about extension names and what they mean.

The rendering of Figure 1.1 by two different browsers is shown in Figures 1.2 and 1.3. All browsers allow you to load and view files created on your own computer, even if you are not connected to the Internet, simply by giving the browser the name of the local file. To view the example using the lynx browser, you type

```
lynx ex1.html
```

at the command prompt. With graphical browsers like Netscape Navigator and Microsoft Internet Explorer, you just start the program and select an "Open File.." or other similar item, usually from the "File" pull-down menu at the top of the window, and then select the file you wish to open.

Figures 1.2 and 1.3 show this document rendered by two different WWW browsers. Figure 1.2 shows the document as displayed by the graphical Netscape Navigator browser, while Figure 1.3 shows what you get from the character-based browser lynx.

Document Structure: The HTML Element

Since HTML is a structural language, the tags and elements are best analyzed by starting from the outside and working in. The outermost element, which encompasses the entire document, is named **HTML**. This element indicates that the enclosed text is an HTML document. This may seem unnecessary, but it is useful in some contexts where the content of a file cannot be determined from the filename. Surprisingly enough (or perhaps not), there are several other markup languages that look superficially like HTML. The HTML tag is then a way to distinguish between these different types of documents.

The Document HEAD

The next element inside the **HTML** element is named **HEAD**. The **HEAD** element is a container for information *about* the document, such as the **TITLE**. **HEAD** information, if it is displayed, is not presented as part of the document. Looking at Figures 1.2 and 1.3, you will see that the content of the **TITLE** element is displayed apart from the text. With Netscape Navigator the title is displayed in the frame of the window, while with lynx, the name is displayed at the top of the screen and to the right.

The **HEAD** must always be the first element inside the document, coming right after the <HTML> tag.

Use Short, Descriptive Titles

Because the **TITLE** is displayed separately from the text, and usually in a restricted space such as a window title bar, a small fixed-size text box, or as a single line at the top of a text screen, you want the **TITLE** to be both descriptive and short. If a **TITLE** is too long, it will simply not fit. The **TITLE** should be descriptive of the document. When users store a visited location in their Web browser's bookmark or hotlist file, they are actually recording the location along with the **TITLE**. The **TITLE** is then the *only* information in the bookmark list that describes the location's content. As an author, you thus want **TITLE**s to be descriptive of your documents, so that they can be easily located in a bookmark list.

The Document BODY

After the **HEAD** comes the **BODY**. This element contains *all* the text and other material that is to be displayed. Notice how this is true in Figure 1.1, where all the displayed material lies between the <BODY> and </BODY> tags.

Figure 1.1 Contents of the example HTML document *ex1.html*. The rendering of this document by different browsers is shown in Figures 1.2 and 1.3.

```
<HTML>
<HEAD>
<TITLE> This is the Title of the Document </TITLE>
</HEAD>
<BODY>
<H1> This is a Heading</H1>

<P>      Hello.  This is not a very exciting document.
I
    bet you were expecting <EM> poetry</EM>, or

some kind of <STRONG> exciting <BR> fact</STRONG> about the Internet and
the World Wide Web.

<P> Sorry.  No such luck.        This document
does
contain examples of HTML markup, for example, here is an "unordered
list":
<UL>
  <LI> One item of the list,
    <LI> A second list item  <LI> A third list item that goes on and on and
    on to indicate that the lists can wrap right around the page and still
    be nicely formatted by the browsers.
    <LI> The final item.
</UL>
<p> Lists are exciting. You can also have ordered lists (the items are numbered)
and description lists.
<HR>
<p> And you can draw horizontal lines, which are useful for dividing
sections.
</BODY>
</HTML>
```

Why a HEAD and BODY?

Why bother with this **HEAD/BODY** separation? Recall that HTML is designed to organize your document in a logical way. It then makes sense to separate the document itself (the **BODY**) from information *about* the document (the **HEAD**). There are several other **HEAD** elements (discussed in Chapter 4) that describe relationships between a document and other documents (the **LINK** element), or that can provide indexing or other meta-information about the document (the **META** element). These can be extremely useful for indexing and cataloging document collections, or for other organizational purposes.

Figure 1.2 Netscape Navigator 3.0 rendering of the HTML document *ex1.html* (the HTML document is listed in Figure 1.1).

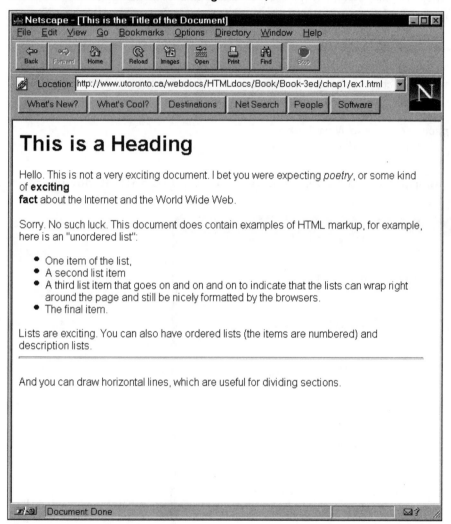

Heading Elements

The first element in the **BODY** of Figure 1.1 is an **H1** element. **H1** stands for a level 1 *heading* element. In HTML, headings come in six levels, **H1** through **H6**, with **H1** being the highest (most important) heading level, and **H6** the lowest. A browser must then take the **H1** element content and display it in a manner appropriate to a major heading. For example, Netscape Navigator shows the heading

```
<H1> This is a Heading</H1>
```

as a large, boldfaced string of characters, left-justified and separated by a wide vertical space from the following text (Figure 1.2). Lynx, on the other hand, shows this as an uppercase text string centered on the page (Figure 1.3). This should remind you of the point made earlier: that different browsers may render the same elements in very different ways. HTML markup instructions are designed to specify the logical structure of the document far more than the physical layout. Thus, the browser is free to find the best way to display items, such as headings, consistent with its own limitations.

Interpretation of Spaces, Tabs, and New Lines

Referring back to Figure 1.1, review the next few lines of text:

Figure 1.3 Lynx rendering of the HTML document *ex1.html* (the HTML document is listed in Figure 1.1).

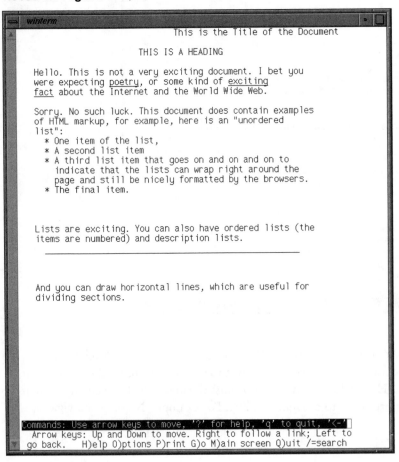

```
<P>     Hello.  This is not a very exciting document.
I
    bet you were expecting <EM> poetry</EM>, or
```

some kind of <STRONG> exciting <BR> fact</STRONG> about the Internet and
the World Wide Web.

You will see in Figures 1.2 and 1.3 that these lines have been rendered as a continuous paragraph of text, ignoring the blank lines, extra spaces, and tabs that are present in the original file. The rendering of an HTML document *ignores* extra spaces, tabs, and blank lines, and treats any combination of these characters as a single word space. This means that you can use extra space characters, line breaks, and indentations to organize the logical layout of an HTML document, and make it easier to see the placement of the tags relative to the text. This is done in the bottom half of Figure 1.1, and in many of the other examples in this book. This concept will be familiar if you have written computer programs or have used typesetting languages such as TeX or Scribe, and is equivalent to using spaces and tabs to make a computer program easier to read.

Character Highlighting

The first sentence in Figure 1.1 contains two additional elements: **EM** for *emphasis* and **STRONG** for *strong* emphasis. Note that these are *logical* descriptions of the enclosed text, and do not directly specify physical formatting styles. The HTML specifications recommend that text marked with **EM** be italicized, if possible, and that text marked with **STRONG** be rendered as bold. This is exactly what is done by Netscape Navigator, as shown in Figure 1.2. Lynx, on the other hand, renders both **EM** and **STRONG** as underlined text (Figure 1.3). Character-based programs such as lynx can really do only four things to text—underline it, boldface it, force it to capital letters, or display it in reverse video. Given these limitations, lynx cannot render as distinct all the different elements in HTML. It therefore renders **EM** and **STRONG** in the same way. On the other hand, a text-to-speech converter would have no problem distinguishing **EM** and **BOLD**, and could simply modify the spoken intonation to account for the specified emphasis. Unfortunately, it is hard to include a text-to-speech example in a book!

Highlighting elements, such as **EM** and **STRONG**, can be placed anywhere you find regular text, except within the **TITLE** element in the **HEAD**. The content of a **TITLE** element can only be text; there can be no HTML elements inside it. Recall that the text inside a **TITLE** is not part of the document, but simply a text string providing information about the document. Thus markup has no meaning here.

HTML has several other logical highlighting elements, such as **CODE** for computer code, **KBD** for keyboard input, **VAR** for a variable, **DFN** for the defining instance of a term, **CITE** for a short citation, and so on. HTML also has *physical* highlighting elements, such as **B** for boldface, **I** for italics, **TT** for typewriter font (fixed-width characters), and **U** for an underlined font. Where sensible, you should specify logical meaning for text strings rather than these physical styles: Logical styles assign true meaning to the associated text, and give a browser more flexibility in determining the best presentation.

Physical highlighting tags are particularly useful when translating from a word processor format, which already contains tags for boldface, italics, or other physical styles, since these styles can be directly converted to their HTML equivalents. They are also useful if you want to specify physical formatting for decorative purposes, but do not want to associate any special meaning to the formatted text.

Paragraphs

Look at the next line, beginning with the string `<P> Sorry.`:

```
<P> Sorry.  No such luck.        This document
does
contain examples of HTML markup, for example, here is an "unordered
list":
<UL>
```

The `<P>` tag marks the beginning of a paragraph, and is best thought of as marking the start of a paragraph *container*. Most browsers interpret the `<P>` that starts a paragraph by skipping a line, as shown in Figures 1.2 and 1.3.

Note that a paragraph mark can be anywhere in a line. For example, the three lines (note the blank line between the two lines of text):

```
the World Wide Web.

<P> Sorry.  No such luck.        This document
```

can equally well be written as:

```
the World Wide Web.  <P> Sorry.  No such luck.  This document
```

Recall that the rendering of an HTML document depends only on where the markup tags are located relative to the text they describe. Of course, putting `<P>` at the beginning of a line makes it easier to read the "raw" HTML, and is thus a good idea.

You will notice in Figure 1.1 that there are no `</P>` ending tags to mark the ends of the paragraphs. In HTML, ending paragraph tags are optional. The rule is that a paragraph is ended by the next `<P>` tag that starts another paragraph, or by another tag that starts another block of text such as a heading tag (`<Hn>`), a quotation tag (`<BLOCKQUOTE>`), or list tags (`<UL>`, `<OL>`, `<DIR>`, `<MENU>`, `<DL>`). Thus, the paragraph ending with the words `unordered list` is ended by the following `<UL>` tag that marks the beginning of an *unordered list* element.

Don't Use Empty Paragraphs

The HTML specification recommends that, if two (or more) adjacent elements describing the logical structure of the document require some special vertical spacing, only one of the spacing values (the larger) should be used, and the other should be ignored. This implies that constructions like:

```
<p><p><p><p>  This is a paragraph
```

should yield at most a single paragraph break. More important, you should avoid doing such things, since, by definition, paragraphs cannot be empty. If you do try constructions like this, you will find that spacing is rendered differently by different Web browsers: Some will leave extra space, some will not, and others will complain that the document is illegal.

Getting Extra Vertical Space

If you really want extra vertical space, try using consecutive line break elements:

```
<BR> <BR> <BR>
```

This is valid HTML, and usually yields the extra spacing you require. The long-term solution for detailed formatting is found in *stylesheets*, discussed in Chapter 5.

Lists

Having beaten paragraphs into the ground, we now move on to the next component, namely the list of items seen in Figure 1.2 and 1.3. HTML supports several types of lists, the example here being an unordered (bulleted) list. An unordered list element begins with the tag `<UL>`, and ends with a `</UL>`:

```
<UL>
    <LI>One item of the list,
    <LI>A second list item  <LI>A third list item that goes on and on and
    on to indicate that the lists can wrap right around the page and still
    be nicely formatted by the browsers.
    <LI>The final item.
</UL>
```

Both the start and stop tags are mandatory—unlike `</P>`, you cannot omit the `</UL>` that ends an unordered list. Other list elements include the *ordered* list element **OL** and the *description* or glossary list element **DL**. **DL** is discussed in Chapter 4, and is illustrated in Figures 4.19 and 4.20.

Like paragraphs, lists cannot be empty. However, unlike paragraphs, UL or OL lists can contain only one thing—**LI** *list item* elements. In turn, **LI** elements cannot be empty, as every list item must consist of some text; however, if you want a blank item, just put in a space character or a **BR** element. The ending `</LI>` tag is not required, however, as the end of a list item is implied by the next `<LI>` or by the `</UL>` tag that finally terminates the list, as illustrated in this example.

An unordered list is simply that—an unordered list of items, each item marked by an indentation of some type and a star or bullet. It is up to the browser to format them nicely. As you can see in Figures 1.2 and 1.3, lynx and Netscape Navigator do very similar things; however, you will also note that these browsers do different things to the spacing that surrounds the lists; such browser-to-browser variations are common.

As mentioned, the only thing that can go inside a **UL** element is an **LI** element. Thus, the following markup

```
<UL>
    here is some non-list text inside a list
    <LI>Here is list item 1.
</UL>
```

is invalid. An **LI** element, however, can contain lots of things. For example, an **LI** element can contain text, the **IMG** element (for inline images), text emphasis (such as the **STRONG** element), another list, paragraphs, and even a fill-in HTML form. However, it cannot contain a heading element. Heading elements can only be directly inside the **BODY**, or inside a **FORM** (for fill-in forms) or a **BLOCKQUOTE** (for quoted text) element. **FORMs** and **BLOCKQUOTEs** are discussed in Examples 4, 6, 7, and 9 in Chapter 2.

Be Careful of Leading Space inside Elements

You should not leave spaces between the `<LI>` tag and the content of the list item. This is because the space will be treated as a whitespace, which will affect the indentation for the particular list item. Thus, the items

```
<LI>  Item 1
<LI>Item 2
```

will be indented differently due to the extra whitespace in front of "Item 1." This is a subtle point, but will come up often when you are trying to format your text. It is always best to omit spaces between the start tags and the enclosed text you wish to mark up.

Lists within Lists

You can include lists within lists. For example, the markup

```
<OL>
    <LI>ordered list Item 1
    <LI>ordered list Item 2
    <UL>
        <LI>unordered item under ordered list item 2
        <LI>unordered item under ordered list item 2
    </UL>
    <LI>ordered list Item 3
</OL>
```

indicates an ordered list that in turn contains an unordered list under the second ordered list item.

Horizontal Rules

The final element in Figure 1.1 is the **HR** or horizontal rule element. This element simply draws a horizontal dividing line across the page, and is useful for dividing sections. This is also an empty element, since it does not act on a body of text.

Lessons from Example 1

1. Titles should be short and descriptive of the document content.

2. HTML is a hierarchical set of markup instructions. The outer layer of this organization, showing the basic document outline, is:

```
  ┌─── <HTML>
  │ ┌─── <HEAD>
  │ │ .. document head ..
  │ └─── </HEAD>
  │ ┌─── <BODY>
  │ │ .. document body ..
  │ └─── </BODY>
  └─── </HTML>
```

The **TITLE** goes inside the **HEAD**, while the text to be displayed goes inside the **BODY**.

3. Extra whitespaces, tabs, and blank lines are irrelevant in the formatting of a document; the only thing that affects the display of the document by the browser is the placement of the HTML markup *tags*. You should, however, avoid spaces between start tags and the text being marked up by the tags.

4. Heading elements (**H1** through **H6**) can only go inside the **BODY, DIV** (discussed later), **FORM,** or **BLOCKQUOTE** elements.

5. **UL** and **OL** lists can contain only **LI** (list item) elements. The **LI** elements can contain text, images, and other lists, but cannot contain headings.

Exercises from Example 1

If you are going to create HTML documents, you might as well start doing so! Using your favorite text or HTML editor (it doesn't matter which one), start creating Web pages—you can use the examples in this book as a starting point, if you wish. All the example documents in this book can be found at the URL:

```
http://www.utoronto.ca/webdocs/HTMLdocs/Book/Book-3ed/
```

Once you've created a page, save it to a disk file, and then view it with your Web browser or browsers—the more the merrier, as this helps you appreciate (and adjust for!) the different capabilities of the different browser packages. Try adding headings, lists, and other elements, concentrating on following the rules of HTML. Chapter 4 gives these rules in detail, so you can check there if you are not sure about the placement of a given element.

Example 2: Images and Hypertext Links

Figure 1.1 illustrated how HTML can be used to mark up the logical organization of a single document. This second example illustrates the hypertext capabilities of HTML. The example consists of two documents, *ex2a.html* and *ex2b.html*, with a hypertext link from one to the other. The documents are shown in Figures 1.4 and 1.9. *Ex2a.html* also includes inline images, to illustrate some of the things to think about when using images in your documents. Notice how space characters and line breaks are used to make the raw HTML easier to read, by indenting the text and aligning the markup tags.

Figure 1.4 Contents of the example HTML document *ex2a.html*. The rendering of this document by the Netscape Navigator, MacWeb and lynx browsers is shown in Figures 1.5–1.8.

```
<HTML>
<HEAD>
<TITLE> Example 2A, Showing IMG and Hypertext Links </TITLE>
</HEAD>
<BODY>

<H1> Example 2A: Image Inclusion and Hypertext Links </H1>

<P> Greetings from the exciting world of HTML Example documents. OK, so text
    is not so exciting.  But how about some pictures!

<P> There are many ways to fit in the image.  For example,
    you could fit it in this way:
    <IMG SRC="home.gif" ALIGN="top">, this way
    <IMG SRC="home.gif" ALIGN="middle"> or this way
    <IMG SRC="home.gif" ALIGN="bottom">.

<P> Another important thing: you can make
    <a href="ex2b.html">hypertext links</a> to other files.
    You can even make hypertext links using images,  for example
    <a href="ex2b.html"><IMG SRC="sright.xbm" ALIGN="middle"></a>.

<P> Lastly, here is a row of images:
    <IMG src="home.gif" alt="[Home Icon]">
    <IMG src="home.gif" alt="[Home Icon]">
    <IMG src="home.gif" alt="[Home Icon]">
    <IMG src="home.gif" alt="[Home Icon]">
    <IMG src="home.gif" alt="[Home Icon]">
    <IMG src="home.gif" alt="[Home Icon]">
    <IMG src="home.gif" alt="[Home Icon]">
```

Figure 1.4 *Continued*

```
<IMG src="home.gif" alt="[Home Icon]">
<IMG src="home.gif" alt="[Home Icon]">

</body>
</html>
```

Figure 1.5 Netscape Navigator rendering of the HTML document *ex2a.html* (the HTML document source is shown in Figure 1.4).

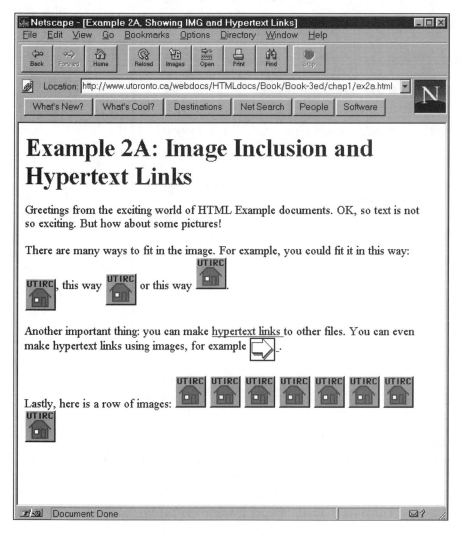

Figure 1.6 Netscape Navigator browser rendering of the HTML document *ex2a.html*, but with image loading disabled (the HTML document source is listed in Figure 1.4).

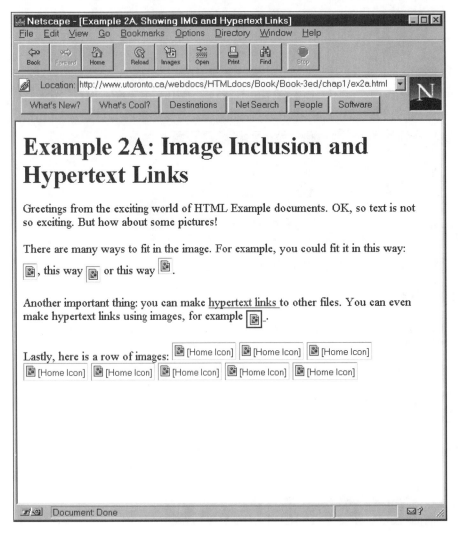

The Example Document

Figure 1.4, the contents of the file *ex2a.html*, will be examined first. The first paragraph contains only text. The second paragraph is similar, except that it contains three images, which are included using the **IMG** element `<IMG SRC="home.gif">`. ***Home.gif*** is an image file in GIF format; I know this by the *.gif* filename extension (and, of course, because I created it). GIF files are one of the common image formats that can be included within HTML documents.

Figure 1.7 MacWeb browser rendering of the HTML document *ex2a.html* (the HTML document source is listed in Figure 1.4).

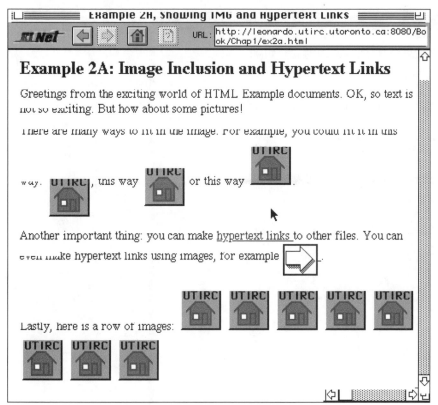

Example Document Rendered

The rendering of the document *ex2a.html* (listed in Figure 1.4) is shown in Figures 1.5 through 1.8. Figures 1.5 and 1.6 show the document as presented by the Netscape Navigator browser, while Figure 1.7 shows the document viewed using the Macintosh MacWeb browser, and Figure 1.8 shows the document as displayed by lynx. Many of the differences amongst them are simply due to the different window sizes and fonts. Still, there are differences that warrant mention.

Inline Images

Note the appearance of the images in Figures 1.5 and 1.7. By default, an image is included as if it were a large letter or word inline with the surrounding text, deforming the line spacing to ensure that no text overlaps the image. Also by default, the bottom of the inserted image aligns with the bottom of the line of text leading up to the image. In this case there is no special wrapping or flowing of the text around the image. You have no way of guaranteeing how the document will

Figure 1.8 Lynx browser rendering of the HTML document *ex2a.html* (the HTML document source is listed in Figure 1.4).

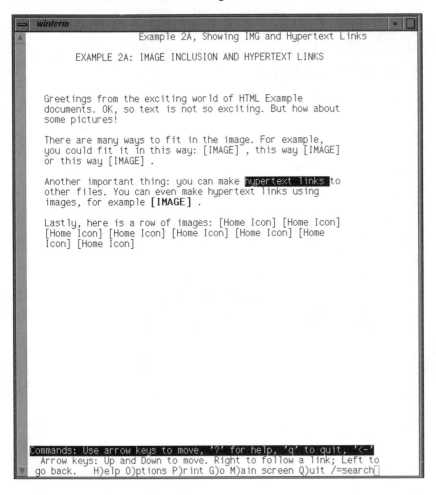

be formatted and displayed and no guarantee that an image embedded in the middle of a sentence will appear in a particular place on the screen. Consequently, the only way to guarantee image placement is to make the image element the first item following a paragraph (or other) break; then, it will always be the first item on a line.

Figure 1.9 Contents of the example HTML document *ex2b.html*. This document is the target of a hypertext link from the file *ex2a.html* shown in Figure 1.4.

```
<HTML>
<HEAD>
<TITLE> Example 2B: Target of example Hypertext Link</TITLE>
</HEAD>
<BODY>

<h2> Target of Hypertext Link </h2>

<p> OK, so now that you are here, how do you get back?  This document
    doesn't have any hypertext links, so you have to use a "back" button (or the
    'u' key if using lynx) to move back to the previously viewed document.

</BODY>
</HTML>
```

Figure 1.10 MacWeb browser rendering of the HTML document *ex2b.html* (the HTML document source is listed in Figure 1.9).

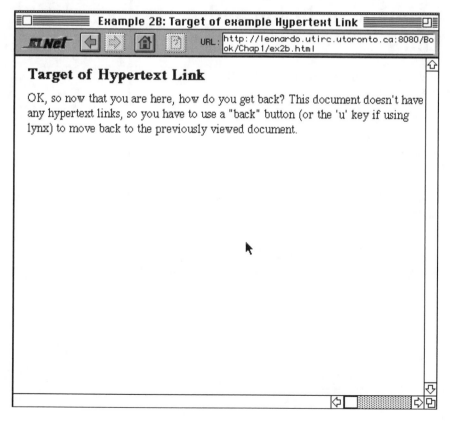

This point is illustrated by the last line of *ex2a.html* (Figure 1.4), which is simply a row of inline images. Note that these wrap to best fit the width of the screen, just as if they were a sequence of words (Figures 1.6 and 1.8). Consequently, if the user changes the size of the browser window, these icons are repositioned. This again points out the wide variation possible between different renderings of the same document.

Figure 1.11 Netscape Navigator 3.0 browser rendering of the HTML document *ex2a.html* after returning from a hypertext jump to the document *ex2b.html*.

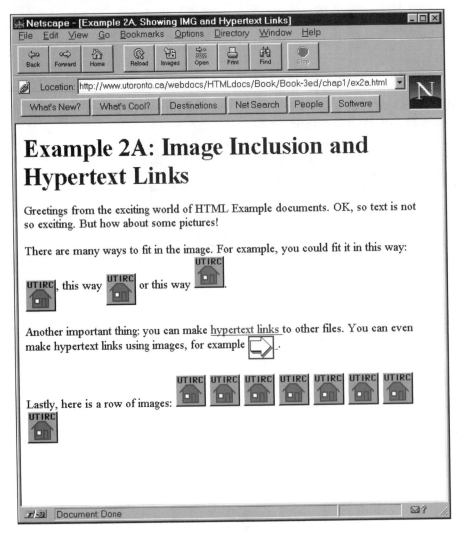

More advanced image placement control is possible, and is discussed later in this example, as well as in Chapter 4.

Aligning Images with Text

The IMG element can take an optional **ALIGN** attribute to specify how the image should be aligned on the page. In HTML 2.0 there were only three allowed values: ALIGN="top", ALIGN="bottom", or ALIGN="middle" (the argument is case-insensitive), ALIGN="bottom" being the default. The three options are illustrated in Figures 1.5 through 1.7 using the three "Home" icons (I am afraid I am not a great graphic artist). The first, ALIGN="top", aligns the top of the image with the top of the text, while ALIGN="middle" aligns the middle of the image with the bottom of the text, and ALIGN="bottom" aligns the bottom of the image with the bottom of the text.

These attribute values only allow for rudimentary control over image placement. HTML 3.2 supports the additional **IMG** alignment attribute values ALIGN="left" and ALIGN="right", which allow images to float on the page and permit text flow around the image, plus several other attributes to control other aspects of image placement. These image features are described in detail in Chapters 2 and 4, and are supported by most current browsers.

No Graphics?—The ALT Attribute

Most graphical browsers let the user disable the loading of images. This can substantially speed up the appearance of a page, since the user does not need to await the arrival of all the images. Figure 1.6 shows the display by Netscape Navigator when image loading is disabled, while Figure 1.8 shows the lynx interpretation. Lynx is a text-only browser and cannot display images. Netscape Navigator replaces the missing images by graphic symbols that denote a missing image, while lynx replaces each occurrence of an image with the text string [IMAGE]. In neither case is the replacement very descriptive, but at least it tells users what they are missing.

A far better choice is to use the **ALT** attribute to the **IMG** element to provide a text alternative to the image. This is essential for any browser that cannot display images, and extremely useful for graphical browsers with disabled image loading. The usage is simply:

```
<IMG SRC="image.file" ALT="[A text alternative to the Image]">
```

The string specified for **ALT** is case-sensitive, thus it should be enclosed in quotation marks. It is common (but not necessary) to enclose the string with square brackets, as is done at the bottom of *ex2a.html*, where the attribute alt="[Home Icon]" is used with all the inline images. The resulting text rendering is shown in Figures 1.6 and 1.8. Note how the text effectively indicates the content of the missing image.

Purely Decorative Image?—Use an Empty ALT

If you have a purely decorative image with no associated underlying meaning, you should use the **ALT** attribute to assign an empty description, that is:

```
<IMG SRC="decoration.gif" ALT="">
```

This means that a user of a non-graphical browser will see nothing. This is far better than seeing `"[IMAGE]"`, or an image symbol, which always leaves a reader wondering if the author forgot to provide a description of an important part of the document.

Loading Images

How does the browser actually obtain images and complete the document? The browser first obtains the HTML document and then looks for **IMG** elements. If it finds **IMG** elements, the browser makes additional connections to the server, indicated by the **SRC** attributes, to obtain the required image files. Thus, a single document containing 10 images will require 11 distinct connections to load the complete document content. Needless to say, this can be slow, particularly if the browser has a slow network connection to the server.

As mentioned previously, most graphical browsers have a "Delay Image Loading" button or pull-down menu selection that disables the automatic loading of inline images, which was the mechanism used to create Figure 1.6. However, often the images are important, or necessary, so it is nice if the browser can format the display before the images arrive—in this way the user can read the text while awaiting the rest of the document. This is possible using the **HEIGHT** and **WIDTH** attributes to the **IMG** element.

Image Size—WIDTH and HEIGHT Attributes

IN HTML 3.2 the **IMG** element supports **HEIGHT** and **WIDTH** attributes to specify the size of the image being included. For example, if you have an image 500 pixels high and 230 pixels wide, you should write

```
<IMG SRC="image.gif" HEIGHT="500" WIDTH="230" ALT="[alt text]">
```

where the **HEIGHT** and **WIDTH** attributes give the image size, in pixels. In this case, the browser retrieving the document knows the size of the image *before* the data are actually received. As a result, it can start drawing the page immediately, leaving an appropriate empty space (500×230 in this example) for the yet-to-arrive image. This significantly speeds up the presentation of the page to the user, and is particularly important for pages containing large, slow-to-download images.

Image Formats

There are many formats for storing digital images, with various advantages and disadvantages. Unfortunately, Web browsers are able to display only a small subset of these, so that images for Web pages must be converted into one of the commonly understood formats.

On the World Wide Web, the most universally accepted image format is the Graphics Interchange Format, or GIF (filename extension *.gif*). This is the main format used in Example 2. GIF images can be displayed inline by all Web browsers. Another common format is JPEG (filename extensions *.jpeg* or *.jpg*), which is a format optimized for storing photographic images. Almost all browsers support JPEG. Both GIF and JPEG store images in a *compressed* format, which means that images can be stored in relatively small files. This is important, as images tend to require big files, which can be very slow to access over the Internet. On the Web, smaller is almost always better!

A third common format is the X-Pixelmap, or its black-and-white X-Bitmap equivalent (filename extensions *.xpm* and *.xbm* respectively). However, these store data in a non-compressed format, and are thus an inefficient way of storing images. Fortunately, such images can easily be converted to GIF or JPEG. The different image formats are discussed in more detail in Chapter 10.

Hypertext Links

The third paragraph in *ex2a.html* shows a hypertext link. The form is straightforward:

```
<A HREF="ex2b.html">hypertext links</A>
```

The element marking a hypertext link is called an **A** or *anchor* element, and the marked text is referred to as a *hypertext anchor*. The area between the beginning `<A>` and ending `</A>` tags becomes a "hot" part of the text. With graphical browsers such as Netscape Navigator or Microsoft Internet Explorer, "hot" text is often displayed with an underline, and usually in a different color (often blue), while with lynx, this region of text is displayed in bold characters. Placing the mouse over this region and clicking the mouse button, or, with lynx, using the tab key to move the cursor to lie over the hot part and pressing Enter, causes the browser to access the indicated document or other Internet resource.

Images in Hypertext Anchors

You can place images as well as text inside hypertext anchors. At the end of the second paragraph in *ex2a.html* (Figure 1.4), the image *sright.xbm* lies inside an anchor (recall that the *.xbm* means this is an X-Bitmap image). The relevant piece of HTML is:

```
<a href="ex2b.html"><IMG SRC="sright.xbm" ALIGN="middle"></a>
```

Graphical browsers often indicate this by *boxing* the image with a colored or highlighted box, while lynx simply bolds the `[Image]` text string it puts in place of the image. With this mechanism you can use small images as *button* icons, as is commonly done in multimedia applications. This doesn't do much good with lynx, of course, so, if you do use images as *navigation icons*, you had better add an **ALT** attribute to let lynx (or Braille browser) users know what's going on.

Text Spaces in Anchor Elements

You will note that there are no spaces between the anchor tags and the surrounded **IMG** element. If you have spaces at either end of the enclosed anchor string, the browser will assume that these spaces are part of the anchor, and will render them accordingly. This is not always pleasing, and can leave an anchored image with small lines sticking out from the bottom, or anchored text with underlines hanging out beyond the beginning or end of the text. The lesson once again is: Use tags around the text you want to mark up, and don't include extra spaces unless specifically intended.

Uniform Resource Locators

The *target* of the hypertext link is indicated by the anchor attribute **HREF**, which takes as its value the *uniform resource locator (URL)* of the target document or resource. As mentioned in the Preface, a URL is a text string that indicates the server protocol (HTTP, FTP, WAIS, etc.) to use in accessing the resource, the Internet domain name of the server, and the name and location of the resource on that particular server. Obviously, the **HREF** attributes in Figure 1.4 do not contain all this information! These URLs are examples of *partial* URLs, which are a shorthand way of referring to files or other resources *relative* to the URL of the document currently being viewed. For Figure 1.4, this means: Use the same protocol, same Internet domain name, and directory path of the present document (*ex2a.html*), and retrieve the indicated file *ex2b.html* from the same directory.

If you click the mouse button over the hypertext anchor, the browser downloads and displays the linked document, as shown in Figure 1.10. To return to the previously viewed document, press the Back button on the browser control panel (with lynx, press the letter "u", for *up*), which takes you back to the previously displayed document, namely *ex2a.html*. Figure 1.11 shows what this document looks like the second time around using Netscape Navigator. The document is subtly different: The portion of text that served as the launching point for the hypertext link, previously underlined in blue, is now underlined by a faded, purple line (this does not show up well in this black-and-white figure). Graphical browsers use such highlighting changes to help keep users oriented, by letting them know where they have already been. Unfortunately, this is not possible with lynx, as there are too few text highlighting modes to allow this level of subtlety. With lynx, users must pay more attention to what they have been doing, and where they have been.

Relative Uniform Resource Locators: Linking Documents Together

As mentioned, the anchor

```
<A HREF="ex2b.html">hypertext links</A>
```

uses a partial URL, which references a location relative to the URL of the displayed document. This partial URL idea is great news, because it means that you need not specify entire URLs for simple links between files on the same computer. Instead, you need only specify their position on the filesystem relative to each other, as done in Figure 1.4.

Partial URLs can point to directories other than the one containing the current document. Specification of these relative directories is done using a UNIX-like path structure, as illustrated in Figure 1.12. Suppose that the example documents *ex2a.html* and *ex2b.html* lie in the indicated directory structure. The files *ex2a.html* and *ex2b.html* are in the directory *Examples/*, while the file *e2c.html* is in *Examples/SubDir/*, and *ex2d.html* is in *Other/*.

How do you reference the files *ex2c.html* and *ex2d.html* from the file *ex2a.html*? To reference *ex2c.html*, you simply create a hypertext link that accesses the partial URL *SubDir/ex2c.html*:

```
<A HREF="SubDir/ex2c.html">hypertext links</A>
```

Notice the UNIX-like directory pathnames in which the forward slash character indicates a new directory. The specification of the URL syntax uses the forward slash to denote directories or any other hierarchical relationship (formally, URLs can reference not just files, but also programs and other resources). You *cannot* use backslashes (\) as you do with DOS and Windows, or colons (:) as you do on Macintoshes.

If you want to create a link from *ex2a.html* to *ex2d.html* in *Other/*, you write the URL as:

```
<A HREF="../Other/ex2d.html">hypertext links</A>
```

since the file is one directory level up (the symbol **..** meaning one directory up), and one level down into the directory *Other/*. A single dot (.) means the current directory, so `HREF="./SubDir/ex2c.html"` and `HREF="SubDir/ex2c.html"` are equivalent.

Special Characters in a URL

Of course, this scheme will cause problems if you actually use a slash character as part of a filename, since the URL convention will try to interpret it as a directory change. You therefore should avoid file or directory names containing this character. The URL specification does have a way of allowing this and other special characters within a URL, without having them interpreted specially. This *encoding* mechanism is discussed in Chapter 6.

There are a lot of other partial URL forms, and, of course, full URLs have yet to be discussed. More URL examples appear later in this chapter as well as in Chapter 2, while a detailed description of the URL syntax is given in Chapter 6.

Effective Hypertext Links: The Good, Bad, and Ugly

As you can see, hypertext links are easy and can be very useful—in fact, it is fair to say that they are the most important feature of HTML documents. However, it is easy to get carried away with hypertext links, and they can quickly become a source of irritation to someone reading a document. The following are a few suggestions for ways to include links in an HTML document

Figure 1.12 Accessing neighboring files using partial URLs. The figure shows some folders and files lying in the *Document Directory*—the directory that contains resources available to clients accessing an HTTP server. Material not under the document directory, such as the file *file.html*, is inaccessible to the server. The dotted lines and the corresponding text strings show partial URLs relating the file *ex2a.html* to the files *ex2b.html*, *ex2c.html*, and *ex2d.html*. The grayed directory, *cgi-bin,* indicates a gateway program directory, which contains programs to be executed by the HTTP server. This directory is kept physically separate from the document directories, since programs present a security risk to the server and must be more tightly guarded—most users will not have access to such program directories.

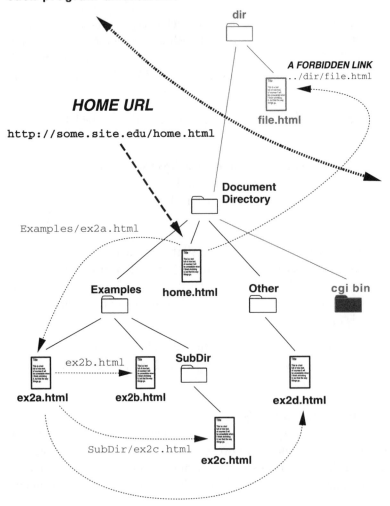

without detracting from the presentation and readability of the text. Most of these issues are illustrated in Figures 1.13 and 1.14.

Create hypertext links that flow naturally from the text. Make the link appear naturally in the text, so as not to interrupt the flow of reading, Thus, it is better to write:

```
<p> The issue of hormone-controlled ostrich-feather
growth has recently been a topic of
intense <A HREF="ostrich-paper.html">interest</A>
```

than:

```
<p> For information about current hormone-controlled
ostrich-feather
growth press <A HREF="ostrich-paper.html"> here </A>
```

Figure 1.13 Listing for the document *badlinks.html*. This document illustrates good and bad examples of hypertext links. A Microsoft Internet Explorer rendering is shown in Figure 1.14.

```
<HTML>
<HEAD>
<TITLE> Examples of Bad Hypertext Links </TITLE>
</HEAD>
<BODY>
<H1> Examples of Good/Bad Hypertext Link Design</H1>

<p> <B> 1) Don't distort the Written Text  </B>
<P> <B> Good: </B>
<BR>The issue of hormone-controlled ostrich-feather growth has recently
    been a topic of intense <A HREF="ostrich-paper.html">interest</A>.

<P> <B> Not So Good: </B>
<BR> For information about current hormone-controlled ostrich-feather
    growth press  <A HREF="ostrich-paper.html">here</A>.
<p> <B> 2) Keep the linked text section short. </B>
<p> <B> Good: </B>
<br> The life cycle of the  <A HREF="animal.html">atlantic polar-bear
    ocelot</A> is a complex and .......

<p> <B> Not So Good: </B>
<br> <A HREF="animal.html">The life cycle of the atlantic polar-bear
    ocelot is a complex</A> and .......

<p> <B> 3) Link Icon and Text Together </B>
<p> <B> Good: </B>
<br> <A HREF="file.html"><IMG SRC="home.gif"> The latest</A> home
    security systems breakdown show......
<p> <B> Not so Good: </B>
```

Figure 1.13 (Continued)

```
<br> <A HREF="file.html"><IMG SRC="home.gif"></A> The latest home
     security systems breakdown show......

</BODY>
</HTML>
```

Figure 1.14 Microsoft Internet Explorer 3.0 rendering of the file *badlinks.html* (shown in Figure 1.13).

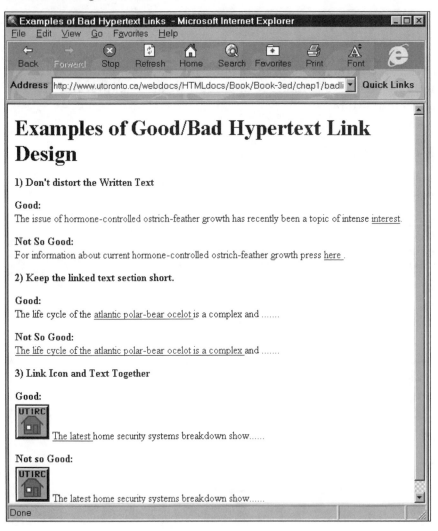

Keep linked text strings short. It is much more effective to link to a single word or selection of words than to a whole sentence. Thus such links as:

```
<p> <A HREF="animal.html">The life cycle of the atlantic polar-bear ocelot</A>
is a complex and interesting example of ...
```

are better written as:

```
<p> The life cycle of the  <A HREF="animal.html">atlantic polar-bear ocelot</A>
is a complex and interesting example of ...
```

Link icon and text together. Sometimes you will use a small icon to indicate a hypertext link. To make this clearer to the reader, it is sometimes useful to include the text adjacent to the icon within the anchor.

There aren't any hard and fast rules for creating bad and good link presentations. In general, if you are adding links within a text document that you want easily read, it is best to make the links as unobtrusive as possible.

Using the URL as the Linked Text

It is sometimes appropriate to include the URLs as part of the text—you don't always have to hide the URL inside **HREF** attributes. This is particularly useful if a document is likely to be printed, since the references are otherwise not visible. For example, the WWW FAQ (Frequently Asked Questions) document, a wonderful repository of useful information about the World Wide Web, contains lines like:

```
<p> ...The original home of the WWW F.A.Q. is
<A HREF="http://www.boutell.com/faq/">http://www.boutell.com/faq/</A>.
```

If you are reading the HTML document containing this markup, just click on the anchored text to view the referenced document. If you are reading the paper version, you can see the printed URL and have all the information you need to access the site when you next have access to the Internet.

Lists, Paragraphs, or Menus of Links

If you are putting together a collection of links, you want to think carefully about their organization. Should they be placed within in a paragraph? Probably not. More likely, they should go in a list or as a menu bar (a horizontal list of text or graphical buttons linked to the desired objects). You will also want to arrange them in a logical and organized manner—a page full of random links is exceedingly frustrating to use. Link-mania pages containing seemingly random collections of links occur quite innocently, often when you have been slowly assembling lists of interesting URLs. The collection may be fine for you, but will be confusing to anyone else.

Figure 1.16 shows a *home* page constructed using some of the features of "bad" anchor design (the source for this document is in Figure 1.15), while Figure 1.18 shows an improved and better organized home page using the suggestions given in the preceding paragraph (the source is in Figure 1.17). By simple comparison, you will see that Figure 1.18 is much easier to understand than Figure 1.16, even though Figure 1.18 actually contains less textual information.

Validate All Hypertext Links

Finally and most important of all: Make sure all your hypertext links work and go to the right place! There is nothing worse than clicking on a hypertext link only to get "ERROR. Requested document not available" in response. Actually, that's not quite true. It is even worse to click on an anchor that indicates a particular destination, only to find that you have actually accessed something completely different and obviously incorrect. Errors like these tell a reader that the document developer did not bother with even the simplest checks of his or her work, and immediately bring into question the accuracy of the documents themselves. It is easy to check your links: Just do it.

Lessons from Example 2

1. Images are included via the **IMG** element:

```
<IMG src="prism-small.gif" ALT="[Text stuff]">
```

   SRC specifies the URL of the image file to be included, while the **ALT** attribute gives a text string to be displayed by browsers that cannot display images. The **ALIGN** attribute specifies how the image should be aligned with the surrounding text, while the **HEIGHT** and **WIDTH** attributes can specify the size (in pixels) of the image.

2. Hypertext links to another document are included using the **A** (anchor) element:

```
<A HREF="SubDir/example1.2B.html">hypertext links</A>
```

   where **HREF** is used to specify the URL of the target of the link. The examples here are of partial URLs: Partial URLs assume the same Internet site and protocol as for the document currently being viewed, and look for the file (or resource) relative to it. In this regard the slash (/) and double dot (..) characters are special, representing relative positions in the directory (or other) hierarchy.

   Images can also be hypertext anchors via constructs such as:

```
<A HREF="someplace.html"><IMG SRC="image.gif"></A>
```

3. Don't use hypertext links gratuitously. If they are embedded in the text, try to make them flow with the text. If a paragraph has many links, try thinking of another way to present the material: Maybe it should be a list or a menu, or perhaps the hypertext anchors could be combined into a less intrusive form. Above all, make sure the links work; links going nowhere or to the wrong place are cardinal sins of HTML authoring.

Exercises for Example 2

Try accessing Web sites containing lots of images, but with image loading disabled on your browser. Preferably choose a site that is far away and slow to access. Note how confusing sites can be when the designers do not bother with **ALT** attributes, and how slowly the page appears if the author did not bother to include **HEIGHT** and **WIDTH** attributes.

Example 3: Home Pages—Headings, ADDRESS, and Anchors

This example, illustrated in Figures 1.15 through 1.19, looks again at the **A** (anchor) and heading elements, and introduces the **ADDRESS** (for address information) element, all in the context of a practical document design problem, namely the construction of a document collection *home page*. A home page is designed to be the first document seen by visitors to a site, and serves as your introduction to guests. It is most often used to direct people to your other interesting resources, and to provide an overview of your material. This particular example is based on a page constructed for the Instructional and Research Computing Group at the University of Toronto. Figures 1.15 and 1.16 illustrate bad design features (don't imitate this page!), while Figures 1.17 through 1.19 exemplify good design. Although this example comes from an academic institution, the model is similar for business, entertainment, or other sites—although their look will not be quite so "academic" (others might called it "stodgy"!).

Figure 1.15 HTML document listing for the file *home_bad.html*, which contains a poorly designed home page. Figure 1.16 shows the rendering of this by the Microsoft Internet Explorer browser.

```
<HTML> <HEAD>
<TITLE> Instructional and Research Computing </TITLE>
</HEAD> <BODY>
<hr>

<h1> Instructional and Research Computing </H1>

This is the home page of the Instructional and Research Computing
Group <STRONG>(IRC)</STRONG>, one of seven departments of the Division
of Computing and Communications.
The IRC group provides support for
<A HREF="MulVis/intro.html"> multimedia and visualization techniques</A>,
access to and support for
<A HREF="HPC/intro.html"> high performance computing</A>,
and support for <A HREF="AdTech/intro.html"> adaptive technology
</A>.  (aids for the physically challenged)  We also have some interesting
links to <A HREF="Lists/Lists.html"> WWW Starting Points </A>,
a big list of <A HREF="Lists/Lists.html"> WWW Search Tools</A>,
another list of hypertext pointers to
```

Figure 1.15 (Continued)

```
<A HREF="Lists/Libraries.html"> Libraries </A> resources, and a
link to the  <A HREF="http://www.utoronto.ca/uoft.html"> Main University
Home Page </A>.

<p>
If you become lost in our documents use the navigation icons.
The <EM> home </EM> icon brings you back here, while the <EM> up </EM>
icon takes up one level in the document hierarchy.  <EM> Info </EM>
and <EM> help </EM> are also useful, while the <EM> letter</EM> icon let
you send us a message, and the <EM> search </EM> icon allows you to do
a textual search of our pages.
<hr>
  <A HREF="home.html"><IMG SRC="home.gif"    ALIGN=TOP ALT="[Home]"  ></A>
  <A HREF="help.html"><IMG SRC="ic_help.gif" ALIGN=TOP ALT="[Help]"  ></A>
  <A HREF="info.html"><IMG SRC="ic_info.gif" ALIGN=TOP ALT="[Info]"  ></A>
  <A HREF="/cgi-bin/mail.pl"> <IMG SRC="ic_mail.gif" ALIGN=TOP ALT="[Mail]"  ></A>
  <A HREF="home.html"><IMG SRC="ic_up.gif"    ALIGN=TOP ALT="[Up]"     ></A>..
  <A HREF="cgi-bin/doc-search.pl"> <IMG SRC="ic_find.gif" ALIGN=TOP
ALT="[Search]"></A>
<hr>
<ADDRESS>
<A HREF="Staff/web_admin.html"> webmaster@site.address.edu </A>
</ADDRESS>

</BODY>
</HTML>
```

Figure 1.17 shows the example HTML home page document, while Figures 1.18 and 1.19 show how this page looks using the Windows Internet Explorer and UNIX lynx browsers.

Appropriate Use of Heading Elements

We start with the **TITLE** and **H1** heading in Figure 1.17. In both cases these are clearly descriptive of the content and origin of this document or document collection. As mentioned previously, the **TITLE** should always be clearly descriptive of a page's content, since it is used to reference a page when a user bookmarks the location. You have much more flexibility with headings, but, in general, the main heading of a home page should also clearly reflect the contents of the collection, as this quickly lets your visitors know that they have reached the right place.

Headings can range from **H1** through to **H6**, in decreasing order of importance. In designing a collection of documents, you should use heading elements that retain this sense of relative importance, as it helps to build organizational structure within and between documents. There are useful programs that can build a table of contents for a large collection of HTML documents based on the contents and relative *levels* of the heading elements. This, of course, will work only if the headings elements were used correctly (i.e., **H1** for major sections, **H2** for subsections, **H3** for sub-subsections, and so on).

Figure 1.16 Microsoft Internet Explorer rendering of the HTML document *home_bad.html*.

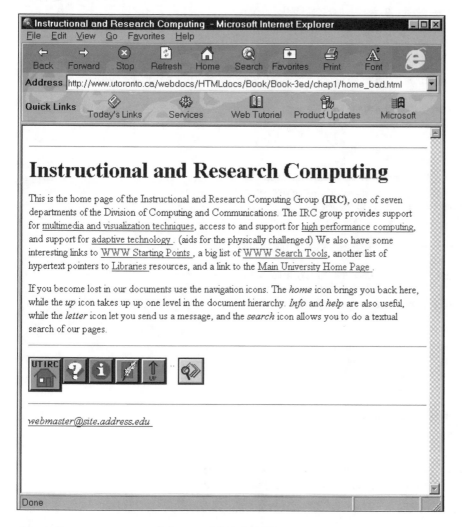

Sign Documents with an ADDRESS

It is always a good idea to sign HTML documents, particularly the home pages or other major pages. This provides information allowing visitors to send feedback or commentary on what they have found at your site. The HTML **ADDRESS** element is specifically designed for address information, and is used for this purpose in Figure 1.17. Here the **ADDRESS** element contains an e-mail address suitable for feedback and/or commentary about the IRC collection. Also, this e-mail address is placed within an anchor element linked to a page (*web_admin.html*) containing additional

Figure 1.17 Listing of the example home page document *home.html*.

```
<HTML> <HEAD>
<TITLE> Instructional and Research Computing </TITLE>
</HEAD> <BODY>
[<A HREF="home.html">              Home   </A>]
[<A HREF="help.html">              Help   </A>]
[<A HREF="info.html">              Info   </A>]
[<A HREF="/cgi-bin/mail.pl">       Mail   </A>]
[<A HREF="home.html">              Up     </A>]
[<A HREF="cgi-bin/doc-search.pl">Search</A>]
<hr>

<h1> Instructional and Research Computing </H1>

This is the home page of the Instructional and Research Computing
Group <STRONG>(IRC)</STRONG>, one of seven departments of the Division
of Computing and Communications.  We provide:

<UL>
<LI> support for <A HREF="MulVis/intro.html"> multimedia and visualization
     techniques</A>
<LI> access to and support for <A HREF="HPC/intro.html"> high performance
     computing</A>
<LI> support for <A HREF="AdTech/intro.html"> adaptive technology </A>
     (aids for the physically challenged).
</UL>
Some other useful University resources are:
<p>
 <A HREF="Lists/Lists.html"> WWW Starting Points </A> |
 <A HREF="Lists/Lists.html"> WWW Search Tools</A> |
 <A HREF="Lists/Libraries.html"> Libraries </A> |
 <A HREF="http://www.utoronto.ca/uoft.html"> Main University Home Page </A>
<p>
If you become lost in our documents use the navigation icons.
The <EM> home </EM> icon brings you back here, while the <EM> up </EM>
icon takes up one level in the document hierarchy.   <EM> Info </EM>
and <EM> help </EM> are also useful, while the <EM> letter</EM> icon let
you send us a message, and the <EM> search </EM> icon allows you to do
a textual search of our pages.
<hr>
  <A HREF="home.html"><IMG SRC="home.gif"    ALIGN=TOP ALT="[Home]"   ></A>
  <A HREF="help.html"><IMG SRC="ic_help.gif" ALIGN=TOP ALT="[Help]"   ></A>
  <A HREF="info.html"><IMG SRC="ic_info.gif" ALIGN=TOP ALT="[Info]"   ></A>
  <A HREF="/cgi-bin/mail.pl">
     <IMG SRC="ic_mail.gif" ALIGN=TOP ALT="[Mail]"   ></A>
  <A HREF="home.html">
     <IMG SRC="ic_up.gif"   ALIGN=TOP ALT="[Up]"       ></A>..
  <A HREF="cgi-bin/doc-search.pl">
     <IMG SRC="ic_find.gif" ALIGN=TOP ALT="[Search]">
```

Figure 1.17 (Continued)

```
   </A>
<hr>
<ADDRESS>
<A HREF="Staff/web_admin.html"> webmaster@site.address.edu </A>
</ADDRESS>

</BODY>
</HTML>
```

Figure 1.18 Internet Explorer rendering of the HTML document *home.html* (the document is listed in Figure 1.17).

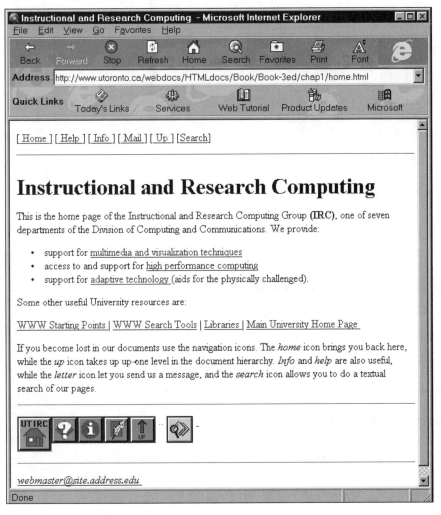

Figure 1.19 Lynx rendering of the HTML document *home.html* (the document is listed in Figure 1.17).

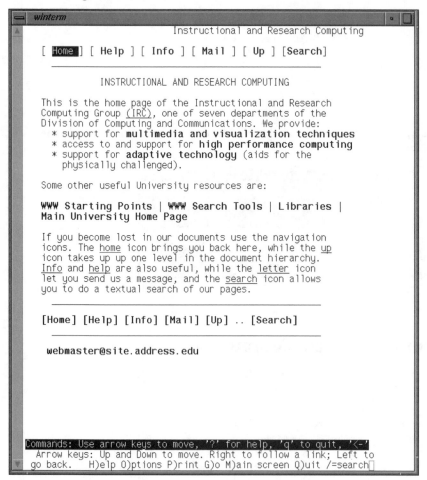

information—for example, about the server and server administrator. For more personal projects, this linked page might be an HTML document containing a brief biography of the document author. The link may also be a **mailto** URL containing the indicated e-mail address—clicking on the link will then allow the reader to directly send mail to the indicated person.

Full Uniform Resource Locators

Looking at Figure 1.17, you will see that most of the URL references are relative references. There is one, however, that is not. This is the URL pointing to the *Main University Home Page*. This is a full URL that specifies the complete information needed to access the main University HTTP server:

`http://www.utoronto.ca/uoft.html`

A complete HTTP URL has three main parts, as in this example:

1. `http:`—*The protocol specifier*. The string `http:` indicates the HTTP protocol. This and other URL schemes are discussed in Chapter 6.

2. `//www.utoronto.ca`—The *Internet domain name* of the server. This gives the Internet name the client should contact. Sometimes, you will see this with a number after the name, for example: `www.somewhere.edu:8080`. The trailing number is a *port number* and specifies the port the server is actually "listening" at. Port numbers are rather like local telephone extensions, and allow a single computer to run several different services (FTP, HTTP, etc.) each "listening" at a different port. Most HTTP servers listen at port 80. You can omit the port number from the URL if contacting the server at the default value.

3. `/uoft.html`—The *path and filename* of the desired file (or other resource). Here, the URL is to the file **uoft.html** that lies right at the top of the server's *document directory* which is the directory under which the HTTP server keeps the documents. If the file were in a subdirectory, then that information would be here, so that paths such as `/Examples/ex2a.html` (as in Figure 1.12) are possible.

The URL scheme allows for all sorts of protocols: `ftp:` for the FTP protocol; `gopher:` for the gopher protocol; `wais:` for the WAIS protocol; and so on. Consequently, using URLs, you can create hypertext links to anonymous FTP servers, Gopher sites, WAIS databases, and many other Internet resources. Web browsers are designed to understand these protocols. When they encounter a hypertext reference in an HTML element such as `HREF="`*`url`*`"`, where *url* points to an anonymous FTP or Gopher site, a browser is able to contact the site, using the appropriate protocol, and access the indicated resource.

General Home Page Design Issues

There are several things to consider when designing Web pages in general, and home pages in particular. Typically:

1. **A home page should be** *small*. A home page should be a small document with a minimum of extraneous graphics or text. Many people have slow Internet connections and don't want to spend many minutes waiting for thousands of kilobytes of gratuitous imagery. Large images (meaning large image files) and the detailed resources of your site should be elsewhere. Also you must ensure that a user can understand your home page without the graphics. Many users will access your site with image loading disabled, or with text-only browsers; thus, if you use icons for navigation buttons, you must use the **IMG** element **ALT** attribute to provide a text-only description of the button.

2. **A home page should be *concise*.** A home page is like an introductory map to a site or to a collection of documents, explaining what the site is and where to find the local resources. Thus, it should *briefly* outline the content of your site and provide hypertext links to those specific content resources. It should also briefly explain (where necessary) the organization of the site, such as the meanings of icons or menus, so that visitors will know how to navigate their way around.

3. **A home page should include *contact information*.** At some point, someone will want to contact you or your Web server administrator, perhaps to point out a problem, or most likely to compliment you on your work. The home page should therefore include contact information for the administrator(s) of the resources. A common, generic e-mail address for the site administrator is **webmaster@*www.domain.name***, where *www.domain.name* is the domain name of your server. Such information should be included on the home page, most commonly at the page bottom.

Clarity of Text Content

To make a home page small and compact, you must make sure that the text component is both clear and concise. The text portion of the example home page document (Figure 1.17) fulfills these criteria, providing a clear and concise description of the site and the material it contains, with a minimum of extraneous detail. This can be written in whatever style you prefer: polite and well mannered, or eclectic and off the wall. In the example in Figure 1.17, the first paragraph explains what the site is and provides links to the major areas of interest. Each of these areas may, in turn, have its own home page, specific to the subject at hand. This hierarchical structure lets people quickly find what they are looking for, and also makes it easy for you to organize your documents. For example, you could have independent subdirectories for each distinct project, with your main home page having hypertext links to introductory home pages located in each of these subdirectories. Other hypertext links can then provide alternative relationships between documents, within this overall hierarchical arrangement.

The home page in Figure 1.17 also contains a second, less detailed list that provides a brief selection of alternative services. These items link to documents or services that are perhaps peripheral to the main purpose of your site, but that may be useful in directing the visitor to his or her destination. Here this is a collection of hypertext pointers to other resources that the group commonly uses.

Referring to Figures 1.18 and 1.19, you can see how clean the organization appears. Since the document is written in correct HTML, both browsers display it clearly, subject to their own limitations. A comparison of Figure 1.19 with the less-well-thought-out version in Figure 1.16 illustrates the importance of good organizational design. A little thought about how the hypertext links should be organized makes an enormous difference in the clarity and readability of the final presentation.

Image-Intensive Home Pages

Alternatively, you might consider an all-graphical home page. Some sites, such as the *Silicon Graphics Inc.* site, use a large *imagemap* as their home page. You can find this home page at the URL:

```
http://www.sgi.com
```

The image on this home page contains imagemapped regions that are linked to the various resources on their Web site, much like the text buttons and links in Figure 1.18. You will note, however, that SGI also provides a menu of text buttons for users who do not have graphical browsers (or who have disabled image loading because of slow Internet connections).

Images: Acceptable Sizes

Although not included in Example 3, decorative images containing, for example, the company or organizational logo are often placed at the top or within a home page document. This can be a very attractive addition, adding appealing graphical impact to your introductory page. You must be careful, however, to ensure that an image is not so large that it frustrates your users by taking a long time to download—as mentioned before, the sizes of all the images on a page should ideally sum to less than 20 KB. Even if the page is attractive, the impact of this elegance will be lost on a user who has had to wait minutes for the image to arrive.

As mentioned in Example 2, you should also use **IMG** element **HEIGHT** and **WIDTH** attributes to specify the size of the images being included. This lets the browser go ahead and format the text, while setting aside space for the images before they arrive. If you don't specify **WIDTH** and **HEIGHT,** many browsers will wait to load the images (and determine the image sizes) before drawing the page. This can be very slow if there are lots of images, during which the user sees nothing at all and curses you for having created such an irritating, slow-to-access page!

Images: Navigation Icons

Look back to the bottom of the HTML document listed in Figure 1.17 and displayed in Figures 1.18 and 1.19. The feature to look at is the group of small *icons*. These icons are attached by hypertext anchors to important reference documents of the collection; the paragraph preceding these icons explains what the icons mean. The intent is to place these icons on every HTML document, to provide a universal cue for navigating through the local document collection. For example, the *home* icon always links back to this main home page, while the *up* icon links up to the top of whatever set of documents you are looking at. Thus, if you had chosen to visit the High Performance Computing section, then the *up* icon would bring you back to the High Performance

Computing home page. In turn, the *Info* icon refers to a page giving a brief description of IRC and its mandate, while the *Help* icon connects to a page that briefly describes the meanings of all the icons. Finally, the *Mail* icon links to a gateway program on the HTTP server that allows the user to send mail to the server administrator, while the *Search* icon links to a different gateway program that allows the user to do keyword searches on the collection of HTML documents. Note that all these icons are equipped with an **ALT** attribute text alternative. If you are going to use icons for navigation, be sure that people using a text-only browser can see what the icons mean!

Having navigation icons is extremely important, particularly when you have a very large number of related hypertext documents. It is very easy to get lost when you are browsing through large collections. Hypertext is not like a book, where you can always tell where you are by the page number or the thickness of the remaining pages. Navigation icons replace these tactile methods of navigation with symbols that link you to reference points within the collection. In addition, icons can direct users to general services that may be useful wherever they are in a collection, such as a search tool for searching a database or a mail tool for sending an electronic message to the site administrator.

The very top of this home page shows a text-only variant of the navigation icons (see Figures 1.17 to 1.19). This was added for contrast with the iconic approach. Text or icons, both add the same functionality, and choosing one or the other is largely a matter of taste. Text-based navigation aids can take up less space on a page and do not require that the client software access the server to obtain the icon images. If you do use icons, the latter problem is mitigated by using the same icons in all your pages. Most Web clients *cache* (retain local) copies of images once they have been accessed, and don't bother to retrieve them from the server when they are required on subsequent occasions.

Image downloading problems can also be alleviated by using small icons and a reduced number of colors per image. Most of the GIF-format icons included in the document shown in Figure 1.17 and displayed in Figure 1.18 are only 36 pixels square and contain only 16 colors each (4 bits/pixel), and as a result, they take up only 280 bytes each. Consequently, downloading the icons to the browser is fast, even over a dial-up connection.

Lessons from Example 3

1. A home page should be small and should not contain many large images. It should also be designed to be usable if accessed by a browser that has image loading disabled.

2. Home pages should clearly and concisely describe the contents of a Web site and should contain hypertext links to these resources.

3. All included images should contain appropriate **ALT** text descriptions, and should use the **HEIGHT** and **WIDTH** attributes to specify the image size.

4. A home page should explain and introduce navigation icons if they are used, and if their function is not obvious to the user.

5. Home pages should contain contact information for the administrator of the documents managed at the site.

Exercises for Example 3

Figure 1.17 was very simple, designed only to illustrate the basic design features of a home page. As an exercise, try visiting several Web sites, examining how they follow (or don't!) these design principles. To test a page properly, you should first access it with you browser's image loading disabled (to check how well it works without images). You can then load in the images, and see how long it takes—and how good it looks! Here are some sample Web sites (from amongst millions):

```
http://home.netscape.com
http://www.microsoft.com
http://www.sgi.com
http://www.cnet.com
http://www.nando.net
```

References

There is much documentation on HTML available on the Web itself. The best place to start is the World Wide Web FAQ. Thanks to Thomas Boutell, the Web Frequently Asked Questions (FAQ) list is one of the most useful collections of information on the Web. Sections of this list are posted regularly on relevant newsgroups, while the entire FAQ is available in hypertext form at the URL given in the following paragraph, and at many mirror sites. USENET newsgroups devoted to World Wide Web and HTML issues are a good place to see announcements of new products or services, to ask questions, or to hear of the latest WWW happenings. There are also several Web sites offering introductions to the Web and HTML, and lists of links to other useful resources.

World Wide Web FAQ List
```
http://www.boutell.com/faq/
```

Web USENET Newsgroups
The following is a list of all the active World Wide Web newsgroups, and their associated subjects. Please, post messages only to the appropriate groups, and *cross-post* when sending the same message to more than one group!

comp.infosystems.www.advocacy	Political and other advocacy issues
comp.infosystems.www.announce	Announcements of new sites or services (moderated)

comp.infosystems.www.authoring.cgi	CGI programming
comp.infosystems.www.authoring.html	HTML authoring issues
comp.infosystems.www.authoring.images	Images in Web documents, including image formats, format conversions, and imagemaps
comp.infosystems.www.authoring.misc	Miscellaneous Web authoring issues
comp.infosystems.www.browsers.mac	Macintosh browsers
comp.infosystems.www.browsers.misc	Miscellaneous browser issues
comp.infosystems.www.browsers.ms-windows	MS-Windows Web browsers
comp.infosystems.www.browsers.x	X-Windows Web browsers
comp.infosystems.www.marketplace	Miscellaneous marketplace musings …
comp.infosystems.www.servers.mac	Macintosh HTTP servers
comp.infosystems.www.servers.misc	Miscellaneous HTTP server issues
comp.infosystems.www.servers.ms-windows	Windows 3.1/95/NT HTTP servers
comp.infosystems.www.servers.unix	UNIX HTTP servers
comp.os.os2.networking.www	Web issues related to IBM OS/2
bionet.software.www	WWW applications in the biological sciences

User Surveys of WWW Resources
http://www.cc.gatech.edu/gvu/user_surveys/

Introductory HTML and Web References
http://www.utoronto.ca/webdocs/HTMLdocs/NewHTML/intro.html
http://oneworld.wa.com/htmldev/devpage/dev-page.html
http://cbl.leeds.ac.uk/nikos/doc/repository.html
http://coney.gsfc.nasa.gov/www/sswg/candy_style.html

Guide to Browser Capabilities—Browsercaps
http://www.pragmaticainc.com/bc/index.html

Yahoo List of HTML-related Web Resources
http://www.yahoo.com/yahoo/Computers/World_Wide_Web/HTML/

HTML and Document Design

Chapter 1 introduced the philosophy behind the HTML language. It also used example documents to illustrate the basic elements of an HTML document: headings, lists, character highlighting, images, horizontal rule dividers, and, most important, hypertext anchors. In this chapter, we look again at these elements, focusing on advanced features and document design issues. Here also, you will find an introduction to some other important HTML elements—**BLOCKQUOTE, OL** (ordered list), **FORM,** and **TABLE** elements—that significantly enrich the vocabulary of HTML document authors.

The examples are again designed to illustrate the proper use of these elements, and to point out some common mistakes. Since most browsers do not check for incorrect HTML, it is easy to write badly formed HTML documents that look fine on one browser, but awful on another—document authors need to be careful to avoid this problem. In addition, these examples reflect design issues that are important when creating a page. For example, what are good and bad ways to include hypertext anchors, or image files? Although there are no perfect ways, the examples are designed to illustrate the characteristics and limitations of the Web, thereby showing why some design choices are better than others.

This chapter is structured as a tutorial to HTML design, so the examples are relatively simple. Chapter 12 presents a discussion of Web site implementation and planning, and includes several complex examples of page design that make use of more advanced aspects of HTML coding.

Example 4: Linear Hypertext—PRE and BLOCKQUOTE

This example, illustrated in Figures 2.1 through 2.6, demonstrates the construction of a hypertext collection of text-based documents. One common use of HTML is to prepare on-line documentation, or on-line collections of reference materials. These can be very large collections of documents, not only with some overall hierarchical structure (such as sections and subsections), but also with many hypertext links *cross-linking* these documents and linking them to other resources on the Internet. Frequently, the root structure of a collection of documents is linear, reflecting its origin as a printed manual, or its logical presentation as a readable, linear collection. This is not necessarily a bad thing—after all, books are a rather successful communication medium. Furthermore, while hypertext allows for nonlinear representations of information, linear models may be the best match for user needs.

The PRE Element

Figures 2.1 and 2.2 introduce the **PRE** element. This element contains preformatted text for presentation as-is, preserving the space characters and carriage returns typed into the HTML document, and displaying the characters using a fixed-width typewriter font. You can use **PRE** to display computer codes, text examples, or verbatim text sequences. This is also one way you can create tables for display in an HTML document, since this element preserves the horizontal spacing needed to align columns.

You can include character emphasis within a **PRE**, so that you can use **STRONG** and **EM** to emphasize certain text strings. You can also include hypertext anchors. Tags do not add width to the displayed text, so you can use them to add highlighting or hypertext anchors without affecting vertical alignment of text. The usefulness of the **PRE** element is illustrated in Figure 4.14 (Chapter 4), where it is used to display both program code and a small table. Anchors and text highlighting elements are the only HTML elements allowed within a **PRE**; other elements, such as **IMG, P**, heading elements, list elements, **BLOCKQUOTE** (for quotations), and **ADDRESS** elements, are prohibited.

The BLOCKQUOTE Element

Figures 2.1 and 2.2, as well as Figures 2.13 and 2.14, illustrate another new element: **BLOCKQUOTE**. This element marks block quotations, such as an extract from a book or speech. Blockquoted text is often indented by browsers, so that HTML authors sometimes use this element simply to indent text (as done in the examples). This is not the true intent of **BLOCKQUOTE**—but it does work, and it is one of the few ways you can currently create indented sections. In the long run, *stylesheets* (discussed in Chapter 5) are the better way to apply indentation or other styles to paragraphs or other blocks of text. Unfortunately, stylesheets are not yet widely implemented.

Document Collections: Some Design Issues

The design of document collections is discussed in more detail in the next chapter. However, some major points are apparent in this example, so it makes sense to discuss them here.

1. **Each document should be small.** Each document should display no more than two or three screens full of data. The advantage of the hypertext model lies in the linking of various components of the document web. This advantage is often lost if you are viewing a single, huge document containing hundreds or thousands of lines of displayed text. Although you can build hypertext links within a document to other points inside the same document, this is generally more difficult to navigate than a collection of smaller files.

2. **Each document should have navigation tools.** These are simply hypertext links that connect the document to other documents in the hierarchy and to general navigation points within the collection. Thus, each page should have links to *next* and *previous* documents (if there is an obvious order to the pages) and to a table of contents or the section heading. If the document is big, say more than two or three screens full of text, then it might be a good idea to place the navigation icons at both the top and bottom of the document, to make them easier to find.

3. **Every document should show a consistent presentation style.** Each document should be consistently designed, with the same heading structure, the same navigation icons, and similar content outlines. This makes it easy to get the *feel* for the collection, and also makes it possible to index or catalog the collection using programs that take advantage of this structure.

Artistic license is, of course, allowed! But these are general guidelines, based on experience, that will help to make your work more pleasing and easier to use.

Figure 2.1 HTML listing for the document *hrule.html*, a typical text-only HTML document.

```
<html>
<head><title> HR element in HTML </title></head>
<body>
[<a href="htmlindex.html">Index</a>]
```

Figure 2.1 (Continued)

```
[<a href="body.html">Up</a>]
[<a href="lists_reg.html">Back</a>]
[<a href="entities.html">Next</a>]


<H1> 4.7 Horizontal Ruled Line </H1>

The HR element is used to draw a horizontal dividing
line completely across the screen. This can be
to logically separate blocks of text, or to separate
icon lists from the body of the text.

<p> The HR element is empty (you don't need a <code>&lt;/HR></code>).

<h2> Example </h2>
The following shows an example of the use of &lt;HR>
and the resulting rendering (on your browser).
<blockquote>
<pre>
The following document is scanned from the back of
a cereal box.  To see the scanned image, press the
icon at the bottom of the text ....
&lt;HR>
&lt;H1> MIGHTY CHOKEE-OS! &lt;/H1>
The cereal of chocolate deprived kiddies everywhere!
&lt;p> Aren't you lucky your parents love you enough
to buy you CHOCKEE-OS!
&lt;p> Remember to ask Mom and Dad for NEW SUPER
CHOCKEE-OS, now with Nicotine!!
</pre>
</blockquote>
<p> <b> This is rendered as:</b>
<p> The following document is scanned from the back of a
cereal box.  To see the scanned image, press the icon at
the bottom of the text ....
<HR>
<H1> MIGHTY CHOKEE-OS! </H1>
The cereal of chocolate deprived kiddies everywhere!
<p> Aren't you lucky your parents love you enough
to buy you CHOCKEE-OS!
<p> Remember to ask Mom and Dad for NEW SUPER CHOCKEE-OS,
now with Nicotine!!!
<hr>
<p> [<a href="htmlindex.html">Index</a>]
[<a href="body.html">Up</a>]
[<a href="lists_reg.html">Back</a>]
[<a href="entities.html">Next</a>]
</body></html>
```

Figure 2.2 (the HTML listing is in Figure 2.1) shows an example HTML document from a large collection of related files. This particular example is one of approximately 70 documents that discuss various aspects of the HTML language. This collection of documents can be accessed at the URL:

```
http://www.utoronto.ca/webdocs/HTMLdocs/NewHTML/htmlindex.html
```

Flat or Serial Document Collections

The documents in Figures 2.1 and 2.3 are a part of a *flat* collection of documents—all the files are linked together in a serial fashion, like pages in a book. However, there are also many hypertext

Figure 2.2 Mosaic For X-Windows display of a typical text-only document (*hrule.html*).

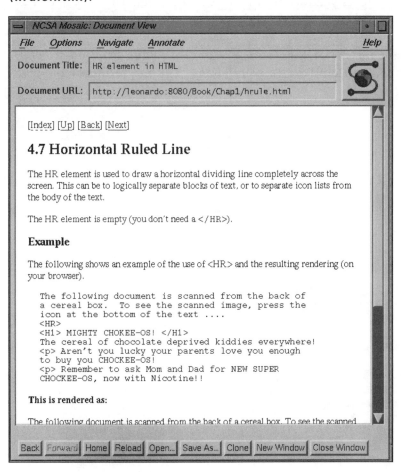

links relating the documents in non-serial ways; for example, one document discussing the **IMG** element has a sentence mentioning URLs, which contains a hypertext link to a document giving a more detailed discussion of URLs. The documents are also ordered hierarchically. Thus, the document discussing the **HR** element is *under* the **BODY** document, which is, in turn, *under* the Table of Contents (see Figure 2.4). The Table of Contents page contains hypertext links to all the documents in the collection and is an easy tool for quickly finding and accessing a particular section.

Navigation Buttons

Note the navigation text icons at the top of the page in Figure 2.2. There are four navigation buttons: *Index*, *Up*, *Back*, and *Next*. The *Index* button takes you directly to a Table of Contents page, while the *Up* button takes you one level up in the hierarchy—in this case, to the **BODY** page. The *Back* button takes you backward to the preceding document in the sequence, while the *Next* button takes you forward to the next document. The *Back* and *Next* buttons are the ones to use if you want to read the document straight through.

Figure 2.3 HTML source document for the Table of Contents Page *htmlindex.html*. Some of this document has been omitted to save space. The rendering of the document is shown in Figure 2.4.

```
<html><head>
<title> HTML Documentation Table of Contents</title>
</head>
<body>
<h1> HTML Documentation Table of Contents </h1>
<dl>
  <dt><a href="htmlindex.html">Table of Contents (this page)</a>
  <dt><a href="about_the_author.html">About the Author</a>
</dl>
<ol>
  <li><a href="intro.html">Introduction to this Document</a>
  <li><a href="html_intro.html">Introduction to HTML </a>
  <ol>
    <li><a href="elements.html">HTML Elements</a>
    <li><a href="doc_struct.html">HTML Document Structure</a>
    <li><a href="naming.html">HTML Document Naming Scheme</a>
  </ol>
  <li><a href="head.html">HEAD</a> of an HTML Document
    <ol>
      <li><a href="title.html">TITLE</a>
      <li><a href="isindex.html">ISINDEX</a>
      <li><a href="nextid.html">NEXTID</a>
      <li><a href="link.html">LINK</a>
      <li><a href="base.html">BASE</a>
    </ol>
  <li><a href="body.html">BODY</a> of an HTML Document
    <ol>
```

Figure 2.3 (Continued)

```
      <li><a href="headings.html">Headings</a> (Hn)
      <li><a href="paragraph.html">Paragraphs</a> (P)
      <li><a href="line_break.html">Line Breaks</a> (BR)
. . .
    </ol>
. . .
</ol>
</body></html>
```

Figure 2.4 Table of Contents page (*htmlindex.html*, listed in Figure 2.3) for the HTML document collection containing the file *hrule.html* (shown in Figure 2.1). This collection of documents can be accessed at:

`http://www.utoronto.ca/webdocs/HTMLdocs/NewHTML/htmlindex.html`

These documents are updated on a regular basis.

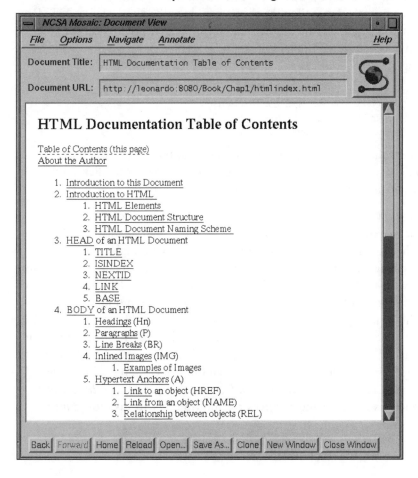

Table of Contents Page

Figure 2.4 shows the HTML Table of Contents document for this collection (the listing is in Figure 2.3), although only a portion appears within the window. Notice how it gives a complete overview of the document tree, including the relative placement of the sections in the hierarchy and the hypertext links to each section. This table of contents was constructed by hand—a tedious process, to say the least. Fortunately, there are programs that can automatically generate a hypertext table of contents directly from the HTML document collection, using the headings embedded in the documents to create both section names and the hierarchical organization. This is another good reason to use appropriate heading elements. Information about these indexing tools is provided in Chapter 11.

General Design Issues: Offering Alternative Formats

There are several other organizational features that you may want to employ. For example, you might want to provide a printable version of a document collection. If so, you can combine the documents and present them as a single, large file that clients can download and read as HTML or print (from their browsers) as a single text file. However, you should let users know what to expect. For example, you can add text in the table of contents or some other page that provides information like the following:

```
<p> This entire archive of documents is also available as a
    single <A HREF="alldocs.html">concatenated HTML document</A>
    (198 Kbytes), suitable for printing.  Note, however, that
    the hypertext links in this document have been removed.</P>
```

This guides users to a document that can be both viewed and printed, but also warns that the file is big, and that certain facilities are not present. They can then choose whether to click on the phrase "concatenated HTML document" and access this resource.

In some cases, you might want to make the entire document collection available as an archive. Then, users who make extensive use of the documents can copy the entire HTML collection and install it on their own machine. If you are using a PC, you might make such an archive using the PKZIP package. This allows you to archive files and directories into a single compressed file, usually with the filename extension *.zip*. Thus, you could pkzip all the files in the document collection into a file called ***alldocs.zip***. StuffIt is a common archiving program on a Macintosh; the resulting archive would be named ***alldocs.sit***. UNIX users will use a program called tar (for tape archiver), which would result in the archive file ***alldocs.tar***. UNIX also has two programs for compressing files: compress, which places a .Z at the end of the compressed filename, and gzip, which places a .z at the end of the compressed filename. This would yield the compressed archive files ***alldocs.tar.Z*** (using compress) or ***alldocs.tar.z***. (using gzip). If you were generous in preparing archives for multiple platforms, you might prepare a document pointing to these files. An example of such a document is shown in Figures 2.5 and 2.6.

Most HTTP server programs let you control access to certain files or directories on the server, and restrict access to authorized users. You might for example choose to control access to archives, should there be copyright problems associated with the archive content.

Nesting of List Elements

As a final HTML aside, note that Figure 2.6 illustrates how different types of lists can be nested. Here, an unordered list element (**UL**) is nested inside an *ordered list* (**OL**):

```
<OL>
    <LI><A HREF="alldocs.zip">.........
    .
    .
    <LI><A HREF="alldocs.html">alldocs.html</A> (523 Kbytes) .....
        Concatenated HTML documents </EM>
    <UL>
        <LI>(This is a concatenation of the .....
    </UL>
</OL>
```

The browser does exactly what you would expect, and simply nests one list inside the other. In HTML, any type of list can be nested within another list. Recall, however, that you cannot put lists inside headings, or headings inside lists.

Lessons from Example 4

1. **PRE** tags surround blocks of text to display the text with a fixed-width font, preserving the spaces, tabs, and line breaks of the actual text. Text emphasis and anchor elements are allowed inside **PRE**; other elements such as **Hn**, and **IMG** are not permitted.

2. **BLOCKQUOTE** is for block quotations, and usually displays the enclosed text with indented margins. This is often used as a trick to introduce text indentation.

3. Collections of documents should have a consistent design to make them easy to navigate. Where appropriate, you should also create a hypertext table of contents. There are programs available that can help you do this, some of which are discussed in Chapter 11.

4. You should use navigation icons (or text keywords instead of pictures) as hypertext links to help the user navigate through the document collection. If you use icons, make sure that you provide a text-only navigation option (use that **ALT** attribute!) for users with non-graphical browsers.

Figure 2.5 Example HTML document *src_link.html* that contains links to alternative formats of a document collection. Clicking on the items retrieves the archives to the client's machine.

```
<HTML>
<HEAD><TITLE> Archives of this Documentation </TITLE></HEAD>
<BODY>
<H2> Document Archives </H2>
<p> Archives of the document collection are available in the following
formats:
<OL>
<LI><A HREF="alldocs.zip">alldocs.zip</A>    (138 Kbytes) -- <EM> DOS PKZIP  </EM>
<LI><A HREF="alldocs.sit">alldocs.sit</A>    (532 Kbytes) -- <EM> Macintosh
     Stuffit</EM>
<LI><A HREF="alldocs.tar">alldocs.tar</A>    (527 Kbytes) -- <EM> UNIX tar </EM>
<LI><A HREF="alldocs.tar.Z">alldocs.tar.Z</A> (133 Kbytes) -- <EM> UNIX tar
     (compressed)</EM>
<LI><A HREF="alldocs.tar.z">alldocs.tar.z</A> (104 Kbytes) -- <EM> UNIX tar
     (gnuzipped) </EM>
<LI><A HREF="alldocs.html">alldocs.html </A> (523 Kbytes) -- <EM> Concatenated
     HTML documents </EM>
     <UL>
        <LI><EM>This is a concatenation of the HTML documents, suitable for
             printing from a browser. The Hypertext links have been removed.</EM>
     </UL>
</OL>
<HR NOSHADE>
<B>Last Update:</B> <EM>12 July 1996</EM> --
&lt;<A HREF="mailto:prof.plum@clue.com">prof.plum@clue.com</a>&gt;
</BODY>
</HTML>
```

5. Single HTML documents should be small and self-contained. Larger documents should be broken up into smaller documents to best take advantage of the hypertext approach.

6. Sometimes a *flat*, printable document is also desirable. You can concatenate your HTML files together to make such a document, and then create a hypertext link to it, but be sure to include information about the size of this file (if it is large) so that the user knows what to expect.

Exercises for Example 4

There are several examples of book-like document collections—have a look at them, and see how they compare with the model described here. Some examples are:

```
http://www.utoronto.ca/webdocs/HTMLdocs/NewHTML/htmlindex.html
http://info.med.yale.edu/caim/StyleManual_Top.HTML
```

Figure 2.6 Rendering of the HTML document *src_link.html* (shown in Figure 2.5) by the Internet Explorer 3.0 browser.

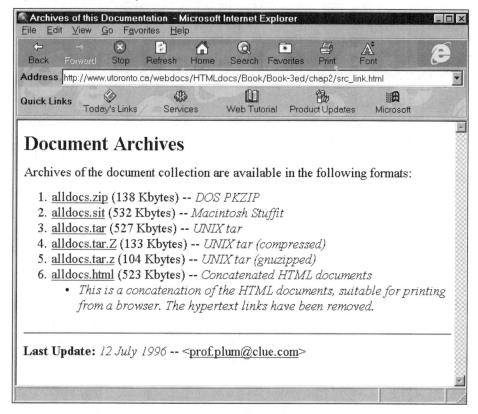

Navigational icons are found in almost all document collections, not just book-like ones. The next time you are on the Web, look for these navigational icons, and note how their presence makes it much easier to navigate within the collection.

Example 5: Linking to Data—Images, Movies, Sound, and Other File Types

As mentioned earlier, WWW browsers can display only certain image formats, and sometimes restrict GIF images to fewer than 50 or so displayed colors per image. It was also pointed out that small images are advantageous, since large images can take a long time to download and are often irritating for that reason alone.

However, sometimes these restrictions are unreasonable. Often you need to include a large image that is an important part of your material, such as a still from a movie (if you are a publicity site for a film), or a campus map that can be *clicked* on to access information about various campus buildings. For both of these cases, a tiny image is unacceptable. Alternatively, you may have truly high-quality GIF images containing 256 colors, or perhaps non-GIF format images, and want to make them available for viewing. Perhaps you even have movie or sound files. How can these be included in a document and presented to your clients?

Large Image—Small File

If you need a large image on a main page, the key is to make the image *file* small. Remember that GIF and JPEG store images in a compressed format. As a result, you can often process images so that the image file is small, even if the image itself is very large. Chapter 10 discusses these and other issues associated with processing images for use on the Web.

Linking to Pages with Large Images

If you have a secondary page containing large image files, good design requires that you warn the user of what to expect, by placing a note near the hypertext anchor pointing to this secondary page. This gives the user the option of accessing the page as is, disabling image loading when accessing the page, or not accessing the document altogether.

Thumbnail Sketches

A *thumbnail sketch* is a particularly useful way of linking to a large image. A *thumbnail* is simply a small icon of the actual image—either a size reduction or some characteristic portion of the image. Thumbnails are easy to make with almost any commercial or public-domain image editing program. You can then include the thumbnail in your document, and make a hypertext link from the thumbnail to the document containing the large image, or to the image itself. This is what was done in Figures 2.7 and 2.8, where the small images are links to larger images or to movie files. In this example, the thumbnail of the larger GIF image is only 1,500 bytes, one tenth the size of the original file. Note that sizes of the linked documents are also given—these are big files! Extra information such as this is useful to readers, as it lets them know what to expect.

Linking to Other Data Types

Anchors can indicate links to anything—not just HTML documents or images. There are many different audio, movie, multimedia, and image formats, and most clients are capable of displaying only a subset of them. Therefore, it is often a good idea to indicate the format of large data files, so that users can avoid accessing files they cannot view or use. In Figure 2.8, for example, the text indicates that the linked image file is a GIF and that the linked movie is in MPEG format.

Helper Applications

So far our hypertext links have been to HTML documents or to HTML documents containing images via the **IMG** element. What happens if these links connect to other media, such as image files, movie files, or sound files? Most World Wide Web browsers are not capable of displaying these data formats. So, what do they do?

When these data are linked using hypertext anchors, the answer lies in so-called *helper* or *viewer* applications. These are programs on the user's computer that can display images, movies, or sounds that cannot be handled by the browser itself. Thus, in Figure 2.8, the large-screen image was produced by clicking on the top image icon in the browser window, which caused the browser to retrieve the data accessed by this link, acknowledge the data to be an image file, and launch the appropriate helper application to display the image (in this case, the UNIX image viewing program xv). In the case of the movie file, the browser knew that the data was an MPEG movie, so it started up the program mpeg_play to display the video information.

Downloaded Data and MIME Types

How does the browser know what a file contains and what to do with it? Whenever data is retrieved from an HTTP server, the server, as part of the HTTP protocol, explicitly tells the browser the type of data being sent. It does this with a special message that is sent to the client just before the actual data, called a *MIME content-type* header. For a GIF image file, it looks like this:

```
Content-Type: image/gif
```

and for an MPEG movie, it looks like this:

```
Content-Type: video/mpeg
```

When the browser receives this message, and if the browser cannot itself display the data, it looks in its database of *helper* applications to find the program that matches this *MIME type*. If it finds a program to help, it passes the data to the program and lets it do its job.

If the data come from an FTP server, or if the browser is accessing the file from the local machine and not from an HTTP server, then the browser has to guess at the data content. It does this from the filename *extension*. Each browser has a database that matches filename extensions to the appropriate MIME type, and uses this database to determine the MIME types of files accessed locally or via FTP. In general, this database will map the *.gif* suffix to the image/gif MIME type, the suffixes *.jpeg* or *.jpg* for JPEG images and the suffixes *.mpeg*, *.mpg*, or *.mpe* to the video/mpeg MIME type. These lists have to be updated if you add a new filename extension. With most Macintosh and Microsoft Windows browsers, the lists can be edited from a pull-down menu.

Figure 2.7 The HTML document *vortex.html*, showing links from image icons to full-size images and video sequences. Figure 2.8 shows the rendering of this document by the Mosaic for X-Windows browser.

```
<HTML>
<HEAD>
<TITLE>Simulated Vortex Dynamics in a Porous-Body Wake</TITLE>
</HEAD>
<BODY>
<H1>Simulated Vortex Dynamics in a Porous-Body Wake</H1>
<P>This video presents the result of a numerical simulation on the wake
generated by a porous body.  The wake flow is simulated by inserting
small-scale discrete vortices into a uniform stream,  and  the colors
in the video represent the magnitude of vorticity.   The initial flow
field is subjected to a small perturbation based on experimental data.
The evolution of the wake flow is  manifested  by the merging  and
interactions of the small-scale vortices.
<P>The objective of this investigation is to study the merging and
inter-action processes of vortices and the formation of large eddies in
the flow.  Such an investigation is of importance to many flow-related
industrial and environmental problems, such as mixing, cooling,
combustion and dispersion of air-borne or water-borne contaminants.<P>
<HR>
<B> <A HREF="legend.gif"><IMG SRC="legicon.gif"
ALIGN=Bottom> Initial flow</A> and color legend for vorticity.</B>
(14.5 KB gif image)<p>
<HR>
<B> <A HREF="flow.mpeg"><IMG SRC="vortex.gif" ALT="[movie icon]"
ALIGN=Bottom> Visualization</A> of the evolution of the wake flow.</B>
(0.38 MB mpeg-1 movie)<p>
</BODY></HTML>
```

There are literally dozens of MIME types for data ranging from images and audio and video clips to compressed archives and executable programs. The use of MIME types is discussed in more detail in Chapter 7, and in Appendix B.

Lessons from Example 5

1. Warn users when you present a link to a large image document or file, so that they can estimate how long it will take to download the data.

2. List the data format in your links to large image, audio, movie, or data archive files so that users can tell if the file is in a format they can actually use.

3. You can use icons to link to larger image or movie files. This lets users know what to expect, and is often a good graphical addition to your document.

Figure 2.8 The Mosaic for X-Windows rendering of the document listed in Figure 2.7, showing thumbnail image icons linked to full-size image files, movie files, and sound files. The picture overlaid on the browser resulted from clicking on the image icon at the top of the screen, while the movie—playing window was launched by pressing on the icon at the middle of the screen. This page and the associated images and movies are courtesy of Rudy Ziegler of the University of Toronto High Performance Research Computing Group, while the data yielding the displayed image and movie frame were provided by Z. Huang, J. G. Kawall, and J. F. Keffer of the Department of Mechanical Engineering at the University of Toronto.

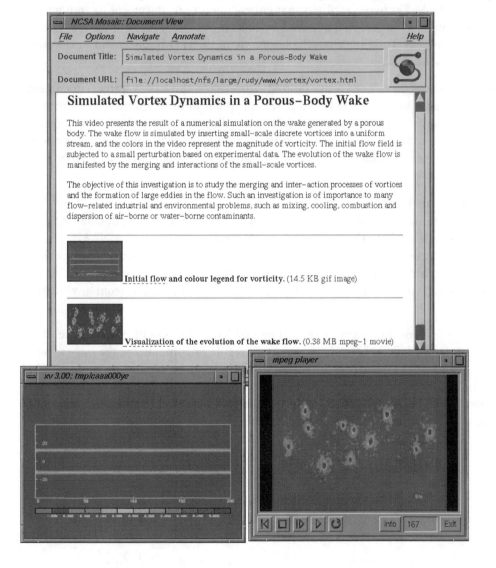

Exercises for Example 5

While you are Web surfing, try and keep track of how long it takes for a file to arrive—if you have a watch, try and time this. You will no doubt grow frustrated after only a few seconds. Now imagine how users will feel if they choose to download one of your files only to discover that they will need to wait *several minutes* for the data to arrive and be displayed. Now try and imagine how happy this makes them feel....

Example 6: Linking within a Document

Up until now, we have looked at hypertext links that either connect one document to another, or a document to other data resources. When one of these links is activated, the browser retrieves the linked object, and displays it starting from the beginning of the HTML document or the start of the data file.

With HTML documents, this is not always desired. Sometimes, the linked (target) document is actually quite long, and you want to link to a particular point in the document, and not to the beginning. Alternatively, you may want to link between different places in the *same* document—for example, from a short list of sections to the beginning of each section. This is possible with HTML, but requires the use of an additional feature of the anchor element—the **NAME** attribute.

Anchor Element: The NAME Attribute

Links to particular locations in a document, or between locations in the same document, are made possible through the **NAME** attribute of the **A** (anchor) element. The **NAME** attribute lets you assign a unique name, called a *fragment identifier*, to a particular place in a document. You can then link to this particular named location using a special form of URL that contains this name. You can do this from within the same document, or from any other document.

Figure 2.9 shows a document containing several named locations, and illustrating one of the common uses of named locations—to create a simple table of contents for the page. The top of the page contains links that access the different sections of the document, while each section contains links that allow you to return to the top of the page, and back to the contents listing. This page was originally developed by the author and Sian Meikle of the University of Toronto Library, and is part of a template document collection we distribute to university departments interested in developing their own document collections. The entire template is located at:

`http://www.utoronto.ca/ian/Template/readme.html`

Figure 2.9 A Typical HTML document, *deptinfo.html,* that contains named anchor elements. Portions of the document have been omitted to save space. Comments are in italics, while markers indicating the named anchors are in boldface italics.

```
<HTML> <HEAD>
   <TITLE> Biology Department: General Information  </TITLE> </HEAD>
<BODY>
<A HREF="depthome.html" NAME="top"><IMG SRC="home.gif" ALT="[home]"></A>
<HR>
<IMG SRC="french2.gif" ALT="[Picture of our Building]">
<H1>Biology at the University of Toronto</H1>
<ADDRESS>
   University of Toronto            <BR>
   150 St George Street, Room 213 <BR>
   Toronto Ontario M5S 1A1 CANADA <BR>
   <B>Tel:</B>     (416)-978-7000  <BR>
   <B>Fax:</B>     (416)-978-9000  <BR>
   <B>E-mail:</B>
<a href="mailto:infobiol@biology.utoronto.ca">infobiol@biology.utoronto.ca</a>
</ADDRESS>
<HR>
<B>On this page:</B>
[<A HREF="#general">General Information</A>]
[<A HREF="#facilities">Research Facilities</A>]
[<A HREF="#history">Department History</A>] [<-- References Named Anchor]
<HR>

<H2><A NAME="general">General</A></H2>
<BLOCKQUOTE>
 <P>
  <EM> This is an example document only.There is no need, for example, to
   have all this information on a single page. There is one advantage,
   however, to keeping this material together -- it allows the user to
   print the entire document for reading away from the computer.</EM>
</BLOCKQUOTE>

<P> The University of Toronto is the largest university in Canada
   with 2500 graduate faculty and more than 9000 full and part-time graduate
   students. Metropolitan Toronto has a population of 3,000,000 people
   who provide a rich multicultural mix and create an interesting and
   stimulating environment outside the University.</P>

        [text deleted ...]
<H2><A NAME="facilities">Research Facilities</a></H2>
```

Figure 2.9 (Continued)

```
<P> The Department provides many facilities to aid astronomical research,
    and students and staff use national and international observatories
    all over the world and in space. The Department has a special fund for
    students to pay for travel to such observatories as the UTSO in Chile,
    CFHT in Hawaii, the VLA in New Mexico, and the IUE satellite
    groundstation in Maryland.</P>

    [text deleted]
[<a HREF="#top">... to top of page</A>
<H2><A NAME="history">History of the Department</A> </H2> [<--Named Anchor]

<P> Biology became a major department in 1905.  The first chair of
    the Department, Dr. Roland Fishburn, introduced several teaching
    programs in aid of the Faculty of Medicine, and went on to
    develop major programs in Bological Research. This led to the
    construction of the Biology Building in 1911, constructed on
.......[more text deleted]
[<a HREF="#top">... to top of page</A>
<HR>
<a HREF="depthome.html"><IMG SRC="icons/home.gif" ALT="[home]"></A>
</BODY> </HTML>
```

NAME Attribute and Fragment Identifiers

There are four named anchors in Figure 2.9, but for this discussion, we will focus on the one for the history section. The relevant hypertext anchor is:

```
<A NAME="history">History of the Department</A>
```

This anchor associates a *fragment identifier*, history, with this location. Looking at Figure 2.10, you will see that this section of text is not rendered by the browser in any special way. In general, an anchor that contains only a **NAME** attribute is not specially displayed. From elsewhere in this document, this location can be referenced using a URL of the form:

```
<A HREF="#history">Department History</A>
```

as seen in Figure 2.9. Note how the fragment identifier is indicated by *prepending* the hash character (#), to distinguish this from a regular URL. If the user clicks on the anchored text *Department History*, the browser will search for the named fragment identifier and scroll the page down to that location, as illustrated in Figure 2.11.

NAME and HREF Combined

A hypertext reference can simultaneously take both **HREF** and **NAME** attributes. An example is shown in the very first anchor in Figure 2.9, namely:

```
<A HREF="depthome.html" NAME="top"><IMG SRC="home.gif" ALT="[home]"></A>
```

Clicking on this anchor links the user to the document ***depthome.html*** (you will note in Figure 2.10, this image is highlighted as a linked hypertext anchor). At the same time, clicking on internal page links of the form:

```
<a HREF="#top">... to top of page</A>
```

Figure 2.10 Netscape Navigator rendering of the document *deptinfo.html* shown in Figure 2.9.

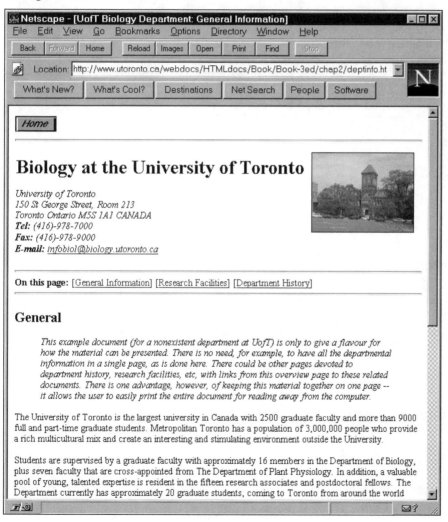

Figure 2.11 Netscape Navigator rendering of the document *deptinfo.html* shown in Figure 2.9 after accessing the internal link referenced by the text string "Department History," shown at the top of Figure 2.10.

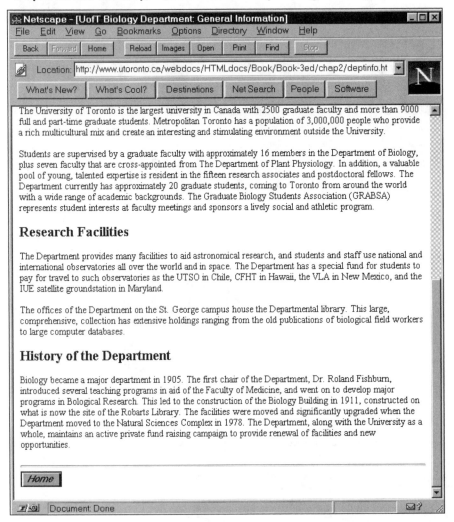

returns the user to the top of the page and to this same linked image. Thus, anchors can be both the start and destination of a hypertext link.

Fragment Identifiers and Full URLs

You can also access named locations from outside the document. This is done by *appending* the fragment identifier to the document's locator string. For example, if the full URL for the document *deptinfo.html* is:

```
http://www.utoronto.ca/ian/Template/deptinfo.html
```

then the URL that explicitly references the history section is just (with the fragment identifier in boldface):

```
http://www.utoronto.ca/ian/Template/deptinfo.html#history
```

Figure 2.12 schematically illustrates some of the more common uses of named anchors. Details about writing valid fragment identifiers and URLs are found in Chapter 6.

Lessons from Example 6

1. The **NAME** attribute assigns a name, called a *fragment identifier*, to an **A** (anchor) element. This allows an anchor to be the *destination* of a hypertext link, and allows for hypertext **HREF** anchors that target specific locations within a given document.

2. You can reference a **NAME**d location from within the same document using an anchor element of the form `<A HREF="#`*frag_id*`">anchor text</A>`, where *frag_id* is the fragment identifier you wish to reference. The hash character is mandatory, and indicates the start of a fragment identifier.

3. You can reference a **NAME**d location from any other document by appending the fragment identifier to the URL of the document, for example:

   ```
   <A HREF="http://bla.bla.edu/Projects/doc2.html#frag_id">anchor text</A>.
   ```

4. You can combine **HREF** and **NAME** anchors in the same anchor element:

   ```
   <A HREF="URL_string" NAME="frag_id" >anchor text</A>.
   ```

   This means that the anchor is both the start of one hypertext link and the possible destination of others.

Exercises for Example 6

Create a long HTML document (e.g., convert a word-processor document to HTML) and build some internal links between a contents list and the various sections. Note how much easier it is to read the document when these internal navigational tools are available.

Figure 2.12 Schematic illustrating the use of NAME and HREF attributes. The dashed lines indicate hypertext links and their destinations. Links (A) and (E) are absolute URLs, while (B) and (D) are partial URLs between two documents in the same directory. (C) is an internal link within the document *deptinfo.html*. The base URL for both documents is:

```
http://www.utoronto.ca/ian/Template/
```

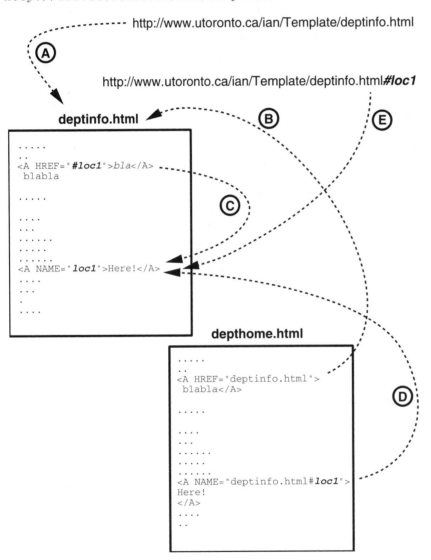

Example 7: Image, Heading, and Paragraph Alignment

As discussed in Example 2, HTML 2.0 allows for rudimentary control over the placement and alignment of images or text on the page. Recent extensions to HTML allow for significant improvement in control over this aspect of document presentation. These extensions occur through the addition of **ALIGN** (alignment) attributes to the **Hn** (heading) and **P** (paragraph) elements, as well as the addition of **ALIGN** attribute values for **IMG**. These new attributes and their effects are shown in Figures 2.13 through 2.16.

Heading and Paragraph Alignment

In HTML 2.0, the **H1** through **H6** and **P** elements do not take attributes. HTML 3.2 supports a new attribute, **ALIGN**, for these elements. **ALIGN** defines the desired alignment for the element on the page, and can take the values "left" (left-justify the text: the default), "center" (center the text between the margins), "right" (right-justify the text), and "justify" (justify text between left and right margins). Currently, only left, center, and right are widely implemented. Figure 2.14 shows the effect of these different alignment options on the heading and paragraph elements. If a browser does not understand the value, it ignores the **ALIGN** attribute and uses the browser's alignment default (usually left-adjusted).

Image Alignment

Image alignment is more problematic than text alignment, since the desire is to let the image "float" to some preferred location, and then let the text flow around it. HTML 3.2 supports the use of **ALIGN** values of "left" and "right" for this purpose, where "left" causes the image to float to the left margin, and "right" causes the image to float to the right margin. Any text following the image, or included in the paragraph containing the image, flows around the image. Figures 2.15 and 2.16 show the effect of the left and right alignment values. Here the images have floated to the indicated margins, with text flowing around them.

Almost all browsers support this type of image alignment; however, some do not and simply place the image inline with the text. It is therefore a good idea to place an **IMG** as the first item in a line, or to precede it by a line break element. This guarantees that the image will appear as the first item in a line, regardless of the browser's limitations.

Image WIDTH and HEIGHT

To format the page, a browser must obviously know the size of the image being inserted. In general, a browser does not know this until the image is loaded, which means that it can't begin displaying the page until after the image has arrived. Because this can significantly delay the construction of the page, HTML 3.2 supports **IMG** element **HEIGHT** and **WIDTH** attributes, to specify the size of the image in pixels. Given this information, the browser can

Figure 2.13 HTML code for the document *align.html*. This document illustrates some of the alignment features possible with the heading and paragraph elements.

```
<HTML>
<HEAD><TITLE>
Heading and Paragraph Alignment Options
</TITLE></HEAD>
<BODY>
<H2 ALIGN="center"> Alignment Options: Headings and Paragraphs</H2>
<HR NOSHADE>
<BLOCKQUOTE>
<H3 ALIGN="left">Left-Aligned Paragraph &amp; Heading</H3>
<P>
Alignment can take the four values "center", "left" (the default), "
right" and "justify". This paragraph is "left" (default) aligned, so that
the text lines up with the left margin, and the right side is ragged.
<H3 ALIGN="right">Right-Aligned Paragraph &amp; Heading</H3>
<P align="right">
Here is a right-aligned paragraph. This can look odd, but is useful for
special emphasis, or if placed against a left-aligned image. Note how
the right margin is straight, and the left is ragged.
<H3 ALIGN="center">Center-Aligned Paragraph &amp; Heading</H3>
<P align="center">
Here is a centered paragraph. In principle, this means both the left
and right margins will be ragged. This is a useful way of centering
images. For example:<BR><IMG SRC="sright.xbm">
<H3 ALIGN="justify">Justified Paragraph &amp; Heading</H3>
<P align="justify">
Here is a justified paragraph. In principle, this means both the left
and right margins should be smooth, with wordspaces being adjusted
to keep it that way.   If your browser does not understand
<CODE>ALIGN="justify"</CODE> (most do not), it will use the default
left-justification.
</BLOCKQUOTE>
</BODY></HTML>
```

begin formatting the page, leaving an empty box for the image to be downloaded. If the image is not of the specified size, the browser will resize the image to fit the defined box. This is illustrated in Figure 2.16, where the little home page icon has been sized to almost twice its actual size. Of course, with an image as ugly as this, shrinking the image might have been a better choice.

Image Padding: HSPACE and VSPACE

When inserting an image into a document, an author may sometimes wish to leave some space between the image and the surrounding text. One way to do this is to create the image with a

Figure 2.14 Netscape Navigator rendering of the document *align.html*. The HTML listing is shown in Figure 2.13.

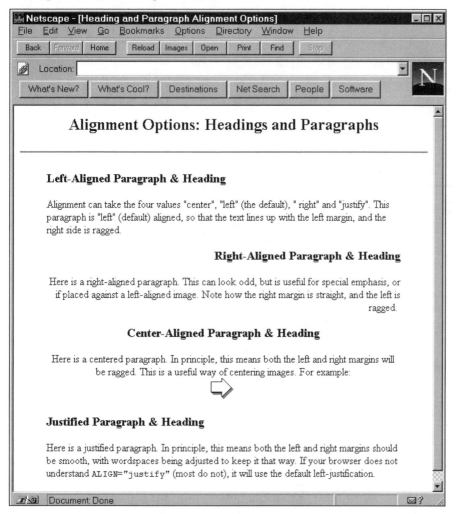

surrounding border, and use this border (perhaps *transparent*—see Chapter 10 for more information on image formats and transparency) to space the image from the text. However, this is not always possible or convenient, so HTML 3.2 supports **HSPACE** and **VSPACE** attributes to define the spacing in pixels to be left around an image. For example, in Figure 2.16 the second image has been inserted using HSPACE="8" and VSPACE="5". This creates padding borders around the image, and makes the surrounding text more readable.

Figure 2.15 HTML code for the document *alignimg.html*. This document illustrates some of the alignment features possible with the image elements.

```
<HTML>
<HEAD><TITLE>
Heading, Paragraph and Image Alignment Options
</TITLE></HEAD>
<BODY>
<A HREF="isindex.html"><IMG SRC="sleft.xbm" ALT="[Previous]"></A>
<A HREF="url.html"><IMG SRC="sright.xbm" BORDER=0 ALT="[Next]"></A>
<HR NOSHADE>
<H2 ALIGN="right"> Alignment Options --<BR>
    <em>Images</em></H2>
<P>
Here is some text that flows around the image. The
<CODE>ALIGN="left"</CODE>
<IMG ALIGN="left" ALT="[Example Image]" SRC="home.gif">
attribute value causes the image to float to the left hand margin, and
allows the text to flow around the image.  This results in much nicer
image—text placement, a better use of the page, and graphically more
attractive documents.
<P>
The following is the same example image, but with <B>HSPACE</B> and
<IMG VSPACE=5 HSPACE=8 ALIGN="left" ALT="[Example Image]" SRC="home.gif">
<B>VSPACE</B> attributes used to add  spacings around the image.
Note how this improves the readability of both text and image. You
could get a similar effect by simply building this border into the image
file itself.
<P> To the right is the image with <B>HEIGHT</B> and <B>WIDTH</B> set
to 100—
<IMG ALIGN="right" HEIGHT=100 WIDTH=100 ALT="[Example Image]"
     SRC="home.gif">
the image is zoomed to this size. To clear text to follow the image,
we need <CODE>&lt;BR CLEAR="right"&gt;</CODE>.
<BR>
<em>after regular <CODE>&lt;BR&gt;</CODE></em>
<BR CLEAR="right">
<em>after  <CODE>&lt;BR CLEAR="right"&gt;</CODE></em>
<HR>
</BODY>
</HTML>
```

Image Borders

Images can also be inside anchor elements, which allows you to turn an image into a clickable icon for accessing another resource. By default, a browser will box an anchored image with a colored or shaded border, just as it underlines anchored text. This is not always desired, as the borders can

Figure 2.16 Microsoft Internet Explorer rendering of the document *alignimg.html*. The HTML listing is shown in Figure 2.15.

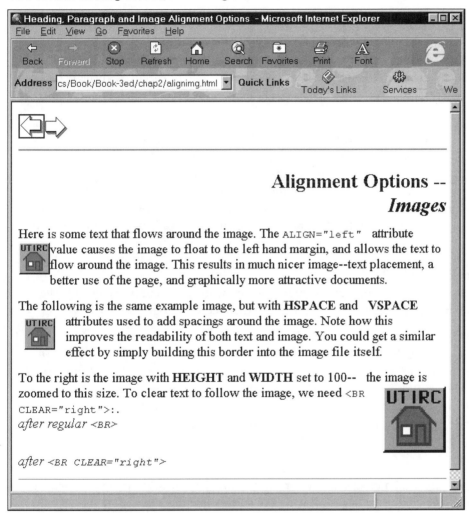

detract from the appearance of the icon. In addition, sometimes the image clearly indicates that the icon is selectable, so that a border is superfluous.

HTML 3.2 supports a **BORDER** attribute to the **IMG** element, to specify the thickness, in pixels, of the border surrounding the image. The default value is **BORDER="1"**. Borderless images can be created using **BORDER="0"**. The navigational buttons at the top of Figures 2.15

and 2.16 illustrate this use for the border attribute: Note how the second arrow does not have a border, although it is an active anchor.

Clearing Margins for Text

Often, you will want text to continue below the bottom of the figure, and not beside it. To do this, you must "clear" the text so that subsequent text moves down unconditionally below the image. Since the image can be to the left or right, you must be able to specify that the text should start only when the left margin is clear, when the right margin is clear, or when both margins are clear.

In HTML 3.2, you accomplish this using the **CLEAR** attribute, available only on the **BR** element. Thus, `<BR CLEAR="left">` ensures that the text following the **BR** is cleared to the left margin, while `<BR CLEAR="right">` ensures that the following text is cleared to the right margin, and `<BR CLEAR="all">` ensures that the following text is cleared to both margins. Figure 2.15 shows the effect of `CLEAR="right"` to clear the text that follows the large right-hand image. This attribute is understood by any browser that allows left- and right-aligned images.

Lessons from Example 7

1. The **ALIGN** attribute on headings and paragraphs can be used to modify the default alignment of the text content. Possible values are "left" (the default), "right", "center", and "justify".

2. On some browsers, the **ALIGN** attribute on **IMG** elements can float an image to the left (`ALIGN="left"`) or right (`ALIGN="right"`) of the display, and allow text to flow around the image. An author can also use the **WIDTH** and **HEIGHT** attributes to specify the dimensions of the image being inserted (in pixels), as well as **HSPACE** and **VSPACE** to specify the horizontal and vertical spacing (also in pixels) to be left at each side of the image. **BORDER** can be used to set the width of (or eliminate) the border drawn around images within anchor elements.

3. When text flows around an image, an author can use the element **BR** with an appropriate **CLEAR** attribute value to clear subsequent text to start below the image.

Exercises for Example 7

Take the example document *align.html* and modify the alignment options. In particular, use the **HEIGHT** and **WIDTH** attributes to modify the size of embedded images—note how you can use these to stretch and deform inline images.

Example 8: Using Tables and Backgrounds

This example looks at HTML tags for modifying the background of the display window and for defining tables of items.

The absence of tables was one of the major weaknesses of HTML 2.0. This has been largely solved in HTML 3.2, which contains a simple yet effective collection of elements for defining tabular structures. Tables are discussed in detail in Chapter 4. A few simple examples are given here.

Background Control

HTML 3.2 supports a **BACKGROUND** attribute to the **BODY** element to indicate an image file that the browser can use as a background for the displayed document. The general form is:

```
<BODY BACKGROUND="url">
```

The value for **BACKGROUND** is the URL of an image file: If capable, the browser will load this image and use it to *tile* the background of the document being displayed. Figure 2.18 shows an example of a loaded background. This can be an attractive change to the document, but should be used with care—remember that not everyone has a good graphics monitor, and that every color you use for the background is one color less for any images you might want to display on top of the background.

Backgrounds can cause problems if the background color is similar to the default color used for the text. All browsers that support the **BACKGROUND** attribute also support the additional attributes **TEXT**, **LINK**, and **VLINK** for specifying the color of regular text, text within hypertext anchors, and text within *visited* hypertext anchors, respectively. In addition, you can use the attribute **BGCOLOR** to specify the color of the background. This is another way of changing the background, and avoids downloading a background image file. These options are discussed in detail in Chapter 4.

TABLEs

Tables are defined using the **TABLE** element, while the content of the table is laid out as a sequence of table rows (**TR**), which in turn contain table headers (**TH**) and/or table data (**TD**). A table can also have a caption, defined by the **CAPTION** element. A caption can contain all forms of character formatting markup, including hypertext anchors. An example is shown in Figures 2.17 and 2.18. Tables can have borders and dividing lines, or can be borderless. The start tag `<TABLE BORDER>` ensures that the table is drawn with borders and dividers—you can adjust the thickness of the border by assigning a value (in pixels) to the **BORDER** attribute.

HTML 3.2 allows tables to be aligned on the page like images. This is illustrated in Figure 2.18, where the second table was allowed to "float" to the right-hand margin. Many current browsers do not support floating tables. In this case, the table always appears alone, with all images and text either above or below it.

Rows and Columns

Tables are defined as a collection of rows, defined by the **TR** element. Each of these rows contains a collection of *cells*, defined by the **TH** or **TD** elements. **TH** (table header) elements are used for column or row headings, while **TD** (regular tabular entry) elements are used for everything else. These are non-empty elements, but the end tags are optional. These elements can take several attributes to define the alignment of the element content (**ALIGN** and **VALIGN**), or the number of rows or columns (**ROWSPAN** and **COLSPAN** respectively) occupied by the element.

Justification of Table Rows and Columns

When you design a table, you must ensure that the number of rows and columns sum to the correct number for your table; that is, all the rows must span the same number of columns, and all the columns must span the same number of rows. For example, compare the markup in Figure 2.17 with the table rendering in Figure 2.18. The table is defined with three columns and six rows. Note how the number of columns in each **TR** element always sums to three—a cell with ROWSPAN=2, such as the first one in Figure 2.18, contributes an extra column to the following row, since this cell "spans" two rows. Keeping track of the rows and columns tends to be a bit tricky the first time you create a table, but you will quickly get the hang of it. If you are doing tables by hand, it is useful to lay out the HTML to show table alignment, as done in Figure 2.17, as this allows you to see the underlying tabular structure. Of course, it is easier if you can find a program that will create HTML tables for you. This is possible with some modern HTML editors.

Alignment within Table Cells

Items within table data or header elements, or along entire rows, can be aligned using the alignment attributes. **ALIGN**, which can take the values **ALIGN**="left", "center", or "right" aligns the cell contents horizontally within the cell. The attribute **VALIGN** is used to vertically align the contents, and can take the values **VALIGN**="top", "middle", or "bottom". The effects of some of these alignment options are illustrated in Figure 2.18. Note that you can set these alignment attributes within a **TR** element, to set the alignment for all the cells in the row.

Row and Cell Properties

Finally, you can use the **BGCOLOR** attribute within a **TR, TD,** or **TH** element to change the background color of the cell or group of cells. This is illustrated in both example tables shown in Figures 2.17 and 2.18, where the background color has been modified to emphasize cell contents.

Rendering by Older Browsers

Tables and background tiling are supported by most, but not all, browsers. What happens if a browser that does not support these features attempts to display tables or backgrounds? There is no problem with backgrounds (provided the background does not contain important information), since the document content will be displayed regardless of the background. The situation with tables is more problematic. If a browser does not understand the **TABLE** element, then table tags are ignored, and the table content is jumbled together in a haphazard and unreadable fashion.

Almost all current browsers understand the **TABLE** elements. However, a few older browsers do not. If you are eager to make sure that everyone can see your tabular data, you might want to create a GIF image of the table as an alternative.

Lessons from Example 8

1. The **TABLE** element permits formally defined tables in HTML documents. A few older browsers do not support this element, so you may want to offer a non-**TABLE** alternative for these users, if this is likely to pose a problem.

2. The **BACKGROUND** attribute to the **BODY** specifies an image file to be used as a background to the displayed text. Care should be taken to make sure that the background does not dominate or otherwise obscure the text or images lying on top. The additional **BODY** attributes **TEXT, LINK,** and **VLINK** allow for control of the color of the text and are described in Chapter 4.

Exercises for Example 8

Tables are complicated to design and are well worth some practice. As a first exercise, try modifying the tables in Figures 2.17 to create your own tables: You can, for example, take tabular information from a printed book or magazine and try to re-create it using HTML. Note that tables need not contain text, but can contain pictures, or even other tables. The examples in Chapters 4 and 12 demonstrate some common uses of **TABLE** that take advantage of this flexibility.

Figure 2.17 HTML code for the document *tables.html*. This document illustrates the TABLE element, as well as the BACKGROUND attribute to the BODY element.

```
<HTML><HEAD>
<TITLE>Table and Background Example</TITLE>
</HEAD>
<BODY BACKGROUND="paper01.jpg" TEXT="#000000"
      ALINK="#ff0000" VLINK="#005050">
<H1> Simple Table Examples </H1>
<BLOCKQUOTE>
<P>This simple example demonstrates simple table layout. Note
how the second table does not have any borders, and is right-aligned
on the page.
<HR>
<TABLE BORDER>
<CAPTION> <B>First Example <A HREF="tables.html">Table</A></B></CAPTION>
  <TR BGCOLOR="#ffffff">
      <TH ROWSPAN=2> Segment </TH>  <TH COLSPAN=2> Total Memory </TH>
  </TR>
  <TR>
                                        <TH>Bytes</TH> <TH> Kbytes </TH>
  </TR>
  <TR>
      <TD> 005B5 </TD> <TD ALIGN=right> 78 </TD> <TD> (0K) </TD>
  </TR>
  <TR>
      <TD> 00780 </TD> <TD ALIGN=right > 175 </TD> <TD> 0K </TD>
  </TR>
  <TR>
      <TD> 020B  </TD> <TD ALIGN=right > 88348 </TD>
      <TD BGCOLOR="#ffffff"> 510K </TD>
  </TR>
  <TR>
      <TD COLSPAN=2 ALIGN=left><A HREF="memory.html">Total Free</A></TD>
      <TD BGCOLOR="#666666"> 510K </TD>
  </TR>
</TABLE>
<HR>
<TABLE BORDER="0" ALIGN="right">
<CAPTION> <B>Second Example <A HREF="tables.html">Table</A>
          </B></CAPTION>
  <TR>
      <TD COLSPAN=2
          ALIGN="center"
          BGCOLOR="#ffff77"><EM><B>Note Well!!</B></EM></TD>
  </TR>
```

Figure 2.17 (Continued)

```
    <TR>
        <TD BGCOLOR="#f1ffff">Here is some<BR>text in a cell
        <TD BGCOLOR="#666666">Here is some<BR>text in the next cell

    </TR>
</TABLE>
<P>Text flows around this right-aligned  table, just as with images.
Thus you can create proper text documents and associated tabular
information (or images) without difficulty.
</BLOCKQUOTE>
</BODY></HTML>
```

Figure 2.18 Netscape Navigator 3.0 rendering of the document *tables.html*. The HTML listing for this document is shown in Figure 2.17.

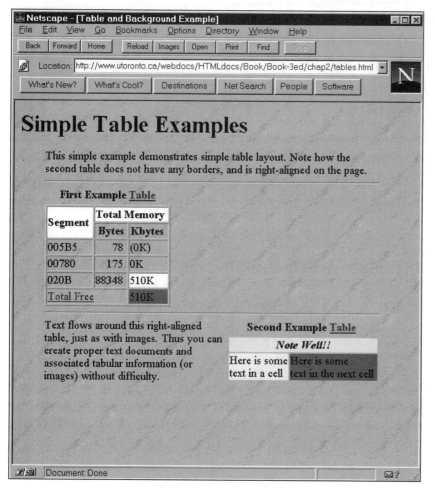

Example 9: Fill-in Forms

This example looks at the HTML **FORM** element, which lets a Web author solicit user input through documents containing fill-in forms. Using this element, a designer can build a document containing checkboxes, radio buttons, pull-down lists, text windows, and menus, and can configure this **FORM** to send the data gathered by the form to a program on an HTTP server. For example, **FORM**s can be used to collect data for a database search; solicit data for an on-line questionnaire; accept electronic text for submission to a database; or solicit electronic messages for forwarding to a particular user.

The example in Figure 2.19 shows this latter case: namely, a **FORM** that lets the user type in a text message for forwarding to a recipient chosen from a selectable list. Figure 2.20 shows this form rendered by Internet Explorer, while Figure 2.21 shows the rendering by lynx.

The FORM Element

Let's first look at Figure 2.19 and the <FORM..> tag beginning with the line:

```
<FORM  ACTION="http://side.edu/cgi-bin/send_note">
```

This line starts the **FORM** element and ties the data of the form to a particular program (*send_note*) on the indicated HTTP server. All a **FORM** element does is collect data: It doesn't do any processing of the data, so the only way you can get a form to do anything useful is to send the gathered data to a program on the server. The **ACTION** attribute tells the browser where to send the data—in this case, the program *send_note* at the indicated HTTP server. Data is sent to this server-side program when the user presses the *Send Message* button at the bottom of the page. The FORM and the program *send_note* must be designed together for the program to understand the message sent by the form.

The program *send_note* takes the data sent by the client and processes it to complete the task. In this example, the program might take the data sent by the form and compose an electronic mail message to be sent to the intended person. The HTTP mechanisms for sending data to a server are described in Chapter 7, while gateway programs and the mechanisms by which data are sent to gateway programs are discussed in the **http** URL section in Chapter 6, and also in Chapter 8.

FORM Input Elements

By comparing the HTML document in Figure 2.19 and its rendering in Figure 2.20, you can see some of the several input items that can go inside a form. This example shows a **SELECT** element pull-down menu (where the user selects the name of the person to whom he or she wishes to send the message—the possible names being given by the **OPTION** element); a single-line text **INPUT** element (here, where the user types in his or her e-mail address); and a **TEXTAREA** element (where the user types the body of the message). Several other input elements are available and are described in Chapter 4. The elements **SELECT**, **INPUT**, **OPTION**, and **TEXTAREA** can appear only inside a **FORM**.

Every FORM input element takes one key attribute. This is the **NAME** attribute, which associates a *variable name* to the data associated with the input element, for example `NAME="mailto_name"` or `NAME="button"`. These names are used to differentiate between the data associated with the different input elements. Some elements, such as the **INPUT** element, can assign a default initial *value* to the named variable using the **VALUE** attribute. An example is the element

`<INPUT TYPE="checkbox" NAME="button" VALUE="on">`

which assigns the value `on` to the name `button`. These values can subsequently be changed by user input, by selecting a different entry from a pull-down menu, typing text into a box, or clicking on checkboxes or buttons.

When the user presses the *Send Message* button (a special **INPUT** element with the attribute `TYPE="submit"`), the data in the form are sent to the server as a collection of strings of the form *name=value*, where *name* is the value assigned to the **NAME** attribute of an element, and *value* is the value assigned by the user's input. For example, the checkbox input element in this illustration would send the string `button=on`. The details of the algorithm used in constructing this string are discussed in Chapter 6, and also in Chapter 8.

The server program sorts out what the data mean by matching the *names* in the message to names the program is designed to recognize. Consequently, a form and the associated server-side gateway program must be designed together.

Like all HTML elements, the **FORM** element has restrictions on where it can be placed. A **FORM** cannot be inside a heading, inside another **FORM,** or inside character emphasis markup, such as a **STRONG** or **EM** element. However, a **FORM** can contain headings, character markup elements, and even lists. Again, the details of the nesting rules are given in Chapter 4.

Figure 2.21 shows the same **FORM** as displayed by lynx. The lynx browser can display all the **FORM** elements, and provides instructions at the bottom of the screen explaining how to fill in the different items.

Notice the little button enclosed in square brackets near the top of Figures 2.20 and 2.21. This button does not actually do anything (note that there is no associated `<INPUT TYPE="submit">` button), and is simply there to test the capabilities of the browser. There are still a few browsers in use that do not understand **FORM**s, and this button (or, rather, its absence) tests for them. If you suspect that this will be an issue for you, you can provide an alternative mechanism for accessing the same data, as indicated in this example.

Figure 2.19 The HTML source code for the document *form.html*.

```
<HTML><HEAD>
  <TITLE> Example of an HTML FORM  </TITLE>
</HEAD>
<BODY>
<H1> Example of an HTML FORM  </H1>
<FORM ACTION="no_action">
Data entered into a FORM is sent to a program on the server
for processing.  If you see a button at the end of this sentence
then your browser supports the HTML FORMs element.
--[<INPUT TYPE="checkbox" NAME="button" VALUE="on">]--
If you do not see a button between the square brackets go to the
<A HREF="text_only.html"> text-only interface </A>. </FORM>
<hr>
<FORM  ACTION="http://side.edu/cgi-bin/submit_abstract">
  <p> <STRONG> 1) Send this note to: </STRONG>
  <SELECT NAME="mailto_name" >
    <OPTION SELECTED> Martin Grant
    <OPTION> Jack Smith
    <OPTION> Bruce Lee
    <OPTION> Anna Mcgarrigle
    <OPTION> Kate Bush
    <OPTION> Spike Lee
    <OPTION> Diane Koziol
    <OPTION> Ross Thomson
    <OPTION> Ann Dean
  </SELECT>

  <p> 2) <STRONG>Give your e-mail address: </STRONG>
      This indicates who sent the letter
  <p> <INPUT TYPE="text"  NAME="signature"
      VALUE="name@internet.address" SIZE=60>

  <p> <STRONG> 3) Message Body: </STRONG>
  <p>
  <TEXTAREA COLS=60 ROWS=8 NAME="message_body">
   Delete this message and type your message into this
   textbox.  Press the "Send Message" button to send it
   off. You can press the "Reset" button to reset the
   form to the original values.
  </TEXTAREA>
  <P>
  <INPUT TYPE="submit" VALUE="Send Message"> <INPUT TYPE="reset"> (reset form)
  </FORM>
  </BODY>
</HTML>
```

Figure 2.20 Microsoft Internet Explorer rendering of the *form.html* document (listed in Figure 2.19). The FORM fill-in elements are clearly evident.

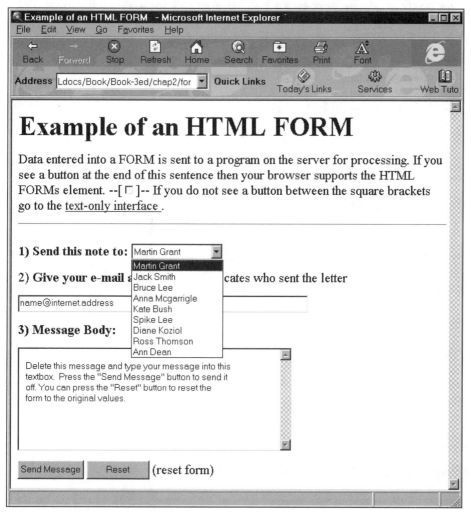

Lessons from Example 9

1. The document developer can use the HTML **FORM** element to solicit user input. However, each FORM document must send the data it gathers to a server-side gateway program designed to analyze the form data. This gateway program is specified by the **ACTION** attribute of the **FORM** element. The program and form must be designed together.

Figure 2.21 Lynx browser rendering of the *form.html* document (listed in Figure 2.19). The FORM fill-in elements are clearly evident. In general, lynx gives written instructions at the bottom of the screen to help the user properly manipulate the form.

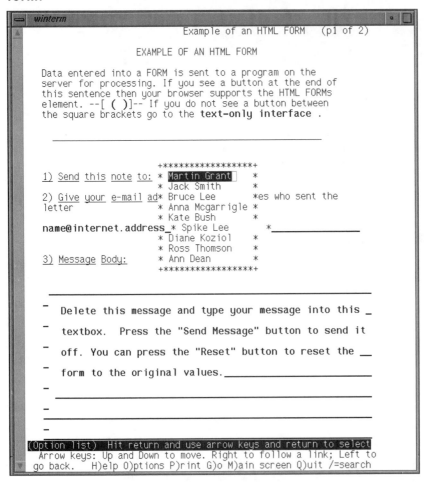

2. An HTML **FORM** can contain several input elements, namely **INPUT, SELECT,** and **TEXTAREA**. These elements can appear only inside a **FORM**.

3. A **FORM** cannot be inside a heading element or inside another **FORM—FORM**s cannot be nested. However, heading, list, character markup, **PRE**, and **TABLE** elements can be inside a **FORM**.

Exercises for Example 9

Constructing **FORMs** is a complicated compromise of structure and ease-of-use: You need to organize the input elements so that they are easy to use and understand, and must keep the form small enough that it does not get confusing. As an exercise, you can try creating HTML versions of some of the form-style interfaces of standard programs. Chapter 4 gives more details about how **FORMs** work. Do not worry, at this point, about the server-side processing of the data, other than to give all the form input items appropriate **NAMEs**.

Example 10: Inline Data Viewers—EMBED Element

In Example 5, we looked at hypertext links to data other than other HTML documents, and discussed how these data could be processed by external helper applications. Sometimes, however, you do not want exotic data types to be displayed away from the document, but rather want them displayed within the text. For example, you might want an audio or movie player to appear right within the page of a text document, or perhaps an Excel spreadsheet to be displayed next to a description of the data.

This is now possible using the **EMBED** element (nonstandardized, but supported by Netscape and, to some extent, other browser vendors) and the newer **OBJECT** element (not yet widely supported, but a proposed universal standard). These are designed for embedding objects of arbitrary data types *within* an HTML document, much in the way that images are embedded using the **IMG** element.

Using the empty **EMBED** element, an author can include one of these nonstandard data types using a tag such as:

```
<EMBED SRC="video/movie1.avi" WIDTH="200" HEIGHT="150">
```

which embeds the file *movie.avi* (a Microsoft AVI-format movie) in the document. How does the browser determine the data type of this file? The type is determined in the same manner described in Example 5: Either the HTTP server explicitly sends a MIME content-type header to indicate the type, or the browser guesses the type based on the filename extension, using its preconfigured database of filenames and MIME types.

The second method only works if the browser knows the filename extension. In fact, there are hundreds of extensions that are not configured by default. Therefore, it is always best to serve data out using an HTTP server, ensuring that the server always sends out the proper content-type MIME header. For example, the following embed element would insert a Corel CMX-format image into a document:

```
<EMBED SRC="cmx/canary.cmx" WIDTH="500" HEIGHT="200">
```

Current browsers do not know, by default, what this filename extension (.cmx) means, and count on the server to provide the proper content-type information.

The **EMBED** element can take the three attributes **SRC, WIDTH,** and **HEIGHT,** which have the same meanings as with the **IMG** element: **SRC** gives the URL for accessing the data, while the **HEIGHT** and **WIDTH** give the size for the box that will display the data within the page. In addition, **EMBED** can take arbitrary user-defined attributes of the form *PARAM_NAME*="*value*", where both *PARAM_NAME* and *value* are arbitrary, and depend only on the particular data type being displayed. This turns out to be a bad way of doing things, and as a result the **EMBED** tag will soon be dropped in favor of the much more flexible **OBJECT** element. **OBJECT** is discussed in detail in Chapter 5.

Figure 2.22 shows a typical HTML document that uses **EMBED** to include a special data type—in this case, a Corel CMX image. Figures 2.23 and 2.24 show the display of this document by the Netscape Navigator browser.

Figure 2.22 Example HTML document *embed.html,* which uses the EMBED element to include arbitrary data types within the HTML document. The rendering of this document by the Netscape Navigator browser is shown in Figures 2.23 and 2.24.

```
<HTML>
<HEAD>
<TITLE> Example of the EMBED Element</TITLE>
</HEAD>
<BODY>
<H1>Example of the EMBED Element</H1>
<BLOCKQUOTE>
<P>These simple examples illustrate the  <B>EMBED</B> element,
as currently implemented on the Netscape Navigator and some other
browsers. <BR>

<EMBED SRC="canary.cmx" WIDTH=200 HEIGHT=150><BR>

<P> Here is another <B>EMBED</B>, this time for an audio file.
The associated plugin is an audio control panel--
<EMBED SRC="sound.au" WIDTH=145 HEIGHT=60 HSPACE=10 VSPACE=5>
 the panel is treated like an image.
<P> You can also left and right-align the plugin,
in the same way as images.
<EMBED SRC="sound.au" WIDTH=145 HEIGHT=60 HSPACE=10 VSPACE=5
 ALIGN=LEFT>
<EMBED SRC="sound.au" WIDTH=145 HEIGHT=60 HSPACE=10 VSPACE=5
 ALIGN=RIGHT>
```

Figure 2.22 (Continued)

```
 Here are two examples: note how the text
wraps around the panels, just as it wraps around regular image
files.
</BODY>
</HTML>
```

Figure 2.23 Rendering of the document in Figure 2.22 by a Netscape Navigator browser that is not equipped with the appropriate plug-in. The browser is consequently unable to display the embedded data.

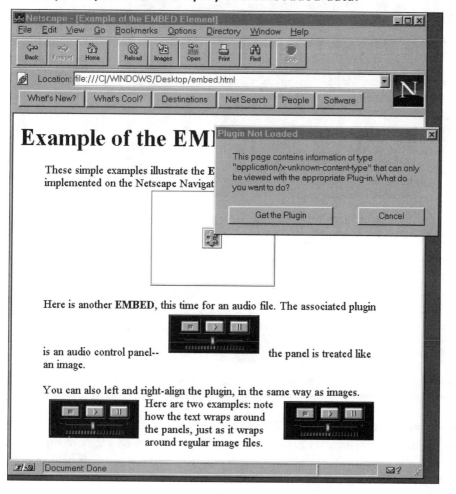

Figure 2.24 Rendering of the document in Figure 2.22 by a Netscape Navigator browser equipped with the appropriate plug-in. The browser can now display the embedded data, with the plug-in also providing a *user interface* that lets the user manipulate the data.

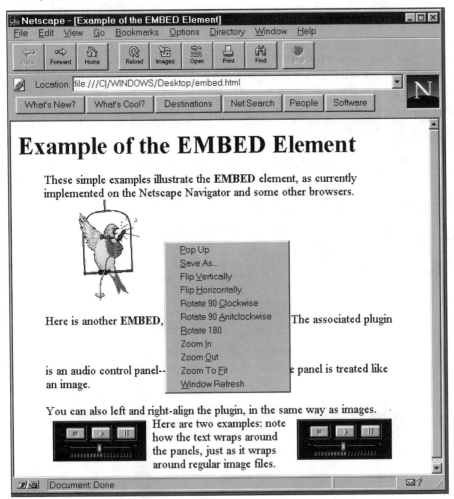

Displaying Embedded Data—Browser Plug-ins

Of course just getting the data to the browser is not sufficient, as you also need a way of displaying it. The problem is that the browser itself does not know how to do this, and needs help. As you may recall from Example 5, this is the same problem we encountered when linking to an arbitrary data type; in that case, the problem was solved by helper applications that processed the

Figure 2.25 Rendering of the document in Figure 2.22 by a beta-version of Internet Explorer 3.0. This early version does not support Netscape plug-ins, although such support should be available by the time you read this.

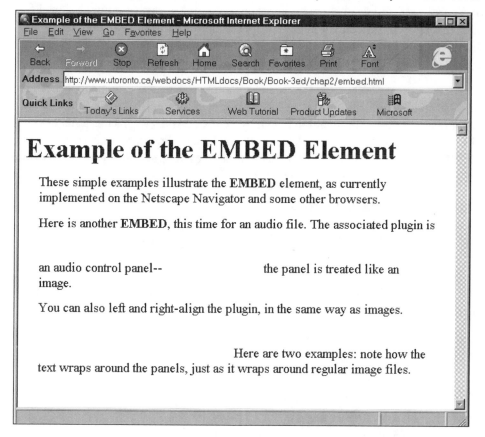

data in place of the browser. For embedded data types, we again need the help of additional software, but in this case the help must be plugged right into the browser. Such software modules are thus called *browser plug-ins*.

Figure 2.23 shows the Netscape Navigator rendering of the page shown in Figure 2.22, but for the case where the browser is not equipped with the special plug-in capable of displaying Corel CMX image files. The browser, unable to display this data type, substitutes a default symbol indicating this failure. Note also the pop-up menu that informs the user that the plugged-in data is of an unknown type (the type would be listed as "image/x-cmx," if the server were properly equipped). Figure 2.24 shows the same document, but after the browser has been equipped with the plug-in—the browser can now display the image. In addition, the box containing the CMX image also supports special right-mouse button menu controls for processing and displaying the image. These controls are provided by the plug-in module.

The bottom of Figures 2.23 and 2.24 show an additional plug-in, in this case one designed for playing audio files. This plug-in is a control panel: The slider on the bottom is a volume control, while the other buttons are for stopping, pausing, and playing the audio file. More sophisticated controls are of course found in other plug-ins.

Finally, Figure 2.25 shows what users see if they are using a browser that does not support plug-ins. In this case they see nothing, which can lead to very confusing and/or misleading documents. The **EMBED** element does not allow for an alternative to the embedded data, which is a major weaknesses of the **EMBED** approach. The new element **OBJECT** does allow for an alternative (perhaps a regular image for the embedded CMX file, or perhaps a text paragraph giving a text description of the audio file). **OBJECT** is discussed in Chapter 5.

Microsoft Plug-ins—ActiveX Controls

Needless to say, Microsoft is also pursuing embedded object technology, and has defined a technology named *ActiveX* for creating plug-ins for Microsoft's Internet Explorer. Plug-in software written according to the Microsoft ActiveX specifications works with Microsoft's Internet Explorer, but not within Netscape Navigator. Also, plug-ins written for Netscape Navigator often do not work with Microsoft's Internet Explorer. Both companies are working to incorporate support for each other's technology, in order to support both families of plug-ins.

Information about plug-ins for the Netscape Navigator and Microsoft Internet Explorer browsers can be found, respectively, at:

```
http://home.netscape.com/comprod/products/navigator/version_2.0/plugins/index.html
http://www.microsoft.com/activex/
```

Plug-ins: Strengths and Weaknesses

Embedded data can richly expand the types of information that can be presented by a Web browser. However, you must keep in mind that not everyone can display the data: Many people will not have the required plug-in, or will be using a computer (e.g., Macintosh or UNIX as opposed to Windows-based) for which there is no appropriate plug-in; or they may simply be using a browser that does not support plug-ins. In addition, many plug-ins require advanced operating systems (Windows 95/NT, Macintosh System 7.5, etc.), fast processors (Pentium or faster), and lots of memory (16 MB or more). If the user's machine has too little memory, or too slow a processor, the plug-ins will be very slow and unresponsive and, with most PCs, may crash the computer.

If you decide to incorporate **EMBED/OBJECT** elements, you should provide instructions to the readers explaining how to obtain the required plug-in. You might also want to provide an alternative to the embedded data, should you want to service clients who simply cannot obtain the required software.

Plug-ins are, at present, most useful in a semi-controlled environment (such as within a company), where you can ensure that users will have the required hardware and software.

Lessons from Example 10

1. Arbitrary data types can be included inline in an HTML document using **EMBED** elements. **EMBED** works like **IMG** elements, and takes the same **SRC**, **HEIGHT**, and **WIDTH** attributes, as well as arbitrary attributes specific to the plug-in. **EMBED** is not supported by all browsers, and is not part of "standard" HTML.

2. HTML is currently standardizing around the **OBJECT** element as a replacement for **EMBED**. **OBJECT**, which is more flexible than **EMBED**, is described in Chapter 5.

3. Embedded data types can only be displayed if the browser is equipped with the appropriate *plug-in*. A plug-in is a platform- and browser-specific software component that "plugs into" the browser, giving it the ability to display the associated data type. Most plug-ins are developed by software vendors responsible for the corresponding data type. Many plug-ins are available for only a limited number of browsers and/or platforms.

Exercises for Example 10

Consider your inventory of data (audio or video, spreadsheets, special image formats, etc.) and think about how these may or may not be incorporated into HTML documents. Then locate and install the required plug-in. Next, write some simple Web pages that embed this data type. If you know your intended audience, try polling them (by e-mail, for example) to find out if they have a browser that supports a plug-in for this data type. This helps you determine whether this will be an effective way to distribute your resources.

Example 11: Embedded Programs and Applets

In addition to allowing you to embed arbitrary data into an HTML document, HTML also supports the embedding of actual *programs*. Embedded programs are downloaded from a remote Web server and then run on the user's local computer. This is an exciting concept, but brings with it a host of security concerns: The user has no idea what the program is going to do when it arrives, and after it arrives, it is too late, since the program could have destroyed files, copied passwords to another computer, or done other despicable things.

This has led to the development of several so-called safe languages, the most well-known of which is *Java*. Java is designed to be a safe language (running a Java program cannot damage your computer or access your computer's files and send them to someone else), as well as platform independent. A compiled Java program can run on any computer, regardless of the processor or operating system. Most browser vendors now include support for Java programs within their Web browsers. HTML authors can then use the **APPLET** element to embed Java programs into their pages: The browser downloads the indicated Java program and executes it, using a built-in browser module that supports Java. For security reasons, the things a Java program can do are tightly restricted. For this and other reasons, the downloaded Java program is not considered a full application, but rather a mini-application, or *applet*.

Current variants of HTML let you include Java applets using the **APPLET** element, as illustrated in Figure 2.26. This is a non-empty element, and can contain two important parts: **PARAMETER** elements that define parameters required by the running applet, and regular HTML markup that is displayed by browsers that do not understand **APPLET** elements, or are otherwise incapable of running Java programs. The **APPLET** element can take several attributes: **HEIGHT, WIDTH, HSPACE, VSPACE,** and **ALIGN** have the same meanings as with images (the Netscape Navigator currently ignores **HSPACE** and **VSPACE** attributes). **CODEBASE** indicates the URL where the applet software comes from, while **CODE** indicates the name of the actual applet program from this URL.

Figure 2.26 Example HTML document *applet.html*, which uses the APPLET element to include a Java-language program within an HTML document. The rendering of this document by the Microsoft Internet Explorer browser is shown in Figures 2.27.

```
<HTML>
<HEAD>
<TITLE>Example of an Embedded Applet</TITLE>
</HEAD>
<BODY>
<H1>Example of an Embedded Applet</H1>
<BLOCKQUOTE>
<P>To the right is a simple example of an embedded
<APPLET
    CODEBASE="http://www.dgp.toronto.edu/people/JamesStewart/378/notes/"
    CODE="bst.class" WIDTH=321 HEIGHT=151 VSPACE=10 HSPACE=10 ALIGN="right">
    <PARAM NAME=keys VALUE="50 42 43 15 6 23 17 30">
    <PARAM NAME=action VALUE="rotate">
    <PARAM NAME=alternate_nodes VALUE="15 42">
    <BLOCKQUOTE>
    <HR> If you were using a Java-enabled Web browser, you would
    see a binary search tree instead of this paragraph. <HR>
    </BLOCKQUOTE>
</APPLET>
applet, in this case a Java applet that demonstrates
<EM>binary search tree (BST) rotations</EM>. This is a
complicated concept in computer science, associated
with data storage and searching algorithms. The
interactive applet (the user can click on the balls
to "select and rotate" the data) helps illustrate the
principles in an easy to use and effective manner.
<P>Note how the HTML <EM>content</EM> of the <B>APPLET</B>
```

Figure 2.26 (Continued)

```
element is not displayed: the content is alternative markup,
that is displayed by browsers that do not understand
the <B>APPLET</B> element or that are unable to run Java
applets.
<P>This applet example is courtesy of James Stewart, an
Assistant professor in the
Department of Computer Science, University of Toronto.
</BLOCKQUOTE>

<HR NOSHADE>
</BODY>
</HTML>
```

Figure 2.27 Rendering of the document in Figure 2.26 by the Microsoft Internet Explorer 3 browser.

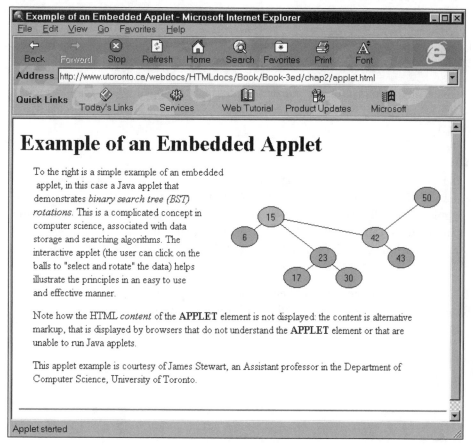

Figure 2.27 shows the resulting document as displayed by the Microsoft Internet Explorer 3.0 browser. Both Microsoft and Netscape support Java in their browsers. The applet appears as the graphic to the right, which is an animation that illustrates binary search tree rotations—an important concept in computer science. The reader can actually click on the balls causing these rotations, and in doing so, learn about this database concept.

The **APPLET** element, although in wide use, is considered experimental and not part of the formal HTML standard. The **OBJECT** element, discussed in Chapter 5, is a likely successor to both **APPLET** and **EMBED**.

Java applets offer enormous promise for building dynamic, interactive Web pages. However, you do need someone to write the programs, and the programs tend to be very large and slow to arrive—it is not uncommon to wait minutes for large applets to download. Also, as with plug-ins, the user needs modern equipment to run applets, and a fast machine with lots of memory—a 100-MHz Pentium processor with 16 MB of memory would be a good start. These are things to think about when considering a Java-based tool.

Document Scripting: JavaScript and VBScript

If you can download programs and run them on the browser, why can't you also incorporate programs right within the HTML documents?

This is now possible using two scripting languages: JavaScript, developed by Netscape and Sun Microsystems, and VBScript (Visual Basic Script), developed by Microsoft. Scripting languages are discussed in Chapter 5.

Lessons from Example 11

1. The **APPLET** element is used to embed a program applet within an HTML document. This element can contain HTML markup, as well as **PARAMETER** elements to define parameters needed by the applet. The **APPLET** element also takes attributes needed to define the location (**CODEBASE**) and name (**CODE**) of the requested applet, and also to specify the size and location for the applet within the window (**HEIGHT, WIDTH, HSPACE, VSPACE,** and **ALIGN**).

2. The **OBJECT** element (see Chapter 5) is a likely successor to the experimental **APPLET** tag. Browsers will, however, be backward-compatible with the **APPLET** element.

Exercises for Example 11

Try visiting some sites containing applets to get a flavor for what they can do, and also to get a flavor for the time it takes to download a large applet over the Internet. A large repository of Java applets can be found at:

```
http://www.gamelan.com/
```

This is a good place for Java examples. You might even find an applet you want to use!

The Design of Web Collections

Chapters 1 and 2 provided a gentle (I hope!) introduction to HTML, and to good design habits for creating HTML documents. This chapter takes a broader approach, and looks at the issues involved in designing *collections* of HTML documents and associated resources. By analogy to the printed world, this is the difference between designing a single page of text, and designing a magazine or book or creating a library. Such "collections" of pages require organizational and design elements that are neither necessary nor apparent from the perspective of a single page. The same is true of hypertext collections, although the required design elements are quite different from those of the purely printed world.

Why such differences? The reasons lie in the different nature of the presentation media: Books are spatial, physical, and static collections, with a fixed *linear* structure, while hypertext is nonspatial and nonphysical, possibly dynamic, and often *nonlinear*. Good hypertext design must reflect these differences, while preserving the easy navigability of printed books. This chapter looks at some ways of accomplishing this goal, and provides references for additional reading on this subject.

Paper and Books

The easiest way to appreciate the important issues is to start with the familiar example of a book. This allows us to introduce, using a familiar model, the ideas behind the construction of a document collection. The issues that arise in hypertext design can then be analyzed with respect to this more familiar paradigm.

In simplest terms, a book simply is a collection of related, printed pages. Of course, there is much more to a book than that! A large collection of unbound and unnumbered pages is, to say the least, awkward and confusing to read or handle (rather like the floor of this author's office, as he sits writing this chapter). Given a bundle of papers, a reader cannot distinguish between pages arising from different books or documents (should there be pages present from more than one collection), and cannot, even within a collection of associated pages, determine the proper reading sequence without explicitly checking for page-to-page continuity.

Book design solves such organizational problems by giving the pages a uniform design (top and bottom page banners, typeface, and so on), so that pages within a given book have a distinctive look; by numbering the pages to give *linear order* to the collection; and by binding the pages together to enforce the correct order. If there are many pages, or if the book has important organizational requirements, there is often a table of contents listing the page numbers of important starting pages, and perhaps an index providing page references to other important locations. By convention, these are placed at the beginning and end of the book (the exact location varies according to linguistic and national conventions), to make them easy to find. Additional cross-referencing is possible through internal page references, footnotes, bibliographies, and so on, while additional components are present within specialty books such as dictionaries. In fact, the organizational technology of printed books is very sophisticated, covering everything from simple pamphlets to multivolume encyclopedias. This is not surprising, given that this technology has been refined over 500 years of practical experience.

Linear Documents

Books and other printed media can all be described as *linear*. By linear, I mean that they have an obvious beginning and end, and a fixed sequence of pages in between. Indexes, tables of contents, or cross-references exist superimposed on this linear framework—they provide added value, and are often critically important, but they do not change the underlying structure. In fact, they depend on the underlying structure (page numbers, etc.) to provide internal references within the book.

The reasons for the near-universality of this linear model are both physical and psychological. Physically, the only reliable way to organize printed pages is as a bound, linear entity—it is hard to create a book as a collection of nonlinearly accessible documents! Psychologically, a linear, well-defined structure is comfortable, familiar, and convenient, since the result is easy to read, easy to reference, and easy to communicate to others. The goal of all publishing is *communication*, and a book is a robust collection that can be reliably communicated to others (through duplicate copies), and reliably referenced and compared (through page number references), since everyone with the same book has the same information, at the same location within the book.

It is also important to note that the physical nature of a book allows a reader to know both the exact size of the book, and where he or she is *in* the book. This makes it easy for a reader to browse a book, for example by jumping from the table of contents to some selected location, or by simply selecting pages at random, all the while retaining a sense of location with respect to the beginning, end, table of contents, or index.

The traditional media of music, video, and film are also linear in this sense, being predetermined sequential presentations of sounds or images created by a musician or director. This, in part, reflects the temporal nature of these media—music and film move dynamically (and usually forward!) in time in a sequential way. This also reflects the technical limitations of the media, as it is almost impossible to make nonlinear presentations with traditional film, video, or audio technology, just as is the case with printed text.

Figure 3.1 illustrates both the structure of a book and how the table of contents and index merely provide referencing on top of the underlying linear structure.

Nonlinear Media

The advent in recent years of inexpensive, yet extremely powerful, computers and graphical displays has made it possible to step beyond the linear, and has opened up enormous—and still largely unexplored—possibilities in the organization and presentation of information. This is because a computer has no preferred organization for stored data, and can easily store, index, relate, and access the data in a number of different ways, subject to the design of the database holding the data and the abilities of the database software. In addition, a computer can create a representation of the underlying data quickly, efficiently, and *inexpensively*, according to instructions provided by software and/or user input. In a sense, you can think of the stored data as a collection of book pages or page components (paragraphs, images, etc.) which can be shuffled and rearranged almost instantaneously by the computer, at practically no cost. This is in stark contrast to the difficulty and high cost of modifying the order of printed material, or material on tape or film.*

---

* The flexibility and speed of computers also apply to audio and video data, which in large part explains why text, audio, and video editing are now commonly performed on computers.

Figure 3.1 The structure of a linear document collection, in this case a book. The ordering is implicit in the page numbering. Tables of contents and indexes simply provide referencing on top of this underlying structure.

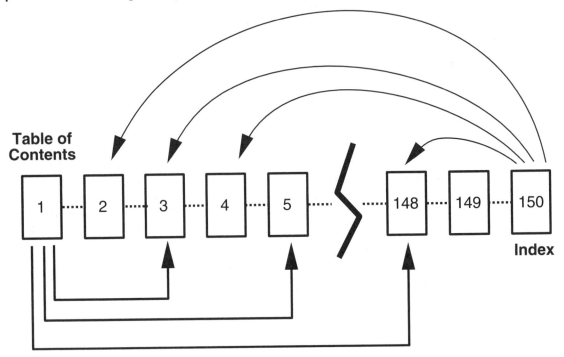

At the same time, modern computer interfaces can directly, and again at low cost, present these data to a user—a Web browser is just one instance of this process. This also is a new phenomenon, since high-resolution computer display systems capable of rapidly displaying finely formatted text and graphics have only recently become affordable. Thus, not only can a computer rapidly organize data, it can also nearly instantly present the data to a user, in almost any format (text, graphics, audio and video, etc.). A computer can consequently act like an infinitely customizable printing press, capable of organizing and presenting data in decidedly nonlinear ways, limited only by the capabilities of the underlying software and the interests of a user.

Computer Games as Media

This has led, in the past fifteen or so years, to the birth of several new media. The first, and possibly still most popular, was video games. Games are inherently nonlinear in the sense described above, since they evolve in an unpredictable way following the input (i.e., "play") of the user.

Video games preserve this model through an environment that incorporates both the game scenario and rules—the user "plays" in this environment, and can explore nearly endless game variants, the number of possible variations depending, of course, on the sophistication of the game. The first computer games were very simple, with primitive graphics and limited scenarios, but today's games, such as **Myst** and **Doom** (still two of my favorites), provide enormously rich environments, and enormous flexibility in the way a player can explore the game's virtual world. Anyone with an interest in the possible directions of these new media should spend time playing with modern computer games—even if it is hard to convince others that this really is "work"!

Hypertext and Multimedia

At the same time, it was apparent from the earliest days of computers that this new technology could realize the long-dreamed notions of hypertext and multimedia.* Inexpensive computers and easy-to-use programs like HyperCard and Macromedia Director opened up exciting new ways of presenting combinations of otherwise weakly connected media. Very quickly, hypertext and multimedia became the hottest new topics in media design, with products ranging from multimedia wine guides and hypertext encyclopedias to multimedia/hypertext training packages. Indeed, today many corporations commission multimedia promotional kits instead of the more traditional videos or films.

Designing linear multimedia is relatively straightforward—it is the design of *hyper*text or *hyper*media collections that introduces enormous design complexities. This is because each hypertext presentation must incorporate, *within* the structure of the presentation, the tools allowing a user to successfully and comfortably explore the collected material. Since in hypertext the components can be related in decidedly nonlinear ways, there are no simple organizational schemes, such as page numbering, that can serve as ubiquitous and commonly understood paradigms of navigation and location. And, you want the rules for hypertext, unlike those for a game, to be nonintrusive and easy to follow, since you want to communicate *content*, without the reader having to worry about navigating through it. Designers and researchers are still exploring ways of designing easy-to-use hypertext and hypermedia, and it is not a surprise that good design is something of an art rather than a science.

Web Collections as Hypertext

Web collections are a form of hypermedia, limited of course by the technologies of the Web and the Internet (a web collection is clearly not as dynamic or multimedia-oriented as a Macromedia Director presentation), but at the same time enriched by the ability to connect with resources around the

---

* *Hypertext*: a collection of text and graphics that can be explored, by the reader, in a nonlinear way; *multimedia*: the mixture of text, graphics, sound, and video in a single presentation. Note that a multimedia presentation is often *linear*. The combination of multimedia in a nonlinear hypertext format is often called *hypermedia*. In this book, the term hypertext can be taken as synonymous with hypermedia.

world. Most important, the Web is inherently nonlinear, since there can be a nearly (and often frustratingly) endless number of ways of getting from one page to another. Figure 3.2 shows a simple figure of a possible Web document collection—as in Figure 3.1, the solid lines indicate the links (in this case, hypertext links) between the pages, with the arrows indicating the directions of the links.

Figure 3.2 A figurative example of a web of documents—the links between the documents are indicated by the arrows. The collection is *nonlinear*, in that there are a number of different routes by which the collection could be visited. It is very easy to get lost in such a web.

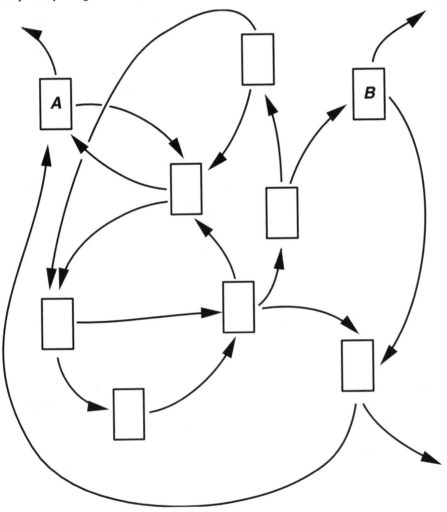

Do you see the inherent problem in Figure 3.2? Suppose you are reading document *A*, and want to proceed to a topic discussed in document *B*. How do you get there? The answer is that you have absolutely no idea. If this collection were to have no structure other than the indicated links, you would be forced to move randomly through the collection until you happened, largely by chance, upon the desired page. In the absence of additional information, you do not know where to find the table of contents (or even if there is one), the index, or the beginning of a section. Even if the links were sequential (the documents connected one after the other, like a book), you would not be able to find places such as these, since with the Web, there is no way to step back, "see" the entire book, and just turn to the "front" for the table of contents. Indeed, a reader has absolutely no idea of the size of the collection: There could be one page or a thousand. A book gives you both a local and global feel for its size and for your location in it: The page number tells you where you are, and where the next and previous pages are, while the feel of the book tells you approximately where you are with respect to the entire book (e.g., halfway through) and also tells you exactly where to find the table of contents (at the front) or the index (at the back). The ability to see the whole picture, plus conventions for the location of contents pages and indexes, are part of the technology of books that makes them so easy to use. It is your goal, in designing a web, to include similar navigational tools, to allow visitors to easily explore and find what they are looking for, without becoming lost or frustrated.

Types of Web Collections

Now that we've given this introductory discussion of design principles, it is time to look at some practical examples of Web collection design, and at the issues that a web designer or *webmaster* must take into account in managing and maintaining such collections.

We will first look at a linear model for a web—just because the Web is nonlinear, doesn't mean you have to give up linearity completely! A linear approach is often appropriate when converting a printed document to hypertext, for on-line documentation, or when you have a particular sequence that you want followed by your readers, such as a sequence of slides.

Of course, most webs are not linear, and the next examples look at nonlinear collections, in particular, at the possible organization of collections of documents at a Web site. This section will include design pointers for larger collections, as well as administrative suggestions for managing large collections developed by several people or groups.

Next, we look at design and planning issues that are independent of the layout of your web: how to plan the web layout, how to organize the documents, how to incorporate multimedia components, and so on.

Finally, we look at tuning a design to make a Web site attractive to visitors, and to encourage their return. This is an issue both of hypertext design and public relations. You must always remember that a Web site is a dynamic place that *encourages* interaction with its visitors. You must be aware, and take advantage of this character, if you are going to develop a site that attracts and retains visitors.

Linear Document Collections

Figure 3.3 shows the schematic layout for a linear document collection—the solid lines with the arrows show the locations and directions of the critical navigational links; Figures 3.4 and 3.5 show a possible design for a page in this collection: Figures 2.2 and 2.4 are other examples of pages from a linear collection. The structure in Figure 3.3 very much follows the book layout shown in Figure 3.1, except that now there are explicit links to places such as the index and table of contents. Recall that in a book, the reader could easily find these components because of their physical placement within the book. This is not possible with hypertext, so the Web collection must have explicit links connecting each page to these important navigational aids.

It is easiest to start by looking at the structure of a single page, such as the example in Figures 3.4 and 3.5. The important navigational features are in the banner at the top and bottom of the pages. The first navigational feature is the title graphic. This quickly identifies the page as part of a particular collection (the "Information Commons" collection), so that users immediately know, from page to page, which collection they are "in." (The text "INFORMATION COMMONS" and "Help With E-Mail" are part of the graphic itself.) Every collection should carry an identifying title graphic such as this, or alternatively, an identifying string of text. It is then possible to use variations of a particular graphic to indicate which section is being examined. For example, the graphic in Figure 3.5 could be varied from section to section—each section would still show the logo and the name "Information Commons," but might also show a smaller-font string with the section name or heading. Some examples of this are shown later in this chapter.

The second navigational feature is the collection of text buttons that link to important related documents. These buttons replace the navigational cues available in a printed book, and let readers quickly find their place in the document. Using the "Prev" and "Next" buttons, the document can be read sequentially; or it can be accessed nonsequentially, using "Table of Contents" or "Index." The "Up" button is linked to the top page of the local section—for example, if this were a page from Section 2 of the collection, the "Up" button might link to the first page of Section 2. Part (B) of Figure 3.3 shows how this could be organized. For convenience, this top-of-section page might contain a brief section introduction, and perhaps a contents listing for the section. This lets the user move "up" for an overview of the section, without having to return all the way to the full table of contents.

Figure 3.3 A linear collection of hypertext documents. The thick solid lines show the main navigational links, while the thin lines illustrate secondary links superimposed on this linear structure. Part (A) shows the underlying linear structure—the links from each page to the *Next* ("Next") and *Previous* ("Prev") pages, as well as to the *Table of Contents* ("ToC") and *Index* ("Index"), with the link names marked in italics. To make the figure easy to follow, the links from the Index to the individual documents have been omitted.

Part (B) shows the possible linking structure when there are section headings within the linear structure. Here the "Up" link connects each page to the top page of this section. For clarity, the "ToC" and "Index" links have been omitted.

(A)

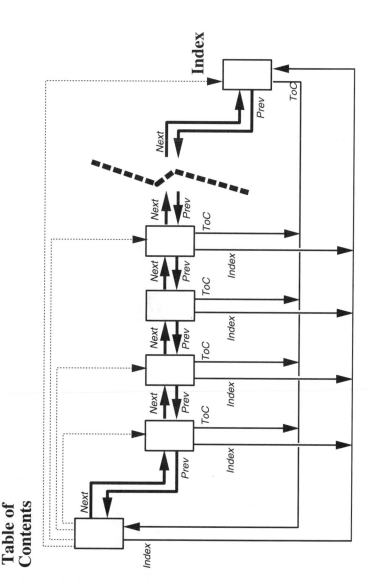

Table of
Contents

Figure 3.3 (Continued)

(B)

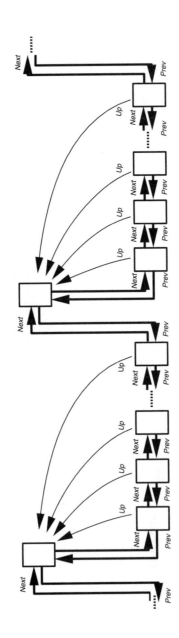

Note how the anchor elements include the **REL** attributes, with values corresponding to the meanings of the links. Although **REL** and the converse, **REV**, do not currently affect the behavior of browsers, they are exceedingly useful in identifying the intent of a link, both to someone editing documents and to someone trying to understand, perhaps through automated web-mapping programs, the overall layout of a collection. Thus, you are advised to include these attributes if you know the relationship(s) defined by the hypertext link. **REL** and **REV** attribute values and their meanings are discussed in Chapter 4.

Adding all this information does not need to be a lot of work. If you are building a large collection, you are best advised to build HTML *templates* for your documents; such templates contain all the generic markup, but not the text, image, or embedded object content. You can then copy the template, edit in your content, and quickly prepare the desired document. Since all your pages will have navigation tools, you can prepare each template to have these tools, including the **REL** and **REV** values; all you need do is add the correct URLs.

Some informational hypertext links are also provided in this example linear collection—these connect to resources that are not really part of the collection, but that provide information useful to the user. For example, the "Feedback" link connects to a gateway program (it could also simply be a **mailto** URL) that lets the visitor send feedback to the document author(s), while the "Info" link provides information explaining what all the navigation buttons mean, and how they work. Both features are useful and should be present in a well-designed collection.

The last thing to stress is the importance of clean design of the page layout, and the use of the same layout for all pages in the collection. Thus, if you decide to use centered **H2** headings for main sections and left-justified **H3** headings for subsections, you should do this for all pages. This reinforces the familiar pattern implied by the graphic and banner design, and makes it easy for a reader to navigate within each page, as well as across the collection.

Note also in Figure 3.5 that the page is dated, and contains a hypertext link to the author or maintainer of the page. Although these items are not necessary on every page, dating pages lets visitors know when the material was last modified, while the feedback mechanism lets you hear what your readers think. You should use a dating scheme that will not be misinterpreted internationally—thus the form 8/9/95 is not ideal, since some countries use the order day/month/year, while others use month/day/year. If you don't want feedback, you can omit the feedback link—but my experience is that feedback is overwhelmingly positive and constructive, and that feedback helps enormously when maintaining large collections.

If you use stylesheets, you can use the stylesheet specification to define layout features that will make your pages both coherent and distinctive. However, this will still only work if you have been consistent in your usage of the HTML elements within your documents.

Figure 3.4 Template HTML document for a linear collection (here, part of a collection of documentation on HTML), illustrating how navigational links can be included within the page design. Each page in a collection will have an identical banner design and labeling graphic that uniquely identifies the collection and allows the user to quickly get used to the look and feel of the pages. Figure 3.5 shows this document as displayed by the Netscape Navigator browser. Note that the text adjacent to the logo ("INFORMATION COMMONS" and "Help With E-Mail") is part of the header graphic.

```
<HTML><HEAD>
<TITLE> REL and REV Attributes for Hypertext Links</TITLE>
</HEAD><BODY>
<P ALIGN="center"><IMG ALIGN="bottom" SRC="iclogo.gif"
        ALT="{Information Commons — HTML Docmentation]"><BR>
[<A HREF="page2_1.html" REL="previous">Prev</A>]
[<A HREF="page2_3.html" REL="next">Next</A>]
[<A HREF="page2_0.html" REL="parent">Up</A>]
. . .
[<A HREF="contents.html"     REL="contents"><B>ToC</B></A>]
[<A HREF="/cgi-bin/index.pl" REL="index"><B>Index</B></A>]
. . .
[<A HREF="info.html"><EM>Info</EM></A>]
[<A HREF="/cgi-bin/feedback.pl"><EM>Feedback</EM></A>]
<HR>
<H2> REL and REV Attributes </H2>
<P> REL and REV attribute are used, with LINK and A (anchor)
elements, to describe the relationship between the document
containing the element, and the document referenced by the
 hypertext link .....
<P> And yet more babble about REL and REV...
<HR>
<CENTER> <EM><A HREF="mailto:ic_html_doc@ic.utor.ca">IC
HTML Documentation</A> . . . . . .</EM>
<EM>Last Update:</EM> 12 September 1995 </CENTER>
</BODY>
</HTML>
```

Structured Treelike Collections

The next hypertext model is that of a tree or hierarchical document collection. An example is given in Figure 3.6, which shows a single, extended tree. A real-world example is the Yahoo collection at http://www.yahoo.com, which is a list of Web-accessible resources. The Yahoo documents are organized hierarchically. For example, the Yahoo page on aids for people with disabilities, shown in Figure 3.7B, lies under the category "Companies," listed in Figure 3.7A. This page in turn lies under the category "Disabilities," which in turn lies under the category

Figure 3.5 Display, by the Netscape Navigator browser, of the document listed in Figure 3.4.

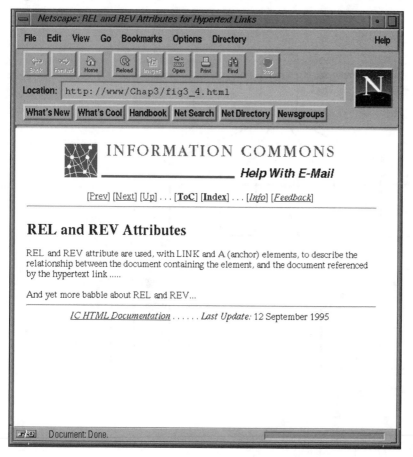

"Health." If you have information that organizes itself in a hierarchical manner, this is your obvious approach. Of course, the hierarchy need not be as large as the Yahoo collection for this approach to be valuable. Another more modest example is presented later in this chapter.

The navigation tools required within a hierarchy are different from those needed in a linear collection. For example, the linear concepts of *next* and *previous* are no longer meaningful, while links to "Up" are usually equivalent to the browser's "back" button, and are often not necessary. Instead, you want links back to a number of locations such as the root of the tree (the link to "Yahoo!" in Figure 3.7—the image is clickable), perhaps a "Search" or "Index" tool (essentially a searchable index), and also to important informational pages. As in the linear collection, the

**Figure 3.6 Schematic diagram of a *hierarchical* document web. The documents
are organized in a tree-like structure, descending from a single home document.**

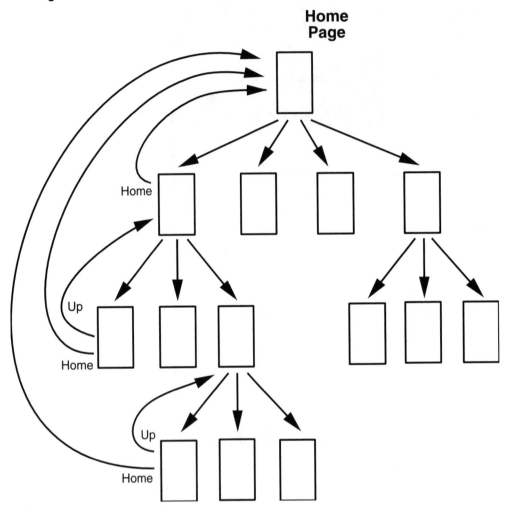

document in Figure 3.7 also has links to a feedback utility ("Write Us") and to general information—hear about the Yahoo hierarchical resource list ("Info"). Finally, the special-purpose link
"Add URL" lets a visitor register new URLs for inclusion in the collection. Obviously, each collection will have its own special-purpose utilities and links, depending on the site's function and
goals.

Figure 3.7 Example page from the Yahoo hierarchical catalog of Web sites. (A) is an example of an index page from this collection—you can find this page by accessing the site: `http://www.yahoo.com/` **and selecting the category "Health," followed by the category "Disabilities." Note the boldface items, which indicate links that go an additional level down the hierarchical tree—the number afterwards gives the number of items in the linked index page. An "@" indicates that the link is to a document that can be reached from more than one Yahoo category page—a "leaf "attached to more than one "branch." (B) shows the document returned by selecting the "Companies (@)" link in the document shown in part (A). These screen captures are courtesy of Yahoo! Inc.**

(A)

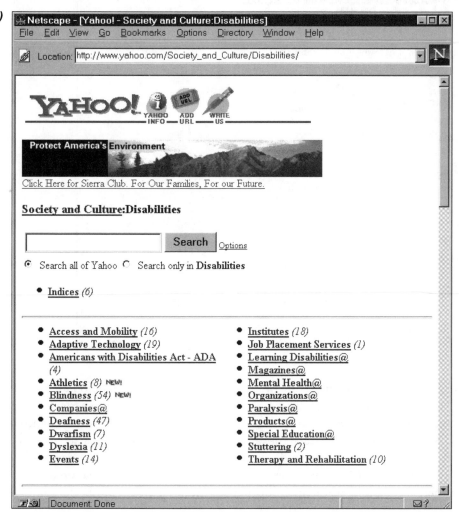

Figure 3.7 (Continued)

(B)

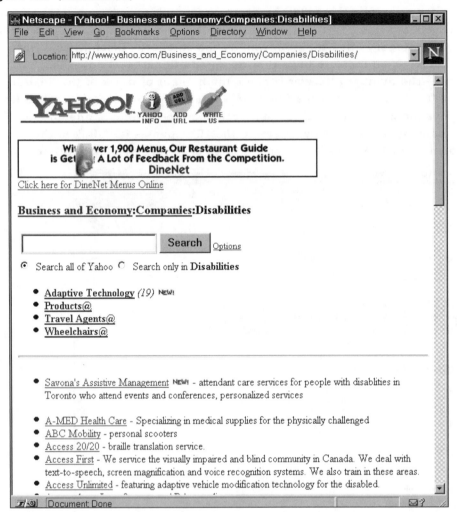

At Yahoo, the page *layout* also contains important information. In all the Yahoo index pages (e.g., Figure 3.7A), links to additional subcategories are indicated by boldface hypertext anchors, while the bracketed number after each such anchor indicates the number of items catalogued in that subcategory. A trailing "at" (@) character means that the subcategory is actually accessible from more than one place in the hierarchy, indicating that the node has *multiple parents*—the hierarchy is not a simple tree, but contains cross-linked branches. In this case, the top of the page lists the primary route through the hierarchy to the document: in Figure 3.7B, "Business and

Economy," followed by "Companies," followed by "Disabilities." The label "Disabilities" is not an active anchor, as this is just a label for the document we are reading; the others provide direct links to these patent pages.

The Yahoo design is undergoing constant evolution, as better page layout models are developed, and as the collection of references grows—the Yahoo tree(s) keep growing new document "branches" and "leaves" to account for the ever-increasing size of the database. Overall, the design has evolved comfortably (at least as far as a user is concerned!) within the original structure, which is a good indication of the robust nature of the approach.

Designing a Good Hierarchy

The hierarchical approach can be extremely useful, but you must be careful to make it easily navigable. In particular, you do not want the hierarchy to be too deep (too many levels), or too shallow (too few). If the hierarchy is too shallow, then there will be too many categories at each level and it will be difficult for visitors to find what they are looking for. At the same time, having too many levels in the hierarchy presents similar problems, as after four or five selections down into the hierarchy, visitors may lose confidence that they are on the right track. You should strive to keep the tree depth as shallow as possible, without making each level too unwieldy. A depth of three to five is ideal, while anything greater than six is likely a bad choice.

Most important, your design—the number of levels, and the names and labels of your categories—must reflect the material you wish to present, and the way you wish to present it: There is no one hierarchical structure that is universally appropriate. Thus the Yahoo layout, which works well for Yahoo, is not where you should start—you should start by looking at *your* data, and determining how you want *it* to be organized and accessed.

A Web Document Hierarchy

Another example of a well-organized hierarchy is found at the URL:

```
http://www.utoronto.ca/webdocs/HTMLdocs/tools_home.html
```

which is the top node for a document collection describing many of the Web browsers, HTML editors, and support tools available on Mac, UNIX, and PC platforms. This collection is organized hierarchically, first by platform (Windows, Macintosh, OS/2, UNIX, Miscellaneous Tools) and second by subcategories based on tool type (TCP/IP Software, WWW Browsers, Browser Helper Applications, HTML Editors, HTML Translators/Filters). Figure 3.8 shows a typical page from this collection—in this case, the top-level page of this hierarchy. Note how this page has navigational links to the documents one level down in the hierarchy, namely "Windows Tools," "Macintosh Tools," "OS/2 Tools," "UNIX Tools," and "Miscellaneous Tools." This organization makes it extremely easy to navigate through the hierarchy and find the desired information. Although not apparent from this page, the hierarchy is only three levels deep.

Figure 3.8 A page from a hierarchical list of Web programming resources, showing the important design features in a hierarchical collection. This page is available over the Web at:

`http://www.utoronto.ca/webdocs/HTMLdocs/tools_home.html`

This page was designed by Michael Lee of the University of Toronto's Information Commons.

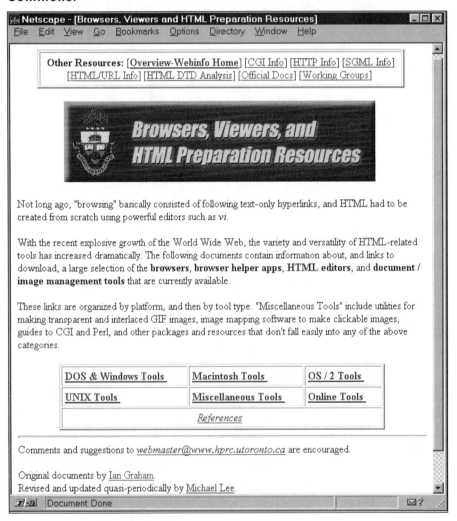

Note also that there is a link from this page all the way back to the home page for this Web site ("Webinfo Home"), which is the top node or home page for the entire local document collection.

The overall design and organization of a Web site is discussed later in this chapter.

Hierarchies and Linear Components Together

Obviously, it is easy to include linear collections, described at the beginning of this section, within this hierarchical model. A particular node within the hierarchy simply becomes the starting page for the linear collection. The hierarchy then gives an overall and easily navigable structure to the entire collection, rather like shelf labels in a library or bookstore.

Web Site Collections

A Web site usually follows the hierarchical approach, but with a few twists. Figure 3.9 illustrates a possible organization of a large site's Web collection. In general, a web has a single top node, or *home page*, which is the publicly advertised location for the document collection. The home page then has links to other pages that lead down to the remaining resources in the collection. In this example, the home page has links to small introductory documents that explain the origins of the site and provide some useful site information; in addition, links to the top-level nodes of the various hierarchical collections beneath the home page are also provided. Figures 3.10 and 3.11 show two example home pages—despite their superficial dissimilarity, both pages follow precisely this model.

Almost all sites on the Web follow this home page design model. As an exercise, explore Web sites and the associated home pages, comparing the home page design and site layout with the model presented here. You will quickly begin to see the overall design similarities.

Distinguishing Branches in a Large Web

Often, a Web site will have many different main sections rooted in the home page, as seen in both the University of Toronto (Figure 3.10) and the Silicon Surf (Figure 3.11) home pages. Often, the web manager will want to use similar document layouts and design models in the different branches, since this makes it easier for users to navigate through the collection. At the same time, the designer will want to give each section a distinctive look, so that the readers have a sense of location, and know where they are.

One way to do this is to modify the banner text graphic at the top of the page to reflect the identity of the site and the specific features of the local tree—this is just what we prescribed for linear collections earlier in this chapter. Consider, for example, the "Information Commons" Web site. For this site, the banner graphic shown in Figure 3.5, which contains the Information Commons logo and name, could be modified for each section at the Web site, retaining the logo

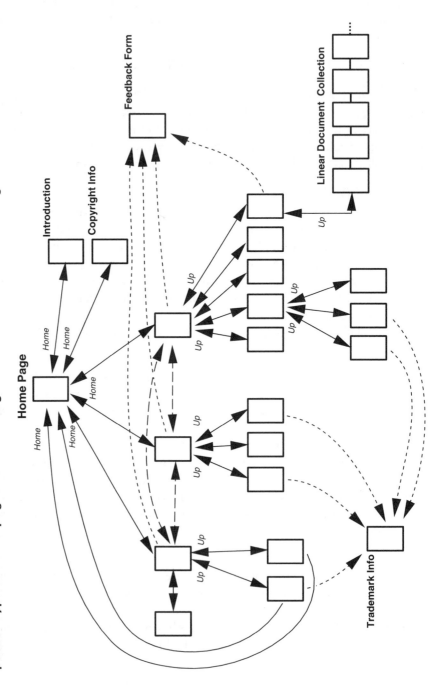

Figure 3.9 Schematic layout of a large Web collection, showing the HTML-coded hypertext relationships between the home page, the top-level organizational nodes, and other elements of the collection. The solid lines indicate main links between items within the hierarchical (or linear) structures, while the long-dashed lines indicate links between "siblings" at the same level in a hierarchy. The arrows indicate the possible directions of the links, as coded into the HTML anchor elements in the documents. The short-dashed links indicate links to general-purpose pages—note that these hypertext anchors are unidirectional, since it is unreasonable to code in all the possible return paths. Typical home pages for such large collections are shown in Figures 3.10 and 3.11.

Figure 3.10 Official home page for the University of Toronto. The page has links to single documents describing the University organization and mandate, as well as links to the main organizational areas. These latter links are to top-level nodes of subsequent hierarchical trees.

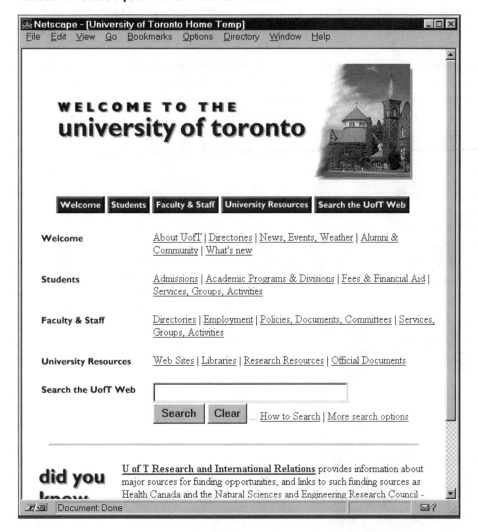

and name but adding a subtitle appropriate to each section. The logo immediately communicates that the page belongs within the Information Commons collection, while the subtitle quickly indicates the particular subsection or topic. In addition, different-sized or differently styled logos

Figure 3.11 Home page of *Silicon Surf*, the electronic publication of Silicon Graphics Inc. This is a graphically oriented home page that contains links to the main information categories at the *Silicon Surf* Web site. Despite the very different visual style, the organization of this page is very similar to that in Figure 3.10. Note that the *Silicon Surf* home page cannot be sensibly viewed by non-graphical browsers, but that the very first text line of the page (hard to read in this figure) provides a link to a text-only version of this home page. You should recall that imagemapped (active) images are *never* functional with a non-graphical browser, so if you use an imagemapped image as a navigational tool, you must offer a text-only menu. Image used by permission of Silicon Graphics (http://www.sgi.com) and copyright 1996 Silicon Graphics Inc. All rights reserved.

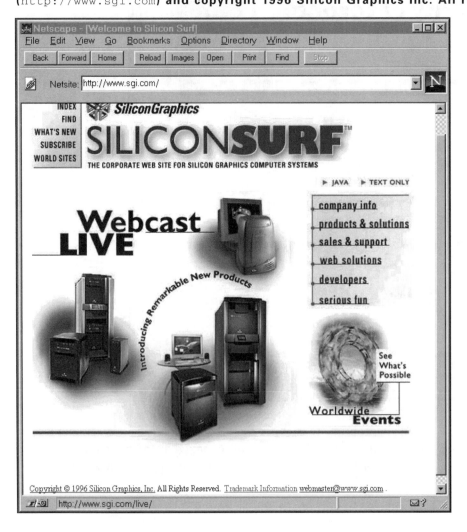

can be used for sections and subsections, to give a graphical feel for the hierarchical location of the document in the overall collection. Finally, the **BACKGROUND** attribute to the **BODY** element can be used to tile the background with a "watermark" reflecting this same information. These graphical approaches are not sufficient on their own, however, as the information provided by the graphics is lost with a non-graphical browser, or if image loading is disabled on the user's browser. You must therefore be sure to use the **ALT** attribute to provide an appropriate text alternative.

Figure 3.12 shows some possible banner designs for the Information Commons, based on the ideas just presented. Note how each preserves the Information Commons look and feel, while quickly communicating the function of the page and its location within the overall hierarchy.

Multiple Document Versions

Ideally, you want to design all your pages, including your home page, so that they can be understood on any Web browser. However, sometimes this is not possible, or is inconvenient—for example, you may be presenting information both to users who have learning disabilities and prefer graphics over text, and to users who are blind and can *only* use text. To deal with this type of conflict, some Web sites offer *multiple* home pages.* A good example of this is found at the University of Toronto's Adaptive Technology Resource Centre home page, shown in Figure 3.13. This page is graphically rich, but offers *two* alternative home pages—one designed for users with screen readers, and the other for users who can use graphics, but who prefer a less graphically intense presentation.

You may also want to offer alternative navigational pages that structure the underlying content of a site from different points of view. For example, the collection of material on Adaptive Technology (aids for persons with disabilities) can be organized as a tree presenting important issues and technologies, but could also be presented as a problem-solving tree, where the various branches represent options in a decision-tree for obtaining technology solutions for particular user disabilities. A schematic for this type of structure is given in Figure 3.14, which illustrates two organizational trees linked to the same underlying content.

You must be careful with this type of design, since the documents at the bottom of the tree (the actual data in your collection) have no way of knowing whether they were accessed from tree *A* or tree *B*. The navigational icons on each document must therefore point to both trees, and to the appropriate places on each tree. This presents difficulties similar to those at the Yahoo site, where several list categories appeared below multiple nodes in the tree. At Yahoo, the referenced page lists all the possible parent nodes. Unfortunately, accessing these alternative parents can be quite disorienting for an inexperienced user, unless their nature as optional routes is well explained.

---

* This is also useful for sites that insist on using active imagemaps, java applets, et cetera, on their home pages. Such resources do not work for visitors using lynx, who have disabled image loading, or who cannot run Java, so these visitors need an alternative, graphics- and applet-free home page. The SGI home page, shown in Figure 3.11, provides these options.

Figure 3.12 Possible page banners for different Web pages at the Information Commons. Note how the banner graphics preserve the identity of the site, while at the same time communicating the subcategory each page belongs to. In addition, major section banners are bigger than minor page banners, allowing for easy determination of place in the hierarchy.

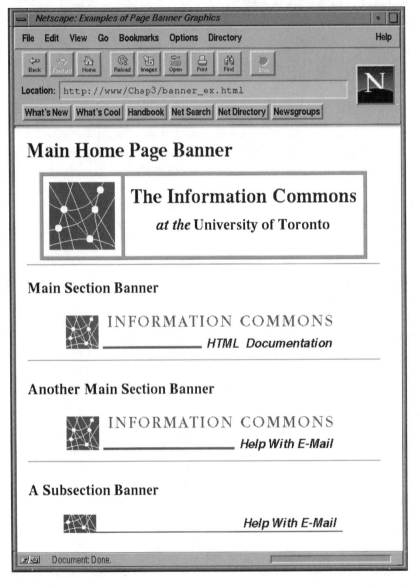

Figure 3.13 Home page for the Adaptive Technology Resource Centre at the University of Toronto. Note how this page offers two alternative home pages, optimized for different audiences. This page is available at the URL:

http://www.hprc.utoronto.ca/AdTech/ATRCmain.html

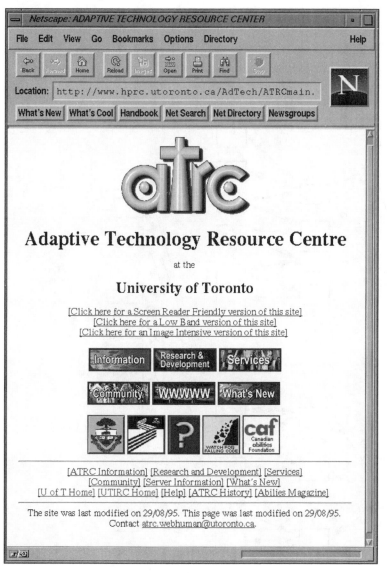

Figure 3.14 Possible structure of a Web site having two home pages and two parallel organizational structures, labeled *A* and *B*. Both trees access the same underlying collection of documents, shown at the bottom of the figure.

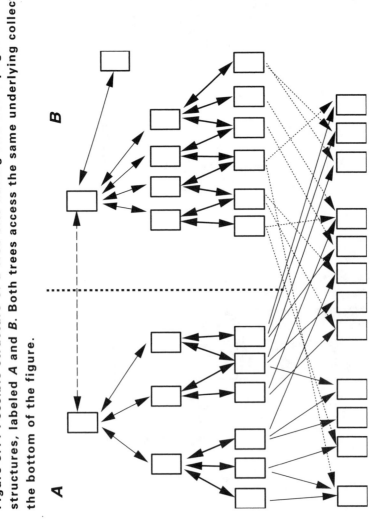

Gateway Filtering of Documents

Although the Web is a dynamic medium, HTML documents by themselves are static and unintelligent—as just noted, a retrieved page contains no information about the history of your interaction, and cannot know, for example, which home (or other) page you used to access it. This means that if you use multiple home pages, then all your documents must have "Go to HOME" buttons for each of these possible home pages, or you have to leave out these links entirely.

You can in part deal with this issue by using a *gateway* program (gateway programs are discussed in Chapters 8 and 9) or some other server-side processing mechanism, to dynamically modify *every* document returned from the server. For example, suppose there are two alternative structures for a document collection, labeled *pathA* and *pathB*, each path starting from a different home page. You can implement this collection so that the home pages do not access the remaining documents directly, but instead access them *through* a gateway program. This program processes the documents so that they include the navigational icons and other information that reflects the path being explored. Suppose the first page to be explored from home page *A* is the document ***monsters.html***. In this example, the page is accessed via the URL:

```
http:/www.we.edu/cgi-bin/docfilter/dir1/dir2/monsters.html?path-a
```

where the gateway filtering program is **docfilter,** the path to the desired document is `/dir1/dir2/monsters.html`, and the query string `path-a` indicates which path is being explored. The `docfilter` program retrieves the indicated document, and edits all URL strings in the document so that they also use **docfilter** to access documents from the local collection, and so that they also contain the query string `path-a` to indicate the path being explored. In addition, **docfilter** could modify the document banner, inserting the navigational icons and hypertext links appropriate to this path.

This is not a trivial exercise, since the filtering process is complicated and must take into account the structure of the entire document collection. Thus, to date, use of this approach has been limited. However, a wonderful (and very sophisticated) example of the power of this approach can be found at the Electronic Books Technology site:

```
http://www.ebt.com/
```

Here, the document collection is entirely served from an underlying database of non-HTML documents—filtering programs dynamically convert the database entries (coded in another SGML language) into HTML, and automatically configure the presentation depending, for example, on the path being explored.

Designing and Managing a Web Site

Large Web sites are usually designed and maintained by more than one person. As a site becomes large, maintenance and development become major issues, so it is useful to have a model for management that allows for scalability with size and for a well-defined delineation of responsibilities.

Site Organization—The Webmaster

A Web site should have an overall web manager, or *webmaster*, who organizes the home page and the main navigational pages. This manager is responsible for ensuring valid links to the top pages of the underlying collections, but cannot be responsible for the internal consistency of those underlying collections. This makes for a reasonable division of responsibilities and obligations, giving the individual project groups full control over their own document collections, while leaving the overall management of the site in the hands of a site manager.

A site manager should prepare a template of HTML documents for use by the groups developing their own resources. This template might contain a generic graphical logo for the site, some document templates that reflect a generic page or collection design, and, finally, a list of URLs that link to the main navigational pages maintained by the site manager. Each project group can then integrate these links into their own project pages to create links back to the site home page. They can also use the logos and page templates to preserve, if they wish (or are mandated) to do so, the site's look and feel.

Individual Project Directories

Each major document subcollection should be placed in its own directory or subdirectory, distinct from the directory housing the Web site home page and main organizational pages. Users responsible for maintaining each collection can then be given permission to create and modify files in their particular directory, but nowhere else. This isolates the projects from each other, and ensures that no one can accidentally modify another group's pages.

Test and Production Directories

In some cases, it may be convenient to give each group two directories—one for the finished and publicly available material, the other as a development or test area. In this way, the development team can develop and modify documents in the test directory, without worrying about affecting the documents being seen by visitors to the site. Once the new material has been fully developed and tested, in can be collectively copied into the public directory, making it available to the general public.

There are several Web development packages—for example, Microsoft's FrontPage and the Silicon Graphics' WebMagic—that support this type of development and "publication," while several HTTP servers integrate database management of the document collection with the server.

Many of the newer *intranet* software suites also include this type of functionality. You can expect more tools such as these to become available in the near future.

Revision Control and Document Management

In many cases, a single collection will be designed collaboratively by many different users. In this case, it is often convenient to use revision control or document management software to manage the collaborative development process. Such software can archive the changes made to a collection, and can also ensure that only a single person can modify a given document at a time. The tools mentioned in the previous section support this functionality, to some degree.

There are also many stand-alone revision and document management packages available on every platform, which can be adapted to Web applications. (Most were originally designed for software development projects, for which similar issues are important.) Some, such as rcs (Revision Control System) and sccs (Source Code Control System), often come bundled with UNIX systems, and were designed to manage large software development projects. If you are developing a large project involving many document developers, you should definitely consider one of these tools. Sites such as Yahoo have links to information about other similar packages. If you are interested in this option, you should search Yahoo (or other) sites, using search strings such as "revision control" or "document management."

In the absence (or even in the presence) of document management software, you will want to take the following points into account when designing and maintaining a large document collection:

- Keep your documents well organized on disk, using subdirectories to appropriately organize the material by topic or workgroup.

- Use HTML comments (`<!-- comment -->`), **META** elements, or some other mechanism, to record modifications to the documents. Document management systems often maintain a secondary database for these data. HTML comments and **META** elements are described in Chapter 4.

- Use partial URLs to reference documents on the same server. This makes the collection transportable, as the relative references will be correct regardless of the absolute location of the collection.

- Preserve the original high-resolution image files you use to create your page graphics, logos, and buttons, so that at a later date you can easily create new document graphics from these original data.

Design and Maintenance of a Web Collection

In designing a collection of any type, there are several general rules you should follow, and these rules are presented in the following sections. Although in most cases these rules will seem like common sense, they are often overlooked or unimplemented unless you (a) incorporate them into your design model and (b) implement them early in the design phase for your web. It is usually very difficult to back up and fix mistakes once a site is up and running, and these simple rules will help you to reduce the number of mistakes you make.

Storyboard the Collection

You have probably noticed the usefulness of schematic drawings in picturing the interrelationships and linkages between Web documents. In fact, such drawings are extremely useful in *designing* Web collections—it is always a good idea to sketch out the web layout and work out the desired relationships *before* you actually begin preparing the documents. Storyboarding is enormously flexible, and lets you experiment with many possibilities before you start preparing the pages. Design and navigation problems quickly become apparent when you lay out the overall organization of the pages, as do the choices for the navigational links that must be built into each page. Storyboarding is easy to do, and will save you time and effort in the long run.

Determine Page Layout and Design

Once you have a Web site design, you now need to implement the technical design elements described in Chapters 1 and 2. Each page must contain the required navigational tools and should have a recognizable and well-designed layout. In the latter regard, you should take advantage of the typographic and design principles well known in the print world. To paraphrase Robin Williams (the designer, not the actor), these principles are:

> **Contrast**—elements on a page that are not the same should be *very different*.

> **Repetition**—elements that repeat through the page or collection should repeat with the *same design layout*, to show the unity of the content and to indicate the organizational structure.

> **Alignment**—page layout is not arbitrary, and everything placed on the page should have a *visual* connection to something else.

> **Proximity**—elements *related* to one another should be placed *close together*.

Some examples that apply these principles are shown in Chapter 12. For additional information on this topic, you are referred to Williams's book, listed in the bibliography at the end of the chapter.

Plan for the Future

This may seem obvious, but it is not—or, at least, many people seem to ignore this aspect of design. A well-designed collection will both age and grow well. Aging well means that pages can be redesigned, with new graphics and better layout, without affecting the underlying hypertext structure. The same is true for growth. A well-designed collection will have room for new nodes, new trees, and new branches, without requiring the pruning, dismemberment, or outright destruction of the original structure. You must plan ahead—you can do this while storyboarding the first version of your collection—because any good Web site will grow quickly, at which time it is exceedingly difficult to go back and fix basic design flaws.

Make Navigation Easy

This may seem mindless repetition, but it is essential that you consistently use good design to make your collection easy to explore. All your pages should have links back to some master navigational page, such as the local linear collection's table of contents, or the home page of the local document tree. Also, all your pages must have obvious exit points—you don't want users guessing at what to do next. And, last, make sure your links work! All the navigation buttons in the world won't help if you made a mistake in the underlying URLs. Chapter 11 lists some useful utilities for testing hypertext links in a collection of documents.

Never Move Main Pages

Once you have built a popular site, your visitors will bookmark your important navigational pages so that they can return directly to these locations. Therefore, once these pages are put in place, you should *never*, *ever*, move them. Doing so will break all your visitor's stored hotlist or bookmark entries, and will cause no end of grief. If you must move pages, make sure to provide server redirection for the main pages, or to provide temporary pages that point to the new location.

When expanding a collection, you should avoid eliminating pages—only add new ones. This avoids the problem just mentioned, and ensures that hotlist entries are not broken. This reiterates the importance of properly thinking out the organization of your collection before you start. A well-organized collection has room for easy expansion, whereas an ill-thought-out jumble of pages will not grow easily, and will lead to problems when you find you must reorganize the pages due to flaws in the initial structure.

You should also assign a special domain name for your HTTP server. Names of the form www.my.domain.edu, web.site.com, or home.pluto.com are quite common, with the strings www, web, or home quickly identifying this as a Web server site. This domain name can then easily be moved from one machine to another, without affecting your site visitors. For example, you might initially have www.pluto.com on a shared machine or some other temporary location. Later on, the server and the domain name can be moved to a machine dedicated to HTTP services, without affecting the URL used to access your resources.

Commercial domain names (ending with .com) are registered through the Internet Network Information Centre (InterNIC). This is accessible over the Web at:

`http://www.internic.net/`

There is currently a registration fee of $US 50. Many Internet providers will help you obtain domain names, for a small additional fee. Given the technical issues involved, this is probably worth the extra expense.

Make Resources Easy to Find

Your collection is there to be read, so make it easy for users to find what they are looking for. A visitor should be able to get to your main resources after only a couple of clicks—most visitors will give up if the resource they are interested in is too far away. This requires a careful analysis of the intent of the site, the available content, and content usage. You can monitor the use of your documents by analyzing the server log files. If you find that a particular resource is very popular, you can always add direct links from your home (or other) page to this resource, and make it more easily accessible.

Making information easy to find *also* means letting people know when resources are *not* available. For example, a visitor to an airline Web site will probably be looking for airline flight information and ticket prices. However, since ticket prices are notoriously variable, it is hard to keep Web-based data up-to-date. The Web site then should have a page discussing fares that says exactly this, and that provides an alternative (maybe a 1-800 number!) for further inquiries.

Indicate Changes and Updates

Indicate on your Web pages when you make changes or additions—adding a date to each page to indicate when it was last modified is one good way of accomplishing this. As a result, it is easy for frequent visitors to find things that are new, and furthermore lets new visitors know that the collection is being continuously improved—visitors will keep coming back if they know you are keeping the site up-to-date.

Keep Your Visitors

No doubt you want people to spend some time at your site once they arrive, and, of course, if you have followed all my design pointers, they are bound to do so! However, one easy way to unwittingly send visitors away is to explicitly give them, just after they have arrived at your site, links to places outside your local web. It is generally a bad idea to include, on your home (or other high-level) pages, links to "KooL SiTEs" or "Important Resources" elsewhere on the Web, as your visitors are likely to head right there and never come back. Instead, put this information further down in your collection, thereby forcing users to step through and see some of your own work before arriving at these external links.

Solicit User Feedback
Your pages should allow for user feedback, so that users can make inquiries, point out problems (broken links, nonfunctional search tools, etc.), or provide commentary. This can be done by using either **mailto** URLs or fill-in feedback forms.

Monitor Utilization
There are many tools for monitoring the usage log files of your Web site, and these can be constructively used to find out which parts of the collection are popular (and which are not), and to find out how people are exploring your collection. If you find that a part is popular but difficult to access, you can rebuild the links to make access easier.

Many commercial servers come with simple analysis tools, while a number of commercial shareware and freeware analysis packages are also available. Chapter 11 lists some of the more popular utilities.

Preserve Individual Privacy
At the same time, you must guard your visitor's privacy. No user would be happy knowing that you were directly monitoring his or her access to information, just as you would be unhappy if your librarian were to monitor the list of books you checked out. If you do access the log files, you should do so in a way that preserves user anonymity: for example, by hiding the domain names of the clients, or by looking at aggregate information averaged over many users.

Creating an *Attractive* Web Site
This is clearly an open-ended section, as the design of a popular and attractive Web site depends enormously on both the material being presented and the intended audience. This section summarizes those features that, in the author's opinion, apply in most cases.

Useful, Timely, and Interesting Information
If your site does not provide something newer than, better than, value-added to, or different from other Web sites, no one will bother coming back. Before you design a site, think about how your material will be novel, different, or better than already existing resources. If you can't, then you should try thinking of something else to do. And, if you are presenting something new and different, be sure to explain why it is better, or different.

Make Your Site Dynamic

The Web is dynamic, and encourages communication. Your site should recognize and embrace these facts by encouraging user feedback and user interaction, and by providing information that is updated on a regular (that is, daily or weekly) basis. Some of the more attractive Web resources, such as daily cartoons ("Dilbert"), Web contests, the amazing Fishcam, browsable archives of mailing lists, and so on, do exactly this (you can find most of these examples by searching the Yahoo index). You should strive to implement similar dynamic and interactive features at your site.

Make Your Site Fast

You must make sure that your visitors can access your information as fast as possible. Thus, you want your site to have a high-speed connection to the Internet, so that any delays in getting your material to your visitors are not due to your own low-speed link. This is particularly important if your site contains a lot of images, which are notoriously big files, and correspondingly slow to download. At a minimum, you should have an ISDN-speed connection (128 Kbps), and preferably something much faster. You don't always need to buy this for yourself—if you are buying space on a commercial HTTP server, just make sure your service provider has a fast Internet connection. You should also check your site's access speed by accessing the site from some other network. This will quickly tell you if visitors to your collection are going to have access problems.

*Make Your Site Accessible—*A.K.A.: *Don't Get Carried Away*

It is easy to get carried away in designing a Web site by incorporating audio and video data, multimedia or other plug-ins, or complicated JavaScript scripts or Java applets. You must always be aware that at best, these objects require high bandwidth to be effective, and at worst, users with older PCs or inappropriate browsers will simply not be able to view these data, regardless of bandwidth. Many sites have started with home pages filled with applets and gorgeous embedded multimedia components, only to remove these components due to complaints from visitors. This is not to say that these components are bad; rather, you should be careful in their use, and aware of the limitations your users may have. If you do use these technologies, be sure to offer alternative pages for those users who cannot view the content.

Listen to Your Visitors

If users bother to write with commentary about your collection, you should pay attention to what they say. Almost universally, such letters either point out problems with your collection (perhaps a broken link), contain suggestions for improvements or changes, or contain requests for additional information. You should respond to these notes—after all, if they have bothered to send you a comment, the least you can do is send a note of thanks. This is polite and will also improve your public relations.

Watch for New Ideas

There are thousands of people creating new and exciting Web collections, every day of the week. Certainly, much of what I have learned has been the result of surfing around the Web and seeing what others are doing. You must do the same! The design possibilities are growing quickly, as a result of novel design by talented individuals, and as a result of new Web technologies that permits new design elements (backgrounds, tables, animation, and so on). You must explore the Web and see how these tools are implemented elsewhere, before you can intelligently implement them yourself.

Planning and Implementation

This chapter has covered basic issues related to the structure of good hypertext collections, but has not discussed the details of Web site planning and implementation. These important issues are discussed in Chapter 12.

Annotated Bibliography

http://info.med.yale.edu/caim/StyleManual_Top.HTML This URL points to an excellent on-line discussion of hypertext design issues, and their relevance to the Web. This excellent resource has a large and very useful annotated bibliography. The author of the collection is Patrick J. Lynch, codirector of the Center for Advanced Instructional Media at the Yale University School of Medicine, and a lecturer in graphic design at the Yale University School of Art.

Multimedia and Hypertext: The Internet and Beyond, by Jacob Nielsen, Academic Press, Cambridge, Mass., 1995. Jacob Nielsen's book is an expansive overview of multimedia and hypertext, with important discussions of usability and design issues. With its almost 70 pages of references, you will never again be at a loss for what to read!

The Non-Designer's Design Book, by Robin Williams, Peachpit Press, 1994. This small, outstanding book covers all the basic elements of good typography, page layout, and book design. Although written for the printed page, this is a must-read book for anyone who wants to design Web pages and who does not have a background in design and/or typography.

Understanding Hypermedia, by Bob Cotton and Richard Oliver, Phaidon Press, 1993. A somewhat glitzy and graphical introduction to hypermedia, and an excellent addition to any coffee table. This will be of particular interest to those with a background in design.

Hypertext, by George P. Landow, Johns Hopkins University Press, 1992. This is a discussion not of the technical aspects of hypertext, but of the literary meaning of hypertext, and of its impact on our understanding of text and literature. If "critical theory" or the name Michel Foucault means anything to you, then this is the book to read!

In a similar, if more readable, vein, see: *The Gutenberg Elegies*, by Sven Birkerts, Fawcett Columbine, 1994.

4

HTML in Detail

This chapter and Chapter 5 provide a detailed exposition of the *HyperText Markup Language,* or *HTML,* written from a document developer's point of view and designed to help authors create well-designed, *valid* HTML documents. The two chapters present detailed descriptions of every HTML element and of allowed hierarchical relationships amongst these elements. Although relatively straightforward, the material is most easily followed if you have a basic understanding of HTML at the level outlined in Chapters 1 and 2 of this book. If things seem confusing, you should probably go back to these earlier chapters, and review some of the examples given there.

Chapter 4 is divided into 14 sections. The first explains the structural rules and design principles behind HTML, and outlines specific features of the HTML markup model. The second section defines the terminology used in the rest of the chapter, for explaining the details of the HTML element specifications. The next 11 sections break down the different elements into the following categories:

- Basic Structure: **HTML, HEAD,** and **BODY** Elements

- Head Meta-Information Elements (**TITLE, LINK, META, BASE, SCRIPT, STYLE, ISINDEX**)

- Body Text Block and Heading Elements (**ADDRESS, BLOCKQUOTE, CENTER, P,** etc.)

- Fill-In Forms (**FORM** and related elements)

- Lists and List-Related Elements (**DL, UL, OL, DIR, MENU, DT, DD, LI**)

- Tables and Tabular Structures (**TABLE** and related elements)

- Inclusion Elements (**APPLET** and **IMG**)

- Hypertext Relationship Elements (**A**)

- Text/Phrase Markup Elements (**STRONG, CITE, B, I,** etc.)

- Character-Like Elements (**BR**)

- Meta-Information Elements (**BASEFONT, MAP, AREA, SCRIPT**)

Finally, the last section provides references to other important on-line and non–on-line (i.e., books!) resources.

This chapter focuses on the markup elements of HTML 3.2, which is the current, definitive version of HTML, and is the language version you should use to design universally viewable documents. However, several extensions to this version of HTML are in common use—some proprietary (Netscape- or Microsoft-specific, for the most part), and some part of the ongoing HTML standardization process. These elements—**EMBED, FRAME, SPACER, BLINK, MARQUEE,** and so on (there *are* a lot of them)—are described in Chapter 5. Chapter 5 also discusses some of the exciting new features coming out of the HTML development process, such as internationalization (redesigning HTML to support non-European languages), connections between HTML and scripting languages such as JavaScript, and stylesheets. Note, however, that these features will not function on many browsers currently in use. This is an important consideration if you want your documents to be accessible to the largest possible audience.

The Basics of Markup Languages

As mentioned in Chapter 1, the HyperText Markup Language is designed to specify the *logical* organization and formatting of text documents, with extensions to include inline images, fill-in forms, embedded objects and programs, and hypertext links to other documents and Internet resources. The goal of this approach is a markup language that:

- is not bound to a particular hardware or software environment

- represents the logical structure of a document, and not its presentation

This approach reflects the fact that in a distributed environment like the Web, individuals viewing a document will use many different "browser" programs with very different formatting capabilities. For example, it is not terribly useful to specify that a portion of text must be presented with a 14-point Times Roman font, if the person viewing the document is using a Braille reader. For this reason, HTML does not specify details of the document typesetting, and instead marks the text according to its logical meaning, such as headings, lists, or paragraphs. The details of the presentation of these *elements* are left to the browser, which uses the logical description of the document, built in using HTML, to present the material in the best possible way. Thus, a well-designed HTML document can be clearly presented by graphical or non-graphical browsers, or by non-visual browsers, such as text-to-speech browsers or Braille readers.

Defining HTML: The Document Type Definition

The rules of HTML are defined via the International Standards Organization's (ISO) *Standard Generalized Markup Language*, or *SGML*. SGML is an extremely sophisticated tool for defining markup languages that describe structured documents—HTML is just one instance of SGML. The details of SGML are complex, and fortunately not critical to an HTML document developer. One component that is particularly useful, however, is the SGML *definition* of the HTML syntax, which is contained in a special SGML document called a *Document Type Definition,* or *DTD*. This is a simple text file, often having an imaginative name like ***html.dtd***. The HTML DTD can be used, in combination with SGML parsing programs such as sgmls, to *validate* the syntax of an HTML document—that is, it can check for HTML markup errors in any HTML document and let the author know where they are. The References section at the end of this chapter suggests places where you can obtain the official DTD file for HTML, while Chapter 11 discusses document validation using SGMLs.

This book is a guide to authoring HTML documents, and although it provides a quite complete description of HTML, it should not be considered the definitive reference for the language. For com-prehensive details, you should read the Internet Engineering Task Force (IETF) and World Wide Web Consortium (W3C) documents listed in the "References" section at the end of this chapter, and at the end of Chapter 5.

Allowed Characters in HTML Documents

As illustrated in Chapter 1, an HTML document is just a text document, and can be created and edited with any text editor. An HTML 3.2 document can contain any of the valid *printable* (i.e., excluding control or undefined) characters from the 8-bit ISO Latin-1 character set (also known as ISO 8859-1—see Appendix A for more information about ISO Latin-1 characters and character sets in general). The 256 characters of the ISO Latin-1 character set include the 128 characters of the 7-bit US-ASCII character set (also known as ISO 646) plus 128 additional characters that use the eighth bit ($2^7 = 128$, $2^8 = 256$). The 128 ASCII characters are essentially those found on

U.S. keyboards, while the extra 128 contain many of the accented and other characters common in Western European languages.

Character and Entity References

With many keyboards and text editors, it is difficult to type non-ASCII characters. Partly for this reason, the HTML language has mechanisms for representing these characters using sequences of 7-bit ASCII characters. These mechanisms are called *character references*, which reference the characters using decimal numbers, and *entity references*, which reference them using symbolic names. For example, the character reference for the character é is `&#233;` (the semicolon is necessary and terminates the special reference), while the entity reference for this same character is `&eacute;`. These references are also useful for sending HTML documents by electronic mail, since some mail programs mishandle (i.e., convert into gibberish) non-ASCII characters. However, this is never a problem when transferring HTML documents from a Web server to a browser, since the HTTP protocol reliably transfers all 8-bit data.

These references are also useful with computers such as Macintoshes or PCs running DOS, which do not use ISO Latin-1 for their internal representation of characters (Microsoft Windows does use ISO Latin-1), and which instead use proprietary mappings between the binary codes and the characters these codes represent. Fortunately, this only affects the 128 non-ASCII characters, so that restricting yourself to ASCII ensures a valid HTML document, while character and entity references let you include characters from the full ISO Latin-1 character set.

The ISO Latin-1 character set restriction is clearly a problem for non–Western European languages. Some of the efforts to generalize the character-set options for HTML documents are discussed in Chapter 5 and Appendix A.

Special Characters

Certain ASCII characters codes are treated as special in an HTML document. For example, the ampersand character (&) indicates the start of an entity or character reference, the left and right angle brackets (< and >) indicate the markup tags, and the double quotation mark (") marks the beginning or end of a string within a markup tag. Since an HTML parser interprets these characters as special commands or directives, you cannot use the characters themselves to display as ampersands, greater than or less than signs, or double quotation marks. If you want these characters to appear as regular text, you must include them as character or entity references. The references for these special characters are given in Table 4.1.

When a browser interprets an HTML document, it looks for the special character strings and interprets them accordingly. Thus, when it encounters the string:

```
<H1> Heading string </H1>
```

Table 4.1 Special Characters in HTML

Character	Character Reference	Entity Reference
Left angle bracket (<)	&#60;	&lt;
Right angle bracket (>)	&#62;	&gt;
Ampersand sign (&)	&#38;	&amp;
Double quotation sign (")	&#34;	&quot;

it interprets the strings inside each pair of angle brackets as markup tags, and renders the text between the tags as a heading. However, when the browser sees the string:

```
&lt;H1&gt; Heading string &lt;/H1&gt;
```

it interprets < and > as entity references, and displays the characters

> *<H1> Heading string </H1>*

as a string of regular text.

Comments in HTML Documents

In most HTML documents *comments* are surrounded by the special character strings <!-- and -->. Here the text between them is a comment, and should not be displayed by a browser. There can be spaces between the -- and the > that ends a comment, but the string <!--that starts the *comment declaration* must have no spaces between the characters. The following is an example of a simple comment:

```
<!-- This is a comment -- >
```

Comments can span more than one line, but cannot nest or overlap. You should also be careful when using comments to *hide* HTML markup that would otherwise be displayed, as some older browsers mistakenly use the greater-than sign (>) of regular HTML markup tags to prematurely end the comment.

Here are some examples of comments:

```
<!-- This is a comment --
   -- This is a second comment within the same comment declaration -- >

<!-- This is also a comment
     This comment spans more than one line. Some old browsers improperly
     interpret comments that span multiple lines.
   -- >
```

Some browsers mishandle these multiline comments, so you are best advised to use simple, single-line comments whenever possible.

TIP: The Truth about Comments Formally, a comment consists of a comment *declaration* (consisting of a start string `<!` and the end string `>`) which, in turn, can contain any number of comments. Each comment is simply a text string surrounded by the strings `--` and `--` (two adjacent dashes). Thus the string `-- this is a comment --` is a single comment when inside a comment declaration. However, there must be no whitespace between the starting string of the comment declaration (`<!`) and the start of the first comment, so that all comment statements must begin with the string `<!--`. (Pathologically, you can have empty comments of the form `<! >`.) However, whitespace is allowed *after* every comment, so that the string `--` marking the end of the last comment inside a comment declaration can be separated by whitespace from the `>` character marking the end of the declaration, for example: `<!-- This is also a comment-- >`.

HTML as a MIME Type

HTML is a proposed *MIME content-type*. MIME, for Multipart Independent Mail Extensions, is a scheme originally designed for sending electronic mail messages with mixed media (containing pictures, text, and other digital data) using the standard Internet mail protocol. The scheme uses MIME *content-type* headers to define the data content of each message, or each part of a message, being sent by e-mail. On the World Wide Web, MIME types are used by the HTTP protocol to communicate the *type* of data being sent out (or received) by a server—the appropriate *content-type header field* is included within the header that precedes the data being sent. For example, a JPEG format image file being sent from an HTTP server to a client would have the message string:

```
Content-Type: image/jpeg
```

as part of the HTTP header that precedes the actual data. Similarly, when an HTML document is served, the header that precedes it contains the string:

```
Content-Type: text/html
```

which indicates that the document is HTML and not just plain text. HTTP and MIME types are discussed in more detail in Chapter 7 and Appendix B.

HTML Public Text Identifier

As mentioned several times, HTML is an evolving language. You can formally specify the version of the language supported by a document by including, as the first line in the text, a string known as a *public text identifier*. The standard declaration for HTML 3.2 is simply (or perhaps not so simply):

```
<!DOCTYPE HTML PUBLIC "-//W3C//DTD HTML 3.2 Draft//EN">
```

where the text inside the double quotation marks is the identifier for the DTD that applies to the document. DOCTYPE specifications should always be placed at the start of a document by any HTML editor (such as SoftQuad's HoTMetaL) that rigorously enforces correct HTML markup as defined by the language DTD.

HTML Elements and Markup Tags

The overall structure of the HTML language was covered in Chapter 1. The following is a review of the basic concepts, using the HTML document in Figure 4.1 (and rendered in Figure 4.2) as an example.

An HTML document is simply a text file in which certain strings of characters, called *tags*, mark regions of the document and assign special meanings to them. In the jargon of SGML, these regions and the enclosing tags are called *elements*. The tags are strings of characters surrounded by the less-than (<) and greater-than (>) characters. For example,

```
<H1>
```

is the *start tag* for an **H1** (a heading) element, while

```
</H1>
```

is the corresponding *end tag*. The entire **H1** *element* is then the string:

```
<H1> Environmental Change Project </H1>
```

Each element has a name, which appears inside the tags, and which is related to what the element means. For example, the **H1** element marks a level 1 heading. Elements that mark blocks of text are often called *containers*. Most elements are similar to this **H1** example, and mark regions of the document into blocks of text, which in turn may contain other elements containing other blocks of text, and so on. You can think of a document as a hierarchy of these elements, with the complete hierarchy defining the entire document.

Empty Elements

Some elements (such as the **IMG** [insert an inline image], **HR,** and **BR** [line break] elements) do not "contain" anything, and are called *empty* elements. In HTML, empty elements cannot have end tags.

Element Attributes

An element may also have *attributes*, which are quantities that specify properties for that particular element. For example, the **A** (hypertext anchor) element can take the **HREF** attribute, which specifies the target of a hypertext link. Most attributes are assigned *values*. For example, **HREF** is assigned the URL of the target document for a hypertext link, as in:

```
<A HREF="http://who.zoo.do/Ozone.html">Ozone</A> layer
```

Figure 4.1 An example of a simple HTML document.

```
<HTML>
<HEAD>
  <TITLE> Environmental Change Project </TITLE>
</HEAD>
<BODY>
<H1> <A NAME="env-change"> Environmental </A> Change Project </H1>

<P>Welcome to the home page of the Environmental Change Project.
This project is different from other projects with similar
names.  In our case we actually wish to change the climate.
For example, we would like hot beaches in Northern
Quebec, and deserts near Chicago.

<P> So how will we do this.  Well we do the following:
<UL>
   <LI><A HREF="burn.html"><EM>Burn down</EM></A> more forests
   <LI>Destroy the <A HREF="http://who.zoo.do/ozone.html">Ozone</A> layer
   <LI>Breed more <A HREF="ftp://foo.do.do/cows.gif">cows</A> (for extra
       greenhouse gas)
</UL>
</BODY>
</HTML>
```

Attributes are always placed inside the start tag, and never the end tag. Attributes are often optional.

In some cases the end tag is optional. This is the case when the end of an element can be unambiguously determined from the surrounding elements. As an example, look at the **LI** element in Figure 4.1. This element defines a single list item inside the **UL** unordered list element and does not require a `</LI>` end tag even though the element is not empty. This is because the end of a given list item is implied by the next `<LI>` start tag, or by the `</UL>` end tag ending the list.

Element Nesting

Elements are always *nested*, with this nesting reflecting the structure of the document (for example, emphasized text inside a paragraph, inside a form, inside the **BODY**). However, elements can *never* overlap. Thus the structure

```
<A HREF=..><EM>Burn down</EM></A> more forests
```

is valid HTML markup, while (comment in italics)

```
<A HREF=..><EM>Burn down</A></EM> more forests <!-- Illegal markup!-->
```

is not. In addition, all elements have restrictions as to what can be nested inside them and where they, themselves, can be nested. Details of allowed nestings are presented later in this chapter as each element is discussed.

Figure 4.2 Display, using the Internet Explorer 3 browser, of the document listed in Figure 4.1.

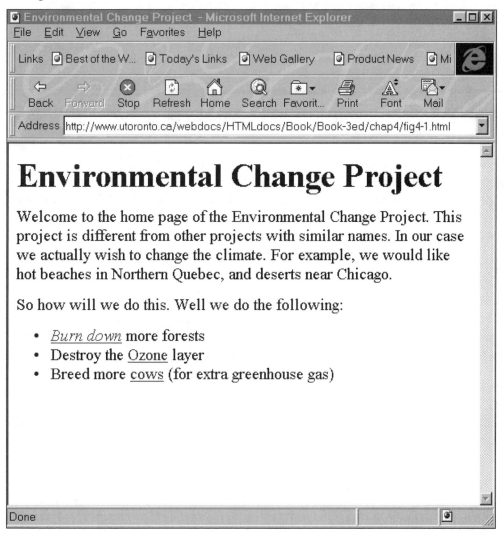

Some browsers are able to recover from simple nesting errors, so your mistakes may not show up on your own browser and will thus be hard to spot. If you are lucky, you will get mail from someone questioning why he or she cannot properly view your document. A better choice is to use a validation tool, such as sgmls, to check your documents for mistakes. This option is discussed in Chapter 11.

Case-Insensitve Element and Attribute Names

Element and attribute names inside the markup tags are *case-insensitive*. Thus, the strings `<H1>` and `<h1>` are equivalent, as are

```
<a HreF="Dir1/foo.html"><EM>Burn down</eM> </a> more forests
```

and

```
<A href="Dir1/foo.html"><em>Burn down</eM> </A> more forests
```

Element and attribute names are nevertheless usually written in uppercase to make the HTML document easier, for the developer, to read.

Case-Sensitive Attribute Values

While element and attribute names are case-insensitive, the *values* assigned to attributes are often case-sensitive. An obvious example is a URL assigned to an **HREF** attribute. A URL can contain both directory and filename information. Many computers distinguish between upper- and lowercase characters in file and directory names, so it is crucial that case be preserved. For a document author, this is ensured by enclosing the attribute argument in double quotes, as done in Figure 4.1.

Attribute Values as Literal Strings

Formally, HTML has two main mechanisms for handling values assigned to attributes: *literal strings* and *name tokens*. A literal string is just that—a string of characters to be accepted literally as typed by the author, including the preservation of case. Literal strings must be surrounded by double quotation marks, since otherwise the string may be prematurely ended at a space or other character. Literal strings can contain any sequence of printable characters, including HTML character and entity references—a browser will turn these references back into the desired characters. Clearly, you must use character or entity references to include the double quotation mark (`&quot;`), since this character would otherwise be interpreted as the end of a literal string.

Most attributes that can be assigned arbitrary, author-defined strings, such as **HREF** and **SRC** (uniform resource locators), **ALT** (**IMG** elements), and **NAME** (fragment identifiers for anchor elements), are handled as literal strings.

Attribute Values as Name Tokens

Name tokens are restricted character strings; name tokens can only contain the letters a–z or A–Z, the numbers 0–9, periods (.), and hyphens (-), and must begin with a letter. Unlike literal strings, name tokens are *case-insensitive*, so that the token abba is equivalent to ABbA. Because they are simple, name token attribute values do not need to be surrounded by quotation marks, as in the case of the string "text" in the assignment TYPE=text. However, since it is never an error to enclose attribute values within quotation marks, it is safer to leave them in. Furthermore, quotation marks are necessary if you want to assign *multiple* name tokens to the same attribute—in this case, you need to use an expression of the form ATTRIBUTE="token1 token2 token3".

Name tokens are used for values defined as part of HTML, such as the value "text" in the element <INPUT TYPE="text"...>.

The HTML DTD specifies whether the value assigned to an attribute should be a literal string or a name token. It also defines the allowed name token values for those attributes that take name tokens. For example, the HTML DTD states that the **ALIGN** attribute of an **H1** element can take the values "left", "right", and "center", but no others. Consequently, HTML *validators* (tools that check the validity of an HTML document) can check for incorrect values of name tokens, but not of literal strings, since a validator has no way of knowing if a particular string is correct.

In this book, attribute values are, in general, placed inside quotation marks, since name tokens are always valid inside quotation marks, and the added quotation marks help to make them stand out from the regular text.

Browser Handling of HTML Errors, Unknown Elements, and Unknown Attributes

On the World Wide Web, browsers are supposed to be generous in their interpretation and presentation of HTML documents. Thus, even if a document is badly constructed, for example with missing or misplaced tags, a browser will do the best it can to present the document content. Sometimes the document will look very odd due to the resulting formatting decisions, but from a user's point of view this is infinitely better than displaying nothing at all. This reiterates the importance, on the author's side, of ensuring a valid HTML document that can be properly viewed by any browser.

At the same time, HTML is an evolving language, and new elements and attributes are constantly being added, either as part of the formal language development process (HTML 2.0, HTML 3.2, etc.), or as customized extensions introduced by browser designers (such as the Netscape HTML extensions). For such an evolution to work, there must be some mechanism for a browser to handle HTML elements, or element attributes, that it does not understand.

In general, a browser is supposed to *ignore* elements, or element attributes, that it does not understand. For example, the **BLINK** element is Netscape-specific: On other browsers, `<BLINK>` ... `</BLINK>` tags are usually ignored, and the enclosed text is rendered as regular text (given whatever other elements the string is inside). Similarly, in HTML 3.2, paragraphs can be centered using the **ALIGN** attribute, that is, `<P ALIGN="center">`. If a browser does not understand this attribute or the value assigned to it, it simply ignores the attribute and use its own default paragraph alignment.

However, many of the newer elements will not produce readable documents if the browser does not understand the relevant tags. Particular examples are the **FRAME** (discussed in the next chapter) and **TABLE** elements. In general, you can assume that any new element that implies both logical and physical structure will be poorly displayed by a browser that does not understand the element.

HTML Structural Overview

Every HTML document can be divided into two main parts: the *body*, which contains the part of the document to be displayed by a browser, and the *head*, which contains information about the document, but which is not displayed in the browser window. These parts are defined by the **BODY** and **HEAD** elements respectively. The resulting overall structure of an HTML document is then (commentary in italics):

```
<HTML>
    <HEAD>
        .... elements valid in the document HEAD
    </HEAD>
    <BODY>
        .... elements valid in the document BODY
    </BODY>
</HTML>
```

Note how Figure 4.1 follows this outline. The outer **HTML** element declares the enclosed text to be an HTML document. Directly inside this lie the **HEAD** and the **BODY**. The **BODY** contains the text and associated HTML markup instructions of the material you want displayed. The **HEAD**, which must appear before the **BODY**, contains elements that define information *about* the document, such as its title or its logical relationships with other documents. Certain elements can only appear in the **HEAD**, while others can only appear in the **BODY**.

Elements Table of Contents

Figure 4.3 summarizes the HTML elements within this overall organization, and provides page references to the sections describing each element—you can use this as an "element-oriented" table of contents to Chapters 4 and 5.

Figure 4.3 Summary of HTML elements described in this chapter, showing their relative locations in the element hierarchy. Proposed but not yet standardized elements are in italics, while proprietary extensions are underlined.

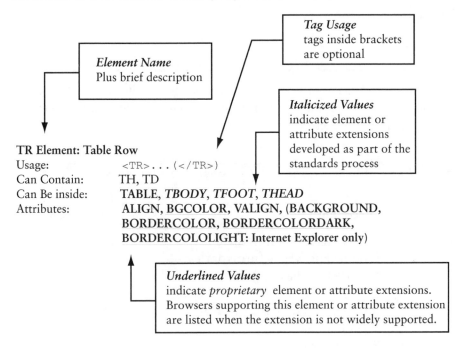

HTML Element Specifications

This section describes each HTML element, with a description of the purpose of the element, a list of where the element can be used, and examples of its use. This section describes elements from the HTML 3.2 specification, although a few non–HTML 3.2 elements and attribute extensions are mentioned, where it seemed more appropriate to mention them here. Most non–HTML 3.2 elements are discussed in Chapter 5.

Specifications Key

Because HTML is a hierarchical language, is it important to know not only *how* to use an element, but also *where* it can be used. This information is given in the four lines at the beginning of each element's description. The format is:

Usage:	<NAME> ... </NAME>
Can Contain:	*element list*
Can Be Inside:	*element list*
Attributes:	*attribute list*

where **element list** is a list of allowed elements, and **attribute list** is a list of allowed attributes. Figure 4.4 shows an example, using the **TR** *table row* element; the four fields in Figure 4.4 define the rules for using the element. The meanings of the fields are given in Table 4.2.

Figure 4.4 Illustration of the abbreviations used to describe elements.

Element	Description	Page Ch 4	Ch 5
HTML	An HTML Document	149	
HEAD	Document Meta-Information	150	
BASE	Base URL of the document	153	
ISINDEX	Searchable document	154	
LINK	Relationships to other resources	155	
META	Meta Information	157	302
SCRIPT	Program scripts	159	313
STYLE	Document stylesheet	160	305
TITLE	Document title	162	
BODY	Document Body	150	
ADDRESS	Address information	163	
BLOCKQUOTE	Block quotation	164	
CENTER	Centered text	168	
DIV	Block division of a document	169	
H1–H6	Headings (1–6)	169	
HR	Horizontal divider	174	
MULTICOL	Multicolumn text		285
P	Paragraphs	175	
PRE	Preformatted text	177	
FORM	User input form	178	324

Figure 4.4 (Continued)

Element	Description	Page Ch 4	Ch 5
FIELDSET	Group related input elements		334
KEYGEN	Generate encrcrypted keys	192	
LABEL	Label for input elements		335
INPUT	Input fields	180	
SELECT	Selectable fields	187	
OPTION	Option in selectable field	190	
TEXTAREA	Text input region	190	
DL	Description/Glossary list	193	
DT	Term	193	
DD	Description	196	
OL	Ordered list	196	
LI	List item	201	
UL	Unordered list	197	
LI	List item	201	
MENU	Menu list (obsolete?)	200	
LI	List item	201	
DIR	Directory list (obsolete?)	200	
LI	List item	201	
TABLE	Table	213	
CAPTION	Table Caption	218	
COL	Column properties specifier	218	336
COLGROUP	Column group specification	219	336
THEAD	Table header grouping	220	336
TBODY	Table body grouping	220	336
TFOOT	Table footer grouping	221	336
TR	Table row	221	336
TD	Table data cell	223	337
TH	Table header cell	223	337
Semantic Phrase Markup			
CITE	Citation	241	
CODE	Typed computer code	242	
DFN	Definition	242	
EM	Emphasized text	243	
KBD	Keyboard input	244	

Continued

Figure 4.4 (Continued)

Element	Description	Page Ch 4	Ch 5
Q	Inline quotation		331
SAMP	Sample text	244	
STRIKE	Struck-out text	244	
STRONG	Strong emphasis	244	
VAR	A variable	244	
Physical Phrase Markup			
B	**Bold**	244	
BDO	Bidirectional override		331
BIG	Bigger text	244	
BLINK	Blinking text		279
FONT	Font size/face/color	244	
I	*Italics*	248	
MARQUEE	Scrolling marquee text		283
NOBR	No line breaks		286
S	~~Strike through~~	248	
SMALL	Smaller text	248	
SPAN	Stylesheet-specified styling		305
SUB	Subscript	248	
SUP	superscript	248	
TT	Fixed-width font	249	
U	<u>Underline</u>	249	
Character Level Elements			
BR	Line break	249	
WBR	Optional Word Break		289
SPACER	Horizontal or vertical space		287
Inclusion Elements			
APPLET	Embedded applet	226	
PARAM	Parameter for applet	227	
IMG	Inline image	228	
IFRAME	Insert floating document frame		272
EMBED	Embed arbitrary data		281
NOEMBED	HTML Alternative to EMBED		286
NOSCRIPT	HTML alternative to SCRIPT		314
OBJECT	Embed data and handler		294

Figure 4.4 (Continued)

Element	Description	Page Ch 4	Ch 5
PARAM	Parameter for object/handler		298
SERVER	Server-side scripting		327
Hypertext Relationships			
A	Hypertext anchor	236	297
Meta-Information Elements			
BASEFONT	Base font for document	250	
BGSOUND	Background audio/sound		277
MAP	Client-side imagemap	251	
AREA	Imagemap data	252	
Netscape FRAME Documents			
FRAMESET	Declare framed regions		265
FRAME	Specify frame contents		269
NOFRAMES	Markup for non-frame browsers		271

Table 4.2 Meanings of Fields in Element Definitions (see also Figure 4.3)

Usage: Shows how the element is used. An end tag indicates that an element is a container (the *Can Contain* field lists what can go inside the element). If the end tag is enclosed by parentheses, then it is optional. If no end tag is given, then the element is empty.

Can Contain: This field indicates what elements can go inside this element. The string "**characters**" indicates elements that can contain text. If the element is empty, the word "empty" appears here. In several places, the **ISINDEX** name appears enclosed by square brackets. This indicates that the element is allowed, but that it should more appropriately appear in the **HEAD**. Elements that are proposed as part the HTML standardization process are shown in boldface italics. Underlined elements are proprietary extensions by browser vendors.

Can Be Inside: Indicates the elements inside which this element can be placed. The example in Figure 4.3 indicates that the **TR** element can be inside **TABLE**, **TBODY**, **TFOOT**, or **THEAD** elements, but nowhere else. Elements that are proposed as part the HTML standardization process are shown in boldface italics. Underlined elements are proprietary extensions by browser vendors.

Attributes: This lists the names of the attributes that can be taken by the element. The word "none" means that the element takes no attributes. Attributes proposed as part the HTML standardization process are shown in boldface italics. Underlined attributes are proprietary extensions by browser vendors.

Special Abbreviations

For ease in reading, several abbreviations are used in the element descriptions; these are illustrated in Figure 4.4 and defined in Table 4.3.

Attribute Value Definitions

Attribute values are either arbitrary strings selected by the user, such as URLs in hypertext anchors, form variable names and values, and so on (generally literal strings); or particular values (generally, but not always, name tokens) defined as part of HTML. To distinguish between these two types, user-definable values are presented in quoted italics (*"value"*), while values defined as part of HTML are presented as quoted regular text ("value"). The notation is summarized in Table 4.4.

In addition, user-defined values are often restricted in some way; for example, color specifications must be given as RGB color codes or as special named colors, while lengths may need to be integer numbers, and so on. Notation used with attribute value assignments to indicate these requirements is outlined in Table 4.5.

Table 4.3 Key to Abbreviations Used in Element Descriptions

Hn	The six heading elements **H1**, **H2**, **H3**, **H4**, **H5**, and **H6**.
characters	Any valid ISO Latin-1 character, character reference, or entity reference.
character highlighting	**CITE, CODE, DFN, EM, KBD, SAMP, STRIKE, STRONG, VAR**, and **B, BIG, FONT, I, S, SMALL, SUB, SUP, TT, U**
	These are the logical (**CITE** through **VAR**) and physical (**B** through **U**) highlighting elements used to mark text for meaning or for formatting purposes.

Table 4.4 Explanation of Attribute Value Assignments

ATTRIBUTE="value"	Non-italicized strings indicate attribute values that are defined as part of HTML, and that are not arbitrary. For example, **ALIGN**="center", or **METHOD**="post".
ATTRIBUTE=*"value"*	Italicized strings indicate arbitrary user-defined values. The value may be limited by context; for example, in **BGCOLOR**=*"#rrggbb"*, the string references an RGB color code, which restricts the allowed value of *rrggbb*.

Table 4.5 User-Specified Attribute Value Assignments and Their Meanings

color	Represents a *named color*. Several browsers support *name token* text strings to indicate particular colors. The commonly supported values are "aqua", "black", "blue", "fuchsia", "gray", "green", "lime", "maroon", "navy", "olive", "purple", "red", "silver", "teal", "white", and "yellow." If a browser does not understand the color name, it will ignore the associated attribute, and use the default color.

Table 4.5 (Continued)

	Color names are not supported by early versions of Netscape Navigator or Internet Explorer (Version 2 or earlier).
#rrggbb	Represents a color as an RGB (Red-Green-Blue) value—this describes the color in terms of its of red, green, and blue components. Each color can be in the range 0–255 (eight bits), and each color is referenced, in the RGB value, by its hexadecimal code. Thus the color red, which is full red (255), zero blue, and zero green, is coded as "`#ff0000`", while white (all colors on full) is "`#ffffff`". The default colors are determined by a browser's internal configuration.
string	Represents an arbitrary user-defined string.
name	Represents an arbitrary user-defined *name token* string. A name token is a string including any combination of letters (a–z), (A–Z), digits (0–9), periods (.),and dashes (-), but it must begin with a letter. Names are usually case-insensitive.
names	Represents an arbitrary, user-defined collection of name tokens, separated by spaces (e.g., "*name1 name2*").
number	Represents an arbitrary *integer number*.
pixels	Represents an arbitrary *integer number* corresponding to a number of pixels, indicating either horizontal or vertical measurement.
real.number	Represents a positive *real number*. Decimals (e.g., 2.3) are allowed but not exponentials.
url	Represents an arbitrary, user-defined uniform resource locator.

Basic Structure: HTML, HEAD, and BODY

The basic structure of an HTML document is laid out by these three elements.

HTML Element: An HTML Document

Usage:	`<HTML> ... </HTML>`
Can Contain:	**HEAD, BODY**
Can Be Inside:	nothing
Attributes:	none

The **HTML** element declares the enclosed text to be an HTML document. It may directly contain only two elements: **HEAD** and **BODY**.

Example of **HTML**:

```
<HTML>
    <HEAD>
    ... head content...
    </HEAD>
    <BODY>
    ... body content...
    </BODY>
</HTML>
```

HEAD Element: Document Meta-Information

Usage:	`<HEAD> ... </HEAD>`
Can Contain:	BASE, ISINDEX, LINK, META, SCRIPT, STYLE, TITLE
Can Be Inside:	HTML
Attributes:	HREF

HEAD contains general information about the document. This information is not displayed as part of the document text; consequently, only certain elements are appropriate within the **HEAD**. These elements, **BASE, ISINDEX, LINK, META, SCRIPT, STYLE,** and **TITLE**, can appear inside **HEAD** in any order. The only mandatory **HEAD** element is **TITLE**; all others are optional. All the head elements except **TITLE, SCRIPT,** and **STYLE** are empty.

The division between the **HEAD** and the **BODY** is important, as there are mechanisms for retrieving just the information in the document **HEAD**. Since the **HEAD** is always much smaller than the body, this is faster than accessing an entire document, and can be extremely useful for quickly generating catalogs or indexes based on **HEAD** content.

BODY Element: Document Text Body

Usage:	`<BODY> ... </BODY>`
Can Contain:	characters, character highlighting, A, APPLET, BR, IMG,
	BASEFONT, MAP, SCRIPT, [ISINDEX], INPUT, SELECT, TEXTAREA,
	DIR, DL, MENU, OL, UL, P, HR, Hn,
	ADDRESS, BLOCKQUOTE, CENTER, DIV, FORM, PRE, TABLE
Can Be Inside:	HTML

Attributes: **ALINK, BACKGROUND, BGCOLOR, LINK, TEXT, VLINK,**

(**BGPROPERTIES**, **LEFTMARGIN**, **TOPMARGIN** Internet Explorer only)

The **BODY** contains the document proper, as opposed to the meta-information found in the **HEAD**. Formally, the **BODY** should not directly contain text; instead, it should contain elements that in turn contain the text. Recall that **BODY** states simply "this is the body of the document" and supplies no additional meaning to its content. It is the job of elements nested within the **BODY** to organize the text and assign it meaning. This is accomplished by the elements that define headings, lists, addresses, paragraphs, and so on.

The contents of the **HEAD** and **BODY** are largely exclusive—elements that belong inside the **HEAD** do not belong inside the **BODY**, and vice versa.

HTML 3.2 supports several optional attributes for specifying properties of the document body, such as the default text colors and page background properties. Some proprietary attributes are supported by Microsoft Internet Explorer. In general, such properties are better (and much more easily) specified by stylesheets, as described in Chapter 5.

BACKGROUND=*"url"* (optional) **BACKGROUND** specifies the URL of an image file (generally GIF or JPEG) that should be used to *tile*, or *wallpaper*, the background of the browser window. A background acts like a watermark, and scrolls with the text.

BGCOLOR=*"#rrggbb"* or *"color"* (optional) **BGCOLOR** specifies the background color for the display window, either as a RGB color value or as a named color. If a **BACKGROUND** image is also specified, the background will first be tiled with this color, and then with the image. If the **BACKGROUND** image is transparent, the color behind the background is given by **BGCOLOR**.

ALINK=*"#rrggbb"* or *"color"* (optional) **ALINK** specifies the color for text within *active* (i.e., selected) links. The default color varies from browser to browser (e.g., it is red with Netscape Navigator).

TEXT=*"#rrggbb"* or *"color"* (optional) **TEXT** specifies the default color for the document text (the default is black).

LINK=*"#rrggbb"* or *"color"* (optional) **LINK** specifies the color for text within unvisited hypertext links (the default is usually blue).

VLINK=*"#rrggbb"* or *"color"* (optional) **VLINK** specifies the color for text within *previously visited* hypertext links (the default is often a pale purple).

The following attributes are only supported by the Microsoft Internet Explorer browser.

BGPROPERTIES="fixed" (optional) (Internet Explorer only) **BGPROPERTIES** takes the single value "fixed", which indicates a fixed (non-scrolling) background. The default is for the background to scroll with the text.

LEFTMARGIN="*pixels*" (optional) (Internet Explorer only) Specifies, in pixels, the left margin to leave for the entire body of the document. If set to zero, the text will be flush with the left-hand border of the browser window.

TOPMARGIN="*pixels*" (optional) (Internet Explorer only) Specifies, in pixels, the margin to leave at the top of the browser window. If set to zero, the text will be flush with the top window border.

HEAD Meta-Information Elements

There are only seven elements that can appear in the document **HEAD**. These elements (and their associated meanings/content) are shown in Table 4.6. All these elements are empty, except for **TITLE, SCRIPT,** and **STYLE**. As you can tell by the descriptions, these elements provide information about the document, such as the title, the relationship to other documents, or a stylesheet that should be *applied* to the document. To support older, less well-designed documents and software, the DTD actually allows **ISINDEX** and **STYLE** elements within the **BODY**, but you are best advised to keep them within the head, where they belong.

Table 4.6 Elements Allowed in the Document HEAD

BASE	Records the original or **base** URL of the document.
ISINDEX	Indicates the document is searchable.
LINK	Defines a relationship between the document and another document.
META	Provides meta-information about the document that cannot be expressed in the preceding elements.
SCRIPT	Embeds executable program scripts, or references an external file that contains a program script. In both cases the script should be applied to the current document.
STYLE	Embeds stylesheet instructions. The stylesheet information should be used to format the document **BODY**.
TITLE	Provides the title of the document.

BASE Element: Base URL

Usage:	`<BASE>`
Can Contain:	empty
Can Be Inside:	**HEAD**
Attributes:	**HREF, <u>TARGET</u>**

BASE is an empty element, and is optional. If present, **BASE** has a single mandatory attribute, **HREF,** which is assigned the *base URL* of the document.

The base URL is a URL indicating where a document was originally located. This is useful for documents moved away from their original URL—after moving the document, partial URLs that referenced neighboring documents are no longer valid. However, if the original URL address is specified in the **BASE** element, then relative URLs from this document are evaluated relative to this "base" URL and are correctly located from the original location.

If the **BASE** element is absent, the browser determines partial URLs with respect to the URL used to access the document.

> **NOTE: Possible Problems with BASE** Be aware that browsers differ in their interpretation of **BASE** when it comes to "bookmarking" a document or to accessing **FORM** or **ISINDEX**-referenced resources: Some browsers use the **BASE** URL, in these cases, while others use the actual URL used in retrieving the displayed document.

The following is an example of the appropriate use of **BASE**. If a document was originally found at the URL:

```
http://somewhere.org/Dir/Subdir/file.html
```

the appropriate **BASE** element to include in this document is:

```
<HEAD>
   <TITLE> some sort of title... </TITLE>
   <BASE HREF="http://somewhere.org/Dir/Subdir/file.html">
</HEAD>
```

Support for Netscape Frames
Browsers that support the Netscape frame elements support *targeted* links—this lets a document author direct the data returned, upon selecting a hypertext link, to a particular *named*

browser window or named pane within a window. Named windows are produced using a **TARGET** attribute to the **A** (anchor) element, or using the **FRAMESET** element, as discussed in Chapter 5.

Browsers that support frames also support a **TARGET** attribute with the **BASE** element. Analogous to the value of **HREF**, **TARGET** defines the default name of the target window for all hypertext links within the document. For example, the element

```
<BASE TARGET="window3">
```

means that all accessed hypertext links will be displayed in (sent to) the window named window3. If a pane by this name does not already exist, then a new browser window will be created, and will be assigned this name.

The base target is always overridden by an explicit **TARGET** within an anchor, such as:

```
<A HREF="/path/file.html" TARGET="window2">anchor text</A>
```

The document returned upon accessing this anchor will be directed to the window named "window2", overriding any target specified by the **BASE** element **TARGET** value.

The default target is always the window or frame containing the document being displayed.

ISINDEX Element: Searchable Document

Usage:	`<ISINDEX>`
Can Contain:	empty
Can Be Inside:	**HEAD [BLOCKQUOTE, BODY, CENTER, DD, DIV, FORM, LI, TD, TH]**
Attributes:	**PROMPT, <u>ACTION</u>**

ISINDEX is an optional, empty element. Because there are many older documents that have **ISINDEX** in the **BODY**, the HTML definition still allows this form. New documents should always place **ISINDEX** inside the **HEAD**. This element informs the browser that the document can be examined using a keyword search, and that the browser should query the user for a search or query string. The attribute **PROMPT**, which takes as its value an arbitrary author-specified string, specifies the prompt that should be presented for this query—for example:

```
<ISINDEX PROMPT="Please enter your favorite ice cream flavor:">
```

ISINDEX does *not* mean a search of the text being read. Documents containing **ISINDEX** elements are usually sent to the client from server-side gateway programs designed for database searches. You can think of such a document as a front end to a gateway program, and the document you search as the database *represented* by the document you see.

By default, **ISINDEX**-accepted data are returned to the same URL that was used to retrieve the document containing the **ISINDEX** element. Several browsers, including Navigator and Internet Explorer, support an **ACTION** attribute that takes as its value a URL to which the query should instead be directed.

The encoding mechanism by which **ISINDEX** query data are appended to a URL is discussed in the HTTP URL section of Chapter 6, and also in Chapter 8.

Example of **ISINDEX**:

```
<HEAD>
  <ISINDEX>
  <TITLE> title text </TITLE>
  ...
</HEAD>
<BODY>
  ... body of document
</BODY>
```

LINK Element: Relationship to Other Documents

Usage:	`<LINK>`
Can Contain:	empty
Can Be Inside:	**HEAD**
Attributes:	**HREF, ID, REL, REV, TITLE**

LINK describes a *relationship* between a document and other documents or objects. For example, **LINK** can indicate a related index, a glossary, or perhaps different versions of the same document. Alternatively, **LINK** can point out likely *next* or *previous* documents. This information could be used by a browser—for instance, to predict and preload documents it is likely to need, or to configure customized navigational buttons or menus. A document may have any number of **LINK** elements to represent these various relationships to other documents.

LINK is an empty element, and is optional. The **HREF** attribute is mandatory, as is at least one of **REL** or **REV**. All other attributes are optional.

NOTE: Using LINK to Reference External Stylesheets The Internet Explorer 3 browser can reference external stylesheets using **LINK** elements. Stylesheets are described in Chapter 5.

Examples of **LINK**:

```
<LINK REL="made" HREF="mailto:igraham@hprc.utoronto.ca">
```

HREF points to information about the creator of the document containing the **LINK**.

```
<LINK REL="next" HREF="another_url">
```

HREF points to the *next* document in some logical document sequence.

```
<LINK REL="previous" HREF="another_url">
```

HREF points to the *previous* document in some logical document sequence.

```
<LINK REL="index" HREF="another_url">
```

HREF points to an *index* related to the collection containing the document.

```
<LINK REL="contents" HREF="another_url">
```

HREF points to a *table of contents* related to the document containing the **LINK**.

```
<LINK REL="navigate" HREF="another_url">
```

HREF points to a *navigational aid*, perhaps a table of contents extract, relevant to the document containing the **LINK**.

LINK takes essentially the same attributes as the anchor (**A**) element, which are discussed in detail in the anchor element section later in this chapter. The only difference is the **ID** attribute, which is used with **LINK** in place of **NAME**. **ID** labels a **LINK** with an identifying label, which must be a name token. Using **ID**, **LINK** elements can themselves be referenced by a hypertext anchor, allowing for a level of indirection in link references.

LINK elements, with **REL** (or **REV**) attributes, are only useful given well-understood meanings for the values assigned to them. The process of defining a set of values is currently underway; some of the commonly understood relationships were given in the previous examples. In the absence of well-defined meanings, **LINK** is largely unused. Current efforts at establishing well-defined **REL/REV** relationships are found at the URL:

```
http:// www.sq.com/papers/Relationships.html
```

The **META** element provides a place to put meta-information that is not defined by the other **HEAD** elements. This allows an author to more richly describe the document content for indexing

META Element: Document Meta-Information

Usage: `<META>`

Can Contain: empty

Can Be Inside: **HEAD**

Attributes: **CONTENT, HTTP-EQUIV, NAME**

and cataloging purposes, as illustrated in the following **META** element discussion. You should not, however, use **META** as a substitute for the other **HEAD** elements.

The **META** element is optional. If present, it must take the **CONTENT** attribute and one of the **NAME** or **HTTP-EQUIV** attributes (but not both). The meanings of the attributes are:

NAME="*name*" (one of **NAME** or **HTTP-EQUIV** must be present) This specifies the meta-information name (ideally as a name token). The client program (browser) must understand what this name means. HTML does not currently define any values for **NAME**. **META** must contain one of **NAME** or **HTTP-EQUIV**, but not both.

HTTP-EQUIV="*name*" (one of **NAME** or **HTTP-EQUIV** must be present) This indicates meta-information equivalent to that communicated by the HTTP protocol within HTTP *response header fields*. HTTP response headers are discussed in Chapter 7. **META** must contain either **NAME** or **HTTP-EQUIV**, but not both.

CONTENT="*string*" (mandatory) This assigns the content associated with the **NAME** or **HTTP-EQUIV** value of the **META** element.

NAME Attribute Usage

An example using the **NAME** attribute is:

```
<META NAME="keywords" CONTENT="pets dogs cats rocks lizards">
```

This might tell the client that words "pets," dogs," cats," rocks," and "lizards" are keywords useful for indexing the current document. The client or indexing program that is accessing the **HEAD** of this document must consequently understand the meanings behind the names.

HTTP-EQUIV Attribute Usage

The **HTTP-EQUIV** attribute lets the document contain HTTP-header information, which can be accessed (and used to generate the HTTP response) either by the server delivering the document, or by the browser receiving the document. An example is:

```
<META HTTP-EQUIV="Creation-Date" CONTENT="23-Sep-94 18:28:33 GMT">
```

which indicates the creation date of the document, in the context of the appropriate HTTP header field `Creation-Date`. If the server actually parses the document head, then it will create an HTTP header field

```
Creation-Date: 23-Sep-94 18:28:33 GMT
```

and include this with the HTTP *response header* that precedes the document during an HTTP transaction (see Chapter 7). Even if the server does not create such a header, a browser or other program can still obtain this information directly from the **META** element in the document **HEAD**.

NOTE: You should not use `<META HTTP-EQUIV...>` to override server response header fields that are normally returned by the server.

Common META Elements

Most servers do not parse a document for **META** elements, although several browsers parse documents for specific **META** content. The most common cases are:

```
<META HTTP-EQUIV="content-type" CONTENT="text/html; charset="EUC-2">
```

This gives the content-type of the document, as the HTTP content-type header field, but also lists the character set in which the document is written. This is useful, as most servers cannot currently indicate character set information relevant to the documents they serve out.

```
<META HTTP-EQUIV="expires" CONTENT="Tue, 01 Jan 1981 01:00:00 GMT">
```

This gives the expiry date for the document. A browser or server will not cache a document past its expiry date. Giving an expiry date in the past (as in the example) guarantees that the document will never be cached by a browser or proxy server.

```
<META HTTP-EQUIV="refresh" CONTENT="10; URL=http://foo.org/bx.html">
```

This proprietary extension by Netscape asks the browser to wait 10 seconds, and then access the indicated URL. Chapter 9 describes this *client-pull* feature in more detail.

```
<META http-equiv="PICS-Label" content="PICS-1.0 label information">
```

This references a PICS (Platform for Internet Content Selection) label for the document. PICS is a rating scheme for Web pages, and provides a way of censoring content that might be unfit for young children. Some browsers understand PICS, and will refuse to display documents that are PICS-rated as unsatisfactory. PICS information is available from the references at the end of this chapter.

```
<META name="keywords" content="space separated keywords list">
```

Several Web-based search engines will preferentially index a document using keywords specified by **META** elements of this form. A careful choice of keywords can make your documents much easier to find at search engines such as Lycos, AltaVista, Yahoo, and OpenText.

```
<META name="description" content="A short resource description">
```

AltaVista indexes the content of **META** elements with **NAME**="keywords" or **NAME**="description". The latter value is also used by the search engine as a brief description of the resource. If this is absent, AltaVista uses the first few sentences of the document.

SCRIPT Element: Include a Program Script

Usage: `<SCRIPT> ... </SCRIPT>`

Can Contain: script program code (**characters**)

Can Be Inside: **HEAD, BODY,** any **BODY** element that allows content

Attributes: *LANGUAGE, SRC, TYPE*

SCRIPT is used to include program scripts within an HTML document. The content of the element is treated as script program code, and is executed, if possible, by the browser. Browsers that do not understand **SCRIPT** elements or the language in which the script is written should ignore this element and its content.

SCRIPT is a non-empty element, the content being the program script. To hide this text from browsers that do not understand **SCRIPT**, the actual text code should be placed inside an HTML comment. This is illustrated in the following example (the dots indicate omitted code):

```
<SCRIPT LANGUAGE="JavaScript">
<!--
.

.
function opentip() {
        str="/comprod/news/todaystip.html";
        tipWin = window.open(str,'tipWin','width=175,height=175');
        window.open(str,'tipWin','width=175,height=175');
        tipWin.opener = self;
}
.

.
// -->
</SCRIPT>
```

SCRIPT is allowed in the body as well as the **HEAD**: **SCRIPT**s in the **HEAD** portion should be used to define any functions used elsewhere in the document, while **SCRIPT**s in the **BODY** should be used to print script-generated text into the HTML document. This is described in more detail Chapter 5.

Inside the **BODY**, the element **NOSCRIPT** can contain HTML markup to use in place of the **SCRIPT** content, should the browser not understand the **SCRIPT** element or the requested scripting language. This is discussed in more detail in Chapter 5.

In HTML 3.2, **SCRIPT** takes no attributes. However, this is clearly insufficient, since there are multiple scripting languages, and hence the need to indicate the language. In addition, developers like to place scripts in files separate from the document itself. The HTML development process has arrived at three attributes to satisfy these needs: (1) **LANGUAGE** to indicate the language of a script placed inside a **SCRIPT** element, (2) **SRC** to specify the **URL** of a file containing a script program, and (3) **TYPE** to specify the MIME-type of this file. Currently, only **LANGUAGE** is supported. The specifications for these attributes are given below. Note that **LANGUAGE** is likely to be dropped in favor of **TYPE**.

LANGUAGE=*"string"* (optional) (Netscape Navigator and Internet Explorer only) Specifies the language of the script contained within the **SCRIPT** element. The only commonly supported values are **LANGUAGE**=*"JavaScript"*, for JavaScript and **LANGUAGE**=*"VBScript"* for Visual Basic Script. Internet Explorer supports both languages, while Netscape Navigator 3 supports only JavaScript.

SRC=*"url"* (optional) (Netscape Navigator only) Specifies the URL of a file that contains a script. The browser should access the file, and load the script as if it were included inline with the document.

TYPE=*"string"* (optional) (not yet supported) Gives the MIME type for the script referenced by the SRC attribute. For example, an external JavaScript program from the file *prog1.js* would be referenced by the markup:

```
<SCRIPT SRC="http://scripts.ian.com/prog1.js"
        TYPE="application/x-javascript">
</SCRIPT>
```

In principle, a **SCRIPT** element can both reference an external script file and contain a script. The handling of such composite programs is not yet specified.

STYLE Element: Stylesheet or Rendering Information

Usage: <STYLE> ... </STYLE>

Can Contain: **characters**

Can Be Inside: **HEAD**

Attributes: none

STYLE contains stylesheet rendering instructions, to be applied to the document when displayed by the browser. **STYLE** allows rendering information to be placed within the document, and not as a second file referenced through a **LINK** element. The latter may be accomplished using **LINK** elements of the form:

```
<LINK REL="stylesheet"
      HREF="http:some.where.dom/path/stylesheet"
      TYPE="mime/type">
```

where *mime/type* is the MIME type of the indicated stylesheet (text/css for Cascading Stylesheets). The **STYLE** element allows for browsers that do not support linked stylesheets. In this instance, **STYLE** is best thought of as an interim mechanism for including stylesheet information, as it has several disadvantages compared with linked stylesheets. In particular, a linked stylesheet can be shared between many documents, while the **STYLE** element forces every document to contain the stylesheet.

However, **STYLE** has a second use—for local customization of an external stylesheet. In this regard, you can use a linked stylesheet to specify the broad details of the layout, with the content in the **STYLE** element providing small-scale, local modifications.

Here is an example **STYLE** element:

```
<HEAD>
<STYLE>
  BODY {
    background: url(waves.gif) black;
  }
H1 {
    margin-top: 10px;
    color: #4F;
    text-align: left;
    font: 30px "Arial Alternative", gill, helvetica, sans-serif;
  }
...
</STYLE>
....
</HEAD>
<BODY>
```

TITLE Element: Document Title

Usage:	`<TITLE> ... </TITLE>`
Can Contain:	**characters**
Can Be Inside:	**HEAD**
Attributes:	none

The title of a document is specified by the **TITLE** element. Every document must have a **TITLE**, and can only have one. The text inside a **TITLE** should indicate the document content in a concise but general way. A **TITLE** serves several purposes:

- To label the display window or text screen

- To serve as a record in a history or bookmark list marking documents the user has viewed

- To allow quick indexing of a document, in place of indexing the entire text

The **TITLE** is not part of the document text, and cannot contain hypertext links or any other markup commands—it can contain only text, including entity or character references.

The **TITLE** should be short—preferably less than 60 characters—so that it can easily label a window or fit in a history list. It should be easy to determine the content of the document from the **TITLE** itself. Otherwise, a person reviewing his/her bookmarks will see the **TITLE** but not know to what it refers. Here are some examples of good **TITLE**s:

```
<TITLE>Paper on Rings by Baggins and Gandalf, 1989,/TITLE>

<TITLE>Introduction to MIME types <TITLE>
```

and bad **TITLE**s:

```
<TITLE>Introduction</TITLE>

<TITLE>A Summary of the Ring-Ring Interaction Cross-Section
Measurement of B. Baggins, et al. in both Low-Temperature and
High-Temperature Studies, including Water Immersion and
Non-Destructive Testing: A Brief Review plus Commentary on
the "Missing Ring" Problem.</TITLE>
```

Body Text Block and Heading Elements

Block elements divide a document into logical blocks of text, such as paragraphs (**P**), block quotations (**BLOCKQUOTE**), lists (see the following section), **ADDRESS** (address information), and so on. In general, other HTML elements appear inside block elements. The elements **FORM**, which defines a fill-in interactive form, and **TABLE**, which defines tabular structures, are more complex than the others and are described in detail later.

Several proprietary block-like elements, such as **FRAMESET, FRAME,** and **IFRAME** (Netscape frame documents), **MULTICOL** (multicolumn text), and **NOBR** (no line breaks), are supported by a number of browsers. These elements are described in Chapter 5.

ADDRESS Element: Address Information

Usage:	`<ADDRESS> ... </ADDRESS>`
Can Contain:	**characters, character highlighting, A, APPLET, BR, IMG, BASEFONT, MAP, SCRIPT, INPUT, SELECT, TEXTAREA, P**
Can Be Inside:	**BLOCKQUOTE, BODY, CENTER, DIV, FORM, TD, TH**
Attributes:	none

ADDRESS denotes information such as addresses, electronic signatures, or lists of authors. Typically, a document author would use **ADDRESS** to sign his or her documents. In this case, the **ADDRESS** is often placed at the bottom of the HTML document to keep it separate from the main text. In a family of documents, the **ADDRESS** may contain just the author's initials or name connected by a hypertext link to a biographical page. Alternatively, a collection of documents may have an introductory document that has **ADDRESS** elements containing detailed contact information for the author or authors, with the remaining documents having **ADDRESS** elements containing hypertext links back to this page.

As with all elements, the rendering of the contents of **ADDRESS** is left up to the browser. Most browsers render **ADDRESS** content in italics.

Figures 4.5 and 4.7 show some typical applications of the **ADDRESS** element. Browser renderings of these documents are shown in Figures 4.6 and 4.8 respectively.

BLOCKQUOTE marks a block of text as a quotation. Browsers can render this in various ways: for example, by indenting the **BLOCKQUOTE** content, and by offsetting it from the preceding and following text. A **BLOCKQUOTE** also causes a paragraph break, and terminates preceding paragraphs.

Figure 4.5 HTML example document illustrating headings, BLOCKQUOTE, and ADDRESS elements. Figure 4.6 shows this document viewed by Internet Explorer 3.

```
<HTML>
<HEAD>
<TITLE> Examples of ADDRESS and BLOCKQUOTE elements</TITLE>
</HEAD>
<BODY>
<H1>The Meaning of Life </H1>

<P> How many times have you sat down and asked yourself "What is
the meaning of life?."  I certainly have.  I've
even read many of the good books, from C.S. Lewis, to Kant, to
Sartre to Zoltan the Magnificent.  But I think the most profound
statement about life was made by Jack Handey, who said:
<BLOCKQUOTE>
<P>I can still recall old Mister Barnslow getting out every morning and
nailing a fresh load of tadpoles to that old board of his.  Then he'd
spin it around and around, like a wheel of fortune, and no matter where
it stopped he'd yell out, "Tadpoles!  Tadpoles is a winner!"
We all thought he was crazy.  But then, we had some growing up to do.
</BLOCKQUOTE>
<P>That pretty well sums it up.
<HR>
<ADDRESS>  <A HREF="about_the_author.html"> C.S.O </A> </ADDRESS>
</BODY>
</HTML>
```

BLOCKQUOTE Element: Block Quotations

Usage: `<BLOCKQUOTE> ... </BLOCKQUOTE>`

Can Contain: **characters, character highlighting, A, APPLET, BR, IMG,**

BASEFONT, MAP, SCRIPT, [ISINDEX], INPUT, SELECT, TEXTAREA,

DIR, DL, MENU, OL, UL, P, HR, Hn,

ADDRESS, BLOCKQUOTE, CENTER, DIV, FORM, PRE, TABLE

Can Be Inside: **BLOCKQUOTE, BODY, CENTER, DD, DIV, FORM, LI, TD, TH**

Attributes: none

Figure 4.6 Display, by the Internet Explorer 3 browser, of the document shown in Figure 4.5.

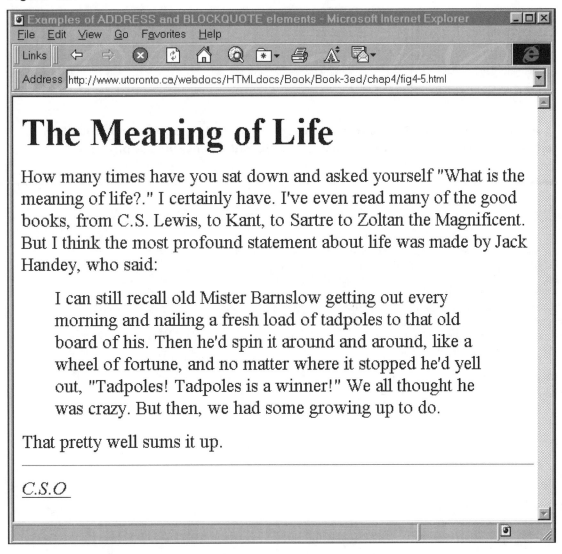

Note that, ideally, you should not place text directly inside a **BLOCKQUOTE**; rather, text should lie inside other elements (such as paragraphs and lists) that are in turn inside the **BLOCK-QUOTE**. Thus, the form:

```
<BLOCKQUOTE>
<P> This is the quotation ...
.....
</BLOCKQUOTE>
```

is better than:

```
 <BLOCKQUOTE>
This is the quotation ...
.....
</BLOCKQUOTE>
```

Figure 4.7 HTML example document illustrating TITLE, heading, and ADDRESS elements. Figure 4.8 shows this document viewed by Internet Explorer 3.

```
<HTML>
<HEAD>
<TITLE> Some examples of ADDRESS and heading elements </TITLE>
</HEAD>
<BODY>

<H1 ALIGN="center"> Example 3: The Truth About Santa  </H1>
<P> Breaking the news to a small child that Santa Claus is
merely a tool of the modern capitalist is one of
the saddest moments in raising children.  Nevertheless, such
truths must be brought to life, for fear that your child
become another Pangloss lost in the idealism so prevalent
amongst our youth. Here are some different methods to
introduce this topic.

<H2 ALIGN="left"> Santa's Exploitation of the Working Class </H2>
<P>  Begin by talking about Santa's enslaved workforce.  How
can those poor gnomes make all those gifts?  Clearly
by driven overwork.....

<H3> Elves and the Union Movement </H3>
<P> and so on.......

<H4> Elf Exploitation </H4>
<P> And still more text.
<HR>
<ADDRESS>
Santa Claus<BR>
Christmas Holiday Specialist <BR>
North Pole, CANADA H0H 0H0<BR>
Tel: (555) 555 POLE
</ADDRESS>
</BODY> </HTML>
```

Figure 4.8 Display, by the Internet Explorer 3 browser, of the document shown in Figure 4.7.

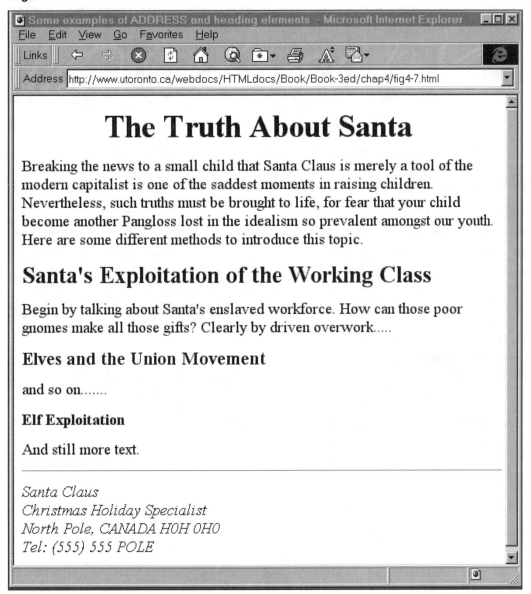

A typical **BLOCKQUOTE** is shown in Figures 4.5 and 4.6. Because **BLOCKQUOTE** usually introduces left-margin indentation, it is often used to indent blocks of text, such as the paragraphs following a heading. An example is shown in Figures 2.17 and 2.18. A much better approach is to use stylesheets, as discussed in Chapter 5.

CENTER Element: Center the Enclosed Text Horizontally

Usage	`<CENTER> ... CENTER>`
Can Contain:	characters, character highlighting, A, APPLET, BR, IMG, BASEFONT, MAP, SCRIPT, [ISINDEX], INPUT, SELECT, TEXTAREA, DIR, DL, MENU, OL, UL, P, HR, Hn, ADDRESS, BLOCKQUOTE, CENTER, DIV, FORM, PRE, TABLE
Can Be Inside:	BLOCKQUOTE, BODY, CENTER, DD, DIV, FORM, LI, TD, TH
Attributes:	none

CENTER center-aligns text enclosed within the element, including any enclosed blocks of text, with the exception of left- or right-aligned images or tables, or block elements for which the alignment is specified by the element's own alignment attribute. In particular, **CENTER** is often used to center a **TABLE** between margins. Note that **CENTER** introduces a line break both before and after the centered text, so that only the enclosed text is centered—**CENTER** does not introduce any extra vertical spacing beyond that of a regular line break.

TIP: Use DIV with ALIGN="center" instead of CENTER
CENTER and **DIV** with attribute value ALIGN="center" are equivalent. The latter is preferred, as **DIV** can be linked easily to stylesheet formatting control, while **CENTER** cannot.

Formally **CENTER** is a block element, equivalent to **DIV** with center. However, you must be careful about assuming that **CENTER** provides a line break, since browsers that do not understand this element will ignore the tags and will neither introduce a break, nor center the text.

CENTER is commonly used between two **HR** elements, as in the following:

```
<hr width=80%>
<center>
  These simple notes form a useful, single document
  explaining the rationale and organization of the Web Document
  template collection. Please print this out for off-line
  reference.
</center>
<hr width=80%>
```

If the browser does not support **CENTER**, the text in this example will still be separated from the preceding and following material because of the **HRs**. Figures 4.9 and 4.10 show how this differs from the following (which includes a **P** element):

```
<hr width=80%>
<center>
  <P> These simple notes form a useful, single document
  explaining the rationale and organization of the Web Document
  template collection. Please print this out for off-line
  reference.
</center>
<hr width=80%>
```

DIV Element: A Block Division of the BODY

Usage:	`<DIV> ... </DIV>`
Can Contain:	characters, character highlighting, A, APPLET, BR, IMG, BASEFONT, MAP, SCRIPT, [ISINDEX], INPUT, SELECT, TEXTAREA, DIR, DL, MENU, OL, UL, P, HR, Hn, ADDRESS, BLOCKQUOTE, CENTER, DIV, FORM, PRE, TABLE
Can Be Inside:	BLOCKQUOTE, BODY, CENTER, DD, DIV, FORM, LI, TD, TH
Attributes:	ALIGN

DIV marks a block of the document as a logical group or *division*, and is used to specify generic properties for the entire block. For example, `<DIV ALIGN="right">` indicates that all the text within the **DIV** element should be right-aligned, unless this alignment specification is overridden by an element within the **DIV**. In particular, `<DIV ALIGN="center">` is equivalent to `<CENTER>`. This form of **DIV** is now the recommended mechanism for horizontally centering blocks of text.

DIV implies the end of any paragraph and will cause a line break in the text. Other than for this, **DIV** does not affect the formatting or presentation of a document (i.e., it does not add any extra vertical spacing), and is simply used to more formally organize the document content. Figure 4.11 shows an example of this use of **DIV**; Figure 4.12 shows the result as displayed by the NetManage WebSurfer 5 browser.

Hn Elements: Headings

Usage:	`<Hn> ... </Hn>`
Can Contain:	characters, character highlighting, A, APPLET, BR, IMG, BASEFONT, MAP, SCRIPT, INPUT, SELECT, TEXTAREA

Can Be Inside:	BLOCKQUOTE, BODY, CENTER, DIV, FORM, TD, TH
Attributes:	**ALIGN**

Figure 4.9 HTML example document illustrating CENTER and HR elements.

```
<HTML>
<HEAD><TITLE>Example of CENTER and HR</TITLE></HEAD>
<BODY>
<H2>Example of CENTER and HR</H2>
It is always better to use <B>ALIGN</B>="center" to align
things, but sometimes <B>CENTER</B> does have advantages.
For example, look at the following: text centered between
two <B>HR</B> elements:
<HR WIDTH="60%">
<CENTER>
  This is a single-page document -- why not <BR>
  print it out for future reference?
</CENTER>
<HR WIDTH="60%">
<P>The <B>CENTER</B> element centers any enclosed, text,
including lists ...
<CENTER>
<UL>
  <LI>Lists
  <LI>Centering the text, and not the bullets
  <LI>Which is sometimes useful
  <LI>But not always.....
</UL>
</CENTER>
<HR NOSHADE>
Note that CENTER tags do not add extra vertical spacing. Observe
what happens when an extra <B>P</B> is added inside a <B>CENTER</B>:
<HR WIDTH="60%">
<CENTER>
  <P>This is a single-page document -- why not <BR>
  print it out for future reference?
</CENTER>
<HR WIDTH="60%">
Note how the extra <B>&lt;P></B> in the second example of text
centred between HR elements  adds extra vertical space between
the text and the rule.
<HR SIZE=2 NOSHADE>
<DIV ALIGN="right">
<I>Another Exciting HTML Example</I>
</DIV>
</BODY>
</HTML>
```

Figure 4.10 Rendering of the HTML document in Figure 4.9 by the Netscape Navigator 3 browser. Note the control of spacing around the HR elements.

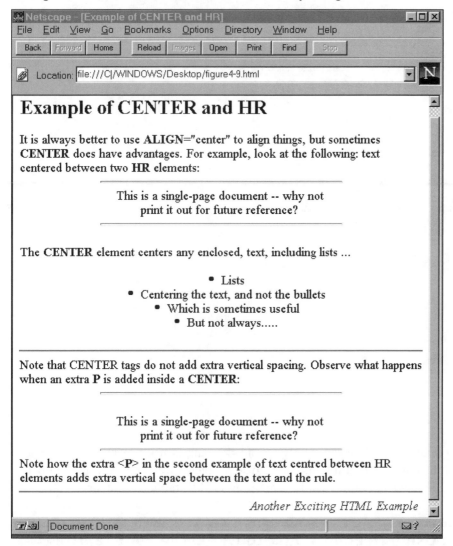

The elements **H1** through **H6** denote *headings*. There is no forced hierarchy in these headings, but for consistency you should use the top level (**H1**) for main headings, and lower levels for

Figure 4.11 Example HTML document illustrating use of the DIV element.

```
<HTML><HEAD><TITLE>Example of DIV</TITLE></HEAD>
<BODY>
<DIV ALIGN="left">
    <H1>A Left-Aligned Heading</H1>
    <P>A left-aligned paragraph....If you actually read this
        example you will realize that that the author is a
        raving idiot.
     ... more paragraph text ...
    </P>
    <DIV ALIGN="right">
        <H2>A right-aligned heading</H2>
        <BLOCKQUOTE>
        <P>A paragraph inside a block quotation -- the entire
            quotation is right-aligned. Note, however, that this
            is a formatting issue, and not a political statement
            on the part of the author.</P>
        </BLOCKQUOTE>
    </DIV>
    <P>Another left-aligned paragraph. Again, this is not a
        political statement.<BR>
        ...
    </P>
</DIV>
<HR NOSHADE>
<DIV ALIGN="right">
<I>Another Incredible HTML Example!</I>
</DIV>
</BODY></HTML>
```

progressively less important ones. You should also avoid skipping heading levels within a document, as this breaks the logical structure and may cause problems when converting the document into another form, or when automatically generating HTML table of contents documents.

NOTE: Avoid Using Headings Just to Get Large Font Text   Because headings are often used to construct document indexes and databases, you should not using headings simply to obtain large-font text. The **FONT** element, or **SPAN** (plus stylesheets) provide much better ways of accomplishing the same thing, without affecting the indexing of your work.

Figure 4.12 Rendering of the document listed in Figure 4.11 by the NetManage WebSurfer 5 browser.

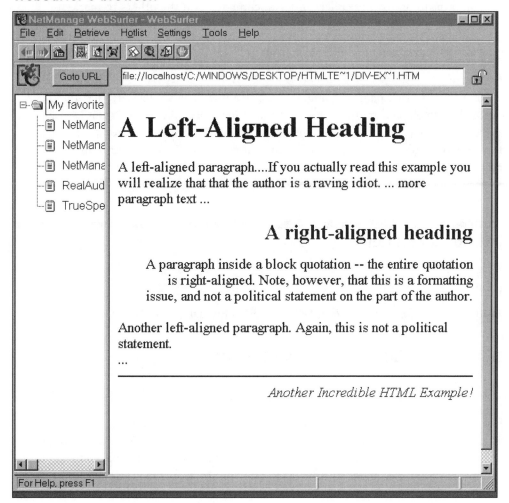

Renderings of headings are very much browser-dependent. Most graphical browsers left-adjust headings and use progressively smaller fonts as heading importance decreases (from **H1** to **H6**). Other browsers, such as lynx render **H1** headings as capitalized strings centered on the page. Examples are shown in figures throughout this chapter.

As a general rule, hypertext documents should be broken up such that each page does not occupy more than one or two browser screen areas. You can then use the **H1** or **H2** heading to mark the main heading for the collection of documents, and the others to mark sub-headings.

Heading elements can take a single, optional attribute:

ALIGN="left", "center", "right" ["justify"—proposed] (optional) **ALIGN** provides a hint to the browser as to the desired page alignment of the heading. The value "left" left-justifies the heading flush with the left margin (this is the default), while the value "right" flushes the heading to the right window margin. The value "center" causes the heading to be centered on the display window. Also proposed is the value "justify" to justify the title between the left and right margins, falling back to left alignment when the heading is too short; this alignment is not widely supported. Examples of aligned headings are shown throughout this chapter.

HR Element: Horizontal Rule

Usage:	`<HR>`
Can Contain:	empty
Can Be Inside:	**BLOCKQUOTE, BODY, CENTER, DD, DIV, FORM, LI, TD, TH**
Attributes:	**ALIGN, NOSHADE, SIZE, WIDTH,** (<u>**COLOR**</u>: Internet Explorer only)

The empty **HR** element draws a horizontal line completely across the screen, and is often used to divide sections within a single document. An `<HR>` terminates any preceding paragraph, so a new paragraph mark should follow an `<HR>` if there is subsequent text that is part of a paragraph. One common design is to place an `<HR>` at the bottom of a document, followed by an **ADDRESS** element containing address information for the document maintainer or owner. This is illustrated in Figures 4.5 through 4.8.

HR supports a number of attributes. These are:

ALIGN="left", "right", "center" (optional) If an **HR** does not span the page, then it can, like a heading, be aligned on the page. The alignment is controlled by the **ALIGN** attribute, which can take the values "left", "right", or "center" (center is the default).

<u>COLOR</u>=*"#rrggbb"* or *"color"* (optional; Internet Explorer only) This attribute specifies the desired color for the horizontal rule, either as an RGB color code or as a color name. If **COLOR** is specified, then the rule takes this color uniformly, and is not shaded.

NOSHADE (optional) By default, browsers usually render an **HR** as a shaded, chiseled bar drawn across the page. The attribute **NOSHADE** (which takes no value) indicates that the bar should be rendered in a solid color (usually black), with no shading.

SIZE=*"number"* (optional) **SIZE** specifies, in pixels, the vertical thickness of the horizontal rule. The default value is 1.

WIDTH=*"number"* or *"number%"* (optional) **WIDTH** specifies the horizontal width of the **HR** element. The form **WIDTH**=*"number"* specifies the absolute width in pixels (note that the displayed result will depend on the screen resolution of the display), while the form **WIDTH**=*"n%"* specifies the width as a percentage of the possible full width of a horizontal rule (e.g., **WIDTH**=*"80%"*).

Note that percentage width is determined relative to the maximum width allowed, which depends on the location of the **HR**. For example, inside a **BLOCKQUOTE** or **TD** (table cell), the full width of an **HR** (**WIDTH**=*"100%"*) is limited to the width of the blockquoted text or the width of the table cell, respectively.

P Element: Paragraphs

Usage:	`<P> ... (</P>)`
Can Contain:	characters, character highlighting, A, APPLET, BR, IMG, BASEFONT, MAP, SCRIPT, INPUT, SELECT, TEXTAREA
Can Be Inside:	ADDRESS, BLOCKQUOTE, BODY, CENTER, DD, DIV, FORM, LI, TD, TH
Attributes:	ALIGN

P marks a paragraph block: `<P>` is treated as a beginning paragraph marker, and implies a paragraph break and the start of a new paragraph. This is different from the **BR** element that represents a simple line break, possibly within a paragraph. Paragraphs should be thought of as logical blocks of text, similar to a **BLOCKQUOTE, ADDRESS,** or **Hn** headings, whereas a **BR** is simply a "character" that causes a line break.

Typically, a paragraph is rendered with extra space separating it from the previous and subsequent blocks of text. Sometimes the first line is also indented.

For historical reasons, an end tag `</P>` is not required. Instead, the end of a paragraph is implied by the start of another paragraph or by the start of another element marking a block of text. However, an end tag definitively marks the end of a paragraph, and is recommended.

P can take the single attribute **ALIGN** to specify text alignment. The specification is:

ALIGN="center", "left", or "right", ["justify"—proposed] (optional) Changes the paragraph alignment (the default is left) or paragraph justification. This option is implemented on most current browsers, although not all alignment options are supported. In particular, the "justify" alignment option (to justify the text between the left and right margins) is a proposed extension, and is not widely supported.

NOTE: `</P>` **Can Introduce Extra Space in Front of Subsequent Elements**   Some browsers use the `</P>` tag to introduce extra vertical spacing after the paragraph and before the following element. For example, the markup

```
... some text
<HR>
```
and
```
 ... some text </P>
<HR>
```

will be rendered differently: In the first case, the text and the following **HR** will be close together, while in the second case, there is extra space between them. With Netscape Navigator and Internet Explorer 3, this occurs when paragraph text is followed by **ADDRESS**, **HR**, **CENTER**, **DIV**, and **TABLE** elements. Internet Explorer 3 also leaves extra space in front of list elements.

TIP: Creating Extra Vertical Spacing If you wish to leave extra vertical space, you should use a paragraph containing multiple <BR> tags—for example:

```
... text
<P> <BR><BR><BR>
<H2>Heading, with lots of space above it</H2>
```
You should not use empty paragraphs to add vertical spacing, as in:
```
....text
<P><P><P>
<H2> And another thing of Interest </H2>
```

Formally, a paragraph cannot be empty, so this is illegal. Most browsers will tolerate it, but their interpretations will vary—some will leave extra spaces, while others ignore the extra <P> tags completely (the latter is formally the recommended behavior).

PRE Element: Preformatted Text

Usage:	`<PRE>` ... `</PRE>`
Can Contain:	**characters, B, CITE, CODE, DFN, EM, I, KBD, S, SAMP, STRIKE, STRONG, TT, U, VAR, A, APPLET, BR, MAP, SCRIPT, INPUT, SELECT, TEXTAREA**
Can Be Inside:	**BLOCKQUOTE, BODY, CENTER, DD, DIV, FORM, LI, TD, TH**
Attributes:	**WIDTH**

The **PRE** element marks text to be displayed with a fixed-width typewriter font. In particular, the **PRE** environment preserves the line breaks and space characters of the original text—this is the only HTML element that does so. **PRE** is therefore useful for presenting text that has been formatted for a fixed-width character display, such as a plain text terminal, or for presenting program code or HTML markup examples that should be presented with a fixed-width font.

PRE can take the optional attribute **WIDTH**, which specifies the maximum number of characters that can be displayed on a single line, and which tells a browser that it can wrap the line at this point. Most graphical browsers ignore the **WIDTH** attribute and never wrap text inside **PRE**—users can use scroll bars to see text that runs off display.

PRE content is restricted to text and character highlighting, and furthermore does not allow character highlighting elements that affect character font size or spacing (**BIG, FONT, SMALL, SUP,** and **SUB**). Most browsers will allow these elements, although different browsers will display such elements in different ways.

TIP: PRE Element—Things to Avoid   You cannot use elements that define paragraph formatting within the **PRE** element. This means you cannot use `<P>`, `<ADDRESS>`, `<Hn>`, and so on. You also cannot use `<BR>`. You should also avoid tab characters, since different browsers interpret the size of a tab differently. Instead, you should use space characters to control horizontal spacing.

TIP: Useful Features of PRE   You can use the **A** (anchor) element to create hypertext anchors inside **PRE**. You can also use the character highlighting elements (**STRONG**, **EM**, etc.), although these highlighting elements may be ignored by the browser if appropriate rendering is not possible.

An example of **PRE** is shown in Figures 4.13 and 4.14. Note the use of character highlighting. Character highlighting elements inside a **PRE** contribute zero character width.

Fill-in Forms

HTML supports interactive forms via the **FORM** element and the special elements **INPUT**, **SELECT**, **OPTION**, and **TEXTAREA**—these four elements define a form's user input mechanisms, and can only appear inside a **FORM**. The **FORM** element, in turn, specifies how the data collected by the form should be encoded, and where the encoded data should be sent.

FORM Element: Fill-in Forms

Usage:	`<FORM> ... </FORM>`
Can Contain:	characters, character highlighting, **A, APPLET, BR, IMG,**
	BASEFONT, MAP, SCRIPT, [ISINDEX], INPUT, SELECT, TEXTAREA,
	DIR, DL, MENU, OL, UL, P, HR, Hn,
	ADDRESS, BLOCKQUOTE, CENTER, DIV, PRE, TABLE
Can Be Inside:	**BLOCKQUOTE, BODY, CENTER, DD, DIV, LI, TD, TH**
Attributes:	ACTION, ENCTYPE, METHOD, <u>TARGET</u>

FORM encompasses the content of an HTML *fill-in form*. This is the element you use to create fill-in forms containing checkboxes, radio buttons, text input windows, and buttons. Data from a **FORM** *must* be sent to server-side gateway programs for processing, since a **FORM** collects data, but does not process it. In general, a **FORM** and the server-side program handling the **FORM** output must be designed together so that the program understands the data being sent from the **FORM**. Some simple examples showing the variety of possible **FORM**s are shown in Figures 4.15 through 4.18.

The **FORM** element takes four attributes. These determine where the **FORM** input data is to be sent; what HTTP protocol to use when sending the data; and the data type of the content (as a MIME content-type). Note that **FORM**s do not nest—you *cannot* have a **FORM** within a **FORM**.

The attributes are:

ACTION=*"url"* (mandatory) Specifies the URL to which the **FORM** content is to be sent. Usually this is a URL pointing to a program on an HTTP server, since only HTTP servers allow significant interaction between the client and the server. However, the **ACTION** can specify other URLs. For example, in the case of a **mailto** URL, the **FORM** content could be mailed to the indicated address. However, in this case the **METHOD** must be set to "POST."

ACTION is formally mandatory, but if it is omitted, some browsers (e.g., Netscape but not Internet Explorer) will attempt to recontact the URL from which the document containing the form was retrieved.

METHOD= "GET" or "POST" (optional) Specifies the **METHOD** for sending the data, the default value being GET. When **ACTION** indicates an **http** URL, the **METHOD** is just the HTTP *method* for sending information to the server. HTTP methods are discussed in Chapter 7. With GET, the content of the form is then appended to the URL in a manner similar to query data from an **ISINDEX** search (as discussed in Chapter 8). With the POST method, the data are sent to the server as a message body and encoded as specified by the **ENCTYPE** attribute value. The situation with **mailto** URLs is not fully specified—in practice you must specify **METHOD**="POST", and the data are sent as a mail message body and encoded as specified by **ENCTYPE**. Many current browsers do not support **mailto** URLs with **FORM**s.

ENCTYPE= *"MIME_type"* (optional) Specifies the MIME-type encoding used for data sent via the POST method. The default value is `application/x-www-form-urlencoded`. The only other supported value is `multipart/form-data`. These encoding formats are described in Chapters 7 and 8.

TARGET= *"string"* (optional) (Netscape and Internet Explorer only) Specifies the name of the *frame* or window to which the data returned by the submitted form should be sent. This attribute is used for the same purpose with the **A** (anchor) element; please see the anchor element section for further details. This attribute is supported only by the browsers that support **FRAME**s.

Figure 4.13 HTML example document illustrating the use of the PRE element.
Figure 4.14 shows this document as displayed by the Netscape Navigator browser.

```
<HTML>
<HEAD>
<TITLE> Example of the PRE Element </TITLE>
</HEAD>
<BODY>
<H1 ALIGN="center"> Example of the PRE Element</H1>
<P ALIGN="center"> <B><I>The PRE element is often used to
include blocks of plain text.  For example you can use it
to include examples of typed code, such as the following
extract from a C program:</I></B>
<HR>
<PRE>
/* main program for fitting program */

extern int *sharv;
static char boggle[100];

main (int argc, char *argv)
double x_transpose, y_transpose, f_ack=2.3;
{
  ....
</PRE>
<HR>
<P> PRE is also useful for simple tables, as in:
<PRE>
   Item            Price    Tax    Total        Category

   fileserver     10000     300   10300           <A HREF="cat_a.html">A</A>
   disk drive       900      30     930           <A HREF="cat_b.html">B</A>
  <STRONG>transmission</STRONG>    4400    110    4510            C
  <EM>fertilizer</EM>      5500    100    5600           F
</PRE>
The markup tags take up no space: if you delete everything alt the tags
inside the <B>PRE</B>, you will see that all the columns line up.
</BODY>
</HTML>
```

INPUT Element: Text Boxes, Checkboxes, and Radio Buttons

Usage: <INPUT>

Can Contain: empty

Can Be Inside: ADDRESS, BLOCKQUOTE, BODY, CENTER, DD, DIV, DT, FORM, LI, PRE, TD, TH, P, Hn,

A, CAPTION, character highlighting

Attributes: *ACCEPT*, ALIGN, CHECKED, MAXLENGTH, NAME, SIZE, SRC, TYPE, VALUE,

<u>HSPACE</u>, <u>VSPACE</u> (Netscape only)

Figure 4.14 Display, by the Netscape Navigator 3 browser, of the document shown in Figure 4.13.

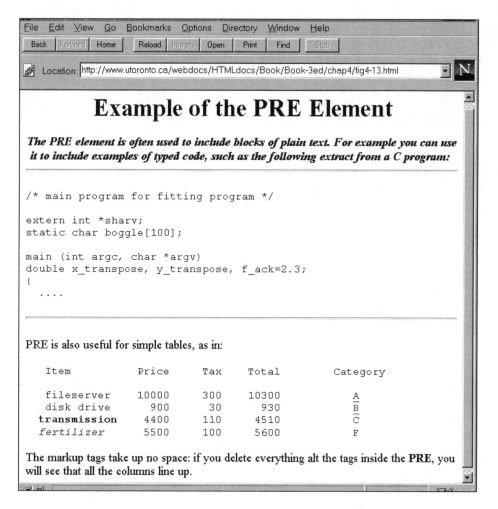

INPUT specifies a variety of *editable fields*, and should appear only inside a **FORM**. It takes several attributes that define the type of input mechanism (text field, buttons, checkboxes, etc.), the *variable name* associated with the input data, and the alignment and size of the input element when displayed. Although the **INPUT** element can appear only inside a **FORM,** many other elements (lists, blockquotes, etc.) are also allowed inside a **FORM,** and can be used to structure **INPUT** elements into a well-organized interface. Some examples of **INPUT** elements, and the organization allowed by other elements, are shown in Figures 4.15 through 4.18.

The most important attribute to the **INPUT** element is **NAME**, which assigns a *variable name* to the *value* entered into the element. The data entered into a **FORM** are sent to the server as a collection of strings of the form *name=value*, where *name* is the variable name and *value* is the value that is input or selected by the user (the *name* and *value* strings are encoded prior to being sent to the server, as discussed in Chapters 6 and 8). The program parsing the **FORM** data uses the variable *name* to interpret the contents of the corresponding *value* and must therefore understand the different *names*. For this reason, a **FORM** and the gateway program that handles the **FORM** data must be designed together.

The other main attribute is **TYPE**, which selects the type of the **INPUT** element. There are several other attributes, but their usage and relevance depends on the **TYPE**.

The attributes are:

ACCEPT = *"string"* (optional) (valid with **TYPE**="file" only) (not widely supported) Specifies a comma-separated list of MIME-types that are acceptable for input by **TYPE**="file" input elements. This proposed attribute is not widely implemented.

NAME = *"string"* (mandatory) Associates the variable name *"string"* with the data content of this **INPUT** element. Values for this attribute are chosen by the document author, and should best be strings that logically relate to the purpose of the user input.

TYPE = "checkbox", "file", "hidden", "image", "password", radio", "reset", "submit", "text" ("button", Netscape/Microsoft extension) (mandatory*)* Determines the type of input element, from amongst a list of nine possible types. The meaning and function of these different types is given below.

TYPE="button" Specifies an input button. The label of the element is obtained from the VALUE attribute value. *Button data are never sent when a FORM is submitted*—the button type is designed purely as an interface between **FORM** content and script programs within the HTML document containing the form. This is discussed in more detail in Chapter 5.

TYPE="checkbox" The input element is a *checkbox*. This is a Boolean (on/off) quantity, the default state being *off* (this is reversed if a **CHECKED** attribute is also present). **VALUE** sets the *value* assigned to an *on* checkbox. When you submit a **FORM**, the *name/value* pair is sent only if the checkbox is *on*. If there is no **VALUE** attribute to a **TYPE**="checkbox" input element, then the browser uses the default value string "on".

Different checkboxes may associate different *values* with the same variable *name*. This is convenient, for example, if you have six different databases to search and want to allow the user to select one, two, or all of them. When the **FORM** is submitted, the browser sends all the *values* from the *on* checkboxes, yielding several *name/value* pairs with the same *name*. An example is shown in Figures 4.15 and 4.16.

TYPE="file" The INPUT element is a file-selection tool or widget with which the user can select an arbitrary file to be sent to the server, as part of the submitted form data. This type is allowed only when the FORM element specifies **ENCTYPE**="multipart/form-data". Note that this may cause problems if the **ACTION** indicates a **mailto** URL and if the file contains binary data: The encoding make no special provisions for binary data, and such data is often corrupted when sent by e-mail.

TYPE="hidden" This **INPUT** element is not displayed to the user, although the content of a "hidden" element (set by the **NAME** and **VALUE** attributes) is always sent to the server when the **FORM** is submitted. This is useful for passing information back and forth between the client and server, and is typically used to record the *state* of the client-server interaction. Recall that the HTTP protocol is stateless, so that without such passed information, the gateway program handling the **FORM** data has no record of any past interaction. Thus, a "hidden" **INPUT** element is typically placed in a **FORM** by a server-side program that assembles the **FORM**. This is discussed in more detail in Chapters 8 and 9.

TYPE="image" The **INPUT** element is an inline active image (analogous to an **ISMAP** active **IMG** element). The **SRC** attribute specifies the URL of the image to include.

Clicking on the image immediately submits the **FORM** data, including the coordinates of the mouse pointer (measured in pixels from the upper left-hand corner of the image). The coordinates are sent in two *name/value* pairs. The *name* is created by taking the **NAME** attribute and appending the strings ".x" and ".y" to indicate the *x* or *y* coordinate. Thus, if the **NAME** is "king", the coordinates are sent as the *name/value* pairs `king.x=xval` and `king.y=yval`, `xval` and `yval` being the pixel coordinates selected by the user.

TYPE="password" The **INPUT** element is a single-line text field, but the text typed into the field is obscured by asterisks or by some other method. This is used for password entry. An example password field is shown in Figures 4.17 and 4.18.

TYPE="radio" The **INPUT** element is a *radio button*. Radio buttons are only meaningful when there are multiple buttons taking the same **NAME** attribute value. Sharing a common **NAME** links the buttons together, such that when a user selects or turns *on* one of the radio buttons, all other buttons associated with the same **NAME** are automatically turned *off*. Thus, only one button can be selected at a time. Each radio button must have a value, so that every **INPUT** element of **TYPE**="radio" must have a **VALUE** attribute.

Figure 4.15 HTML example document illustrating several FORM INPUT elements and the SELECT element. Figure 4.16 shows this document as displayed by the Netscape Navigator 3 browser.

```
<HTML>
<HEAD>
<TITLE> Example of an HTML FORM </TITLE>
</HEAD>
<BODY>
<H1>HTML FORM Example </H1>
<BLOCKQUOTE>

<FORM  ACTION="http://side.edu/cgi-bin/script">

<P><B>Search String:</B> <INPUT TYPE="text" NAME="search_string" SIZE=24>
<P><B>Search Type:</B>
<SELECT NAME="search_type">
  <OPTION> Insensitive Substring
  <OPTION SELECTED> Exact Match
  <OPTION> Sensitive Substring
  <OPTION> Regular Expression
</SELECT>
<P><B> Search databases in:</B>
  [<INPUT TYPE="checkbox" NAME="servers" VALUE="Canada" CHECKED>Canada]
  [<INPUT TYPE="checkbox" NAME="servers" VALUE="Russia">Russia]
  [<INPUT TYPE="checkbox" NAME="servers" VALUE="Sweden">Sweden]
  [<INPUT TYPE="checkbox" NAME="servers" VALUE="U.S.A.">U.S.A.]
  <BR><SMALL><EM>Multiple items can be selected.)</EM></SMALL>
<P><B>Niceness: </B>
<MENU>
<LI> <INPUT TYPE="radio" NAME="niceness" VALUE="nicest" CHECKED > Nicest
<LI> <INPUT TYPE="radio" NAME="niceness" VALUE="nice" >    Nice
<LI> <INPUT TYPE="radio" NAME="niceness" VALUE="not nice"> Not Nice
<LI> <INPUT TYPE="radio" NAME="niceness" VALUE="nasty" >  Nasty
</MENU>
<P> <INPUT TYPE="submit" NAME="sub" VALUE="Start Search">
    <INPUT TYPE="reset" VALUE="Reset Form">

</FORM>
</BLOCKQUOTE>
<HR>
<ADDRESS>  Form by <A HREF="about_the_author.html"> I.S.G</A> </ADDRESS>
</BODY> </HTML>
```

TYPE="reset" The **INPUT** element is a reset button. When this element is selected, all the fields in the **FORM** are reset to the values given by their respective **VALUE** attributes, thereby erasing all user input. **RESET** can itself have a **VALUE** attribute, the value of which

Figure 4.16 Display of the document shown in Figure 4.15 by the Netscape Navigator 3 browser.

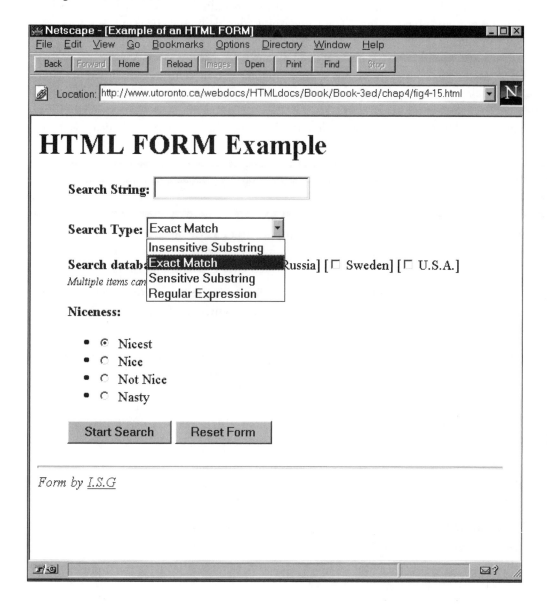

is used as the button label. Data from a **TYPE**="reset" button are *not* sent to the server when the form is submitted.

TYPE="submit" The **INPUT** element is a submit button. Pressing the submit button sends the **FORM** data to the specified URL. A form can have more than one such button, each with different **NAME** and **VALUE** attributes; the **FORM** sends only the *name/value* pair associated with the pressed submit button. The *value* is not editable by the client and is displayed as the button label.

NOTE: Some older browsers do not support multiple submit buttons with different *name/value* pairs.

TYPE="text" The **INPUT** element is a single-line text entry field. The physically displayed size of the input field is set by the **SIZE** attribute.

NOTE: In general, undefined **TYPE** values are treated by browsers as if they were of **TYPE**="text".

ALIGN="bottom", "left", "middle", "right", "top"(optional) (**TYPE**="image" only) Specifies the alignment of the image with respect to the surrounding text. The meanings are the same as with the **ALIGN** attribute to the **IMG** element (described later in this chapter).

CHECKED (optional) (**TYPE**="checkbox" or **TYPE**="radio" only) Indicates that a checkbox or radio button is selected (turned on). If **TYPE**="radio", then only one of the collection of linked radio buttons can be **CHECKED**.

MAXLENGTH="*number*" (optional) (**TYPE**="text" or **TYPE**="password" only) Specifies the length of the character buffer for a text box, where "*number*" is the buffer length. **MAXLENGTH** can be larger than the displayed text box, in which case, arrow keys may be used to scroll the text. The default buffer length is unlimited. **MAXLENGTH** simply restricts the maximum size of the string input by the user. This may also apply to **TYPE**="file", if the browser presents a type-in field for entering filename information.

SIZE=" *number*" (optional) (**TYPE**="text" or **TYPE**="password" only) Specifies, in characters, the actual size of the displayed text input field. This may also apply to **TYPE**="file", if the browser presents a type-in field for entering filename information.

SRC="*url*" (mandatory with **TYPE**="image") Specifies the URL of the image to be included *inline*—valid only with **TYPE**="image".

VALUE="*string*" (mandatory with **TYPE**="radio") Specifies the initial value of the input element. If absent, a null value is assumed.

Netscape supports two additional attributes for **INPUT** elements. These are:

<u>HSPACE</u>=*"pixels"* (optional) (valid only with **TYPE**=*"image"*) Specifies the space to be left to the left and right of the image, in pixels.

<u>VSPACE</u>=*"pixels"* (optional) (valid only with **TYPE**=*"image"*) Specifies the space to be left above and below the image, in pixels.

Figures 4.15 through 4.18 give typical examples of **INPUT** element usage. **FORM**s are also discussed in Chapters 2 and 8.

SELECT Element: Select from among Multiple Options

Usage:	`<SELECT> ... </SELECT>`
Can Contain:	**OPTION**
Can Be Inside:	**ADDRESS, BLOCKQUOTE, BODY, CENTER, DD, DIV, DT, FORM, LI, PRE, TD, TH, P, Hn,**
	A, CAPTION, character highlighting
Attributes:	**MULTIPLE, NAME, SIZE**

SELECT contains a list of selectable string values, the *values* of which are specified by **OPTION** elements lying within the **SELECT**. A browser provides a way for the user to select from amongst these values: for example, a selectable list or pull-down menu. The attribute **MULTIPLE** permits selection of multiple values; otherwise, only one value can be chosen. As with **INPUT** elements, the selected data are sent as *name/value* pairs.

The attributes are:

MULTIPLE (optional) Allows the user to select multiple items from a single **SELECT** element. If **MULTIPLE** is absent, the user can select only a single item.

NAME=*"string"* (mandatory) Specifies the variable name associated with the **SELECT** element.

SIZE=*"number"* (optional) Specifies the number of displayed text lines to be presented. The default value is 1 and, consequently, a list is often presented as a pull-down menu. For other values, the list is usually presented as a scrollbox. If **MULTIPLE** is present, browsers choose a default **SIZE** greater than 1 (so that multiple selections are possible) and will not permit a smaller value, regardless of the value assigned to **SIZE**.

Figures 4.17 and 4.18 show typical examples of **SELECT** (and **OPTION**) elements.

Figure 4.17 HTML example document illustrating FORM INPUT, SELECT, and TEXTAREA input elements. Figure 4.18 shows this document as displayed by the Netscape Navigator 3 browser.

```
<HTML>
<HEAD>
<TITLE> HTML FORM Example (2)</TITLE>
</HEAD>

<BODY>

<H2>HTML FORM Example (2) </H2>
<P>Submit your abstract for registration in the appropriate databases.
<FORM  ACTION="http://side.edu/cgi-bin/submit_abstract">
<B>1. Please give Name and Password </B>
<BLOCKQUOTE>
   <B>Name:</B>       <INPUT TYPE="text"     NAME="userid" VALUE="guest" SIZE=20>
   <B>Password:</B> <INPUT TYPE="password" NAME="password" VALUE="bozo..." SIZE=8>
</BLOCKQUOTE>
<B>2. Select Appropriate Database(s)</B> <BR>
<BLOCKQUOTE>
    <B>Physics: </B>
     <SELECT NAME="physics_database" MULTIPLE SIZE=3>
        <OPTION SELECTED> Condensed-Matter
        <OPTION> High Energy
        <OPTION> Solid-State
        <OPTION> Quantum Cosmology
        <OPTION> Astrophysics
    </SELECT>
    <B>Chemistry: </B>
    <SELECT NAME="chemistry_database" MULTIPLE SIZE=3>
        <OPTION> Surface Dynamics
        <OPTION> Quantum Chemistry
        <OPTION SELECTED> Polymer Dynamics
        <OPTION> Biochemistry
        <OPTION> Nuclear Chemistry
    </SELECT>
</BLOCKQUOTE>
<B>3. Enter Abstract: </B>
<BLOCKQUOTE>
    <TEXTAREA NAME="abstract" COLS=50 ROWS=4>
If you are submitting an abstract, select the
desired databases from the above list, delete
this text, type (or paste) the abstract into
this box and press the "Deposit Abstract" button.
    </TEXTAREA>
</BLOCKQUOTE>
<B>4. Submit Form or Reset --</B>
<INPUT TYPE="submit" NAME="depo" VALUE="Deposit Abstract">
<INPUT TYPE=reset VALUE="Reset Form">
```

Figure 4.17 HTML (Continued)

```
</FORM>
<HR>
<ADDRESS>   Form by <A HREF="about_the_author.html"> I.S.G</A> </ADDRESS>
</BODY>
</HTML>
```

Figure 4.18 Display of the document shown in Figure 4.17 by the Netscape Navigator 3 browser.

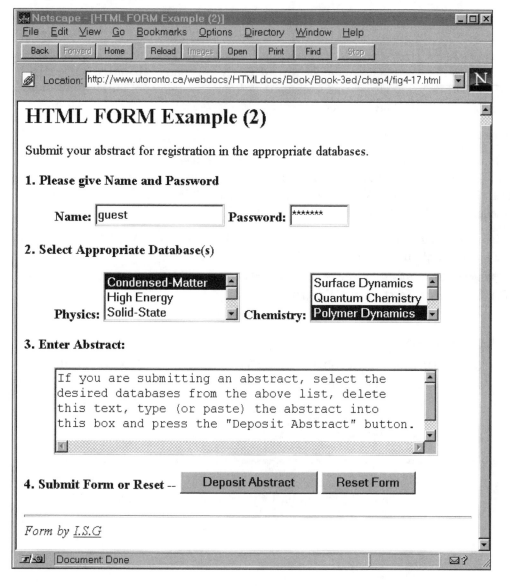

OPTION Element: List of Options for SELECT

Usage: `<OPTION> ... (</OPTION>)`

Can Contain: **characters**

Can Be Inside: **SELECT**

Attributes: **VALUE, SELECTED**

OPTION sets the character-string options for a **SELECT** element. This element is not empty, but the terminating `</OPTION>` is optional, as the element is by default terminated by the next `<OPTION>` tag or by the `</SELECT>` tag ending the list. **OPTION** can contain characters, character references, or entity references only; it cannot contain markup. The content of **OPTION** is used as the *value* unless a **VALUE** attribute is explicitly set.

The attributes are:

SELECTED (optional) This marks the **OPTION** as selected—by default, items are not selected. If the **SELECT** element has the **MULTIPLE** attribute, more than one **OPTION** can be marked as **SELECTED**. Figures 4.17 and 4.18 show examples. **SELECTED** items can be deselected by the user. Consequently, **SELECTED** is often used to set default selection values.

VALUE= *"value"* (optional) Specifies the *value* assigned to the **OPTION**. If **VALUE** is absent, then the text content of **OPTION** is used as the *value*.

TEXTAREA Element: Text Input Region

Usage: `<TEXTAREA> ... </TEXTAREA>`

Can Contain: **characters**

Can Be Inside: **ADDRESS, BLOCKQUOTE, BODY, CENTER, DD, DIV, DT, FORM, LI, PRE, TD, TH, P, Hn,**

                    A, CAPTION, character highlighting

Attributes: **COLS, NAME, ROWS, <u>WRAP</u>** (Netscape only)

TEXTAREA provides a mechanism for the user to input a block of text; usually this is done by providing a text input window. The text input by the user can grow to almost unlimited size, and is not limited, either horizontally or vertically, by the size of the displayed input window. Scroll bars are often presented if the text entered into a **TEXTAREA** grows to be (or initially is) bigger than the displayed region.

The size of a **TEXTAREA** is set by the **COLS** and **ROWS** attributes (the default size in the absence of these attributes is browser-specific). Since **TEXTAREA** windows usually display characters using a fixed-width font, **COLS** specifies the input box width as a number of characters, while **ROWS** specifies the height as the number of displayable text rows. **TEXTAREA** input can include any printable characters; the **TEXTAREA** data are simply characters to be sent elsewhere. Thus a person typing text into a **TEXTAREA** can in principle send an entire HTML document to a server by typing (or cutting and pasting) the document into a **TEXTAREA**.

By default, text in a **TEXTAREA** does not wrap—lines can be as long as desired, with line wrapping only occurring at carriage returns explicitly typed in by the user. In some cases, it is more convenient if the **TEXTAREA** element itself automatically wraps the text, either virtually (the lines are displayed with wrapping, but the software-imposed new-line characters are not sent as part of the **TEXTAREA** data) or physically (the new-line characters introduced by the **TEXTAREA** formatting are sent as part of the **TEXTAREA** data). Netscape Navigator supports a special **WRAP** attribute that allows for these options.

The attributes are:

COLS=*"number"* (mandatory) **COLS** specifies the display width of a **TEXTAREA**, in columns.

NAME=*"string"* (mandatory) **NAME** specifies the variable name associated with a **TEXTAREA** contents.

ROWS=*"number"* (mandatory) **ROWS** specifies the display height of a **TEXTAREA**, in rows.

WRAP="off", "virtual", "physical" (optional) **WRAP** specifies the handling of word-wrapping within the **TEXTAREA** element. **WRAP**="off" disables word-wrapping completely—the only new-line characters are those explicitly typed or included with the input data. **WRAP**="virtual" causes virtual word-wrapping—new-line characters are introduced to ensure that the text fits within the specified area, but these characters are *not* included with the data when the **FORM** is submitted. According to the Netscape specifications, **WRAP**="physical" should cause word-wrapping equivalent to **WRAP**="virtual", but in this case the extra new-line characters should be included with the data when the **FORM** is submitted. The default behavior is **WRAP**="off", which reproduces the behavior of most current browsers.

> **NOTE:** With Netscape Navigator 3 and Microsoft Internet Explorer 3, the attribute **WRAP**="physical" *does not* introduce line breaks in the transmitted data at the wrap points. Instead, both programs treat **WRAP**="physical" in the same manner as **WRAP**="virtual."

Text placed inside a **TEXTAREA** element is displayed as an initial value; a browser provides some way to edit the displayed text. Note that HTML markup tags are not interpreted inside a **TEXTAREA**, and are displayed as plain text. However, entity and character references inside the **TEXTAREA** element *are* interpreted, and are converted to their respective characters prior to being displayed.

Figures 4.17 and 4.18 show a typical example of a **TEXTAREA** element.

KEYGEN Element: Generate Encrypted Keys (Netscape Navigator Only)

Usage:	<KEYGEN>
Can Contain:	empty
Can Be Inside:	ADDRESS, BLOCKQUOTE, BODY, DD, DIV, DT, FORM, LI, PRE, TD, TH, CENTER, Hn, P, A, APPLET, CAPTION, character highlighting
Attributes:	*CHALLENGE, NAME*

KEYGEN is used to generate encrypted user key certificates for submission to remote sites—the remote site can use this key to authenticate the user through a third-party authentication service. The mandatory **NAME** attribute specifies the name to use with the encrypted keystring: The associate *value* will be the encrypted string calculated by the browser's encryption software. The optional **CHALLENGE** attribute specifies a challenge string, which is encrypted along with the public key. This is used to verify that the request comes from the appropriate document. The default **CHALLENGE** value is an empty string.

When present inside a **FORM, KEYGEN** produces a selectable list of keys. When the **FORM** containing a **KEYGEN** is submitted, the user is prompted for a password, which is used to create the certificate key. The key is added to the submitted request as a standard name/value pair.

Lists and List-Related Elements

There are two broad categories of list elements: description lists and regular lists. Description lists (DL) define glossary-like lists, and can only contain two elements: **DT** (description term) and **DD**

DL Element: Glossary List

Usage:	`<DL> ... </DL>`
Can Contain:	**DT, DD**
Can Be Inside:	**BLOCKQUOTE, BODY, CENTER, DD, DIV, FORM, LI, TD, TH**
Attributes:	**COMPACT**

(the description). There are four types of regular list elements—**DIR, MENU, OL,** and **UL**—which can in turn only contain one thing: **LI** list items. However, **DD** and **LI** elements can in turn contain any of the five list elements, thereby allowing for nested lists.

This list type, also known as a definition list, is designed for a list of items each with an associated, descriptive paragraph. This can be used, for example, for traditional glossaries. A **DL** list can contain two elements:

DT The term being defined

DD The definition of the term

Logically, **DT** and **DD** elements should appear in pairs; however, the specification does not require this, so that you can have **DT** and **DD** elements in any order you like. In general, **DT** elements are rendered flush with the left margin, while **DD** elements are slightly indented.

DL can take a single optional attribute, **COMPACT,** to signify that the list should be rendered in a physically compact way. This is useful for compacting a list of small items, or to compact a large list that would be easier to read if rendered in a compact manner. This tends to close up text and reduce spacing between items. While **COMPACT** will compact the formatting on Netscape Navigator, it is not understood on most other commercial browsers.

Figures 4.19 and 4.20 show an example of a **DL** list.

DT Element: Term in a Glossary List

Usage:	`<DT> ... (</DT>)`
Can Contain:	**characters, character highlighting, A, APPLET, BR, IMG, BASEFONT, MAP, SCRIPT, INPUT, SELECT, TEXTAREA**
Can Be Inside:	**DL**
Attributes:	none

Figure 4.19 HTML example document illustrating the DL glossary list elements, and a UL unordered list nested inside a glossary list. Figure 4.20 shows this document as displayed by the NetManage WebSurfer browser.

```
<HTML> <HEAD>
<TITLE> Example of Glossary List elements </TITLE>
</HEAD>
<BODY>
<H1>Example of Glossary Lists </H1>

<P> Here is an example of a glossary list. The third item in the list
has a regular, unordered list nested within it. Note that the first
term (marked by the <B>DT</B> element) does not have a matching
description (marked by the <B>DD</B> element). This is perfectly legal.
You can also use <B>BR</B> elements to add extra line spacing, where
desired -- here it is done after the first <B>DT</B>.
<DL>
   <DT>Things to do: <BR><BR>
   <DT>Things to Avoid:
   <DD>You should not use elements that define paragraph
       formatting within the PRE element. This means you should
       not use <code> &lt;P>, &lt;ADDRESS>, &lt;Hn> </code> and so on.
       You should avoid the use of tab characters -- use single blank
       characters to space text apart.
   <DT>Things That are OK:
   <DD>You <EM> can </EM> use the anchor element A.  A typed carriage
       return will cause a new line in the presented text.
       People you should never let format lists include:
       <UL>
          <LI>Bozo the Clown
          <LI>Uncle Fester
          <LI>Knights who go nii
       </UL>
       as they generally do a poor job.
</DL>
</BODY>
</HTML>
```

The **DT** element contains the term part of a glossary or description list entry. The contents of a **DT** element should be short: typically, a few words, and certainly shorter than a line. The element can contain standard character markup, images, line breaks, and hypertext anchors, as well as form input elements.

Figure 4.20 Display, by the NetManage WebSurfer 5 browser, of the document shown in Figure 4.19.

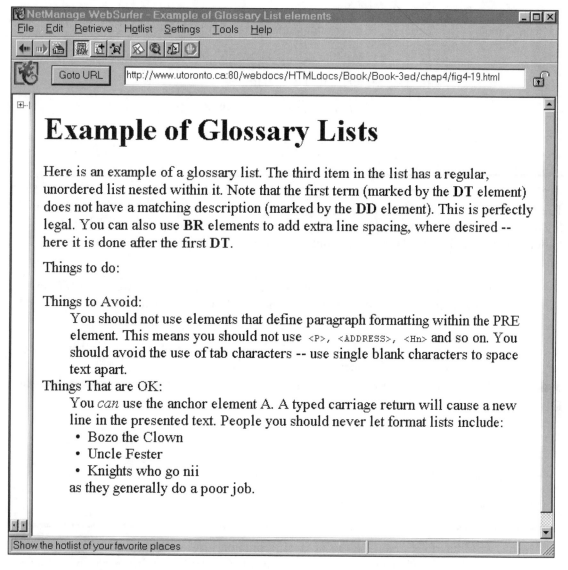

The **DT** element is not empty, but the terminating `</DT>` is optional, as it is implied either by the start of another `<DT>` or `<DD>` element, or by the `</DL>` ending the list.

DD Element: Description in a Glossary List

Usage:	`<DD> ... (</DD>)`
Can Contain:	characters, character highlighting, A, APPLET, BR, IMG, BASEFONT, MAP, SCRIPT, [ISINDEX], INPUT, SELECT, TEXTAREA, DIR, DL, MENU, OL, UL, P, HR, BLOCKQUOTE, CENTER, DIV, FORM, PRE, TABLE
Can Be Inside:	DL
Attributes:	none

The **DD** element gives the description corresponding to the previous **DT** element or elements. It can be a long description, broken into paragraphs and containing other lists, **FORMs**, quotations, and so on. A **DD** element should follow a **DT** element and should not occur alone.

Most browsers render **DD** content a line below and slightly indented relative to the **DT** content. This may be changed if the **DL** element took the **COMPACT** attribute—in this case the **DD** content may be tab-indented relative to the **DT** content, and on the same line.

DD is not empty, but the terminating `</DD>` is optional, since the end is implied either by the `<DT>` or `<DD>` tag starting another element, or by the `</DL>` tag terminating the list.

OL Element: Ordered List

Usage:	`<OL> ... </OL>`
Can Contain:	LI
Can Be Inside:	BLOCKQUOTE, BODY, CENTER, DD, DIV, FORM, LI, TD, TH
Attributes:	COMPACT, START, TYPE

OL defines an ordered list. Each item in the list is contained within an **LI** (list item) element— **LI** elements are the *only* elements that can appear inside **OL**. Items can be paragraphs of text, but should be kept reasonably short; otherwise, the idea of a list is lost. If the list items are big, perhaps it is not really a list: Try paragraphs with appropriate section headings. A typical ordered list is show in Figures 4.21 and 4.22.

A browser indicates item ordering by numbering the items, by assigning them ascending letters, et cetera. **OL** can take three attributes: **COMPACT** to render the list in compact format, and **TYPE** and **START** to control how items are numbered and ordered.

COMPACT (optional) Indicates that the list should be rendered in a compact format, for example by reducing the space between items or by arranging the items horizontally across the display. This attribute is not widely supported.

START="*number*" (optional) **START** specifies the starting number for the first item in the list, where *number* is an integer specifying the starting number.

TYPE="A", "a", "I", "i", "1" (optional) **TYPE** specifies the type of the marker by which the items should be numbered. Thus, **TYPE**="A" and **TYPE**="a" indicate ordering via capital or lowercase letters respectively, while **TYPE**="I" and **TYPE**="i" indicate ordering with uppercase or lowercase roman numerals respectively. **TYPE**="1" invokes standard numerical ordering, and is the default.

UL Element: Unordered List

Usage:	`<UL> ... </UL>`
Can Contain:	**LI**
Can Be Inside:	**BLOCKQUOTE, BODY, CENTER, DD, DIV, FORM, LI, TD, TH**
Attributes:	**COMPACT, TYPE**

UL defines an unordered list of items. A graphical browser will present each list item with a special leading symbol, such as a bullet or asterisk. Each *item* in a UL list is contained within an **LI** (list item) element—**LI** elements are the *only* things that can appear inside a **UL**. Items can be paragraphs of text, but should be kept reasonably short; otherwise, the idea of a list is lost. If the list items are big, perhaps it is not really a list: Try paragraphs with appropriate section headings.

The **UL** element can take two optional attributes:

COMPACT (optional) Requests that the list be presented in a compact way, for example, by reducing whitespace between list entries. This attribute is not widely supported.

TYPE="circle", "disc", "square" (optional) Specifies the desired type of bulleting symbol. The allowed values are **TYPE**="disc" (for a small circular disc), **TYPE**="circle" (for a small, open circle), or **TYPE**="square" (for a small square). The default value varies, depending on the level of the list: Most browsers use different symbols for list items nested inside other list items.

Figures 4.21 to 4.24 show examples of unordered lists.

Figure 4.21 HTML example document illustrating UL and OL lists, and the nesting of list elements. Figure 4.22 shows this document as displayed by the Internet Explorer browser.

```
<HTML>
<HEAD>
<TITLE> Example of Regular List elements </TITLE>
</HEAD>
<BODY>
<H2> Examples of Regular Lists </H2>
<H3> Ordered Lists </H3>
<P>This shows an ordered list, with another ordered list nested
   within it.
<OL>
   <LI>First item -- items can contain images, blockquotes, and
       other lists, among other things
   <LI>A Second item in the list
   <LI VALUE="6">And a third item (but a <B>VALUE</B> attribute sets it
   to numeral 6). And now.... a nested ordered list, with the type
   attribute <B>TYPE</B>="i":
       <OL TYPE="i" START="2">
          <LI>The first sub-item
          <LI>The second sub-item, and so on.....
       </OL>
</OL>
<H3> Unordered Lists </H3>
<P>This examples illustrates and unordered list containing another
unordered list.
<UL>
   <LI>A list item
   <LI>Another list item; again these can contain IMG elements,
       paragraphs, and so on
   <LI>List items can also contain lists, for example:
       <UL>
        <LI TYPE="circle">An item in the list
        <LI TYPE="square">Something else that is
            important, and so on
       </UL>
       Which is simply a list within a list
</UL>
</BODY> </HTML>
```

Figure 4.22 Display, by the Internet Explorer 3 browser, of the document shown in Figure 4.21.

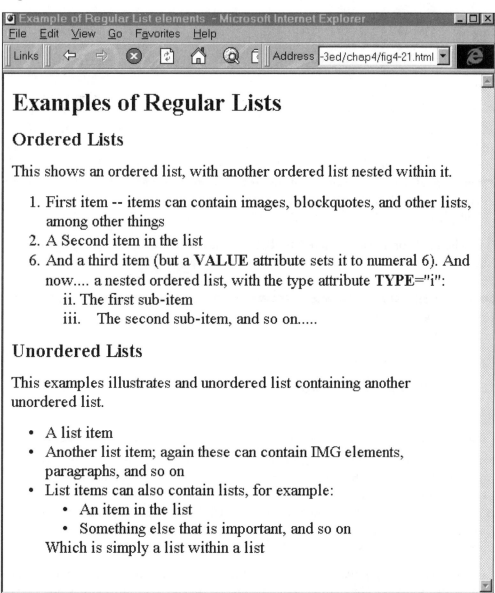

DIR Element: Directory List

Usage: `<DIR> ... </DIR>`

Can Contain: **LI**

Can Be Inside: **BLOCKQUOTE, BODY, CENTER, DD, DIV, FORM, LI, TD, TH**

Attributes: **COMPACT**

DIR defines a directory list—a list of short items, each usually no more than about 20 characters. If possible, a browser may display the items in columns across the screen, rather than one above the other (most browsers do not do this, however, and format **DIR** and **UL** lists identically). Each item in a **DIR** list is contained within an **LI** (list item) element—**LI** elements are the *only* things that can appear inside a **DIR** list. An example of a directory list is shown in Figures 4.23 and 4.24.

DIR can take the single optional attribute **COMPACT**. This attribute does not take a value, and simply directs the browser to render the list in a compact manner. This attribute is not widely supported.

MENU Element: Menu List

Usage: `<MENU> ... </MENU>`

Can Contain: **LI**

Can Be Inside: **BLOCKQUOTE, BODY, CENTER, DD, DIV, FORM, LI, TD, TH**

Attributes: **COMPACT**

MENU defines a list of short menu items, each item preferably less than a sentence long. **MENU** is designed to work like **UL** but to be formatted in a more compact manner similar to a `<UL COMPACT>` list, except that formatting may be optimized to favor short list items. (Most browsers do not do this, however, and format **MENU** and **UL** lists identically.) Each item in a **MENU** list is contained within an **LI** (list item) element—**LI** elements are the *only* things that can appear inside a **MENU** list. Figures 4.23 and 4.24 give an example of a **MENU** list.

MENU can take the single optional attribute **COMPACT**. This attribute does not take a value, and simply directs the browser to render the list in a compact manner. This attribute is not widely supported.

LI Element: List Item

Usage: `<LI> ... (</LI>)`

Can Contain: **characters, character highlighting, A, APPLET, BR, IMG,**

                       BASEFONT, MAP, SCRIPT, [ISINDEX], INPUT, SELECT, TEXTAREA,

                       DIR, DL, MENU, OL, UL, P, HR,

                       BLOCKQUOTE, CENTER, DIV, FORM, PRE, TABLE

Can Be inside: **DIR, MENU, UL, OL**

Attributes: **TYPE, VALUE**

LI marks a list item within a **DIR, MENU, OL,** or **UL** list. The item can contain text, character markup, and hypertext anchors, as well as subsidiary lists and text blocks. Note, however, that **LI** cannot contain **ADDRESS** or **Hn** heading elements.

LI supports two attributes for defining the type of the bullets in unordered lists, and for controlling numbering in ordered lists. These are:

TYPE="disc", "circle", "square" (within **UL** unordered lists), or "I", "i", "A", "a", "1" (within **OL** ordered lists)

TYPE determines the manner in which list items are marked. In unordered lists, the values "disc", "circle", and "square" produce closed discs, open circles, and squares respectively. In ordered lists, "I" and "i" produced uppercase and lowercase roman numerals respectively; "A" and "a" produce uppercase and lowercase alphabetized lists, and "1" produces numbered lists. Note that selecting a **TYPE** for a list item sets this type for all subsequent list items, unless another **TYPE** attribute is present.

NOTE: Internet Explorer 3 does not support **TYPE** attributes for **LI** elements inside **UL, MENU,** or **DIR** lists.

VALUE="*number*" **VALUE** sets the numeric counter for the current list item, where *number* is an integer. Thus **VALUE**=5 sets the current list item to be item number 5. Subsequent numbered items are incremented from this value.

Some examples of list items are shown in Figures 4.21 and 4.24.

**Figure 4.23 HTML example document illustrating MENU and DIR lists.
Figure 4.24 shows this document as displayed by the Netscape Navigator
browser.**

```
<HTML><HEAD>
<TITLE> More Examples of Regular Lists </TITLE>
</HEAD>
<BODY>
<H2 ALIGN="center"> Lists, Lists and Yet More Lists </H2>

<H3> Regular UL Lists </H3>
<UL>
    <LI>A list item.
    <LI>another list item
    <LI>and still more items
    <LI>What ... still more?
</UL>
<HR SIZE="5" WIDTH="20%">
<H3> DIR Lists </H3>
<DIR>
    <LI>Abraham - Carbon
    <LI>Cardshark - Elegant
    <LI>Elegiac - Food
    <LI>Foot - Hogs
</DIR>
<HR SIZE=5 WIDTH="20%">
<H3> MENU Lists </H3>
<MENU>
    <LI>First item    <LI>Second item
    <LI>Third item    <LI>Fourth item
</MENU>
</BODY></HTML>
```

Tables and Tabular Structures

The HTML **TABLE** element and the elements allowed inside **TABLE** are used to define tables or
other tabular structures. This section provides a brief overview of the table model, and introduces
some of the basic elements. The two sections that follow describe additional details and features,
and introduce some advanced features from the next-generation table specification.

The design of HTML **TABLE**s will be familiar to those who have used tabular environments
in typesetting languages such as LaTeX. A table is defined as a collection of *cells,* where a cell is
simply an item (a box) within the table. For regular tables, the content of a cell might be a number, a word, or a small image. However, the HTML table model allows paragraphs, headings,
blockquotes, and even other tables within a table cell, so that **TABLE** is not limited to describing

Figure 4.24 Display of the document shown in Figure 4.23 by the Netscape Navigator 3 browser. Note how the UL, MENU, and DIR lists are rendered in the same way. Very few browsers distinguish between these three list types.

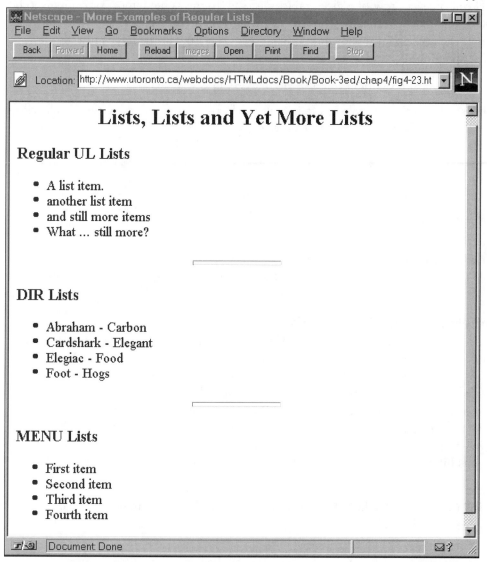

ordinary tabular structures. Indeed, **TABLE** is commonly used to create multicolumn text, sidebar notes within multicolumn tables, and so on. Some examples of these uses are illustrated in the next few pages.

Individual table cells are specified using the **TD** (table data) and **TH** (table header) elements, which contain the contents of a cell. Cells are, in turn, organized into *rows*, each row defined by a **TR** (table row) element. A table row can contain any number of **TD** and **TH** elements; however, the **TD** and **TH** cells in every row of a given table must sum to the same number of *columns*, otherwise the table will not align vertically. Thus, if the first row contains two **TD** and two **TH** elements (by default, each cell spans one column), then every other row in the table must also contain cells that span four columns.

Finally, a table can take an optional caption, via the **CAPTION** element.

The following small, captioned table has four rows, each row containing three cells, each cell spanning one column. This table is shown in Figures 4.25 and 4.26.

```
<TABLE BORDER>
<CAPTION>Here is the caption to this exciting table</CAPTION>
  <TR>  <th> Heading 1 </th>  <th> Heading 2 </th>   <th> Heading 3</th> </TR>
  <TR>  <td> item 1    </td>  <td> item 2    </td>   <td> item 3   </td> </TR>
  <TR>  <td> item 4    </td>  <td> item 5    </td>   <td> item 6   </td> </TR>
  <TR>  <td> item 7    </td>  <td> item 8    </td>   <td> item 9   </td> </TR>
</TABLE>
```

Note how each row contains three cells, defined either by **TH** header or **TD** data cells. In this example the first row contains the three headings, while subsequent rows contain the data.

Multirow or Multicolumn Table Cells

Tables are made somewhat more interesting by letting a **TH** or **TD** cell occupy more than one row or column. This is accomplished through two special attributes. The **ROWSPAN** attribute specifies how many *rows* are occupied by a cell, counting to the right of the cell, while the **COLSPAN** attribute specifies how many *columns* are occupied by a cell, counting downwards. A multicolumn or multirow cell means that some **TR** row definitions will contain fewer **TD** or **TH** items in the row than you might expect, since some of the cells are occupied by the cell "hanging down" from the row above, or pushing over from the cell to the left. It is the table designer's responsibility to make sure that all the items in a row sum to the correct number of columns.

The use of **ROWSPAN** and **COLSPAN** is illustrated in the following example and is also shown in Figures 4.25 and 4.26.

```
<TABLE BORDER>
<TR>  <th colspan="2"> Heading 1                   </th>  <th> Heading 3</th> </TR>
  <TR>   <td rowspan="2"> item 1</td> <td> item 2  </td>  <td> item 3   </td> </TR>
  <TR>                                <td> item 4  </td>  <td> item 5   </td> </TR>
  <TR>  <td> item 6            </td>  <td> item 7  </td>  <td> item 8   </td> </TR>
```

```
<TR>  <td> item 9          </td>  <td rowspan=2 colspan=2>  item 10   </td> </TR>
<TR>  <td> item 1          </td>                                            </TR>
<TR>  <td colspan=3> a big wide item 11  </td>                              </TR>
</TABLE>
```

The first row indicates that this table has three columns, although the first **TH** cell spans two of these columns, so that there are only two **TH** elements in this row. The second row contains the required three cells, but the **ROWSPAN="2"** attribute, in the first cell, indicates that this cell spans two rows, and hence hangs down into the next row. Consequently, there are only two cells declared in the third row, since the first column is occupied by the cell that started in the preceding row.

The fourth row is a regular row with three single-column and single-row cells. The fifth row, however, contains only two cells; the second of these occupies two rows and two columns. Consequently, the sixth row contains only one cell, as the remaining columns are occupied by the two-column-wide cell hanging down from row 5. Finally, the last row contains a single cell that spans the entire table.

Finally, Figures 4.27 and 4.28 show some convenient uses of tables, such as for boxing images and text, and creating double-column text. Although the latter looks quite nice here, just imagine how it would look with a larger font size or a smaller display window!

Table Border and Presentation Controls

The display and rendering of tables is controlled through several **TABLE** attributes. The universally supported attributes are **BORDER, CELLSPACING,** and **CELLPADDING,** which specify, in pixels, the border width, the cell dividing line width, and the padding space around table cell content. Many browsers also support a **BGCOLOR** attribute, to specify the background color for the table cells. This, however, is not part of HTML 3.2. Internet Explorer supports some proprietary attributes for more refined control of cell border coloration; these attributes, described later, are not supported by other browsers.

Alignment of Cell Content and Cell Properties

The alignment of data within table cells can be controlled using the **ALIGN** (horizontal alignment) and **VALIGN** (vertical alignment) attributes. These attributes are supported by TD and TH elements, as well as **TR** elements; in the latter case, the alignment is applied to all cells in the row. However, any attribute specified in a **TR** element is overridden by the value specified in a **TD** or **TH.** Thus you can use **TR** attributes to describe overall row properties, and attributes within each **TD** or **TH** to set properties specific to a cell.

Most browsers support the nonstandardized **BGCOLOR** attribute, which specifies the background color for a cell or group of cells. When supported, this attribute is allowed within **TR,**

Figure 4.25 HTML example document illustrating the TABLE elements. Figure 4.26 shows this document as displayed by the Internet Explorer browser.

```
<HTML><HEAD>
<TITLE> HTML TABLEs </TITLE>
</HEAD><BODY>

<H2 ALIGN="center"> HTML Tables</H2>
<P> The following two examples look at basic HTML tables.
<H3> First Example -- A Simple Table </H3>
<TABLE BORDER>
 <TR>  <TH> Heading 1 </TH>  <TH> Heading 2 </TH>   <TH> Heading 3 </TH> </TR>
 <TR>  <TD> item 1    </TD>  <TD> item 2    </TD>   <TD> item 3    </TD> </TR>
 <TR>  <TD> item 4    </TD>  <TD> item 5    </TD>   <TD> item 6    </TD> </TR>
 <TR>  <TD> item 7    </TD>  <TD> item 8    </TD>   <TD> item 9    </TD> </TR>
</TABLE>
<HR NOSHADE>
<H3>Second Example with COLSPAN and ROWSPAN </H3>

<TABLE BORDER ALIGN="right">
<CAPTION>Here is the caption to this exciting table</CAPTION>
 <TR>  <TH COLSPAN=2> Heading 1             </TH>  <TH> Heading 3 </TH> </TR>
 <TR>  <TD ROWSPAN=2> item 1 </TD>  <TD> item 2 </TD>  <TD> item 3    </TD> </TR>
 <TR>                              <TD> item 4 </TD>  <TD> item 5    </TD> </TR>
 <TR>  <TD> item 6        </TD>  <TD> item 7 </TD>  <TD> item 8    </TD> </TR>
 <TR>  <TD> item 9        </TD>  <TD ROWSPAN=2 COLSPAN=2> item 10 </TD> </TR>
 <TR>  <TD> item 1     </TD>                                         </TR>
 <TR>  <TD COLSPAN=3> a big wide item 11  </TD>                      </TR>
</TABLE>
</BODY></HTML>
```

TH, or **TD** elements. Internet Explorer supports some proprietary attributes for more refined control of cell border color.

Cell Heights and Widths

By default, a browser chooses cell heights and widths according to an internal table-generation algorithm. Often, however, an author desires more control over the layout of the table: for example, to force a particular cell to occupy 50 percent of the entire table width, or perhaps a group of columns to all be of the same width, or to specify a column with an explicit absolute width, in pixels.

Cell widths are controlled by the **WIDTH** attribute, which can specify the width in three ways: absolute width (pixels), percentage width (percentage of total table width), or relative width (width

Figure 4.26 Display, by the Internet Explorer 3 browser, of the document shown in Figure 4.25.

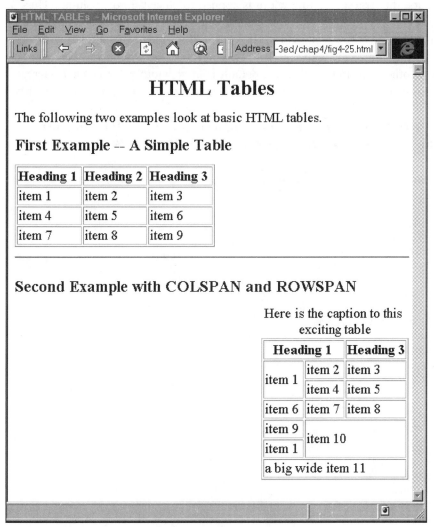

relative to other cells in the table). Cell heights are specified by the **HEIGHT** attribute, which takes as a value the height, in pixels, for the cell. Some examples of the use of these attributes are shown in Figures 4.29 and 4.30. The allowed **WIDTH** values are summarized in Table 4.7. The specification for the allowed values (and their meanings) are:

WIDTH="*number*", "*number%*", "*real.number**" (optional) Specifies the width of a cell. Note that all cells in a column must have the same width, so that if more than one cell in a column takes a **WIDTH** attribute, the largest resulting width is applied to all cells in the column. The value "*number*" specifies an absolute cell width, in pixels, while the value "*number%*" specifies the width as a percentage of the entire table width. (If you specify percentage widths for all cells in a row, be careful that the sum of the widths is 100%). The value "*real.number**" determines the cell width relative to other cells in the table, the default relative width value being 1. Here, *real.number* is a decimal or integer value (e.g., 1, or 1.5), but cannot be an exponential quantity.

Figure 4.27 A second HTML example document illustrating the TABLE elements. Figure 4.28 shows this document as displayed by the NetManage WebSurfer 5 browser.

```
<HTML><HEAD>
<TITLe> HTML TABLEs (part 2)</TITLE>
</HEAD><BODY>
<H2 ALIGN="center"> More Table Examples</H2>

<H3>First Example: Images in Tables</H3>
<TABLE BORDER=5 CELLSPACING=5 CELLPADDING=10>
<TR><TD>
    <IMG SRC="./logo.gif" ALT="[Information Commons Logo]" ><BR>
</TD><TD>
    <H2 ALIGN="center">The Information Commons
    <BR><EM>at the</EM>
    <BR>University of Toronto </H2>
</TD></TR>
</TABLE>

<H3 ALIGN="center">Second Example: Text in two columns</H3>
<TABLE CELLPADDING=5>
<TR> <TD>
  <P> Here is the first column of text. This could go on, and on, and on
  and on, and on, and on, which is to say that I have completely lost any
  any sense of what to type for these examples. Oh, I know --
  how about throwing in a list:
  <UL>
    <LI> here's a nice item
    <Li>and here's another
  </UL>
  <P> But that's enough, now for the second column.
</TD><TD>
  <P> Here we go with the second column. This column sits nicely next to
  the other one, and is separated by the invisible cell border. Cells can
  contain all sorts of markup elements, so you can create very sophisticated
  things inside these cells, such as:
  <H3>Heading</H3>
```

Figure 4.27 (Continued)

```
<P> If a browser does not understand tables, then this will be presented as
a single page of single-column text: this is one example where things will
still be readable, even if the browser does not understand tables.
</TD></TR>
</TABLE>
</BODY> </HTML>
```

Figure 4.28 Display, by the NetManage WebSurfer 5 browser, of the document shown in Figure 4.27.

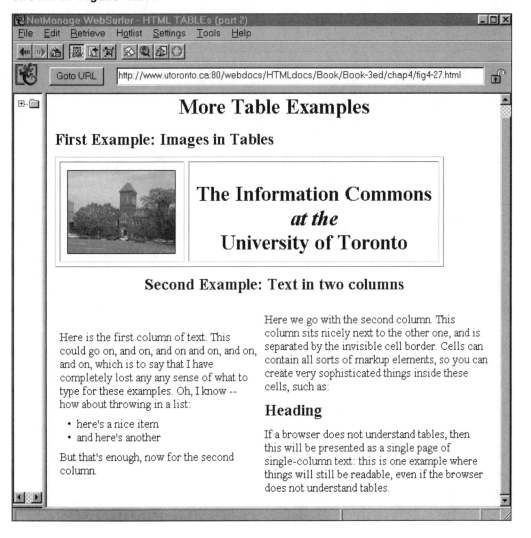

Figure 4.29 Example tables illustrating use of HEIGHT, WIDTH, ALIGN, and BGCOLOR attributes. The rendering of this document by the Netscape Navigator browser is shown in Figure 4.30.

```
<HTML><HEAD>
<TITLE> HTML TABLEs (part 3)</TITLE>
</HEAD><BODY>
<H2 ALIGN="center"> Yet More Table Examples</H2>

<H3>Simple Table</H3>
<TABLE BORDER=2>
<TR>
   <TD>Item 1
   <TD>A
   <TD>Item 3 is much longer than the other items
</TR>
<TR>
   <TD>Fred
   <TD>B
   <TD>Wilma!
</TR>
</TABLE>

<H3>Same Simple Table with WIDTH, HEIGHT, ALIGN and BGCOLOR</H3>
<TABLE BORDER=2>
<TR>
   <TD WIDTH="20%">Item 1
   <TD WIDTH="20%">A
   <TD WIDTH="190">Item 3 is much longer than the other items
</TR>
<TR>
   <TD HEIGHT="80" VALIGN="top">Fred
   <TD ALIGN="middle" BGCOLOR="#bbbbbb">B
   <TD VALIGN="bottom">Wilma!
</TR>
</TABLE>

<H3>Another Simple Table with Table Alignment</H3>
In this case, the simple table is right-aligned: consequently
<TABLE BORDER=0 BGCOLOR="#dddddd" ALIGN="right" VSPACE="5" HSPACE="5">
<TR>
   <TD ALIGN="center"><B><I>NOTE!</I></B>
</TR>
<TR>
   <TD>My Dog Has Fleas!
</TR>
</TABLE>
the text flows around the table, just as it can flow around
left or right-aligned images. This is very useful for embedding
```

Figure 4.29 (Continued)
```
text in the document the text relates with, and is also
useful for embedding notes, sidebars, etc. within regular
text.


</BODY> </HTML>
```

Figure 4.30 Display, by the Netscape Navigator 3 browser, of the document listed in Figure 4.29

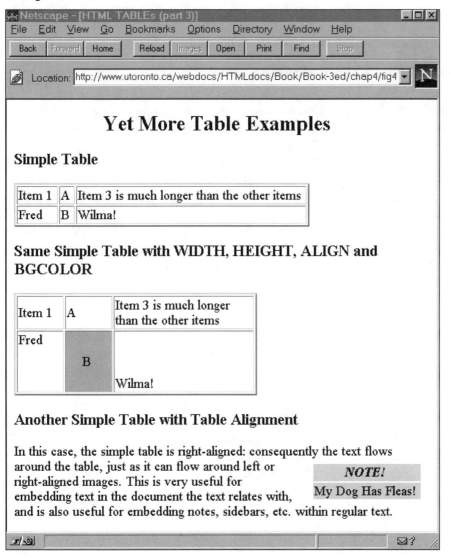

Table 4.7 Supported Table Cell WIDTH Values

Notation	Meaning
number	cell width, in pixels
number%	cell width as a *percentage* of total table width
real.number*	cell width *relative to* other cells in the table (the default relative width value is 1)

HEIGHT=*"number"* (optional) Specifies, in pixels, the height of the cell. Note that all cells in a row must have the same height, so that if more than one cell in a row takes a **HEIGHT** attribute, the largest value will be applied to all cells in the row.

Advanced Tables—Border Layout Control

The HTML development process has proposed a number extensions to **TABLE**s, several of which are implemented on the Internet Explorer browser. Notable among these extensions are the additional **TABLE** element attributes **FRAME** and **RULES**. **FRAME** specifies how the external border of the table should be rendered (all borders, or only some of them), while **RULES** specifies how the internal borders between cells should be drawn. The use of these attributes is illustrated in Figures 4.31 and 4.32. The **RULES** attribute uses structural information about the table to decide where to draw dividing lines; this extra structural information is provided by the **TBODY**, **TFOOT**, and **THEAD** elements, which divide the rows into body rows (the table body), footer rows (the table footer), and header rows (the table header), as well as the **COL** and **COLGROUP** elements, which group columns. The function of t hese newer elements is described in the next section. Their use is illustrated in Figures 4.31 and 4.32.

Advanced Table Structure

In the basic table model, a **TABLE** contained **TR** (table rows) elements and optionally a **CAP-TION**. In the newer table model, a **TABLE** does not directly contain table rows, but instead should contain **THEAD**, **TFOOT**, and **TBODY** elements, which in turn contain **TR** elements, grouped into a header (**THEAD**), footer (**TFOOT**), and table body (**TBODY**). In addition, the **TABLE** element can contain the elements **COL** and **COLGROUP**, which define properties such as cell alignment and/or width for particular columns or groups of columns. **COL** and **COLGROUP** elements must precede all table rows, since the program rendering the table must know this column—grouping information before it can begin formatting the table. These elements are employed by the example tables in Figures 4.31 and 4.32.

TABLE Element: Tables and Tabular Structures

Usage   <TABLE> ... </TABLE>

Can Contain: **CAPTION**, *COL*, *COLGROUP*, *TBODY*, *TFOOT*, *THEAD*, **TR**

Can Be Inside: **BLOCKQUOTE, BODY, CENTER, DD, DIV, FORM, LI, TD, TH**

Attributes: **ALIGN**, <u>BGCOLOR</u>, **BORDER, CELLPADDING, CELLSPACING**, *FRAME*, **HSPACE**, *RULES*, <u>VSPACE</u>, **WIDTH**, (<u>BACKGROUND</u>, <u>BORDERCOLOR</u>, <u>BORDERCOLORDARK</u>, <u>BORDERCOLORLIGHT</u>: Internet Explorer only)

TABLE specifies a table or other tabular structure. A basic **TABLE** can only contain two elements: a single **CAPTION**, to define a table caption, and one or more **TR** elements, which define the table rows. The **TR** element, in turn, can contain **TD** (table data) and **TH** (table header) elements that contain the actual content of the table. The construction of tables using this model is discussed later in the **TD** and **TH** sections.

By default, tables are drawn without borders, with a predetermined spacing between items in the table, and with a table width that depends on the table content and that is calculated by the table-generation program. Finally, tables are, by default, left-aligned on the page, and break all text flow. This means that text preceding a **TABLE** appears above the rendered table, and text following a **TABLE** appears below it.

TABLE can take several optional attributes that modify these presentation details of the table. **BORDER, CELLPADDING**, and **CELLSPACING** describe how borders should be drawn around the table, and how much spacing should be left between items in the table. **WIDTH** specifies the desired width of the table, either as an absolute width in pixels or as a percentage of the full window width. Last, **ALIGN** allows for *floating tables*, which can float to the left or right margins, and can have text flow around them. The details of these five attributes are provided in this section.

The more advanced table model, currently only supported by Internet Explorer, supports additional attributes, **FRAME** and **RULES**, for further specifying how borders should be drawn. The use of these attributes is also explained in the following descriptions.

Proprietary extensions to **TABLE** allow for control of the table cell background color (**BGCOLOR**). Microsoft supports additional extensions to control the color of the table borders, and to apply a background image for the table.

Figure 4.31 Example HTML table illustrating the use of COL and COLGROUP elements and the FRAME and RULES attributes to the TABLE element. The rendering of this document by the Internet Explorer browser is shown in Figure 4.32.

```
<HTML><HEAD>
<TITLE> Advanced HTML TABLEs (part 4)</TITLE>
</HEAD><BODY>
<H2 ALIGN="center">Advanced Table Examples</H2>
<H3 ALIGN="center">THEAD, TFOOT, COL and COLGROUP</H3>

<H3>The Table</H3>
<TABLE WIDTH="80%" BORDER=2>
<THEAD>
<TR><TH ROWSPAN=2>
    <TH ROWSPAN=2>Heading1
    <TH ROWSPAN=2>Heading2
    <TH COLSPAN=2> Main Heading </TR>
<TR> <TH>Subhead1 <TH>Subhead2    </TR>
<TBODY>
<TR><TH>Title1 <TD>Item 1    <TD>Item2      <TD>Item 3    <TD>  SubT-1
<TR><TH>Title2 <TD>Item 5    <TD>Item6      <TD>Item 7    <TD>  SubT-2
<TFOOT>
<TR><TH>MAIN-T <TD>MAIN-A    <TD>MAIN-B     <TD>MAIN-C    <TD>SubMAIN
</TABLE>

<H3>Same Table, With:<BR>
   - COL and COLGROUP Elements<BR>
   - TABLE element FRAME and RULES Attributes</H3>
<TABLE FRAME="hsides" RULES="groups" WIDTH="80%" BORDER=2>
<COLGROUP>
  <COL ALIGN="left">
<COLGROUP>
  <COL SPAN="3" ALIGN="middle">
<COLGROUP>
  <COL ALIGN="right">
<THEAD>
<TR><TH ROWSPAN=2>  
    <TH ROWSPAN=2>Heading1
    <TH ROWSPAN=2>Heading2
    <TH COLSPAN=2> Main Heading </TR>
<TR> <TH>Subhead1 <TH>Subhead2    </TR>
<TBODY>
<TR><TH>Title1 <TD>Item 1    <TD>Item2      <TD>Item 3    <TD>  SubT-1
<TR><TH>Title2 <TD>Item 5    <TD>Item6      <TD>Item 7    <TD>  SubT-2
<TFOOT>
<TR><TH>MAIN-T <TD>MAIN-A    <TD>MAIN-B     <TD>MAIN-C    <TD>SubMAIN
</TABLE>
</BODY> </HTML>
```

Figure 4.32 Display, by the Internet Explorer browser, of the document listed in Figure 4.31.

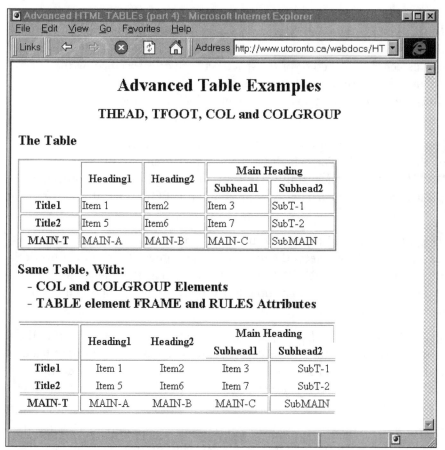

ALIGN="center", "left", "right" (optional) Allows for floating tables, analogous to floating images as described in the **IMG** element section. **ALIGN**="left" floats the table to the left margin and allows subsequent text to flow to the right of the table. **ALIGN**="right" floats the table to the right margin and allows subsequent text to flow to the left of the table. **ALIGN**="center" should float the table to the center of the window, with text flowing around it. However, most browsers do not support this attribute value, and assume in its place the default alignment (left-aligned, with no text flow around the table). Center-aligned tables are currently possible by placing a **TABLE** inside a **DIV** element with **ALIGN**="center".

If **ALIGN** is absent, the table is left-aligned, and text flow around the table is not allowed.

BACKGROUND=*"#url"* (optional) (Internet Explorer only) Specifies a background image to be used to tile the background of the table. This attribute is only supported by the Microsoft Internet Explorer 3 browser.

BGCOLOR=*"#rrggbb"*, or *"color"* (optional) Specifies a background color for the table. With Netscape Navigator this only changes the background color for the table cells, while with Internet Explorer this also changes the color of the space between cells specified by the **CELLSPACING** attribute (the width of the dividing lines and border). Be careful that you allow sufficient contrast between the text and background color, or else the text will not be legible.

BORDER=*"number"* (optional) Tells the browser to draw a box around each cell in the table, and a border around the entire table. The default behavior in the absence of **BORDER** is a table without borders. The value assigned to **BORDER** specifies the width of the borders, in pixels—if the value is not specified, the default is assumed to be 1. **BORDER**="0" also draws a borderless table.

BORDERCOLOR=*"#rrggbb"* or *"color"* (optional) (Internet Explorer only) Specifies the desired color for the cell border. This affects the outer, chiseled border of the table (outside the border width affected by the **CELLSPACING** attribute), as well as the thinly chiseled lines drawn around the edge of each cell. It has no effect if there are no borders. This is only supported by the Internet Explorer browser.

BORDERCOLORDARK=*"#rrggbb"* or *"color"* (optional) (Internet Explorer only) Specifies the desired color for the darker portion of the cell border. This affects the bottom and right-hand side of the outer border of the table, and the upper and left-hand sides of the thinly chiseled lines drawn around each cell. It has no effect if there are no borders. This is only supported by the Internet Explorer browser.

BORDERCOLORLIGHT=*"#rrggbb"* or *"color"* (optional) (Internet Explorer only) Specifies the desired color for the lighter-colored portion of the cell border. This affects the top and left-hand side of the outer border of the table, and the bottom and right-hand borders drawn around each cell. It has no effect if there are no borders. This is only supported by the Internet Explorer browser.

CELLPADDING=*"number"* (optional) Specifies the horizontal and vertical space, in pixels, to leave between the edge of a table cell and the cell contents (image or text). The default value is 1.

CELLSPACING=*"number"* (optional) Specifies the horizontal and vertical space, in pixels, left between individual cells in a table—this is the "width" of the dividing lines. The default value is 2.

HSPACE=*"number"* (optional) (Netscape Navigator only) Specifies the horizontal padding, in pixels, to leave to the left and right of the table. This is useful for providing spacing around tables that are left- or right-aligned.

FRAME=*"void"*, *"above"*, *"below"*, *"hsides"*, *"lhs"*, *"rhs"*, *"vsides"*, *"box"*, *"border"* (optional) **FRAME** specifies which sides of the framing border should be rendered—this does not affect the borders drawn between table cells. The possible values, and their meanings, are:

above	Draw a border only at the top of the table frame.
below	Draw a border only at the bottom of the table frame.
box (or border)	Draw borders on all four sides of the table frame.
hsides	Draw borders only at the top and bottom of the table frame.
lhs	Draw a border only at the left-hand side of the table frame.
rhs	Draw a border only at the right-hand side of the table frame.
void	Draw no borders for the table frame.
vsides	Draw borders on the left- and right-hand sides of the table frame.

RULES=*"none"*, *"basic"*, *"rows"*, *"cols"*, *"all"* (optional) Specifies which cell dividing lines should be drawn within the table—this does not affect the external table border. The meanings of the five values are:

all	Draw dividing lines between all rows and all columns. This is the default. A browser may use heavier lines between groups of columns, or between **THEAD, TFOOT,** and **TBODY.**
cols	Draw vertical dividing lines between all columns. A browser may use heavier lines between columns grouped within a **COLGROUP** grouping.
groups	Draw borders between all table groups—groups are specified by **THEAD, TBODY, TFOOT,** and **COLGROUP.**
none	Do not draw any interior dividing lines.
rows	Draw horizontal dividing lines between all table rows. A browser may use heavier lines between **THEAD, TFOOT,** and **TBODY** than between regular cells.

VSPACE=*"number"* (optional) (Netscape Navigator only) Specifies the vertical padding, in pixels, to leave above and below the table. This is useful for providing spacing around tables that are left- or right-aligned.

WIDTH=*"number"* or *"number%"* (optional) Prescribes the desired width of the table, in pixels, either as a percentage of the width of the display window (*number%*, ranging from 0% to 100%) or as an absolute width, *number*. Note that fixing a table to a particular pixel width may introduce formatting difficulties, should the table not fit easily within the specified size.

CAPTION Element: Table Caption

Usage:	`<CAPTION> ... </CAPTION>`
Can Contain:	**characters, character highlighting, A, APPLET, BR, IMG, BASEFONT, MAP, SCRIPT, INPUT, SELECT, TEXTAREA**
Can Be Inside:	**TABLE**
Attributes:	**ALIGN**

CAPTION specifies an optional table caption or title. A **TABLE** can have at most one **CAPTION**. A **CAPTION** can contain text, character highlighting, **IMG**, and hypertext anchors elements, but not block elements. **CAPTION** takes the single optional attribute **ALIGN** to specify how the caption is aligned relative to the **TABLE**.

ALIGN=*"top"*, *"bottom"* (*"left"*, *"right"*: Internet Explorer only) (optional) **ALIGN** specifies the desired location for the caption relative to the table. **ALIGN**=*"top"* (the default) places the caption above the table, while **ALIGN**=*"bottom"* places the caption below it. Internet Explorer 3 supports the additional values *"left"* and *"right"*, which place the caption on top of the table, but aligned to the left or right edge of the table.

Figures 4.25 and 4.26 show an example of a table caption.

COL Element: Specify Properties of a Column

Usage:	`<COL>`
Can Contain:	empty
Can Be Inside:	*COLGROUP*, **TABLE**
Attributes:	*ALIGN, SPAN,* (*WIDTH*: not currently supported)

COL, an optional element, specifies default properties for a column or a group of columns. A table will generally have multiple **COL** elements to specify properties of the different columns. For example,

```
<COL ALIGN="left">
<COL ALIGN="right">
<COL ALIGN="center">
```

indicates that the first column content should be left-aligned, the second column content right-aligned, and the third column content center-aligned. The number of columns affected by a **COL** is set by the **SPAN** attribute. Thus, **SPAN="3"** means that the properties specified by the **COL** element apply to three adjacent columns. For example,

```
<COL ALIGN="left">
<COL SPAN=3 ALIGN="center">
<COL ALIGN="right">
```

indicates that the second, third, and fourth columns should be center-aligned, and that the fifth column content should be right-aligned. The value **SPAN="0"** is special, and indicates that the properties should be applied to all columns from the current column up to the last column in the table.

The **WIDTH** attribute can be used to specify the desired width of a column, using any of the values defined below in the **TD** section. There are no commercial browsers that support the **WIDTH** attribute to the **COL** element.

COLGROUP Element: Properties of a Collection of Columns

Usage:	`<COLGROUP> ... (</COLGROUP>)`
Can Contain:	*COL*
Can Be Inside:	**TABLE**
Attributes:	*ALIGN,* (*VALIGN*: not widely supported)

It is often useful to *group* columns together in situations where there is logical structure associated with the group. For example, you might want to group the leftmost two columns as a vertical collection of subject headings, or the two rightmost columns as spreadsheet totals. Such groupings are possible using **COLGROUP**. This element allows you to group columns, and assign default alignment settings to this group. An example is

```
<COLGROUP  VALIGN="baseline">
   <COL ALIGN="left">
   <COL ALIGN="center">
</COLGROUP>
<COLGROUP ALIGN="center">
   <COL SPAN="2">
<THEAD> ....
```

which defines two column groups: the first with baseline vertical alignment, the second with horizontal centering. Note that **COLGROUP** properties apply to *all* columns specified within the **COLGROUP**.

Recall also that the **RULES** attribute of the **TABLE** element allows for special rendering of the borders between grouped columns. This points out the utility of using **COLGROUP** to group columns that logically belong together.

An example table illustrating the use of **COLGROUP** is shown in Figures 4.31 and 4.32.

THEAD Element: Table Header

Usage:	`<THEAD> ... (</THEAD>)`
Can Contain:	**TR**
Can Be Inside:	**TABLE**
Attributes:	none

THEAD defines the table header. A table header consists of table rows that make up the header of the table (for example, a **THEAD** might contain one or more rows of **TH** table header cells). **THEAD** content may act as a non-scrolling header, so that if the table is longer than the display, the **THEAD** cells stay at the top of the displayed table as the user scrolls through the table body. There are no browsers that currently implement **THEAD** and **TFOOT** in this way.

THEAD must precede the **TBODY**, which in turn must precede the **TFOOT**. An example employing **THEAD** is shown in Figures 4.31 and 4.32.

TBODY Element: Table Body

Usage:	`(<TBODY>) ... (</TBODY>)`
Can Contain:	**TR**
Can Be Inside:	**TABLE**
Attributes:	none

TBODY defines the body of the table. Formally you do not need the start and stop tags in the absence of **THEAD** or **TFOOT** elements, but it is better to put them in. An example employing **TBODY** is shown in Figures 4.31 and 4.32.

TFOOT Element: Table Footer

Usage: `<TFOOT> ... (</TFOOT>)`

Can Contain: **TR**

Can Be Inside: **TABLE**

Attributes: none

TFOOT defines the table footer. A table footer consists of table rows that make up the footer of the table. **TFOOT** content is designed to act like a **BANNER**, so that if the table is longer than the display, then the **TFOOT** cells stay at the bottom of the displayed table as the user browses through the table body.

TFOOT must be the final element in a table, just after **TBODY**. An example employing **TFOOT** is shown in Figures 4.31 and 4.32.

TR Element: Table Row

Usage   `<TR>...(</TR>)`

Can Contain: **TH, TD**

Can Be Inside: **TABLE,** *TBODY, TFOOT, THEAD*

Attributes: **ALIGN, <u>BGCOLOR</u>, VALIGN, (<u>BACKGROUND</u>, <u>BORDERCOLOR</u>, <u>BORDERCOLORDARK</u>, <u>BORDERCOLORLIGHT</u>:** Internet Explorer only)

The **TR** element denotes a row of a table. Thus, a row in a table might be coded:

```
<TR>
    <TH> Heading <TD> data 1 <TD> data2 <TD> data3 <TD> data4
</TR>
```

which indicates a row containing five columns, the first column being a table heading, and the rest containing table data. Every row must be terminated by a `</TR>`, except for the final row, where the final `</TR>` can be inferred from the `</TABLE>` tag ending the table.

The **TR** element can take two optional attributes, **ALIGN** and **VALIGN**. These attributes define the horizontal (**ALIGN**) and vertical (**VALIGN**) alignment for all cells within the row. These settings can be overridden by alignment attributes specific to a cell. The specific meanings of the attributes are:

ALIGN = "left", "right", "center" (optional) Specifies the *horizontal* alignment of the cell content within every cell in the row. **ALIGN**="left" aligns the content flush left within the cell, **ALIGN**="right" aligns the content flush right within the cell, while **ALIGN**="center" centers the content between the left and right cell borders. This is overridden by **ALIGN** attributes specific to a cell.

NOTE: Internet Explorer 3 Bug   With Internet Explorer 3, **ALIGN** in a **TR** element does not properly override the default center-alignment of enclosed **TH** cells.

<u>**BACKGROUND**</u>="#*url*" (optional) (Internet Explorer only) Specifies a background image to be used to tile the background of the row. This attribute is only supported by the Internet Explorer 3 browser.

<u>**BGCOLOR**</u> = "#*rrggbb*", "*color*" (optional) Specifies the background color to use for the cells in the row. This overrides any color specified by a **BGCOLOR** attribute to the **TABLE** element, but can, in turn, be overridden by any **BGCOLOR** attribute of a specific **TD** or **TH** cell.

<u>**BORDERCOLOR**</u>="#*rrggbb*" or "*color*" (optional) (Internet Explorer only) Specifies the desired color for the cell border: the thinly chiseled lines drawn around the edge of each cell. It has no effect if there are no borders. This can be overridden by **BORDERCOLORDARK** and **BORDERCOLORLIGHT,** or by color specification within a given cell.

<u>**BORDERCOLORDARK**</u>="#*rrggbb*" or "*color*" (optional) (Internet Explorer only) Specifies the desired color for the darker portion of the cell border. This affects the bottom and right-hand side of the outer border of the table, and the upper and left-hand sides of the thinly chiseled lines drawn around each cell. It has no effect if there are no borders. This is overridden by color specification within a given cell.

<u>**BORDERCOLORLIGHT**</u>="#*rrggbb*" or "*color*" (optional) (Internet Explorer only) Specifies the desired color for the lightened portion of the cell border. This affects the top and left-hand side of the outer border of the table, and the bottom and right-hand borders drawn around each cell. It has no effect if there are no borders. This is overridden by color specification within a given cell.

VALIGN = "top", "middle", "bottom", "baseline" (optional) Specifies the *vertical* alignment of the content within every cell in the row. The values "top", "middle", and "bottom" vertically align the cell content at the top, middle or bottom of the cell, respectively, while **VALIGN**="baseline" specifies that the baseline of the cell content should be vertically aligned with the baseline of the text in adjacent cells from the same row.

TD and TH Elements: Table Data and Table Headers

Usage:	`<TD> ... (</TD>)`
	`<TH> ... (</TH>)`
Can Contain:	**characters, character highlighting, A, APPLET, BR, IMG, BASEFONT, MAP, SCRIPT, [ISINDEX], INPUT, SELECT, TEXTAREA DIR, DL, MENU, OL, UL, P, HR, Hn, ADDRESS, BLOCKQUOTE, CENTER, DIV, FORM, PRE, TABLE**
Can Be Inside:	**TR**
Attributes:	**ALIGN, COLSPAN, NOWRAP, ROWSPAN, VALIGN, (BACKGROUND, BORDERCOLOR, BORDERCOLORDARK, BORDERCOLORLIGHT**: Internet Explorer only)

TD and **TH** elements specify the cells in a table. The only difference between the two is their meaning: TD specifies a Table Data cell—a cell containing table data—while **TH** specifies a Table Header cell—a cell containing a table heading. In both cases, the element is not empty but the end tag is optional, as the end is implied by the next `<TH>`, `<TR>`, or `<TD>` tag. A cell can have empty content, which simply means that the cell is blank.

TD or **TH** elements have several optional attributes that define the centering of the contents of the cell (**ALIGN, VALIGN**), how many columns or rows of the entire table are spanned by the cell (**ROWSPAN, COLSPAN**), and whether wordwrapping is allowed within the cell (**NOWRAP**). Finally, the attributes **HEIGHT** and **WIDTH** can specify the desired width or height of a cell. Note that all cells in a row must have the same height, while all cells in a column must have the same width; thus, if there are two **WIDTH** or **HEIGHT** specifications in the same column or row respectively, the largest value is used. (These attributes can be used to specify the width of an entire column or the height of an entire row.)

The specifications for the attributes are:

ALIGN = "left", "right", "center" (optional) Specifies the alignment of the table cell content within the cell. **ALIGN**="left" aligns the content flush left within the cell, **ALIGN**="right" aligns the content flush right within the cell, while **ALIGN**="center" centers the content within the cell. The **ALIGN** attribute of a **TD** element overrides any **ALIGN** attribute value set in the surrounding **TR** element. The default value is "left" for **TD** elements and "center" for **TH** elements.

BACKGROUND="*#url*" (optional) (Internet Explorer only) Specifies a background image to be used to tile the background of the cell. This attribute is only supported by the Internet Explorer 3 browser.

BGCOLOR = "*#rrggbb*", "*color*" (optional) Specifies the background color to use in the cell. This overrides any color specified by a **BGCOLOR** attribute to the **TABLE** or TR elements.

BORDERCOLOR="*#rrggbb*" or "*color*" (optional) (Internet Explorer only) Specifies the desired color for the cell border—the thinly chiseled lines drawn around the edge of each cell. It has no effect if there are no borders. This can be overridden by **BORDERCOLORDARK** and **BORDERCOLORLIGHT**.

BORDERCOLORDARK="*#rrggbb*" or "*color*" (optional) (Internet Explorer only) Specifies the desired color for the darker portion of the cell border. This affects the bottom and right-hand side of the outer border of the table, and the upper and left-hand sides of the thinly chiseled lines drawn around each cell. It has no effect if there are no borders.

BORDERCOLORLIGHT="*#rrggbb*" or "*color*" (optional) (Internet Explorer only) Specifies the desired color for the lightened portion of the cell border. This affects the top and left-hand side of the outer border of the table, and the bottom and right-hand borders drawn around each cell. It has no effect if there are no borders.

COLSPAN = "*number*" (optional) Specifies how many table *columns* are spanned by the cell—the default value is 1. Counting of columns starts from the left side of the table. It is the author's responsibility to ensure that the cells in each row sum to the correct number of columns.

HEIGHT = "*number*" (optional) Specifies the desired height for the cell, in pixels. Note that all cells in a row must have the same height; thus, if two cells in a row specify different heights, the larger value will be used for the entire row. Care must be taken to ensure that the cell content will fit within the specified region.

In the absence of a **HEIGHT** value, the browser will (hopefully) determine an appropriate height.

NOWRAP (optional) Indicates that text lines within a cell may not wrap; the browser may not use soft line breaks. You can use **BR** elements to force hard line breaks, where desired. **NOWRAP** should be used with caution, as it can lead to extremely wide cells.

ROWSPAN = *"number"* (optional) Specifies how many table rows are spanned by the cell—the default value is 1. Counting of rows is downward from the top of the table. It is the author's responsibility to ensure that the cells in each column sum to the correct number of rows.

VALIGN = "top", "middle", "bottom", "baseline" (optional) Specifies the vertical alignment of the content within the cell. The values "top", "middle", and "bottom" vertically align the cell content at the top, middle, or bottom of the cell respectively, while **VALIGN**="baseline" specifies that the baseline of the cell content should be vertically aligned with the baseline of the text in adjacent cells of the same row. The **VALIGN** attribute of a **TD** or **TH** element overrides any **VALIGN** attribute value set in the surrounding **TR**. The default value is "middle".

WIDTH = *"number"*, *"number%"* (optional) Specifies the desired width for the cell, either as an absolute width (in pixels), or as a percentage relative to the total table width. Note that all cells in a column must have the same width; thus, if two cells in a column specify different widths, the larger value will be used for the entire column. Care must be taken with absolute widths to ensure that the cell content will fit within the specified region.

In the absence of a **WIDTH** value, the browser will (hopefully) determine an appropriate width.

NOTE: Internet Explorer 3 Bug Internet Explorer 3 does not properly determine widths of table cells when percentage widths are specified.

Here is a simple example of a **TD** element:

```
<TD align="center" colspan=1 rowspan=2> 23.22 </TD>
```

This specifies a table data cell that spans one column and two rows, and that contains the data value 23.22. **TD** cells need not contain numbers, or even simple text strings—they can also contain other **TABLE**s, lists, images, hypertext anchors, and so on.

Inclusion Elements

These elements include other content or data within an HTML document. In HTML 3.2 the relevant elements are **IMG** (include an image) and **APPLET** (include a program applet). The proprietary element **EMBED** (include an arbitrary data object) and the proposed new standard element **OBJECT** also fall into this category. These latter two elements are discussed in Chapter 5. Both are implemented on some current browsers.

APPLET Element: Include an Embedded Applet

Usage:	`<APPLET> ... </APPLET>`
Can Contain:	characters, character highlighting, A, BR, IMG, BASEFONT, MAP, SCRIPT, INPUT, SELECT, TEXTAREA, PARAM
Can Be Inside:	ADDRESS, BLOCKQUOTE, BODY, CENTER, DIV, FORM, PRE, DD, DT, LI, P, TD, TH, Hn, A, CAPTION, character highlighting
Attributes:	ALIGN, ALT, <u>ARCHIVE</u>, CODE, CODEBASE, HEIGHT, HSPACE, NAME, VSPACE, WIDTH

APPLET is used to include an inline applet—at present, only Java applets are supported. The attribute **CODE** specifies the URL at which the applet is located (analogous to the **SRC** attribute of the **IMG** element), while the attributes **WIDTH** and **HEIGHT** specify the height and width required by the applet, in pixels. Parameter values required by the applet are obtained from **PARAM** elements contained within the **APPLET** element. An example showing the use of **APPLET** was given in Example 11 in Chapter 2. The supported attributes are:

ALIGN="top", "middle", "bottom", "left", "right" (optional) Specifies the alignment of the applet with respect to the surrounding text. The values "top", "middle", and "bottom" align the top of the applet with the top of the text, the middle of the applet with the middle of the text, and the bottom of the applet with the bottom of the text, respectively. The values "left" and "right" let the applet float to the left and right margins, respectively, and enable text flow around the applet frame.

ALT="*string*" (optional) Specifies a text string to be use in place of the applet by browsers that are unable to run the applet.

ARCHIVE="*url*" (optional) (Netscape Navigator 3 only) Specifies an *uncompressed* ZIP-format archive of classes. If specified, the browser will download the specified ZIP file and will search there for the **CODE**-specified applet and supporting classes (code libraries). Classes not in the ZIP file will still be accessed from the server, following the traditional manner.

CODE="*url*" (mandatory) Specifies the URL of the applet to be run.

CODEBASE="*url*" (optional, depending on situation) Specifies the *code base* for the applet selected by the **CODE** attribute, where the code base is simply the directory or location containing any supporting class libraries required by the applet. If the supporting libraries are at the same location as the program itself, then **CODEBASE** is superfluous and can be omitted.

HEIGHT="*number*" (mandatory) Specifies the *height* required by the embedded applet, in pixels. This is mandatory, as a browser has no other way of knowing how big a display area the applet requires.

HSPACE="*number*" (optional) Specifies a padding space, in pixels, to be left to the left and right of the applet. This creates an extra space between the applet and the surrounding document. This is not supported by Netscape Navigator.

NAME="*string*" (optional) Specifies a name that identifies the applet for external reference. This lets other programs, such as script programs within the document, reference and communicate with the named applet.

VSPACE="*number*" (optional) Specifies a padding space, in pixels, to be included above and below the applet. This creates an extra space between the applet and the surrounding document. This is not supported by Netscape Navigator.

WIDTH="*number*" (mandatory) Specifies the *width* required by the embedded applet, in pixels. This is mandatory, as a browser has no other way of knowing how big a display area the applet requires.

Example of an **APPLET**:

```
<APPLET CODE="HuntingMammoths.class" WIDTH="300" HEIGHT="300">
    <PARAM NAME="x_offset" VALUE="0.224">
    <PARAM NAME="image" VALUE="images/hairy_mammoth.gif">
    <PARAM NAME="weapon" VALUE="rubber biscuit">
</APPLET>
```

NOTE: APPLET to Be Replaced by OBJECT APPLET has some annoying limitations, and is destined to be replaced by the **OBJECT** element. This element, currently supported by Internet Explorer 3, is discussed in Chapter 5.

PARAM Element: Define an Applet Parameter

Usage: <PARAM>

Can Contain: empty

Can Be Inside: **APPLET**

Attributes: **NAME, VALUE**

PARAM assigns a value to any required applet-dependent variable. The variable name is specified via the **NAME** attribute, while the value for this variable is specified by **VALUE**. **NAME**s and **VALUE**s are, of course, entirely specific to the applet being invoked. The specifications for the attributes are:

NAME=*"name"* (mandatory) Specifies the *name* to be associated with this parameter. **NAME**s must be understood by the associated applet.

VALUE=*"string"* (optional) Specifies the *value* to associate with the given name. Again, the value must be meaningful to the specified applet. If a value is not needed, this attribute can be left out.

IMG Element: Inline Images

Usage:	`<IMG>`
Can Contain:	empty
Can Be Inside:	ADDRESS, BLOCKQUOTE, BODY, CENTER, DIV, FORM, DD, DT, LI, P, TD, TH, Hn, A, CAPTION, character highlighting
Attributes:	ALIGN, ALT, BORDER, HEIGHT, HSPACE, ISMAP, (<u>LOWSRC</u>: Netscape Navigator only), SRC, USEMAP, VSPACE, WIDTH, (<u>CONTROLS</u>, <u>DYNSRC</u>, <u>LOOP</u>, <u>START</u>: Internet Explorer only)

IMG includes an image file *inline* with the document text, the image file being specified by the **SRC** attribute. There are currently four common image formats used for inline images: GIF format (with the filename suffix *.gif*), X-Bitmaps (with the filename suffix *.xbm*); X-Pixelmaps (with the filename suffix *.xpm*), and JPEG format (filename suffix *.jpeg* or *.jpg*). A fifth format, Portable Network Graphics or PNG (with the filename suffix *.png*), is expected to be widely supported by the next generation of browsers.

To a large extent, images within a document are treated like words or characters, and you can place an image almost anywhere you have regular text—the exception is the **PRE** (preformatted text) element, which should not contain **IMG** elements. In addition, images can also "float" on the page, allowing text to flow around the images. This is facilitated with special **ALIGN** attribute options, outlined in this section.

The **IMG** element can take three main attributes. **SRC** is mandatory and specifies the URL of the image file to be included. **ALIGN** specifies the alignment of the image with respect to the surrounding text, and **ALT** gives an alternative text string for browsers that cannot display images.

Some examples of **IMG** elements and image alignment are shown in Figures 4.33 and 4.34. There are several other attributes, as well as some Netscape- and Microsoft-specific extensions as discussed in this section. In particular, Internet Explorer supports **DYNSRC** attribute for including inline AVI-format video or VRML data. The additional attributes **CONTROLS, LOOP, LOOPPLAY,** and **START** then determine how the associated side or video is displayed.

ALIGN="bottom", "left", "middle", "right", "top, ("texttop", "absmiddle", "baseline", "absbottom": Netscape extensions) (optional) **ALIGN** specifies the alignment of the image with the neighboring text. "Bottom" aligns the bottom of the image with the baseline of the surrounding text—this is the default. "Middle" aligns the middle of the image with the baseline of the text, and "top" aligns the top of the image with the top of the largest item in a line (including other images). Note that in general, text does not wrap around an image aligned using the "top", "middle", or "bottom" attribute values, so that images within a sentence can create big gaps between adjacent lines.

The values "left" and "right" allow for text flow around an image. **ALIGN**="left" floats the image down and over to the left margin, and allows subsequent text to flow around the right side of the image. **ALIGN**="right" floats the image to the right side of the window, and allows subsequent text to flow around the left side of the image. Browsers that do not understand these values assume the **ALIGN**="bottom" default.

Netscape Navigator (and several other browsers) support additional align values to better control alignment within a line of text. **ALIGN**="texttop" aligns the top of an image with the top of the surrounding text (the same as **ALIGN**="top"). **ALIGN**="absmiddle" aligns the middle of an image with the middle of the line of text, while **ALIGN**="baseline" aligns the bottom of an image with the baseline of the line of text (the same as **ALIGN**="bottom" but with a clearer meaning). **ALIGN**="absbottom" aligns the bottom of the image with the absolute bottom of the line (for example, the bottom tip of a letter such as "q").

ALT="*string*" (optional) **ALT** gives a text alternative for the image, for use by text-only browsers. *This should always be included* to let users with text-only browsers know what they are missing, or to let graphical browsers preview the image using this text description. If the image is purely decorative and warrants no description, you should enter a null string using the form **ALT**="".

BORDER="*number*" (optional) Specifies the border width, in pixels, around images that are marked as hypertext anchors (recall that images are generally surrounded by a colored border if they are inside an anchor). **BORDER**=0 indicates no border around the image. **BORDER** is illustrated in Figures 4.35 and 4.36. With Netscape Navigator, **BORDER** will also place borders around images that are not inside **A** elements.

Figure 4.33 HTML example document illustrating the IMG *inline* image element. Figure 4.34 shows this document as displayed by the Netscape Navigator browser.

```
<HTML>
<HEAD>
<TITLE> Example of IMG Element </TITLE>
</HEAD>
<BODY>
<H1>Examples of IMG Elements</H1>

<P> <IMG SRC="icon-help.gif" ALT="[Test image]" ALIGN=TOP> Here is
some text related to the test image.   The text is aligned with the
top of the image. Note that the text does not flow around the image.

<P> <IMG SRC="icon-help.gif" ALT="[Test image]" ALIGN=MIDDLE> Here is
some text related to the test image.   The text is aligned with the
middle of the image. Note that the text does not flow around the image.

<P> <A HREF="http://www.bozo.edu/test.html"><IMG SRC="icon-help.gif"
ALT="[Test image]" ALIGN=BOTTOM> Here is some text</A>   related
to the test image.   The text is aligned with the bottom of
the image, and is also part of the <EM> hypertext link</EM>.

<P>  Here is a <IMG SRC="icon-help.gif" ALT="" ALIGN="left">
left-aligned image. Note how the text flows around this image,
unlike the top, middle and bottom aligned images shown above. The
element <CODE>&lt;BR CLEAR="left"></CODE> (there is one just
coming up, right after the closing bracket....)
<BR CLEAR="left">
(....there it was) creates a line break that clears the text to
follow the left-flushed image.
</BODY>
</HTML>
```

CONTROLS (optional) (Internet Explorer only) Indicates that a set of video or VRML controls should be displayed along with the inline viewer. If **CONTROLS** is absent, then the controls are not displayed.

DYNSRC=*"url"* (optional) (Internet Explorer only) Specifies the URL of an AVI-format video clip or a VRML world description file to be included inline with the document. The attributes **CONTROLS, LOOP, LOOPDELAY,** and **START** are used to control the behavior of the video clip or VRML scene. Both **DYNSRC** and **SRC** can be specified in the same **IMG** element, so that a **DYNSRC**-incapable browser can display a regular image file in place of the VRML data or video sequence.

Figure 4.34 Display, by the Netscape Navigator 3 browser, of the document shown in Figure 4.33.

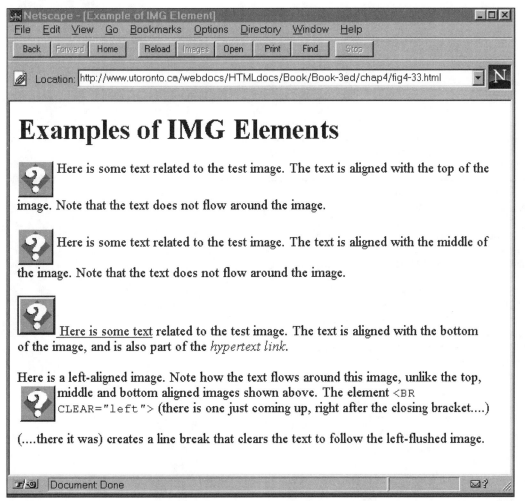

HEIGHT="*number*" (optional) **HEIGHT** specifies the height of the image to be displayed, in pixels. The **HEIGHT** and **WIDTH** attributes let the browser format the text before actually loading the image. Browsers will *rescale* the image to fit this height. This use of **WIDTH** is illustrated in Figures 4.35 and 4.36.

Figure 4.35 Example HTML document illustrating IMG border, image size rescaling, and spacing control. Browser rendering of this document is shown in Figure 4.36.

```
<HTML>
<HEAD>
<TITLE> More Example of IMG Element </TITLE>
</HEAD>
<BODY>
<H2 ALIGN="center"> More Examples of IMG Elements</H2>

<P>Here is a left-aligned image
<IMG SRC="icon-help.gif" ALT="[Test image]" ALIGN="left"> with
text flowing around it.  Note how tight the text is to the image.
The next example has attributes <B>HSPACE</B>="15" and
<B>VSPACE</B>="15": <BR CLEAR="all">

<P>Here is a left-aligned image
<IMG SRC="icon-help.gif" ALT="[Test image]" ALIGN="left"
HSPACE="15" VSPACE="15"> with text flowing around it.
Note how there is extra space around the image, due
to the <B>HSPACE</B> and <B>VSPACE</B>
attributes added to the IMG element. <BR CLEAR="all">

<P>Here is a right-aligned image
<IMG SRC="icon-help.gif" ALT="[Test image]" ALIGN="right"
HEIGHT="60" WIDTH="120"> with the image size rescaled
using the <B>HEIGHT</B> and <B>WIDTH</B> attributes.
Note that you <EM>must not</EM> use these attribute to
resize imagemapped images.
<BR CLEAR="all">

<P>Here are three images inside anchor elements:
Note how the <B>BORDER</B> attribute controls the
border drawn around the images</P>
<CENTER>
<TABLE WIDTH="60%" CELLPADDING=5>
<TR>
  <TD ALIGN="center"> No Specification
  <TD ALIGN="center"> <TT>BORDER="0"</TT>
  <TD ALIGN="center"> <TT>BORDER="8"</TT>
</TR>
<TR>
  <TD ALIGN="center"><A HREF="icon-help.gif"><IMG SRC="icon-help.gif"
                     ALT="[Test image]"></A>
  <TD ALIGN="center"><A HREF="icon-help.gif"><IMG SRC="icon-help.gif"
                     ALT="[Test image]" BORDER="0"></A>
  <TD ALIGN="center"><A HREF="icon-help.gif"><IMG SRC="icon-help.gif"
                     ALT="[Test image]" BORDER="8"></A>
```

Figure 4.35 (Continued)

```
</TR>
</TABLE>
</CENTER></BODY></HTML>
```

Figure 4.36 Display, by the Internet Explorer 3 browser, of the document shown in Figure 4.35.

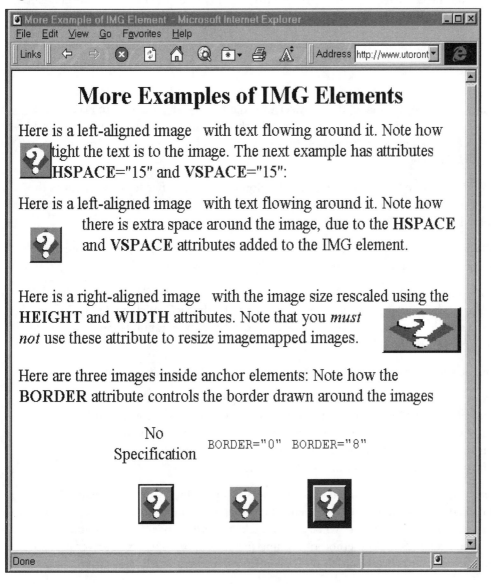

HSPACE=*"number"* (optional) **HSPACE** is used by floating images, and specifies, in pixels, the horizontal space to be left between the image and the surrounding text. The use of this attribute is illustrated in Figures 4.35 and 4.36.

ISMAP (optional) This attribute marks the image as an *active* image. When the user clicks the mouse over the image, the coordinates of the mouse pointer are sent back to the server. The **ISMAP**-activated **IMG** element must, consequently, be enclosed within an anchor element, specifying the URL to which the data should be sent. Typical markup for an active image is:

```
<A HREF="http://www.utirc.ca/cgi-bin/imagemap/map_bozo">
    <IMG SRC="bozo.gif" ISMAP>
</A>
```

where **imagemap** is a server-side gateway program that can interpret the map coordinates. When the user clicks on the image, the browser uses the HTTP GET method to access the URL, indicated by the anchor element, and appends the coordinates of the mouse click (relative to the upper left-hand corner of the image) to the accessed URL. The details of this procedure are discussed in Chapter 10.

LOOP=*"number"*, "infinite" (optional) (Internet Explorer only) Specifies how many times the video clip should be looped before stopping. **LOOP**="–1" or **LOOP**="infinite" means that the loop will play indefinitely. The default value is 1.

LOOPDELAY=*"number"* (optional) (Internet Explorer only) Specifies the delay, in milliseconds, between subsequent replays of the video clip. The default value is 0.

LOWSRC=*"url"* (optional) (Netscape only) Specifies the URL of an image file to be loaded and displayed prior to loading and displaying the image indicated by the **SRC** attribute. **LOWSRC** usually references a placeholder image that can be loaded and displayed more rapidly than the full resolution version (specified by **SRC**).

SRC=*"url"* (mandatory) Specifies the URL of the image file to be included inline.

START="fileopen", "mouseover" (optional) (Internet Explorer only) Indicates when a video clip should begin playing: **START**="fileopen" specifies that it play as soon as the video file is downloaded, while **START**="mouseover" specifies that it play when the mouse pointer is moved over the viewing window. Both can be specified, separated by commas: **START**="fileopen,mouseover" will invoke both behaviors.

USEMAP=*"url"* (optional) Almost all current browsers support client-side imagemaps, whereby a document can contain, within a **MAP** element, imagemap coordinate data. This lets a browser itself determine which link to access when a user clicks the mouse over an active image, in contrast to the traditional (**ISMAP**) method of sending the click coordinates to a server gateway program for subsequent processing. An **IMG** element references a **MAP** element via the

USEMAP attribute, which takes, as its value, either a fragment identifier (the **MAP** is in the same file as the **IMG** element) or in principle a full URL plus a fragment identifier. (The **MAP** is in a separate document: Note, however, that this form is not currently supported.) Each **MAP** element must consequently be identified by an appropriate **NAME** attribute value.

A developer can specify both **USEMAP** and **ISMAP** in the same **IMG** element, with **USEMAP** having precedence. Thus, if a browser understands **USEMAP**, it will use the local **MAP**, while if the browser does not understand **USEMAP**, it will access the standard server-side imagemap program referenced by the surrounding hypertext anchor. In the example:

```
<A HREF="/cgi-bin/imagmep/mapfile1"><IMG SRC="image.gif"
        USEMAP="#map1"  ISMAP></A>
...
<MAP NAME="map1">
<AREA SHAPE="rect" COORD="10,20,50,50" HREF="stuff.html">
<AREA SHAPE="rect" COORD="30,40,60,60" HREF="otherstuff.html">
...
</MAP>
```

if the browser interpreting this document understands **USEMAP**, it will use the local map `<MAP NAME="map1">` when the user clicks on the active image. If the browser does not understand **USEMAP**, it will revert to **ISMAP**, and will send the click coordinates to the referenced server-side program, as per standard practice.

VSPACE=*"number"* (optional) **VSPACE** is used by floating images, and specifies, in pixels, the vertical space to be left between the image and the surrounding text (above or below). The use of this attribute is illustrated in Figures 4.35 and 4.36.

WIDTH=*"number"* (optional) **WIDTH** specifies the height of the image to be displayed, in pixels. The **HEIGHT** and **WIDTH** attributes let the browser format the text before actually loading the image. Browsers will scale the image to fit this width if the image is actually a different size. This use of **WIDTH** is illustrated in Figures 4.35 and 4.36.

NOTE: Percentage WIDTH and HEIGHT Values? The Netscape Navigator 3 and Internet Explorer 3 browsers support, albeit unreliably, **WIDTH**s and **HEIGHT**s specified as percentage values, taken as a percentage of the available width or height. This does not work reliably, however.

Hypertext Relationship Elements

These elements define active hypertext relationships between document content and another resource. There is only one such element in HTML, namely **A**.

A Element: Hypertext Anchors

Usage:	`<A> ... </A>`
Can Contain:	characters, character highlighting, APPLET, BR, IMG, BASEFONT, MAP, SCRIPT, INPUT, SELECT, TEXTAREA
Can Be Inside:	ADDRESS, BLOCKQUOTE, BODY, CENTER, DIV, FORM, PRE, DD, DT, LI, P, TD, TH, Hn, CAPTION, character highlighting
Attributes:	HREF, NAME, REL, REV, <u>TARGET</u>, TITLE

The **A** or *anchor* element marks a block of the document as a hypertext link. This block can be text, highlighted text, or an image. More complex elements, such as headings, cannot be inside an anchor. In particular, note that an anchor element *cannot* contain another anchor element.

A can take several attributes. At least one *must* be either **HREF** or **NAME**—these specify the destination of the hypertext link (**HREF**), or indicate that the marked text can itself be the destination of a hypertext link (**NAME**). Both can be present, indicating that the anchor is both the beginning and end of a link.

Text or images within anchors containing **HREF**s are usually rendered differently than plain text. Often, such text is underlined, boldfaced, or rendered with a different color. Some browsers change this rendering once a link has been accessed, to inform the user that the link has been *explored*. Anchors with only a **NAME** attribute are usually not rendered in a special way.

Some examples of **A** elements are given in Figures 4.1 and 4.2, as well as 4.33 and 4.34.

The element attributes are:

HREF=*"url"* (mandatory if **NAME** is absent) Gives the target of a hypertext link, where *"url"* is the uniform resource locator referencing the target object.

NAME=*"string"* (mandatory if **HREF** is absent) Marks the anchored text as a possible, specific destination of a hypertext link. The value *"string"* identifies this destination. For example, the element

```
<A NAME="poison"> Deadly Toadstools </A>
```

marks "Deadly Toadstools" as a possible hypertext target, referenced by the string `poison`. This string is called a *fragment identifier*. Within the same document, the location is referenced by the hypertext anchor:

```
<A HREF="#poison"> Poisonous non-mushrooms </A>
```

where the hash character indicates that the remaining text is a fragment identifier. Selecting "Poisonous non-mushrooms" links the user back to the place in the document marked by the `<A NAME="poison">...</A>` anchor.

This location can be accessed from another document via an anchor of the form:

```
<A HREF="http://www.site.edu/slimy/toads.html#poison">Poisonous </A>
```

assuming `http://www.site.edu/slimy/toads.html` to be the URL of the document in question. Clicking on the word "Poisonous" then links the user to the document ***toads.html*** and to the location marked by the `<A NAME="poison">...</A>` anchor. This need not be a full URL, but can be a partial URL should the two documents lie on the same server. These issues are discussed in more detail in Chapters 2 (Example 6) and 6.

REL="*string*" (optional) (valid with **HREF** only) **REL** attribute values describe the relationship(s) associated with the hypertext link—consequently, **REL** is only valid if **HREF** is also present. The relationship is defined between the two entire documents and is not just related to the particular link. As an example, **REL** could indicate that the linked document is an index for the current one, or is an annotation to the current one (which a browser might want to display as a pop-up). It is a pity that the **REL** (and **REV,** which is the converse of **REL**) attribute is so little used, as it can impart significant meaning and organization to large sets of related documents.

The value for **REL** is a space-separated list of case-insensitive relationship values (preferably a collection of name tokens). An example is:

```
<A HREF="http://foo.edu/fe.html" REL="next">sdfsddf</a>
```

This would mean that the document ***fe.html,*** at the given URL, is the next document in some author-defined document sequence. Values for the relationships and their semantics are currently being defined; the current status is summarized at the Web site associated with this book, and also at the URL:

```
http://www.sq.com/papers/Relationship.html
```

Some other examples are:

```
<A HREF="http://foo.edu/note1.html" REL="annotation">related notes </a>
```

The information in the document ***note1.html*** is additional and subsidiary to the current document. A browser might display this as margin notes.

```
<A HREF="http://foo.edu/vers2.html" REL="supersedes">previously </a>
```

The document *vers2.html* is an earlier version of the document.

At present, the **REL** and **REV** attributes are rarely used, and most browsers do not understand them. They will be of growing importance as HTML documents and document development environments become more sophisticated.

REV="*string*" (optional) **REV** is like **REL** but with the relationship reversed. For example,

```
<A HREF="http://foo.edu/vers2.html" REV="supersedes"> later </a>
```

means that the document *vers2.html* is a later version of the document containing this link. Most browsers do not understand **REV** or **REL**.

TARGET="*string*" This attribute is part of the Netscape frames technology, which supports multiple browser windows and multiple *frames* within a given browser window, each frame or window with its own *name*. The **TARGET** attribute lets a document author direct data to be returned, upon selecting a hypertext link, to one of these *named* windows. If a window of the given name does not exist, the browser will create it. For example:

```
<A HREF="/path/file.html" TARGET="win-2">anchor text</A>
```

indicates that the retrieved document, upon accessing the anchor, should be directed to the window named "win-2." If a window or window frame with this name does not yet exist, the browser will clone a new copy of the browser, assign the name "win-2" to this new window, and direct the returned data to it.

In the absence of a **TARGET**, a document is retrieved to the window from which the link was accessed, as per standard practice.

TARGETs are most often *named frames* or panes within a given browser window. These are created by the **FRAMESET** and **FRAME** elements, which permit multiple, independent document viewing panes within the same browser window. If a frame is declared via `<FRAME SRC="url" NAME="frame1">`, then an anchor of the form:

```
<A HREF="/path/file.html" TARGET="frame1">anchor text</A>
```

will direct the returned document to the designated **FRAME**. **FRAME**s are discussed in Chapter 5.

Several target names are predefined, with useful special meanings. These names (all beginning with the underscore character) and the associated meanings are defined in Table 4.8.

TITLE="*string*" (optional) Gives a title for the linked resource—valid only if **HREF** is present. This can in principle be used by a browser to *preview* the title before retrieving a document—but note that you cannot guarantee that the **TITLE** is correct until you actually access the resource. Alternatively, **TITLE** can provide a title for a document that would otherwise

Table 4.8 Predefined Target Names and Their Meanings

TARGET Value	Meaning
_blank	Load the referenced data into a new, unnamed window.
_self	Load the referenced data in place of the current document.
_parent	Load the referenced data into the window containing (or that contained) the *parent* of the current document (the document from which the current document was accessed). If there is no parent document, default to **TARGET="_self"**.
_top	Load the referenced data into the window containing (or that contained) the "top" document (the document obtained by iteratively searching through successive parent documents until arriving at the initial, starting document). If there is no top document, default to **TARGET="_self"**.

NOTE: All other names beginning with an underscore (_) are ignored by the browser.

not have a title, such as a plain text file, an image file, or a directory. If the referenced URL is a **mailto**, some browsers (e.g., lynx) will use the title content as the default subject line for the message. However, most browsers do not understand **TITLE** and ignore it.

Text/Phrase Markup Elements

Text markup elements specify special properties for a phrase or a string of characters. Such elements do not cause line breaks or otherwise affect block layout of the text. HTML supports two types of text-level markup: *logical highlighting* (also called information-type formatting or idiomatic phrase markup), and *physical highlighting* (also called character or typographic formatting). Logical highlighting is more in keeping with the markup language model. You can use it to mark a block of text as a piece of typed computer code, a variable, or something to be emphasized; the rendering details are then left to the browser, although hints as to appropriate renderings are part of the HTML specifications. You are strongly encouraged to use logical highlighting elements as opposed to physical ones, whenever possible.

Physical highlighting requests a specific physical format, such as boldface or italics. This, of course, gives no clue to the underlying meaning behind the marked-up phrase. Thus, if a browser is unable to implement the indicated markup (e.g., because the display cannot do italics), it cannot easily determine an alternative logical highlighting style.

Logical styles are not necessarily rendered in distinct ways (i.e., different logical styles may be rendered in the same way). Also, some browsers do not support all physical styles. For example, lynx does not support italics, and renders it as underlined.

The different logical formatting elements are summarized in Table 4.9, and the physical formatting elements in Table 4.10. Figures 4.37 through 4.40 illustrate their use.

Content Model for Highlighting Elements

The content model for all the character highlighting elements is largely the same, so to avoid needless repetition, it is given here. In the following, **NAME** is one of CITE, CODE, DFN, EM, KBD, SAMP, STRIKE, STRONG, VAR, B, BIG, FONT, I, S, SMALL, SUB, SUP, TT, or U.

Usage:	<**NAME**> ... </**NAME**>
Can Contain:	**characters, character highlighting,**
	A, APPLET, BR, IMG, BASEFONT, MAP, SCRIPT,
	INPUT, SELECT, TEXTAREA
Can Be Inside:	**ADDRESS, BLOCKQUOTE, BODY, CENTER, DIV, FORM, PRE,**
	DD, DT, LI, P, TD, TH, Hn,
	A, CAPTION, character highlighting
Attributes:	none (except for **FONT**—see below)

Table 4.9 Logical Highlighting Elements and Their Recommended Formatting

Element	Meaning	Recommended Formatting
CITE	A citation	italics
CODE	An example of typed code	fixed-width font
DFN	A definition	italics
EM	Emphasized text	italics
KBD	Keyboard input—for example, in a manual	fixed-width
SAMP	A sequence of literal characters	fixed-width
STRIKE	Struck-out text, e.g., text marked as deleted	text with line drawn through (struck through)
STRONG	Strong emphasis	boldface
VAR	A variable name	italics

Table 4.10 Physical Highlighting Elements and Their Recommended Formatting

Element	Meaning
B	boldface
BIG	bigger text
FONT	font size, face, or color
I	italics
S	strike-through
SMALL	smaller text
SPAN	stylesheet-specified formatting information (*see Chapter 5*)
SUB	subscript
SUP	superscript
TT	fixed-width font
U	underlined

There are two exceptions to this content model:

1. The elements **BIG**, **FONT**, **SMALL**, **SUB**, and **SUP** are not allowed inside **PRE**.

2. The **FONT** element can take attributes, as discussed in the **FONT** element description.

You can nest logical highlighting modes inside one another; however, this is often not sensible, given the rather specific meanings assigned to them—be careful that you are nesting things in a meaningful way! Note also that different browsers may interpret complicated nestings in different ways, and that the resulting rendering can be unpredictable.

Physical highlighting elements can be nested, and these nestings often make sense. Requesting that a block of text be rendered in *underlined, boldfaced italics* is entirely reasonable. However, be aware that some browsers mishandle these nestings, and render them in unexpected ways—for example, rendering `<B><I>text</I></B>` in boldface, and not boldface italics.

Examples of the different elements are shown in Figures 4.37 and 4.38.

CITE Element: Citation

CITE marks a small *citation*—for example, a book or other document reference. Typically, this block of text will be rendered in italics, subject to the capabilities of the browser.

Figure 4.37 HTML example document illustrating the different text highlighting elements. Figure 4.38 shows this document as displayed by the Netscape Navigator browser.

```
<HTML>
<HEAD>
<TITLE> Example of Highlighting Markup elements </TITLE>
</HEAD>
<BODY>
<H2 ALIGN="center"> Highlighting Elements </H2>
<H3> Examples of Logical Highlighting </H3>
<UL>
   <LI> CITE - This is <CITE>citation</CITE> text
   <LI> CODE - This is <CODE>typed computer code</CODE> text
   <LI> DFN - This is <DFN>a defining instance</DFN> text
   <LI> EM - This is <EM>emphasized</EM> text
   <LI> KBD - This is <KBD>keyboard input</KBD> text
   <LI> SAMP - This is <SAMP>literal character</SAMP> text
   <LI> STRIKE - This is <STRIKE>strike-out</STRIKE> text
   <LI> STRONG - This is <STRONG>strongly emphasized</STRONG> text
   <LI> VAR - This is <VAR>a variable</VAR> text
</UL>

<H3> Examples of Character Highlighting </H3>
<UL>
   <LI> B - This is <B>boldfaced</B> text
   <LI> BIG - This is <BIG>bigger</BIG> text
   <LI> I - This is <I>italicized</I> text
   <LI> S - This is <S>strike-through</S> text
   <LI> SMALL - This is <SMALL>small</SMALL> text
   <LI> SUB - This is sub<SUB>script</SUB> text
   <LI> SUP - This is super<SUP>script</SUP> text
   <LI> TT - This is <TT>fixed-width typewriter font</TT> text
   <LI> U - This is <U> underlined </U>text
</UL>
</BODY> </HTML>
```

CODE Element: Typed Code

The **CODE** element marks a selection of typed computer code—for example, a single line of code from a program. Large selections of code should be displayed using a **PRE** element, which properly reproduces space characters and line breaks. **CODE** element contents should be rendered in a fixed-width typewriter font.

DFN Element: Defining Instance or Definition

DFN marks a selection of text as the *defining instance* of a term. The text content should be rendered in italics, as demonstrated by Internet Explorer. Netscape Navigator, however, renders **DFN** content with an unmodified font.

Figure 4.38 Display, by the Netscape Navigator 3 browser, of the document shown in Figure 4.37.

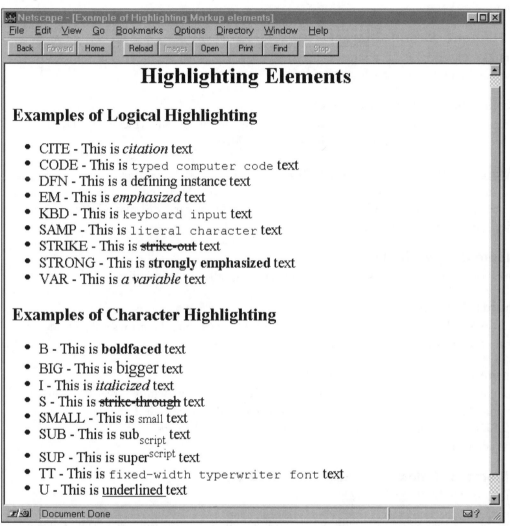

EM Element: Emphasis

EM marks a block of text for *emphasis*. Typically, the marked block of text is rendered in italics, subject to the capabilities of the browser; lynx represents **EM** emphasized text by an underline.

KBD Element: Keyboard Input

KBD marks a block of text as `keyboard input`. Typically, this is displayed with a fixed-width typewriter font.

SAMP Element: Literal Characters

SAMP marks a block of text as a sequence of literal or `sample` characters. Typically, this is rendered in a fixed-width typewriter font.

STRIKE Element: Struck-out Text

STRIKE marks a block of text to be ~~struck out~~ for some logical reason (typically, to indicate text that has been deleted). Lynx may render this is reverse-video.

STRONG Element: Strong Emphasis

STRONG marks a block of text for **strong** emphasis. Typically, this is rendered in boldface, although text-only browsers such as lynx use an underline (with lynx, **EM** and **STRONG** emphasis are displayed in the same way).

VAR Element: A Variable

VAR marks a *variable name*. This is typically rendered in italics or bold italics.

B Element: Boldface

B marks a textblock to be rendered in **boldface**. If this is impossible, the browser can render it in some other way (lynx uses an underline).

BIG Element: Text with Enlarged Font

BIG marks text that should be rendered, when possible, with a font slightly larger than the font of the surrounding text. Enclosed images are not affected. **BIG** is ignored if a larger font is not available. **BIG** is equivalent to a **FONT** element with `<FONT SIZE="+1">`. Note that **BIG** is not allowed inside **PRE**.

FONT Element: Select Text Font Size and Color

Attributes: COLOR, <u>FACE</u>, SIZE

FONT marks text that should be rendered in modified color, size, or font face. **FONT** has no effect on enclosed **IMG** elements. **FONT** can take three attributes: **SIZE** for the font size, **COLOR** for the font color, and **FACE** for the font face. Note that **FONT** is not allowed inside **PRE**.

TIP: Stylesheets Are Better   If you are really worried about using the details of the **FONT** element to obtain absolutely precise control over formatting and presentation, then you should read the stylesheets section in Chapter 5. **FONT** is a very crude tool for typesetting documents; the stylesheet mechanisms provide much better and more reliable ways of accomplishing the same things.

Examples showing the use of **FONT** are given in Figures 4.39 and 4.40. The supported attributes and their meanings are:

SIZE=*"+number"*, *"-number"* or *"number"* (optional) Specifies the desired font size for the text, either as an absolute size (*"number"*) or as a size relative to the size of the surrounding font— *"+number"* for a bigger font, *"-number"* for a smaller font. Absolute font sizes range from 1 (the smallest) to 7 (the largest), with the default value being 3. For example, <FONT SIZE="1"> requests the smallest possible font, while <FONT SIZE="-2"> requests a font two sizes smaller than the current font. The default font size (with respect to which relative sizes are calculated) can be reset via the **BASEFONT** element.

COLOR=*"#rrggbb"* or *"color"* (optional) Specifies the desired color for the text, either as a hexadecimal RGB code or as a named color. If using this attribute, be careful that the text color contrasts well with the display background.

FACE=*"string"* (optional) (Microsoft and Netscape, and some others) This attribute, added by Microsoft, lets an author specify the desired typeface (**FACE**=*"Arial"*, *"Times"*, etc.) to be used for the displayed text. Supported names depend on the fonts installed on the user's computer, and on the browser; for example, on a typical Windows 95 system, the name "Helvetica" works with Netscape Navigator 3 but not Internet Explorer 3. Note also that the names are tied to the Microsoft font names, and many fonts are not found by these names on other platforms (Macintosh or UNIX) or other PC operating systems (OS/2). On any system, **FACE** only works if the designated font is installed on the system.

FACE names are *space-sensitive*. Thus to request the Arial black font you need **FACE**=*"Arial black"*, and not **FACE**=*"Arialblack"*. Names are not, however, *case-sensitive*.

You can specify multiple fonts by separating the font names by commas. Thus **FACE**=*"Arial,helvetica,times"* asks the browser to first try the Arial font, followed by Helvetica (if Arial is not present), and finally the times font (if Helvetica is not present).

Some font faces are shown in Table 4.11 and displayed by a browser in Figure 4.40 (the HTML document is shown in Figure 4.39). Note that most computers do not have all of these fonts.

Figure 4.39 Example HTML document illustrating the use of the FONT element. Browser rendering of this document is shown in Figure 4.40.

```
<HTML><HEAD>
<TITLE> The FONT Element </TITLE>
</HEAD><BODY>
<H2 ALIGN="center"> The FONT Element </H2>

<FONT SIZE="+1"><B>Font Size</B> --</FONT>
You can use <B>FONT</B> to control font size. For example,
<FONT SIZE=2>t<FONT SIZE=3>h<FONT SIZE=4>i<FONT SIZE=5>s
<FONT SIZE=6>i</FONT>s </FONT>o</FONT>d</FONT>d </FONT>
looking, as I adjusted the size of each letter.
You can use this for large capital letters in
headings:
<p><FONT SIZE="+1">I</FONT>AN <FONT SIZE="+1">G</FONT>RAHAM'S
   <FONT SIZE="+1">H</FONT>OME
   <FONT SIZE="+1">P</FONT>AGE -- (with size change on
   leading letters)
<HR SIZE=4>
<FONT SIZE="+1"><B>Font Color -- </B></FONT>
You can can also control text color. For example,
the default text is black, but the following words are
<FONT COLOR="red">bright red</FONT>,
<FONT COLOR="#00ff00">bright green</FONT>, and
<FONT COLOR="#cccccc">light gray</FONT>. This of course, loses
some of its impact when printed in black and white....
<HR SIZE=4>
<FONT SIZE="+1"><B>Font Face -- </B></FONT>
Some browsers support font face control. This is nonstandardized,
and depends on (a) browser support for this extension, and (b) the
presence of the font on your computer. Here is a table of
some examples:
<BR><BR>
<CENTER>
<TABLE WIDTH="80%" CELLPADDING=2 CELLSPACING=3
       BGCOLOR="#cccccc" BORDER>
<TR>
  <TD><FONT FACE="arial">Arial</FONT>
  <TD><FONT FACE="Book antiqua">Book antiqua</FONT>
  <TD><FONT FACE="Helvetica">Helvetica</FONT>
</TR>
<TR>
  <TD><FONT FACE="modern">modern</FONT>
  <TD><FONT FACE="times">times</FONT>
  <TD><FONT FACE="arial black">arial black</FONT>
</TR>
<TR>
  <TD><FONT FACE="bookman">bookman</FONT>
  <TD><FONT FACE="garamond">garamond</FONT>
```

Figure 4.39 (Continued)

```
  <TD><FONT FACE="helvetica-narrow">helvetica-narrow</FONT>
</TR>
<TR>
  <TD><FONT FACE="palatino">palatino</FONT>
  <TD><FONT FACE="lucida sans">lucida sans</FONT>
  <TD><FONT FACE="helvetica narrow">   </FONT>
</TR>
</TABLE>
</CENTER>
</BODY> </HTML>
```

Figure 4.40 Rendering, by the Netscape Navigator 3 browser, of the document shown in Figure 4.39. Note that these font names are not supported on all browsers, as discussed in the text.

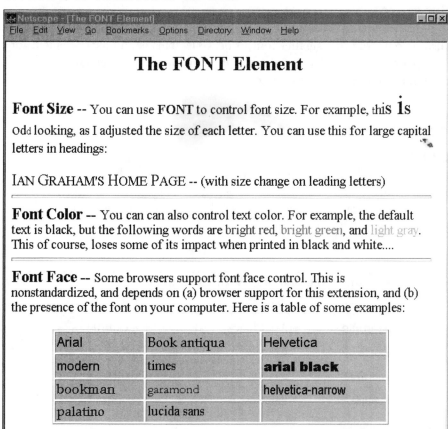

I Element: Italics

I marks a section to be rendered in *italics*. If this is impossible, the browser can render it in some other way (lynx uses an underline). Note that most computers do not have all of these fonts.

S Element: Strike-Through

S marks a section to be rendered with a line ~~struck through~~ the text. If this is impossible, the browser can render this in some other way (lynx currently ignores this element).

SMALL Element: Superscripts (Text with Reduced Size Font)

SMALL marks text that should be rendered, when possible, with a font slightly smaller than the font of the surrounding text. Enclosed images are not affected. SMALL is ignored if a smaller font is not available. SMALL is equivalent to a FONT element with `<FONT SIZE="-1">`. Note that SMALL is not allowed inside PRE.

SUB Element: Subscript

SUB marks text that should be rendered as a subscript relative to the preceding text. The content of a SUB may also be rendered in a smaller font, if possible. This is an unsafe element for browsers that do not support it, since subscripted text will be incorrectly presented by a browser that does not understand SUB. An example is:

```
CaCO<SUB>3</SUB>
```

Note that SUB is not allowed inside PRE.

SUP Element: Superscript

SUP marks text that should be rendered as a superscript relative to the preceding text. The content of a SUP may also be rendered in a smaller font, if possible. This is an unsafe element for browsers that do not support it, since superscripted text will be incorrectly presented by a browser that does not understand SUP. An example is:

```
x<SUP>2</SUP>
```

Table 4.11 Some Supported Font Face Names, With Examples

Font Name	Example	Font Name	Example
Arial	example	Arial black	**example**
Bookman	example	Courier	`example`
Garamond	example	Helvetica	example
Helvetica-narrow	example	Palatino	example
Times (Times New Roman)	example		

Note that **SUP** is not allowed inside **PRE**.

TT Element: Fixed-Width Typewriter Font

TT marks a section to be rendered with a `fixed-width typewriter` font.

U Element: Underline

U marks a section to be rendered with an <u>underline</u>. This element is understood by some, but not all, browsers.

Character-Like Elements

These elements provide character-like behavior within the document. The only such element defined in HTML 3.2 is **BR**. The proprietary HTML extensions **WBR** (word break) and **SPACER** (an arbitrary text spacing) are described in Chapter 5. (Note that **HR** [horizontal rule] was discussed previously in the Body Text Block section.)

BR Element: Line Break

Usage:	` `
Can Contain:	empty
Can Be Inside:	ADDRESS, BLOCKQUOTE, BODY, CENTER, DIV, FORM, PRE, DD, DT, LI, P, TD, TH, Hn, A, CAPTION, character highlighting
Attributes:	CLEAR

BR indicates a line break. This is fundamentally different from a paragraph element—`<BR>` is treated as a character (like a *hard* carriage return), while **P** defines a text block as a paragraph. An example of **BR** is shown in Figures 4.7 and 4.8, where it is used to break lines in an **ADDRESS**. **BR** can also break lines in a poem, with **P** elements marking the different verses.

In the case of text flow around right- and left-aligned images or tables, an author must be able to specify how the text should break; that is, should the text simply continue at the next line that runs alongside the image, or should it break until the next line can be flush with the left, right, or both margins? In HTML, the optional **CLEAR** attribute is used with **BR** to make this specification. The possible **CLEAR** values are:

CLEAR="left", "right", "all" (optional) `<BR CLEAR="left">` breaks the line and moves the following text down until it can be flush with the left margin. `<BR CLEAR="right">` breaks the line and moves the following text down until the right margin is clear. `<BR CLEAR="all">` breaks the line and moves the following text down until both margins are clear.

An example is given in Figures 4.33 and 4.34.

Meta-Information Elements

These elements provide information used by the document but not explicitly presented to the reader/user. The four relevant elements are **MAP** and **AREA,** which provide image-mapping data used by client-side imagemaps; **BASEFONT,** which toggles default font characteristics; and **SCRIPT,** which includes a program script within an HTML document. Note that **SCRIPT** should more appropriately be placed in the **HEAD,** and is described previously in this chapter in the **HEAD** element section.

BASEFONT Element: Set Default Font Characteristics

Usage:	`<BASEFONT>`
Can Contain:	empty
Can Be Inside:	ADDRESS, BLOCKQUOTE, BODY, CENTER, DIV, FORM, PRE,
	DD, DT, LI, P, TD, TH, Hn,
	A, CAPTION, character highlighting
Attributes:	COLOR, FACE, SIZE

BASEFONT specifies the default font characteristics—primarily font size—for all text following **BASEFONT.** Internet Explorer also supports text color and font face control, but this is not supported by other browser vendors. With Internet Explorer, **BASEFONT**-specified colors and faces override any selections by **BODY** attributes.

The **BASEFONT** attribute specifications are:

SIZE="*number*" (optional) Specifies the default font size, as a value from 1 to 7 (the default is 3). Note that **BASEFONT** does not affect the size of text inside heading elements.

COLOR="*#rrggbb*", "*color*" (optional) (Internet Explorer only) Specifies the default text color, either as an RGB value or as a named color.

FACE="*string*" (optional) (Internet Explorer only) Specifies the default font face for the document, either as a font name or as a sequence of comma-separated font names. The browser will try all fonts from left to right, and will choose the first supported font.

BASEFONT should ideally appear prior to any displayed text in the **BODY** of the document. Localized changes to the font size should be implemented using the **FONT** element or—better yet—by using **SPAN** and stylesheets, as discussed in Chapter 5. The following is a simple example of **BASEFONT**:

```
<BASEFONT SIZE=4>
```

MAP Element: Client-Side Imagemap Database

Usage:	`<MAP> ... </MAP>`
Can Contain:	**AREA**
Can Be Inside:	**ADDRESS, BLOCKQUOTE, BODY, CENTER, DIV, FORM, PRE, DD, DT, LI, P, TD, TH, Hn, A, CAPTION, character highlighting**
Attributes:	**NAME**

A **MAP** element contains *client-side imagemap* mapping data. Each **MAP** must be uniquely identified by a **NAME** attribute: for example, `<MAP NAME="map1">`. Such a map is referenced from an **IMG** element using the **USEMAP** attribute, for example:

```
<IMG SRC="image.gif" ... USEMAP="#map1">
```

A single document can contain any number of **MAP** elements, each uniquely identified by a **NAME**. In principle, a **MAP** need not be in the same document as the **IMG** from which it is referenced, so that the above reference should also be possible via:

```
<IMG SRC="image.gif" ... USEMAP="http://some.where.ca/maps/maps.html#map1">
```

where the file *maps.html* contains **MAP** elements used in several different documents. There are, however, no browsers that currently support such external **MAP** elements.

A **MAP** element must contain **AREA** elements—these are the only elements allowed within a **MAP**. **AREA** elements mark out the regions of an image and the URLs to which these regions are linked—for example:

```
<MAP NAME="map1">
  <AREA SHAPE="rect" COORD="10,20,50,50" HREF="stuff.html">
  <AREA SHAPE="rect" COORD="30,40,60,60" HREF="otherstuff.html">
...
</MAP>
```

SHAPE and coordinate specifications are discussed in the next section.

AREA Element: Client-Side Imagemap Mapping Areas

Usage: <AREA>

Can Contain: empty

Can Be Inside: **MAP**

Attributes: **ALT, COORDS, HREF, NOHREF, SHAPE, <u>TARGET</u>**

The **AREA** element specifies shaped regions in a mapped image and the URLs associated with the shape. The meanings and uses of the six attributes are:

ALT=*"string"* (optional) Gives a text description of the mapped region that can be presented to the user as a description of the linked region; or it can be used by browsers that cannot display the image. This attribute is not widely supported.

SHAPE="rect", "circle", "poly", "default" (optional) Indicates the type of shape being specified in the **AREA** element—the only currently supported shape is "rect", for rectangle. If **SHAPE** is not specified, a browser assumes the default **SHAPE**="rect". "Default" specifies no area, and corresponds to the default behavior should none of the specified regions be selected.

NOTE: Internet Explorer 3 Bug   Internet Explorer 3 does not support the **SHAPE**="default" attribute value.

COORDS=*"x1,y1,x2,y2..."* (mandatory) Specifies the comma-separated coordinates of the defined **SHAPE**, as a sequence of *(x,y)* pairs—the required number of pairs depends on the specified **SHAPE**. Coordinates are specified in pixels measured from the upper left-hand corner of the image. The coordinate specifications are:

SHAPE="rect" **COORDS**=*"x1,y1,x2,y2"*—where $(x1,y1)$ are the coordinates of the upper left-hand corner, and $(x2,y2)$ are the coordinates of the lower right-hand corner.

SHAPE="circle" **COORDS**=*"xc,yc,r"*—where (xc,yc) is the circle center, and (r) is the circle radius.

SHAPE="poly" **COORDS**=*"x1,y1,x2,y2 ... xn, yn"*—where $(x1,y1)$ ... (xn,yn) are the coordinates of the vertices of the polygon.

SHAPE="default" No coordinates are specified. This is the default behavior if the mouse is clicked in an undefined region.

AREAs can overlap—in this case, the browser searches sequentially down through the different **AREA** elements, and selects the first acceptable entry.

NOHREF (one of **HREF** and **NOHREF** is required) **NOHREF** indicates that the browser should take no action if the user clicks inside the specified region, and should continue to display the current document.

HREF="*url*" (one of **HREF** and **NOHREF** is required) Specifies the URL to which the region is linked. Note that partial URLs are evaluated relative to the URL of the **MAP** file—and recall that the **MAP** need not be in the same document as the **IMG** element referencing the **MAP**. Similarly, if the document containing the **MAP** element also contains a **BASE** element, relative URLs specified by the **HREF** will be evaluated relative to the base URL.

<u>**TARGET**</u>= "*string*" (optional) (Netscape and Internet Explorer only) Specifies the name of the *frame* or window to which the data returned by the submitted form should be sent. This attribute is used to the same purpose with the **A** (anchor) element. Please see the anchor element section for further details.

References

Web-based SGML Resources

http://etext.virginia.edu/bin/tei-tocs?div=DIV1&id=SG	(Gentle SGML Introduction)
http://www.lib.virginia.edu/etext/tagging-intro.html	(Gentle SGML Introduction)
ftp://www.ucc.ie/pub/sgml/p2sg.ps	(The above, but in PostScript)
http://www.sil.org/sgml/sgml.html	(SGML Reference Collection)
http://www.w3.org/pub/WWW/MarkUp/SGML/Activity	(W3C SGML Activites summary)
ftp://ftp.ifi.uio.no/pub/SGML/	(Eric Naggum's SGML archive)

Books on SGML

The SGML Handbook, by Charles F. Goldfarb, Oxford University Press, 1990 (the SGML "bible"—not for the faint of heart!)

The SGML Implementation Guide, by B. Travis and D. Waldt, Springer-Verlag, 1995

HTML Specifications

http://ds.internic.net/rfc/rfc1866.txt	(HTML 2.0 specifications)
http://www.w3.org/pub/WWW/MarkUp/Wilbur/	(HTML 3.2 information)
http://www.w3.org/pub/WWW/MarkUp/html3/	(Expired HTML 3 draft)
http://www.w3.org/pub/WWW/MarkUp/	(W3C HTML overview)

PICS Document Rating System

http://www.w3.org/pub/WWW/PICS/ (W3C PICS information and specifications)

HTML Document Type Definitions *(Used by programs such as sgmls to validate HTML document syntax)*

HTML 2.0

http://www.java.utoronto.ca/DTDs/HTML/html.decl (SGML declaration for HTML)
http://www.java.utoronto.ca/DTDs/HTML/html2.dtd (HTML 2.0 DTD)
http://www.java.utoronto.ca/DTDs/HTML/HTML2.catalog (HTML 2.0 catalog)
http://www.java.utoronto.ca/DTDs/HTML/ISOlat1.sgml (Entity definitions)

"Strict" HTML 2.0—Restrictive Use of Elements

http://www.java.utoronto.ca/DTDs/HTML/html.decl (SGML declaration for HTML)
http://www.java.utoronto.ca/DTDs/HTML/html2-strict.dtd (Strict HTML 2.0 DTD)
http://www.java.utoronto.ca/DTDs/HTML/HTML2-strict.catalog (Catalog for strict DTD)
http://www.java.utoronto.ca/DTDs/HTML/ISOlat1.sgml (Entity definitions)

HTML 3.2

http://www.java.utoronto.ca/DTDs/HTML/html.decl (SGML declaration for HTML)
http://www.w3.org/pub/WWW/MarkUp/Wilbur/HTML32.dtd (HTML 3.2 DTD)
http://www.w3.org/pub/WWW/MarkUp/Wilbur/HTML32.cat (HTML 3.2 catalog)
http://www.w3.org/pub/WWW/MarkUp/Wilbur/ISOlat1.ent (Entity definitions)

5

Advanced HTML—
Proprietary Extensions
and New Features

Chapter 4 gave an overview of the markup model, and provided a detailed description of the current, "official" version of HTML, known as HTML 3.2. However, there is more to practical HTML authoring than that. Most commercial browsers support popular proprietary extensions, such as **FRAMESET, FRAME,** and **EMBED,** while some newer standards-derived elements, such as **OBJECT** and **SPAN,** are also gaining support. A Web author not only needs to know how to use these elements, but also needs to be aware of their status and possible utility—after all, there's no point using an element if it is not supported by browsers used by many of your customers.

This chapter describes these newer HTML features. Also covered are more advanced issues, such as stylesheets, internationalization, and document scripting.

Note that the descriptions of the new elements presented here follow the layout used in Chapter 4, and you are referred there for details. Recall that in Chapter 4, the elements grouped under the name "Character Highlighting" consisted of the physical (**B, I, U,** etc.) and logical (**EM, STRONG, CITE,** etc.) highlighting elements. In this chapter, the definition is extended to include the appropriate new elements. The revised definition is:

character highlighting: CITE, CODE, DFN, EM, KBD, SAMP, STRIKE, STRONG, VAR, and B, BIG, FONT, I, *S*, SMALL, SUB, SUP, TT, U, (<u>BLINK</u>, <u>NOBR</u>, *SPAN*, *BDO*, *Q*, <u>MARQUEE</u>)

where the added elements are enclosed in parentheses.

Chapter Organization

For ease of use, the material in this chapter is divided into eight sections. These are:

1. **FRAME and Framed Documents**

   Describes the **FRAMESET, FRAME,** and **IFRAME** elements for creating framed documents. These elements let a single browser window contain multiple, independent frames, each frame containing a different HTML document. Most—but not all—commercial browsers support these elements.

2. **Common HTML Extensions**

   Describes other elements currently in common use but not part of the HTML3.2 standard discussed in Chapter 4. These include the Netscape **EMBED, MULTICOL,** and **SPACER** elements, the Microsoft **MARQUEE** and **BGSOUND** elements, among others. These elements are understood by several browsers. As Netscape Navigator and Microsoft Internet Explorer are the two most popular browsers, the section notes those elements that are supported by one and not the other of these programs.

3. **Embedding Objects in HTML**

   The HTML standardization process has developed a new element, **OBJECT,** to replace and augment the current embedding elements **APPLET, EMBED,** and **IMG.** This element, and related changes to **A** and **PARAM,** are discussed here.

4. **Stylesheets and HTML**

   Describes the concept behind stylesheets and how stylesheets are linked to the text of an HTML document. At present, a subset of one proposed stylesheets language is supported by the Internet Explorer browser; both Netscape and Microsoft promise full support for stylesheets in 1997.

5. **Scripting in HTML Documents**

   Describes the new attributes and elements added to HTML to allow interaction between HTML elements and script programs, and briefly describes the nature of these document scripting languages, using JavaScript as an example.

6. **Internationalization of HTML**

A description of the new elements and attributes to be added to HTML in support of non-European languages. These new features are not yet widely supported, but are part of the standards process and are expected to be incorporated into the next generation of Web browsers.

7. **Next-Generation HTML**

Outlines new elements and attributes proposed for the next version of HTML, not discussed in the previous sections. These elements are more speculative, but are expected to be integrated into HTML in the near future.

8. **Mathematics, and Other Missing Features**

This final section discusses some of the obvious missing features of HTML, and describes what is possible now, and what may be possible in the near future.

At present, very few browsers support the more advanced multilingual or next generation HTML features, although this situation will soon change. If you want to experiment with these more advanced aspects of HTML you should obtain the noncommercial emacs-w3, arena, amaya, or grail browsers. Information about these browsers is provided in the references at the end of this chapter.

FRAME and Framed Documents

With Navigator 2, Netscape introduced a new form of document, known as an HTML *frame* document. Such documents use a new type of markup that lets the document author divide the browser window into a number of independent *frames*, where each frame contains its own, unique HTML document. In a frame document, the traditional **BODY** element is replaced by a **FRAMESET** element, which defines the layout of the different frames within the browser window. The initial *content* of a frame is defined by **FRAME** or **FRAMESET** elements located inside the **FRAMESET**. **FRAME** elements define the content and properties of a particular frame, while additional **FRAMESET** elements simply further divide a frame into subframes.

The only other element allowed inside a frame document is **NOFRAMES**. This non-empty element can contain a **BODY** element that, in turn, contains regular body content HTML markup. Browsers that understand **FRAMESET** ignore the **NOFRAMES** content, while browsers that do not understand **FRAMESET** ignore all of the **FRAMESET**, **FRAME**, and **NOFRAMES** tags, and take the **BODY** element content as the document to be displayed. An example of such a document is shown in Figure 5.1.

Figure 5.1 A simple example document illustrating the use of the FRAMESET, FRAME, and NOFRAMES elements. Also listed are the contents of the documents initially referenced by the FRAME elements.

fig5-1.html

```
<HTML>
<HEAD><TITLE>Simple Frame Test Document</TITLE></HEAD>

<FRAMESET ROWS="90, *">
  <FRAME NAME="topbar" SRC="direct.html">
  <FRAMESET COLS="10%, 45%, 45%">
    <FRAME NAME="navi-bar" SRC="left.html">
    <FRAME NAME="main-l" SRC="middle.html">
    <FRAME NAME="main-r" SRC="right.html">
  </FRAMESET>
</FRAMESET>

<NOFRAMES>
  <BODY>
  <H2 ALIGN="center">So, You Don't Support Frames, Eh?</H2>
  <BLOCKQUOTE>
    <P>So you don't like frames. Well, too bad for you!
  </BLOCKQUOTE>
  <HR>
  <DIV ALIGN="right">
    <EM>Stupid Document Trick Number 13</EM>
  </DIV>
  </BODY>
</NOFRAMES>
</HTML>
```

direct.html

```
<HTML>
<HEAD><TITLE>Simple Frame Test Document</TITLE></HEAD><BODY>
<DIV ALIGN="center">
<TABLE CELLPADDING=0 CELLSPACING=0 WIDTH="100%">
<TR><TD COLSPAN="6" ALIGN="center">
      <B><FONT SIZE="+1">C</FONT>ATEGORIES</B>
</TR><TR>
  <TD ALIGN="center">Beasts
  <TD ALIGN="center"><A HREF=".">Birds</A>
  <TD ALIGN="center"><A HREF=".">Fish</A>
  <TD ALIGN="center"><A HREF=".">Parrots</A>
  <TD ALIGN="center"><A HREF=".">Cheese</A>
  <TD ALIGN="center"><A HREF=".">Piston Engines</A>
</TR>
</TABLE>
</DIV></BODY></HTML>
```

Figure 5.1 (Continued)

left.html

```
<HTML>
<HEAD><TITLE>Category Navigation</TITLE></HEAD>
<BODY>
<B>Beasts</B><BR><BR>
<A HREF="dogs.html" TARGET="main-l">Dogs</A><BR><BR>
<A HREF="cats.html" TARGET="main-r">Cats</A><BR><BR>
<A HREF="nada.html">Frogs</A><BR><BR>
<A HREF="nada.html" TARGET="blobby">Deer</A><BR><BR>
<A HREF="nada.html">Snakes</A><BR><BR>
<A HREF="nada.html">Mice</A><BR><BR>
<A HREF="nada.html">Rats</A><BR><BR>
<A HREF="nada.html">Snakes</A><BR><BR>
</BODY></HTML>
```

middle.html

```
<HTML>
<HEAD><TITLE>Middle Frame Placeholder</TITLE></HEAD>
<BODY>
<BR><BR><BR><BR><BR><BR><BR><BR>
<H2 ALIGN="center">Placeholder For Middle Frame</H2>
</BODY></HTML>
```

right.html

```
<HTML>
<HEAD><TITLE>Right Frame Placeholder</TITLE></HEAD>
<BODY>
<BR><BR><BR><BR><BR><BR><BR><BR>
<H2 ALIGN="center">Placeholder For Right Frame</H2>
</BODY></HTML>
```

An HTML document containing a **FRAMESET** cannot contain **BODY** content, other than within a **NOFRAMES**. If regular **BODY** element tags occur prior to the first **FRAMESET**, the Netscape Navigator browser will entirely ignore the **FRAMESET** elements, and will display the **NOFRAMES** content instead.

FRAME elements are supported by many, but not all, Web browsers—you should always provide **NOFRAMES** alternatives for this significant minority.

Figure 5.1 shows a simple example of a frame document (*fig5-1.html*) containing markup that specifies four framed regions. The resulting document is shown in Figure 5.2, while Figure 5.3 shows the same document viewed by a browser that does not understand frames. First, a few words about the content of Figure 5.1 and about how the frame outline is created.

The frames are created by the **FRAMESET** elements. The first **FRAMESET** divides the window vertically into two frames, the top one 90 pixels high, the second occupying the remain-

Figure 5.2 Display, by Netscape Navigator 3, of the document listed in Figure 5.1. Note how the frames are laid out, each frame containing its own distinct document.

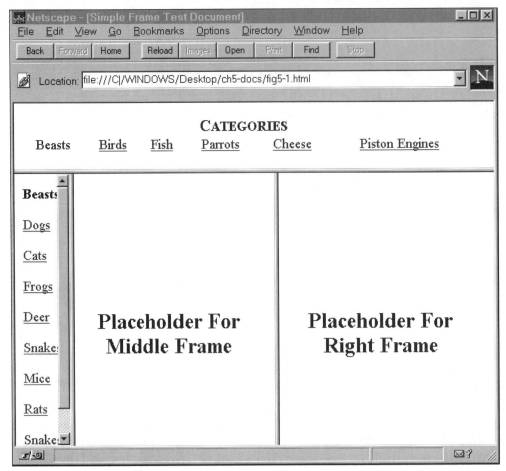

der of the window height. A second **FRAMESET** subsequently vertically divides the second of these frames into three parts, the first occupying 10% of the available width, the remaining two 45% each, for a total of 100%. Note how a **FRAMESET** can divide a region either horizontally (**ROWS**) or vertically (**COLS**), but not both at the same time. The **FRAME** elements indicate, via the **SRC** attributes, which HTML documents should be loaded and displayed in each of these frames—the result is shown in Figure 5.2. Note how each frame is given a unique name via the **NAME** attribute. This allows each frame to be uniquely addressed by elements invoking hypertext links. This is discussed in more detail later in this section.

Figure 5.3 Display, by the NCSA Mosaic 2.1.1 browser, of the document listed in Figure 5.1. NCSA Mosaic does not understand frames, and consequently displays the NOFRAMES content instead.

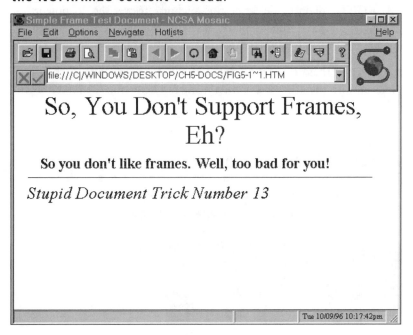

Some browsers do not understand the frame elements and ignore all these elements and attributes. The frame mechanism uses the **NOFRAMES** element to provide an alternative for these browsers. A browser that understands **FRAMESET** will completely ignore the content of the **NOFRAMES** element—you can see in Figure 5.2 that Netscape Navigator 3 does exactly this. However, browsers that do not understand frame elements will ignore everything but the **NOFRAMES** content. An example is shown in Figure 5.3: The noncommercial Mosaic browser does not understand frames, and displays the **NOFRAMES** content instead.

Targeting Data to Named Frames

Frames are only useful if their content (such as the placeholders shown in Figure 5.2) can be updated and replaced by other documents or data. This is, of course, only possible if you can *identify* which frame you want to update or replace. This identifier is provided by the **FRAME** element **NAME** attribute value. These names, which must be unique within a collection of framed documents, *identify* each individual frame. In the example in Figures 5.1 and 5.2, the top frame is named "topbar," the right-hand frame "main-r," and so on. These names are arbitrary, but should be chosen to be easy to remember—as an author you will refer to these names often, so it is best to choose short, meaningful names.

Individual frames can be *targeted* by **A** (hypertext anchor) or **FORM** elements taking a **TARGET** attribute. This attribute takes, as its value, the *name* of the frame to which the data should be sent. Looking to Figure 5.1, you will note that the anchor surrounding the word "Dogs" in the file *left.html* contains the attribute **TARGET**="main-l." Selecting this anchor retrieves the document *dogs.html* and displays it in the left-hand large frame. Similarly, selecting the link "Cats" retrieves the file *cats.html*, but directs this file to the frame labeled "main-r".

The document resulting from selecting these two links is shown in Figure 5.4. Indeed, the two documents were retrieved and placed into the specified named frames. The listing for linked documents are shown in Figure 5.5.

Figure 5.4 Display, by Netscape Navigator 3, of the document listed in Figure 5.1, after selecting the links underlying the words "Dogs" and "Cats". Note how the returned documents are retrieved to the named frames as indicated in Figure 5.1. The listings for the linked documents *dogs.html* and *cats.html* are given in Figure 5.5.

Figure 5.5 HTML documents *dogs.html*, *cats.html*, and *nada.html* referenced by the hypertext links in the framed document listed in Figure 5.2.

dogs.html

```
<HTML>
<HEAD><TITLE>My Wife Loves Dogs</TITLE></HEAD>
<BODY>
<H1 ALIGN="center"><FONT FACE="arial black">
My Wife Loves Dogs!</FONT></H1>
<BLOCKQUOTE>
<FONT FACE="arial">
She loves dogs, and I want to get a cat. This leads
to enormous debates over the advantages and disadvantages
of each of these wonderful animals. But as yet, there is
no resolution to this difficult question.
</FONT>
</BLOCKQUOTE>
</BODY></HTML>
```

cats.html

```
<HTML>
<HEAD><TITLE>Cats are Best</TITLE></HEAD>
<BODY BGCOLOR="#cccccc">
<H1 ALIGN="center"><FONT FACE="verdana">
Cats are King</FONT></H1>
<BLOCKQUOTE>
<FONT FACE="courier">
So what's the problem with cats? They eat mice,
which is probably good, given all the mice in
our house. They purr and like to sleep by the
hot radiators. They are generally friendly.
So -- what's the problem?
</FONT>
</BLOCKQUOTE>
</BODY></HTML>
```

nada.html

```
<HTML>
<HEAD><TITLE>Nothing</TITLE></HEAD>
<BODY>
<BLINK><CENTER><B><FONT FACE="arial">
N<BR>O<BR>T<BR>H<BR>I<BR>N<BR>G<BR>
<BR><BR>
H<BR>E<BR>R<BR>E<BR>
</FONT></B></CENTER><BLINK>
</BODY></HTML>
```

No TARGET Specified

If no **TARGET** is specified, the retrieved document replaces the frame containing the selected anchor (or **FORM**). Thus, if the link "Frogs" is selected, the document *nada.html* is retrieved and replaces the left-hand side navigational bar. The document resulting from selecting this link is shown in Figure 5.6.

Nonexistent TARGET Name

If an anchor or **FORM** references a **TARGET** name that is not defined, then the browser needs to create a frame with this name. However, there is no way to place an otherwise undefined frame

Figure 5.6 Document generated by selecting the link to the word "Frogs" in the document shown in Figure 5.4. The selected anchor had no TARGET attribute, so the retrieved page simply replaces the frame from which the link was selected—and hence replaces the leftmost framed window.

within a framed document, so the browser instead creates a new browser window and gives this entire window the new name. For example, the anchor surrounding the word "Deer" references the target name "blobby," which was not defined in *fig5-1.html*. Thus, when this link is accessed there is no frame defined for this document, so it is retrieved and placed in a new browser window, as shown in Figure 5.7.

Predefined TARGET Names

There are four special target names defined as part of the frame specification. These values, all of which begin with the underscore (_) character, were defined in Table 4.8; to reiterate, these values are:

Value	Meaning
_blank	Load the referenced data into a new, unnamed window.
_self	Load the referenced data in place of the current document.
_parent	Load the referenced data into the window containing (or, that contained) the *parent* of the current document (the document from which the current document was accessed). If there is no parent document, default to **TARGET**="_self".
_top	Load the referenced data into the window containing (or, that contained) the "top" document (the document obtained by iteratively searching through successive parent documents until arriving at the initial, starting document). If there is no top document, default to **TARGET**="_self".

NOTE: All other names beginning with an underscore (_) are ignored by the browser.

The next sections provide detailed specifications for the various frame-related elements.

FRAMESET Element: Declare a FRAME Document

Usage: `<FRAMESET> ... </FRAMESET>`

Can Contain: **FRAME, FRAMESET, NOFRAMES**

Can Be Inside: **HTML**

Attributes: **BORDER, BORDERCOLOR, COLS, FRAMEBORDER, FRAMESPACING, ROWS**

FRAMESET divides a region of a framed document into frames. An HTML document containing a **FRAMESET** cannot contain **BODY** content, other than within a **NOFRAMES**. If you include regular **BODY** element tags prior to the first **FRAMESET**, Netscape Navigator browsers will entirely ignore the **FRAME** and **FRAMESET** elements, and will display the **NOFRAMES** content (if any).

Figure 5.7 Document generated by selecting the link "Deer" in Figure 5.4. The target name is not defined, so a new window with this name is created for this content.

The layout and size of the frames defined by a **FRAMESET** are specified by the **COLS** or **ROWS** attribute. **COLS** indicates that the frames are laid out in columns, with the comma-separated values assigned to **COLS** specifying the number and widths of the columns. **ROWS** indicates that the frames are laid out in rows, with the comma-separated value assigned to **ROWS** specifying the number and heights of the rows. A **FRAMESET** must have one of **ROWS** or **COLS**, but cannot take both.

The *number* of comma-separated values assigned to **ROWS** or **COLS** specifies the number of frames contained within the **FRAMESET**, while the *values* determine the frame sizes. The values can take the three possible forms described in Table 5.1.

Table 5.1 Frame Size Value Specifications for FRAMESET, COL, and ROW Attribute Values

Type	Format	Description
Fixed Pixel	*number*	Specifies the absolute frame size, in pixels, where *n* is the integer number of pixels.
Percentage	*number%*	Specifies the frame size as a percentage of the total available height (or width), where *n* is an integer. If the total of all specified frames is greater than 100%, then all frames are rescaled until the total is 100%. If the total is less than 100%, and there are no relative frames (see below), then all frames are rescaled until the total is 100%. If the total is less than 100% and there are relative-sized frames, the space is assigned to the relative frames.
Relative Size	*number**	Specifies the size as a free-floating, relative value—all space remaining after allocating fixed pixel or percentage frames is divided amongst all relative-sized frames. An optional integer preceding the asterisk weights the space contribution; thus, the string "2*,3*,*" would allocate 2/6 of the remaining space to the first frame, 3/6 to the second frame, and 1/6 to the third frame.

Finally, the attributes **BORDER**, **BORDERCOLOR**, **FRAMEBORDER**, and **FRAMESPACING** control presentation aspects of the frame borders.

BORDER="*number*" (optional) (Netscape Navigator only) Specifies the width of the frame border, in pixels, the default being 5. **BORDER** can only be set on the outermost **FRAMESET** element. Scroll bars, if needed in a frame, are placed inside the frame border. This attribute is not supported by Internet Explorer. Figure 5.8 shows an example of a borderless frame document.

BORDERCOLOR="*#rrggbb*", "*color*" (optional) (Netscape Navigator only) Specifies the color of the frame borders. This is overridden by a **BORDERCOLOR** specification of a **FRAMESET** lying inside another **FRAMESET**, or by a **BORDERCOLOR** specification of a specific **FRAME**. This attribute is not supported by Internet Explorer.

COLS="*comma-separated frame widths*" (one of **ROWS**, **COLS** is mandatory) Specifies the widths of a selection of *vertically* oriented frames, where the terms specifying the width are separated by commas. The widths are specified as described in Table 5.1, while the number of comma-separated entries gives the number of frames within the **FRAMESET**. An example (see Figure 5.1) is **COLS**="10%, 45%, 45%", which declares three columnar frames—the first frame occupies 10% of the available width, and the second and third occupy 45% each.

FRAMEBORDER="yes", "no" (optional) Specifies how the frame borders should be drawn. **FRAMEBORDER**="yes" draws three-dimensional borders (the default), while "no" draws a plain border. If **BORDER**="0" then no borders are drawn regardless of the **FRAMEBORDER** setting.

Figure 5.8 The same document as displayed in Figure 5.4 but with BORDER="0" applied to the outer FRAMESET (see Figure 5.1). Note that the frame borders are now invisible. In addition, the frames are not resizable—the user cannot use the mouse to grab and move the frame edges.

TIP: Internet Explorer 3 and Netscape Navigator 3 Incompatibility

Navigator and Internet Explorer both support **FRAMEBORDER**, but with incompatible values: Explorer requires numbers (0 or 1) instead of the "yes"/"no" values required by Netscape Navigator 3. However, the following will work with both browsers: to obtain three-dimensional borders, omit the **FRAMEBORDER** attribute. If you want plain borders, use **FRAMEBORDER**="no".

FRAMESPACING="*number*" (optional) (Internet Explorer only) Specifies the spacing to leave between internal frames, in pixels. This attribute is not supported by Netscape Navigator.

ROWS="*comma-separated frame heights*" "(one of **ROWS**, **COLS** is mandatory) Specifies the heights of a selection of *horizontally* oriented frames. Heights are specified as described in Table 5.1, and are separated by commas, while the number of entries gives the number of **FRAME**s within the **FRAMESET**. An example is **ROWS**="80, 3*, *, 100" which declares four frame rows—the first (top) frame is 80 pixels high, while the fourth (bottom) frame is 100 pixels high. The second frame will occupy 3/4 of the remaining height, while the third frame will occupy the final 1/4 of the remaining height.

FRAME Element: A FRAME within a FRAMESET

Usage:	<FRAME>
Can Contain:	empty
Can Be Inside:	**FRAMESET**
Attributes:	BORDERCOLOR, FRAMEBORDER, MARGINHEIGHT, MARGINWIDTH, NAME, NORESIZE, SCROLLING, SRC

FRAME defines the content of a frame within a **FRAMESET** element. The **SRC** attribute references the HTML document to be placed within the **FRAME**. The attributes **MARGINWIDTH**, **MARGINHEIGHT**, **NORESIZE**, and **SCROLLING** define the physical properties of the frame. The **NAME** attribute assigns a specific name to the **FRAME**, and allows the frame to be targeted using the **TARGET** attribute of anchor elements. All attributes are optional, including **SRC**; if **SRC** is absent, the frame is simply left empty. **FRAME** is an empty element, as the content of the frame is defined via the **SRC** attribute.

The **ROWS** or **COLS** attribute specifies the number of frames that must be inside the **FRAMESET**. It is an error if a **FRAMESET** does not actually contain this number of **FRAME** and/or **FRAMESET** elements.

The following is an example of correctly defined **FRAME**s (comments in italics):

```
<FRAMESET ROWS="10%, 80%, 10%>              3 rows, narrow top and bottom
   <FRAME SCROLLING="no" SRC="logo+buttonbar.html">   1'st frame
   <FRAMESET COLS="20%, 80%">               2'd frame is a FRAMESET
      <FRAME NAME="navigation" SRC="navigate.html">     containing 2 frames
      <FRAME NAME="main" SRC="main/start.html">
   </FRAMESET>
   <FRAME SCROLLING="no" SRC="credits.html">   3'd frame
</FRAMESET>
....
```

In this example, the display is first divided into three rows: The top and bottom rows are narrow (10% of the available height) and contain non-scrolling documents, while the middle row takes up the remaining 80% of the window height. The middle row is further divided by the second **FRAMESET** into two columns: The first takes up 20% of the window width, the second the remaining 80%. Both these frames are scrollable, and are named using **NAME** attributes.

The following is an example of incorrectly defined **FRAME**s (comments in italics):

```
<FRAMESET ROWS="10%, 80%, 10%>              3 rows, narrow top and bottom
   <FRAME SCROLLING="no" SRC="logo+buttonbar.html">   1'st frame
   <FRAMESET COLS="20%, 80%">               2'd frame is a FRAMESET
      <FRAME NAME="navigation" SRC="navigate.html">    containing 2 frames
      <FRAME NAME="main" SRC="main/start.html">
   </FRAMESET>
   <FRAME SCROLLING="no" SRC="credits.html">  3'd frame
   <FRAME SRC="oops.html">                  ERROR-- FRAMESET declares
                                            3 rows, but this is the
                                            fourth FRAME!!

</FRAMESET>
```

BORDERCOLOR = "#*rrggbb*", "*color*" (optional) Sets the color for the frame borders. This overrides any border colors specified by a surrounding **FRAMESET** element. The color is undefined if two neighboring **FRAME**s try to set different colors to an adjacent boundary. **BORDERCOLOR** is only valid with 3D frame borders—if **FRAMEBORDER**="no", then the borders are invisible.

FRAMEBORDER = "yes", "no" (optional) Sets the display mode for the frame border—the value "yes" (the default) creates borders with a 3D effect, while "no" produces plain borders. The border width is set by the **BORDER** attribute of the outermost **FRAMESET** element. Note that Internet Explorer and Navigator treat frame bordering differently, so make sure to test your frame designs on both browsers.

MARGINHEIGHT="*number*" (optional) Specifies the height, in pixels, of the top and bottom margins for the frame; the default value is approximately 10, and is browser-specific. **MARGINHEIGHT** cannot be less than 1, to ensure that there is some blank space left between the frame content and the frame borders. If this attribute is absent, the browser will itself determine a (hopefully) appropriate margin height.

MARGINWIDTH = "*number*" (optional) Specifies the width, in pixels, of the left and right margins inside the frame; the default value is approximately 10, and is browser-specific. **MARGINWIDTH** cannot be less than 1, to ensure that there is some blank space left between the frame content and the frame borders. If this attribute is absent, the browser will hopefully determine an appropriate margin width.

NAME=*"name "* (optional) Assigns a *symbolic name* to the particular frame; the **TARGET** attribute of a **FORM** or **A** element can then direct retrieved documents or data to this named frame. If **NAME** is absent, the frame name is undefined. Values for names must be name tokens, as defined previously in this chapter.

NORESIZE (optional) Informs the browser that the frame size is fixed and cannot be modified by the user—this also restricts resizing of adjacent frames in the same window. If this attribute is absent and if frame borders are present (see **FRAMEBORDER**), the frame can be resized, usually by using the mouse to drag a border of the frame.

SCROLLING="yes", "no", "auto" (optional) Specifies the status of scroll bars for the frame. A value of "yes" means that the frame must always have scroll bars, while "no" means that the frame should never have scroll bars. If you use this latter value, you must be sure that the frame is large enough to contain the desired document. The value "auto" lets the browser include scroll bars when necessary. The default value is "auto".

SRC=*"url"* (optional) Specifies the URL of the HTML document to be displayed within the frame. **SRC** can be absent, in which case the frame is initially blank.

NOFRAMES Element: Markup for FRAME-Incapable Browsers

Usage:	`<NOFRAMES>` ... `</NOFRAMES>`
Can Contain:	**characters, character highlighting, A, APPLET, BR, IMG, MAP, SCRIPT, CENTER, Hn, P, HR, [ISINDEX], DIR, DL, MENU, OL, UL, ADDRESS, BLOCKQUOTE, DIV, FORM, PRE, TABLE, BODY**
Can Be Inside:	**FRAMESET**
Attributes:	none

NOFRAMES contains HTML markup to be displayed by browsers that do not understand the **FRAMESET** and **FRAME** elements. **NOFRAMES** content will not be displayed by a **FRAME**-capable browser. A **FRAME**-incapable browser, however, ignores the **FRAMESET**, **FRAME**, and **NOFRAMES** elements, and displays the **NOFRAMES** content as if it were the **BODY** of a regular HTML document.

NOFRAMES should contain a **BODY** element and regular **BODY** content. The following is an example of the use of **NOFRAMES**:

```
<HTML>
<HEAD>
<TITLE>Test of the NOFRAMES Element</TITLE>
</HEAD>
<FRAMESET ROWS="50%, 50%">

   <FRAME SRC="top_part.html" NAME="wind1">
   <FRAME SRC="bot_part.html" NAME="wind2">

<NOFRAMES>
<BODY BACKGROUND="greywhale.gif">
<H1 ALIGN="center"> Warning! </H1>
<P ALIGN="center"><EM>If you are reading this text, you are viewing this
   document with a FRAMEs-incapable browser—this document was designed
   to be viewed by a FRAME-capable browser, such as Netscape Navigator
   2.0. If you do not have such a browser, please access the alternative
   <A HREF="noframes.html">noframes</A> collection.
</BODY>
</NOFRAMES>
</FRAMESET>
</HTML>
```

IFRAME Element: A Floating FRAME (Internet Explorer only)

Usage: `<IFRAME> ... </IFRAME>`

Can Contain: empty

Can be Inside: Unspecified; probably: **ADDRESS, BLOCKQUOTE, BODY, CENTER, DIV, FORM, PRE, Hn, DD, DT, LI, P, TD, TH,**

A, CAPTION, character highlighting

Attributes: **ALIGN, FRAMEBORDER, HEIGHT, HSPACE, MARGINHEIGHT, MARGIN-WIDTH, NAME, SCROLLING, SRC, VSPACE, WIDTH**

Not to be outdone, Microsoft created an entirely different type of frame, called a *floating frame*. A floating frame is just that: a frame that can float anywhere inside an HTML document. Thus, **IFRAME** can be placed inside the regular document **BODY** and, in a sense, acts like an embedded object or image. Figures 5.9 and 5.10 illustrate such use of an **IFRAME**.

The content of a floating frame is specified by a **SRC** attribute. The remaining attributes **FRAMEBORDER, MARGINWIDTH, MARGINHEIGHT, NORESIZE,** and **SCROLLING** definethe physical properties of the frame, while **HEIGHT** and **WIDTH** define the size, and

ALIGN the alignment on the display. The **NAME** attribute assigns a specific name to the **FRAME**, which allows the frame to be targeted (using the **TARGET** attribute) by **A** or **FORM** elements.

IFRAME is non-empty, and the content of **IFRAME** is for use by browsers that do not understand **IFRAME** elements. A browser that understands **IFRAME** will ignore the **IFRAME** element content. Figure 5.11 shows the rendering of the document listed in Figure 5.9 by an **IFRAME**-incapable browser.

Currently, Internet Explorer is the only browser that supports **IFRAME**. The attribute specifications are:

ALIGN="top", "middle", "bottom", "left", "right" (optional) Specifies the alignment for the floating frame on the page. The meanings are the same as for the **IMG** element. The values "left" and "right" produce floating frames. The default value is "bottom".

FRAMEBORDER = "1", "0" (optional) Sets the display mode for the floating frame border. The value "1" (the default) creates borders with a 3D effect, while "0" produces no borders.

HEIGHT="*number*", "*number*%" (optional; must be specified if **WIDTH** is specified) Specifies the height of the displayed floating frame, either in pixels, or as a percentage of the available window height. If **HEIGHT** is specified, then **WIDTH** must also be specified, otherwise Internet Explorer will improperly display the document.

NOTE: You Must Specify *Both* HEIGHT and WIDTH If you specify a floating frame **WIDTH**, you must specify a **HEIGHT**, and vice versa.

HSPACE="*number*" (optional) Specifies a spacing margin, in pixels, to leave to the left and right of the floating frame. The default margin is zero pixels. This is only relevant for "left" and "right" aligned frames.

MARGINHEIGHT="*number*" (optional) Specifies the height, in pixels, of the top and bottom margins within the frame; the default value is approximately 10, and is browser-specific. **MARGINHEIGHT** cannot be less than 1, to ensure that there is some blank space left between the frame content and the frame borders. If this attribute is absent, the browser will itself determine a (hopefully) appropriate margin height.

MARGINWIDTH = "*number*" (optional) Specifies the width, in pixels, of the left and right margins within the frame; the default value is approximately 10, and is browser-specific. **MARGINWIDTH** cannot be less than 1, to ensure that there is some blank space left between the frame content and the frame borders. If this attribute is absent, the browser will hopefully determine an appropriate margin width.

NAME="*name* " (optional) Assigns a *symbolic name* to the particular frame. The **TARGET** attribute of a **FORM** or **A** element can then direct retrieved documents or data to this

Figure 5.9 An example document illustrating the use of the IFRAME element. Figures 5.10 and 5.11 show the rendering of this document by Internet Explorer 3 and Netscape Navigator 3 respectively.

```
<HTML>
<HEAD><TITLE>Test of Microsoft IFRAME</TITLE></HEAD>
<BODY>
<H2>A Test of Microsoft's IFRAME</H2>
This is not a terribly exciting example -- which is
not suprising, given that I am writing this at
around 2:30AM, afterapproximately 14 hours at the
computer. Book writing seems to take forever....
<IFRAME  SRC="dogs.html" BORDER="20"
         FRAMEBORDER="1" ALIGN="left"
         WIDTH="350" HEIGHT="200">
<HR NOSHADE>
<H3>Alternative Content</H3>
Ok, So you don't understand <B>IFRAME</B>. Well, this
block of text is for you!
<HR NOSHADE>
</IFRAME>
</DIV>
<P> Writing a book is a slow process, much slower than I
first expected -- there are always small things to do,
such as correcting Figure numberings, checking spelling, or
fixing poor wordings and explanations. The truth, however
is that most writers <em>enjoy</em> this process.
Perhaps 14 hours at a stretch is a bit too much -- and I will
admit that I would prefer less onerous hours (a publisher's
deadline does tend to focus one's efforts) -- but I do enjoy
the process, and feel great satisfaction at producing
informative, readable, and accurate prose.
</BODY>
</HTML>
```

named frame. If **NAME** is absent, the frame name is undefined. Values for names must be name tokens, as defined previously.

SCROLLING="yes", "no", "auto" (optional) Specifies the status of scroll bars for the frame. A value of "yes" means that the frame must always have scroll bars, while "no" means that the frame should never have scroll bars. If you use this latter value, you must be sure that the frame is large enough to contain the desired document. The value "auto" lets the browser include scroll bars when necessary. The default value is "auto".

SRC="*url*" (optional) Specifies the URL of the HTML document to be displayed within the frame. **SRC** can be absent, in which case the frame is initially blank.

Figure 5.10 Internet Explorer 3 rendering of the document illustrated in Figure 5.9. Note how the IFRAME is left-aligned with surrounding text flow, just as if it were an embedded image.

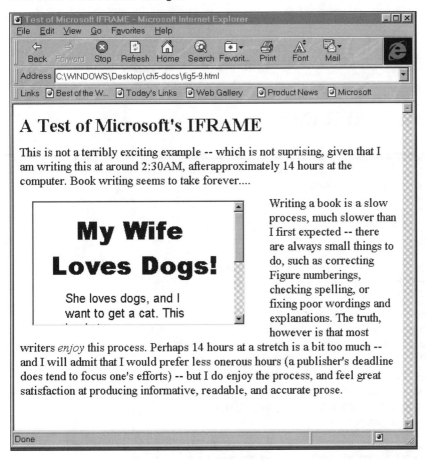

VSPACE="*number*" (optional) Specifies a spacing margin, in pixels, to leave above and below the floating frame. This is only relevant for "left" and "right" aligned frames. The default margin for floating frames is zero pixels.

WIDTH="*number*" (optional; must be specified if **HEIGHT** is specified) Specifies the width of the displayed floating frame, either in pixels, or as a percentage of the available window width. If **WIDTH** is specified, then **HEIGHT** must also be specified, as otherwise Internet Explorer will improperly render the document.

Figure 5.11 Netscape Navigator 3 rendering of the document illustrated in Figure 5.9. Navigator does not understand the IFRAME element, and instead displays the alternative content contained inside the IFRAME.

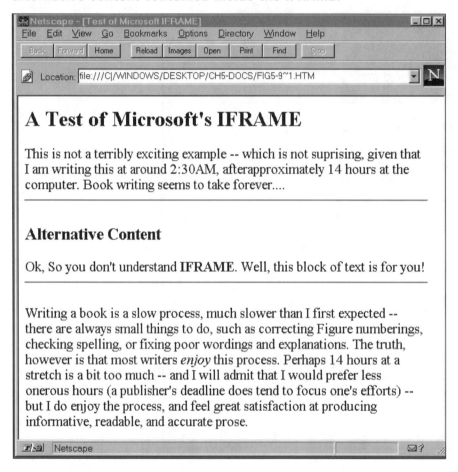

Common HTML Extensions

In addition to the frame-related elements, Netscape and Microsoft have implemented a number of other proprietary elements. Some of these (e.g., **WBR, NOBR**) have been widely adopted by other browser vendors, while other elements (e.g., **BLINK, MARQUEE**) are far less widely supported, and are unlikely to be supported in the future. These elements can be useful in certain contexts, but you should always be aware of their lack of universality. If you do use these elements, be sure to check your documents on several different browsers, to make sure that users see the content you intend.

BGSOUND Element: Inline Audio Snippets (Internet Explorer only)

Usage: `<BGSOUND>`

Can Contain: empty

Can Be Inside: unclear: can apparently appear inside the **HEAD**, or inside any non-empty **BODY** element

Attributes: **SRC, LOOP**

BGSOUND inserts an inline audio snippet—the URL location of the audio file is specified by the **SRC** attribute. By default, the sound is loaded and played once; this can be modified by the **LOOP** attribute. Thus, **LOOP**="10" instructs the browser to play the sound file 10 times before stopping. The values **LOOP**="–1" or **LOOP**="infinite" instruct the browser to continuously play the sound file until the user selects another document. The following is an example of **BGSOUND**:

```
<BGSOUND SRC="/project1/sounds/bubbles.wav" LOOP="-1">
```

BGSOUND can appear in the head or the body, although the **HEAD** seems a more reasonable location.

TIP: Embedding Sound for Both Internet Explorer and Netscape Navigator
These browsers use different mechanisms for embedded audio—thus you need to include markup appropriate to both. The trick for doing this is as follows:

```
<EMBED SRC="sndfile.au" HEIGHT="1" WIDTH="1" AUTOSTART="true" HIDDEN="true">
<NOEMBED>
       <BGSOUND SRC="sndfile.au">
</NOEMBED>
```

Netscape Navigator will use the **EMBED** element, and invokes the default Netscape Navigator LiveAudio player. Setting **HEIGHT** and **WIDTH** to 1 ensures that the embedded object takes no space, while **AUTOSTART** automatically starts the audio, and **HIDDEN**="true" hides the plug-in control panel from the user (Figure 2.23 shows an unhidden LiveAudio control panel). Alternatively, Internet Explorer understands both **EMBED** and **BGSOUND**, but the extra **NOEMBED** tags let the browser select which approach to take. In this instance, Internet Explorer is designed to choose **BGSOUND**, which is part of the basic browser program, and thus faster to load than the plug-in. Note that if you omit the **NOEMBED** elements, the sound will be played twice—once by **BGSOUND** and once by **EMBED**!

Figure 5.12 Demonstration HTML document illustrating the MULTICOL, SPACER, NOBR, WBR, and MARQUEE elements. These elements do not work on all browsers.

```
<HTML>
<HEAD><TITLE>Common HTML Extensions</TITLE></HEAD>
<BODY>
<H2>Common HTML Extensions</H2>
<B><I><MARQUEE ALIGN="middle" HSPACE="10" LOOP="-1"
          SCROLLAMOUNT="3"
          SCROLLDELAY="4"
          BGCOLOR="yellow">
 Look out -- Falling Aardvarks!!
</MARQUEE></I></B><BR>

Here is some regular text -- note how the lines are
broken to best fit the page. This is not an exciting
example but, as I have pointed out, the imagination
starts to fade at around 3:00AM.
<HR WIDTH="80%" ALIGN="left">
<NOBR>
Here is some regular text, but placed inside a <B>NOBR</B>
so that lines are<WBR><EM>*wbr*</EM> not broken, except
at BR or WBR elements -- I have placed the string
<EM>*wbr*</EM> right after every ocurrence of an &lt;WBR>
tag. This is rather  boring but, hey -- <WBR><EM>*wbr*</EM>
whadaya want at these prices?</NOBR>
<HR NOSHADE SIZE=4>
<H3>MULTICOL Example</H3>
<MULTICOL COLS=2 GUTTER=15>
<P>There are three types of spacers, "block", "horizontal",
and "vertical". The first exmaple is a block spacer, with a
height of 40 pixels, a width of 60 pixels, and left-alignment.
Here it is --
<SPACER ALIGN="left" WIDTH="60" HEIGHT="40" TYPE="block">
-- and there it was. Notice how it floats like an image, with
text flowing around it. Of course, a blank, fully transparent
image works just as well--and also works on other browsers.
<H3>Horizontal and Vertical</H3>
Horizontal spacers are like tabs: here is one of SIZE=40
(40 pixels long)--|
<SPACER TYPE="horizontal" SIZE="40">|--
see how it tabs across. Vertical spacers moves text down
and also cause a line break. Here is an example
with a vertical spacing of 40 pixels.
--|<SPACER TYPE="vertical" SIZE="20">|--there it was.
</MULTICOL>
</BODY>
</HTML>
```

Figure 5.13 Rendering, using Netscape Navigator 3, of the HTML document shown in Figure 5.12. This browser does not understand the MARQUEE element.

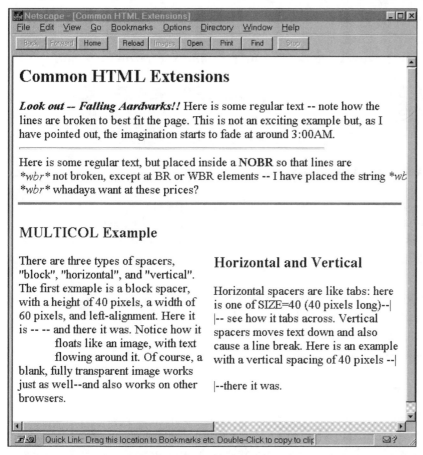

BLINK Element: Blinking Text (Netscape Navigator Only)

Usage: `<BLINK> ... </BLINK>`

Can Contain: Unspecified; probably: **characters, character highlighting, A, BASEFONT, BR, IMG, MAP, <u>NOSCRIPT</u>, SCRIPT, <u>SPACER</u>, <u>WBR</u>,**

                APPLET, <u>EMBED</u>, <u>NOEMBED</u>, *OBJECT*

Can Be Inside: Unspecified; probably: **ADDRESS, BLOCKQUOTE, BODY, CENTER, DIV, FORM, <u>MULTICOL</u>, PRE,**

                Hn, DD, DT, LI, P, TD, TH, APPLET, <u>NOEMBED</u>, *OBJECT*

A, CAPTION, character highlighting

Attributes: none

Figure 5.14 Rendering, using Internet Explorer 3 browser, of the HTML document shown in Figure 5.12. This browser does not understand the MULTICOL and SPACER elements.

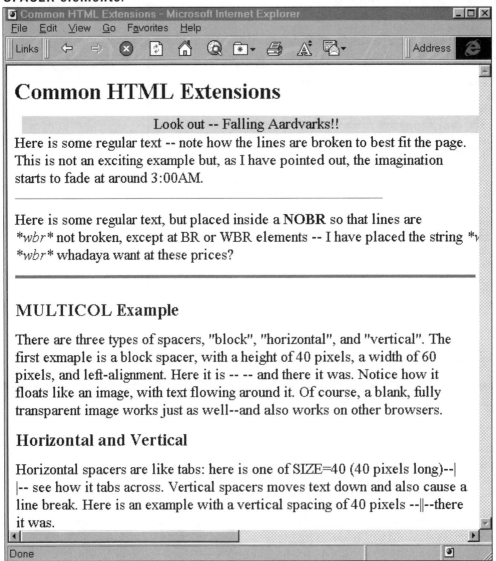

BLINK marks the enclosed text as blinking—browsers generally flash this text on and off. **BLINK** affects only enclosed text, and has no effect on enclosed images, **FORM** input elements (although regular text inside a **FORM** can be rendered as blinking), or list item markers (bullets, numbers, etc.).

NOTE: BLINK Not Supported by Internet Explorer In principle, you should explicitly mark each block of text (paragraph, list item, etc.) for blinking, as opposed to marking large blocks (several paragraphs and lists) of the document. In practice, you can use a single <BLINK> tag to mark an entire document as blinking, and thereby drive your readers crazy.

The slightest mention of the **BLINK** element causes formal HTML language designers to pull out crosses, garlic, and wooden stakes and begin chanting, in rising voices, "evil, evil, horrible evil!!" It is, therefore, unlikely that **BLINK** will be integrated into the official HTML specification.

For obvious reasons, there are no **BLINK** examples given in the figures.

EMBED Element: Embed an Arbitrary Data Object

Usage:	<EMBED>
Can Contain:	empty
Can Be Inside:	ADDRESS, BLOCKQUOTE, BODY, CENTER, DIV, FORM, <u>MULTICOL</u>, PRE, Hn, DD, DT, LI, P, TD, TH, NOEMBED, *OBJECT*, A, CAPTION, character highlighting
Attributes:	ALIGN, BORDER, FRAMEBORDER, HEIGHT, HIDDEN, HSPACE, NAME, PALETTE, PLUGINSPAGE, *P_NAME* (arbitrary name value), SRC, TYPE, VSPACE, WIDTH

EMBED specifies an arbitrary data object to be embedded within the document—for example an audio file, a special-format graphic file, or a spreadsheet. Display of embedded objects requires extra functionality on a browser, usually provided by browser *plug-ins*—product- or data-format-specific modules that are loaded into the browser whenever the corresponding data format is accessed.

The **NOEMBED** element can be used to provide an HTML alternative to the embedded data for use by browsers that do not support the **EMBED** element or that cannot process the specified embedded data type. The use of **NOEMBED** is described later in this section.

NOTE: EMBED to Be Replaced by OBJECT The **EMBED** element design has many problems; in particular its violation of important SGML syntax rules and the inability to specify alternative or preferred plug-ins for handling a given data type. **EMBED** will very soon be replaced by the more sophisticated **OBJECT** element, described later in this chapter.

Some examples of plug-ins were shown in Example 10 in Chapter 2. The attributes supported by **EMBED** are:

ALIGN="top", "middle", "bottom", "left", "right" (optional) Specifies the alignment of the embedded object on the page. The meanings are the same as for the **IMG** element, as described in Chapter 4.

BORDER="*number*" (optional) Specifies the size, in pixels, of the border to be drawn around the displayed object. The default is to have no border.

HEIGHT="*number*" (mandatory) Specifies the height of the embedded object, in pixels. This is mandatory, as the browser has no other way of knowing the size of the object. Most standard plug-in modules are distributed with recommended heights and widths—if you don't know the correct size, just try experimenting until you find appropriate values.

HIDDEN="true", "false" (optional) Specifies whether the plug-in is displayed in the document ("false") or is hidden from view ("true"). The default value is "false".

HSPACE="*number*" (optional) Specifies a horizontal spacing, in pixels, to be left to the left and right of the plug-in. The default value is zero.

NAME="*string*" (optional) Specifies a *symbolic name* for the embedded object. This allows the object to be referenced by other objects, scripts, or applets embedded in the document, thereby allowing objects to communicate with each other.

PALETTE="background", "foreground" (optional) Specifies the color palette to use in rendering the object, in terms of the default colors used by the browser. This is relevant only for Microsoft Windows platforms.

PLUGINSPACE="*url*" (optional) Specifies the URL of a document containing instructions as to how to obtain the plug-in required by the **EMBED**ded object. If the browser does not have an appropriate plug-in, it will inform the user of this fact and will optionally link to this supporting resource.

P_NAME="*string*" (optional) Specifies names and values required by the embedded object. ***P_NAME*** is an arbitrary name, and "*string*" is a value to associate with the name. These names and values are passed to the plug-in program that displays the object, so that the names and values must have meaning for that plug-in.

SRC=*"url"* (one of **TYPE** or **SRC** mandatory) Specifies the URL for the data object to be inserted into the document.

TYPE=*"MIME_type"* (one of **TYPE** or **SRC** mandatory) Specifies the MIME type for the embedded object. This is used in place of **SRC** when the plug-in requires no data, or when the plug-in obtains the data itself.

VSPACE=*"number"* (optional) Specifies a vertical spacing, in pixels, to be left above and below the plug-in. The default value is zero.

WIDTH=*"number"* (mandatory) Specifies the height of the embedded object, in pixels. This is mandatory as the browser has no other way of knowing an object's size. Most standard plug-in modules are distributed with recommended heights and widths—if you don't know the correct size, just try experimenting until you find appropriate values.

MARQUEE Element: A Scrolling Text Marquee (Internet Explorer only)

Usage:	`<MARQUEE> ... </MARQUEE>`
Can Contain:	**characters**
Can Be Inside:	Unspecified; probably: **ADDRESS, BLOCKQUOTE, BODY, CENTER, DIV, FORM, <u>MULTICOL</u>, PRE,**
	Hn, DD, DT, LI, P, TD, TH, APPLET, <u>NOEMBED</u>, *OBJECT*,
	A, CAPTION, character highlighting
Attributes:	**ALIGN, BEHAVIOR, BGCOLOR, DIRECTION, HEIGHT, HSPACE, LOOP, SCROLLAMOUNT, SCROLLDELAY, VSPACE**

MARQUEE denotes a text string to be scrolled horizontally on the display; the content of the element is the text to be scrolled. **MARQUEE** takes a number of attributes to control the size and placement of the marquee on the page (**ALIGN, HEIGHT, HSPACE,** and **VSPACE**), and to control the behavior of the scrolled text (**BEHAVIOR, DIRECTION, LOOP, SCROLLAMOUNT, SCROLLDELAY**). **BGCOLOR** specifies a background color specific to the marquee text.

Example of **MARQUEE**:

```
<MARQUEE ALIGN="middle" HSPACE="10" LOOP="-1" SCROLLAMOUNT="1"
   SCROLLDELAY="4">Look out -- Falling Aardvarks!!</MARQUEE>
```

This marquee is shown in Figures 5.12 through 5.14. Figure 5.14 catches the scrolling marquee in action—pretty boring in print, isn't it? Figure 5.13 shows what happens when a browser does not understand **MARQUEE**. In this case there is no marquee, but the browser can use any surrounding emphasis elements (here **B** and **I**) to mark the marquee text in a special way.

ALIGN="top", "middle", "bottom" (optional) Specifies the alignment of the text following **MARQUEE** with the marquee itself. **ALIGN**="top" means that the top of the text following **MARQUEE** should align with the top of the **MARQUEE**. **ALIGN**="middle" means that the middle of the text following the **MARQUEE** should be aligned with the middle of the MAR-QUEE. **ALIGN**="bottom" means that the bottom of the text following the **MARQUEE** should be aligned with the bottom of the **MARQUEE**. The default alignment is "bottom".

Note that a **MARQUEE** is treated like a large word or character, so that at most there is one line of text to the right of a marquee—subsequent text flows below the marquee element. **MARQUEE** is also always left-aligned, unless it is inside a **CENTER**.

BEHAVIOR="scroll", "slide", "alternate" (optional) Specifies how the marquee text should scroll. The value "scroll" means that the text should start from beyond one margin (left or right) and scroll completely across to the other margin, and disappear completely, while "slide" means that the text should start from beyond one margin (left or right) and scroll onto the screen until it touches the other margin, whereupon it should cease scrolling. "Alternate" means that the text should bounce back and forth between the left- and right-hand margins of the **MARQUEE**. The default is **BEHAVIOR**="scroll".

BGCOLOR="#rrggbb", "color" (optional) Specifies the background color for the marquee, either as an RGB code or by using a color name. **MARQUEE** only supports the basic 16 colors names given in Table F.1

DIRECTION="left", "right" (optional) Specifies the scrolling direction for the text: "left" means that the text will scroll from left to right, while "right" means the text will scroll from right to left. The default value is "left".

HEIGHT=" number", "number%" (optional) Specifies the height of the marquee. This height can be specified either in pixels or as a percentage of the display window height. You should be careful not to make the **MARQUEE** too thin, as this will obscure the marquee text. The default will be just tall enough to contain the text in the selected font and font size.

HSPACE="number" (optional) Specifies the margin, in pixels, to leave to the left and right of the **MARQUEE**. The default value is 0.

LOOP=" number", "infinite" (optional) Specifies the number of times the marquee will loop before stopping. The values **LOOP**="–1" or **LOOP**="infinite" cause the marquee to loop forever. The default is "–1".

SCROLLAMOUNT="number" (optional) Specifies the number of pixels between subsequent redraws of the marquee text—a large value yields a marquee that jumps rapidly across the screen, while a small value yields smoothly scrolled text.

SCROLLDELAY=*"number"* (optional) Specifies the time delay, in milliseconds, between subsequent redraws of the marquee text—a small value results in a rapidly scrolling marquee.

VSPACE=*"number"* (optional) Specifies the margin, in pixels, to leave above and below the **MARQUEE**. The default value is 0.

WIDTH=*" number"*, *"number%"* (optional) Specifies the width of the marquee. This width can be specified either in pixels or as a percentage of the display window width. You should be careful not to make the **MARQUEE** too narrow, as the text content may then be hard to read.

MULTICOL Element: Multicolumn Text (Netscape Navigator only)

Usage:	`<MULTICOL>...</MULTICOL>`
Can Contain:	Unspecified; probably: **characters, character highlighting, A, <u>BASEFONT</u>, BR, IMG, MAP, <u>NOSCRIPT</u>, SCRIPT, <u>SPACER</u>, [ISINDEX], <u>WBR</u>,**
	INPUT, SELECT, TEXTAREA,
	APPLET, <u>EMBED</u>, <u>NOEMBED</u>, *OBJECT*,
	CENTER, Hn, P, HR, DIR, DL, MENU, OL, UL,
	ADDRESS, BLOCKQUOTE, DIV, FORM, <u>MULTICOL</u>, PRE, TABLE
Can Be Inside:	Unspecified; probably: **ADDRESS, BLOCKQUOTE, BODY, CENTER, DIV, FORM, <u>MULTICOL</u>,**
	DD, LI, TD, TH, APPLET, <u>NOEMBED</u>, *OBJECT*
Attributes:	**COLS, GUTTER, WIDTH**

MULTICOL specifies text to be displayed in multicolumn format, with the attributes specifying the number of columns to use and the spacing to leave between columns. Almost any **BODY** element can appear inside **MULTICOL**, but some, such as **BLOCKQUOTE,** can lead to odd formatting due to the browser's miscalculation of text lengths within the columns. Note also that embedding an image or object within columnar text will cause problems if the object is larger than the column width.

MULTICOL is allowed inside **MULTICOL**—but don't get carried away, or the text will look ridiculous! An example of **MULTICOL** is shown in Figures 5.12 and 5.13. Figure 5.14 shows how this document looks when viewed by a browser that does not understand **MULTICOL**. The text is still easy to read, although displayed in only one column.

COLS=*"number"* (mandatory) Specifies the number of columns to use. The default value is 1.

GUTTER=*"number"* (optional) Specifies the space to leave between the columns, in pixels. The default value is 10.

WIDTH=*"number"*, *"number%"* (optional) Specifies the width for the entire collection of columns, either as an absolute width, in pixels (*number*) or as a percentage of the available width (*number%*).

NOBR Element: No Line Break

Usage	`<NOBR>...</NOBR>`
Can Contain:	Unspecified; probably: **characters, character highlighting**
	A, BASEFONT, BR, IMG, MAP, <u>NOSCRIPT</u>, SCRIPT, <u>SPACER</u>, <u>WBR</u>,
	INPUT, SELECT, TEXTAREA,
	APPLET, <u>EMBED</u>, <u>NOEMBED</u>, *OBJECT*
Can Be Inside:	Unspecified; probably: ADDRESS, BLOCKQUOTE, BODY, CENTER, DIV, FORM, <u>MULTICOL</u>,
	Hn, DD, DT, LI, P, TD, TH, APPLET, <u>NOEMBED</u>, *OBJECT*,
	A, CAPTION, **character highlighting**
Attributes:	none

NOBR marks a block of text that cannot contain line breaks. Thus, a block of text enclosed by a **NOBR** will be presented as a single line of text with no word wrapping, even if it scrolls off the edge of the screen. This is useful for strings of text that you do not wish broken at word spaces, regardless of the page layout.

In this context, however, an author may wish to allow word breaks, but only at specific locations. This is the role of the **WBR** element, which is used inside **NOBR** to mark places where line breaking is allowed. **WBR** is essentially a conditional **BR** element, in that it does not force a line break, but instead permits one where a break would otherwise be forbidden.

NOEMBED Element: HTML Alternative to EMBED

Usage	`<NOEMBED>...</NOEMBED>`
Can Contain:	Unspecified; probably: **characters, character highlighting**, A, BR, IMG, MAP, <u>NOSCRIPT</u>, SCRIPT, <u>SPACER</u>, [ISINDEX], <u>WBR</u>,
	INPUT, SELECT, TEXTAREA,

APPLET, EMBED, NOEMBED, *OBJECT,*

CENTER, Hn, P, HR, DIR, DL, MENU, OL, UL,

ADDRESS, BLOCKQUOTE, DIV, FORM, PRE, TABLE, MULTICOL

Can Be Inside: Unspecified; probably: ADDRESS, BLOCKQUOTE, BODY, CENTER, DIV, FORM, MULTICOL,

DD, LI, TD, TH, APPLET, *OBJECT*

Attributes: None

When the Netscape programmers introduced the **EMBED** element, they realized that many browsers would be unable to process the element, or might not have a plug-in capable of processing the embedded object or data type. Consequently, they introduced a second element, **NOEMBED**, to contain HTML markup to be used in place of the **EMBED** object should the browser be unable to process **EMBED**. A browser that understands **EMBED** and that can process the referenced data will display the **EMBED**ded object, and will hide the content of **NOEMBED**. On the other hand, a browser that does not understand **EMBED** will ignore the **EMBED** and **NOEMBED** tags, and will treat the content of the **NOEMBED** element as additional HTML markup to be displayed with the document.

The appropriate use of **NOEMBED** is to place the **NOEMBED** element just after the associated **EMBED**—for example:

```
<EMBED SRC="screaming-penguins.au" HEIGHT="100" WIDTH="200">
<NOEMBED>
    <H3> The Sound of The Screaming Penguins</H3>
    <P>If you are reading this text, then your browser does not support EMBED, and
    is unable to play the embedded audio snipped. You are missing the exciting
    musical texturings of the new jazz quintet <EM>The Screaming Penguins</EM>.
    You can pick up their debut album at a record store near your.
</NOEMBED>
```

Recall that **EMBED** is soon to be replaced by **OBJECT**. **OBJECT** provides much better mechanisms for embedding arbitrary data or program objects, and also has a better mechanism for providing alternative HTML content for browsers that do not support the specified embedded object.

SPACER Element: Horizontal and Vertical Spacing (Netscape Navigator only)

Usage: `<SPACER>`

Can Contain: empty

Can be Inside:	Unspecified; probably: **ADDRESS, BLOCKQUOTE, BODY, CENTER, DIV, FORM, <u>MULTICOL</u>,**
	Hn, DD, DT, LI, P, TD, TH, APPLET, <u>NOEMBED</u>, *OBJECT,*
	A, CAPTION, character highlighting
Attributes:	ALIGN, HEIGHT, SIZE, TYPE, WIDTH

SPACER introduces arbitrary horizontal or vertical spacing within typed text. **TYPE**="block" spacing is analogous to inserting a transparent (invisible) image of size **HEIGHT** and **WIDTH**, and allows insertion of horizontal and vertical space at the same place. **TYPE**="horizontal" spacers introduce simple horizontal tab-like spacings of length specified by **SIZE**. **TYPE**="vertical" introduces a vertical tab, again with size specified by **SIZE**. In this case, however, the tab also implies a line break.

Some examples of **SPACER** are shown in Figures 5.12 through 5.14. Note in particular Figure 5.14, which shows the page as displayed by a browser that does not understand **SPACER**. Because **SPACER** so strongly affects formatting, pages that depend on **SPACER** can be almost unreadable by browsers that do not understand this element.

TIP: Use Fully Transparent Images Instead of SPACER A fully transparent image can be used to create indents similar to **SPACER**, but in a way that is understood on many browsers, not just Netscape Navigator. Simply create a fully transparent (blank) GIF image of some small size, for example 20 by 20 pixels. You then use **IMG** elements to create spacers of any size, simply by using the **HEIGHT** and **WIDTH** attributes to reshape the image. For example, to create a horizontal spacer 60 pixels long, use the tag:

```
<IMG SRC="blank.gif" HEIGHT="1" WIDTH="60">
```

which resizes the image to be 1 pixel high and 60 pixels wide.

The allowed **SPACER** attributes are:

ALIGN="top", "middle", "bottom", "left", "right" (mandatory: **TYPE**="block" only) Specifies the page alignment for the spacer, relevant for **TYPE**="block" spacers only. Such spacers are treated in the same manner as images, so that the alignment options have the same meanings as for the **IMG** element.

HEIGHT="*number*" (mandatory: **TYPE**="block" only) Specifies the height, in pixels, of the spacer. This is relevant only for **TYPE**="block".

SIZE="*number*" (mandatory: **TYPE**="horizontal" or "vertical" only) Indicates the horizontal or vertical dimension of the spacer, in pixels: This attribute is relevant only for **TYPE**="horizontal" or "vertical" spacers. The effect is similar to a horizontal or vertical tab.

TYPE="block", "horizontal", "vertical" (mandatory) Specifies the type of the spacer. A "block" spacer is analogous to an invisible image; you must also specify the **HEIGHT, WIDTH,** and desired **ALIGN**ment of this type of spacer. **TYPE**="horizontal" or **TYPE**="vertical" are analogous to tabs—in these cases, the only required attribute is **SIZE**, which specifies the tab size. Note that a "vertical" spacer also introduces a line break.

WIDTH="*number*" (mandatory: **TYPE**="block" only) Specifies the width, in pixels, of the spacer. This is relevant only for **TYPE**="block".

WBR Element: Word Break

Usage:	<WBR>
Can Contain:	empty
Can Be Inside:	Unspecified; probably: **ADDRESS, BLOCKQUOTE, BODY, CENTER, DIV, FORM, <u>MULTICOL</u>, PRE,**
	Hn, DD, DT, LI, P, TD, TH, APPLET, <u>NOEMBED</u>, *OBJECT*,
	A, CAPTION, character highlighting
Attributes:	none

WBR marks a word space, within a **NOBR** element, where a word break is allowed. **WBR** does not force a break, but simply tells the browser where a word break is allowed, should one be needed. **WBR** is only meaningful within a **NOBR**.

Embedding OBJECTs in HTML

The **OBJECT** element is a proposed standards-based element designed to augment and replace the current embedding elements **IMG, EMBED,** and **APPLET. OBJECT** is still under development, although the specification appears quite stable, so that the following description is likely to reflect the properties of the standardized element. To assist you further, URLs referencing the specification documents are listed at the end of the chapter.

OBJECT can take most HTML elements as content. In particular, **PARAM** elements within an **OBJECT** specify parameters that are passed to the object when it is invoked, as was the case for **PARAM** elements inside an **APPLET**. Almost all other markup inside **OBJECT** is ignored by a browser that supports **OBJECT,** and that also supports the object being embedded. However, if a browser does not understand **OBJECT,** or does not support the particular embedded object, it should take the HTML content and display it instead. Thus the content of **OBJECT** serves as an HTML alternative for users who are unable to view the object itself.

Note, in particular, that you can currently code documents using the **OBJECT** element, while including the old pre-**OBJECT** markup inside. Thus if you already have markup using **EMBED** elements, you can include these elements inside an **OBJECT**. Browsers that do not understand **OBJECT** will then, if capable, implement the **EMBED** instructions.

It is easiest to give a flavor of the **OBJECT** element using some simple examples, and that is the approach we shall take here. A detailed description of the **OBJECT** element and attributes follows this overview.

NOTE: Limited Support for OBJECT Elements At time of publication, **OBJECT** is only supported by Internet Explorer 3, and even then only partially—Internet Explorer 3 does not support **OBJECT** embedding of simple data types (e.g., video or images), and does not support **OBJECT**-based client-side imagemaps, as described in the following paragraph. However, note that *all* major browser vendors have announced that they will support the full **OBJECT** element specification by early 1997.

OBJECT-Based Imagemaps—The SHAPES Attribute

There are several ways **OBJECT** can be used to create client-side imagemaps. The recommended form makes use of a proposed extension to the anchor element. An example of this is shown in the HTML document listed in Figure 5.15.

As with **IMG**, the **OBJECT** element **ALIGN, HEIGHT,** and **WIDTH** attributes specify the desired alignment, height, and width for the displayed object (the image). The **SHAPES** attribute tells the browser that this object is an imagemap—as a result, the browser looks inside the **OBJECT** element for anchor elements containing the new **SHAPE** and **COORDS** attributes, which in turn contain the map coordinate information. If a browser does not support **OBJECT**, then the user will see the enclosed list of hypertext anchors as regular HTML markup. Thus the approach provides fully functional links or imagemaps regardless of the browser's capabilities.

OBJECT-Based Imagemaps—The USEMAP Attribute

For compatibility with the **MAP** element approach to client-side imagemaps (see Chapter 4), **OBJECT** also supports a **USEMAP** attribute, equivalent to the **USEMAP** attribute of the **IMG** element. Figure 5.16 shows a **USEMAP** equivalent to the client-side imagemap first given in

---

Figure 5.15 Client-side imagemaps using OBJECT and special A element attributes.

```
<OBJECT DATA="activeimage.gif" SHAPES  ALIGN="left" HEIGHT="200" WIDTH="180">
    <A HREF="intro.html" SHAPE="rect" COORDS="20,20,60,40">Introduction</A> |
    <A HREF="welcome.html" SHAPE="circle" COORDS="70,70,10">Welcome</A> |
    <A HREF="blobby.html" SHAPE="poly"
        COORDS="100,100, 100,110, 110, 120, 90, 130">Visit Mr. Blobby!</A> |
    <A HREF="help.html" SHAPE="default">Help</A>
</OBJECT>
```

Figure 5.16 Client-side imagemaps using OBJECT and MAP elements.

```
<OBJECT DATA="activeimage.gif" USEMAP="#mapref" ALIGN="left"
        HEIGHT="200" WIDTH="180"> >
... alternative markup ...
</OBJECT>
<MAP NAME="mapref">
    <AREA HREF="intro.html" SHAPE="rect" COORDS="20,20,60,40"
        ALT="Introduction">
    <AREA HREF="welcome.html" SHAPE="circle" COORDS="70,70,10"
        ALT="Welcome">
    <AREA HREF="blobby.html" SHAPE="poly"
        COORDS="100,100, 100,110, 110, 120, 90, 130"
        ALT="Visit Mr. Blobby!">
    <AREA HREF="help.html" SHAPE="default"
        ALT="help">
</MAP>
```

Figure 5.15. The imagemap results are essentially the same as those described in the previous section, although this approach does not provide a simple HTML text alternative for browsers that do not support **OBJECT**.

OBJECT-Based Imagemaps—Mixed Client-Side and Server-Side

The **OBJECT** element proposals also add an **ISMAP** attribute to the anchor element, for use only when an **A** is inside an **OBJECT** taking the **SHAPES** attribute. **ISMAP** indicates that this anchor is associated with a *server-side* imagemap—if the shape corresponding to this anchor is selected, the data should be encoded and sent to the server as per a traditional **ISMAP** active image. For example, Figure 5.17 shows the same image map example as Figure 5.15, modified so that one of the anchors (**SHAPE**="poly") takes the **ISMAP** attribute.

If the user selects a point inside the rectangle or circle, or outside all of the declared shapes, the browser retrieves the indicated URL. However, if the user selects a region inside the polygon, the browser will measure the coordinates of the selection and send these coordinates to the indicated URL, encoded as per the server-side imagemapping approach discussed in Chapters 4 and 10.

Figure 5.17 Mixed client-side and server-side imagemaps using OBJECT and special A element attributes.

```
<OBJECT DATA="activeimage.gif" SHAPES ALIGN="left" HEIGHT="200" WIDTH="180">
  <A HREF="intro.html" SHAPE="rect" COORDS="20,20,60,40">Introduction</A> |
  <A HREF="welcome.html" SHAPE="circle" COORDS="70,70,10">Welcome</A> |
  <A HREF="cgi-bin/imagemap/database" SHAPE="poly"
     COORDS="100,100, 100,110, 110,120, 90,130"
     ISMAP >Visit Mr. Blobby!</A> |
  <A HREF="help.html" SHAPE="default">Help</A>
</OBJECT>
```

OBJECT Embedding of Arbitrary Data

Prior to **OBJECT**, the **EMBED** element was used to embed arbitrary data types, such as audio files, VRML scenes, and so on. These are all possible using **OBJECT**. For example, to include anExcel spreadsheet within a document, the markup could be:

```
<OBJECT  DATA="spreadsheet.xls" HEIGHT="400" WIDTH="300" HSPACE="5" VSPACE="4"
         TYPE="application/vnd.ms-excel">
   <P>Sorry, but your browser is unable to display the embedded Excel
   spreadsheet. If you wish, you can choose to
   <A HREF="spreadsheed.xls">download</A> the spreadsheet and view it
   externally.</P>
</OBJECT>
```

The **HSPACE** and **VSPACE** attributes provide a padding space around the object, as with **IMG** elements. Note that the **HEIGHT** and **WIDTH** must be specified here, as otherwise the browser has no idea of the space it needs to assign for the embedded data. The **TYPE** attribute indicates the MIME type of the data to be downloaded—in principle, a browser could choose not to download the data, should it know it is not capable of displaying it.

OBJECT Embedding of Applets

Applets are included in a similar manner, but require different attributes. A simple example is:

```
<OBJECT CLASSID="./applets/Testapp.class" ALIGN="left">
 .... HTML alternative to applet ...
</OBJECT>
```

Here **CLASSID** specifies the class ID for the applet to be run—this can either be a regular URL pointing to a file (as in this example) or a special class-related URL that specifies a generic class ID for the desired applet. In the latter case, the actual location of the code is specified by the **CODEBASE** attribute. If **CODEBASE** is absent, the value defaults to the same URL as that of the document containing the **OBJECT** element. An example showing this approach is:

```
<OBJECT CLASSID="java:program.start" ALIGN="left"
        CODEBASE="./applets/"
        CODETYPE="application/java-vm">
 .... HTML alternative to applet ...
</OBJECT>
```

Here **CODETYPE** specifies the MIME type of the code, and can be used by the browser to skip loading the referenced applet, should the browser not support this code type.

OBJECT Referencing Both Data and Data Handler

Finally, an object can reference both the code to be executed and the data that should be processed by the code. For example, the following **OBJECT** element specifies both a data file and a special Java applet that should process the data:

```
<OBJECT  DATA="http://www.whoopee.com/test/frogs.cpt"
         TYPE="application/hdf"
         CLASSID="java:dataanal.hdf.start"
         CODEBASE="http://hdf.ncsa.uiuc.edu/java-apps/"
         CODETYPE="application/java-vm">
  <P>Sorry, but the browser was unable to load the Java applet that
  processes the referenced HDF data file. If you have local software
  to analyze HDF data files, please select
  <A HREF=" http://www.whoopee.com/test/frogs.cpt">here</A>
  to directly download the data.</P>
</OBJECT>
```

In this case, the referred handler (a Java program) is located on a remote server. This need not be the case, and **CLASSID** could just as easily reference software on the client (i.e., plug-ins), or it could reference a generic handler, which might be local or on a remote server—the browser would then use some appropriate mechanism to locate the required package. This reiterates the flexibility offered by **OBJECT**.

Nested OBJECTS

OBJECT elements can be nested, allowing a cascade of possible object embeddings and handlers. An example of the associated **OBJECT** markup is (commentary in italics):

```
<OBJECT  ... (preferred data/handler) >
  <OBJECT ... (second choice ...) >
    <OBJECT ... (third choice ...) >
       HTML alternative to OBJECT ...
    </OBJECT>
  </OBJECT>
</OBJECT>
```

The browser would then work its way in through the **OBJECT**s, stopping when it finds one it can successfully process, and ignoring any subsequent **OBJECT**s.

Backward Compatibility

To a large extent, **OBJECT** elements are backward-compatible with browsers that do not understand **OBJECT**. For example, **OBJECT** elements used to invoke imagemaps can contain, as an alternative, the regular **IMG** element markup, while more complex **OBJECT**s might contain **EMBED** elements with similar or equivalent functionality. These options, however, hinge on proper support of **OBJECT**—at present, the Microsoft Internet Explorer 3 implementation is incomplete, such that this approach is not yet possible.

The specification for **OBJECT** is presented below. This is followed by an overview of the changes to the **PARAM** and **A** elements introduced to support **OBJECT**.

OBJECT Element: Embed an Arbitrary Data/Program Object

Usage:	`<OBJECT>...</OBJECT>`
Can Contain:	Unspecified; probably: **characters, character highlighting**, A, BASEFONT, BR, IMG, MAP, <u>NOSCRIPT</u>, SCRIPT, <u>SPACER</u>, <u>WBR</u>,
	INPUT, SELECT, TEXTAREA,
	APPLET, <u>EMBED</u>, <u>NOEMBED</u>, *OBJECT*,
	ADDRESS, BLOCKQUOTE, BODY, CENTER, DIV, FORM, <u>MULTICOL</u>, PRE, TABLE
Can Be Inside:	Unspecified; probably: ADDRESS, BLOCKQUOTE, BODY, CENTER, DIV, FORM, <u>MULTICOL</u>, PRE,
	Hn, DD, DT, LI, P, TD, TH, <u>NOEMBED</u>, *OBJECT*,
	A, CAPTION, **character highlighting**
Attributes:	*ALIGN, BORDER, CLASSID, CODEBASE, CODETYPE, DATA, DECLARE, HEIGHT, HSPACE, NAME, SHAPES, STANDBY, TYPE, USEMAP, VSPACE, WIDTH*

ALIGN="baseline", "middle", "textbottom", "textmiddle", "texttop", "center", "left", "right" (optional) Specifies the desired alignment of the object. The values are different from the standard **IMG** element alignment attributes, but provide the same general functionality. The default value is "middle".

TYPE="baseline"—Vertically aligns the bottom of the object with the baseline of the text surrounding the object.

TYPE="middle"—Vertically aligns the middle of the object with the baseline of the text surrounding the object. This is the default value.

TYPE="textbottom"—Vertically aligns the bottom of the object with the bottom of the text surrounding the object.

TYPE="textmiddle"—Vertically aligns the middle of the object with the middle of the text surrounding the object.

TYPE="texttop"—Vertically aligns the top of the object with the top of the text surrounding the object.

TYPE="center"—Centers the object between the left and right margins. Text before the object appears above the object, and text after the object appears below.

TYPE="left"—Floats the object downwards and to the left margin. Subsequent text can flow around the object, to its right. **HSPACE** and **VSPACE** specify a padding space to leave between the object and the surrounding text.

TYPE="right"—Floats the object downwards and to the right margin. Subsequent text can flow around the object, to its left. **HSPACE** and **VSPACE** specify a padding space to leave between the object and the surrounding text.

BORDER="*number*" (optional) Specifies the thickness of the border to be drawn around the object, should it be within an active anchor element. The thickness can be specified in any of the supported length units—at present, the only supported unit is pixels (the default), in which case the thickness is simply given as an integer. The value of "0" indicates that the object should be drawn without borders.

CLASSID="*string*" (optional) (one of **DATA** or **CLASSID** is required) Specifies the URL of the program code that will implement the object. In some cases, this is simply a class identifier, such as the **clsid** URL scheme supported by Microsoft for identifying Component Object Model (COM) objects.

CODEBASE="*string*" (optional) Specifies a URL that references program code required by the code specified by **CLASSID**, and which otherwise cannot be located by the **CLASSID** value. An example is a **CLASSID** that references an applet, with a **CODEBASE** that references the associated class/code library.

CODETYPE="*string*" Specifies the MIME type of the code referenced by the **CLASSID** attribute (**CLASSID** references the program object to be loaded). This is a hint to the browser—a browser can use this information to avoid downloading objects the browser does not support.

DATA="*string*" (optional) (one of **DATA** or **CLASSID** is required) Specifies the URL of the data to be loaded. This can, for example, be an image file, a spreadsheet data set, or a VRML world scene. **TYPE** can specify the MIME type of the data referenced by **DATA**. If **CLASSID** is absent, the browser will use the MIME type specified by **TYPE**, or the type determined by downloading the actual data file, to establish a program to handle the data type. In other words, the data type is used to determine an appropriate default value for **CLASSID**.

DECLARE (optional) Indicates that the object should be declared, but not *instantiated*. That is, the object is made available to the system, but not started until invoked by some other resource. This allows objects to be loaded for future use.

HEIGHT="*length*" (mandatory) Specifies the desired height of the box enclosing the object. This can be specified in any of the length units mentioned in the "Next-Generation HTML" section later in this chapter. At present, the only supported units are pixels (the default), in which case the height is simply given as an integer.

In principle, **HEIGHT** can be used to rescale the object to the specified height. Whether or not this is possible depends on the object being embedded.

HSPACE=*"length"* (optional) Specifies the desired horizontal spacing to leave to the left and right of the object. This can be specified in any of the length units mentioned in the "Next-Generation HTML" section later in this chapter. At present, the only supported units are pixels (the default), in which case the width is simply given as an integer.

ID=*"name"* (optional) Specifies a name token identifier for the object. This identifier can be used by the browser, script programs, or other objects embedded in the document to identify and communicate with the **ID**-labeled object.

NAME=*"string"* (optional) Specifies a variable name, analogous to the **NAME** attribute of the **SELECT, INPUT,** and **TEXTAREA** elements. This is only relevant if the **OBJECT** is inside a **FORM**. In this case, the presence of a **NAME** tells the browser that data from the object should be included with the form data when the form is submitted (it is the responsibility of the object author to ensure that the data is made available to the **FORM**, and in the correct format). If **NAME** is absent, then the object and the form are unrelated.

SHAPES (optional) Indicates that the content of the **OBJECT** contains anchor elements with hypertext links associated with regions ("shapes") within the area displayed by the object. This provides an **OBJECT**-based replacement for the active imagemap mechanisms of the **IMG** element.

STANDBY=*"string"* (optional) Specifies a short text string (including character and entity references, but not HTML markup) that can be displayed to the user while the object is loading.

TYPE=*"string"* (optional) Specifies the MIME type of the data referenced by the **DATA** attribute. This is a hint to the browser—a browser can in principle use this information to avoid downloading data types it does not support. In practice, however, a browser cannot definitively know the type until the data are actually accessed.

CLASSID can reference the code to properly handle the indicated data type. If **CLASSID** is absent, then **TYPE** is used to select an appropriate data handler.

USEMAP=*"string"* (optional) Specifies the URL of a client-side imagemap **MAP** element, as specified in Chapter 4. This gives **OBJECT** the same functionality as client-side imagemapped **IMG** elements.

VSPACE=*"length"* (optional) Specifies the desired vertical spacing to leave above and below the object. This can be specified in any of the length units mentioned in the "Next-Generation HTML" section later in this chapter. At present, the only supported units are pixels (the default), in which case the height is simply given as an integer.

WIDTH=*"length"* (mandatory) Specifies the desired width of the box enclosing the object. This can be specified in any of the length units mentioned in the "Next-Generation HTML" section later in this chapter. At present, the only supported units are pixels (the default), in which case the width is simply given as an integer.

In principle, **WIDTH** can be used to rescale the size of the object to the specified width. Whether or not this is possible depends on the object being embedded.

A Element: Hypertext Anchors

Usage: `<A> ... </A>`

Can Contain: probably: **characters, character highlighting, BASEFONT, BR, IMG, MAP, NOSCRIPT, SCRIPT, SPACER, WBR,**

                    APPLET, EMBED, NOEMBED, *OBJECT*

Can Be Inside: probably: **ADDRESS, BLOCKQUOTE, BODY, CENTER, DIV, FORM, PRE,**

                    Hn, DD, DT, LI, P, TD, TH, APPLET, NOEMBED, *OBJECT,*

                    CAPTION, character highlighting

Attributes: *CLASS, COORDS, DIR,* HREF, *ID, LANG,* NAME, *ONCLICK, ONMOUSEOUT, ONMOUSEOVER,* REL, REV, *SHAPE, STYLE,* TITLE

As in HTML 3.2, **A** marks a text or image block as the beginning and/or target of a hypertext link. However, within an **OBJECT**, **A** can support three new attributes that relate the anchor reference to regions within an image referenced by the **OBJECT**. The details of this mechanism were discussed previously in this section. The important attributes and their meanings are:

SHAPE="circle", "default", "poly", "rect" (optional: used inside **OBJECT** only; if present, then **COORDS** is also mandatory) **SHAPE** is valid only for anchor elements within **OBJECT** elements, as discussed previously. **SHAPE**, in combination with the **COORDS** attribute, defines active regions of the image referenced by an **OBJECT**, and attaches these regions to the remote resource indicated by the **HREF** attribute. **SHAPE** simply specifies the type of shape, the possible values being "circle", "default", "poly", and "rect".

COORDS="*string*" (optional: mandatory if **SHAPE** is present and if **SHAPE** is not equal to "default") Specifies the coordinates associated with the designated **SHAPE**, measured from the upper left-hand corner of the image. Coordinates can either be integer quantities, in which case they are measurements in pixels from the upper-left hand corner, or percentage values in the range (0%,0%) (the upper left-hand corner) to (100%, 100%) (lower right-hand corner).

The following table illustrates the appropriate use of coordinates for the different possible **SHAPE**s:

SHAPE	COORDS
"circle"	"*x, y, r*"—A circle centered at (*x,y*) and of radius *r*.
"rect"	"*x_top, y_top, x_bot, y_bot*"—A rectangle with upper-left hand coordinates (*x_top, y_top*) and lower right-hand coordinates (*x_bot, y_bot*).
"poly	"*x1, y1, ... xn, yn*"—A polygon, where the coordinates (*x1,y1*) ... (*xn,yn*) are the *vertices* of the polygon (minimum of three vertices). The polygon is closed by connecting the point (*x1,y1*) to (*xn, yn*).

ISMAP (optional: only valid inside **OBJECT**; if present, then **SHAPE** is also mandatory) Indicates that the shaped region is associated with a server-side imagemap. If a user selects within the region associated with this anchor, the user-selected coordinates (in pixels relative to the upper left-hand corner of the image) should be appended to the URL specified by the **HREF** attribute, and the resulting URL should be accessed using the GET method. This permits an **OBJECT** to reference, depending on the region of the image, client-side or server-side imagemap handlers.

The attributes **ONCLICK, ONMOUSEOVER**, and **ONMOUSEOUT** are described in the "Scripting in HTML Documents" section later in this chapter.

PARAM Element: Parameter inside an OBJECT

Usage:	<PARAM>
Can Contain:	empty
Can be Inside:	**APPLET**, *OBJECT*
Attributes:	**NAME**, *TYPE*, **VALUE**, *VALUETYPE*

The advanced **OBJECT** model supports extra attributes to **PARAM** elements inside an **OBJECT**. **VALUETYPE** specifies the type of the string being assigned to **VALUE**, and can take the three possible values "data", "object", or "ref". "Data" means that the **VALUE** string is data to be passed to the object, and that HTML entity and character references must be replaced by the referenced characters before the string is sent. The value "object" means that the assigned string is a reference pointing to another (possibly running) **OBJECT** within the same document. The value "ref" indicates that the value is a proper URL referencing a resource. If VALUETYPE="ref", then the optional **TYPE** attribute can be used to specify the MIME type of the referenced object.

NOTE: TYPE and VALUETYPE Not Widely Supported   At present, Microsoft Internet Explorer 3, the only browser to support **OBJECT**, does *not* support the **TYPE** and **VALUETYPE** attributes.

Stylesheets and HTML

Stylesheets are a mechanism for adding formatting and other typographic information to an HTML document, but in such a way that the HTML markup is largely unaffected. Stylesheets are supported by HTML through the addition of two new elements and three new general purpose attributes. This section describes the stylesheet mechanism, and how it is related to an HTML document.

Summary—New HTML Elements and Attributes

Stylesheet support requires the following new HTML elements and attributes. The uses of these new elements and attributes are discussed later in this section.

New HTML Elements	**STYLE** (introduced in Chapter 4), *SPAN*
New HTML Attributes	*CLASS*, *ID*, *STYLE*—supported by all **BODY** content elements *except* **AREA, CENTER, FONT, MAP, PARAM,** and **SCRIPT**
	REL="stylesheet"—supported by **LINK** element
	HTTP-EQUIV="Content-style-type"—supported by **META** element
Attribute Specifications	**CLASS=**"*string*" (optional)—*Subclasses* the element
identifier	**ID=**"*name*" (optional)—Gives the element a unique name token
element	**STYLE=**"*string*" (optional)—Provides stylesheet instructions for an

Stylesheets Overview

As mentioned throughout this book, HTML is a semantic markup language designed to describe the *meaning* and structure of a document, and not the physical presentation. And, as noted repeatedly, there are many advantages to this approach. First, semantic markup *adds* information about the text, by explaining what the text is for (e.g., headings, figures, or paragraphs) or what the text means (e.g., block quotations, address, or emphasis). In addition, the language model allows for alternate information content, for presentation by non-graphical or non-visual displays—examples include the **ALT** attribute content of **IMG** elements, or text contained within an **APPLET**. The net result is that carefully crafted HTML documents can, in principle, be presented by many different technologies, ranging from graphical displays to text-only displays to Braille readers to text-to-speech converters, with little loss of information content.

At the same time, no author wants to be limited to a semantic description alone. Authors and readers alike care how a document is presented or what it looks like, be it on paper, on a computer display, or in any other format. Each author or designer will have preferred ways of representing things such as headings, quotations, or emphasis, as well as background colors or textures, graphics, and so on. These issues fall under the general category of *style*—how do the different parts of the document look or feel? To be a fully functional markup language, HTML must support a mechanism whereby authors (or readers!) can specify the styles they want applied to the written words.

Up until recently, HTML largely ignored these issues. Browser software often gave the user limited control over the display (for example, users could select preferred background colors, font faces and sizes, and so on), while limited author-side control was possible through elements such as **FONT** or **BASEFONT,** or through attributes such as **ALIGN, BGCOLOR,** and so on. However, using elements and attributes to specify formatting details is not a good long-term solution—the documents soon become big, cumbersome, and impossible to maintain, largely because HTML simply was not designed to specify the page layout descriptions required for detailed layout control.

With HTML, as with all modern document systems, the preferred solution is to create a *second* mechanism for specifying formatting, separate from the markup. This is known as the *stylesheet* mechanism. Since a stylesheet is a separate piece of information, it can be maintained as a separate document. Indeed, multiple, different stylesheets can be written, with each display device (graphic display, printer, text-to-speech, etc.) selecting the style information appropriate for its display format.

As an example, a stylesheet might contain instructions such as:

```
H1 { font-size=24pt; font-family=arial; text-align: center; }
H2 { font-size=18pt; font-family=arial; text-align: left; }
EM {font-style=italics; }
```

which says:

> *"Center H1 headings on the page and display them using a 24-point Arial font"*
> *"Left-align H2 headings, and display them using 18-point Arial font"*
> *"Format text inside EM using an italics version of the current font"*

If a browser understands the stylesheet mechanism, as it loads an HTML document, it accesses the associated stylesheet information (mechanisms for finding this information are discussed later), and applies the stylesheet instructions to format the document. This lets authors suggest, through author-specified stylesheets, the preferred formatting prescriptions for their documents. I use the word "suggest" because the browser, or the user, always has the option of ignoring the style information, should it be inappropriate for some reason.

There are additional benefits to the stylesheet model. First, an author can develop a single stylesheet and apply it to all documents in a given collection. As a result, the work of developing a style can be shared amongst a number of documents, making life easier for the author, and giving the collection a common look and feel. Also, separating the style information from the HTML document means that the HTML document stays compact and easy to understand—it does not become cluttered with lots of device-specific formatting tags. It is far more difficult to write an HTML document if the author, each time, has to add all sorts of physical formatting hints. The author need only create a single stylesheet, and can then forget about this part of the problem and get back to creating the desired content.

Stylesheet Languages

So if stylesheets are so good, why are they not in active use? The answer is like the fable of the chicken and the egg. First, until recently there were no accepted *stylesheet languages*. Second, there was a lack of browser support for a stylesheet language—which makes sense, given the lack of such a language. These issues have finally been resolved, with two proposed stylesheet languages, and with several browsers vendors already developing support for them.

The language now being implemented on the Web is know as *cascading stylesheets*, or *CSS*. CSS was designed to be very simple to use and understand, so that most HTML authors should find it easy to construct CSS stylesheets. The second language is *DSSSL-Lite*, or *DSSSL-Online*. This is a "lite" version of *Document Style Semantics and Specification Language* (*DSSSL*), an extremely advanced (and complicated!) stylesheet language. DSSSL-Online is significantly more complicated than CSS, and in the long run may provide a more powerful approach to stylesheets than CSS.

At present, Internet Explorer 3 provides limited support for CSS stylesheets, while Netscape has promised support for CSS with the next release (Version 4) of their browser. CSS is still being refined, and the first version, known as CSS Level 1 or CSS1, should be formally released by early 1997. The following discussion is based on the current, preliminary, CSS1 specification.

Linking Stylesheets to HTML Documents

There are two ways to include stylesheet information in a document: either by using **LINK** to reference an external stylesheet, or by including stylesheet information within a **STYLE** element inside the document itself.

Linking to an External Stylesheet

In this approach, the stylesheet information is placed in a file separate from the HTML document. An HTML document then references the desired stylesheet using our old and underutilized friend, the **LINK** element. The relevant markup is

```
<LINK REL="stylesheet" TYPE="mime/type" HREF="url">
```

where the value **REL**="stylesheet" indicates that the target resource is a stylesheet, *url* is the URL pointing to the stylesheet document, and *mime/type* is the MIME type for the stylesheet—this allows for different stylesheet languages, each with its own MIME type. The currently supported CSS stylesheet language has the MIME type `text/css`; the type `application/dsssl` has been proposed for the DSSSL-Online language.

Stylesheets within the Document HEAD

Stylesheets can be also placed inside a **STYLE** element, which is, in turn, found in the document **HEAD**. A simple CSS example is:

```
<STYLE>
  BODY {
      font-family: times, serif;
      color: black ;
      margin-left: 10%;
      margin-right: 10%;
  }

  A:link { color: black; text-decoration: underline }
  A:visited { color: black; text-decoration: none }
</STYLE>
```

As far as formatting is concerned, there is no difference between placing the stylesheet in a separate file or in the **HEAD** of an HTML document. The advantage of the former, of course, is that the same stylesheet can be used by many different files, without the need for duplicating the information in the **HEAD** of every document.

Hiding Stylesheets from Older Browsers

Older browsers that do not understand stylesheets will think the **STYLE** content is body-content text, and will try to display the stylesheet instructions as document text—needless to say, this can look rather messy. The CSS specification lets authors enclose the entire stylesheet within an HTML comment, hiding the stylesheet from these older browsers and avoiding this problem. For example, the stylesheet in the previous example is hidden by using the markup (the extra comment tags are given in boldface):

```
<STYLE>
<!--
  BODY {
      font-family: times, serif;
...
  A:visited { color: black; text-decoration: none }
-->
</STYLE>
```

where the dotted lines indicate text omitted to save space.

META Specification of a Default Language

Of course, the **STYLE** element does not indicate the stylesheet language used by the enclosed data. It is currently proposed that **META** elements be used for this purpose. Using META, the default stylesheet language for a document is specified by:

```
<META HTTP-EQUIV="Content-style-type" CONTENT="type/subtype">
```

where *type/subtype* is the type of the stylesheet language. For CSS, this is simply:

```
<META HTTP-EQUIV="Content-style-type" CONTENT="text/css">
```

In the absence of this element, a browser may guess at the language, with unpredictable results.

Note that this **META** element format implies that the default stylesheet type can also be indicated by an HTTP server response header field of the form:

```
Content-style-type: type/subtype
```

(see Chapter 7 for more information about HTTP headers and the HTTP protocol). At present, there are no browsers that understand this particular header field or the associated **META** element.

Attaching Formatting to Elements

There are then several ways of associating stylesheet formatting information with HTML elements. Typically, stylesheet instructions specify the element to which the style should be applied. For example, the statement EM {font-style=italics;} says that all **EM** elements should be rendered in italics, while the statement A:visited {color:purple} says that the text inside *visited* hypertext anchors should be in the regular font, but purple in color. This simple mechanism lets CSS stylesheets easily specify generic characteristics for all elements of a particular type.

Stylesheets and the CLASS Attribute

In some cases, however, an author may wish to specify formatting specific to one particular instance of an element, and not another. For example, text within standard **DIV** elements may have no special formatting, whereas text within another **DIV** should be indented and in a slightly smaller font, to mark the fact, for example, that the enclosed text is part of an abstract.

Such element-specific variation is supported through element *subclassing*, made possible by the new **CLASS** attribute. **CLASS** is allowed with all **BODY** content elements (including **SPAN**—discussed later) except **AREA, CENTER, FONT, MAP, PARAM,** and **SCRIPT.** The elements in this exception list either do not affect the document presentation (**AREA, MAP, PARAM, SCRIPT**) or are formatting-specific elements (**FONT, CENTER**) that stylesheets are designed to replace. **CLASS** is intended for defining special logical characteristics associated with an element. For example, to indicate that a block of text is part of an abstract, the markup could be written:

```
<DIV CLASS="abstract">
<P>The spiny-bifurcated oyster is one of the most interesting, if poorly
 understood mollusks of the Eastern seaboard. In this overly long and tedious
paper, we ....
</DIV>
```

In a stylesheet, the author can then specify abstract-specific formatting with an instruction of the form:

```
DIV.abstract {
    font-size: 10pt;
    color: black ;
    margin-left: 15%;
    margin-right: 15%;
}
```

where the notation `DIV.abstract` relates these instructions to **DIV** elements with **CLASS**="abstract".

Nested Elements and CLASS Inheritance

An important characteristic of CSS is *inheritance*—unless a stylesheet states otherwise, an element *inherits* the characteristics of the element it is inside. Thus, in the preceding example, **P** elements (paragraphs) inside the **DIV** inherit the extra indents and 10-point font size specification from the surrounding **DIV**. This is possible because, in general, default formatting for elements is specified as rules *relative to* the elements they are contained within. For example, the default specification for **EM** is `EM {font-style:italics}`; which just italicizes whatever font face, size, or color the surrounding text may have.

Stylesheets and the ID Attribute

With stylesheets also comes the **ID** attribute: **ID** specifies a unique *name token* identifier for an element (no two **ID** values in a given document can be the same) and is actually intended as a general purpose replacement for the **NAME** attribute of anchor elements. However, **ID** is also used by CSS to provide a second way of associating style specifications with a specific element.

The mechanism is as follows. If an element is marked by an **ID** attribute, for example

```
<P ID="nut12"> A nutty paragraph, which will be
    rendered in a nutty way ....
...</P>
```

then style information can be tied to this specific paragraph through a CSS instruction of the form:

```
#nut12 {font-size: 42pt; color: #22FF3b;
        text-decoration: underline;
}
```

Note how similar this is to the fragment-identifier notation of URLs—the hash character, followed by the name, denotes an element **ID** value, and relates the associated stylesheet instruction to a particular and unique **ID**-labeled element.

You should preferentially use the **CLASS** mechanism to control styles, particularly if your styling has real structural meaning, such as "abstract", "product-name", product-info", and so on.

As with **CLASS**, **ID** is allowed with all elements (including **SPAN**—see below) except **AREA, CENTER, FONT, MAP, PARAM,** and **SCRIPT.** The more general purpose of **ID** is to act as an element label. In principle, a hypertext anchor can link to any **ID**-labeled element by using the **ID** value as a URL fragment identifier. For example, a paragraph labeled with the start tag `<P ID="gfx23">` could be referenced by the URL `http://some.where/path/document.html#gfx23`. This functionality is not supported by most current browsers.

STYLE Attribute—Element-Specific Formatting

Sometimes an author wants to apply style just to one element, and does not have the luxury of modifying the stylesheet document. In this case, the author can use a **STYLE** attribute to add element-specific formatting information within the element itself. An example is:

```
<P STYLE="font-family: times; font-size: 12pt">
    paragraph text ....</P>
```

The value of **STYLE** is simply a set of applicable stylesheet instructions, to be applied to the content of the element. **STYLE** is supported by all body-content elements (including **SPAN**) except **AREA, CENTER, FONT, MAP, PARAM,** and **SCRIPT.**

SPAN Element—Text-Specific Formatting

Last, the new **SPAN** element allows formatting to be tied to individual phrases, words, or letters, independent of any element-specific formatting. For example, the markup

```
<SPAN STYLE="color: red; text-decoration: line-through">
    some text </SPAN>
```

requests that the text inside the **SPAN** be rendered in red, with a line drawn through. **SPAN** is intended for use in setting stylistic features that have no logical meaning, in the sense of HTML markup elements. **SPAN** is discussed in the next section.

SPAN: Select a Span of Text for Special Formatting

Usage: `<SPAN> ... </SPAN>`

Can Contain: **characters, character highlighting A, BR, IMG, BASEFONT, MAP, <u>NOSCRIPT</u>, SCRIPT, <u>SPACER</u>, <u>WBR</u>,**

APPLET, <u>EMBED</u>, <u>NOEMBED</u>, *OBJECT*,

INPUT, SELECT, TEXTAREA

Can Be Inside: **ADDRESS, BLOCKQUOTE, BODY, CENTER, DIV, FORM, <u>MULTICOL</u>, PRE,**

Hn, DD, DT, LI, P, TD, TH, APPLET, <u>NOEMBED</u>, *OBJECT*,

A, CAPTION, character highlighting

Attributes: *CLASS, DIR, ID, LANG, STYLE*

SPAN marks text for special formatting by a stylesheet, and can be thought of as a general-purpose replacement for **FONT**. **SPAN** can take three optional attributes: **CLASS, ID,** and **STYLE**. The specifications are:

CLASS=*"string"* (optional) Specifies a subclass name for the element. *Subclassing* is used to define the special nature of an element, as in `<DIV CLASS="introduction">`, `<DIV CLASS="verse">`, and so on. Stylesheets can specify different formatting for different classes of the same element.

ID=*"name"* (optional) Specifies a unique identifier for the element, as a name token. Within a given document, no two elements can have the same **ID** value. In principle, **ID**-labeled elements can be the targets of hypertext links, as **ID** plays the same role as the **NAME** attribute of the anchor element. This aspect of **ID** is not supported by current browsers. Stylesheets can also reference **IDs**, and can apply formatting instructions to specific **ID**-labeled elements.

STYLE=*"string"* (optional) Contains stylesheet instructions that should be applied to the content of **SPAN**. There is no way of specifying the stylesheet language of the **STYLE** value.

DIR and **LANG** (optional) **DIR** and **LANG** are language-specific attributes, related to the internationalization of HTML. These are discussed in the Internationalization section later in this chapter.

Cascading Stylesheets Overview

The CSS specification is long, and this brief discussion is not intended as a replacement for the full CSS specification. However, some simple examples will help to give a feel for how the system works, and are useful for understanding how the CSS mechanism relates to HTML documents.

The following discussion refers to the example stylesheet shown in Figure 5.18. Lines 1 through 6 set the default document properties: left and right margins 10% in from the full width of the display, and black text. The `font-family` specification gives a list of preferred fonts, from left to right. Thus this stylesheet requests Gill font, followed by Times-Roman (if Gill is not available), followed by any serifed font should Times-Roman be absent. These font family names are specified in the CSS specifications. Lines 7 and 8 specify properties of anchored text: Line 7 indicates that unvisited links should be black, and with an underline, while line 8 indicates that visited links should be gray, and without an underline.

Lines 9 through 11 specify properties for headings. Line 9 states that **H1, H2,** and **H3** headings should all be in Arial font, or alternatively in a sans-serif font should Arial not be available.

Figure 5.18 Portion of a demonstration *cascading* stylesheet (CSS). The meanings of the various lines are discussed in the text. The italicized line numbers on the left are not part of the stylesheet, and are there for reference purposes only.

```
1      BODY {
2             font-family: gill, times, serif;
3             color: black ;
4             margin-left: 10%;
5             margin-right: 10%;
6      }
7      A:link          { color: black; text-decoration: underline }
8      A:visited       { color: gray; text-decoration: none }
9      H1 H2 H3        { font-family:  arial, sans-serif }
10     H2 H3           { margin-left:  2% }
11     H1              { text-align: center }
12     DIV.abstract    { margin-left: 15%;
13                       margin-right: 15%;
14                       font-size: smaller }
15     .goofy          { color: #FFFF00;
16                       font-family: arial;
17                       background: blue;
18                     }
19     @import url(http://www.java.utoronto.ca/styles/special.css)
```

Line 10 states that **H2** and **H3** headings should have only a 2% indent, so that they will hang to the left of the regular text, while line 11 states that **H1** headings should be centered between the margins.

Lines 12 through 14 specify the properties for text within **DIV**isions of **CLASS**="abstract". Inside such a **DIV**, the margins should be wider (15% of the display width), while the text should be in a font smaller than the regular font. Lines 15 through 18 state that *every* element of **CLASS**="goofy" should have text in the indicated color (as an RGB value—this is bright yellow), should be rendered in the Arial font, and should have the indicated background color (blue). Finally, line 19 imports an external stylesheet from the indicates URL, for inclusion with the current style specifications.

The HTML document in Figure 5.19 helps to demonstrate the effect of this stylesheet. Figure 5.20 shows this document formatted without the benefit of stylesheet formatting instructions, while Figure 5.21 shows the effect of the stylesheet instructions. Notice how the headings and indents in Figure 5.21 are just as specified by the stylesheet. The font size of the abstract, however, is actually larger than the regular font, even though the stylesheet requests a smaller font. This is simply a bug in this early Internet Explorer implementation of stylesheets.

Figure 5.19 Simple HTML document that includes the stylesheet listed in Figure 5.18. The rendering of this document by Web browsers is shown in Figures 5.20 and 5.21.

```
<HTML><HEAD>
<STYLE>
BODY {
    font-family: gill, times, serif;
            color: black ;
            margin-left: 10%;
            margin-right:10%;
       }
       A:link        { color: black; text-decoration: underline }
       A:visited     { color: gray; text-decoration: none }
       H1,H2,H3      { font-family:  arial,  sans-serif }
       H2,H3         { margin-left:  2% }
       H1            { text-align: center }
       DIV.abstract{ margin-left:  15%;
                        margin-right: 15%;
                        font-size: smaller; }
        .goofy       { color: #FFFF00;
                        font-family: arial;
                        background:  blue;
                     }
      @import url(http://www.java.utoronto.ca/styles/special.css)
</STYLE>
<TITLE>Test Of Stylesheets Document </TITLE>
</HEAD>
<BODY>
<H1>Big Stylesheets test</H1>
<DIV CLASS="abstract">
<P>This document tests stylesheet support. There are
   various stylesheet elements to modify presentation
   based on CLASS, or simply SPANning a group of letters.
<P>For example, if
   <A HREF="test.html">stylesheets are working</A>, this
   abstract should be in a slightly smaller font, with
   a slightly larger indent than the following paragraphs.
</DIV>
<H2>Level 2 Heading</H2>
<P>So, what did we get there?  Now, we will try doing some
   word specific formatting with the goofy style, as in
   <EM CLASS="goofy"> this line of text </EM>
<P>Was that interesting, or not?
<H3>A Level 3 Heading</H3>
<P>At this point, I will bring this example to an end. It
   is nothing terribly fancy, but it should illustrate the
   main features of stylesheets. We will see
```

Figure 5.19 (Continued)

```
<SPAN STYLE="{font-family: arial; font-size:60pt;
  background=url(testimg.gif)}"> HELLO</SPAN>
</BODY>
</HTML>
```

The last feature of interest is the word "Hello" at the bottom of Figure 5.21. This is in a large Arial font, on an image background. Looking to Figure 5.19, you will see that this is accomplished using a **SPAN** element with local **STYLE**-attribute stylesheet instructions.

It is clear that the stylesheet can strongly affect the presentation, and much more easily than simply by adding special, browser-specific HTML tags. Without doubt, this new technology will come to play an ever more important role in designing Web pages.

Figure 5.20 Rendering, by the Netscape Navigator 3 browser, of the document listed in Figure 5.19. This browser does not support stylesheets.

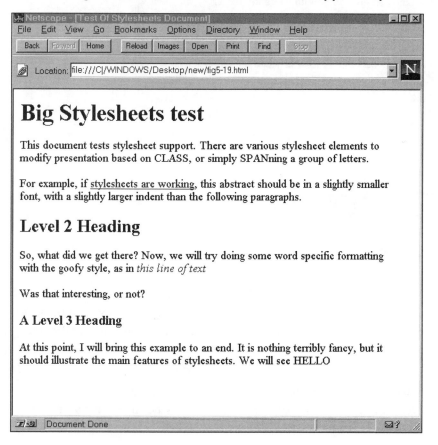

Figure 5.21 Rendering, by the Internet Explorer 3 browser, of the document listed in Figure 5.19. This browser does support stylesheets.

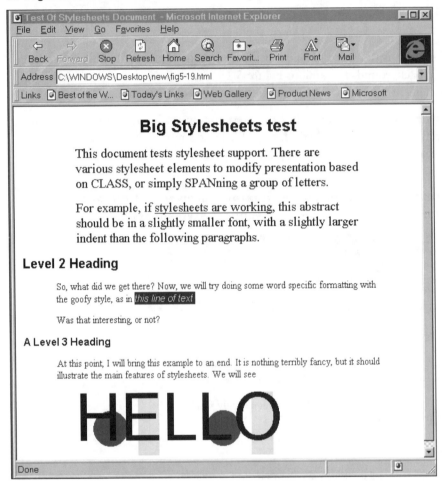

Cascading Properties

The above sections illustrated some of the cascading properties—styles cascade down from one element to other elements contained within it (e.g., from a **DIV** to all paragraphs within the **DIV**), until overridden by a specific declaration relevant to one of the interior elements (e.g., **DIV** content may be in Times-Roman, while a paragraph-specific instruction may override this font to Arial).

However, this does not cover the case where there are multiple stylesheet specifications for the same element. There are several ways this might happen. First, there may be an external stylesheet linked to the document, as well as internal stylesheet information within a **STYLE** element. Also, users may have their own default stylesheets, specified via a browser configuration file. Finally, there may be element-specific style information specified by **STYLE** attribute content, or by an **ID** label with corresponding style information in the stylesheet.

The CSS handles this kind of conflict through a sequence of complex cascading rules, which involve weighting different types of specifications and applying the formatting instructions in the order of increasing weights. In general, the instructions closer to a specific block of text override those further from it—that is, text-specific instructions will override block-specific instructions, which override generic document instructions. If two equivalent instructions are found, then the last one found is used. Finally, author-specified formatting instructions will override reader-specified stylesheet instructions, which in turn override a browser's default behavior.

There are many aspects of CSS that have been omitted from this brief discussion: CSS also supports style specifications for nested elements (e.g., how to format list items within a list that lies within another list), drop-cap lettering, horizontal and vertical spacing control, backgrounds, floating elements, boxing of elements, and so on. For details, you are referred to the CSS specifications, referenced at the end of this chapter.

Scripting in HTML Documents

New HTML Elements	**SCRIPT** (discussed in Chapter 4), <u>**NOSCRIPT**</u>, <u>**SERVER**</u>
New Attributes	**onBlur, onChange, onClick, onFocus, onLoad, onMouseOver, onMouseOut, onReset, onSelect, onSubmit, onUnload** (usage discussed later in this section)
	NAME (for **FORM** elements)
	MAYSCRIPT (for **APPLET** elements)
Modified Attributes	**TYPE**="button" supported for HTML **INPUT** elements

With the Navigator 2 browser, Netscape introduced the concept of *scripted* HTML documents. These are documents that contain, in addition to regular HTML markup, script programs that can process data passed from the HTML document (i.e., from **FORM** input, hypertext anchor selections, etc.) and also return output for inclusion within the HTML document, as it is rendered for display. To implement this functionality, Netscape developed a new scripting language, called JavaScript. This an object-derived language, similar in look and feel to Java or C but designed expressly for Web and HTML document-related scripting—the object model of JavaScript is based on the component structure of the browser (windows, status bars, document URLs, etc.) and of HTML documents (applets, embedded objects, forms, anchors, document body, images, etc.).

Microsoft quickly followed up Netscape's launch of scripted HTML, by implementing JavaScript support in their Internet Explorer 3 browser. However, Microsoft did not have access to all the internal details of the JavaScript language, so that their browser is not entirely compatible with the version of JavaScript supported by Netscape. Thus, if you are working in a mixed-platform environment, it is important to check your JavaScript programs with all possible browsers.

NOTE: Navigator 2/Navigator 3 Incompatibility   With Navigator 3, Netscape introduced several enhancements to JavaScript. Consequently, scripts that work with Navigator 3 may not function with Navigator 2.

Microsoft also implemented a second scripting language, known as VBScript (or Visual Basic Script). In terms of functionality, VBScript is similar to JavaScript, although the language is closer in design to Visual Basic, from which it is derived. However, the *interaction* between a document and a scripting language is largely independent of the language used, so that the information presented here is also largely applicable to VBScript programs.

In this section, we focus on the interaction between HTML documents and scripts, using some JavaScript programs as simple examples. Note, however, that this chapter is *not* a guide to JavaScript programming—the language is far too complex for this short section to do it justice. For details about the language, you are referred to the references listed at the end of the chapter.

General Scripting Issues

As mentioned in Chapter 4, document scripts are included within an HTML document via the HTML **SCRIPT** element. These elements can be in the **HEAD** or **BODY** of a document. It is strongly recommended that the bulk of the script appear in the **HEAD**; this is because of they way scripts are interpreted and executed. When a browser parses a document for script components, it starts at the beginning of the file and works downwards. As a result, any required functions must be defined *before* they are used—if this is not done, and the function is not defined at the time of its intended invocation, then the script will fail, claiming that the function is undefined. Consequently, function definitions are best placed in the **HEAD** of a document—that way they are guaranteed to be defined before the browser begins to lay out the document **BODY**.

Script programs can be included directly within an HTML document, or they can be included from external files. Some examples illustrating these two mechanisms are given in the following sections.

Including a Script within a SCRIPT Element

Figure 5.22 illustrates a simple JavaScript function definition, defined in a **SCRIPT** element that typically would lie in the document **HEAD** (since it defines a general-purpose function). This simple example illustrates a few of the important points that are relevant whenever a script is included within an HTML document.

Figure 5.22 Example SCRIPT element containing a single function definition. Note the use of the HTML comment tags (in boldface) to "hide" the element content from old browsers that do not understand the SCRIPT element.

```
<SCRIPT LANGUAGE="JavaScript">
<!-- Use Comments to "hide" script from old browsers
//     that don't understand scripts
//     The symbol // starts a comment line
function validate(obj, minV, maxV)) {
  var value = parseInt(obj.value);
  if( value < minVal || value > maxVal) {
     alert(obj.name + ' Not in range ('+minV+','+maxV+')' );
  }
}
//  End HTML comment that hides the script from old browsers  -->
</SCRIPT>
```

There are three critical things to note in Figure 5.22:

1. **JavaScript comment lines**—Comments in JavaScript begin with two successive forward slashes. All text after these slashes is a comment, and is ignored by the JavaScript parser.

2. **Hiding a script using an HTML comment**—A script can be placed inside an HTML comment, safely hiding it from any browsers that do not understand **SCRIPT** elements. Note that the string `-->` ending the comment must be placed at the end of a JavaScript comment line, as otherwise it is interpreted as JavaScript program code.

3. **Use of single quotes for strings**—In JavaScript, single quotes can be used to delimit strings (e.g.: 'this is a string'). This allows HTML markup inside a string, as any double quotes in the HTML markup will not prematurely end single quote–delimited JavaScript strings.

With respect to the actual JavaScript language, this example illustrates how variables (`var`) and functional methods (`function()`) are defined, and shows how alerts (pop-up alert notifications) are invoked (`alert()`). JavaScript variables are *untyped*—as with several other scripting languages (e.g., perl), variable type is determined by context.

Using SCRIPT within the BODY

Script components in the document **BODY** can actually print out text for inclusion with the displayed HTML. A simple HTML document example that uses the JavaScript `Date()` function to print the current time and date is shown in Figure 5.23. Figure 5.24 shows the resulting document displayed by Netscape Navigator, while Figure 5.25 shows the document displayed by a browser that does not understand **SCRIPT** elements.

Looking to Figure 5.23, you should note how the single-quote string delimiters allow HTML elements to be easily included in the write statement. Note also the presence of a new element, NOSCRIPT, immediately following the SCRIPT. NOSCRIPT can contain regular

Figure 5.23 A simple HTML document containing a JavaScript block that prints a line of HTML into the displayed document.

```
<HTML><HEAD>
<TITLE>Scripting Test</TITLE></HEAD>
<BODY>
<H2>Scripting Test</H2>
<SCRIPT>
 <!--
document.write('<H3 ALIGN="right">' + Date() + '</H3>');
 // -->
</SCRIPT>
<NOSCRIPT>
 <P>Sorry, no Scripting Support...
</NOSCRIPT>
</BODY></HTML>
```

HTML markup, as an alternative to **SCRIPT** for those browsers that do not understand the scripting language or the **SCRIPT** element. Browsers that understand **SCRIPT** and **NOSCRIPT** will hide the **NOSCRIPT** content. Figure 5.25 shows the utility of this new element. **NOSCRIPT** is understood by Netscape Navigator 3 and Internet Explorer 3, but not by earlier versions of these browsers—these early versions display the **NOSCRIPT** content in addition to that produced by **SCRIPT**.

NOSCRIPT Element—*HTML Alternative to SCRIPT*

Usage:	`<NOSCRIPT> ... </NOSCRIPT>`
Can Contain:	Unspecified; apparently depends on context
Can Be Inside:	Unspecified; apparently depends on context
Attributes:	none

NOSCRIPT is a container for HTML markup to be used in place of **SCRIPT** element output by browsers that do not understand **SCRIPT**. **NOSCRIPT** can apparently contain any **BODY**-content markup, provided that content is permitted at the location occupied by **NOSCRIPT**. For example, a **NOSCRIPT** inside an **EM** can only contain text or character highlighting elements, whereas a **NOSCRIPT** inside a **BLOCKQUOTE** can contain these elements in addition to **P**, **BLOCKQUOTE**, headings, and so on.

A **NOSCRIPT** must immediately follow the **SCRIPT** with which it is associated. Thus the appropriate markup for a **SCRIPT/NOSCRIPT** pair is:

```
<SCRIPT>
 ... script element content ...
```

Figure 5.24 Netscape Navigator 3 rendering of the document listed in Figure 5.23. Note the JavaScript-produced date on the right of the page.

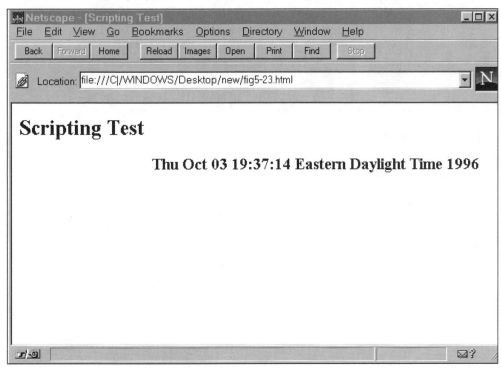

```
</SCRIPT>
<NOSCRIPT>
   ... HTML alternative to the preceding script ...
</NOSCRIPT>
```

Dynamic Scripting

Usually, scripting programs are more dynamic than the example shown in Figures 5.24 and 5.25, with many script programs including a level of user interaction. However, the dynamic character of the document is actually quite limited. In the current version of JavaScript, text, once drawn to a frame or window, can only be modified by replacing the entire frame or window by a new document. Fortunately, **FORM** element text input fields can be dynamically updated by JavaScripts, without reloading the entire document, thereby allowing for far more dynamic and interactive scripts. This is discussed a bit later when we describe how JavaScript handles events generated by *active* HTML elements such as anchor elements or forms.

Figure 5.25 NetManage WebSurfer 5 rendering of the document listed in Figure 5.23. This browser does not understand JavaScript, and hence displays the alternative NOSCRIPT content.

External Script Files

Script programs can be kept in external files, and from there included into an HTML document. Currently, remote script programs are included using **SCRIPT** elements of the form:

```
<SCRIPT LANGUAGE="lang_name" SRC="URL">
</SCRIPT>
```

where *lang_name* is the name of the scripting language (JavaScript or VBScript), and where *URL* is the URL referencing the script file. Note that the end tag `</SCRIPT>` is required—if you leave it out, the script will not load properly. Figure 5.26 shows how the document listed in Figure 5.23 can be rewritten to use an external script, and also shows the content of the referenced script file *script.js*.

NOTE: Netscape Navigator Ignores LANGUAGE Attribute   Netscape Navigator 3 ignores the **LANGUAGE** attribute, and interprets all scripts, external or otherwise, as being written in JavaScript.

Figure 5.26 HTML document illustrating external JavaScript files. This document is equivalent to the one listed in Figure 5.23, except for the placement of the JavaScript program in the external file *script.js*.

script1.html

```
<HTML><HEAD>
<TITLE>Scripting Test</TITLE></HEAD>
<BODY>
<H2>Scripting Test</H2>

<SCRIPT LANGUAGE="javascript" SRC="script.js">
</SCRIPT>
<NOSCRIPT>
  <P>Sorry, no Scripting Support...
</NOSCRIPT>
</BODY></HTML>
```

script.js

```
document.write('<H3 ALIGN="right">' + Date() + '</H3>');
```

Note in Figure 5.26 how the program within external script file is not placed within an HTML comment—obviously this hiding mechanism is not needed for a script outside an HTML document. However, you can include the HTML comments within a script file, as they will be ignored by the script parser. This can be convenient if you are moving scripts back and forth between HTML documents and external script files.

MIME Types for Script Files

An HTTP server distributing script files must be configured to send the correct MIME type associated with the script—otherwise the browser will not know the language of the arriving program. The currently supported MIME types are listed in Table 5.2.

You should note, however, that there is currently an interest in changing these to be subtypes of the primary media type "text", as in text/javascript and text/vbscript. The advantage is that users can then easily view the script source listing as a text file—otherwise browsers are generally configured to treat "application" primary media types as non-viewable without special supporting software.

Mixing Local and Remote Scripts

A document can contain both local and remote **SCRIPT** declarations. This can make for sensible separation of program modules, with generic script libraries included via external files, and

Table 5.2 Scripting Languages and Associated MIME Types

Language	Typical Filename Extension	MIME Type
JavaScript	js	application/x-javascript
VBScript	?? (unspecified)	application/x-vbscript

document-specific scripting placed within the documents. However, you cannot use the *same* **SCRIPT** element to reference local and remote script components at the same time. Thus markup of the form:

```
<SCRIPT LANGUAGE="javascript" SRC="/path/to/prog.js">
    <!--
    document.write('Here is some internal JavaScript...');
    // -->
</SCRIPT>
```

must be avoided. Netscape Navigator 3 will use the external script but will ignore the internal one. However, if the URL referencing the external script is invalid, Netscape Navigator will use the local script. Internet Explorer, on the other hand, always ignores the externally referenced JavaScript program, and only executes the local one.

Proposed Changes to SCRIPT

Although not currently supported, there is currently much interest in replacing **LANGUAGE** by a **TYPE** attribute that specifies the MIME content-type for the script. This brings the naming scheme in line with that used throughout the Web, and avoids the need for two parallel naming schemes for script languages. As a result, script elements would be written as:

```
<SCRIPT TYPE="application/x-javascript" SRC="/path/to/prog.js">
</SCRIPT>

<SCRIPT TYPE="application/x-javascript">
<!--
 ... script content ...
// -->
</SCRIPT>
```

In practice, **SCRIPT** elements could contain both **LANGUAGE** and **TYPE** attributes: Browsers that support **TYPE** would ignore **LANGUAGE**, while older browsers that do not understand **TYPE** would still understand **LANGUAGE**.

Specifying the Default Language

If neither **TYPE** nor **LANGUAGE** is given, then the browser needs to guess at the language used by the document script. To avoid confusion that may arise from this process, an author can specify, using a **META** element, the default scripting language used in the document. The specification is:

```
<META HTTP-EQUIV="Content-Script-type" CONTENT="type/subtype">
```

where *type/subtype* is the MIME type of the default document scripting language. Note that this format indicates that the default script type can also be indicated by an HTTP server response header field of the form

```
Content-script-type: type/subtype
```

(see Chapter 7 for more information about HTTP headers and the HTTP protocol). At present, there are no browsers that understand this HTTP header field or the associated **META** element content.

Script Interaction with HTML Elements

Scripting languages become much more dynamic when they are bound to user input elements. In HTML, the basic user input elements are the anchor element **A** and the various **FORM** input elements. Both JavaScript and VBScript provide these bindings through the special *event handlers* listed in Table 5.3, which are triggered by the events described in the table. For example, an *onClick* event is triggered when a hypertext link is "selected" (clicked), while the *onLoad* event is triggered whenever a document or frame is loaded onto the display.

Table 5.3 HTML Event Handler Attributes
Italicized event handlers were introduced as of Netscape Navigator 3.

Attribute	Description
onAbort	Triggered when the browser user aborts the loading of an image file.
onBlur	Triggered when the associated **FORM** input element *loses focus* (i.e., the user selects text outside the element, or selects another input element).
onChange	Triggered when a **FORM** element both loses focus *and* has been modified (for example, by user input of text, or by selecting a button).
onClick	Triggered when a **FORM**-element button or a hypertext link has been selected ("clicked").
onError	Triggered by an error in a JavaScript program. This event is *not* available as an HTML attribute, since the event is not specific to a particular element.
OnFocus	Triggered when a **FORM** input element is selected, usually by clicking the mouse button within the element, or by using the Tab key to advance to a new item.
OnLoad	Triggered when the document is loaded.
onMouseOut	Triggered when the associated *hypertext link* is deselected (e.g., the mouse moves off the link).
onMouseOver	Triggered when the associated hypertext link is selected (e.g., the mouse moves on top of the link).
onReset	Triggered when a **FORM** reset button is pressed.
onSelect	Triggered when text is selected within a **TEXTAREA** or within an **INPUT** element that accepts text input (**TYPE**="text" or "password"). This is different from **onFocus**, as **onFocus** is triggered by selecting the element, even if text has not been selected.
onSubmit	Triggered when a **FORM** is submitted.
OnUnload	Triggered when the document is unloaded (e.g., the user selects to move to another page).

Event handlers are attached to specific elements via special event handling *attributes*. These attributes have the same names as the events they handle (recall, however, that the attribute names are *case-insensitive*), and take as their value the *function* that should be invoked when the event takes place. Consider, for example, the following markup:

```
<INPUT TYPE="button" NAME="butt1" VALUE=foo
     ONCLICK="alert('Uh oh -- you pressed the Foo Button!' );" >
```

The **ONCLICK** attribute binds this button (named "butt1") to the indicated JavaScript—here a simple alert pop-up window. When the user presses this button, the *onClick* event is triggered, and the browser will pop-up an alert window containing the given message string.

To support client-specific form processing and user interaction, Netscape introduced a **TYPE**="button" **INPUT** element. This type is intended for controlling client-side actions only—the name and value associated with a **TYPE**="button" element are *never* sent with the form data when a **FORM** is submitted to a remote server. This is illustrated in Figure 5.27, which shows a **FORM** containing two **INPUT** elements: one of **TYPE**="button", (taken from our previous example) and the other of **TYPE**="submit".

Figure 5.28 shows the document displayed after the user has selected the button labeled "Foo." This button is tied by the *onClick* event handler to the JavaScript `alert()` function, so that pressing this button causes the visible pop-up alert menu. If, instead, the user presses the submit button, the accessed URL is (omitting the leading part of the URL):

```
.../cgi/prog.pl?submit=Submit+It%21
```

which contains only the encoded data from the **TYPE**="submit" button—note that the name and value from the **TYPE**="button" element are absent.

Figure 5.27 Example HTML document illustrating the TYPE="button" input element and event handling. The display of this form by Netscape Navigator 3 is shown in Figure 5.28.

```
<HEAD><TITLE>
Scripting Test</TITLE></HEAD>
<BODY>
<H2>Buttons and More Buttons</H2>
<BLOCKQUOTE>
<FORM ACTION="/cgi/prog.pl" METHOD="get">
  <H3> A Simple FORM Example</H3>
  <INPUT TYPE="button"
      NAME="butt1" VALUE="foo"
      ONCLICK="alert('Uh oh — you pressed the Foo Button!' );" >
   — <B>The FOO BUTTON!</B><BR>
  <INPUT TYPE="submit" NAME="submit" VALUE="Submit it!">
</FORM>
</BODY></HTML>
```

Figure 5.28 Display, by the Internet Explorer 3 browser, of the document listed in Figure 5.27. Note the JavaScript alert window displayed as a result of clicking on the button labeled "Foo."

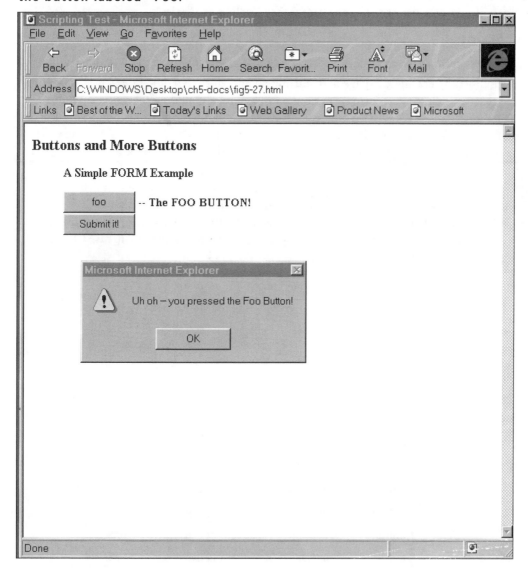

HTML Elements and Event Handlers

There are 13 different event handlers (listed in Table 5.3), and 15 different HTML elements that can take event-handling attributes. However, there are only a few event handlers appropriate for any given element—for example, the *onUnload* event, triggered when the user leaves a document, is irrelevant to the **AREA** (client-side imagemap data) element, but appropriate to **BODY** and **FRAMESET**. To help keep track of which handlers go where, Table 5.4 lists elements that take event handlers, alongside a list of the supported event-handling attributes.

Dynamic Scripts

As mentioned, HTML output generated by scripts is static—once it is displayed on the page, it can only be modified by erasing the page and starting again. More dynamic interaction is possible using **FORM** text-level elements—script programs can dynamically update the value content of **INPUT TYPE**="text" and **TEXTAREA** elements (they can actually modify the content of any **VALUE** attribute). This allows for auto-tabulating forms (for example, summing a column of elements, as in a spreadsheet) or dynamic generation of form field data using data derived from user input or other sources.

Table 5.4 HTML Elements and Supported Event Handling Attributes
Italicized handlers and handled elements were added as of Netscape Navigator 3.
Handlers inside dashed-line boxes are currently unreliable and should not be used.

Element Type	Supported Event Handlers			
AREA (Navigator 3+ only)		*onMouseOut*	*onMouseOver*	
A	onClick	*onMouseOut*	onMouseOver	
IMG (Navigator 3+ only)	*onAbort*	onLoad		
INPUT TYPE="button"	onClick			
INPUT TYPE="checkbox "	onClick			
INPUT TYPE="radio"	onClick			
INPUT TYPE="submit"	onClick			
INPUT TYPE="reset"	onClick			
BODY	*onBlur*	*onFocus*	onLoad	onUnload
FRAMESET	*onBlur*	*onFocus*	onLoad	onUnload
SELECT	onBlur	onChange	onFocus	
TEXTAREA	onBlur	onChange	onFocus	onSelect
INPUT TYPE="text"	onBlur	onChange	onFocus	onSelect
INPUT TYPE="password"	onBlur	onChange	OnFocus	onSelect
FORM	onSubmit	*onReset*		
INPUT TYPE="password"	N/A			

This dynamic functionality is illustrated by the simple JavaScript example listed in Figure 5.29. This small script uses a **FORM** text input element to display the local time and date, updated every second. Figure 5.30 shows the result of this script as rendered by the Netscape Navigator 3 browser, while Figure 5.31 shows the script rendered by Internet Explorer 3.

Figure 5.29 Example HTML JavaScript document illustrating dynamic updating of text input element. This example creates a single text input element that acts as a real-time clock. The line numbers, in italics, are not part of the document.

```
1    <HEAD>
2    <TITLE>Clock Test Script</TITLE>
3    <SCRIPT>
4    <!-- hide the script
5
6    var timer_id   = 0;              // reference to timer
7    var form_name  = 0;              // Instance label for form
8    var delay      = 1000;           // Delay between updates (1 sec)
9
10   function updater(){
11                                    // Initialize timer interrupt
12                                    // to re-call clock_updater()
13                                    // after 'delay' milliseconds
14                                    // Then calculate new time/date,
15                                    // and put results in the VALUE
16                                    // attribute of the FORM
17                                    // field with NAME="result".
18                                    // Then copy time/date into the
19                                    // form field with NAME="result2"
20                                    // and NAME="result3"
21       timer_id=window.setTimeout("updater()", delay);
22       form_name.result.value  = new Date();
23       form_name.result2.value = form_name.result.value;
24       form_name.result3.value = form_name.result.value;
25   }
26   function start(element_id) {
27       form_name = element_id;      // Attach time_field to
28                                    // form element named as argument.
29       updater();                   // Then call clock_updater()
30                                    // to start the clock
31   }
32   function stop() {
33      window.clearTimeout(timer_id);   // Remove Timer reference
34   }
35
36   // End script -- end of comment that hides the script -->
37
38   </SCRIPT></HEAD>
39
```

Continued

Figure 5.29 (Continued)

```
40   <!--       ONLOAD   triggers    start(), passing the named form
41             ONUNLOAD triggers    stop (), which deletes the timer
42   -->
43   <BODY ONLOAD="start(document.forms.clock)"
44        ONUNLOAD="stop()">
45
46   <H2 ALIGN="center">Dynamic Clock Script</H2>
47
48   <FORM NAME="clock">
49     <CENTER>
50     <B>Clock Output</B> (updates every second)<BR>
51     <BR>
52     <INPUT TYPE="text" NAME="result"  SIZE=18>  <BR><BR>
53     <INPUT TYPE="text" NAME="result2" SIZE=39>  <BR><BR>
54     <INPUT TYPE="text" NAME="result3" SIZE=50>
55     </CENTER>
56   </FORM>
57   </HTML>
```

The script inside the document **HEAD** defines three methods: start() (lines 26–31), called when the page is loaded; stop() (lines 32–34), called when the page is unloaded (the user moves to another page); and updater() (lines 10–25), which actually runs the timer.

How are these invoked? When the document is loaded, the **BODY** element **ONLOAD** attribute (line 43) invokes the start() method, to start the timer. The argument of start() is the object name for the **FORM** element with which the timer output will be associated. The notation document.forms.clock references the **FORM** element, lying in the current document, with the attribute **NAME**="clock".

The start() method first assigns a reference variable to this object (the variable form_name) and then calls updater(). Updater() does all the work. The first line (line 21) calls the window method window.setTimeout(), with two arguments: the name of a method to run (updater()), and the time delay (delay) before the next call. As a result, the system will awaken after one second and re-invoke updater(). This procedure then continues until this timer, labeled by timer_id, is explicitly deleted.

Labeling FORMs: The NAME Attribute

After setting the wake-up call, the function creates a new instance of the Date() object (line 22) and assigns this to the **VALUE** attribute of one of the **FORM** input elements. The particular element is addressed as an object; for example, line 22 references the **FORM** with **NAME** given by the form_name variable (the value is "clock"), and references this particular form's **INPUT** element with **NAME**="result." This is simply the first of the three text input elements, starting at line 52. Lines 23 and 24 assign this same object to the two other input elements within the **FORM**.

Figure 5.30 Rendering of the document listed in Figure 5.29 by the Netscape Navigator 3 browser.

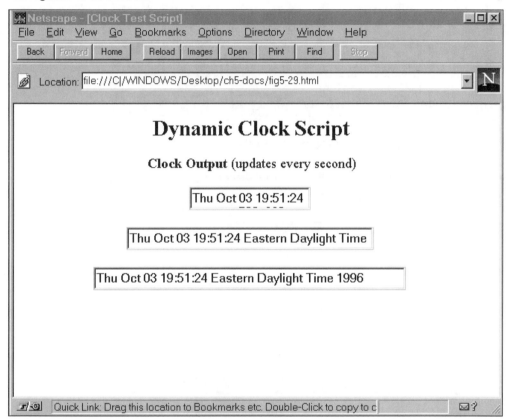

When the document is generated, the contents of these elements are replaced by the `Date()` object, giving rise to the dates displayed in Figure 5.30. This field is updated every second, for every invocation of the `updater()` method.

Microsoft/Netscape Incompatibilities

The script shown in Figure 5.29 does not work under Internet Explorer 3, and produces the following error message:

```
Error at line 22: Object doesn't support this property or method.
```

Internet Explorer does not treat the `Date()` object in the same manner as Netscape Navigator. If, however, line 22 is replaced by

```
form_name.result.value = Date()
```

Figure 5.31 Rendering of the document listed in Figure 5.29 by the Internet Explorer 3 browser.

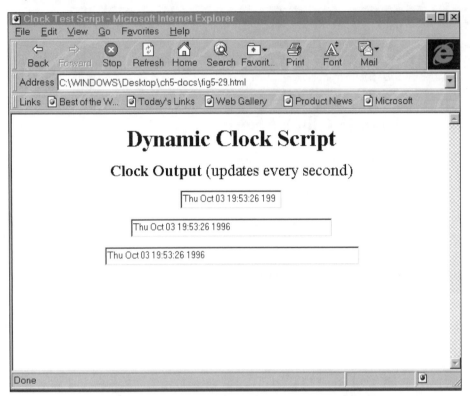

then the script functions under Internet Explorer 3 and also Navigator 3, with the result shown in Figure 5.31. Note how the time fields display differently than in Netscape Navigator 3 (Figure 5.30), since the two browser display text input fields (and the text within those fields) in different ways. You thus cannot reliably use a **SIZE** attribute to clip the date and display specific leading portions of the time/date field.

Of course, this brief introduction has left out many important scripting language features, such as the ability to reference and retrieve remote URLs, to communicate between multiple frames or windows, or, as of Netscape Navigator 3, to mediate communication between local scripts, embedded Java applets, and plug-ins. (With Navigator 3, the **APPLET** element can take an optional **MAYSCRIPT** attribute [which takes no value]. The presence of **MAYSCRIPT** gives the applet permission to communicate with JavaScript programs.) For additional information on these topics, you are directed to the JavaScript references listed at the end of this chapter.

Server-Side Scripting—Netscape LiveWire

Document scripting is a powerful tool for creating dynamic and interactive documents. However, it is also useful to have similar scripting capabilities at the HTTP server. This would allow servers to process documents and to dynamically include content, client-side scripts, and data generated by a script run on the server. This is similar to the facilities offered by server-side includes and CGI programs, although a well-designed scripting language, designed with the nature of browsers, HTML documents, and the Internet in mind, would provide an easier framework for writing Web-related applications.

Netscape supports this type of scripting in its *Netscape LiveWire* server packages. In LiveWire, documents delivered by the server can contain scripts that are preprocessed by the server, prior to the delivery of the document. These scripts are placed inside a special Netscape-specific element called **SERVER**. **SERVER** acts just like **SCRIPT** (that is, it is a container for a JavaScript program), except that the content is executed on the server, and not on the client. For instance, the following example document contains both client and server scripts:

```
<HTML>
<HEAD>
<SERVER>
     .... JavaScript to be executed by the server
</SERVER>
<SCRIPT>
<!--  Begin hiding
     .... JavaScript to be passed through to, and executed on,
              the client
//  end hiding -->
</SCRIPT>
<TITLE> Some title -- may be generated by Script </TITLE>
</HEAD>
<BODY>
     .... body HTML content ...
<SERVER>
     .... additional server-executed script ...
</SERVER>
</BODY></HTML>
```

When this document is requested, the server executes the JavaScript contained within the **SERVER** elements, which can result in the dynamic generation of document content, the modification of server database entries, and so on. LiveWire includes special methods for database access on the server, and for communicating with custom-written server modules authored in Java or other languages.

There is unfortunately very little on-line or print documentation on LiveWire. If looking for additional information, you are best advised to visit the Netscape (*www.netscape.com*) home page, and search the site for information.

Internationalization of HTML

Internationalization refers to the process of modifying software and software systems to support the world's languages, and operate with an interface customizable for any of these languages. For HTML, this means giving HTML the ability to use character sets other than ISO Latin-1, as well as the ability to support truly multilingual documents—that is, documents containing more than one language.

This requires several modifications to HTML. First, the character set for HTML must be changed from ISO Latin-1 to another set that supports more of the characters used by the world's languages. The required number of characters or symbols (*glyphs*) runs to the tens of thousands, a far cry from the 200-odd characters possible with ISO Latin-1. Second, new elements and attributes are needed to specify the language used within a particular element, or the direction in which the characters should be drawn on the display. Additional details and explanations about these changes are given in this section. First, however, we present a brief summary of the required changes to HTML.

Summary—New HTML Elements and Attributes

Internationalized HTML requires the following new HTML elements and attributes. The use of these new elements and attributes are discussed in later sections.

New HTML Elements	*BDO, Q*
New Attributes	*DIR, LANG*
	Allowed with all **BODY** content elements *except*: **AREA, CENTER, FONT, HR, MAP, PARAM** and **SCRIPT**
	Allowed with **HEAD**-content elements: **ISINDEX, STYLE, TITLE**
Attribute Specifications	DIR="ltr", "rtl" (optional)—Specifies directionality for character layout, as "ltr" (left to right) or "rtl" (right to left)
	LANG="*lang-sub*" (optional)—Specifies the *language* of enclosed text (see Appendix E for language specifications)
Modified Attributes	ALIGN: Must support values "left", "right", "center", and "justify". **ALIGN** must also be supported by the elements **ADDRESS, BLOCKQUOTE, DIR, MENU, OL, UL,** and **LI**

Internationalized Character Sets

To support truly international applications, HTML must support a character set that in turn supports all the characters and symbols of all the world's languages. This is a tall order!

Unfortunately, the specified character set of HTML 3.2 is ISO Latin-1, an 8-bit character set that supports on the order of 200 characters common in Western European languages. This is, to say the least, insufficient—ISO Latin-1 is useless for non-European languages, while any standard 8-bit character set is clearly insufficient for languages, such as Chinese or Japanese, where the required repertoire of characters far exceeds the 256 character limit of an 8-bit character set.

Over the years, literally dozens of character sets have sprung up to support non–Anglo-centric requirements (some of these are mentioned in Appendix A). However, most of these were designed to support a particular language (Greek, Arabic, Korean, etc.) and not for more general use. A truly internationalized specification of HTML needs a single character set that encompasses all the required characters, within a single standard.

There is such a character set, and it goes by the romantic name ISO-10646. The most important part of ISO 10646 is contained within a 16-bit (65,536-character) subset known as the *Basic Multilingual Plane*, or *BMP* (this subset is equivalent to the Unicode character set, as noted in Appendix A). The HTML internationalization effort has chosen this character set as the *document character set* for HTML. The phrase "document character set" means that the rules for processing HTML documents are composed in terms of this character set, and that a document must in some way be convertible into this character set to be properly processed. It further means that HTML character references in HTML refer by default to this character set; for example, ֘ refers by default to character number 1432 of the Unicode character set.

However, this does not mean that a document need be *encoded* using this character set (although that would be the preferred choice). Documents can still be written in any desired character set, known as a *character encoding* (in reflection of the fact that a digital document is simply an encoding of the characters as binary data), but any entity references must be defined as part of HTML, while numeric character references must refer to the Unicode character at the indicated numerical position.

Communicating Character Encoding

When an HTML document is sent by a server to a browser, the server should indicate the character set encoding for the document being sent. The mechanism for this is to send, with the header that precedes the document, a MIME content-type header of the form

```
Content-type: text/html; charset=charset_name
```

where *charset_name* is the name of the character set in which the document is encoded.

Unfortunately, many current browsers do not understand charset strings, and assume the string to be part of the MIME-type declaration; they consequently think the document is of some unknown type, and cannot display it. As a way of circumventing this problem, internationalized

HTML supports an HTML-based mechanism for indicating the character encoding of a document. This is through **META** elements of the form:

```
<META HTTT-EQUIV="Content-type"
         CONTENT="text/html; charset=charset_name">
```

A browser that reads a document can then search for this header to determine the charset encoding of the document. Of course, this is a bit of a chicken-and-egg problem, as the browser must first assume a character set (typically ISO Latin-1) in order to start reading the text. This will work provided that up to the aforementioned **META** element, the document, is encoded in bytes that correspond to ASCII characters, since then the text can be understood assuming the standard default encoding.

The general algorithm for determining the encoding character set is as follows:

1. Use the character set specified in the header sent by the server.

2. If there is no charset value sent by the server, check for **META** element content specifying a character set.

3. If there is no detectable **META** element, then use heuristic algorithms to determine the character set (i.e., guess).

Issues Related to Language and Character Set

Once you have an internationalized document, you confront several important formatting problems not encountered with simple European text. For example, several languages read from right to left, and not left to right—and in a truly international document, many languages may appear in the same document, even in the same paragraph! Thus internationalized HTML needs a way of specifying the language of a particular piece of text, as well as the desired directionality for the layout of the characters.

These features are enabled through the new attributes **LANG** and **DIR**. **LANG** specifies the language for a block of text, while **DIR** specifies the text directionality. Browsers that understand these attributes use the **LANG** value to control text formatting, and the **DIR** value to change the direction of the text layout. There may also be a need to locally override the directionality of a block of text, and this fine control is provided by the **BDO**, or Bi-Directional Override element, described later.

Last, the internationalization efforts introduced a new element, **Q**, for use with short inline quotations. The purpose is similar to **BLOCKQUOTE**, except that text inside **Q** will be inline with the regular text flow, and will be surrounded by quotation symbols appropriate to the language indicated by the **LANG** attribute.

BDO Element: Bidirectional Override Element

Usage:	`<BDO> ... </BDO>`
Can Contain:	characters, character highlighting, A, BR, IMG, BASEFONT, MAP, NOSCRIPT, SCRIPT, SPACER, WBR,
	APPLET, EMBED, NOEMBED, *OBJECT*,
	INPUT, SELECT, TEXTAREA
Can Be Inside:	ADDRESS, BLOCKQUOTE, BODY, CENTER, DIV, FORM, MULTICOL, PRE,
	Hn, DD, DT, LI, P, TD, TH, APPLET, NOEMBED, *OBJECT,*
	A, CAPTION, character highlighting
Attributes:	*CLASS, DIR, ID, LANG, STYLE*

BDO is text-level markup that marks a section of text for *bidirectional override*. The purpose is to force a particular directionality to the characters within the element, regardless of their intrinsic directional properties. **DIR** is thus a mandatory attribute for **BDO**, while all other attributes are optional. The attributes for **BDO** are identical to those attributes taken by **Q**—please see the **Q** element description for details of their meaning and use.

Q Element: Short Quotation

Usage:	`<Q> ... </Q>`
Can Contain:	characters, character highlighting, A, BR, IMG, BASEFONT, MAP, NOSCRIPT, SCRIPT, SPACER, WBR,
	APPLET, EMBED, NOEMBED, *OBJECT*,
	INPUT, SELECT, TEXTAREA
Can Be Inside:	ADDRESS, BLOCKQUOTE, BODY, CENTER, DIV, FORM, MULTICOL, PRE,
	Hn, DD, DT, LI, P, TD, TH, APPLET, NOEMBED, *OBJECT*,
	A, CAPTION, character highlighting
Attributes:	*CLASS, DIR, ID, LANG, STYLE*

Q marks a short quotation, in contrast to **BLOCKQUOTE,** which marks large blocks of quoted text. The content of **Q** will typically be rendered in quotation marks appropriate to the language context (as set by the **LANG** attribute). For example, in an English language context the text would be surrounded by single or double quotation marks. This is a *partially* safe element for older browsers, as the browser will display the text content, but without modified formatting— the quoted nature may no longer be obvious. The possible attributes are the same as for **BDO.** These are:

CLASS=*"string"* (optional) Specifies a subclass name for the element. Subclassing is used to define the special nature of an element, such as CLASS="introduction", CLASS="verse", and so on. Stylesheets can bind to these specific classes, so that an author can specify special formatting for different classes of the same element.

DIR="ltr", "rtl" (optional) Specifies the base directionality for the text flow within the element, where the default is inherited from the surrounding elements. The possible values are "ltr" (left to right) and "rtl" (right to left). This attribute allows for what is known as *bidirectional text*, or *BIDI*—that is, text segments that read left to right in some places, right to left in others.

ID=*"name"* (optional) Specifies a unique identifier for the element, as a name token. In principle, **ID**-labeled elements can be the targets of hypertext links, as **ID** plays the same role as the **NAME** attribute of the anchor element. This aspect of **ID** is not supported by most current browsers. Stylesheets can also reference **ID**-labeled elements, and can use **ID** to apply formatting instructions to specific elements.

STYLE=*"string"* (optional) Contains stylesheet instructions that should be applied to the content of **SPAN.** There is no way of specifying the stylesheet language of the **STYLE** attribute content.

LANG=*"name"* (optional) Specifies the language of the document, and possibly the national variant of that language. This is done using a collection of special codes for languages, along with a second collection of codes for individual countries: for example, fr-ca for Canadian French. These codes are summarized in Appendix E. The country code is optional, so that you can have just a language code.

This attribute allows the browser to choose appropriate language and national formatting for things such as monetary symbols, decimal point characters, hyphenation rules, text directionality, and punctuation for quoted text.

Added Entity References

To support certain special relationships between adjacent characters, internationalized HTML has an additional four entity references corresponding to four special Unicode characters. These are:

Entity Reference	Character Reference (UCS)	Description
&zwnj;	&#8204;	zero-width non-joiner
&zwj;	&#8205;	zero-width joiner
&lrm;	&#8206;	left-to-right mark
&rlm;	&#8207;	right-to-left mark

The first two entities control cursive joining behavior between adjacent letters: a ‌ after a letter means that the cursive joining form of the letter should be used, regardless of the following letter, while a ‍ after a letter means that the cursive non-joining form should be used, again regardless of the letter that follows. The other two entity references specify text directionality in situations where the directionality is not obvious. For example, in the case of a double quotation mark between an Arabic (right-to-left) and a Latin (left-to-right) character, it is unclear if the mark should belong with the Arabic or Latin letter. If the double quote is surrounded by characters of the same directionality (one of these characters being either ‎ or ‏), then this deadlock is broken, and the quotation mark knows which way to point.

The details of internationalized text are complex, and the preceding discussion has only touched on some of the main issues. For more information, you are referred to the HTML Internationalization RFC and the references quoted therein.

Next-Generation HTML—Anticipated Features

As mentioned earlier in this book, HTML 3 was an ambitious but, in the end, unsuccessful effort to add many important new features to HTML. Many of these features are still in the works or have been implemented to a limited degree—several were mentioned in this chapter, in the context of stylesheets, internationalization, and document scripting. This section summarizes the more experimental features now in development. Note that most of these proposed enhancements are not implemented on current commercial browsers.

Length Measurements

In HTML 3.2, length quantities are generally given in pixels, or in some cases as a percentage of an available length (e.g., **WIDTH**s expressed as a percentage of the accessible region). However, neither of these units is ideal—in many cases, it would be better to specify absolute lengths in units independent of the display resolution (pixel size varies from computer to computer, while percentage widths depend on the size of the displayed region). Current proposals suggest allowing length measurements in points, picas, centimeters or millimeters, and inches—the different units to be indicated by adding the suffix *in* (inches), *pi* (picas), *pt* (points), *cm* (centimeters), or *mm* (millimeters) after the number. In the context of Web applications, the relative sizes of these units to 1 inch are:

Inches	Picas	Points	Centimeters	Millimeters
1in	6pi	72 pt	2.54cm	25.4mm

which also illustrates the use of suffixes to indicate the units being used. Real numbers are allowed—for example, a length of 5 millimeters can be specified as "5mm" or "0.5cm"—but exponential notation (e.g., 5e-1) is not allowed. Pixel units are assumed if the suffix is left off.

At present there are no Web applications that accept length measurements in these units.

Within **TABLE** elements, lengths can also, in some cases, be expressed relative to other lengths—indicated by appending the asterisk symbol "*" after the number. This is useful when defining relative widths of columns, and where you do not know the absolute width of the table. For example, the element <COL WIDTH="3*"> indicates a column with a width three times that of a column specified by <COL WIDTH="1*"> (or <COL WIDTH="*">), and six times that of a column specified by <COL WIDTH="0.5*">.

FORM Element Extensions—Grouping and Sub-Forms

In addition to the extra attributes introduced to link **FORM** elements to scripting programs, there are also plans for new elements to *group* form content into logical collections, and to assign formal labels to these collections. These proposed elements are described below. These are, admittedly, very speculative changes, and have not been implemented on any current browsers. There is much work underway on improving the **FORM**-based interface, and you can expect considerable evolution of the **FORM** element model before a new specification arises.

FIELDSET Element: Grouping of Related FORM Fields

Usage:	<FIELDSET> ... </FIELDSET>
Can Contain:	Undefined; probably: **characters, character highlighting, A, BR, IMG, BASE-FONT, MAP, NOSCRIPT, SCRIPT, SPACER, WBR,**
	APPLET, EMBED, NOEMBED, *OBJECT,*
	INPUT, SELECT, TEXTAREA,
	ADDRESS, BLOCKQUOTE, BODY, CENTER, DIV, FORM, MULTICOL, PRE
Can Be Inside:	Undefined; probably: **BLOCKQUOTE, BODY, CENTER, DIV,** *FIELDSET,* **FORM, MULTICOL, PRE,**

DD, LI, TD, TH, <u>NOEMBED,</u> *OBJECT*

Attributes: *CLASS, DIR, ID, LANG, STYLE,* TITLE

FIELDSET groups together a selection of related **FORM** input elements. The group rendering of these elements may be specified by stylesheets, or by some other mechanism. A **FIELDSET** can be given a *label* via a **LABEL** elements—the **FOR** attribute of the **LABEL** references the **ID** value of the associated **FIELDSET**. There are currently no browsers that implement the **FIELDSET** or **LABEL** elements.

LABEL Element: Label for a FORM Input Element

Usage: `<LABEL> ... </LABEL>`

Can Contain: probably: **characters, character highlighting,** A, BASEFONT, BR, IMG, MAP, <u>NOSCRIPT,</u> SCRIPT, <u>SPACER,</u> <u>WBR,</u>

APPLET, <u>EMBED,</u> <u>NOEMBED,</u> *OBJECT,*

INPUT, SELECT, TEXTAREA

Can Be Inside: probably: BLOCKQUOTE, BODY, CENTER, DIV, *FIELDSET,* FORM, <u>MULTICOL,</u> PRE,

Hn, DD, DT, LI, P, TD, TH, APPLET, <u>NOEMBED,</u> *OBJECT,*

A, CAPTION, **character highlighting**

Attributes: *CLASS, DIR, FOR, ID, LANG, ONCLICK, ONMOUSEOVER, REL, STYLE,* TITLE

LABEL specifies a label for a given group of form input elements, grouped using a **FIELDSET** element—consequently, a **LABEL** should only be placed inside a **FORM**. The **FOR** attribute relates a label to the corresponding **FIELDSET**: The value of the **FOR** attribute should be the same as the **ID** label (name token) of the **FIELDSET** to which it is related. There are no current browsers that implement **FIELDSET** and **LABEL**.

TABLE Element Extensions

Several enhancements to table layout, designed to improve control of the structure and layout of tables, are visible on the horizon. These changes are over and above the addition of support for the **CLASS, DIR, ID, LANG,** and **STYLE** attributes required to support internationalization and stylesheets. These enhancements are at the attribute level—there are no proposals that involve additional table-level elements.

The most important changes involve the new alignment option **ALIGN**="char", which allows for character-based text alignment, such as alignment on a decimal point. The character-specific alignment rules are specified by the **CHAR** and **CHAROFF** attributes, as discussed in the following. Note, however, that there are no current browsers that support **ALIGN**="char".

ALIGN="center", "char", "justify", left", "right" (optional) Specifies the horizontal alignment of the content of the indicated table cell or cells, relative to adjacent cells in the row or column. The alignments "center", "left", "right", and "justify" have their obvious meanings ("justify" reverts to left-aligned, should right *and* left justification not be possible), while "char" indicates alignment upon a particular character. The default alignment is "left." The default character for character alignment is the decimal point character implied by the **LANG** value (a period in English). Other alignment characters are specified by the **CHAR** attribute. The **CHAROFF** attribute specifies the horizontal offset of the alignment character.

CHAR="*c*" (optional) Specifies the character upon which the cell content should be aligned. This overrides the default value (the decimal point character implied by the current language). This is only meaningful with **ALIGN**="char".

CHAROFF="*number*" (optional) Specifies the horizontal offset of the alignment character. If a text line does not contain the alignment character, then the *end* of the text line should be aligned with this position. The offset is measured from the left or right side of the cell, depending on **DIR**. The length can be specified in the standard physical units, or as a percentage offset, the latter being calculated as a percentage of the cell width. This is only meaningful with **ALIGN**="char".

New COL and COLGROUP Attributes

New Attributes: **ALIGN**, *CHAR*, *CHAROFF*, **WIDTH**, **VALIGN** (optional)

Current browsers do not support alignment attributes for **COL** and **COLGROUP**. In the extended table model, all table grouping elements can specify alignment or width characteristics for the indicated columns.

New THEAD, TBODY, and TFOOT Attributes

New Attributes: **ALIGN**, *CHAR*, *CHAROFF*, **WIDTH**, **VALIGN** (optional)

Current browsers support grouping via **THEAD**, **TFOOT**, and **TBODY**, but do not let these elements take attributes. The advanced table model lets these elements take all the standard attributes (**CLASS, DIR, ID, LANG, STYLE**) as well as alignment attributes, to specify the default alignment characteristics for all cells within the element.

New TR Element Attributes

New Attributes: *CHAR*, *CHAROFF* (optional)

These new attributes let a **TR** element specify the default character-based alignment for an entire table row.

New TH and TD Element Attributes

New Attributes: *AXES, AXIS, CHAR, CHAROFF* (optional)

The new **AXIS** and **AXES** attributes provide text-only descriptions of rows and columns, and are designed for making the table data understandable when accessed via Braille or text-to-speech interfaces. The meanings of the new attributes are:

AXIS=*"string"* (optional) **AXIS** specifies an abbreviated name for a header cell, for use by software that renders a table into speech. In the absence of this element, the browser will use the cell content as a spoken label.

AXES=*"string"* (optional) **AXES** specifies a comma-separated collection of **AXIS** names, which then specify the row and column headers appropriate to the cell. A header cell may have both an **AXIS** and **AXES**, which indicates that the cell is actually a subheading.

Mathematics, and Other Missing Features

HTML is currently missing a number of useful hypertext document description features. Notably absent is a way of expressing mathematical symbols and equations. The absence of mathematical expressions is particularly surprising, given the origin of HTML in the scientific community. At present, mathematical equations can only can be included by using a separate application to create GIF images of mathematical expressions, which are then included within the HTML document.

Using TeX and LaTeX on the Web

In the mathematics and scientific community, the LaTeX typesetting/document formatting language is almost universal for preparing scientific and mathematical texts. For this community, Nikos Drakos of the University of Leeds produced a sophisticated program that can convert a LaTeX document into a hypertext collection of HTML documents, automatically converting mathematical expressions into inline GIF images. This remarkably useful package, called latex2html, is available at:

`http://cbl.leeds.ac.uk/nikos/tex2html/doc/latex2html/latex2html.html`

Of course, this means you need to learn LaTeX as well. For less sophisticated needs, there is a convenient collection of GIF-format Greek letters and other mathematical symbols, which authors can include in their documents to create simple mathematical equations or scientific expressions. A crib sheet for these icons, plus access and licensing information (there is a charge for commercial use—read the license agreement for more information), can be found at:

```
http://donald.phast.umass.edu/latex/tutorials/kicons.html
http://www.anachem.umu.se/graphics/symbols/symbols.html
http://donald.phast.umass.edu/kicons/license.html
```

TeX/LaTeX Viewer Plug-in

A third alternative is to use a browser plug-in that can format and display TeX/LaTeX documents. IBM has developed such a tool, named techexplorer, available for download and evaluation at:

```
http://www.ics.raleigh.ibm.com/ics/techexp.htm
```

Note, however, that this package does not support the full set of TeX/LaTeX markup commands—rather, it supports a large subset, plus special extensions for hypermedia and windowing support. Thus, LaTeX documents originally prepared for print publication often need some reworking to be viewed via techexplorer. The documentation at this URL describes the techexplorer-supported TeX/LaTeX language, as well as some of the steps that this adaptation process may entail.

Other Mathematical Alternatives

The current preference of the HTML language design community is to leave mathematical expressions out of HTML, and to design an entirely separate markup language for this purpose. The goal here is to create a language that is mathematically parsable—that is, a markup language that contains sufficient understanding of the meaning of the expression that the expression can be used as input to mathematical analysis programs such as Mathematica or Maple, or spreadsheets such as Lotus 1-2-3 or Excel. This is a difficult problem, and it is unlikely that the world will soon see an easy-to-use method for expressing mathematics on the World Wide Web.

Missing HTML Features

Other annoyingly missing features are page banners (non-scrolling headers or footers for documents—these can be mimicked by frame documents, but not completely reproduced), footnotes (perhaps displayable as pop-up items above the regular text), tabbing control, and the ability to mark arbitrary spots in a document (for linking or referencing purposes), or a range of text in a document (for selective retrieval of document fragments). Several elements in support of these functions (**FN, TAB, SPOT, RANGE**) were proposed in HTML 3, but have subsequently been dropped from the W3C proposals for the next generation of HTML. With luck they will be reintroduced sometime in the future, as such functionality is clearly needed. For additional reading on these topics, you are referred to the expired HTML 3 draft document, and to the "Next-Generation HTML" starting places listed in the References at the end of this chapter.

Keeping Up-to-Date

Many of the details about upcoming features of HTML are found at the World Wide Web Consortium Web site, listed at the beginning of the References section. If you're burning to know what's up and coming, or just being thorough, this is the place to look.

References

Next-Generation HTML—General Starting Place

```
http://www.w3.org/hypertext/WWW/MarkUp/MarkUp.html
http://www.w3.org/pub/WWW/TR/
```
(W3C HTML notes)
(W3C technical reports/publications)

Netscape Frame Documentation

```
http://home.netscape.com/assist/net_sites/frames.html
```

Microsoft and Netscape HTML Documentation

```
http://developer.netscape.com/library/documentation/htmlguid/index.htm
http://www.microsoft.com/workshop/author/other/htmlfaq1.htm
http://www.microsoft.com/workshop/author/newhtml/
```
(Netscape HTML)
(Microsoft Internet Explorer 3.0 HTML FAQ)
(Microsoft HTML references)

Object Embedding and Mobile Code Issues

```
http://www.w3.org/pub/WWW/TR/WD-object.html
http://www.w3.org/hypertext/WWW/MobileCode/
http://www.microsoft.com/intdev/inttech/comintro.htm
http://www.osf.org/dce
```
(OBJECT element draft)
(Mobile code proposals)
(Microsoft COM—Common Object Model)
(Open Software Foundation DCE—Distributed Computing Environment)

Cascading Stylesheets

```
http://www.w3.org/pub/WWW/Style/
http://occam.sjf.novell.com:8080/docs/dsssl-o/
http://www.falch.no/people/pepper/DSSSL-Lite/
http://www.w3.org/pub/WWW/TR/WD-css1
```
(General stylesheet information)
(DSSSL-Online—look at latest file in this directory)
(DSSSL-Lite overview)
(CSS1 specifications)

SCRIPT and HTML-Related Scripting Languages

```
http://www.w3.org/pub/WWW/TR/WD-script.html
http://home.netscape.com/eng/mozilla/3.0/handbook/javascript/index.html
http://www.microsoft.com/vbscript/default.htm
http://www.microsoft.com/intdev/vbs/default.htm
http://www.microsoft. com/intdev/sdk/
```
(SCRIPT element discussion paper)
(JavaScript documentation)
(VBScript documentation)
(VBScript documentation)
(Active-X dcripting documentation)

Internationalization and Character Set Issues (see also Appendix A):

```
http://www.w3.org/pub/WWW/International/
http://www.w3.org/hypertext/WWW/MarkUp/html-spec/charset-harmful.htm
http://www.alis.com:8085/ietf/html/index.en.html
```
(Internationalization overview)
(Discussion of main issues)

Experimental Web Browsers

```
http://www.w3.org/pub/WWW/Amaya/
http://www.w3.org/pub/WWW/Arena/
file://moose.cs.indiana.edu/pub/elisp/w3/
http://monty.cnri.reston.va.us/grail/
```
(Amaya browser)
(Arena browser)
(Emacs-w3 browser)
(Grail browser)

HTML 3 Specification (Expired Draft)

```
http://www.w3.org/hypertext/WWW/MarkUp/html3/
```

Uniform Resource
Locators (URLs)

Uniform resource locators, or *URLs*, are a scheme for specifying Internet resources using a single line of characters: A URL simply indicates where a resource is, and how to access it. The scheme is very flexible, and supports all the major Internet communications protocols, including FTP, Gopher, e-mail, HTTP, and WAIS. Within HTML documents, URLs are used to reference the target of a hypertext link. However, URLs are not restricted to the World Wide Web, and can be used to communicate information about Internet resources in e-mail letters, handwritten notes, or even books.

This chapter begins with a general overview of URL properties and the rules for constructing valid URLs. This is followed by a detailed specification of the currently supported URL schemes. The chapter concludes with a discussion of some proposed, but not widely implemented, schemes, along with some more general addressing issues important to the World Wide Web.

URL Overview and Syntax Rules

As mentioned, a URL is simply a scheme for referencing a particular Internet resource. In general, a URL contains the following pieces of information, some of which are optional depending on the specified protocol:

- The *protocol* to use when accessing the server (e.g., HTTP, Gopher, WAIS). This is always required.

- The Internet *domain name* of the site on which the server is running, along with any required username and password information. This is not required for some protocols.

- The *port number* of the server, which can be present (it is optional) only if the URL requires a domain name. If absent, the browser assumes a default value based on the protocol. For example, the default value for HTTP is 80.

- The *location* of the resource on the server—often a file or directory specification. This is sometimes optional, depending on protocol.

Here is a typical example, in this case for the HTTP protocol:

```
http://www.w3.org/pub/WWW/People/W3Cpeople.html
```

This references the file *W3Cpeople.html* in the directory */pub/WWW/People* accessible at the server *www.w3.org* using the HTTP protocol.

Allowed Characters in URLs

Although a URL can contain any ISO Latin-1 character, every URL must be *written* using only the *printable ASCII* characters that compose the bottom half of the ISO Latin-1 character set (as discussed in Appendix A, excluding control characters), and *cannot* be written using the full ISO Latin-1 character set. This restriction ensures that URLs can be sent by electronic mail, as many electronic mail programs mishandle (the polite way of saying it) messages containing characters from the upper half of the ISO Latin-1 character set.

In a URL, non-ASCII characters can be represented using a *character encoding* scheme, which is analogous to the character entities used with HTML. However, the schemes are distinctly different—the URL encoding scheme is understood as one of the rules for writing URLs, whereas character entities are only understood in the context of an HTML document.

For ISO Latin-1 characters, the encoding is simple: Any character can be represented by the encoding

```
%xx
```

where the percent sign is the special character indicating the start of the encoding, and where *xx* is the *hexadecimal code* for the desired ISO Latin-1 character (the x represents a hexadecimal digit in the range [0-9,A-F]). Table A.1 (Appendix A) lists all the ISO Latin-1 characters alongside their hexadecimal codes. As an example, the encoding for the character *é* (the letter *e* with an acute accent) is %E9.

Disallowed ASCII Characters

Several ASCII characters are disallowed in URLs, and can be present only in encoded form. This is so because these characters often have special meanings in a non-URL context, and their presence can lead to misinterpretation of the URL. For example, HTML documents use the double quotation mark (") to delimit a URL in a hypertext anchor, so that a quotation mark inside the URL would cause the browser to end the URL prematurely. Therefore, the double quote is disallowed. The space character is also disallowed, since many programs will consider the space as a break between two separate strings. Space characters often appear in Macintosh file or folder names, as in the filename "Network Info," where there is a single space between the words "Network" and "Info." In a URL, this name must be encoded as:

`Network%20Info`

Finally, all 33 control characters (hex codes 00 to 1F, and 7F) are disallowed. Table 6.1 summarizes the disallowed printable characters, including TAB (although TAB is formally a control character). You will sometimes see disallowed characters in a URL, without any special encoding. The URL may work, but to avoid possible problems you are best advised to use the encoded forms of these characters.

Special ASCII Characters

In a URL, several ASCII characters have special meanings. In particular, the percent character (%) is special, since it starts a URL character encoding sequence, while the forward slash character (/) is also special, and denotes a change in hierarchy, such as a directory change. These special characters must be encoded if you want them to appear as regular, uninterpreted characters. Thus, to include the string:

`ian%euler`

in a URL you must encode it as:

`ian%25euler`

where `%25` is the encoding for the percent character. If you do not do this, a program parsing the URL will try to interpret `%eu` as a character encoding. Conversely, you must not encode a special character if you require its special meaning. For example, the string:

`dir/subdir`

indicates that `subdir` is a subdirectory of `dir`, while:

`dir%2Fsubdir`

is just the character string `dir/subdir`(`%2F` is the encoding for the slash).

Table 6.1 Disallowed ASCII Characters in URLs

Character	Hex	Character	Hex
TAB	09	SPACE	20
"	22	<	3C
>	3E	[	5B
\	5C	]	5D
^	5E	`	60
{	7B	|	7C
}	7D	~	7E

TIP: URL Encoding Rule   Encode any character that might be special if you do not want to use its special meaning.

The most common special characters are:

- The percent sign (%). This is the escape character for character encodings, and is special in all URLs.

- The hash (#). This separates the URL of a resource from the *fragment identifier* for that resource. A fragment identifier references a particular location within a resource. This character is special in all URLs.

- The slash (/). This indicates hierarchical structures, such as directories.

- The question mark (?). This indicates a *query string*; everything after the question mark is query information to be passed to the server. Special in Gopher, WAIS, and HTTP URLs only.

Other characters that are special in certain URL schemes are the colon (:), semicolon (;), at (@), equals (=), and ampersand (&). These special cases will be noted as they arise.

Examples of Uniform Resource Locators

Figure 6.1 illustrates three typical URLs showing the different parts and the associated meanings. The parts are discussed in the following.

Protocol Specifier   The first string in the URL, of the general form *string:*, specifies the Internet *protocol* to use in accessing the resource—the examples here being for the HTTP (http:), Internet mail (mailto:), and telnet (telnet:) protocols. The protocol is indicated by the name

Figure 6.1 Three example URLs (here http, telnet, and mailto URLs), showing the main components. Not all URLs follow these models, as discussed in the text.

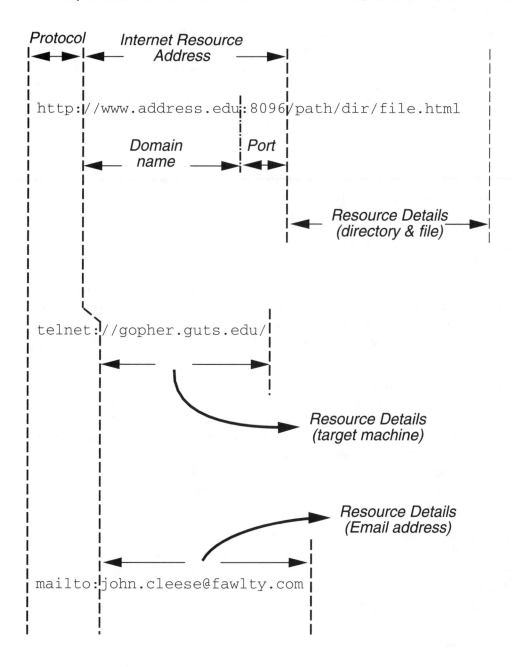

before the colon. The string specifying the protocol can contain only *lowercase letters* (a-z) and numbers (0–9). URL schemes are defined for most Internet protocols. The details of the different schemes are presented later on.

Domain Name and Port Number (Address) The second part of a URL is usually the Internet address of a server; this information lies between the double forward slash (//) and a terminating forward slash (/). This region contains the *domain name* of the server and, optionally, the *port number* to contact, the general form being //dom.name.edu:port/. Omitting the port number (and the colon before it) implies the default port for the given protocol. Numeric IP addresses can be used instead of domain names, for example:

```
//132.206.9.22:1234/
//128.100.100.1/
```

You can sometimes (depending on protocol) include username and password information, if this is needed to access a resource. The form then is:

```
//username:password@www.address.edu:port/
```

Note that the password can be read by anyone who sees the URL, so this is not a secure way to allow access to a resource.

For some URL schemes, Internet domain names are not required. This is the case for protocols that do not depend on a particular server, such as those for sending electronic mail (**mailto**) or accessing USENET newsgroup (**news**) articles. In these cases, each user has his or her own default mail or news server. The domain names for these servers are usually set using a browser's configuration menus.

Resource Location The forward slash after the host and port number field indicates the end of the address field and the beginning of the information required to locate the resource on the server. This field varies considerably, depending on the service being accessed. Often, it resembles a directory path leading down to a file, as in the **http** URL in Figure 6.1. In this context, the forward slash character (/) defines a change in hierarchy or directory, and is used in place of *all* system-dependent symbols defining such relationships, such as the backslash (\) on DOS, OS/2 or Windows computers, the colon (:) on Macintoshes, and the [dir.subdir.subsubdir] expressions on VAX/VMS systems.

Query Strings in URLs

The URL syntax allows you to encode query strings to be passed to the designated Internet resource, in situations (typically Gopher, HTTP, or WAIS) that support such service. This is accomplished by appending the query strings to the URL, separated from it by a question mark, as indicated by boldface in these examples:

```
gopher://gopher.somewhere.edu/77/searches.phone?bob+steve
http://www.somewhere.edu/cgi-bin/srch-data?archie+database
```

The question mark is a special character in HTTP, Gopher, and WAIS URLs, and must be encoded if you do *not* want to indicate a query string.

Encoding of Query Strings

Of course query strings, since they are part of a URL, must also be encoded. However, query string data takes an additional level of encoding, over and above the regular character encodings discussed to this point. These mechanisms are discussed later on, in the section on **http** URLs.

Some Simple URL Examples

The following examples illustrate the basics of URL design.

`http://www.w3.org/pub/WWW/Addressing/URL/Overview.html` References the file *Overview.html* in the directory */pub/WWW/Addressing/URL/* obtainable from the server *www.w3.org* using the HTTP protocol at the default port number (80 for HTTP).

`gopher://gumby.brain.headache.edu:151/7fonebook.txt` References the searchable index *fonebook.txt* from the Gopher server at *gumby.brain.headache.edu* running on port number 151.

`news:alt.rec.motorcycle` References the newsgroup *alt.rec.motorcycle*, to be accessed from any accessible newserver (to be selected by the user).

`mailto:ross@physics.mcg.ca` References sending an electronic mail message to the indicated e-mail address.

Partial URLs—From within an HTML Document

From within a given HTML document, you do not always need to specify the full URL of a second document. This is because being *in* a document already implies knowledge of the current URL, which allows you to reference neighboring documents or resources using a *partial* URL that gives the location *relative* to that of the current document. To put it another way, the URL need only indicate the part of the URL *different* from that used to access the current document.

For example, suppose a user accesses the document *file.html* using the full URL:

`http://www.stuff.edu/main/docs/file.html`

and that within this document, there is a hypertext reference containing the *partial* URL:

`<A HREF="stuff.html">anchor text</A>`

Where is this file? From *file.html,* any information not present in a URL reference is considered the *same* as that used to access the current document. Thus, the partial URL `stuff.html` is transformed into a full URL by appropriating the required URL components from the URL used to access *file.html*. The completed URL is then:

`http://www.stuff.edu/main/docs/stuff.html`

which indicates, as expected, that *stuff.html* is on the same server and in the same directory as *file.html*. Other equivalent partial URLs would then be:

```
/main/docs/stuff.html
//www.stuff.edu/main/docs/stuff.html
```

The former appropriates `http://www.stuff.edu` from the current URL to complete the reference, while the latter appropriates only the `http:` part from the *base* URL of the current document.

You can also use partial URLs to reference resources in other locations on the server. For example, from the *file.html*, the relative URL:

```
../../main.html
```

references the file *main.html* in the root HTTP directory, namely:

```
http://www.stuff.edu/main.html
```

Note how with partial URLs the symbol "`..`" indicates a change one level up in the directory hierarchy, just as it does in DOS or UNIX.

Partial URLs and the BASE Element

Partial URLs are very useful when constructing large collections of documents that will be kept together. However, relative URLs become invalid for a single document from the collection if the document is moved to a new directory or a new Internet site. This problem can be mitigated by using a **BASE** element within the moved document. **BASE** is used to record the *base* URL of a document—a URL recording the original location of the document. Partial URLs are evaluated *relative to* this recorded base URL. Thus, when the document is moved, all partial URLs are determined relative to the URL recorded by **BASE**, and the linked resources are correctly accessed from the original server.

Fragment Identifiers

In some cases, you will see locator strings of the form:

```
http://some.where.edu/Stuff/Path/plonk.html#location
```

The portion of the URL following the hash (#) character is called a *fragment identifier*, which references a particular location *within* the designated URL. Within the targeted HTML document, this location must be marked by an anchor element of the form:

```
<A NAME="location">text marker</A>
```

where the string `location` is the text string marking the location.

When a browser accesses a resource specified by a URL, it first strips off *all* characters following and including an unencoded hash (#), and uses the remaining string as the resource URL; consequently, a fragment identifier must be the very last substring on a URL. The browser preserves the fragment identifier as local information and, after retrieving the indicated resource, looks for the indicated location. The browser will present the document to the user such that the location is prominently displayed, either by placing the location at the top of the screen, or by highlighting it in some way.

You can also reference a named location from within the same document that contains the location. The general form for this is:

```
<A HREF="#location">anchor text</A>
```

That is, you reference just the fragment identifier, and nothing else. A browser should then scroll the document to prominently display the targeted location.

The use of fragment identifiers was discussed in detail in Example 6 of Chapter 2, and you are referred there for additional information.

URL Specifications

We now look at the details of the different URL forms. The protocols that can be referenced by URLs are listed in the Table 6.2; italicized entries indicate schemes that are not widely supported.

Table 6.2 URL Protocol Specifier Strings and Associated Protocols
Italicized entries are not widely supported.

Protocol Specifier	Protocol
ftp:	FTP (File Transfer Protocol)
gopher:	Gopher protocol
http:	HTTP (HyperText Transfer Protocol)
https:	Secure HTTP
mailto:	Internet mail address
news:	NNTP USENET protocol
telnet: (*rlogin:*, *tn3270:*)	Telnet protocol
wais:	WAIS protocol
file:	Local file access (various protocols)
ldap:	*Lightweight Directory Access Protocol*
nntp:	*NNTP USENET Protocol*
prospero:	*Prospero directory services protocol*

Ftp URLs

Ftp URLs designate files and directories accessible using the FTP protocol. In the absence of any username and password information, anonymous FTP access is assumed (implying a connection to the server as username ***anonymous,*** and using a user's Internet mail address as the password). The general form for this type of **ftp** URL is:

```
ftp://int.domain.nam:port/resource
```

where `int.domain.nam` is the domain name to access, `:port` specifies the optional port number (the default is 21), and `resource` is the local resource specification. Here is a typical example, referencing the file ***splunge.txt*** located in the directory ***path*** at the Internet site ***internet.address.edu*** at the default port:

```
ftp://internet.address.edu/path/splunge.txt
```

You can specify an FTP access of a directory using a URL such as:

```
ftp://internet.address.edu/path/
```

in which case the server sends a directory listing. Browsers display this information as a menu, allowing the user to navigate through the filesystem or select particular files for downloading.

Special Characters in Ftp URLs

The forward slash (/) and semicolon (;) characters are special in an **ftp** URL. The forward slash indicates directory or other hierarchical structures, while the semicolon is used to indicate the start of a *typecode* string. Typecode strings, discussed later in this section, must be the last string of the URL (not including any fragment identifier).

Non-Anonymous FTP Access

You can reference non-anonymous FTP resources by specifying, within the URL, the username and password of the account you wish to access. For example, the URL

```
ftp://joe_bozo:bl123@internet.address.edu/dir1/Dir2/file.gz
```

references the indicated file on the machine ***internet.address.edu***, accessible by logging in as user `joe_bozo` with password `bl123`. This is obviously not a secure way of giving access, since anyone who reads the URL then knows `joe_bozo`'s password. An alternative is to give only the username, as in:

```
ftp://joe_bozo@internet.address.edu/dir1/Dir2/file.gz
```

Many user agents (Netscape Navigator, for example) will connect to the remote machine using the indicated username, and will prompt the visitor for an appropriate password. Certainly, this is not ideal if you wish to publicly distribute large quantities of information. It would be better to set up a proper anonymous FTP service, or make the data available via HTTP.

FTP Directory Paths

Directory paths during FTP accesses are defined relative to a specific *home directory*, where this home directory differs depending on how the user accomplishes the FTP connection. A user who connects via anonymous FTP is placed in the anonymous FTP home directory, and has restricted access to the server filesystem. This is a security feature that permits making certain files publicly available without exposing the rest of the system to unauthorized users. On the other hand, if a visitor connects to the same machine as a registered user, the home directory will be that of the registered user, entirely different from that attained via anonymous FTP.

Consequently, the path you use to access a file as a regular user can be quite different from the path used to access the same file by anonymous FTP. You must keep this in mind when placing data in anonymous FTP archives, and when creating URLs that reference these data.

Modes for File Transfers

The FTP protocol allows several modes for transferring files. The most important is *image* or *binary* mode, which makes a byte-by-byte copy of the file. This is the mode to use when transferring programs, compressed data, or image files. Also common is *ASCII* mode, which is designed for transferring plain, printable text files. This mode is useful because it "corrects" for the fact that PCs, Macintoshes, and UNIX computers use different characters to mark the end of a line of text. In particular, Macintoshes use the carriage-return character CR; UNIX computers use the line-feed character LF; and DOS/Windows computers use both CR and LF (often written CRLF). In ASCII mode, FTP automatically converts between these three end-of-line markers to ensure that the received file has the new line codes appropriate to the local system. You cannot use this mode to transfer programs, however, since programs and data files contain bytes with the same codes as CR or LF characters—under ASCII mode, these codes will be converted into the new line codes appropriate to the local system, thereby destroying the data content of binary data files.

The FTP protocol has no knowledge of the data content of a file and must be told what mode to use in a file transfer. Thus, your WWW browser must have some way of determining the data type of a file being accessed via an **ftp** URL. Some browsers "guess" the type from the suffix of the filename, using a local database that maps filename extensions onto data types. This is not ideal, since the true type is only known by the author who constructed the URL and who created the resource referenced by the URL.

FTP Typecode Strings

Authors can now use URL *typecode strings* to specify the desired transfer mode. For example, the following URL:

```
ftp://internet.address.edu/path/splunge.txt;type=a
```

indicates that the designated resource (the file *splunge.txt*) should be retrieved using ASCII mode. The special semicolon character is used to separate the end of the resource locator string from the type indicator. Other possible type indicators are `type=i` for image (binary) transfers, or `type=d` for directory listings. Typecode strings are optional, the default being binary data transfers. Fragment identifiers, if used, must be placed after the typecode string:

```
ftp://internet.address.edu/path/goof.html;type=a#location
```

TIP: Problems with Typecode Strings? Typecode strings are supported by Netscape Navigator 3.0 and Microsoft Internet Explorer 3, but not by some other browsers, or by earlier versions of these programs. Browsers that do not understand a typecode string assume it to be part of the filename, and cannot locate the resource. If you have problems accessing a URL that has a typecode string, delete the typecode portion and try again.

TIP: Troubleshooting Ftp URLs At times, an **ftp** URL request may fail, either because the network is down or because the machine you are trying to access is overloaded with FTP accesses and refuses your request. Alternatively, the server may be configured to restrict access to requests from certain Internet sites. Web browsers are notoriously terse in handling FTP connections, and say very little about why a connection has failed. You can check for the cause of the problem by using an FTP program outside of your Web browser. A stand-alone FTP session can provide much more commentary on the state of the connection and will often give you a message explaining why the connection cannot be made.

Gopher URLs

Gopher servers can be accessed via URLs that look superficially similar to **ftp** or **http** URLs but that are, in fact, quite different. This is because Gopher resources are referenced using a combination of *resource identifier* codes and *selector strings*, and not directories and files. Resource identifiers are single-digit codes that specify the *type* of the Gopher resource—for example, that it is a text file, a directory, or a searchable index. The Gopher selector string is just a symbolic name associated with this resource. This can be a directory or file name, but it can also be a redirection to a database search procedure, or to a telnet session. Sometimes the selector string has, as its first character, a duplicate of the single-character resource type identifier. This can lead to hair-pulling confusion, with resource identifiers appearing alone, or in pairs, seemingly at random. Table 6.3 summarizes the Gopher resource identifier codes.

Table 6.3 Gopher Resource Identifier Codes

Code	File or Resource Type
0	Text file
1	Directory
2	CSO name/phone book server
3	Error
4	Macintosh binhexed (*.hqx) file
5	Dos binary file of some type
6	UNIX uuencoded file
7	Full text index search
8	Telnet session
9	Binary file

General Form of a Gopher URL

The general form for a basic **gopher** URL is:

```
gopher://int.domain.nam:port/Tselector_string
```

Where the port number is optional (the default value is 70), T is the Gopher type code from Table 6.3, and *selector_string* is the Gopher selector string. The root information of a Gopher server can be obtained by leaving out all type and selector string information. Thus, the root information of the Gopher server at *mr.bean.org* is available at:

```
gopher://mr.bean.org/
```

Hierarchical relationships are possible. For example:

```
gopher://mr.bean.org/1stuff
```

indicates that `stuff` behaves like a directory, and will retrieve the Gopher contents of `stuff`. The URL:

```
gopher://mr.bean.org/7stuff/index
```

indicates access to the *index* search in the directory *stuff*. Accessing this URL would cause the browser to ask the user for query string information to be used in the search.

Query Strings for Searches

Search information is sent to the Gopher server by appending the search strings to the URL, separated from the URL by a question mark. Thus, to pass the strings `tad`, `jill`, and `joanne` to the Gopher search index noted in the previous section, the URL is:

`gopher://mr.bean.org/7stuff/index?tad+jill+joanne`

Note that the URL syntax for Gopher queries uses a plus (+) sign to separate different search strings. Therefore, if you want to include a literal plus sign within a string, it must be encoded (the encoding for a plus sign is `%2B`).

Client Construction of Query Strings

Inserting plus sign separators and converting plus signs in query strings into encoded values is done by the Web browser. When a user accesses a Gopher search from a Web browser, he or she is prompted for search strings. These are generally entered in a text box, using space characters to separate the different strings. When the search information is submitted, the search strings are appended, with appropriate encodings, to the URL. The client software is responsible for replacing space characters by plus signs and for encoding characters in your search string that might otherwise be incorrectly interpreted.

The Gopher protocol supports additional features not discussed here. Please see the references at the end of this chapter for additional information.

Http URLs

Http URLs designate files, directories, or server-side programs accessible using the HTTP protocol. An **http** URL must always point to a file (text or program) or a directory. The general form is:

`http://int.dom.name:port/resource`

where the port number is optional (the default value is 80) and where *resource* specifies the resource. Resources are usually (but not always) files or directories. A directory is indicated a terminating forward slash, as in:

`http://www.utoronto.ca/webdocs/HTMLdocs/`

The following reference to this directory is an error, as it implies a reference to a file, not a directory:

`http://www.utoronto.ca/webdocs/HTMLdocs`

However, you can omit the trailing slash when you are referencing the root of a Web site and are not specifying any path information. Thus the following two URLs are equivalent and correct:

```
http://www.utoronto.ca/
http://www.utoronto.ca
```

Special Characters in Http URLs

The forward slash (/), semicolon (;), question mark (?), and hash (#) are special characters in the path and query string portions of an **http** URL. The slash denotes a change in hierarchy (such as a directory), while the question mark ends the resource location path and indicates the start of a query string. The hash denotes the start of a fragment identifier. The semicolon is reserved for future use, and should therefore be encoded in all cases where you intend a literal semicolon.

Query String Encodings

Http URLs can contain query data to be passed to the server. These data are appended to the URL, separated by a question mark, as with Gopher queries. However, in addition to the character encodings required within URLs, query strings undergo additional levels of encoding to preserve information about the *structure* of the query data. This is necessary because certain characters in a query string are assigned special encoded meanings as part of the query—for example, the plus character (+) used to encode spaces, as noted earlier. There are several different ways these encodings are done, depending on the mechanism by which the data are input by the user.

Document authors do not usually have to worry about the encoding phase; browsers take **ISINDEX** or **FORM** data and do the encoding automatically. However, a gateway program author must explicitly *decode* these data; thus, he or she must understand the encoding, in order to reverse the procecure and recover the original data. The following is a brief review of the encoding steps, and you are referred to Chapters 4 (discussion of **FORM** elements) and 8 for more details.

ISINDEX and FORM Query Encodings

The following is the query string encoding process, elaborated to illustrate the important points. If the data are from an **ISINDEX** query, then the entire string input as the query is encoded as follows. If the data are from **FORM**-based input, then each *name* and *value* string from the **FORM** user-input elements is encoded as follows:

1. Percent characters (%) are converted into their URL encodings (%2f).

2. Plus signs (+) are converted into their URL encodings (%2b).

3. Ampersands (&) are converted into their URL encodings (%26).

4. Equals signs (=) are converted into their URL encodings (%3d).

5. The possibly special characters—namely, # ; / ? : $! , ' ( )—are converted into their URL encodings.

6. Space characters are encoded as plus signs (+).

7. All non-ASCII characters (hex codes greater than 7f), all ASCII control characters (hex codes 00-31, and 7f), and the unsafe ASCII characters listed in Table 6.1, are converted into their URL encodings (note that spaces have already been converted into plus signs).

At this point, every ASCII punctuation character has been encoded, except for the characters

_ - . * @

If the data are from an **ISINDEX** query, the encoding is complete. If they are from a **FORM**, there are additional stages. In the case of a form, the *name* and *value* strings from each **FORM** input element are encoded as described in steps 1 through 7. These strings are then combined according to the following rules:

8. Each name and value pair is combined into a composite string of the form *name=value*. Note that the first encoding phase (steps 1–7) encoded all equals signs in the name and value strings, so that the only *un*encoded equals signs in the string are those used to separate a name from its associated value.

9. The *name=value* strings from all the **FORM** elements are combined into a single string, separated by ampersand (&) characters. For example:

```
name1=value1&name2=value2
```

Note that the first encoding phase (steps 1–7) encoded all ampersands in the name and value strings, so that the only unencoded ampersands are those used to separate name/value pairs.

Query string data encoded according to this algorithm are said to be *URL-encoded*. In fact, this encoding mechanism is assigned its own MIME type, namely

```
Content-type: application/x-www-form-url-encoded
```

Note that you can easily tell if the data are from a **FORM** or **ISINDEX** query just by checking for an unencoded equals sign. For example, the first of the following two URLs is from an **ISINDEX** query, the second is from a **FORM** (the query string portion is in boldface):

```
http://some.site.edu/cgi-bin/foo?arg1+arg2+arg3
http://some.site.edu/cgi-bin/program?name1=value1&name2=value2
```

NOTE: Proposed Replacement of Ampersand (&) by Semicolon (;)

The **FORM** encoding use of the ampersand (&) to separate name/value strings was a bad choice, because of the second use of the character to denote HTML character and entity references. The current specification recommends using an unencoded semicolon (;) instead of ampersands. Thus the strings would be combined as

```
name1=value1;name2=value2
```

There are no current browsers that do this when processing **FORM** data. However, a gateway program author should write programs to interpret either the ampersand or semicolon character as possible delimiting characters, so that the program is compatible with next-generation browsers.

Encoding of ISMAP Active Image Queries

A typical active image is written, in an HTML document, as:

```
<A HREF="http://some.where.edu/cgi-bin/program"><IMG
     SRC="funny_image.gif" ISMAP>
</A>
```

The **ISMAP** attribute makes the **IMG** element active, while the surrounding anchor element gives the URL to which the image coordinates should be sent. **ISMAP** active image queries are composed by taking the integer (x,y) pixel coordinates of the mouse click, with respect to the upper left-hand corner of the active image, and appending them to the URL of the enclosing anchor, using the format (query string in boldface):

```
http://some.where.edu/prg-bin/program?x,y
```

The only valid characters in the query string are the integer coordinates (x, y) and the comma separating the two values.

Server Issues: Server Processing of Queries

In general, HTTP servers do not handle queries themselves, but instead pass query data on to other gateway programs for further processing—the path /cgi-bin/ in a URL often indicates that process is taking place. The name need not be /cgi-bin/—this is a configurable symbolic name, and other names (or many different names) are possible. This book generally uses the name cgi-bin to indicate this functionality.

The name following the path /cgi-bin/ is the name of the program to be run by the server. Any information following this name that is not a query string is known *as extra path* information: This is an additional parameter that can be passed to a gateway program. An example is given below.

When a server is contacted via a URL referencing a gateway program, the server launches the program and passes to it any data sent from the client (if any) for further processing. In addition, it passes on any query string data, along with any extra path information. This is discussed in more detail in Chapter 8; here are two simple examples:

http://some.site.edu/cgi-bin/srch-example The server executes the program *srch-example* found in the *cgi-bin* directory. Any output from *srch-example* is sent back to the client.

http://www.site.edu/cgi-bin/srch-example/**path/other?***srch_string* The server again executes the program *srch-example* found in the *cgi-bin* directory. The *extra path* information **path/other** is passed as a parameter to *srch-example*, as is the query information *srch_string*.

Server Issues: Personal HTML Directories

Users who have accounts on a machine running the NCSA HTTP, Apache, Netscape, and most other servers can have world-accessible HTML documents in their own home directories, distinct from those files in the server document hierarchy. These "personal" HTTP document directories are indicated in a URL by a tilde (~) character prepended in front of the path information (the first item in the path hierarchy following the tilde must be the account name of the user). The tilde tells the server that this is not a regular directory, but a *redirection* to a personal document archive of the user with the indicated account. For example, if the user iang has a personal document directory, this could be accessed using the URL:

```
http://site.world.edu/%7Eiang/
```

where %7E is the encoding for the tilde character. You will often see a real tilde in such URLs, since the tilde is safe in most situations.

Http URL Examples

The following are some simple example **http** URLs, illustrating the points mentioned in the preceding discussion.

`http://www.myfrog.com:3232/crunchy/frog/bolt.html#cheeks` References the document *bolt.html* in the directory *crunchy/frog/* accessible from the server *www.myfrog.com* at port 3232 via HTTP. Once retrieved, the browser will look for an anchor with the **NAME** attribute value "cheeks", and will display the text labeled by this anchor.

`http://mr.grumpy.edu/cgi-bin/barf.pl/bad/mood?bad-day#greeting` References the program *barf.pl*, accessible via the HTTP server running on the machine *mr.grumpy.edu*. When accessed, the extra path information bad/mood is passed to the program, along with the query string bad-day. Once the data from the gateway program are returned to the browser, the browser will look for an anchor with the **NAME** attribute value "greeting", and will display the text labeled by this anchor.

```
http://www.hprc.utoronto.ca/
http://www.hprc.utoronto.ca
```

Accesses the root directory of the indicated HTTP server. A server can be configured to deliver a standard HTML document, a listing of the directory contents, or an error message. Since there is no directory or file specified in the URL, the trailing slash is optional.

Https URLs—Secure HTTP

Commercial HTTP servers from several vendors support a variant of the **http** URL, known as **https. Https** and **http** URLs are composed in exactly the same way. The only difference between these protocols is that HTTP uses default port number 443 and the connection between client and server is encrypted using Secure Sockets Layer (SSL) encryption technology.

As a result, data can pass securely between client and server without being intercepted and read by a third party. SSL is discussed in more detail in Chapter 7.

Ldap URLs

LDAP, or Lightweight Directory Access Protocol, is a technology being developed by Netscape to provide corporate directory services—this will provide directory-like information about staff, resources, facilities, addresses, et cetera, accessible on directory servers that can be searched using LDAP-format requests. As a component of implementing LDAP, Netscape has proposed a URL scheme for referencing LDAP directory information from an LDAP server. The general form is:

```
ldap://int.domain.nam:port/ldap-query
```

where `int.domain.nam` is the machine running the LDAP server at the indicated `port` (default value is 389), and `ldap-query` is a query string requesting information from the server. The syntax for such queries is complex and is not reproduced here. An example query might be:

```
ldap://ldap.utoronto.ca/o=University%20of%Toronto,c=CA
```

which requests directory information about the University of Toronto, in Canada.

NOTE: At the time of writing, LDAP URLs are not supported, but are under active development at Netscape. Initial implementations should be available by early 1997.

Mailto URLs

The **mailto** URL designates an Internet-format mail address to which mail can be sent. The format for **mailto** is

```
mailto:mail_address
```

where `mail_address` is the Internet mail address (as specified in RFC 822, the document that specifies the format for Internet mail) to which the message should be sent. Typically, this is of the form `name@host`, where `name` is the username of the person and `host` is the name of the machine at which the user receives mail. A browser that supports **mailto** will provide a mechanism for users to compose and send a letter to this destination.

Some mail addresses contain the percent character. This character must be encoded, since it is a special character (marking the beginning of a character encoding string). As an example, the e-mail address:

```
jello%ian@irc.utoronto.ca
```

must be converted into the **mailto** URL:

```
mailto:jello%25ian@irc.utoronto.ca
```

A **mailto** URL does not indicate how the mail should be sent. In general, a client mail program must contact a *mail server*, a program which validates the mail and forwards it to its destination. **Mailto** URLs do not specify a mail server, so that this information must be separately configured into a browser. A Web browser usually provides a configuration menu allowing users to provide this information.

Setting a Mail Message Subject Line

When composing a URL to use in an HTML document for sending a mail message, an author may want to include information beyond the destination address: for example, a default subject line, or perhaps additional (CC'd) mail destinations for the letter.

One proposed approach for accomplishing some these goals is to place the message subject in a **TITLE** attribute of the element containing the **mailto** reference (typically an **A** or **FORM**). Thus elements of the form

```
<A HREF="mailto:address" TITLE="This is the title"> .....
<FORM ACTION="mailto:address" ... TITLE="Mail message title"> ...
```

would use the **TITLE** value as the subject when composing the message. This approach, within the context of **A**, is supported by the lynx browser.

Netscape Navigator developers took a different approach, and decided to include the information as query string information within the **mailto** URL itself. This is done by appending any required mail header in URL-encoded format, using strings of the form *header=value*, where *header* is the mail header name (URL-encoded) and *value* is the (URL-encoded) string to associate with the name. For example, to send a message to the address address, specifying a given title and a list of CC recipients, the URL would be:

```
mailto:address?subject=test%20mail%20message&cc=address1%2caddress2
```

This associates the subject line "test mail message" to the indicated address, as well as the two indicated CC'd addresses. Notice how the different values are separated by the ampersand character (as with **FORM** data encoding) and that all special characters in the fields are encoded via their URL-encoded values.

There is an obvious problem with this approach—it does not work with most other browsers, which assume the extra text to be part of the mail address. Fortunately, the address fields will appear in the pop-up e-mail form and can be hand-edited by the user before sending the letter— provided the user understands the problem, and how to fix it.

Additional information about this URL format is described in the references at the end of this chapter. The Netscape approach is entirely experimental, and is not part of the URL standard. It is likely that certain aspects of it will change prior to its implementation by other browser vendors, so you should be cautious in using this format.

News URLs

News URLs reference USENET newsgroups or individual USENET news articles. There are several ways to compose **news** URLs. Particular newsgroups are specified using the form:

```
news:news.group.name
```

where `news.group.name` is the name of a particular newsgroup. The special form:

```
news:*
```

references *all* available newsgroups. Note that this does not specify a news (NNTP) server from which news can be accessed; it must be specified elsewhere, in a browser-specific manner. Most browsers let the user set the name of the news server using a pull-down menu, while on UNIX systems it is usually set by defining the server domain name in an NNTPSERVER environment variable.

Referencing Particular News Articles

An alternative form is used to request particular news articles. The form is:

```
news:message_id@domain.name.edu
```

where `message_id` is the unique ID associated with a particular article originating from the machine `domain.name.edu` (this is all discussed in gruesome detail in RFC 1036, referenced at the end of the chapter). The at (@) character is special in a **news** URL, and indicates this alternative form of reference. This format is not generally useful, since most news servers delete articles after a few days or weeks, so that any referenced article is soon unavailable.

Referencing Both Server and Newsgroup

A third form, not part of the official URL standard but widely supported, references both the newsgroup and the server from which the articles should be retrieved, or both the server and a particular article. The two forms are

```
news://int.dom.name:port/news.group.name
news://int.dom.name:port/message_id@domain.name.edu
```

where `int.dom.nam` is the domain name of the server to be contacted, `:port` is the optional port number (the default value is 119), `news.group.name` is the desired newsgroup, and *message_id@domain.name.edu* is the message ID for a particular message posted from the machine at ***domain.name.edu***. Note that these are essentially the same as the default forms, save the addition of a specified NNTP server.

Nntp URLs

The **nntp** URL scheme in principle provides a way of explicitly referencing a news article from a particular NNTP news server. An example **nntp** URL might be:

`nntp://news.server.com/alt.rubber-chickens/12311121.121@foo.org`

which references *article number* `12311121.121@foo.org`, in the newsgroup `alt.rubber-chickens`, from the NNTP server running on the machine ***news.server.com*** (at the default port number 119). The NNTP protocol is described in RFC 977, should you want additional details.

> **NOTE: Nntp Functionality within News URLs**   Essentially all the functionality of **nntp** URLs has been added to **news** URLs by allowing server domain name specification in the news URL, as described above. At present, there are few browser vendors who support NNTP URLs.

Prospero URLs

This scheme references resources accessible using the Prospero Directory Service, which is a sophisticated caching and proxying service for directory, file, and other data. A **prospero** URL takes the form:

`prospero://int.domain.name:port/string/stuff`

which indicates a prospero server running at the indicated machine and port (the default port is 1525), with the remaining string indicating the desired resource.

> **NOTE: Prospero URLs Not Widely Supported**   Very few Web browsers (i.e., practically none) support **prospero** URLs, so that this form is not discussed in detail here. Further information is found in the references at the end of the chapter.

Telnet URLs

You can use a **telnet** URL to reference a telnet link to a remote machine. An example is:

`telnet://int.domain.nam:port`

where *ind.domain.nam* is the machine to which a connection should be made and the optional *:port* specifies the desired port (the default value is 32). A more general form is

```
telnet://username:password@int.domain.nam:port/
```

to indicate the *username* and *password* that the user should employ (the *:password* is optional). The colon (:) and at (@) characters are special in a **telnet** URL, since they designate the different fields in this form. In general, the username and password information is not directly used by a browser to complete the connection. Rather, this information may be presented to users as a hint as to what they should do once the connection is made. Obviously you do not want to use this more general form if you want to keep your passwords secret!

Some browsers support a variant of a **telnet** URL, called a **tn3270** URL. This indicates a connection that requires IBM 3270 terminal emulation on the part of the client. In general, this is only useful if the client computer supports a tn3270 client program (tn3270 clients are rarely built into a Web browser), and provided the WWW client is configured to know about this program. If not, most browsers default to a regular telnet connection.

A few browsers support rlogin connections via **rlogin** URLs. The specification is

```
rlogin://username@int.domain.name
```

where *username* is the account name for the rlogin. You will be prompted for a password in the resulting window unless one is not required. Most browsers that support this emulate **rlogin** URLs using a telnet connection. As **login** URLs are not widely supported, it is best to stick to telnet URLs.

WAIS URLs

WAIS servers can be accessed via URLs in a manner similar to HTTP servers. The major difference is in the file specification: Here, the URL must pass the correct search instructions to the WAIS server, in addition to information about what is to be searched.

The standard form for accessing a WAIS server is

```
wais://int.domain.nam:port/database?search
```

where *int.domain.nam* is the Internet domain name of the host running a WAIS server at the indicated port (the default port is 210); *database* is the name of the WAIS database to be searched; and *search* is a list of search instructions to pass to the database. Another form is (leaving out the port number for brevity):

```
wais://int.domain.nam/database
```

which designates a particular searchable database. A browser will understand that this URL references a searchable database and will prompt for query string input.

Finally, **wais** URLs can reference individual resources on a WAIS database. The form for this URL is:

```
wais://int.domain.nam/database/wais_type/resource_path
```

where *wais_type* is a type indicator, which gives the type of the object being accessed, and *resource_path* is the document ID, used internally by the WAIS database. In general these strings are generated by the WAIS server itself, and it is rare that a user will actually compose the *wais_type* and *resource_path* fields. However, if you are burning to do it yourself, you should read the WAIS documentation listed at the end of this chapter.

File URLs

File URLs are specific to a local system and should not be used in documents to be publicly accessed over the Internet. A **file** URL represents access of files from computers on a network but does not specify a protocol for accessing these files. The general form for a **file** URL is

```
file://host.name/path/file
```

where *host.name* is the domain name for the system and *path/file* is the locator of the file. Note that there is no specified port number. **File** URLs are most commonly used to represent local file access. All browsers allow local file access, often with a pull-down menu, and represent the location using a **file** URL. The domain name for local file access can be either the special string `localhost`, or an empty field (i.e., `file:///...`). For example, if you are accessing the local file */big/web/docs.html*, the file URL could be either of the following:

```
file://localhost/big/web/docs.html
file:///big/web/docs.html
```

where the file could be on a local disk, or on a filesystem mounted on the local system from elsewhere.

NOTE: Don't Use File URLs for Internet Publishing   Since **file** URLs are designed to specify local files, and the general public will not have access to your filesystem, **file** URLs should not be used for documents to be published on the Internet.

Coming Attractions?

Several additional general-purpose URL schemes have been proposed. Some examples are **afs** (global file access using the Andrew File System), **cid** (content identifiers for MIME message parts), **mailserver** (access to data from mail servers, as opposed to just sending mail), **mid** (message identifiers for electronic mail), and **z39.50** (access to ANSI standard Z39.50 database and searching services). These are in most cases not fully specified, and are not widely implemented.

Of particular interest are several URL types proposed in conjunction with the new **OBJECT** element (for including program, data, or other "objects" within an HTML document, as discussed in Chapter 5). Notable among these are **data** URLs, for inclusion of small data items as "immediate" data, as if it had been included externally, **clsid** URLs, for referencing class IDs of Microsoft Common Object Model (COM) classes, and **java,** for referencing Java program object classes. Some references to information about these types are given at the end of this chapter. They are also briefly discussed in the **OBJECT** element section in Chapter 5.

Generalized Naming Schemes for the Web

The URL scheme is the only naming scheme currently used on the Web, but several other naming schemes have been proposed, and are likely to be implemented in the future. This brief section summarizes the names and general features of the different proposed schemes. The "Main Addressing References" section at the end of this chapter provides pointers to additional discussion on these topics.

Uniform Resource Names: URN
Uniform resource names, or URNs, are designed to be a location-independent way of referencing an object. A URN would not specify the location of the desired resource, but would specify a generic name. The software processing the name would then locate the named object at the closest or most accessible location, using a name lookup service. The specification of URNs is incomplete, and they are not in current use.

Uniform Resource Locator: URL
Uniform resource locators, or URLs, are protocol- and location-specific schemes for referencing resources on the Internet. This is currently the only implemented mechanism for referencing resources on the Internet.

Uniform Resource Identifier: URI
Uniform resource identifiers, or URIs, generically represent any naming schemes used to reference resources on the Internet. Thus, both URLs and URNs fall under the category of URIs. The names URI and URL are often used synonymously, but this is only correct in the absence of a defined naming scheme for URNs.

Uniform Resource Citation: URC

Uniform resource citations, or URCs, are designed to be collections of attribute/value pairs that describe a particular object (referenced using a URI). Some of the values in these pairs may also be URIs. A URC can act in many ways, for example as a cross-indexing resource for a large resource collection, or simply as a collection of references to related data. The specification for URCs is not complete, so that they are not in current use.

References

The URI specifications originate from the various working groups currently developing Internet and Web standards. In most cases, the Internet protocols or standards are formalized in documents known as Requests for Comments, or RFCs. Once approved by the appropriate Internet Engineering Task Force (IETF), these documents are officially numbered, giving rise to the referenced RFC numbers quoted here.

Main Addressing References

`http://www.w3.org/hypertext/WWW/Addressing/Addressing.html`	(Overview of issues)
`ftp://ds.internic.net/rfc/rfc1738.txt`	(Standard URL specifications)
`ftp://ds.internic.net/rfc/rfc1808.txt`	(Relative URL specification)
`http://www.w3.org/pub/WWW/Addressing/schemes.html`	(Catalog of URL schemes)

Netscape Mailto URL Extensions (Draft Only)

`http://www.utoronto.ca/webdocs/HTMLdocs/Book/Book-3ed/chap6/mail.html`

LDAP URL Specification (Draft Only)

`ftp://ds.internic.net/internet-drafts/draft-ietf-asid-ldap-format-xx.txt` (Look for the most recent 0 version—largest *xx* value)

Proposed URL Schemes (Draft Specifications Only)

`http://www.w3.org/pub/WWW/Addressing/clsid-scheme`	(CLSID URLs)
`ftp://ietf.cnri.reston.va.us/internet-drafts/draft-masinter-url-data-01.txt`	(DATA URLs)
`http://www.w3.org/pub/WWW/Addressing/draft-mirashi-url-irc-01.txt`	(IRC URLs)
`http://www.w3.org/pub/WWW/Addressing/draft-ietf-mhtml-cid-00.txt`	(CID and MID URLs)

Protocol and Data Format Specifications

`ftp://ds.internic.net/rfc/rfc822.txt`	(Internet mail message)
`ftp://ds.internic.net/rfc/rfc1036.txt`	(Usenet messages)
`ftp://ds.internic.net/rfc/rfc977.txt`	(NNTP protocol)
`http://ingis.acn.purdue.edu:9999/WAIS/orgWAISdoc/wais-corp.txt`	(WAIS overview)
`ftp://ds.internic.net/rfc/rfc1625.txt`	(WAIS protocol)
`ftp://prospero.isi.edu/pub/prospero/doc/prospero-protocol.PS.Z`	(Prospero protocol)

URI Specification (RFC 1630)

```
ftp://ds.internic.net/rfc/rfc1630.txt
http://www.w3.org/hypertext/WWW/Addressing/URL/URI_Overview.html
```
(HTML version of early draft)

URNs: Uniform Resource Names

```
http://union.ncsa.uiuc.edu/~liberte/www/path.html
http://www.w3.org/pub/WWW/Addressing/rfc1737.txt
```
Proposed PATH specification)
(Functional requirements for URNs)

URCs: Uniform Resource Characteristics

```
http://union.ncsa.uiuc.edu/HyperNews/get/www/URCs.html
http://www.acl.lanl.gov/URI/ExtRep/urc0.html
http://www.w3.org/pub/WWW/Addressing/citations.html
```
(General issues)

7

The HTTP Protocol

To develop interactive HTML-based applications, a Web designer must understand how a Web client program, such as a browser, interacts with an HTTP server. This interaction involves two distinct but related issues. The first is HTTP—the protocol by which a client program sends information to an HTTP server, and vice versa. HTTP supports mechanisms for communicating information about the transaction, such as the status (successful or not) and the nature of the data being sent (i.e., what is the MIME type of the data) on top of mechanisms for sending data from client to server or from server to client. The protocol also supports several communication *methods* (for example, *GET, POST,* or *HEAD*) for specifying *how* message data is being sent by the browser, or how the request should be handled by the server. This chapter presents a detailed description of these mechanisms and of how they work.

The second issue is the manner in which an HTTP server handles a request. If the requested resource is a file, the server locates the file and sends it back to the client, or sends a relevant error message if the file is unavailable. However, in some cases the requested resource (as specified by the accessed URL) implies special processing on the server machine, such as access to a database. In general, servers do not themselves do this processing, since such tasks are largely customized to the applications running at a particular Web site, and do not reflect "generic" functionality that can be easily incorporated into a "universal" server. Instead, most servers "hand off" these complex tasks to other programs, called *gateway programs*, which are designed explicitly for this special processing and which run as processes separate from the HTTP server. The *common gateway interface (CGI)* specification, described in the next chapter, defines the mechanisms by which HTTP servers communicate with these gateway programs.*

This chapter first outlines the general principles of the HTTP protocol, and then illustrates its operation using seven example transactions. The chapter concludes with a detailed list of the control messages that can be sent from client to server and vice versa.

Like HTML, HTTP is evolving, with significant enhancements due to appear over the next year. The current standard version is known as HTTP 1.0 (Version 1.0); the specifications for the next standard version, HTTP 1.1, are nearly completed. This chapter primarily discusses standard HTTP 1.0, but also mentions the HTTP 1.1 features that have been incorporated into HTTP 1.0 servers as "experimental" but commonly implemented extensions. The chapter also discusses some other HTTP 1.1 features likely to be implemented in the near future.

HTTP Protocol Overview

HTTP is an Internet client-server protocol designed for the rapid and efficient delivery of hypertext materials. HTTP is a *stateless* protocol, which means that once a server has delivered the requested data to a client, the client-server connection is broken, and the server retains no memory of the event that just took place.

All HTTP communication transmits data as a stream of 8-bit characters, or *octets*. This ensures the safe transmission of all forms of data, including images, executable programs, and HTML documents.

A basic HTTP 1.0 session has four stages:

1. **Client opens the connection**—The client program (usually a Web browser) contacts the server at the specified Internet address and port number (the default port is 80).

2. **Client makes the request**—The client sends a message to the server, requesting service. The request consists of an HTTP *request header,* specifying the *HTTP method* to be used during the transaction and providing information about the capabilities of the client and about the

---

*Many servers now support compiled modules that can be dynamically linked to the server and that support gateway-like functionality, with significant performance improvements over the standard CGI mechanism. This is also discussed in Chapter 8.

data being sent to the server (if any); followed by the data actually being sent by the client. Typical HTTP methods are *GET*, for getting an object from a server, and *POST*, for posting data to a resource (e.g., a gateway program) on the server.

3. **Server sends a response**—The server sends a response to the client. This consists of a *response header* describing the state of the transaction (e.g., whether the transaction was successful) and the type of data being sent (if any), followed by any data being returned (if any).

4. **Server closes the connection**—The connection is closed; the server does not retain any knowledge of the transaction just completed.

This procedure means that each connection processes a single transaction, and can therefore only download a single data file to the client, while the stateless nature means that each connection knows nothing about previous connections. The implications of these features are illustrated in the following two example HTTP sections.

NOTE: HTTP 1.0 Keep-alive   Some browsers and HTTP 1.0 servers support an experimental feature called *keep-alive*, that can keep the client-server connection open when a client requests multiple resources from the same server. This means that the closing of the connection at step 4 of the four-step scheme is deferred—instead, the next request starts at step 2, since there is no need to reopen the connection. The server still does not retain knowledge of a transaction once it is finished.

A. Single Transaction per Connection

Assume that HTTP is used to access an HTML document containing 10 inline images via the **IMG** element. Composing the entire document requires 11 distinct connections to the HTTP server: one to retrieve the HTML document itself and 10 others to retrieve the 10 image files.

If this transaction is repeated using keep-alive, the browser still retrieves 11 distinct files, but the connection between browser and server is only broken after the last image has been downloaded. This saves several stages of connection opening and closing, and can significantly speed up the downloading of composite documents. However, as far as the browser and server are concerned, each request is a single transaction, and the server does not retain knowledge of a transaction after it is completed, even if the connection to the client is still open.

B. Stateless Connections

Assume that a user retrieves, from a server, a fill-in HTML **FORM** that contains a fill-in field for a product name, where the entered name lets the user access product-specific information from a database. When the user submits the **FORM**, the name (and any other information gathered by the **FORM**) is sent to a gateway program residing on the server, which in turn processes the request; the URL of the gateway program is specified as an attribute to the **FORM** element, as discussed in Chapter 4.

This gateway program processes the data and returns the results to the user, as a second HTML document that contains another **FORM** allowing further requests of the database. But, in this case, the **FORM** does not contain a place to type a product name. Since the server is stateless, and thus has no memory of the first connection, how does it know the name of the product the second time around?

The answer is that it does not. Instead, gateway programs must explicitly keep track of this information, for example by hiding the name information *inside* the HTML document returned to the user. This can be accomplished through special **FORM** *hidden* input elements of the form `<INPUT TYPE="hidden" ...>`, which are commonly used to record the *state* of the client-server transaction. For this example, the element might be:

```
<INPUT TYPE="hidden" NAME="name_of_product" VALUE="product_name">
```

Then, when the user submits the second **FORM**, the content of the hidden element is sent along with any new input, thereby returning the product name to the server. Using hidden elements, state information can be passed back and forth between client and server, preserving knowledge of the name for each subsequent transaction.

Example HTTP Client-Server Sessions

The easiest way to understand HTTP is through simple examples. The following sections present seven examples covering the most common HTTP methods. Each presentation shows both the data sent from the client to the HTTP server and the data returned from the server to the client. First, a few words about how this "eavesdropping" was accomplished.

Monitoring Client-Server Interaction
It is easy to monitor the interaction between HTTP servers and Web clients, since the communication is entirely in character data sent to a particular port. All you need do is *listen* at a port, or *talk* to a port. You can listen at a port using the program **listen** or **backtalk**, given in Appendix D, while you can talk to a port using **backtalk**, or the standard Internet program **telnet**.

Client Sending to Server
You can use **listen** to find out what a Web client sends to a server. To do this, you run the **listen** program on a computer, and then make a Web client talk to **listen**. As an example, suppose **listen**

is started up on a computer with domain name *leonardo.subnet.ca*. When started, **listen** prints out the port number it is listening at, for example:

```
listening at port 1743
```

It then falls silent, waiting to print any data that arrives at port 1743. The next step is to configure a Web client to send HTTP requests to this port. This is done by accessing a URL that *points* to port 1743 on *leonardo.subnet.ca,* such as:

```
http://leonardo.subnet.ca:1743/Tests/file.html
```

(the port number is marked in boldface). The client dutifully sends the HTTP request headers to port number 1743 on *leonardo.subnet.ca*, whereupon **listen** receives the data and prints them to the screen.

Server Sending to Client

Determining what the server sends back to the client takes a bit more work. In this case, you can use **telnet** to connect to the server, but you must now enter by hand the HTTP request headers that are sent by a "real" client (and which you fortunately intercepted using the **listen** program, following the procedure described in the previous section). Suppose, for example, that a server is running at port 80 on *leonardo.subnet.ca*. You can connect to this server by simply making a telnet connection to this port. On a UNIX system, you would type:

```
telnet leonardo.subnet.ca 80
```

Telnet gives three lines of information to explain what it is doing and then falls silent:

```
Trying 128.100.121.33...
Connected to leonardo.subnet.ca
Escape character is '^]'.
```

Whatever you now type is sent to the server running on *leonardo.subnet.ca*. Type in the required request headers. Whatever the server sends in response is sent to the telnet program and printed on the screen.

A third useful tool is the program **backtalk**, listed in Appendix D. **Backtalk** is a derivative of **listen** that allows you both to monitor data arriving at a port, and send data to the remote program talking to that port. When launched, **backtalk** allocates a port and, like **listen**, prints out the port number, for example:

```
listening at port 1743
```

Thereafter, **backtalk** prints to the display anything a remote program sends to port 1743, while anything typed into the console is sent out through port 1743 back to the remote program. Thus you can use **backtalk** to mimic the response of an HTTP server, albeit by hand. This is useful for examining client response to special server response headers, such as a request for user authentication.

Overview of Examples

These tools were used to determine the information passed between the client and server in several typical HTTP transactions. The examples look at:

1. a simple GET method request

2. a simple GET method request, illustrating some newer header fields

3. a HEAD method request for file meta-information

4. a GET method request with a query string within the URL

5. a GET method request arising from an HTML **FORM** submission

6. a POST method request arising from an HTML **FORM** submission

7. a file access request requiring "Basic" user authentication

To get the most out of these examples, you will need a basic understanding of URLs and of the way data are gathered by an HTML form and composed as a message for the server. These topics were covered in Chapters 4 (**FORMs**) and 6 (construction of query strings).

Basic Elements of an HTTP Session

When a client contacts a server, it sends a *request header* defining the details of the request, followed by any data the client may be sending. In response, the server returns a *response header* describing the status of the transaction, followed in turn by any data being returned. The first example illustrates the basics of this flow of information.

Example 12: A Simple GET Method Request

This example looks in detail at how a client makes a GET request for a document resource from an HTTP server, and how a server responds to the request. In practice, such a transaction would be initi-ated on a browser by clicking on a hypertext anchor pointing to the server and the desired file. For example:

```
<A HREF="http://smaug.middle.earth.ca:2021/Tests/file.html">
   anchor text
</A>
```

For this example (and for Examples 13 and 14), we assume this anchor was accessed from a document previously retrieved from the URL:

```
http://www.utoronto.ca/webdocs/webinfo.html
```

The analysis is broken into the two basic parts: the passing of the request to the server, and the response sent by the server back to the client.

The Client Request Header

Figure 7.1 shows the actual data sent by a Netscape Navigator 1.01 client to the server. Other clients send qualitatively the same information (we will look at some others later on). The dots indicate Accept header fields omitted to save space.

This request message consists of a *request header* containing several *request header fields*. Each field is a line of ASCII text, terminated by a carriage-return linefeed character pair (CRLF). A blank line containing only a CRLF pair marks the end of the request header and the beginning of any *data* being sent from the client to the server. This example transaction does not send data to the server, so the blank line is the end of the request.

The request header contains two parts. The first part—the first line of the header—is called the *method* field. This field specifies the HTTP *method* to be used, the location of the desired resource on the server (as a URL), and the version of the HTTP protocol the client program would like to use. This is followed by several HTTP *request* fields, which provide information to the server about the client, and about the nature of the data (if any) being sent by the client to the server.

Client Request: The Method Field

The method field contains three text fields, separated by whitespace (whitespace is any combination of space and/or tab characters). The general form for this field is:

```
HTTP_method   identifier   HTTP_version
```

which, in our example, was

```
GET /path/file.html HTTP/1.0
```

Figure 7.1 Data sent from a Netscape Navigator 1.01 client to an HTTP server during a simple GET request. *Comments are in italics*.

```
GET /Tests/file.html HTTP/1.0
Accept: text/plain
.
.
Accept: */*
If-Modified-Since: Wed, 25 Sep 1996 17:23:31 GMT
Referer: http://www.utoronto.ca/webdocs/webinfo.html
User-Agent: Mozilla/1.01
          [a blank line, containing only CRLF ]
```

The three components of this method field are:

HTTP_method The HTTP method specification—GET in this example. The method specifies what is to be done to the object specified by the URL. Some others common methods are HEAD, which requests header information about an object, and POST, which is used to send information to the object.

identifier The identifier of the resource. In this example the identifier, /path/file.html, is the URL stripped of the protocol and Internet domain name strings. If this were a request to a *proxy server*, it would be the entire URL. Proxy servers are discussed later in this chapter.

HTTP_version The HTTP protocol version used by the client, currently HTTP/1.0.

Client Request: The Accept Field

In addition to the method field, the example shows several additional request header fields. The Accept fields contain a list of data types, expressed as MIME content-types, that tell the server what type of data the client is willing to accept. MIME types are discussed in more detail in Appendix B, and later in this chapter. The meanings for simple requests are relatively straightforward. For example, Accept: text/plain means that the client can accept plain text files, while Accept: audio/* means that the client can accept any form of audio data.

A client can include information in accept fields stating the relative desirability of particular types of data. This is expressed through two quantities: the q or quality factor (a number in the range 0.0 to 1.0, where 0.0 is equivalent to not accepting a type, and 1.0 is equivalent to always accepting a type), and mxb, which stands for the maximum size in bytes. If the resource is bigger than the mxb value, then it is not acceptable to the client. The default values are q=1.0 and mxb=undefined (that is, any size is acceptable). Thus the following

```
Accept: image/*
Accept: image/jpeg; q=0.7; mxb=50000
Accept: image/gif; q=0.5
```

mean that the client prefers image/jpeg files, provided they are smaller than 50 KB. If there is a JPEG file but it is too big, then the client would prefer a GIF. If there are no GIF files, then the client will take any available image file.

Accept types can be combined in a single field if they are separated by commas. For example, the above three fields could be written:

```
Accept: image/*, image/jpeg; q=0.7; mxb=50000, image/gif; q=0.5
```

NOTE: Unreliability of Accept Header Information   In principle, a server or a server-side gateway program can use Accept information to decide what type of data to send back to the client. However, very few servers have this capability, while most browsers send the field Accept: */*, which indicates that they will accept anything.

Client Request: User-Agent Header Field

There are several other common request header fields. The `User-agent` field, of the form `User-agent: ascii_string`, provide information about the client making the request. The example gave:

```
User-Agent: Mozilla/1.01
```

to indicate the Netscape 1.01 browser (code-named "Mozilla"). Two other examples are:

```
User-Agent: Mozilla/3.0b5 (Win95; I)
User-Agent: Mozilla/2.0 (compatible; MSIE 3.0B; Windows 95;1024,768)
```

The first is from a Netscape Navigator browser, with the text in brackets providing additional information about the browser (version, platform, etc.)—this is the proper syntax for including additional user-agent specific information. The second example is from a Microsoft Internet Explorer browser, although note that it is claiming to be a Netscape browser—many server gateway programs use the browser name to select the type of data to return, so that Microsoft has used the Mozilla name to convince server software to treat the Microsoft product as being equivalent to Netscape's.

Client Request: Referer Header Field

Another common field is `Referer`, which takes the general form `Referer: URL`. This field gives the URL of the document from which the request originated. In the example, we noted that the user first accessed the document:

```
http://www.utoronto.ca/webdocs/webinfo.html
```

and from there accessed the link that produced the request shown in Figure 7.1. Thus, the header field:

```
Referer: http://www.utoronto.ca/webdocs/webinfo.html
```

is part of the request header sent to the server.

Client Request: If-Modified-Since Header Field

A third common header is `If-modified-since`. This contains a time and date, in Greenwich Mean Time, and is used to retrieve a document (or data) only if it has been modified since the specified time and date. This is usually sent by a client that has a local copy of the data and that knows the time and date at which this copy was last modified. In Figure 7.1, the client sent the header:

```
If-Modified-Since: Wed, 25 Sep 1996 17:23:31 GMT
```

If the requested resource */path/file.html* has been modified since this time and date, then the server will send a new copy to the client. However, if the resource has not been modified since this time and date, the server will not send a new copy, but will instead send a special message indicating that the resource has not changed, and that the client should use its existing copy. These messages are discussed in the upcoming section on server response.

Request Headers and Gateway Programs

In this example, the request header fields are used by the server to determine whether or not a data file should be sent to the server, and if so, what type of data to send. (Servers can use the `Accept` fields to decide from amongst a variety of different possible return types. At present this feature, known as *content* or *format negotiation*, is implemented on some servers, including the CERN and Apache packages.) If the request is to a gateway program, and not for a file, then the server cannot make this decision. Instead, the server passes *all* the request header information to the gateway program (as a collection of environment variables) and lets the gateway program decide what to do. Thus, a gateway program author must understand the meanings of these header fields, since he or she will have to write gateway programs that interpret them. A complete list of the possible request header fields is given at the end of this chapter.

The Server Response: Header and Data

When the server receives the request, it tries to apply the designated method to the specified object (file or program), and passes the results of this effort back to the client. The returned data are preceded by a *response header* consisting of *response header fields*, which communicate information about the state of the transaction back to the client. As with the request header fields sent from the client to the server, these are single lines of text terminated by a CRLF, while the end of the response header is indicated by a single blank line containing only a CRLF. The data of the response follow the blank line.

Figure 7.2 shows the data returned by the server in response to the request of Figure 7.1. The first seven lines illustrate the response header. The end of the response header is indicated by the single blank line. The data response of the request (in this case, the requested HTML document) follows this blank line.

Figure 7.2 Data returned from the server to the client subsequent to the GET request of Figure 7.1. *Comments are in italics*.

```
HTTP/1.0 200 OK
Date: Mon, 07 Oct 1996 16:04:09 GMT
Server: NCSA/1.5.2
MIME-version: 1.0
Content-type: text/html
Last-modified: Thu, 03 Oct 1996 16:03:27 GMT
Content-length: 139
     [a blank line, containing only CRLF ]
<html><head>
<title> Test HTML file </title>
</head><body>
<h1> This is a test file</h1>
<p> So what did you expect, art?
</body></html>
```

Server Response: The Status Line

The first line in the response header is a status line, which lets the client know what protocol the server uses, and whether or not the request was successfully completed. The general format for this line is:

```
http_version  status_code  explanation
```

which in the example was:

```
HTTP/1.0 200 OK
```

The three components of this status line are:

HTTP_version The protocol version being used by the server, currently `HTTP/1.0`. If a client requests HTTP/1.1 but the server is only capable of HTTP/1.0, then the server can return a version field of `HTTP/1.0` to indicate this fact.

status_code The *status code* for the response, as a number between 200 and 599. Values from 200 and 299 indicate successful transactions, while values 300–399 indicate *redirection*—the resource at the requested URL has moved. In this case, the server must also send the new URL of the object, if it is known (sent within a `Location` response header field). Numbers 400–599 are error messages. When an error occurs, the server usually sends a small HTML document explaining the error, to help the user understand what happened and why. The status codes and their meanings are summarized in Table 7.2 at the end of this chapter.

explanation A text string that provides descriptive information about the status. Explanation strings vary from server to server, whereas status codes and their meanings are explicitly defined by the HTTP specification.

In this example, the code 200 means that everything went fine, and that the server is returning the requested data.

The remaining response header fields contain information about the server and about the response being sent. The example in Figure 7.2 returns six lines of response header information. The first three, the `Date`, `Server`, and `MIME-Version` fields, describe the server and the MIME version used to encode the response, while the `Content-type`, `Last-modified`, and `Content-length` fields pass information specific to the document or data being returned. The formats and meanings of these header fields are described in the following sections.

Server Response: Date Header Field

This field, of the format `Date: date_time,` contains the time and date when the current object was assembled for transmission. Note that the time *must* be Greenwich Mean Time (GMT) to ensure that all clients and servers share a common time zone. In the example, this field was:

```
Date: Thu, 07 Oct 1996 16:04:09 GMT
```

Also note that this is not necessarily the date at which the resource was created (see Last-modified.) Details about allowed time formats are given at the end of the chapter.

Server Response: MIME-Version Field

This field of format `MIME-version: version_number` gives the MIME protocol version used by the server in composing the response. The current version is 1.0, so this field is:

```
MIME-version: 1.0
```

Unfortunately, many servers send this header even though their responses are not MIME-compliant.

Server Response: Server Field

This field, of the format `Server: name/version`, returns the name and version of the server software, with a slash character separating the two—for example:

```
Server: Apache/1.1.1
Server: CERN/3.0
```

Server Response: Content-Length

This field, of the format `Content-length: length`, gives the length in bytes of the data portion of the message. If the length is unknown (for example, if it is output from a gateway program), this field is absent. In this event, the client will continue to read data until the server breaks the connection. If no data are returned, this field is also absent. In the example, the message is 139 bytes long, so the header field is:

```
Content-length: 139
```

Server-Response: Content-Type

This field, of the format `Content-type: type/subtype`, indicates the MIME Content-type of the data being sent from the server to the client. In this example, the returned data is an HTML document, so the returned header field is:

```
Content-type: text/html
```

MIME types are discussed in Appendix B. If no data are returned, this field is absent.

Server Response: Last-Modified

This field, of the format `Last-modified: date_time`, gives the date and time that the document was last modified. As with the Date field, the information must be given in Greenwich Mean Time. In the example, this field was

```
Last-Modified: Thu, 03 Oct 1996 16:03:27 GMT
```

If the server does not know the date on which the resource was last modified, this field is absent.

Server Generation of Response Header

How is the response header generated by the server? If the requested resource is a file, the HTTP server constructs the header itself. If the request is to a gateway program, then the gateway program must provide header fields that specify details about the returned data, such as the `Content-type`, since these cannot otherwise be determined by the server. The server parses the gateway-provided header fields, and adds some of its own, to construct a complete server response header. Alternatively, the gateway program can return a complete response header and bypass server processing, using a special CGI form known as a *non-parsed header* gateway program. Both approaches are described in Chapter 8.

Server Response If File Not Modified

How would the server respond if the requested file was not modified subsequent to the time specified in the `If-modified-since` field in the request header? In this case, the server responds with a short message of the form:

```
HTTP/1.0 304 Not Modified
Date: Mon, 07 Oct 1996 16:04:09 GMT
Server: NCSA/1.5.2
MIME-version: 1.0
    [Blank line, containing CRLF]
```

This contains the status code 304, which tells the client that the file was unchanged and that the client should use its cached copy of the data.

Lessons from Example 12

1. When a client contacts an HTTP server, it sends the server a *request header* composed of *request header fields*. The first of these fields is the *method field*, which specifies the HTTP method being requested by the client and the *location* on the server of the resource being requested. This is followed by other header fields that pass information about the capabilities of the client. The request header is terminated by a single blank line, containing only a carriage-return linefeed (CRLF) character pair.

2. The server responds with a message consisting of a *response header* followed by the requested data. The response header fields communicate information about the state of the transaction, including a MIME *content-type* header that explicitly tells the client the type of data being sent. The response header is terminated by a single blank line. The data being sent to the client follow this blank line.

Example 13: Other Common Request Header Fields

Modern browsers have extended the repertoire of request header fields, incorporating some fields proposed in HTTP 1.1 and others not part of the "official" HTTP 1.0 specification. For example, Figure 7.3 shows the request header produced by the Microsoft Internet Explorer 3.0 browser

---

Figure 7.3 Request header sent by the Microsoft Internet Explorer 3.0 browser. New fields are shown in boldface.

```
GET /Tests/file.html HTTP/1.0
Accept: */*
Referer: http://www.utoronto.ca/webdocs/webinfo.html
Accept-Language: en
User-Agent: Mozilla/2.0 (compatible; MSIE 3.0B; Windows 95;1024,768)
Host: smaug.middle.earth.ca
    [a blank line, containing only CRLF ]
```

when making a request identical with that shown in Figure 7.1, while Figure 7.4 shows the header sent by the Netscape Navigator 3.0 browser. Both cases assume the request is made as described at the beginning of Example 12. New header fields are shown in boldface.

Aside from somewhat cleaner header presentation (there are fewer superfluous accept header fields), there are three new fields, as well as extra information in one of the User-agent fields. The purpose of these additions is described in the following sections.

Client Request: Accept-Language Field

The accept-language field, of the form Accept-language: *lang1*, *lang2* ..., gives a list of languages supported by the browser. It is similar to an accept field, but its function is to allow for selection of different language versions of the same document. Some servers support this field, depending on how the request is made. Language specifications are described in Appendix E. Here, the field accept-language: en means that the client will accept English-language documents.

Client Request: Host Field (HTTP 1.1)

The host field, of the form Host: *domain_name:port*, gives the domain name and port to which the client has directed its request—if the port is absent, the default value (80) is assumed. This field may seem superfluous, but it is useful if the request passes through a proxy server or is directed to a server that has more than one domain name. Most current browsers send this field. Note the bug in the early version of Internet Explorer 3 as shown in Figure 7.3—the port number (2021) is missing.

Figure 7.4 Request header sent by the Netscape Navigator 3.0 browser.

```
GET /Tests/file.html HTTP/1.0
Referer: http://www.utoronto.ca/webdocs/webinfo.html
Connection: Keep-Alive
Cookie: good=bad; apples=oranges
User-Agent: Mozilla/3.0b5 (Win95; I)
Host: smaug.java.utoronto.ca:2021
Accept: image/gif, image/x-xbitmap, image/jpeg, image/pjpeg, */*
Accept-Language: en-US, fr
    [a blank line, containing only CRLF ]
```

Client Request: User-Agent Field

Note how the user-agent field in Figure 7.3 indicates that the browser (MSIE 3.0B) is compatible with Netscape 2.0 (Mozilla). The field also gives the display resolution of the computer (1024 by 768). The placement or inclusion of such data is not standardized, so you cannot count on this information being present.

Client Request: Connection Field (HTTP 1.1)

Figure 7.4 illustrates the connection field, of the form `Connection: Keep-Alive`. This is used to keep the TCP/IP connection from breaking after the requested resource has been uploaded to the client. As mentioned in the introduction to this chapter, HTTP 1.0 was designed to break this connection as soon as the data was sent to a client. This can be very inefficient if a browser requests several subsequent files from the same server (as happens when requesting an HTML document plus all the inline graphics). If the browser sends a keep-alive header field, servers that understand this field will keep the connection open for a short time (usually 10–15 seconds), in anticipation of the next request.

As you can see in Figures 7.3 and 7.4, not all browsers support keep-alive. Similarly, not all servers support this feature; many simply ignore this field. Finally, a server will use keep-alive *only if* it can return a `content-length` response header field for the data it returns—with keep-alive, the content-length field is the only way a client can tell if all the data has been sent by the server, whereupon it can make another request.

Client Request: Netscape Cookie Fields

The Netscape Navigator browser (and, presently, most others) supports a special feature called *Netscape cookies*. This mechanism lets a server store limited pieces information on a browser, sent to the client using a `Set-cookie` server response header field. A browser that understands cookies will store the data on the client machine's hard disk, and will return these data to the server from which the cookie originated within a `cookie` request header field.

Cookies are useful for storing state information (when the user last visited the site, which resources they last used, etc.) on the browser, in such a way that the information is not lost when the user leaves the site or shuts down the browser. However, not all browsers support Netscape cookies, while browsers that do support cookies give the user the option of disabling this feature, so that this is not a guaranteed way of preserving state.

Detailed information about the cookie mechanism is found in Chapter 8.

Lessons from Example 13

1. Most browsers send a `Host` request field, which gives the domain name and port number to which the request is being directed. Some also send an `accept-language` field, to indicate the language(s) preferred by the user.

2. The `User-agent` field may contain browser-specific information, such as the monitor display resolution. There is no standardized way for including this information.

3. Some browsers also send a `Connection:` `keep-alive` header field to stop the server from breaking the connection after the server has sent the requested data. Not all browsers or servers support this feature.

4. Using `Set-cookie` response header fields and the Netscape cookie mechanism is a useful way of storing state information about the client-server session. However, not all browsers support this mechanism.

HEAD Method: Information about a Resource

In some cases, it is useful to gather information about a resource without explicitly retrieving the resource itself. For example, a link-checking program does not always need to retrieve a resource to verify that the resource exists, while an indexing package may only want to know if a resource has changed since it was last catalogued, prior to deciding if it should be retrieved.

This role is satisfied by the HTTP HEAD method, which requests that a server send the response header relevant to the requested URL, but not the content of the referenced object. As the following example indicates, this is a quick way of seeing if a document or gateway program is actually present and of obtaining some general information about it, such as its MIME content-type or the date it was last modified, without downloading the entire resource.

Example 14: Using the HEAD Method

In this example, we suppose that the user (or some automated program, such as a robot or spider) wants to access HEAD information about the document referenced in Example 12. The request that would be sent to the server is simply:

```
HEAD /Tests/file.html HTTP/1.0
User-Agent: HEAD Test Agent
From: name@domain.name.edu
```

The request does not need `accept` header fields, since no data are being retrieved. The `From` field gives the server the electronic mail address of the user making the HEAD request—it is particularly important to give this information if the request comes from an automated program. A typical response (in this case, from an Apache 1.1.1 HTTP server) is:

```
HTTP/1.0 200 OK
Date: Wed, 09 Oct 1996 23:10:55 GMT
Server: Apache/1.1.1
MIME-version: 1.0
```

```
Content-type: text/html
Content-length: 139
Last-modified: Fri, 20 Sep 1996 19:44:28 GMT
```

This indicates that the document exists (the status code 200 indicates a valid URL), and includes information about the document type and the date it was last modified. If this URL referenced a dynamic resource, such as program or a parsed HTML document (see Chapter 8), the `Content-length` and `Last-modified` headers would be absent, to indicate that the length is unknown *a priori*, and that the document is essentially new every time it is accessed.

If the HEAD request references an HTML document, some servers will parse the document **HEAD,** and will extract **META** element information for inclusion in the response header. This feature is not widely implemented.

Lessons from Example 14
1. A HEAD request retrieves only the response header for the indicated URL—the document itself is not retrieved. If the HEAD request is for an HTML document, some servers parse the *document* **HEAD** for information to include in the response headers, but this feature is not widely implemented.

Sending Data to a Server: GET and POST

The HTTP protocol supports several methods for sending data from client to server. The most common are GET and POST, which are commonly used as the interface between HTML **FORM**s and **ISINDEX** queries from the client, and server-side processing programs. The PUT method, on the other hand, is used to create new resources (such as files) on a server. PUT is described later in this chapter.

Example 15: GET Method with a Query String
Example 15 is a GET method request, but with query information appended to the URL. As discussed in Chapters 2 and 6, query information is appended to the URL following a question mark. This encoding is done automatically by Web browsers when you submit **ISINDEX** queries or, depending on the mechanisms used, when you submit an HTML **FORM**. An example URL is

```
http://www.stuff.ca/cgi-bin/srch-example?item1+item2+item3+item4
```

which passes four items from an **ISINDEX** query to the program *srch-example*.

Figure 7.5 shows the request header fields sent by the Internet Explorer 3.0 browser when accessing this URL. This request header is essentially the same as that in Figure 7.3, the only important difference being the query string appended to the locator string. The server's handling of query strings is described in the next chapter.

Figure 7.5 Data sent from the Internet Explorer 3.0 Beta 1 browser to an HTTP server during a GET request with query strings appended to the URL. *Comments are in italics.*

```
GET /cgi-bin/srch-example?item1+item2+item3+item4 HTTP/1.0
Accept: */*
Accept-Language: en
User-Agent: Mozilla/2.0 (compatible; MSIE 3.0B; Windows 95;1024,768)
Host: smaug.middle.earth.ca
    [a blank line, containing only CRLF ]
```

Lessons from Example 15

1. Query data appended to a URL during a GET request to a server are passed as part of the locator string in the HTTP *method field* of the request headers. All other request header fields are the same as those for a standard GET request, as described in Examples 12 and 13.

Example 16: Submitting a FORM Using the GET Method

This example examines how an HTML **FORM** submits the form data content to a server when the GET method is used. The example HTML **FORM** is shown in Figure 7.6. The actual rendering of this form by a Web browser is shown in Figure 7.7.

Figure 7.6 Example HTML FORM that uses the GET method to submit data to a server.

```
<FORM ACTION="http://smaug.java.utoronto.ca:2021/cgi-bin/form1"
      METHOD=GET>
<p> Search string: <INPUT TYPE="text" NAME="srch" VALUE="dogfish">
<p> Search Type:
  <SELECT NAME="srch_type">
    <OPTION> Insensitive Substring
    <OPTION SELECTED> Exact Match
    <OPTION> Sensitive Substring
    <OPTION> Regular Expression
  </SELECT>
<p> Search databases in:
  <INPUT TYPE="checkbox" NAME="srvr" VALUE="Canada" CHECKED> Canada
  <INPUT TYPE="checkbox" NAME="srvr" VALUE="Russia"  > Russia
  <INPUT TYPE="checkbox" NAME="srvr" VALUE="Sweden" CHECKED> Sweden
  <INPUT TYPE="checkbox" NAME="srvr" VALUE="U.S.A."  > U.S.A.
  <em>(multiple items can be selected.)</em>
<P> <INPUT TYPE="submit"> <INPUT TYPE=reset>.
</FORM>
```

The **FORM** element was discussed in detail in Chapter 4. This **FORM** defines the three variable names *srch*, *srch_type*, and *srvr*. These have been assigned, by user input, the values *srch=dogfish*, *srch_type=Exact Match*, *srvr=Canada* and *srvr=Sweden*. Figure 7.8 shows the data sent by to the server when the **FORM** is submitted.

As discussed in Chapters 4 and 6, the default method of submitting a **FORM** sends the data to the server as a collection of encoded *name/value* pairs. The names and values from each FORM input element are encoded and composed into strings of the form name=value, while ampersand characters (&) are used to separate the composite strings (e.g., name1=value1&name2=value2&...). With the GET method, this string is appended to the URL as a *query string*, separated from it by a question mark. When the HTTP server receives these data, it forwards the entire query string to the gateway program *form1*, as indicated by the **FORM** element. These details are discussed in Chapter 8.

Figure 7.7 Netscape Navigator 3 browser rendering of the FORM example in Figure 7.6.

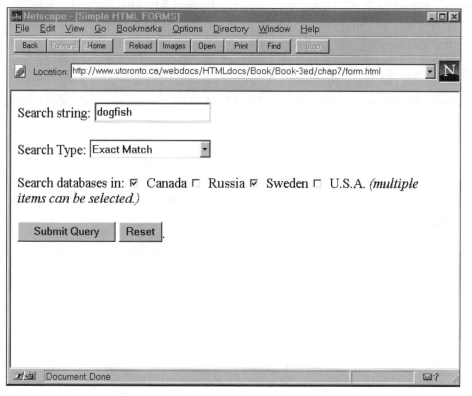

Lessons from Example 16

1. When an HTML **FORM** submits data to an HTTP server using the GET method, the **FORM** data are appended to the URL as a query string. Consequently, the **FORM** data are sent to the server in the query string part of the locator string, in the request header method field. The **FORM** data are encoded according to the **FORM-URL** encoding scheme discussed in Chapters 4 and 6.

Example 17: Submitting a FORM Using the POST Method

This example uses the **FORM** shown in Figure 7.7 to submit the same data to the server, but with one subtle modification: The form requests the POST method instead of GET. This is done by changing the first two lines in Figure 7.6 to (the change is in boldface):

```
<FORM ACTION="http://smaug.java.utoronto.ca:2021/cgi-bin/form1"
      METHOD=POST>
```

As in Example 15, this form has variable names *srch*, *srch_type*, and *srvr*. These have been assigned values *srch=dogfish*, *srch_type=Exact Match*, *srvr=Canada*, and *srvr=Sweden*. Figure 7.9 shows the data sent to the server, again from the Netscape Navigator 3.0 browser.

The POST method sends data in a message body, and not in the URL. The difference is indicated in Figure 7.9 in the four places noted in boldface: the method header, which now specifies the POST method and which has no data appended to the URL; the additional request header fields Content-type and Content-length, which give the type and length of the data message being sent; and last, the actual data following the header.

There are currently two valid content-types for sending **FORM** data to a server. In this example, the type is:

```
Content-type: application/x-www-form-urlencoded
```

to indicate that the data is from a **FORM** and that it is encoded in the same manner as when appended to a URL. You can compare the message body at the bottom of Figure 7.9 with the data appended to the URL in Figure 7.8 to verify this equivalence. The details of how the data are passed from the server to a CGI program are described in Chapter 8.

Figure 7.8 Data sent from a client to an HTTP server during a FORMs-based GET request.

```
GET /cgi-bin/form1?srch=dogfish&srch_type=Exact+Match&srvr=Canada&srvr=Sweden HTTP/1.0
Connection: Keep-Alive
User-Agent: Mozilla/3.0b5 (Win95; I)
Host: smaug.java.utoronto.ca:2021
Accept: image/gif, image/x-xbitmap, image/jpeg, image/pjpeg, */*
Accept-Language: en-US, fr, fr-CA
    [a blank line, containing only CRLF ]
```

Figure 7.9 Data sent from a client to an HTTP server during a FORMs-based POST request. Fields and data specific to the POST method are shown in boldface.

```
POST /cgi-bin/form1 HTTP/1.0
Connection: Keep-Alive
User-Agent: Mozilla/3.0b5 (Win95; I)
Host: smaug.java.utoronto.ca:2021
Accept: image/gif, image/x-xbitmap, image/jpeg, image/pjpeg, */*
Accept-Language: en-US, fr, fr-CA
Content-type: application/x-www-form-urlencoded
Content-length: 58
    [a blank line, containing only CRLF]
srch=dogfish&srch_type=Exact+Match&srvr=Canada&srvr=Sweden
```

Alternatively, **FORM** data sent via the POST method can be encoded as a MIME *multipart/form-data* message. On a browser, this encoding is selected by changing the first two lines in Figure 7.6 to (the changes are in boldface):

```
<FORM ACTION="http://leonardo.utirc.utoronto.ca:8080/cgi-bin/form1"
      METHOD=POST ENCTYPE="multipart/form-data">
```

Figure 7.10 shows the data sent to the server by the Netscape Navigator browser. The important changes from Figure 7.9 are noted in boldface. Once again the method is POST—content-type and content-length header fields are again present, and data are sent following the header. Note, however, the encoding of the data: The FORM data are encoded as a special multipart MIME type, with each block of the message corresponding to a different form input element.

Figure 7.10 Data sent from a client to an HTTP server during a FORMs-based POST request using the multipart/form-data encoding mechanism.

```
POST /cgi-bin/form1 HTTP/1.0
Connection: Keep-Alive
User-Agent: Mozilla/3.0b5 (Win95; I)
Host: smaug.java.utoronto.ca:2021
Accept: image/gif, image/x-xbitmap, image/jpeg, image/pjpeg, */*
Accept-Language: en-US, fr, fr-CA
Content-type: multipart/form-data; boundary=------------------80006273428
Content-Length: 443
    [a blank line, containing only CRLF]
------------------80006273428
Content-Disposition: form-data; name="srch"
    [a blank line, containing only CRLF]
dogfish
------------------80006273428
Content-Disposition: form-data; name="srch_type"
    [a blank line, containing only CRLF]
Exact Match
------------------80006273428
```

Continued

Figure 7.10 (Continued)

```
Content-Disposition: form-data; name="srvr"
    [a blank line, containing only CRLF]
Canada
------------------80006273428
Content-Disposition: form-data; name="srvr"
    [a blank line, containing only CRLF]
Sweden
------------------80006273428-
```

This encoding type has several advantages. In particular, you can use multipart/form-data encoding to upload data files from a client to a server; you can also send user text input that is not coded in the ISO Latin-1 character set (recall that URLs must use ISO Latin-1). These issues are discussed in more detail in Chapter 8 and Appendix B.

Lessons from Example 17

1. When an HTML **FORM** submits data to an HTTP server using the POST method, the **FORM** data are sent to the server as a *message body* that follows the request header. This message body is encoded in the same manner as when appended to the URL. Additional request header fields tell the server the content-type and the length of the arriving message. No data are appended to the URL.

Sending Data to a Server: PUT and DELETE

The methods PUT and DELETE are designed for sending data to and deleting data from an HTTP server. For example, the HTTP request:

```
PUT /project/dir1/file.html HTTP/1.0
Content-type: text/html
Content-length: 103
    [a blank line, containing only CRLF]
<HTML><HEAD><TITLE>Silly Test Stuff</TITLE></HEAD>
<BODY><H1>Really Silly Test Stuff</H1></BODY><HTML>
```

instructs the server to create the file *.../project/dir1/file.html* (the root location is determined by the server configuration files) and *put* the sent message data into this file. If this file already exists, it should be replaced by the new file. If successful, the response status field line should be:

```
HTTP/1.0 201 created
```

to indicate that the resource was created. The DELETE method is the reverse operation. Thus, the HTTP request

```
DELETE /project/dir1/file.html HTTP/1.0
    [a blank line, containing only CRLF]
```

asks that the server delete the resource at the indicated URL.

There are currently no major browsers that implement PUT or DELETE. Some servers do implement these methods, usually through special gateway programs or application-specific server plug-ins. Obviously, PUT and DELETE are not terribly practical without mechanisms for controlling how objects are put onto, modified, or deleted from a server. In this regard, there are several document management systems (e.g., Microsoft FrontPage and MKS Web Integrity) that use PUT and DELETE to manage server document archives.

Access Control, User Authentication, and Data Encryption

So far, we have not discussed controlling access to an HTTP server, or the encryption of data for transmission between client and server. There are several mechanisms available for doing these things. This section briefly discusses the options that are available.

For low-level security, most servers can be configured such that only machine domain names (or numeric IP addresses) belonging within a particular domain (for example, within `.middle.earth.edu`) are permitted access. In general, this restriction can be applied on a per directory basis, although some servers can apply restrictions file-by-file. This is not very secure, however, since a clever cracker can *spoof* (mimic) a domain name and access the data. It is also not very specific, since anyone who can log in on a machine inside the domain can access the restricted material.

Finer, user-specific control is possible using *user authentication*. The "Basic" user-authentication scheme is part of the HTTP protocol, and lets a server restrict access to users who can provide verifiable usernames and passwords: The user is prompted for this information, which is sent to the server, and the server checks the name and password against a designated password file. However, in the Basic authentication scheme, the username and password are sent over the Internet in an essentially unencrypted format, so it is easy for anyone sniffing the network traffic to extract the username and password. Thus, the Basic scheme is not secure, unless the underlying data are also encrypted. And, of course, you need some way to get the usernames and passwords onto the server in the first place.

A second user authentication method, known as *digest* authentication, has recently been proposed, and is implemented experimentally by NCSA's Mosaic browser and the NCSA HTTP server. This is similar to the Basic scheme, but passes usernames and passwords as encrypted strings. This is a significant improvement over Basic authentication, but still has the problem of getting the username and password information on the server. Experimental in HTTP 1.0, digest authentication is an integral part of HTTP 1.1.

Secure communication and user authentication require encryption of the data being sent between client and server. The most common mechanisms employ *negotiated encryption*. Negotiated encryption means that the server and client exchange encryption keys that allow each to send encrypted information that can only be decoded by the other. This requires that client and server support the same encryption and decryption software, and that they both understand the encryption protocol used to send messages between the two.

There are two main encryption schemes currently in use, but as yet no common standard. In addition, all of the encryption algorithms used by these schemes are regulated by U.S. trade and security restrictions (the algorithms are considered "munitions," with tight export controls), which place onerous limits on the quality of encryption software that can be exported outside the United States. This significantly restricts the deployment of highly secure, international Web-based applications.

Example 18: The "Basic" Authentication Scheme

The Basic authentication scheme is the only user authentication scheme universally available on the World Wide Web. This scheme is *not* secure, as username and password information are not encrypted when sent from client to server (they are encoded, however, which at least hides them from nonexperts). You should not think of this as a secure authentication scheme, unless combined with an encryption mechanism such as the Netscape SSL technology (discussed later).

The Basic scheme uses special HTTP request and response header fields. In the following example, we follow a request for a resource that requires user authentication, and illustrate how these fields negotiate the request for authentication information.

Step 1: Client Requests the Resource

The client first makes a regular request for the resource (here, an HTML document). A typical request header is shown in 7.11.

Step 2: Server Response—Authentication Required

The response message is shown in Figure 7.12. The server status message:

```
HTTP/1.0 401 Unauthorized
```

tells the client that the resource was not returned because the resource requires user authentication. In this regard, the server sends the additional header field:

```
WWW-Authenticate: Basic realm="SecRealm1@server.dom.edu"
```

This tells the client which authentication scheme to use (`Basic`), and also what *realm* is involved; here, `realm="SecRealm1@server.dom.edu"` (realms are discussed a bit later on). The response message includes a short HTML document that is displayed by the browser if it does not understand `WWW-Authenticate` headers, or if the user chooses not to provide authentication information.

Figure 7.11 Typical GET request from the Netscape Navigator browser.

```
GET /SecDir1/foo.html HTTP/1.0
User-Agent: Mozilla/1.1N (X11; I; IRIX 5.3 IP22)
Accept: */*
Accept: image/gif
Accept: image/x-xbitmap
Accept: image/jpeg
```

Figure 7.12 HTTP server response upon a request for a resource protected by the Basic authentication scheme. The authentication-related fields are shown in boldface.

```
HTTP/1.0 401 Unauthorized
Date: Thursday, 03-Aug-95 14:38:57 GMT
Server: NCSA/1.3
MIME-version: 1.0
Content-type: text/html
WWW-Authenticate: Basic realm="SecRealm1@server.dom.edu"

<HEAD><TITLE>Authorization Required</TITLE></HEAD>
<BODY><H1>Authorization Required</H1>
Browser not authentication-capable or
authentication failed.
</BODY>
```

Step 3: Client Requests Resource

The client, upon receipt of a 401 HTTP response header, prompts the user for his or her username and password. The client takes the username and password and forms the string:

username:password

This strings is then *uuencoded* into a pseudo-encrypted string (I say pseudo-encrypted, because it is trivial to decode). The client then tries, once again, to access the resource, this time passing the encoded username and password information within an Authorization request header field of the form:

Authorization: Basic *aWFuOmJvb2J5*

where the string *aWFuOmJvb2J5* is the encoded username and password. Figure 7.13 shows a typical request header containing this authentication information.

Figure 7.13 Typical client request for a resource protected by the Basic authentication scheme. The Authorization: **Field indicates the authentication scheme being used (**Basic**) along with the encoded username and password. The authentication-related field is shown in boldface.**

```
GET /SecDir1/foo.html HTTP/1.0
User-Agent: Mozilla/1.1N (X11; I; IRIX 5.3 IP22)
Accept: */*
Accept: image/gif
Accept: image/x-xbitmap
Accept: image/jpeg
Authorization: Basic aWFuOmJvb2J5
```

The server takes the contents of the `Authorization` field and checks its own list of usernames and passwords against the encrypted string sent by the client. If there is a match, then this authenticates the user, and the server returns the resource. If there is no match, then the server again returns the response shown in Figure 7.12, to indicate this failure, and to ask the user to try again.

The Meaning of a Realm

A `Realm` is simply a way of grouping username and password information so that the browser need not prompt the user for a new username and password if subsequent requests access the same realm. For example, suppose that a server administrator creates two secure directories, *SecDir1* and *SecDir2*, and controls access to them using the password files *pass1* and *pass2,* respectively. The administrator must also assign realm names to these directories, so that in communicating with a client, the server can inform the client which realm is involved, without giving away the name of the password file. In this example, we assume the administrator assigned the name "SecRealm1@server.dom.edu" to the directory *SecDir1*, and the name "SecRealm2@server.dom.edu" to the directory *SecDir2*.

The first time a user accesses a document in *SecDir1,* he or she is prompted for a username and password. The browser stores this name/password string under the realm name "SecRealm1@server.dom.edu." On subsequent accesses to this directory, the server sends the header indicating that authentication is again required for the realm "SecRealm1@server.dom.edu." The browser simply returns the authentication password already stored under this name, and does not prompt the user for this information.

If, on the other hand, the user requests a document from *SecDir2*, the server sends back the header:

```
WWW-Authenticate: Basic realm="SecRealm2@server.dom.edu"
```

to tell the browser that authentication is required for this new, as yet unentered, realm. As the browser has never accessed this realm, it has no record of an appropriate username and password, and therefore prompts the user for this information. This information is then stored on the browser under the additional realm keyword.

Note how all the realm names in these examples contain the domain name of the server housing the access-controlled documents. This is useful, as it helps guarantee that realm names are unique.

NOTE: Security Issues with the Basic Password Scheme   With most browsers, usernames and passwords are retained until the user quits the browser. This can create security concerns for public-area terminals, since once a user has entered his or her username, this information can be reused by the next user of the machine.

Client-Server Data Encryption

As mentioned in the previous section, any authentication scheme is insecure if the messages and data passed between client and server are unencrypted: If the username and password are not encrypted, then they can be copied and used by someone else, while if the transported data are not encrypted, then the data can be intercepted and read regardless of any password protection. There are two main approaches to encryption currently being deployed on the Web, and these are summarized in the following sections. Detailed information about these schemes is found in the references at the end of this chapter.

Netscape's Secure Sockets Layer (SSL)

The *Secure Sockets Layer* protocol is designed as an encryption layer *below* the HTTP protocol. Thus, HTTP messages are unaffected, with encryption occurring just prior to converting the messages into TCP/IP packets for transmission over the Internet. To indicate the special nature of this connection, Netscape created the new URL **https** (HTTP-Secure), identical to **http** URLs save for the initial string https:. The default port for **https** URLs is 443, not 80, so that a single machine can run both secure and nonsecure HTTP servers.

In principle, SSL can be used for any Internet tool that uses the underlying TCP/IP protocol for data communications. For example, Netscape markets news and other servers employing SSL.

SSL works at several levels. At the encryption level, SSL employs a sophisticated security hand-shake protocol: When a client contacts a secure server, they exchange encryption keys, which are subsequently used to encrypt all data passed between the server and client. Encryption keys are never reused, to ensure that keys cannot be intercepted and used by an unauthorized party. The server also sends the client a cryptographic certificate that tells the client which server it is in contact with, and that is used to validate that the server is indeed who it claims to be. Finally, the client and server each send, ahead of the transmitted data, a message digest calculated from the data; the receiving party uses this message digest to ensure that the data content has not been modified by any intervening party.

Netscape recently announced Version 3 of SSL. This includes mechanisms for client certificates, which allow users to authenticate themselves using digital signatures, just as servers are currently authenticated. This feature is not yet in wide use.

Most commercial Web browsers have integrated support for SSL, but only for short (40-bit) encryption keys—this is the maximum size allowed for encryption products that can be easily exported outside the United States. By default, their commercial server products also support 40-bit keys. Most browser vendors distribute U.S.-only versions of their programs that support 128-bit keys. The SSL protocol can negotiate the size of the keys, so that if a browser is only capable of 40-bit keys, encryption will be reduced to that level.

At present, almost all commercial browsers and servers support SSL.

Secure HTTP Protocol (S-HTTP)

Secure HTTP or *S-HTTP* is the second Web encryption and authentication scheme. S-HTTP is implemented as part of the HTTP protocol, and involves additional HTTP request and response headers that *negotiate* the type of encryption being used, the exchange of encryption keys, the passing of message digest information, and so on. This is roughly similar to the Basic authentication scheme, except that S-HTTP allows the client and server to exchange cryptographic certificates and encryption keys within the HTTP headers, allowing each party to authenticate the other and to encrypt data it is sending to the other.

S-HTTP and SSL are complementary schemes. SSL has the advantage of encrypting all underlying communication, but the disadvantage that the same encryption is applied to all messages. There is no easy way to change the encryption scheme based, for example, on the personal encryption key of a user (some variation is possible in SSL Version 3, however). S-HTTP, on the other hand, allows for this type of flexible encryption, since the keys can be passed in the HTTP headers. With luck, the different vendors will arrive at a compromise that adopts the best features of both approaches.

Several browser and server vendors support S-HTTP, although the most popular browsers (Netscape, Microsoft Internet Explorer) do not.

Security Enhanced Transactions—SET

Financial transactions over the Web require additional levels of encryption and authentication, to allow users to send credit card information—or even digital money—over the network safely and reliably. Visa and MasterCard, in association with Microsoft, Netscape, and others, are developing a secure transaction technology called SET. This scheme will allow the use of credit cards on the Net, with automatic validation of the card information and debiting of the transaction from the user's account. Additional efforts are underway to develop digital cash—the ability to send real money, in digital format, over a computer network. These technologies are in the development and testing stages, and are likely to be deployed sometime over the next two years. The references section at the end of this chapter provides links to additional readings on these subjects.

Proxy Servers and Server Caching

Proxy servers are often used by local area networks (LANs) to protect their network from unauthorized entry via the Internet. Such protection can be accomplished by installing *firewall* software on the gateway machine that links the local network to the outside world. A firewall keeps TCP/IP packets from entering the local network from outside, and thereby protects the LAN from intruders.

Unfortunately, a firewall means that users inside the LAN cannot access WWW resources outside the LAN, since incoming data are blocked at the firewall. The solution is to install a *proxy server* on the firewall, and to configure the users' Web browsers to refer all outgoing requests to the proxy server instead of to the real servers outside the LAN. A proxy server has access to both the inside and outside worlds, and can safely pass information back and forth across the firewall. When a browser wants to request information from outside the firewall, it instead sends the request to the proxy server on the firewall. The proxy server then *proxies* the request—that is, it makes the request on the user's behalf, and returns the *proxied* results.

This two-stage process can be slow. To speed up service, proxy servers can *cache* retrieved files. Thus, the first time a user requests a document, the server goes to the outside world and fetches it. But, the server then keeps a copy of the file on its own local disk. If a user then makes a subsequent request for the same file, the proxy server returns the locally cached copy, rather than accessing the original server to re-fetch it. This saves time, and can also significantly reduce the load on the network connection.

The use of cached files can be a problem, however, if the files change with time. This is the case for pages containing periodically updated data, or for documents created dynamically by CGI programs: Obviously, such files should not be cached, or should be removed from the cache after some fixed time. These problems are mitigated by Expires and pragma server response header fields. Expires contains an expiry time and date (in one of the standard time/date formats described at the end of this chapter) which tell a proxy server (or a browser) how long it can keep a cached copy of a document before it expires and should be replaced. An even stronger statement is made by the Pragma field, which takes the form:

Pragma: no-cache

When a client (or a proxy server) sends a request header containing this field to a server, the targeted server must always access a new copy of the requested URL, and can never use a cached version. This ensures that the requesting client always gets the most up-to-date version, regardless of which proxy server(s) the requests pass through.

Finally, most servers do not send a last-modified header for documents that should not be cached. A browser that retrieves a document that does not contain a last-modified header field will assume that the document is not cacheable, and will not save a local copy.

The HTTP 1.1 proposals contain a number of protocol enhancements designed to make proxy caching more effective, efficient, and reliable. However, as HTTP 1.1 is not yet implemented, these issues are not discussed here. You are referred to the references at the end of the chapter for additional information on this subject.

HTTP Proxy Servers

There are two ways of implementing proxy support. The first is to use a full HTTP server that has proxying and caching capabilities. Several commercial HTTP servers, as well as the Apache and CERN noncommercial servers, have these capabilities.

A proxy server is of course useful only if a browser can be configured to use it. At present, almost all browsers have this capability.

Format Negotiation

The last topic for this chapter is *format negotiation*. As mentioned in the discussion of accept request headers, a client can send information to a server explaining the types of data it prefers, and the order of preference. The example request headers given were:

```
Accept: image/*
Accept: image/jpeg; q=0.7; mxb=50000
Accept: image/gif; q=0.5
```

which indicate a preference for image/jpeg files, provided they were smaller than 50 kilobytes; followed by GIFs (if the JPEGs were too big), followed by any format of image if the first two were unavailable. However, the HTTP requests described in this chapter were directed at specific files, and not a collection. So, how can alternative formats be allowed?

At present, mechanisms for doing this are server-specific. The CERN server, for example, implements this via server configuration *map* directives. These permit requests for files with particular filename extensions to be mapped onto a special-purpose gateway program.* Suppose you wish to generically refer to images using the filename extension *.image*, and want to use the special gateway program **select** to decide which image format to return to a given client. The appropriate map directives in the server configuration file would be:

```
Pass    *.image      /select/*.image
Exec    /select/*    /path/to/gateways/cgi-bin/select/*
```

The Pass line maps all filenames with extension *.image* onto the gateway program **select**, while the Exec line provides the absolute path to this gateway program (similar to the ScriptAlias command of the NCSA or Apache servers, for those familiar with these servers).

When a browser requests a file with the extension *.image*, the URL, the HTTP accept headers, and other related data (as discussed in Chapter 8) are passed to the program **select**, which determines which image file to return. The remainder of the problem is a programming exercise (there

---

* Thanks to Chris Lilley for this explanation—any errors are, of course, mine.

is no generic **select** program, and the server manager has to either write one, or find a suitable program elsewhere). The gateway program could, for example, directly return the correct format image data (as determined from the `accept` or `User-agent` headers, and from knowledge of what formats actually exist on the server), or it could return a *redirect* header to redirect the client to the correct file.

The Apache server implements format negotiation using two non-CGI-based mechanisms, both somewhat different from the above (the Apache documentation refers to the process as *content negotiation*). The first method requires that the Web or document administrator create a special map file containing information about the different data variants. As an example, consider the following map file *monty_python.image*:

```
URI: monty_python; vary="type"

URI: monty_python.jpeg
Content-type: image/jpeg; qs=0.85

URI: monty_python.gif
Content-type image/gif; qs=0.5

URI: monty_python.xpm
Content-type: image/xpm; qs=0.2
```

The content indicates that there are three different image variants for this file, and describes the relative qualities of the images (through the parameter `qs`). A URL pointing to the file *monty_python.image* will retrieve the appropriate image file from amongst the three possible formats, depending on the `accept` headers sent by the client.

The second method is known as *MultiViews*. This method lets a user request a generic resource *minus* the filename extension, for example `http://.../path/monty_python`, whereupon the server locates all files with this suffix `monty-python` in the indicated directory, and dynamically creates a map file similar to the one above (but without `qs` parameters). The server then uses the `accept` headers to determine which file to return to the client.

The CERN and Apache techniques provide additional features, such as the ability to specify the content-language of a document and/or the content-encoding of the data (e.g., compressed). Other servers offer similar capabilities.

HTTP Methods and Header Fields Reference

The following sections summarize the HTTP methods, request headers, response headers, and server error messages currently defined and in use. These are predominately HTTP 1.0 values, but some HTTP 1.1 values are in common use on experimental HTTP servers, and are also presented here.

HTTP Methods Specification

Table 7.1 summarizes the defined HTTP methods. The commonly implemented methods are GET, HEAD, and POST, which were discussed in detail in this chapter.

Table 7.1. HTTP Methods and Their Meanings

Method	Description
GET	Retrieves the indicated URL. Data can also be sent to the URL by including a query string with the URL. This is the situation for data sent from **ISMAP** active imagemaps, from **ISINDEX** queries, and from **FORM** elements with the **FORM** attribute **METHOD="GET"**.
HEAD	Retrieves the HTTP header information for the indicated URL.
POST	Sends the data to the indicated URL. The URL must already exist; it is an error to POST to a nonexistent URL. This method is used by HTML **FORM** elements with the attribute value **METHOD="POST"**.
PUT	Places the data sent by the client in the indicated URL, replacing the old contents if the URL already exists. Some servers support PUT.
DELETE	Deletes the resource located at the indicated URL. Some servers support DELETE.

Largely Unimplemented Methods

LINK	Links an existing object to another object. For an HTML document, this would imply editing the document and adding **LINK** information to the document **HEAD**. This method is not implemented on most servers.
UNLINK	Removes the link information inserted, for example, by a LINK method. This method is not implemented on most servers.

HTTP 1.1 Methods

OPTIONS	Similar to HEAD, this requests that the server return a list of all communication or processing options available for the requested object. The server should return a list of all such options, without actually accessing the object. This method is not implemented on most servers.
PATCH	Like PUT, but the data consist of a list of differences with respect to the referenced object. The server should apply these differences and update the object. This method is not implemented on most servers.
TRACE	This method requests that the server receiving the request simply return the entire request header within the body of a `message/http` MIME-type message. This is intended for diagnosing HTTP communications problems. This method is not implemented on most servers.

HTTP Request Header Field Specifications

Request header fields can be divided into two broad categories: (A) those that describe the status and properties of the client and of the client-server connection, and (B) those that describe the status and properties of the data (if any) being sent by the client.

(A) Client and Connection Status Header Fields

These header fields define properties about the requesting client, and about the client-server connection, such as the client capabilities, authentication information required by the connection, and so on.

`Accept:` *`type/subtype, type/subtype2`*

Contains a list of MIME content-types acceptable to the client, separated by commas. Types can also contain parameters describing their relative merit (q=0.0 to q=0.1), and the maximum allowed size for a resource (mxb=*num_bytes*). The use of these terms was discussed earlier in this chapter.

`Accept-Charset:` *`charset1, charset2`*

Lists the character sets preferred by the browser, other than the default (ASCII or ISO Latin-1). Thus the server, if capable, can deliver the resource using the character set preferred by the browser. This is not widely supported.

`Accept-Encoding:` *`enc_type1, enc_type2`*

Lists the data encoding types acceptable to the client. For example,

`Accept-Encoding: x-compress`

tells the server that the client can accept compressed data in the `compress` format. Currently understood encoding types are `x-compress` and `x-gzip`, which may also be seen under the names `compress` or `gzip`. Other possible (but largely unimplemented) encoding types are `base64` and `quoted-printable`. If a server sends a document in one of these encodings, it must include the appropriate `Content-encoding` response header.

`Accept-language:` *`lang1, lang2`*

This field lists the languages preferred by the browser. The languages are specified using the schemes discussed in Appendix E. For example, the field:

`Accept-language fr-ca, fr, en`

would mean that the browser prefers Canadian French, will accept standard French if Canadian French is not available, and lastly, will accept English if the other two are not available.

`Authorization:` *`scheme scheme_data`*

This passes user authentication and encryption scheme information to the server. *Scheme* indicates the authorization scheme to be used, with *`scheme_data`* containing scheme-specific authorization data. If authentication is not required, this field is absent.

`Connection:` *`connection_state`* (HTTP 1.0 extension, and HTTP 1.1)

Several HTTP 1.0 servers support keep-alive connections. If a browser sends the header field

`Connection: keep-alive`

a server that supports keep-alive will *not* close the client-server link immediately, allowing the client to send several requests down the still-open connection.

In HTTP 1.1, *all* connections are by default kept alive, and are consequently called *persistent connections*. Thus, in HTTP 1.1, the connection field is used to *close* the connection rather than keep it open. The `connection` header field that closes a connection is:

`Connection: close`

Only browsers that understand HTTP 1.1 persistence will send this header.

`Cookie:` *`name=value cookie_info`* (Netscape Extension)

This passes stored state information from the client to server. Servers can use a special `Set-Cookie:` response header to place state information, in the form of name/value pairs, on a client. The client will then return this information, but only to the server that originally sent the "cookie." This Netscape extension is supported by some, but not all, clients. Details of the mechanism are found in Chapter 8.

`Date:` *`date_time`*

Gives the time and date when the current object was assembled for transmission. Note that the time must be Greenwich Mean Time (GMT) to ensure that all servers share a common time zone. Possible formats for the *`date_time`* string are discussed at the end of this chapter.

`From:` *`mail_address`*

Contains the address, in Internet mail format, of the user accessing the server. In general, a browser does not send this information, out of concern for a user's privacy.

`Host: server.domain.name:port` (HTTP 1.1)

Contains the domain name and port number (optional if port 80) to which the request is being directed. This is useful if the request is passing through a proxy server, or if the request is to a server that has more than one domain name or IP address. This is not sent by all browsers.

If-Modified-Since: *date*

> Sent with a GET request to make the GET conditional—if the requested document has not changed since the indicated time and date, the server does not send the document. Possible formats for the *date_time* string are discussed at the end of this chapter. If the document is not sent, the server should send the response header message 304 (not modified).

Pragma: *server_directive*

> Pragma directives pass special-purpose information to servers. Currently, there is only one server directive, Pragma: no-cache, which tells a proxy server (or servers, if it takes multiple proxy servers to reach the resource) always to fetch the document from the actual server, and never to use a locally cached copy.

Referer: *URL*

> Gives the URL of the document from which the request originated. This can be a partial URL, in which case it is interpreted *relative* to the URL of the document being requested. If a document contains an HTML **BASE** element, then the URL referenced by this element should be sent instead.

User-Agent: *program/version comments*

> Provides information about the client software making the request.

(B) Message Properties Header Fields

Those header fields define specific properties of the message being sent (or about the requested resource, if the request method is HEAD). Certain fields may be absent if they are inappropriate for the response data (e.g., content-language is irrelevant for an image file).

Content-language: *lang*

> Gives the language in which the document is written. Note that this is not the same as the character set. At present, this field is not widely used with request headers.

Content-length: *length*

> Gives the length, in bytes, of the message being sent to the server. If no message is sent, then this field is absent.

Content-type: *type/subtype; parameters*

> Gives the MIME content-type of the message being sent to the server, with optional parameters for this type. If no message is sent, then this field is absent.

MIME-version: *version_number*

> Gives the MIME protocol version used to encode the message, the current version being 1.0. Many browsers, unfortunately, send this even if the message is not MIME-compliant.

Other, uncommon message property header fields:

In principle, a client could also send the message property header fields `allow`, `content-encoding`, `expires`, `last-modified`, `link`, `title`, or `URI`. However, these are rarely used in a request header, and so are not described here.

HTTP Response Header Field Specifications

The following is a list of currently implemented HTTP response headers. These fields can be divided into two broad categories: (A) those that describe the status and properties of the server and the client-server connection, and (B) those that describe the status and properties of the data (if any) being returned by the server.

(A) Server and Connection Status Header Fields

These headers define properties about the server, and about the client-server connection, such as the server capabilities, the date the message was sent, requests for authentication data required by the connection, and so on.

`Date: date_time`

Contains the time and date when the current object was assembled for transmission. The time must be Greenwich Mean Time (GMT) to ensure a common time zone for all users and servers. Possible time formats are discussed at the end of this chapter.

`Location: URL`

Contains a URL to which the client should be redirected. This is returned by a server if the requested document was not found on the server, but the server knows the correct (moved) location of the resource. A `Location` header is included when a *redirection* HTTP status field (status 301 or 302) is returned.

`Public: method1, method2 ...` (HTTP/1.1)

Contains a comma-separated list of non-standard (experimental) methods supported by the server. This header is not implemented on most current servers.

`Retry-after: date_time (or seconds)`

Contains a time and date (or a time in seconds) after which a client should retry to access a resource that was temporarily unavailable. This field is appropriate when the status header 503 (service unavailable) is being returned. It might be returned by a server, or gateway program, that is temporarily unable to comply with a request. Typical forms are:

```
Retry-after: Thursday, 10-Aug-95 12:23:12 GMT
Retry-after: 60
```

the latter indicating that the client should retry after a 60-second wait. Most browsers (and proxy servers) do not understand the `retry-after` field.

Server: *program/version*

Contains information about the server software from which the resource originated. The program and version information fields are separated by a slash.

Set-Cookie: *cookie-information* (Netscape extension)

Contains cookie data sent by the server. A browser that supports cookies will save these data to disk, and will return them to the server that originally deposited the data. The mechanism is discussed in detail in Chapter 8.

WWW-Authenticate: *scheme scheme_message*

Tells the client stating the encryption and authorization schemes the server wants to use. This is only used for directory, file, or CGI program access that requires user authentication. *Scheme* gives the name of the authorization scheme (e.g., Basic), while *scheme_message* gives related data.

(B) Message Properties Header Fields

These headers define specific properties of the message or resource being sent. If no message is sent, these fields will be absent.

Allow: *methods_list*

Contains a comma-separated list of HTTP methods supported by the resource. This must be returned if the status code 405 (HTTP method not allowed) is being returned. This field can contain any supported method, including nonstandard ones supported by the server. It is not in common use.

Content-Encoding: *encoding_type*

Specifies the encoding type mechanism appropriate to the data. The only currently valid types are compress and gzip, and their synonyms x-compress and x-gzip (the latter are obsolete, and are being phased out). You can only have one content-encoding type per header. This allows compressed files to be uncompressed on-the-fly by the client.

Content-language: *lang*

Gives the language of the message being sent to the client.

Content-length: *length*

Gives the length in bytes of the message being sent to the client.

Content-type: *type/subtype; parameters*

Gives the MIME content-type of the message being sent to the client. The content-type can contain optional parameter fields, separated from the type/subtype by a semicolon. For example

```
Content-type: text/html; charset=ISO-10646-1
```

indicates that the message is an HTML document, written using the ISO 10646-1 character set. Parameter fields are ignored by most current browsers.

`Content-Version:` *version_info* (HTTP 1.1)

Indicates the version of the resource being sent. It is used in version control for document management purposes. This is implement by some version control systems, but is not implemented by most current browsers.

`Derived-From:` *version_info* (HTTP 1.1)

Indicates that the version of the resource from which the enclosed data (being sent by the client to the server) was derived. This is used in version control of collaboratively developed resources, and is required if the method is PUT. This field is not implemented on current browsers.

`Expires:` *date_time*

Gives the time and date after which the information being sent should be considered invalid. This tells clients when to refresh data in their local cache. Proxy servers can use this field to determine when a cached copy of a document should be refreshed.

`Last-modified:` *date_time*

Gives the date and time that the document was last modified, here in the format `Thu, 03 Aug 1995 16:02:27 GMT`. As in the `Date` field, the date must be given in Greenwich Mean Time.

`Link:` *link_information*

This is similar to the HTML **LINK** element, and defines relationships between the data being returned by the server and other resources. If derived for an HTML document, this field (or multiple fields) should contain the information from the **LINK** elements in the document. This allows the HTTP header to contain **LINK** information about a resource, and allows a client, using HEAD methods, to access information about the document that is useful for cataloguing, organizational, or indexing purposes. `Link` is not currently implemented.

`MIME-version:` *version_number*

See same entry in the request header fields specification section.

`Title:` *title*

The title of the document. This should be identical to the content of the document's **TITLE** element.

URI: *uri_of_resource*

Contains a URL for the resource being sent—sometimes this is an alternate URL (as per the Location field). In general, the meaning of the URI header is not well defined, and it will be dropped in HTTP 1.1 in favor of other headers with better-defined meanings.

HTTP Status Codes Specification

Table 7.2 describes the meanings of the different HTTP status codes. In general, codes 200 through 299 indicate a successful transaction, while codes 400–599 indicate an error of some type. Codes 300–399 imply redirection: Either the resource has moved and the server is returning the URL of the new location to the client, or the resource has not changed since it was last requested by the client, in which case the server does not need to resend the document.

Table 7.2 HTTP Status Codes
Codes introduced in HTTP 1.1 are italicized and right-aligned.

Successful Transactions

200   The request was completed successfully.

201   The request was a POST (or PUT) method and was completed successfully. 201 indicates that data was sent to the server, and that the server created a new resource as a result of the request.

202   The request has been accepted for processing, but the results of this processing are unknown. This would be returned, for example, if the client deposited data for batch processing at a later date.

203   The GET (or HEAD) request was fulfilled, but has returned partial information.

204   The request was fulfilled, but there is no new information to send to the client. The browser should do nothing, and should continue to display the document from which the request
originated.

Redirection Transactions

300   The requested resource is available from more than one location, but the server could not determine which version to return to the client. The response should contain a list of the locations and their characteristics. The client should then chose the one that is most appropriate. This is not currently supported.

301   The data requested has been permanently moved to a new URL. If this status is returned, the server should also send the client the URL of the new location via the header

Continued

Table 7.2 (Continued)

Location: `URL comments`

where `URL` is the new document URL. Browsers that understand the `Location` field will automatically connect to the new URL.

302   The data was found but it actually resides at a different URL. If this status is returned, the server should also send the client the correct URL via the header

Location: `URL comments`

Browsers that understand the `Location` field will automatically connect to the new URL. The user will get a 302 redirection if a URL pointing to a directory is missing the trailing slash character.

303   The response is available at a different URL, and should be retrieved using a GET method. This lets a server, accessed via a POST method request, redirect the client to a second resource that should be accessed using the GET method.

304   A GET request was sent that contained the `If-Modified-Since` field. However, the server found that the document had not been modified since the date specified in this field. Consequently, the server responds with this code and does not resend the document.

305   The request must be accessed through a proxy server; the response must also contain a `Location:` field specifying the location of the proxy. This is not currently supported.

Client Error Messages

400   The request syntax was wrong.

401   The request required an `Authorization:` field, and the client did not specify one. The server also returns a list of the allowed authorization schemes using a `WWW-Authenticate` response header. This mechanism is used by a client and server to negotiate data encryption and user authentication schemes.

402   The requested operation costs money and the client did not specify a way to pay. There is no specification for payment methods, so this is not currently implemented.

403   The client has requested a resource that is forbidden. No explanation is provided for this refusal.

404   The server cannot find the requested URL.

405   The client tried to access a resource using a method that is not allowed for that resource. The response must include a list of allowed methods, contained within an `Allow:` field. This is not widely implemented.

406   The resource was found, but could not be delivered because the *type* of the resource is incompatible with the acceptable types indicated by the `accept` or `accept-encoding` headers sent to the server by the client.

Table 7.2 (Continued)

407 The request was to a proxy server, and the proxy server requires authentication information; the proxy server must also return a `Proxy-authenticate` header field to indicate the authentication scheme required by the server. This is not currently supported.

408 The client did not produce a request in a timely manner, and the server has timed out and is breaking the connection. This is not currently supported.

409 The request could not be completed due to a conflict; for example, a PUT is not allowed because someone else has locked the resource. This is not currently supported.

410 The resource is no longer available at the server and no forwarding information is available.

411 The server is refusing access because the client tried to access the server and send data to the server, but did not use a `content-length` header to give the size of the data stream. This is not currently supported.

412 The server is refusing access because one of the conditions in the request header field was not satisfied. This is not currently supported.

413 The server is refusing access because the request is too large in some way. The server should include a `Retry-after` response header field to indicate when the client should try again. This is not currently supported.

414 The server is refusing access because the URL of the request is too long. This is not currently supported.

415 The server is refusing access because the client is trying to send data in a MIME type not supported by the server. This is not currently supported.

Server Error Messages

500 The server has encountered an internal error and cannot continue with the request.

501 The request made is legal, but the server does not support this method.

502 The client requested a resource from a server that, in turn, attempted to access the resource from another server or gateway. In this case, the secondary server or gateway did not return a valid response to the server.

503 The service is unavailable, because the server is too busy. The server may also send a `Retry-After` header, which tells the client how long to wait before trying again.

504 The client requested a resource from a server that, in turn, attempted to access the resource from another server or gateway. This is similar to *502*, except that in this case, the transaction failed because the secondary server or gateway took too long to respond.

505 The server does not support the HTTP protocol version in which the request was posed. This is not currently supported.

Time and Date Formats Specification

The HTTP protocol supports three formats for time and date fields, with one of the three being the preferred choice. All applications that return time and date information should use this preferred form.

Preferred Format

This format is specified in RFC 1123. An example is:

```
Wed, 09 Aug 1995 07:49:37 GMT
```

where the first field is the day of the week (`Mon`, `Tue`, `Wed`, `Thu`, `Fri`, `Sat`, or `Sun`), the second is the day of the month (`01` to `31`), the third is the month (`Jan`, `Feb`, `Mar`, `Apr`, `May`, `Jun`, `Jul`, `Aug`, `Sep`, `Oct`, `Nov`, or `Dec`); the remaining hours (`0` to `24`), minutes, and seconds fields are obvious. The time must be in Greenwich Mean Time (GMT), so that all Web applications share a common time zone.

First Alternative Format

An alternative (and common) format is defined in RFC 850. An example is:

```
Wednesday, 09-Aug-94 07:49:37 GMT
```

where the first field is the day of the week (`Monday`, `Tuesday`, `Wednesday`, `Thursday`, `Friday`, `Saturday` or `Sunday`), the third is the month (as given above), and the remaining fields are obvious. This second format will clearly cause chaos at midnight, December 31, 1999.

Second Alternative Format

This format is defined by the ANSI C language `asctime()` format. An example date is:

```
Wed Aug 9 07:49:37 1994
```

Note that this format does not specify a time zone—the assumption is that the time is in GMT.

Any Internet software (including gateway programs) should return time and date values using the first of these three time formats, but should be able to understand the other two.

References

Overview of HTTP

```
http://www.w3.org/hypertext/WWW/Protocols/Overview.html
```

HTTP Specifications

```
http://ds.internic.net/rfc/rfc1945.txt                          (HTTP 1.0)
http://www.w3.org/pub/WWW/Protocols/                            (HTTP 1.1)
http://www.w3.org/pub/WWW/Protocols/HTTP-NG/Overview.html       (HTTP-NG)
```

User Authentication and Data Encryption

```
http://www.w3.org/pub/WWW/Security/                             (Overview)
http://home.mcom.com/info/security-doc.html                     (Netscape overview)
http://ds.internic.net/internet-drafts/draft-ietf-http-digest-aa-04.txt   (Digest authentication)
http://home.netscape.com/newsref/std/SSL.html                   (SSL specification)
ftp://ds.internic.net/internet-drafts/draft-ietf-wts-shttp-03.txt   (Secure HTTP - S-HTTP)
http://www.genome.wi.mit.edu/WWW/faqs/www-security-faq.html     (Web Security FAQ)
```

Secure Financial Transactions

```
http://www.visa.com/cgi-bin/vee/sf/standard.html?2+0            (SET)
http://www.mastercard.com/set/set.htm                          (SET)
http://www.mondex.com/mondex/glance.htm                        (Mondex—digital cash)
http://www.digicash.com/                                       (Digicash—digital cash)
http://ganges.cs.tcd.ie/mepeirce/project.html                  (Digital cash overview)
```

Browser and Server Comparisons and Benchmarks

```
http://webcompare.iworld.com/                      (Server comparisons and benchmarks)
http://www.openmarket.com/browsertest/             (Browser tests and benchmarks)
```

Apache Server Content Negotiation

```
http://www.apache.org/docs/content-negotiation.html
```

Time and Date Formats

```
ftp://ds.internic.net/rfc/rfc1123.txt
ftp://ds.internic.net/rfc/rfc850.txt
```

Data Processing on an HTTP Server

Having an HTTP server to deliver documents is all well and good, but the true power of the Web is only unleashed when you add dynamic content and user interaction. This means that the server must do more than just deliver data: It must be able to dynamically process and deliver content, and respond to complex data sent to the server by a user.

The HTTP protocol, through the GET, POST, and PUT methods, provides many mechanisms for sending user-selected data to the server. But, what to do with the data when it arrives? As mentioned earlier, an HTTP server generally does not know how to process these data; in fact, it would be impossible to write a server that was able to do all the special processing everyone would want. Instead, servers come with generic tools that let local server administrators add data processing functionality in a locally customizable way. The traditional method is via the *common gateway interface*, which is a mechanism that can link a running HTTP server with completely separate programs, known as *gateway programs*, that do this second level of processing. This is still the most commonly used mechanism, and is the main topic of this chapter. Many modern servers also support server programming interfaces, which allow for special processing modules that can be compiled and linked to the server. This is a bit like adding CGI right into the server, eliminating the separation between server and gateway processes. The comparative advantages and disadvantages of this alternative approach are also discussed in this chapter.

The Common Gateway Interface

The common gateway interface (CGI) is the specified Web standard for communication between an HTTP server and server-side gateway programs. When a URL is accessed that references a gateway program, the server launches this gateway program *as a separate running process*, and passes to it any **ISINDEX, FORM,** or other data sent by the client. When the gateway program finishes processing the data, it sends the results back to the server, which in turn forwards these data to the client that made the initial request. The CGI specifications define how these data are passed from the server to the gateway program, and vice versa. This data flow is schematically illustrated in Figure 8.1.

Server Applications Programming Interfaces

Gateway programs are ideal for many problems, as they can be easily added without requiring a rewrite of the HTTP server software. However, this flexibility comes at the expense of speed, as starting up a gateway program involves a lot of operating system overhead, which can significantly slow server response. Most modern servers now support linked-in modules, written in C or other compiled languages, to incorporate gateway-like processing right into the server. In a similar vein, certain Netscape HTTP servers support compiled Java modules, through a special Java interface incorporated into the server.

In all cases, these modules are written using a special server *applications programming interface*, or *API*, which is the software interface that links the modules to the underlying server. Unfortunately, each server vendor (e.g., Netscape, Microsoft, Apache, or Open Market) uses a different and incompatible API, so that modules written for one server do not work with another. However, this is the approach to use if you want fast server response for things like transaction processing, or if you have generic and commonly used CGI functionality (such as imagemapping) that can be easily incorporated into the server. This chapter does not discuss module programming and design—the references section lists online documentation relevant to these topics.

Gateway Programming Languages

Gateway programs can be compiled programs written in languages such as C, C++, or Pascal, or they can be executable scripts written in languages such as perl, tcl, and the various shell programs. In fact, many gateway programs are perl scripts, since these are easy to write and modify and are easily transportable from machine to machine. In addition, execution speed is often not an important factor with gateway programs, since the slowest component is often the resource

Figure 8.1 Schematic diagram illustrating the data flow between a client browser, an HTTP server, and a server-side CGI program. The use of compiled-in server modules in place of CGI is also illustrated.

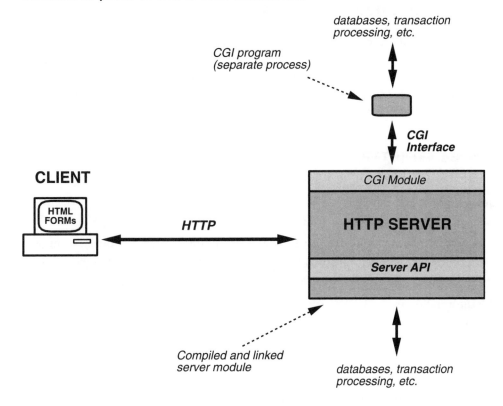

the gateway connects to, and not the gateway program itself. After all, if a database takes many seconds to complete a query, it does not matter if the gateway program takes an extra millisecond to start up!

This chapter first reviews how data are communicated between a client and server (using the HTTP protocol) and then discusses how data are then communicated between the server and a gateway program (the CGI mechanisms). This is followed by five examples that explore the details of the CGI mechanisms for the relevant HTTP methods, namely GET and POST, and for different HTML user input tools, namely **ISINDEX** and **FORM** elements. Lastly, there are brief discussions of how data sent by a client are decoded in gateway programs, and of security issues you should be aware of when writing gateway programs.

Chapter 9 follows up this overview with several CGI programming examples, and also provides a list of CGI utility programs and libraries available over the Internet.

Communication with Gateway Programs

With HTTP, there are three ways a client can send data to an HTTP server. From there, the CGI mechanisms describe how data are passed from a server to a server-side gateway program and back. In general, all data that a client sends to a server are made available, using three CGI mechanisms, to a referenced gateway. In turn, a gateway program has two CGI mechanisms for returning data to the server, and from there to the client. These mechanisms are discussed below.

Client Sends to Server (HTTP)

There are three ways data can be sent from a client to a server. These are:

1. **As a URL query string**—For example,

   ```
   http://some.site.edu/cgi-bin/ex_prog?query_info
   ```

   passes the query string `query_info` to the server. The server, in turn, places the query string within an *environment variable*, and then launches the gateway program *ex_prog*, which in turn obtains the query string from the environment variable.

2. **As *extra path* information in the URL**—*Extra path* information is placed in the URL by adding directory-like information to the URL, just after the name of the gateway program. An example is:

   ```
   http://some.site.edu/cgi-bin/ex_prog/dir/file?query_info
   ```

   If the server knows that `/cgi-bin/ex_prog` references a gateway program, then the string `/dir/file` is interpreted by the server as extra path information, while `query_info` is again the query string. When the server launches the gateway program *ex_prog*, it passes both the query string `query_info` and the extra path string `/dir/file` to *ex_prog*. These data are passed to the gateway program within environment variables.

3. **As data sent to the server in a message body**—This is possible with the HTTP POST method, and is commonly used with HTML **FORM**s. When a server receives a POST method message from a **FORM**, it sends the POSTed data to the designated gateway program. The gateway program reads the data from its standard input.

Server Sends to Gateway (CGI)

The CGI specifications define the mechanisms by which data are forwarded by a server to a gateway program. There are three mechanisms:

1. **Command-line arguments**—The server launches the gateway program, and passes data to the program as command-line arguments. This occurs only with a GET method request arising from an **ISINDEX** query.

2. **Environment variables**—The server puts information in *environment variables* before starting the gateway program: The gateway program can then access these variables and obtain their contents. *Everything* contained in the HTTP header sent by a client is passed program via environment variables to the gateway. Thus, environment variables contain the query string and the extra path information discussed previously, as well as the content of *every* request header field sent by the client to the server. There are also environment variables containing information about the server, such as the home directory for the documents, the type of server, and the server's domain name.

3. **Standard input**—The gateway program reads in data from standard input. This is how message data, sent by a client using the POST HTTP method, are passed to the gateway program.

The mechanisms relevant during a particular transaction depend on the HTTP method of the request (GET or POST), and on the nature of the query string appended to the URL (**ISINDEX** versus non-**ISINDEX** queries). Examples are given later in this chapter.

Gateway Sends to Server (CGI)

There are two mechanisms by which a CGI program communicates information back to the server:

1. **By writing to standard output**—A gateway program passes results back to the server by writing to standard output—this is the *only* way a gateway program can return data. In general, the returned data has two parts. The first part is a collection of *server directives*, which are parsed by the server and are used to compose the response header that the server sends ahead of the returned data. The second part is the actual data being returned by the gateway program. The two parts are separated by a blank line containing only a CRLF (carriage return linefeed) pair.

2. **By the *name* of the gateway program**—Gateway programs with names beginning with the string *nph-* are called *non-parsed header* programs and are treated specially by the server. As mentioned in (1), the server usually parses the output of a gateway program, and uses the *server directives* to create the HTTP response header that is sent to the client ahead of the returned data. If a gateway program name begins with *nph-*, the server sends the gateway program output directly to the client without this extra processing, which means the server does *not* add any header information. In this case, a gateway program must itself provide *all* required HTTP response header fields.

These methods are illustrated in the following five examples. Example 19 looks at an HTML **ISINDEX** document request. Example 20 demonstrates non-parsed header gateway programs, which send data directly back to the client, bypassing any server processing. Example 21 shows how environment variables are passed to the gateway program, and explains the contents of these variables. Examples 22 and 23 show how data from HTML **FORM**s—using the GET and POST methods, respectively—are passed to a gateway program. These examples also explain how the data are decoded by a gateway program.

Example 19: ISINDEX Searches

ISINDEX queries are the *only* query method that pass data to a gateway program as command-line arguments. It is a simple technique, and a useful starting point for understanding client-server-gateway interactions.

This example accesses the gateway program *srch-example* listed in Figure 8.2, which is a Bourne-shell script designed to search a phone-number database via the search program *grep*. The script uses the **ISINDEX** element to prompt for the search string. In this example, the search string is just the list of names you want to search for. When the script receives this data, it searches the database for the indicated names and returns the names and phone numbers of any matches. The script is designed both to prompt for search strings and to return the results of the search.

Chapters 2 and 4 discussed how **ISINDEX** queries send data to the server by appending the query data to the URL of the document being viewed, and then accessing the newly composed URL. An example of such a URL is:

```
http://some.where.edu/cgi-bin/srch_program?string1+string2
```

When this information reaches the server, and if it is an **ISINDEX** query, the server decodes the URL (converts plus (+) signs back into spaces, and converts URL character encodings back into the correct 8-bit characters), uses the space characters to break the query string into individual terms, and then passes these terms to the indicated gateway program as command-line arguments.

Detecting ISINDEX Queries

How does the server know if a GET method request comes from an **ISINDEX** query? The answer is that an ISINDEX query string *never contains* unencoded equals signs (=). As pointed out in Chapter 6 (which gave the details of the URL encoding mechanism), and in Example 15 of Chapter 7, **FORM** data are encoded as a collection of strings of the form name=value, which always contains at least one unencoded equals sign (any literal equals signs originally present in the name or value strings are encoded as %3d). Therefore, the presence of a "real" equals sign in the query string means that the data came from a **FORM**, and not from an **ISINDEX**.

Figure 8.2 Bourne-shell script CGI gateway program srch-example.

```
01 #!/bin/sh
02 echo Content-TYPE:  text/html
03 echo
04
05 if [ $# = 0 ]           # is the number of arguments == 0 ?
06 then                    # do this part if there are NO arguments
07  echo "<HEAD>"
08  echo "<TITLE>Local Phonebook Search</TITLE>"
09  echo "<ISINDEX>"
10  echo "</HEAD>"
11  echo "<BODY>"
12  echo "<H1>Local Phonebook Search</H1>"
13  echo "Enter your search in the search field.<P>"
14  echo "This is a case-insensitive substring search: thus"
15  echo "searching for 'ian' will find 'Ian' and Adriana'."
16  echo "</BODY>"
17 else                    # this part if there ARE arguments
18  echo "<HEAD>"
19  echo "<TITLE>Result of search for \"$*\".</TITLE>"
20  echo "</HEAD>"
21  echo "<BODY>"
22  echo "<H1>Result of search for \"$*\".</H1>"
23  echo "<PRE>"
24   for i in $*
25   do
26      grep -i $i /vast/igraham/Personnel
27  done
28  echo "</PRE>"
39  echo "</BODY>"
40 fi
```

Step 1. First Access of the URL

In this example, the script *srch-example* is initially accessed via the URL:

```
http://leonardo.utirc.utoronto.ca:8080/cgi-bin/srch-example
```

Note that there is no query information attached to the URL; this is an important factor in the initial behavior of the script.

Server Directives in Gateway Programs

Line 1 tells the computer to interpret this script using the */bin/sh* program, which is the traditional location and name for the Bourne shell. The next line prints an HTTP *server directive*, which gives the server information about the data to come (echo is the Bourne-shell command that prints to standard output). This is absolutely necessary, as the server has no other way of knowing what type of data the program will return. This line prints

```
Content-TYPE: text/html
```

to tell the server that the data to follow is an HTML document. The next line prints a blank line. This denotes the end of the headers; subsequent output is the actual data. This output is sent back to the server, and from there, back to the client.

Several other server directives are possible—they are summarized in Example 20.

Line 5 tests the *number* of command-line arguments. In this case, there was no query string, so there are no command-line arguments and the first branch of the `if` is executed. This branch prints, to standard output, a simple HTML document explaining the nature of the search; this is shown in Figure 8.3. This document contains an **ISINDEX** element, to tell the browser to prompt for search information—this gives rise to the query box in Figure 8.3. The names `ian` and `bradley` are typed into this box (the author always likes to look for his own name), separated by a single space. These are the names that will be used in the search.

Figure 8.3 Document returned from the script *srch-example* when accessed *without* a query string appended to the URL.

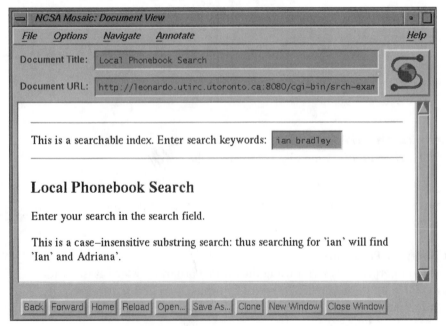

Step 2: Second Access of the URL

Submitting this **ISINDEX** search information accesses the same URL, but appends the names *ian* and *bradley* to the URL as a query string. Thus, in this second phase, the accessed URL is

```
http://leonardo.utirc.utoronto.ca:8080/cgi-bin/srch-example?ian+bradley
```

where the space between `ian` and `bradley` has been encoded as a plus sign, as required by the URL query string encoding scheme described in Chapter 6.

When the server receives this URL, it parses the query string and finds that there are no unencoded equals signs, so it knows that this is an **ISINDEX** query. It therefore takes the query string and breaks it into individual strings, using the plus signs to mark the string separators. This yields the two strings `ian` and `bradley`. The server next launches the gateway program *srch-example*, using the names `ian` and `bradley` as command-line arguments. If you were to run the program by hand, you would type:

```
srch-example ian bradley
```

Figure 8.4 shows the results of this second access to the Bourne-shell program; by following Figure 8.2, you can see how it was generated. As before, the first two lines print the MIME

Figure 8.4 Document returned from the script *srch-example* when accessed *with* a query string appended to the URL.

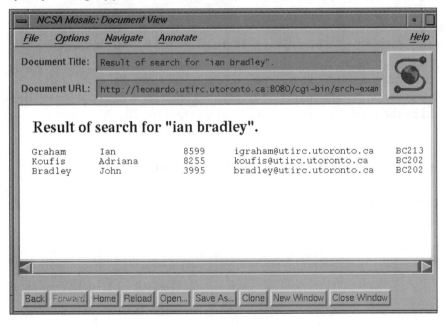

content-type of the message and the blank line separating the HTTP headers from the data. At line 5, the program checks for command-line arguments. This time there are arguments, so the second branch of the script is executed, starting at line 18. This section prints a different HTML document, this time including output from the program *grep*. Lines 24 through 27 loop the variable i through all the command-line arguments. The content of the variable i (denoted by $i) is used as an argument to the program *grep*, which scans the file */vast/igraham/Personnel* for names matching the pattern given by $i. *Grep* prints the matches to standard output. The result of the searches is shown in Figure 8.4. Note that there is no query box, as the second branch of the script in Figure 8.2 did not return an **ISINDEX** element.

Example 20: Gateway Program Server Directives

The second example looks at how HTTP servers compose a response header for data returned by a gateway program. Consider first the actual data sent by a server (here, the Apache 1.1.1 server) upon the client's first access of the program *srch-example* (Figure 8.5; these are the data that produced Figure 8.3).

Comparing Figure 8.5 with Figure 8.2, you will see that the headers are *not* those returned by the script: the content-type headers are typographically different (Content-TYPE versus Content-type). In fact, the headers returned to the client were generated by the HTTP server, with help from server directives returned by the gateway program.

Server Directives

The server takes the header data returned by the gateway program and parses each of the header fields. Most of these headers are passed through unaltered, and are included as part of the server response header returned to the client. Some, however, are treated as *server directives* and are used by the server to *modify* the HTTP response header fields the server normally returns in the response. The three valid server-directive headers are listed and described in Table 8.1.

Figure 8.5 Data returned to the client upon accessing the URL:

```
http://leonardo.utirc.utoronto.ca:8080/cgi-bin/srch-example
```

These are the data that produce Figure 8.3.

```
HTTP/1.0 200 OK
Server: Apache/1.1.1
Date: Thu, 01 Aug 1996 16:43:53 GMT
Content-type: text/html

<HEAD>
<TITLE>Local Phonebook Search</TITLE>
```

Figure 8.5 (Continued)

```
<ISINDEX>
</HEAD>
<BODY>
<H1>Local Phonebook Search</H1>
Enter your search in the search field.<P>
This is a case-insensitive substring search: thus
searching for 'ian' will find 'Ian' and Adriana'.
</BODY>
```

In addition to these special server directives, a gateway program can return most regular server response header fields—they will simply be forwarded to the client as part of the response header, following those headers generated by the server itself. For example, if a gateway program returns results from a database that is updated on a regular basis, the program could return an Expires header field as part of the server directives to indicate when the data will be stale, thereby allowing clients to reliably cache copies until the specified expiration date.

Limitations of Server Directives

You *must not* use server directives to produce duplicates of the headers ordinarily returned by the server—such headers usually describe generic characteristics of the server, and cannot be

Table 8.1 CGI Server Directives and Their Allowed Content

Content-type: *type/subtype (; parameters)*

> Gives the MIME type for the data being returned by the gateway program. The server will use this value to compose the content-type header field returned with the HTTP response header.

Location: *URL*

> Specifies a URL to which the client should be *redirected*. A server will add this Location: field to the server response header and will also modify the server response status line to return:
>
> HTTP/1.0 302 Redirection

Status: *code string*

> Contains an HTTP status code (*code*) and arbitrary descriptive status string (*string*) to be used by the server in place of the standard value. A server will modify its default status field to return the server response header field:
>
> HTTP/1.0 *code string*

altered by a gateway program. For example, the `Server`, `Date`, and `MIME-Version` header fields are server-specific and should never be returned by a gateway program. But, as with spelling, there is an exception to every rule—and the exception here is for *non-parsed header* gateway programs.

Non-Parsed Header Gateway Programs

It is possible to return gateway program output directly to the client without any processing by an HTTP server—in this case, the gateway can return any header fields it wants, regardless of the rule presented above. This is accomplished by appending the string *nph-*, for *non-parsed header*, to the name of the script. When the server sees gateway program names beginning with *nph-*, it passes the gateway program output directly to the client, without any processing. For example, Figure 8.6 shows the data returned from the gateway program ***nph-srch-example***—this is an exact duplicate of the program ***srch-example*** listed in Figure 8.2, the only change being the string *nph-* added to the front of the filename.

Comparing Figure 8.6 with the program listing in Figure 8.2 shows that the response now contains just the data printed by the gateway program, with nothing added or modified by the server. The advantages of non-parsed header gateway programs are speed and flexibility, since the server is not required to parse the returned data and generate appropriate headers, and since the programmer is not limited in what can be placed within the response header. In exchange, the gateway program itself must produce *all* the required header fields. Note how the returned data in Figure 8.6 are an *invalid* server response, as the response does not contain a status line, nor does it indicate the date or server type. Thus an *nph-* script must print, at a minimum, the following response headers, with values appropriate to the script and the data being returned (the portions that must be customized to the situation are shown in italics; these are just sample values):

```
HTTP/1.0 200 OK
Date: Thu, 01 Aug 1996 16:50:57 GMT
Server: NCSA/1.5.2
Content-type: text/x-babelfish
```

Non-parsed header programs are useful, but are obviously more complicated to use.

Example 21: Environment Variables

The preceding examples would imply that the server passes very little information to a gateway program. In fact, the server is not so ungenerous. Before launching a gateway program, the server initializes several *environment variables* that are subsequently accessible to the gateway. In particular, this mechanism is used to pass *extra path* and *query string* information to a gateway program. Table 8.2 lists all the environment variables defined as part of the CGI standard, while Figures 8.7 and 8.8 illustrate the most common variables as used in an example application. Figure 8.7 shows the gateway script *srch-example-2;* this is the same **ISINDEX** script listed in

Figure 8.6 Non-parsed header output returned upon accessing the URL:

```
http://leonardo.utirc.utoronto.ca:8080/cgi-bin/nph-srch-example
```

```
Content-TYPE: text/html

<HEAD>
 <TITLE>Local Phonebook Search</TITLE>
<ISINDEX>
</HEAD>
<BODY>
<H1>Local Phonebook Search</H1>
Enter your search in the search field.<P>
This is a case-insensitive substring search: thus
searching for 'ian' will find 'Ian' and Adriana'.
</BODY>
```

Figure 8.2, modified to print out environment variable contents. The HTML document generated upon accessing this script at the URL:

```
http://leonardo.utirc.utoronto.ca:8080/cgi-bin/srch-example-2/dir/file?ian+bradley
```

is shown in Figure 8.8. Accessing this URL passes both query string (`ian+bradley`) and extra path information (`/dir/file`) to the referenced gateway program.

Figure 8.7 Bourne-shell script *srch-example*-2. This is essentially the same script shown in Figure 8.2, but modified to explicitly print out the environment variables and the command-line arguments.

```
#!/bin/sh
echo Content-TYPE:  text/html
echo
 if [ $# = 0 ]    # is the number of arguments == 0 ?
then              # do this part if there are NO arguments
       echo "<HEAD>"
       echo "<TITLE>Local Phonebook Search</TITLE>"
       echo "<ISINDEX>"
       echo "</HEAD>"
       echo "<BODY>"
       echo "<H1>Local Phonebook Search</H1>"
       echo "Enter your search in the search field.<P>"
       echo "This is a case-insensitive substring search: thus"
       echo "searching for 'ian' will find 'Ian' and Adriana'."
       echo "</BODY>"
else              # this part if there ARE arguments
       echo "<HEAD>"
       echo "<TITLE>Result of search for \"$*\".</TITLE>"
```

Figure 8.7 (Continued)

```
        echo "</HEAD>"
        echo "<BODY>"
        echo "<P> Number of Command-line Arguments = $#.  They are:"
        for i in $*
        do
                echo " <code> $i </code> "
        done
        echo "<h2> The Environment Variables </h2>"
        echo "<pre>"       # print the environment variables
        echo " SERVER_SOFTWARE = $SERVER_SOFTWARE"
        echo " SERVER_NAME = $SERVER_NAME"
        echo " GATEWAY_INTERFACE = $GATEWAY_INTERFACE"
        echo " SERVER_PROTOCOL = $SERVER_PROTOCOL"
        echo " SERVER_PORT = $SERVER_PORT"
        echo " REQUEST_METHOD = $REQUEST_METHOD"
        echo " HTTP_ACCEPT = $HTTP_ACCEPT"
        echo " PATH_INFO = $PATH_INFO"
        echo " PATH_TRANSLATED = $PATH_TRANSLATED"
        echo " SCRIPT_NAME = $SCRIPT_NAME"
        echo " QUERY_STRING = $QUERY_STRING"
        echo " REMOTE_HOST = $REMOTE_HOST"
        echo " REMOTE_ADDR = $REMOTE_ADDR"
        echo " REMOTE_USER = $REMOTE_USER"
        echo " AUTH_TYPE = $AUTH_TYPE"
        echo " CONTENT_TYPE = $CONTENT_TYPE"
        echo " CONTENT_LENGTH = $CONTENT_LENGTH"
        echo "</pre>"
        echo "<H2>Result of search for \"$*\".</H2>"
        echo "<PRE>"
        for i in $*
        do
            grep -i $i /vast/igraham/Personnel done
        echo "</PRE>"
        echo "</BODY>"
fi
```

Most of the environment variables in Figure 8.8 are easy to understand. Some are set by default and do not depend on the nature of the request, while others are set only when particular client-server-gateway interactions are involved.

Gateway Program Environment Variables

Table 8.2 lists all the environment variables that can be passed to a gateway program by an HTTP server. Not all variables are defined in all cases: for example, the variables associated with user authentication are only defined when authentication is required.

Figure 8.8 Document returned from the script in Figure 8.7 after accessing the URL:
http://leonardo.utirc.utoronto.ca:8080/cgi-bin/srch-example-2/dir/file?ian+bradley

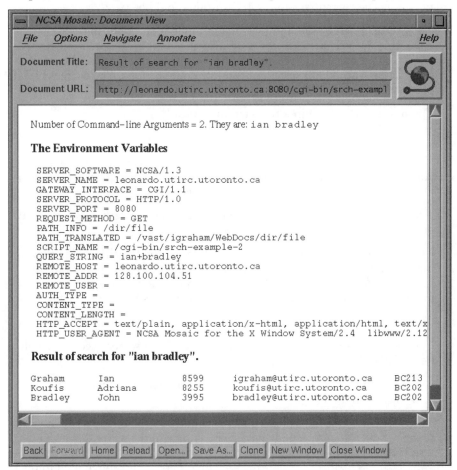

Table 8.2 Environment Variables Available within a Gateway Program

Server Properties

SERVER_SOFTWARE	The name and version of the server software answering the request, in the format *name/version*—for example, NCSA/1.5.2 or Apache/1.1.1.
SERVER_NAME	The Internet domain name of the server; if the domain name is not known, this is the numerical IP address.

Table 8.2 (Continued)

GATEWAY_INTERFACE	The version of the CGI specification used by the server, in the format CGI/*version*. The current version is 1.1, so this should be CGI/1.1.
SERVER_PROTOCOL	The protocol being used and the version number, in the format *protocol/version*. This permits gateway programs that support different protocols (e.g., Gopher and HTTP) or different protocol versions, as the program can use this variable to select appropriate code sections. The current HTTP protocol version is 1.0, so this is usually HTTP/1.0.
SERVER_PORT	The port number used in a transaction (typically 80).

Client Properties

REMOTE_HOST	The Internet domain name of the host making the request. If the domain name is unavailable, this variable is undefined. The numerical IP address is always available in the REMOTE_ADDR variable.
REMOTE_ADDR	The numeric IP address of the remote host accessing the server. This is always defined.
HTTP_*NAME*	The contents of *all* the request header fields sent by the client. The environment variable name is composed of the string HTTP_ followed by the capitalized *header field name*, with all dashes in the name converted to underscores—for example, HTTP_USER_AGENT for the User-Agent field.

Request Properties

REQUEST_METHOD	The method associated with the request. For HTTP server access this will be GET, HEAD, POST, PUT, and so on.
PATH_INFO	Extra path information present in the URL; undefined if there is no such information in the URL.
PATH_TRANSLATED	The PATH_INFO path translated into an *absolute path* on the server's filesystem; undefined if PATH_INFO is undefined. For example, if the server document directory is **/vast/igraham/WebDocs**, and PATH_INFO=dir/file, then PATH_TRANSLATED=/vast/igraham/WebDocs/dir/file. This is often used to reference gateway program configuration files. Note that this is *not* related to the location of the gateway program.
SCRIPT_NAME	The *path* and *name* of the script being accessed as it would be referenced in a URL—for example, /cgi-bin/prog.pl. This can be used to construct URLs that refer back to this same gateway program, for insertion in script-generated HTML documents. For example, the string http://$SERVER_NAME:$SERVER_PORT$SCRIPT_NAME generates the full URL to the program using information contained in the environment variables ($NAME refers to the *content* of the environment variable NAME).

Table 8.2 (Continued)

QUERY_STRING   The query string portion of the URL, in encoded form. A gateway program must decode this string to extract the data sent by the client. If this string results from an **ISINDEX** search request, then QUERY_STRING data are also passed to the program as *decoded* command-line arguments.

Authentication Information

AUTH_TYPE   The *authentication method* required to authenticate the user requesting access. This is defined only for scripts that are access protected. The only currently implemented value is Basic, for the Basic authentication scheme.

REMOTE_USER   The *authenticated name* of the user; defined only when authentication is required.

REMOTE_IDENT   The remote user name, retrieved by the server from the client machine using the **identd** protocol and the remote identification daemon. This is largely unused.

Client Data Properties

CONTENT_TYPE   The MIME content-type of the data sent by the client to the server (POST or PUT method). This is undefined if no data are sent. The actual data are available to the gateway program by reading from standard input. The currently implemented types for POST requests are application/x-www-form-urlencoded and multipart/form-data.

CONTENT_LENGTH   The length, in bytes, of the data message sent to the server by the client (POST or PUT methods). If no data are being sent, this is undefined. A gateway program does not have to read all the data before returning a response, or before exiting.

Request Header Fields as Environment Variables

As noted in Table 8.2, *every* piece of information in the HTTP request header (the headers sent from the client to the server) not contained within a standard CGI environment variables is passed instead within an environment variable of the form HTTP_*NAME*, where *NAME* is related to the *name* of the request header fields. These environment variable names are constructed by:

1. *capitalizing* the name in the request header field (e.g., User-agent to USER-AGENT)

2. *converting* dash (-) characters into underscores (_) (e.g., USER-AGENT to USER_AGENT)

3. *adding* the prefix HTTP_ (e.g., USER_AGENT to HTTP_USER_AGENT)

Some of the more common environment variables of this type are listed in Table 8.3. Note in particular the construction of the HTTP_ACCEPT header.

Table 8.3 Common CGI Environment Variables Derived from HTTP Request Header Fields

Variable	Content
HTTP_ACCEPT	A comma-separated list of all MIME types acceptable to the client, as indicated by the Accept headers sent to the server. An example is shown in Figure 8.8. Gateway programs can use this to determine which type of data to return to the client.
HTTP_COOKIE	A semicolon-separated list of *Netscape cookies*. Netscape cookies are described later in this chapter.
HTTP_IF_MODIFIED_SINCE	Gives the time and date, in the standard format described at the end of Chapter 7, of data held by the client. The gateway program can then decide if the server has data that are newer than this, and if it should forward updated data or not.
HTTP_REFERER	Contains the URL which referred the user to the current request; undefined if there is no Referer header field.
HTTP_USER_AGENT	The contents of the User_Agent request header field. An example is shown at the bottom of Figure 8.8.

Server-Side Include Environment Variables

Several servers support a feature known as *server-side includes*, or SSI. SSI allows for parsable HTML documents: The documents contain special server directives that are processed by the server, and that are replaced by text from a second document, or by the output of a designated CGI program. SSI supports additional environment variables not mention in Tables 8.3 and 8.4. Chapter 9 contains a thorough discussion of SSI, while Tables 9.2 and 9.3 list special environment variables provided by the SSI mechanism.

NOTE: Customized Environment Variables   Some servers permit local customization of CGI enviroment variables. You should check with your local server administrator to find out about any special-purpose CGI environment variables available at your site.

Example 22: HTML FORMs via a GET Request

This example examines the data passed, by an HTML **FORM,** to the program shown in Figure 8.9. The **FORM** used is the same one employed in Example 15 in Chapter 7, which uses the GET method to send the data to the program (The **FORM** document is shown in Figure 7.6

and, as rendered by a browser, in Figure 7.7). The Bourne-shell program in Figure 8.9 prints out the relevant environment variables, and also reads in data from standard input (using the `read var` command, on the seventh line from the bottom) and prints this input data to standard output.

Figure 8.9 Test script *form1* accessed by the HTML FORM in Figure 7.6. This script returns an HTML document listing the script command-line arguments (if there are any), the contents of all the environment variables, and any data read from standard input (if any exists).

```sh
#!/bin/sh
echo Content-TYPE:  text/html
echo
# is a FORMs test script — it prints the environment variable
# contents generated by a FORM access to this script.
echo "<HEAD>"
echo "<TITLE>FORMs Test Page </TITLE>"
echo "</HEAD>"
echo "<P> Number of Command-line Arguments = $#. They are:"
for i in $*
do
    echo " <code> $i </code> "
done
echo "<h2> The Environment Variables </h2>"
echo "<pre>"
echo "SERVER_NAME = $SERVER_NAME"
echo "SERVER_PORT = $SERVER_PORT"
echo "REQUEST_METHOD = $REQUEST_METHOD"
echo "PATH_INFO = $PATH_INFO"
echo "PATH_TRANSLATED = $PATH_TRANSLATED"
echo "SCRIPT_NAME = $SCRIPT_NAME"
echo "QUERY_STRING = $QUERY_STRING"
echo "CONTENT_TYPE = $CONTENT_TYPE"
echo "CONTENT_LENGTH = $CONTENT_LENGTH"
echo
if [ -n "$CONTENT_LENGTH" ]; then # Read/print input data (if any).
        echo "<H2>data at Standard Input is:</h2>"
        echo "<PRE>"
        read "var"  # read data from standard input into "var"
        echo "$var" # print var to standard output
        echo "</PRE>"
else
        echo "<h2> No Data at standard input </h2>"
fi
echo "</BODY>"
```

The data sent to the server (and to the gateway program listed in Figure 8.9) by the form listed in Figure 7.6 are:

```
GET /cgi-bin/form1?srch=dogfish&srch_type=Exact+Match&srvr=Canada&srvr=Sweden HTTP/1.0
Accept: text/plain
Accept: application/x-html
Accept: application/html
Accept: text/x-html
Accept: text/html
Accept: audio/*
.
.
Accept: text/x-setext
Accept: */*
User-Agent: NCSA Mosaic for the X Window System/2.4 libwww/2.12 modified
   [a blank line, containing only CRLF ]
```

The dots indicate Accept headers omitted to save space. You will note that these data were sent by the Mosaic for X-Windows browser.

Figure 8.10 shows the document returned by the script listed in Figure 8.9. You will note that there are no command-line arguments. In parsing the URL, the server detected "real" equals signs in the query string. This indicates a non-**ISINDEX** query, so the server does not create command-line arguments. The remaining quantities are obvious. The REQUEST_METHOD environment variable is set to GET, and the query string is placed in the QUERY_STRING environment variable. The CONTENT_TYPE and CONTENT_LENGTH variables are empty, since there is no data sent in a GET method, while the PATH_INFO and PATH_TRANSLATED variables are also empty, since there was no extra path information in the query.

Further processing requires more sophisticated programming tools to parse the QUERY_STRING and break it into its component parts. This is not difficult, recalling that the ampersand character divided the different segments; the equals sign is used to relate FORM variable names to the assigned values; and spaces in the query strings are encoded as plus signs. Finally, you must decode all the special characters that may have been encoded using the URL encoding scheme discussed in Chapter 6. The perl code extract in Figure 8.11 illustrates how this decoding can be done.

Example 23: HTML FORMs via a POST Request

This example again accesses the program shown in Figure 8.9 using a **FORM** equivalent to the one in Figure 7.6, but, this time, using the POST method. The data sent to a server (again using the Mosaic for X-Windows browser) are:

```
POST /cgi-bin/form1 HTTP/1.0
Accept: text/plain
Accept: application/x-html
```

```
Accept: application/html
Accept: text/x-html
Accept: text/html
Accept: audio/*
  .
  .
Accept: text/x-setext
Accept: */*
User-Agent: NCSA Mosaic for the X Window System/2.4 libwww/2.12 modified
Content-type: application/x-www-form-urlencoded
Content-length: 58

srch=dogfish&srch_type=Exact+Match&srvr=Canada&srvr=Sweden
```

Figure 8.10 Data returned from the script shown in Figure 8.9 when accessed, using the GET method, by the FORM shown in Figure 7.6.

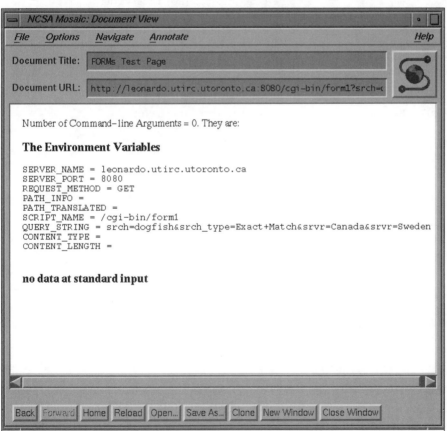

Figure 8.11 Perl code extract for decoding FORM data passed in a query string. Note that this is not a functional piece of code and that the extracted name and value strings must be place in a permanent storage location (such as an associative array) for subsequent processing.

```perl
if( !defined($ENV{"QUERY_STRING"})) {    # Check for Query String environment
    &pk_error("No Query String\n");       # Variable -- if absent, then error.
}
$input=$ENV{"QUERY_STRING"}               # get FORM data from query string

                                          # Check for unencoded equals sign -- if
                                          # there are none, the string didn't
if( $input !~ /=/ ) {                     # come from a FORM, which is an error.

    &pk_error("Query String not from FORM\n");
}
                                          # If we get to here, all is OK. Now
@fields=split("&",$input);                # split data into separate name=value
                                          # fields(@fields is an array)

#   Now loop over each of the entries in the @fields array and break
#   them into the name and value parts. Then decode each part to get
#   back the strings typed into the form by the user

foreach $one (@fields) {
    ($name, $value) = split("=",$one);    # split, at the equals sign, into
                                          # the name and value strings. Next,
                                          # decode the strings.
    $name  =~ s/\+/ /g;                   # convert +'s to spaces
    $name  =~ s/%(..)/pack("c",hex($1))/ge; # convert URL hex codings to Latin-1
    $value =~ s/\+/ /g;                   # convert +'s to spaces
    $value =~ s/%(..)/pack("c",hex($1))/ge; # convert URL hex codings to Latin-1

    #    What you do now depends on how the program works. If you know that each
    #    name is unique (your FORM does not have checkbox or SELECT items that
    #    allow multiple name=value strings with the same name) then you can place
    #    all the data in an associative array (a useful little perl feature!):

    $array{"$name"} = $value;

    #    If your form does have SELECT or <INPUT TYPE=checkbox..> items,
    #    then you'll have to be a bit more careful...

}
```

In this case, the data are sent to the server as an encoded message following the headers. There are two extra header fields: the content-length field, which tells the server the length of the following message; and the content-type field, which tells the server that this is an application/x-www-form-urlencoded MIME type—a special MIME type that indicates **FORM** data that have been encoded using the URL encoding scheme.

Figure 8.12 shows the results returned by the script in Figure 8.9, and displays the data that arrived at the script. There are no command-line arguments—this time, because there is no query string. Most of the environment variables are the same as with the GET request shown in Figure 8.10. Obvious differences are the REQUEST_METHOD variable, which is now POST instead of GET, and the null QUERY_STRING. In addition, the CONTENT_TYPE and CONTENT_LENGTH are not empty but contain the length of the message and the content-type, as indicated in the fields sent by the client.

Figure 8.12 Data returned from the script shown in Figure 8.9 when accessed by the FORM shown in Figure 7.6, modified to use the POST HTTP method.

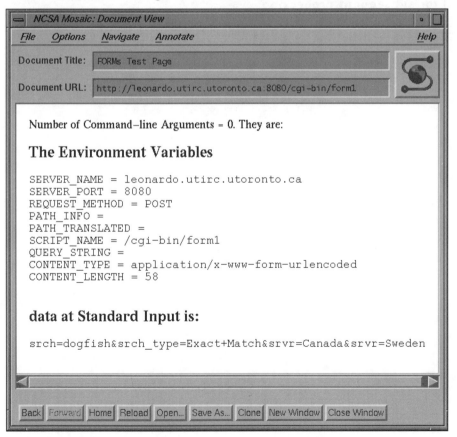

Where are the **FORM** data? With the POST method, these data are sent to the gateway program as an input stream, which the program reads from standard input. The script in Figure 8.9 reads data from standard input, and prints the results back to standard output. The result is printed at the bottom of Figure 8.12, which clearly shows the query data sent by the client. These data are encoded using the same URL encoding mechanisms employed with the GET query in Figure 8.10. To further process these data, you must parse it and separate the fields. Figure 8.13 shows an extract of a perl program that illustrates how this decoding can be done. This is similar to the code in Figure 8.11—the differences occur only at the beginning of the script, and are marked in italics. There are CGI libraries, mentioned in Chapter 9, that can help in the processing of these data.

Figure 8.13 Perl code extract for decoding FORM data passed to the program via standard input. Differences from the extract in Figure 8.11 are shown in italics. Note that this is not a functional piece of code, and that the extracted name and value strings must be place in a permanent storage location (such as an associative array) for subsequent processing.

```perl
$input=<STDIN>;                         # read FORM data from stdin
chop($input); chop($input);             # chop CR/LF trailing characters:
                                        # recall that the data sent by a client
                                        # is always terminated by a single line
                                        # containing only a CRLF pair. This
                                        # must be removed, since it is not
                                        # part of the message body.
                                        # Check for unencoded equals sign — if
                                        # there are none, the string didn't
if( $input !~ /=/ ) {                   # come from a FORM, which is an error.
    &pk_error("Query String not from FORM\n");
}
                                        # If we get to here, all is OK. Now
@fields=split("&",$input);              # split data into separate name=value
                                        # fields(@fields is an array)

#   Now loop over each of the entries in the @fields array and break
#   them into the name and value parts. Then decode each part to get
#   back the strings typed into the form by the user

foreach $one (@fields) {
    ($name, $value) = split("=",$one);  # split,at the equals sign,into
                                        # the name and value strings. Next,
                                        # decode the strings.

    $name  =~ s/\+/ /g;                 # convert +'s to spaces
    $name  =~ s/%(..)/pack("c",hex($1))/ge;   # convert URL hex codings to Latin-1
    $value =~ s/\+/ /g;                 # convert +'s to spaces
    $value =~ s/%(..)/pack("c",hex($1))/ge;   # convert URL hex codings to Latin-1
```

Figure 8.13 (Continued)

```
#   What you do now depends on how the program works. If you know that each
#   name is unique (your FORM does not have checkbox or SELECT items that
#   allow multiple name=value strings with the same name) then you can place
#   all the data in an associative array (a useful little perl feature!):

$array{"$name"} = $value;

#   If your form does have SELECT or <INPUT TYPE=checkbox..> items,
#   then you'll have to be a bit more careful...

}
```

Example 23 may seem similar to Example 22, but it is, in fact, different in important ways. First, many computer operating systems have a finite data space for environment variables, so that large messages passed via GET URLs can be truncated. In addition, the POST method in principle allows for complicated MIME messages to be sent from client to server, something that is impossible with GET. In this regard, data can be POSTed to a server using the *multipart/form-data* encoding scheme, discussed in Example 17 in Chapter 7. This scheme supports file upload (the ability to upload arbitrary data files from the client to the server) as well as the encoding of text input using any character set—recall that URLs, and hence URL-encoded FORM data, are restricted to the ISO Latin-1 character set.

Relative Advantages of GET and POST

The GET and POST methods for handling **FORM** input have different strengths and weaknesses. POST is clearly superior if you are sending large quantities of data to the server or data encoded in character sets other than ISO Latin-1. If you are sending small quantities of data, and only ISO Latin-1 characters, the choice is less clear. One useful criterion is to ask if you want the user to be able to store ("bookmark") a URL that will return the user to this particular resource. If the answer is yes, then you must use the GET method, since the relevant data will be placed in the query string portion of a URL, which is stored when a URL is recorded. If, on the other hand, you do not want the user to be able to quickly return to this resource, or if you want to hide the **FORM** content as much as possible, then you should use POST.

HTML Encoding of Text within a FORM

With gateway programs, you often need to place data inside the **FORM** sent to the client—this might be initial field values assigned to the **VALUE** attributes of **INPUT** or **OPTION** elements or within the body of a **TEXTAREA** element, or it might be state information preserved within the **VALUE** attributes of **TYPE**="hidden" **INPUT** elements. However, in doing so, you must remember that the text received by the client will be *parsed*. This means that any entity or character references embedded in the **VALUE** (or **NAME**) strings, or within the body of a **TEXTAREA** element, will be automatically converted into the correct ISO Latin-1 characters. For example, if a document sent to a client contains the hidden element:

```
<INPUT TYPE="hidden" NAME="stuff" VALUE="&lt;BOO&quot;&gt;">
```

the client will *parse* the **VALUE** string and convert it into the string `<BOO">`. When the **FORM** containing this hidden element is submitted, the string `<BOO">` will be URL-encoded and sent to the server, so that the entity references in the original data are lost.

This is sensible if you recall that, as far as the browser is concerned, entity references and character references *are* no different from the characters they represent. This can be a problem, however, if the data within the hidden form contains HTML markup, since then you often need to *preserve* entity references distinct from the characters they represent, for example so that simple character strings (`&lt;tag&gt;`) do not get converted into markup tags (`<tag>`) by the conversion process. Thus, if you need to preserve entity references, you must do the following encodings of the string prior to placing it within a **VALUE** or **NAME** attribute, or inside a **TEXTAREA** element:

1. encode all ampersand characters in the text string as `&amp;`

2. encode all double quotation symbols as `&quot;`

3. encode all right angle brackets (>) as `&gt;`

The second and third steps are necessary, as any raw double quote characters (`"`) will prematurely terminate a **VALUE** or **NAME** string, while some browsers mistakenly use an unencoded greater-than symbol (`>`) to prematurely end **INPUT** elements. The first step encodes the leading character of each entity or character reference—for example, the original string `&eacute;` becomes `&amp;eacute;`. This is processed by the client browser back to the string `&eacute;`, which brings you back full circle when the data are returned to the server.

State Preservation in CGI Transactions

In a complex gateway application, a complete session may require a series of interactions between the client and server. Since the HTTP protocol is stateless, the server, and any gateway program on the server, retain no knowledge of any previous transaction. Thus you, the gateway program designer, must build in mechanisms for keeping track of what happened in any previous stage. There are two strategies for doing this. The traditional way is to use **TYPE**="hidden" **INPUT** elements within HTML forms, to pass state information back and forth between client and server. A second, newer method is to use Netscape cookies to store state information on the client, for future reference.

State Preservation by Hidden Elements

There are two ways to use **TYPE=**"hidden" **INPUT** ("hidden", for short) elements to preserve state information. First, the gateway program can place all the data received from the client within "hidden" elements returned with the **FORM** used for the next stage of a transaction. Then, the subsequent access to a server will resend the data from the previous interaction(s), since all the data are preserved in the "hidden" elements. The second method is to create a temporary file on the server and store the transaction data within this file. In this case the gateway program need only return a single "hidden" element containing the *name* of this temporary file, so that the gateway program, on subsequent requests, is told where to find the state information. This reduces the amount of data that must be sent from client to server (and back again), but also means that the gateway programs must carefully manage these temporary files. For example, many remote users may not complete the transaction, which will leave temporary files in place unless there are auxiliary routines for deleting "stale" entries.

State Preservation by Netscape Cookies

The "hidden" form element mechanism works, but is not ideal. Problems arise if a user does not move through the sequence exactly as planned, and in a single session. For example, a user might get halfway through a process, shut off the computer, and go home, hoping to resume the next morning. This is not possible with hidden form elements, since all the state information is lost when you shut down the browser.

As a partial solution to this problem, Netscape introduced a mechanism commonly known as *Netscape cookies*. The idea behind cookies is to have the browser store, on its local hard disk, specific state information sent by the server. In a sense, this is like storing "hidden" element data, but outside the document and in such a way that they can be retrieved whenever needed. The cookie content is then sent to the server, as part of the HTTP request header, when appropriate.

Cookies are sent to a browser using a `Set-Cookie` HTTP response header field or fields (the server can send multiple cookies in a single transaction). In turn, the browser sends cookies to a server using a `Cookie` HTTP request header field.

NOTE: Netscape Cookies Are Not Universal
The Netscape cookie mechanism works on the Netscape and Internet Explorer browsers, but not on others, such as lynx or most versions of Mosaic.

Putting a Cookie on the Browser

An HTTP server places cookie information on a browser by sending a special `Set-Cookie` HTTP response header field—which is often returned by CGI programs via a server directive.

The `Set-Cookie` field contains the cookie content as a name/value pair, and can also contain information explaining when the cookie will no longer be valid (expires), the Internet domain for which the cookie is valid (domain), and the path portion of the URL within this domain for which the cookie is valid (path).

Cookie Parameter Values

The general form of a `Set-Cookie` header field is:

```
Set-Cookie: name=value; expires=date;  path=val_path; domain=dom_nam; secure
```

namely, a semicolon-separated collection of values. Most of these parameters are optional. The meanings and uses of the parameters are described in Table 8.4.

Table 8.4 Definition of Parameters for Netscape `Set-Cookie` Header Fields

`name=value` (mandatory)

> This mandatory parameter specifies the name and value for the cookie. Both name and value must be strings of printable ASCII characters, and cannot contain semicolons (;), commas (,) or space characters. There is no encoding mechanism specified for cookies. Both the `name` and `value` are arbitrary, given the above restrictions; the similarity to the name and value portions of a FORM **INPUT** element is intentional.

`domain=domain.name` (optional)

> This parameter specifies the Internet domain for which the cookie is valid, and to which the cookie content can be sent. This can be a *subdomain*, for example `.java.utoronto.ca`, in which case the valid domains will be any domain names ending in this string. For domain names ending in country codes (e.g., .ca, .us—see Appendix E) the *subdomain* specification must contain at least three periods, as in this example. In the case of the special top-level domains .com, .edu, .net, .org, .gov, .mil, or .int, only two periods are needed. An example subdomain specification is `.netscape.com`.

> The server sending the `Set-Cookie` request must reside in the domain specified by the `domain` parameter. Thus the machine `home.netscape.com` can specify `domain=.netscape.com`, while my machine at `smaug.java.utoronto.ca` cannot.

> If not specified, the default value is the full hostname for the server sending the `Set-Cookie` request.

`path=valid/path` (optional)

> Specifies the set of URLs at the allowed domain(s) for which the cookie is valid.

> If not specified, the default value is the URL path to the resource being returned with the `Set-Cookie` header.

Table 8.4 (Continued)

`expires=date` (optional)

> Sets the date at which the cookie expires and should be deleted. The allowed value is a date string of the format
>
> `Day, dd-Mon-yyyy hh:mm:ss GMT`
>
> or any of the date formats described at the end of Chapter 7. If absent, the cookie expires when the user exits the browser session (or when the browser crashes).

`secure` (optional)

> Indicates that the cookie content should only be communicated down a secure HTTP connection, such as **https**. If this parameter is present and the connection is not secure, then the cookie content is not sent. If this parameter is absent, the cookie is sent regardless of security issues.

TIP: No Quotation Marks in Parameter Fields Unlike HTML attributes, cookie parameter values must not be enclosed in quotation marks. Thus, you must type `domain=.sub.domain.edu` and not `domain=".sub.domain.edu"`—the latter will not work. Similarly, you must not surround the `name=value` portion with quotes, as the quotation marks will be taken as the first character of the name and the last character of the value.

Sending Cookies to a Server

When a browser that supports cookies accesses a URL, it checks in its cookie jar for all cookies that are appropriate to the specified domain and path. If there are no relevant cookies, the transaction proceeds normally. If there are relevant cookies, then the browser combines all the cookie *name=value* strings together, separated by semicolons, and modifies the request to include an HTTP request header field of the form:

`Cookie: name1=value1; name2=value2; ...`

A CGI program parsing this request should look to the `HTTP_COOKIE` environment variable and extract the cookie information.

Finite Number of Cookies

Cookies do not live forever, nor do browsers support an infinite number of them—for example, Netscape Navigator allows at most 300 cookies, each cookie no longer than 4 KB. At the same time, there can be no more than 20 cookies per server or per domain. If these limits are exceeded, the client will delete cookies, starting with the one least recently used. A gateway program can delete unneeded cookies by sending a new `Set-Cookie` header that contains an `expires` value that has already "expired." This is a useful way of cleaning up cookies that are no longer required. Note that this will only work if the replacement `Set-Cookie` header field uses the same cookie name.

Cookies and JavaScript

Cookies and cookie content can also be modified, created, or destroyed by JavaScript scripts within HTML documents. This is useful for recording user actions from within navigational tools.

Refusing Cookies

As mentioned, not all browsers support cookies, so this is not a universal mechanism for preserving state. In addition, browsers that support cookies often let the user turn off this feature: Netscape Navigator, for example, can be configured to prompt the user whenever a server tries to send a cookie, giving the user the option of refusing the cookie.

CGI Program Security Issues

There is always a security risk associated with running a gateway program on a server, since a rogue program can easily corrupt the data files being managed by the server. Most HTTP servers restrict executable programs to special URLs (typically those pointing to the directories */cgi-bin* or */htbin),* and do not permit executable gateway programs in the area where regular documents are kept. The server administrator can then maintain strict control over the installation of programs in these areas, and can verify that installed gateways are not dangerous to the integrity of the server.

The details of security management depend on the server that you are using. In general, most servers allow significant customization of these features. You should check with your server manager—or with your server documentation, if you are the server manager—to determine how your server can be customized.

Designing Safe Gateway Programs

Of course few people set out to write unsafe gateway programs. Nevertheless, it is easy to do so unless you are careful. Although it is hard to give definitive rules for writing safe programs, here are three points you should particularly consider:

1. **Guard system information.** Gateway programs should never return to the client any information about the local system that could compromise system security, such as absolute paths to files, system usernames, password information, and so on. If you must return directory information, pass it as a path *relative* to a location unknown to outside users: This gives away only limited filesystem information.

2. **Never trust client data.** A gateway program should never trust data sent by a client—the data could be in error, either due to a simple typing mistake, or due to an intentional effort on the part of the client to break into your system. As a relatively benign example, you should never blindly trust the e-mail address (either *From:* or *To:*) typed into a fill-in HTML **FORM**, since you could be mailing data to the wrong user, or to a nonexistent mail address.

More important, you should be extremely careful about using strings, derived from user input, as arguments to system calls such as the C or perl `system()` and `popen()` calls, or the perl or shell `eval` commands. Blindly passing strings to these calls or commands is a classic mistake, since commands executed by these calls can easily delete files, mail your password file to a remote user, and commit other cardinal sins. If you must execute strings passed by the user, be sure to check them for dangerous commands, and to *unescape* special shell characters that can cause grievous problems:

`` ` ~ ! # $ ^ & * ( ) = | \ { } [ ] ; : ' " < > , . ? ``

3. **Execute in a secure environment.** You can often run a script under a secure, or restricted, shell that takes proactive action to prevent problems. For example, if you are using perl gateway programs you should use *taintperl* instead of perl. This version of perl treats all quantities that come from environment variables or external input as *tainted*, and refuses to pass these quantities, unprocessed, to system calls.

Chapter 9 describes some CGI programming interfaces that are designed to protect you from these sorts of security problems. However, you should still strive to design programs to be as secure as possible.

Server Application Programming Interfaces

The gateway mechanism is simple and effective. However, it can be slow, since the gateway program must be started up, as a distinct running process, each time it is referenced. As mentioned earlier, this is often not a problem, particularly if the resource behind the gateway program is itself not speedy. Nevertheless, there are many occasions when speed is of the essence, and where it would be useful if the gateway designer could bypass the CGI mechanisms completely, and build the interface routines directly into the server.

A few servers support this feature through custom-designed gateway *applications programming interfaces*, or *APIs*. Notable among these are the Netscape Netsite server's NSAPI (Netscape API), the Microsoft IIS Web server ISAPI, and an API under development as part of the Apache server project. The Netscape (http://www.netscape.com) home page maintains some online documentation on the API (just search for the string "nsapi"), but this is badly organized and poorly written (Netscape does, however, sell an NSAPI manual, should you be so bold!). On the other hand, the apache (`http://www.apache.org/`) documentation site maintains somewhat better online information on their own API, which is distinctly different from the Netscape variant.

Gateways built using an API are much faster than those built using the CGI interface. However, they gain this speed at the expense of portability—APIs are strongly server-specific, so if you write an API-based gateway for the Netscape Netsite server, you will be tied to that server, as no other vendor supports that interface specification.

References

The following URLs provide documentation on CGI, Netscape cookies, and server-specific APIs. References to CGI utilities and libraries and to online CGI tutorials are given at the end of Chapter 9.

CGI Specification

```
http://hoohoo.ncsa.uiuc.edu/cgi/overview.html
ftp://ds.internic.net/internet-drafts/draft-robinson-www-interface-01.txt
http://hoohoo.ncsa.uiuc.edu/cgi/examples.html
```
(CGI demo scripts)

Netscape Cookies

```
http://www.netscape.com/newsref/std/cookie_spec.html
```

Server APIs

```
http://www.apache.org/docs/API.html
```
(Apache API)
```
http://solo.dc3.com/wsapi/index.htm
```
(O'Reilly WebSite API)
```
http://website.ora.com/wspro/wsapi/html/
```
(O'Reilly WebSite API)
```
http://home.netscape.com/comprod/server_central/config/nsapi.html
```
(NSAPI)
```
http://home.netscape.com/newsref/std/server_api.html
```
(NSAPI)

CGI Examples, Programs, and Tools

This chapter presents some illustrative examples of CGI programming. The first issues addressed are the Netscape *client push/server pull* HTML and HTTP extensions, which are currently implemented by most browser vendors. These extensions allow for rudimentary animation of Web presentations. Examples are provided that illustrate how these extensions work. Next is a discussion of *server-side includes*. This is a special HTTP server feature that allows for *parsable* HTML documents, which are processed by the server prior to being delivered to a client. The third section gives a detailed presentation of three gateway programming examples, illustrating some of the important issues in gateway program design.

The chapter concludes with sections listing CGI utility programs and CGI database interface programs, and, finally, a listing of archive sites containing collections of gateway programs and/or information related to CGI-database interface routines.

Netscape CGI Animation Techniques

Most modern browsers support special mechanisms that allow for slide show—like presentations and for a rudimentary form of animation. The animation scheme, called *server push*, uses a special *multipart* MIME type to let a server send a client a series of images or documents, which are in turn displayed by the browser as an animated sequence or slide show. This requires a gateway program that sends the data to the client using this special MIME type. The second mechanism, called *client pull*, uses a new HTTP response header, called `Refresh`, which instructs the browser, after a specified delay, either to actively refresh the displayed document, or to access another document at a specified URL. Again, a gateway program is needed to produce the `Refresh` HTTP header field. However, HTML authors can instead include, in their documents, **META** elements containing the `Refresh` header field content (using the **HTTP-EQUIV** attribute value, as discussed in Chapter 4)—the browser parses the documents for the **META** element, and understands `Refresh` header information. This method is particularly useful for creating document slide shows.

Client Pull

In *client pull*, the server sends the client a special HTTP `Refresh` response header field. The field has the general form

```
Refresh: xx; URL=url_string
```

where *xx* is an integer giving the time, in seconds, that the browser should wait before *refreshing* the document, and *url_string* is the *full* (not relative) URL that the browser should access when it is time to do the refresh. For example, the header

```
Refresh: 10; URL=http://www.hprc.utoronto.ca/home.html
```

tells a browser to wait 10 seconds, and to then access the indicated URL. The URL portion can be left out, in which case the browser will re-access the URL it just retrieved. Thus, the field

```
Refresh: 30
```

tells a browser to refresh the currently displayed URL after a 30-second delay. The refresh time can be set to zero, in which case the browser will refresh the display as soon as the requested data are fully loaded.

There are several things to note about this procedure. First, this response header field is understood by most, but not all, browsers; those that do not understand it will simply ignore the header, display the accessed document, and then stop. Second, the `Refresh` field must be returned by a gateway program—servers themselves do not return refresh header fields. Third, each request by the client counts as a separate HTTP transaction, since the connection is broken between refresh requests.

Client Pull via META Elements

As an alternative to using HTTP and CGI programs, `Refresh` can be placed inside a **META** element in an HTML document. This lets authors easily add refresh capability into already existing parsed HTML documents (parsed HTML documents are discussed later in this chapter), or build slide shows into a sequence of regular HTML documents, using the URL references in the `Refresh` fields to reference consecutive documents. The **META** element equivalent to the general form of the `Refresh` HTTP response header is

```
<META HTTP-EQUIV="Refresh" CONTENT="xx; URL=url_string">
```

while **META** elements equivalent to the two examples just given are:

```
<META HTTP-EQUIV="Refresh" CONTENT="10; URL=http://www.hprc.utoronto.ca/home.html">
<META HTTP-EQUIV="Refresh" CONTENT="30">
```

Most browsers understand these **META** elements and interpret their content as HTTP response header fields (this is the purpose of the **HTTP-EQUIV** attribute, as discussed in Chapter 4). This is, of course, only possible with HTML documents; if you are returning other forms of data, you will need to write a gateway program that returns the `refresh` header field.

Server Push

Server push is a second and fundamentally different way of creating dynamic documents. When a client accesses a resource delivered using server push, the client-server connection remains open, and the server sends a sequence of data objects, one after the other, over an open connection—the connection does not close until the sequence is finished. This is done using a special MIME *multi-part* message format, discussed below. There are two advantages to this method. First, you do not need to recontact the server to get the second (or subsequent) data objects. As a result, the data are delivered more quickly, since the client does not need to renegotiate a connection for each part. Second, you can use server push to download a sequence of images into an `<IMG SRC="...">` element. This allows you to embed an *animation sequence* into an HTML document by referencing, from an **IMG** element, a gateway program that delivers a sequence of image files using server push. The disadvantage is that you absolutely need to write a special-purpose gateway program—unlike client pull, you cannot implement server push using **META** elements.

NOTE: Efficiency of Server Push   Server-push animations are far less efficient than animated GIFs—you should use the latter whenever possible. Server-push is appropriate when the animation must be dynamically generated by a gateway program.

Server push is implemented using the MIME type `multipart/x-mixed-replace`. By employing this type, a server can deliver a sequence (in principle, an endless sequence) of data files, one after the other. This is done by defining a *boundary* string as part of the MIME type header. A boundary string is a string of ASCII characters used to separate each part of a multipart message from the preceding and following parts. The MIME content-type declaration takes the form:

```
Content-type: multipart/x-mixed-replace;boundary=RandomAsciiString
```

where *RandomAsciiString* is a random string of ASCII characters used as the separator between the different parts of the message. The general form for this MIME multipart message is shown in Figure 9.1, with comments in italics.

Note how the boundary between different parts of the multipart message are denoted by the string `RandomAsciiString` preceded by two dashes, that is:

`--RandomAsciiString`

The end of the multipart message is denoted by the same string but with two additional trailing dashes:

`--RandomAsciiString--`

In practice, you can leave out this termination string, and send an unending sequence of messages. A user can end this sequence by selecting the browser's "Stop" button, or by explicitly selecting an alternate URL.

The following two gateway program examples illustrate how server-push works.

Figure 9.1 Structure of a `multipart/x-mixed-replace` **MIME message. Here,** `RandomAsciiString` **represents a random string of ASCII characters used to mark the separator between the message parts, and** `type/subtype` **is the data type of the data being sent. Comments are in italics.**

```
Content-type: multipart/x-mixed-replace;boundary=RandomAsciiString
                                  [blank line, containing a CRLF pair ]
--RandomAsciiString               [marker denoting boundary between parts]
Content-type: type/subtype
    [blank line, containing a CRLF pair ]
.... content of first chunk ....
.... and more content ....
--RandomAsciiString
Content-type: type/subtype
    [blank line, containing a CRLF pair ]
.... content of second chunk ....
.... and more content ....
--RandomAsciiString
Content-type: type/subtype
    [blank line, containing a CRLF pair ]
.... content of third chunk ....
.... and more content ....
--RandomAsciiString
.
.
. [and so on....]
.
--RandomAsciiString--              [The end of the multipart message]
```

Example 24: A Simple "Server Push" Shell Script

This simple shell script, listed in Figure 9.2, repeatedly returns a document listing the "top" process running on the computer. This first thing to note is that this is a *non-parsed header* script—this is usually necessary with server push, as many servers *buffer* the data returned from a gateway program, and only forward data when the buffer is full or when the gateway program terminates. In this case we want each part of our multipart message delivered immediately to the client, without any delay. We ensure this by using a non-parsed header script, which bypasses the server buffering and dumps data directly down the port to the client.

As a result, lines 2 through 6 return *all* the required HTTP response headers: namely, the status header (response 200, implying success), the date (the format instructions provide a date in the correct format), the server type (obtained from the environment variable), and the MIME version, followed by the content-type declaration for the type multipart/x-mixed-replace. In this example, the multipart boundary string is `a11pRf5fgFd1dr`. Note that there are no space characters in this content-type header. Ordinarily, you can have spaces before and after the semicolons separating the type/subtype from the associated parameters, but this is incorrectly processed by some servers (in particular, early versions of the NCSA HTTP server), so it is safest to remove all unnecessary

Figure 9.2 The Bourne shell script *nph-top-list.sh*, which returns, every 10 seconds, a list of the top 10 running processes on the computer. *Line numbers are in italics.*

```
1   #!/bin/sh
2   echo "HTTP/1.0  200 OK"              # [ Server
3   date -u '+Date: %A, %d-%b-%y %T GMT'  #    Response
4   echo Server: $SERVER_SOFTWARE         #    Headers ]
5   echo MIME-Version: 1.0
6   echo "Content-type: multipart/x-mixed-replace;boundary=a11pRf5fgFd1dr"
7   echo ""
8   echo "--a11pRf5fgFd1dr"          # [initial boundary for first part]
9   while true
10  do
11      echo "Content-type: text/html"
12      echo ""
13      echo "<HTML><HEAD>"
14      echo "<TITLE> Top Running Processes </TITLE></HEAD><BODY>"
15      echo "<H1 ALIGN=center> Top Running Processes at time: <BR>"
16      date                     # [date prints the current time and date]
17      echo "</H1><HR>"
18      echo "<PRE>"
19      /usr/local/bin/top -d1  # Print out "top" running processes
20      echo "</PRE></BODY></HTML>"
21      echo "--a11pRf5fgFd1dr"
22      sleep 10
23  done
```

whitespace. Finally, line 7 returns a blank line, which indicates the end of server directives and the start of the data stream.

Line 8 prints the first boundary marker—this indicates the start of the first *part* of the message. The script then executes a loop, starting from line 10, which is executed every 10 seconds (see the `sleep 10` command at the bottom of the loop). The loop returns a content-type header (here text/html) followed by a blank line—the mandatory blank line marks the end of the headers and the beginning of the data. This is followed by the HTML document which includes, inside a **PRE**, the output from the program **top**. The last thing returned is the boundary marker "`--a11pRf5fgFd1dr`", which tells the client that the message is complete and that it can stop waiting for more data. It also tells the client to keep the connection to the server open, in anticipation of the next part of the message.

This program will in principle run forever, sending information every 10 seconds. A user can interrupt this by simply pressing the "Stop" button, or by selecting another URL. The server should detect the broken connection and issue a kill signal to the gateway program. Unfortunately, this does not work on some servers, so it is a good idea to have gateway programs check for a broken connection, and gracefully quit if this is found to have occurred. Shell languages, such as the Bourne shell used in this example, are notoriously bad at this—they often "forget" to die—so you should write server push scripts in languages such as perl or C, which properly terminate when the connection breaks. The script in Figure 9.2, for example, does not always terminate when the client breaks the connection—this has, on occasion, left a dozen of these scripts happily running on our server, long after the browser that started them has broken the connection to the server.

Example 25: A C Program for "Pushing" Images

The example C program **nph-doit-2**, shown in Figure 9.3, uses server push to send a sequence of GIF images. Assume that this CGI program is located in the server's *cgi-bin/* directory. Then, to insert an animated image in an HTML document, you would write the following HTML markup:

```
<IMG SRC="/cgi-bin/nph-doit-2">
```

which assumes that the HTML document and gateway program are served out of the same server. The client will then access the indicated URL to download the requested image. A browser that understands multipart messages will play the image sequence as a simple animation. Browsers that do not understand the multipart MIME type will display nothing, or will display a symbol representing a missing or broken image.

The first part of the program (between the *GET LIST* and *GOT LIST* comments) gets a list of all the image files in the directory */abs/path/image_dir*, and creates an array (`files[]`) of absolute path filenames pointing to these files. The program then writes out the necessary server response headers, as well as the initial multipart headers and message dividers required by the multipart message (just after the **PRINT SERVER RESPONSE HEADERS** comment). The subsequent loop iterates over the different image files, sending them one after the other to the client, each file followed by the required multipart boundary marker (after the **WRITE THE PART BOUNDARY** comment). When the program is finished with the list, it exits, writes out the final boundary marking the end of the multipart message, and ends the connection.

Figure 9.3 Simple C program *nph-doit-2.c*, for pushing a sequence of images to a client. The files are read from the indicated directory. Commentary not originally in the program listing is in boldface italics.

```
/*
 * doit-2.c
 * Based on doit.c --
 *    Quick hack to play a sequence of GIF files, by Rob McCool.
 *       This code is released into the public domain. Do whatever
 *       you want with it.
 *
 * Doit-2.c Modifications by By Ian Graham, July 23 1995
 * to make it a simpler demonstration example -- or so I thought!
 */

#include <sys/types.h>
#include <unistd.h>
#include <stdlib.h>
#include <fcntl.h>
#include <sys/stat.h>
#include <dirent.h>
#include <stdio.h>

/* Define the server directives and response headers              */

#define HEADER1  "HTTP/1.0 200 OK\r\n"      /* Nph-response header      */
#define HEADER2 \
   "Content-type: multipart/x-mixed-replace;boundary=aRd4xBloobies\r\n"

/* Define the boundary strings, the Content-type header, and the     */
/* path to the directory containing the images                       */

#define BOUNDARY      "\r\n--aRd4xBloobies\r\n"
#define END_BOUND     "\r\n--aRd4xBloobies--\r\n\r\n"
#define CONTENT       "Content-type: image/gif\r\n\r\n"
#define IMG_DIR       "/abs/path/image_dir"   /* where the files are      */

int main(int argc, char *argv[])
{
```

Continued

Figure 9.3 (Continued)

```
static char    *file;
char           *files[1024], *tmp, buf[127];
caddr_t        fp;
int            fd, i, ndir=0;
DIR            *dirp;
struct dirent  *dp;
struct stat    fi;

/* Get list of all files in image directory -- we will        */
/* spit them out in alphabetical order                        */
                                    /* ** GET LIST    ** */
dirp = opendir(IMG_DIR);
while ( ((dp = readdir(dirp)) != NULL) && (ndir < 1024) ) {
    if( strncmp(dp->d_name,".", 1)) {
        files[ndir] = malloc(strlen(dp->d_name)+1+strlen(IMG_DIR));
        sprintf(files[ndir], "%s/%s", IMG_DIR, dp->d_name);
        ndir++;
    }
}
closedir(dirp);
                                    /* ** GOT LIST    ** */
/* Write out server directives, and first multipart boundary  */

                        /* ** PRINT SERVER RESPONSE HEADERS    ** */
if(write(STDOUT_FILENO, HEADER1, strlen(HEADER1)) == -1)   exit(0);
if(write(STDOUT_FILENO, HEADER2, strlen(HEADER2)) == -1)   exit(0);
if(write(STDOUT_FILENO, BOUNDARY, strlen(BOUNDARY)) == -1) exit(0);

/* Now loop over all files, and write to client               */
for (i=0; i<ndir; i++)  {
    fprintf(stderr, "Doing output loop -- i=%i\n", i);
    sleep(1);
                                /* ** WRITE PART CONTENT-TYPE  ** */
    if(write(STDOUT_FILENO, CONTENT, strlen(CONTENT)) == -1) exit(0);
    if( ( fd=open(files[i],O_RDONLY)) == -1 ) {
        fprintf(stderr,"Unable to open file %s\n", files[i]);
        continue;
    }
    fstat(fd, &fi);                 /*  find size of file and   */
    tmp=malloc(fi.st_size*sizeof(char));  /*  allocate memory for it   */
    read(fd, tmp, fi.st_size);
                                /* ** WRITE THE IMAGE DATA ** */
    if(write(STDOUT_FILENO, tmp, fi.st_size) == -1) exit(0);
                            /* ERROR: unable to write image     */
    free(tmp);
    close(fd);
                                /* ** WRITE THE PART BOUNDARY ** */
```

Figure 9.3 (Continued)

```
    if(write(STDOUT_FILENO, BOUNDARY, strlen(BOUNDARY)) == -1) exit(0);
                                /* ERROR unable to write boundary     */
}

/* Write out the boundary marking the end of the multipart          */
/* message. Then we are done.                                       */

write(STDOUT_FILENO, END_BOUND, strlen(END_BOUND));
exit(0);
}
```

Because this is a gateway program, you can pass variables to the program using the usual tricks. Thus you can use extra path information in a URL (the PATH_INFO environment variable) to pass the location of the image directory, instead of using a hard-wired location as was done in this example.

Both of the techniques just mentioned are not terribly efficient, and are likely to be replaced by more sophisticated methods. For example, HTML **LINK** elements can in principle be used to indicate "Next" and "Previous", allowing the browser to produce a slide show, if desired. Animation is also better handled through alternate mechanisms, such as animated GIFs for simple animations, Macromedia Director plug-ins, or Java applets.

Server-Side Document Includes

A recurring HTML authoring question is: "Can I include a file within my HTML document in the same way I include an image?" The answer is, in general, no, as there are no elements in HTML that allow arbitrary document inclusions. If you want to have documents that are created dynamically (which is what is implied by inclusion), you are supposed to use a CGI program. Needless to say, this can be annoying if all you want to do is patch a small piece of text into an otherwise stable document. Some kind of *include* HTML command would be far easier than a full-blown CGI script.

Most HTTP servers support file inclusion via a mechanism called *server-side includes*, or *SSI*. With SSI, a server parses specially marked documents (called *parsable* HTML documents, often with the filename extension *.shtml*) looking for specially encoded HTML comment strings containing SSI directives. The server replaces these comments by the output generated by processing the directive.

This mechanism lets an author include server directives that "include" other text or HTML files, or that can execute server programs and include the program output within the document.

This powerful feature should not be overused, however, as every parsable file must be specially processed by the server, which can significantly slow server response.

By default, most servers come with this feature disabled by default—you have to explicitly turn it on. Your server's documentation package will explain how this is done, if it is supported.

Server-side includes are well documented in the NCSA HTTPD server online manuals, referenced at the end of this chapter. Also referenced are several sites on the Web that provide useful interactive tutorials illustrating server-side includes.

Include Command Format

The server-side include mechanism is framed inside an HTML comment string:

```
<!--#include_command -->
```

When parsed by a server supporting this feature, the entire comment string is replaced by the output of `include_command`. Because the command is inside a comment string, this will not cause problems if the document is processed by a server that does not support this feature, or that has this feature disabled. Such servers will simply deliver the document, including the comment line, and the client will treat the string as a comment and ignore it.

The general form for the include command is:

```
<!--#command arg1="value1" arg2="value2" -->
```

where `command` is the name of the command to be executed and `arg1` and `arg2` are arguments passed to the command. There must be no space between the hash sign *(#)* and the command name, or between the hash sign and the leading double dash *(--#)*. The number and name of the argument(s) depend on the actual command; most commands take a single argument. Note that, despite its structure, this is *not* a comment statement. You *cannot* include comment descriptions inside an include command. Consequently, lines like:

```
<!--#command arg1="value1" This prints the time of day  -->
```

are invalid.

There are six possible commands: `config`, `include`, `echo`, `fsize`, `flastmod`, and `exec`. `Config` configures the way the server parses the document. `Include` includes another text document (*not* a CGI program) at the indicated location, while `echo` includes the contents of one of the special environment variables set for parsed documents. `Fsize` and `flastmod` are similar to `echo`; `fsize` prints the size of a specified file, while `flastmod` prints the last modification date of a specified file. Finally, `exec` executes a single-line Bourne-shell command, or a CGI program. For security reasons, the `exec` facility can be disabled in the server configuration files while leaving the other features operational.

The next sections describe each of these commands, and how they work. Entries in italics are variables to be set by the document author. Table 9.1 summarizes the commands and the allowed forms.

Include

This directive includes another document (or another parsed document) at the given location in the current document—it cannot include CGI program output. Include takes two arguments to specify the file to be included. These are:

virtual="*virtual/file*"—Specifies the *virtual* path to the document, relative to the server's document directory or to a user's personal server directory. For example, user fosdick with his or her own public HTML area would access files in this area with the virtual path:

```
<!--#include virtual="~fosdick/path/file.html"-->
```

Table 9.1 Server-Side Include Commands. Items in italics are user-selectable strings.

Include Command	Function and Behavior
<--#config errmsg="*err_str*" -->	Set error message to be returned upon error
<--#config timefmt="*format_str*" -->	Set format for times and dates
<--#config sizefmt="bytes" -->	Set format for printing file sizes to "bytes"
<--#config sizefmt="abbrev" -->	Set format for printing file sizes—bytes, kilobytes, or megabytes, depending on size
<--#echo var="*variable*" -->	Print contents of given environment variable
<--#exec cmd="*cmd_string*" -->	Execute the given Bourne-shell command string and include the output inline
<--#exec cgi="*path/cgi_prog*" -->	Execute the indicated CGI program, and include the output inline
<--#flastmod virtual="*virt/file*" -->	Print last-modification date of file at indicated virtual location
<--#flastmod file="*path/file*" -->	Print last-modification date of file at indicated relative location
<--#fsize virtual="*virt/file*" -->	Print size of file at indicated virtual location
<--#fsize file="*path/file*" -->	Print size of file at indicated relative location
<--#include virtual="*virt/file*" -->	Include document from indicated virtual location
<--#include file="*path/file*" -->	Include document from indicated relative location

`file="`*`relative/file`*`"`—Specifies the path to the document relative to the current URL. You cannot use this form to move up in the hierarchy, only down (i.e., you can't use `../stuff.html`). For example, to include the file *junk.html* from the same directory, or the file *blog.html* from the subdirectory *muck*, you would use:

```
<!--#include file="junk.html" -->
<!--#include file="muck/blog.html" -->
```

Echo

This includes the contents of a named environment variable, where the variable is indicated by the argument `var="`*`variable_name`*`"`. *Variable_name* can be any of the CGI environment variables listed in Tables 8.2 and 8.3 (except `QUERY_STRING` and `PATH_INFO`—see the discussion of the exec include later in this section), and can also be one of the special environment variables listed in Table 9.2, valid only in parsable files or in CGI programs called from a parsable file.

Fsize

This includes the size, in bytes, of a file specified using either the `file` or `virtual` arguments, as described with the `include` command. `Fsize` is useful for presenting information about a file to be downloaded, particularly when the size varies often (it might, for example, be a mail archive). For example:

```
... Download</A> the mail archive: (<!--#fsize file="main.html"  --> bytes)
```

The output format is set by the `sizefmt` argument of the `config` command.

Flastmod

This includes the last modification time of a file specified using the `file` or `virtual` arguments, as described with the `include` command. Like `fsize`, `flastmod` is useful for providing up-to-date information about files that are periodically changed. For example:

```
This file was last changed on:
<!--#flastmod virtual="/path/dir1/dir2/main.html"  -->
```

The output format is set by the `timefmt` argument of the `config` command.

Exec

This directive executes the indicated Bourne-shell command or CGI program, and includes the program output inline in the document. The two possible arguments are:

`cmd="`*`cmd_string`*`"`— Causes the string "*cmd_string*" to be executed using the Bourne shell (**sh**). *Cmd_string* can be a simple one-line shell program that does simple tasks such as listing directory contents or running a program to filter data for inclusion.

Table 9.2 Environment Variables Defined Only within Parsed HTML Documents
Items after the dashed divider are not universally available on all servers. These
variables are also available to CGI programs executed from within a parsed HTML
document.

Variable Name	Content
DOCUMENT_NAME	The name of the document being parsed. This is the raw name, stripped of any leading path information, extra path information, or query string data. For example, if the accessed URL were of the form `/path/to/file.shtml/extra/path?foo`, DOCUMENT_NAME would be simply `file.shtml`.
DOCUMENT_URI	The virtual (relative to the server document directory) path to the document, such as `~fosdick/path/file.shtml`, or `/path/subpath/templates/template2.html`. This will include any extra path information in the requesting URL, but not appended query string data.
DATE_LOCAL	The current date, using the local time zone. The format of this date is controlled using the `timefmt` argument of the `config` command.
DATE_GMT	Same as DATE_LOCAL, but in Greenwich Mean Time.
LAST_MODIFIED	The last modification date of the current document. The format is specified by the `timefmt` configuration setting.
DOCUMENT_PATH_INFO	Contains any extra path information in the requesting URL. For example, if the requesting URL were `/path/to/file.shtml/extra/path?foo`, the DOCUMENT_PATH_INFO would be `/extra/path`.

`cgi="cgi_program"`– Executes the given CGI program, the location of the program being given by the *virtual* path to the program. Note that the script must return a valid MIME type. You cannot pass query strings or path information to the script using the standard URL mechanisms. Thus expressions like

```
<!--#exec cgi="/cgi-bin/script.cgi/path1/path2?query" -->
```

are invalid. The only way you can access the script is with the command:

```
!--#exec cgi="/cgi-bin/script.cgi" -->
```

However, suppose the parsable script *stuff.shtml* contained the command:

```
<!--#exec cgi="/cgi-bin/script.cgi" -->
```

and you access the file *stuff.shtml* via a URL of the form:

```
.../stuff.shtml/extra/path?query_string
```

In this case, the query_string and /extra/path information *are* available to the script *script.cgi* called from *stuff.shtml*. This is illustrated in an example at the end of this section.

Environment Variables within Exec'ed CGIs

The variables defined in Table 9.2 are also available to gateway or shell programs executed using the exec command. In addition, any extra path or query information appended to the parsed HTML document name are passed to the CGI program within the PATH_INFO and QUERY_STRING variables, as per standard practice. At the same time, several servers define additional environment variables to provide information about the executing script. The most common of these additional variables are given in Table 9.3. These variables are defined by the Apache servers (Version 1 and greater), but not by the NCSA server prior to version 1.5.

NOTE: Possible Problems with Environment Variables   Some servers do not set the environment variables listed in Table 9.2 or at the bottom or Table 9.1, while others improperly set their content. To be safe, you should verify the data content of all environment variables prior to installing any CGI program invoked using server-side includes.

Config

This directive controls aspects of the output of the other parsed commands, such as the formats of the date and size output strings, or the error message string to include if parsing fails. Config can take three different arguments, one argument per command. These are:

errmsg="*error_string*"—Sets the error message to use if there is an error in parsing the parsable commands.

timefmt="*format*"—Sets the format for printing dates. This format is specified as per the C strftime library call (strftime is commonly found on UNIX computers).

Table 9.3 Environment Variables Defined Only within CGI Programs Invoked by a Parsed HTML Document. These variables are not universally available on all servers.

Variable Name	Content
SCRIPT_NAME	The name of the script being executed, including the virtual path information needed to locate the script.
SCRIPT_FILENAME	The complete absolute name of the file, including the path to the file from the root of the filesystem.

`sizefmt="bytes","abbrev"`—Sets the format for the specification of file sizes. The value `bytes` prints file sizes in bytes, while `abbrev` uses kilobytes or megabytes as abbreviated forms, where applicable.

Some examples are:

```
<!--#config sizefmt="abbrev"  -->
<!--#config timefmt="%m%d%y"  -->
<!--#config errmsg="Unable to parse scripts"  -->
```

Example 26: Server-Side Includes

The following example (shown in Figures 9.4 and 9.5) shows the use of server-side includes. The example consists of a main document *stuff.shtml* (the suffix *.shtml* is often used to indicate parsable HTML documents) that includes a second parsable document *inc_file.shtml*, and that also executes the CGI program *test_script.cgi*. The listings for these examples are shown in Figure 9.4, while the browser rendering of the document *stuff.shtml* is shown in Figure 9.5.

Figure 9.4 Example of server-side includes, showing the listings for three example documents. The main file is stuff.shtml, which *includes* the file inc_file.shtml and also the output of the CGI program test_script.cgi. The resulting HTML document upon accessing the URL:

`http://leonardo:8080/stuff.shtml/extra/path/info?arg1+arg2`

is shown in Figure 9.5.

1. stuff.shtml

```
<html>
<head>
<title> Test of NCSA Server-side Includes </title>
<body>
<h1> Test of NCSA Server-side Includes </h1>
<pre>
Stuff.shtml was last modified:   <!--#flastmod virtual="/stuff.shtml"  -->.
Size of stuff.shtml is:          <!--#fsize file="stuff.shtml"  -->.
DOCUMENT_NAME =                   <!--#echo var="DOCUMENT_NAME" -->
DOCUMENT_URI =                    <!--#echo var="DOCUMENT_URI" -->
DATE_LOCAL =                      <!--#echo var="DATE_LOCAL" -->
QUERY_STRING =                    <!--#echo var="QUERY_STRING" -->
PATH_LOCAL =                      <!--#echo var="QUERY_STRING" -->
DATE_GMT =                        <!--#echo var="DATE_GMT" -->
LAST_MODIFIED =                   <!--#echo var="LAST_MODIFIED" -->
</pre>

<!--#config errmsg="Unable to parse scripts"  -->
```

Continued

Figure 9.4 (Continued)

```
<p><em>....now include inc_example.shtml....</em>

<!--#include file="inc_file.shtml" -->

<p> <em>..... now include test_script.cgi CGI program output...... </em>

<!--#exec cgi="/cgi-bin/test_script.cgi" -->
</body>
</html>
```

2. inc_file.shtml

```
<pre>
Inc_file.shtml last modified:    <!--#flastmod virtual="/inc_file.shtml"-->.
Size of inc_file.shtml is:       <!--#fsize file="inc_file.shtml"  -->.
DOCUMENT_NAME:                   <!--#echo var="DOCUMENT_NAME" -->
DOCUMENT_URI:                    <!--#echo var="DOCUMENT_URI" -->
DATE_LOCAL:                      <!--#echo var="DATE_LOCAL" -->
DATE_GMT                         <!--#echo var="DATE_GMT" -->
LAST_MODIFIED                    <!--#echo var="LAST_MODIFIED" -->

</pre>
```

3. test_script.cgi (in the cgi-bin directory)

```
#!/bin/sh

echo "Content-type: text/html"
echo
echo "<pre>"
echo "This is  CGI script output."
echo "QUERY_STRING is \"$QUERY_STRING\"."
echo "PATH_INFO =  \"$PATH_INFO\". "
echo "</pre>"
```

In this example the document *stuff.shtml* is accessed using the URL:

```
http://leonardo:8080/stuff.shtml/extra/path/info?arg1+arg2
```

Note that this passes query strings and extra path information to *stuff.shtml*, as if it were a gateway program (see Chapter 8 for more information about CGI programs and passed variables). All the example documents are designed to print these environment variables. As seen in Figure 9.4, these variables are empty inside the parsable HTML document. However, the bottom of Figure 9.5 shows that these variables *are* present inside the CGI program (in the environment variables QUERY_STRING and PATH_INFO) executed from within the parsable document. You can, therefore, access a parsable document and, through it, pass query information to a CGI program, just as if you were accessing the CGI program directly.

Figure 9.5 Browser rendering of the server-side executable document stuff.shtml when accessed using the URL:

```
http://leonardo:8080/stuff.shtml/extra/path/info?arg1+arg2
```

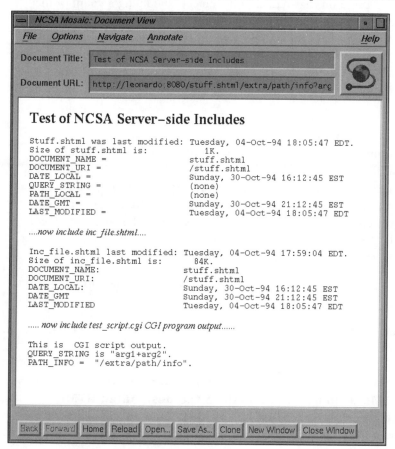

Figures 9.4 and 9.5 also illustrate the `include` and `echo` commands. These are useful for printing information about local files. However, you really want to do this as sparingly as possible, as every such request slows down the server. For example, it is a waste of server resources to use the `LAST_MODIFIED` variable to display the last time you edited a simple HTML document, since you could just as easily place this information in the file directly.

For additional information about server-side includes, and for information on how to configure the NCSA server to support server-side includes, please consult the NCSA on-line documentation, at:

```
http://hoohoo.ncsa.uiuc.edu/docs/tutorials/includes.html
```

Some Example CGI Programs

This section presents a few example CGI programs, representing some of the common uses of the CGI facility. The first example is a program that returns a document containing a count of the number of times the page was accessed. The second looks at using a gateway program and server-side includes to insert a randomly selected HTML snippet into an HTML document. The third and last example looks at WebNotice, a large-scale gateway-program application designed by the author. This package integrates 28 gateway programs, 19 HTML document templates, and 10 HTML documents to create a Web-based system for depositing and viewing notices to be made available to the public.

Example 27: Page Access Counter

The simple perl script of this example answers the common question, "How do I include, within my page, a number indicating how many times the document has been accessed?" This program reads in the document to be returned to the client and edits it, replacing a dummy comment string in the document (the string `<!-- counter -->`) by the desired count. The count is obtained from a log file that keeps track of the number of times the file has been accessed. The gateway program opens this log file and increments the counter by 1. The program listing is found in Figure 9.6.

To use this gateway program, you must access a document using a URL of the form:

`http://some.where.edu/cgi-bin/counter.pl/path/file.html`

where `path/file.html` is the path to the document, relative to the root of the server document directory.

Figure 9.6 Listing of the perl gateway program *counter.pl*, which inserts an access count into a designated HTML document. The path to the designated HTML document is passed as *extra path* information in the URL used to access this program. Line numbers, in italics, are added for reference purposes only—they are not present in the original program.

```
1    #!/usr/local/bin/perl
2    if (defined($ENV{"PATH_TRANSLATED"}) ) {
3        $path = $ENV{"PATH_TRANSLATED"}      # get file from extra path info
4    }
5    else {
6        &f_error("No file specified\n");
7    }
8    $file     = $path;                       # Path to file to be processed
9    $cnt_file = $path;
10   $cnt_file =~ s/.*\///;                   # Extract substring for counter filename
11   $path     =~ s/\/[\w-.;~]*$/\///;        # get path to directory
12
```

Figure 9.6 (Continued)

```
13  $cnt_file = $path.".".$cnt_file;        # counter filename = path/.filename
14
15  if( !(-e $cnt_file) ) {                 # If count file doesn't exist, create it
16     open(CNTFILE, "> $cnt_file") ||
17              &f_error("Unable to create count file\n");
18     print CNTFILE "0";
19     close(CNTFILE);
20  }
21  $loops = 0;                             # try 4 times to lock the count file
22  while ( flock($cnt_file,2) == -1 )  {
23     $loops++;
24     if( $loops > 4) {
25        $cnt = "-1 (Unable to lock counter)\n";
26        goto PROCESS;                     # If unable to lock, skip it.
27     }
28        sleep 1;
29  }
30  open(CNTFILE, "+< $cnt_file")           # open the counter file
31           || &f_error("Unable to open counter file\n");
32  $cnt = <CNTFILE>;                        # get the current count
33  $cnt++;                                  # increment count by one
34  seek(CNTFILE, 0, 0);                     # rewind to start of file
35  print CNTFILE "$cnt";                    # write out new count
36  close(CNTFILE);                          # close the count file
37  flock($cntfile, 8);                      # Unlock the count file
38
39  PROCESS:
40  open(FILE, $file)                        # Open file to process
41        || &f_error("Unable to open file for processing\n");
42  @array= <FILE>;                          # Read in the file
43  close(FILE);
44                                           # Print out the document
45  print "Content-type: text/html\n\n";
46  foreach (@array) {                       # scan for special string, and
47     s/<!-- counter -->/ $cnt /i;          # replace it by the count
48     print $_;
49  }
50  # Error Handling Subroutine
51  sub f_error {
52     print "Content-type text/plain\n\n";
53     print "<HTML><HEAD>\n<TITLE>Error In Counter Script</TITLE>";
54     print "\n</HEAD><BODY>\n<h2>Error</h2>\n<P>Error message: $_[0]";
55     print "\n<P> Please report this problem to someone.";
56     print "\n</BODY></HTML>";
57     die;
58  }
```

The specific location of the file to be returned is contained within the PATH_TRANSLATED environment variable; this value is placed into the local variable $path at line 3. Line 2 checks to make sure this variable actually exists—if it does not, this means that there was no extra path information in the URL, meaning that the author forgot to reference a file. Lines 8 through 11 process the variable $path, to extract the path to the directory containing the document being returned ($path) as well as the name of the file being returned. The count file is given the same name as the file, but preceded by a dot. Thus if the file being returned is *home.html*, then the count file will be named *.home.html*. Every file has its own distinct count file, with a matching name.

Line 15 checks to see if the count file exists—if it does not, lines 16 through 19 create it, and give it an initial value of 0.

Lines 22 through 29 attempt to *lock* the file (flock($cntfile,2)). Locking the file means that the running perl program is the *only* program that can modify the file, and ensures that two users cannot simultaneously attempt to change it. The program tries four times to lock the file, waiting one second between attempts. If it fails, it sets a default value for the string containing the counter value ($cnt) and skips the part of the program that actually reads the count file. If it succeeds in locking the file, it proceeds to the next phase, beginning at line 30, where the count file is opened, the count is read and incremented by 1, and the count is rewritten to the file, overwriting the old value. The file is then closed and the lock is released (flock($cntfile, 8)), freeing it for use by other users.

Line 39 begins the processing of the file returned to the client. The file is opened at line 40 and read, at line 42, into the array @array. When finished, the file is closed (line 43).

Line 45 prints the required content-type header. Lines 46 through 48 print the data to standard output, replacing *every* occurrence of the string <!-- counter --> by the counter string (line 47)—this is either the counter value from line 33, or the error string from line 25.

And that is it. The count is inserted, the document is returned, and the counter has been incremented by 1.

There are several limitations to this program. First, it is slow, since the program has to check every line for the string <-- counter -->. A second problem is associated with file permissions: The server that launches a gateway program usually runs with very limited ability to create and modify files, and thus this gateway program, when launched by the server, will probably not be able to create or modify the count file. If this is the case, the document author will have to create the count file by hand, and change the file characteristics so that the gateway program can modify it. Finally, we note that this program only counts accesses that pass through the gateway program—if the document is accessed via the URL:

```
http://some.where.edu/path/file.html
```

then the access is not counted. In this regard, it is far better to invoke a counter using a parsed HTML document and a server-side exec.

There are also several features you might want to add. For example, you might want to exclude your own machine or domain from the counting process; you may also prefer keeping all the count values in a single counter database file, as opposed to having one file per document.

These and other variations on page counters are available in a number of counter programs, many of which are far more sophisticated than this example. Some popular implementations are found at:

```
http://melmac.corp.harris.com/access_counts.html
http://www.best.com/~kroberts/acc_kntr.html
```

You will find many other examples by searching the Yahoo, Lycos, or other sites using the string "page counter." Yahoo, I believe, devotes an entire page to this topic.

Example 28: Inserting a Randomly Selected HTML Fragment

One useful parsed HTML trick is to use a gateway program to insert a randomly selected HTML text snippet into an HTML document. The perl program **rot-new.pl** is a simple implementation that selects a file at random from a specified directory and inserts it inline within the parsed document. Assuming that the program is located in the server's *cgi-bin/* directory, the relevant server-side include instruction is:

```
<!--#exec cgi="/cgi-bin/rot-new.pl" -->
```

When the server parses this document, it replaces this string by the output of the program **rot-new.pl**.

Figure 9.7 gives the listing for the program **rot-new.pl**. The ideas are very simple. At line 8, the program prints a text/html content-type header—recall that this is required of programs returning data to a parsed HTML document. The second block, at line 12–14, gets a directory listing for the directory /svc/www/InsTest—this is the directory that contains the insertions. Lines 15–17 convert the filenames into absolute paths, excluding non-data files (i.e., directories), and store the list of files in the array @filenames. The subsequent if statement at line 22 checks to see if there are any files in this list—the program exits if there are none. The alternate block of the if, beginning at line 25, selects a filename at random (line 28), opens the file (line 29), reads in the file content and then closes the file (line 31), and prints the content to standard output (line 32). The output is the text included within the HTML document.

Figure 9.7 Listing for the program *rot-new.pl*, which randomly selects an HTML document segment for insertion within an HTML document. Line numbers (in italics) are added for illustration only, and are not present in the original program. The boldfaced comments are referred to by the text.

```perl
1   #!/usr/local/bin/perl
2   # rotator.pl
3   # Author:  Ian Graham
4   #          Information Commons, University of Toronto
5   #          <igraham@hprc.utoronto.ca>
6   # Version: 0.1b.   Date:   July 13 1995
7
8   print "Content-type: text/html\n\n";          # print content-type header
9
10  $include_path="/svc/www/InsTest";             # Directory containing include files
11                                                # Second Block: Get listing for
12  if( !opendir(DIR, $include_path)) {           # the directory containing the inserts
13      &f_error("Unable to open notices directory\n", __LINE__, __FILE__); }
14  @tmp = readdir(DIR);                          # Read list of filenames; then check
15    foreach (@tmp) {                            # to see if they are files, and not
16                                                # directories (-T tests for "real" files
17        push(@filenames, $include_path."/".$_) if -T $include_path."/".$_; }
18  close(DIR);
19  $last_index = $#filenames;                    # Get index of last entry
20  $last_index += 1;                             # in array of filenames
21
22  if($last_index < 0) {
23      print " no files to insert ....\n"; die;  # no stuff, so don't do nuthin'
24  }
25  else {                                        # If there are files to be
26                                                # inserted, select one at random
27      srand(time);                              # and print it to stdout.
28      $rand_index = int(rand($last_index));
29      open(TEMP, $filenames[$rand_index]) ||    # Open selected file --
30          &f_error("Unable to open insertion file.\n", __LINE__,__FILE__);
31      @insertion = <TEMP>; close(TEMP);
32      print @insertion;                         # Print contents to standard output
33  }
34  # -------------- FINISHED ----------- FINISHED --------------
35  # Error Handling Subroutine
36
37  sub f_error {                                 # What to do if there is an error
38    print "Content-type text/html\n\n";
39    print "Fatal error  at line $_[1] in file $_[2].\n";
40    print "Please send mail to: <BR>\n";
41    print "<A HREF=\"mailto:webmaster@comm.ut.ca\">webmaster@comm.ut.ca</A><BR>\n";
```

Figure 9.7 (Continued)

```
42    print "to inform us of this error. If you can please, quote the URL\n";
43    print "of the page that gave this error.\n<HR>\n";
44    die "Fatal Error: $_[0] at line $_[1] in file $_[2] \n";
45 }
```

Example 29: WebNotice—A Web-Based System for Distributing Notices

WebNotice is a Web-based package for posting and distributing notices on the World Wide Web. WebNotice uses the **FORM** interface to collect information from users, and uses gateway programs to process the submitted data, to archive that data in a server-side database, and to extract data from the database for return to the user. Any user can access the database to retrieve posted notices, but only authorized users can add new notices to the system—authorization is accomplished using the Basic authentication scheme, discussed in Chapter 7. The stored notices are organized into *groups*, so that notices can be posted under different group categories (in this example, the groups are different university departments). Each group has its own distinct set of authorized users, and a user can only post under groups for which he or she is authorized.

WebNotice consists of 28 gateway programs, 19 HTML document templates (read in by the gateway programs, and processed into complete HTML documents), 10 HTML documents, and a 30-page instruction manual, so it is clearly impossible to explain the whole package in this short section. The following will simply give an outline of the package, with an explanation of how the important parts work. The intent here is not to explain the detailed functioning of any particular component, but to give an idea of how the design of a large gateway system takes place.

The WebNotice system is currently running at a number of sites. To see how it works, you can visit the original home of the package at:

```
http://www.utoronto.ca/reg/notices_main.pl
```

Figure 9.8 shows the organization of the different gateways, with the arrows showing the flow as the user traverses the system. Everything begins with the program **notices_main.pl**, which returns a simple HTML document describing the various options. The program generates this document by reading in a simple HTML template document, which it customizes according to the local configuration of the WebNotice system. An example of the resulting document is shown in Figure 9.9.

Adding a Notice with WebNotice

There are several possible options shown in Figure 9.9. As an example, we will follow the link to "Add a notice." Selecting this link accesses the gateway program **add_notice.pl**. This program checks a server-side database to obtain a list of all the groups registered with the system, and

Figure 9.8 A schematic diagram showing some of the different perl programs in the WebNotice notice distribution system. The arrows show the possible hypertext links that relate the different documents. The loops following the process_form.pl and process_modify.pl programs indicate that the results returned by these programs can produce HTML FORMs that have ACTIONs linked to either of the two destinations, depending on the data.

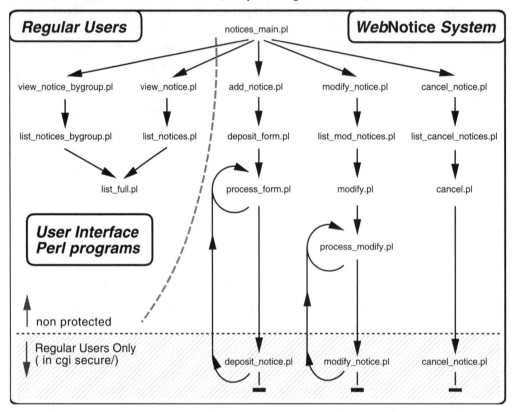

returns a page containing this list. This page is shown in Figure 9.10. The list of groups (here, a list of university departments) is presented as a list of selectable items (radio buttons) in a fill-in FORM. The user selects the group under which he or she wishes to submit a notice, and presses the *Submit* button—in this example, the user has selected the *Department of Statistics*. Pressing the *Submit* button sends the **FORM** data to the server, and to the program **deposit_form.pl** (see Figure 9.8 to follow the flow).

Figure 9.9 The HTML document returned by the program notices_main.pl. This is the home page for the WebNotice system and provides links to all the functional components of the system.

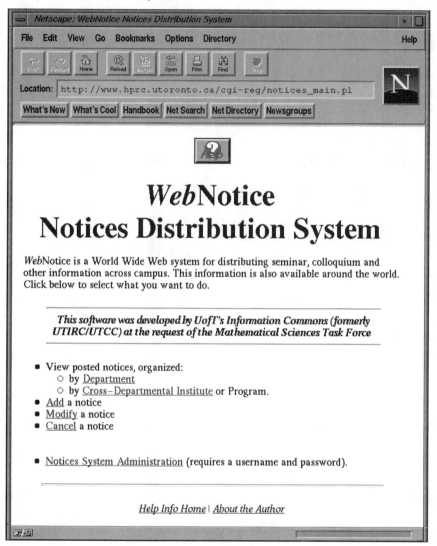

The Notice Fill-in FORM—deposit_form.pl

Figure 9.11 shows the document returned by the program **deposit_form.pl**. Note how this gateway program was accessed using the GET method—you can tell this by the encoded group

Figure 9.10 The HTML document returned by the program add_notice.pl. This page lists, within an HTML FORM, all the groups under which notices can be deposited. The program add_notice.pl obtains this information by reading a server database.

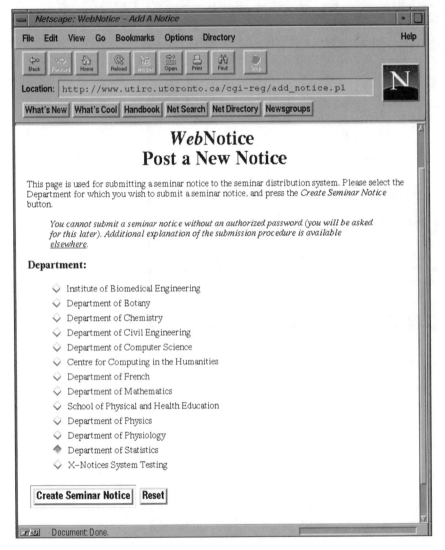

information appended to the URL. This lets the user *bookmark* this page, so that he or she can return here without having to restart at **notices_home.pl**. This judicious choice of the GET method makes it possible for users to bookmark pages they are likely to access often.

Figure 9.11 The HTML document returned by the program deposit_form.pl. This document contains a FORM into which the user enters the information required by the notice system. This program is accessed using the GET method (see the URL in the "Location" window), so that this fill-in FORM document can be bookmarked for future reference.

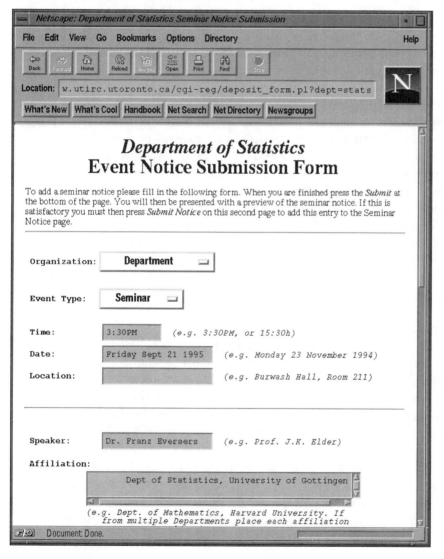

The document returned by **deposit_form.pl** contains an extensive fill-in **FORM**, into which the user enters the information required of a notice announcement—there are fields for the time, date, and location of the event (this system is designed for notifications of events, such as concerts or seminars), the name of the presenter, and so on. Not obvious here is that the **FORM** also contains the "hidden" input element:

```
<INPUT TYPE="hidden" NAME="dept" VALUE="stats">
```

This was inserted into the **FORM** by the program **deposit_form.pl,** using the data passed in the query string. Thus, when the data in this new **FORM** are sent the server, they will still include the name of the group under which the notice is to be recorded.

Processing and Checking the FORM Data—process_form.pl

When the user completes the **FORM**, he or she presses the *Submit* button at the bottom of the page. This **FORM** uses the POST method to send the data to the gateway program **process_form.pl. Process_form.pl** processes the data and checks for obvious errors, such as missing fields, errors in the time and date, and so on. If there are no errors, the program returns a preview of the posted notice, for confirmation by the user—an example preview document is shown in Figure 9.12. Notice the "Accept?" yes-or-no checkboxes, and the associated *Submit* button. The *entire* data content of the notice is stored within `<INPUT TYPE="hidden" ...>` elements contained inside the "Yes/No" acceptance **FORM**. The **ACTION** of this **FORM** points to the program **deposit_notice.pl,** which actually adds the notice to the notices database. If the user decides the notice is acceptable, selects "Yes", and presses *Submit*, the data contained within the hidden elements are sent to **deposit_notice.pl.**

Processing an Error-Free FORM

As indicated in Figure 9.8, the program **deposit_notice.pl** is located in a directory (here labeled *cgi-secure*) different from that containing **process_form.pl, deposit_form.pl,** and so on— **deposit_notice.pl** is located in a directory *protected* by the Basic authentication scheme. As soon as a user accesses **deposit_notice.pl,** he or she is challenged for an authorization username and password. If the username and password information entered by the user are in error, access is immediately refused. If the username/password pair is acceptable because it is a valid pair, the program **deposit_notice.pl** then checks to make sure this particular user is authorized to deposit under the group being considered—the username and password may be valid, but only for *another* departmental group (e.g., for the Department of Physiology). The WebNotice system checks the username against a database that matches usernames with groups—if the user is *not* authorized to submit notices under the Department of Statistics, the program **deposit_notice.pl** returns the server directive:

```
Status: 401 Not authorized
```

which is the HTTP status message indicating authorization failure. The server subsequently returns the 401 header message to the client. In general, the client will tell the user that

Figure 9.12 If the FORM in Figure 9.11 is properly completed and submitted, the user is presented with this "preview" of the notice. It contains a small FORM, which the user uses to accept or reject the notice. This FORM contains `<INPUT TYPE="hidden"...>` **elements that contain the entire data content of the fill-in FORM shown in Figure 9.11.**

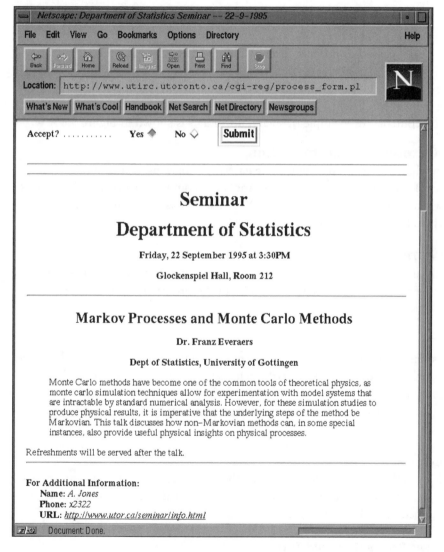

authorization failed, and will give the user the option of trying again with another username and password.

Finally, if the username/password pair is acceptable, and the particular user is allowed to deposit notices under the given department, then the notices data are stored in the notices database. The deposited notice can then be retrieved for viewing (**list_notices.pl** and **list_notices_bygroup.pl**), modification (**modify.pl**), or deletion (**cancel.pl**). The process of modification and cancellation both pass through programs in the *cgi-secure* directory, ensuring that authentication is again required before changes are permitted.

Processing a FORM Containing Field Errors—process_form.pl

It is also possible that the data passed to **process_form.pl** contained errors in the time, date, or other fields. In this case, **process_form.pl** creates a table of the errors and returns a document containing both a list of these errors and a duplicate fill-in **FORM**. However, the input fields of this **FORM** contain the data from the user's first attempt, so the user need only correct the mistakes, and not re-enter the entire content. An example of such a document is shown in Figure 9.13.

General Issues in Gateway Program Design

There are many problems that will crop up as you write gateway programs, as is the case with any programming project. This section describes four of the more common errors, in this author's experience, that occur when writing gateway programs. Your list will assuredly be different, but hopefully this section will help you avoid some basic pitfalls!

Check for the Correct HTTP Method

The environment variable REQUEST_METHOD indicates the method being used to access the script. If the method is incorrect (the request used the GET method, but the program expects POST), you should return an appropriate error message.

Check for Input

Your gateway program should always check for the existence of input (if input is expected), either in the QUERY_STRING environment variable or standard input, depending on the HTTP method. Programs often behave very badly if they attempt to read nonexistent environment variables, or an empty standard input stream. You should check for this error, and return an appropriate error message.

Check for Errors in Input Fields

Check the input fields for obvious errors—and never trust the data that has been sent. Innocuous errors, such as an unexpected negative number where a positive one was anticipated, can lead to havoc if you haven't "trapped" for all possibilities.

Remember that the Client Parses Returned Text

Remember that text returned to a browser inside a **NAME** or **VALUE** string or inside a **TEXTAREA** region will be parsed, and that all character and entity references will be converted

Figure 9.13 The FORM returned by the program *process_form.pl* if there were errors in the FORM input fields. This document lists the errors at the top, and then reproduces the fill-in FORM for correction by the user. This FORM, when submitted, once again accesses the program *process_form.pl*. The issues involved in ensuring that FORM data are safely returned in this second form, and in "hidden" elements within a FORM, are discussed in the text, and in Chapter 8.

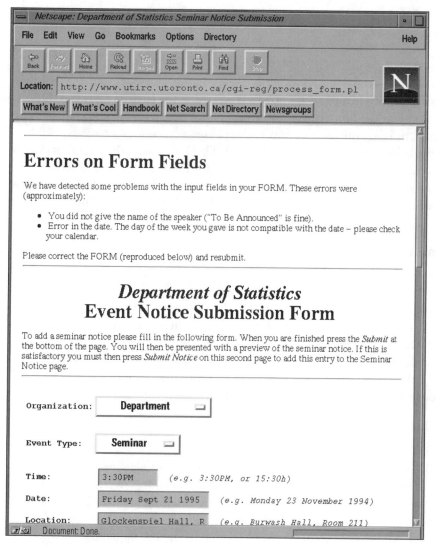

into the corresponding ISO Latin-1 characters. If you do not want this to happen, you must *encode* the ampersand characters in the original data prior to placing the data in the **FORM** being sent to the client.

Want to Obtain WebNotice?

The WebNotice software package is, like many World Wide Web applications, freely available over the Internet. If you want to find out more about WebNotice, and perhaps obtain your own copy of the software, just access the URL:

```
http://www.utoronto.ca/ian/Software/webnotice.html
```

CGI Programming Libraries

One of the most tedious aspects of writing a CGI program is parsing the environment variables, command-line arguments, or standard input data to the program. These data are encoded using the URL encoding schemes, or using the multipart/form-data approach, so that a gateway program must first decode the information before it can be used. There are currently several packages that can help in this process, by providing a library of routines for doing these basic tasks, and some that can do much more. This section summarizes some of these tools, although the list is not complete. You are advised to look to the references section at the end of the chapter for additional information.

CGI.pm—The Ultimate Perl 5 CGI Library

```
http://www-genome.wi.mit.edu/ftp/pub/software/WWW/cgi_docs.html
http://victim.earthlink.net/~websupport/CGI.pm
```

CGI.pm, by L. Stein, is by far the best publicly available perl 5 library for CGI programming. There are modules for parsing and processing form data, including those sent using the multipart/form-data encoding, for generating FORM-based HTML documents to return to the client, and for error checking and reporting. The package is complicated and complete, and is recommended for serious CGI programmers. The package can be thought of as a more sophisticated (and complicated) successor to the cgi-lib.pl package (see later).

Cgic—An ANSII C Library

```
http://www.boutell.com/cgic/
```

Cgic, by Thomas Boutell, is a free (noncommercial use only) library of C-language routines for parsing and manipulating **FORM** data sent to a server via the application/x-www-form-urlencoded encoding. Cgic contains modules for exception and error handling, and for handling standard processing functions, such as bounds checking and multiple-choice selection; and it can even check for well-known browser errors. There is also a debugging mode, useful when developing new CGI applications. The package can run under UNIX, and also under DOS/Windows.

Cgi-lib.pl Perl Library

http://www.bio.cam.ac.uk/cgi-lib/

Cgi-lib.pl, by Steven Brenner, is one of the most popular perl libraries for CGI program development. It is simple, compatible with both perl 4 and 5, and can handle data sent using the multipart/form-data encoding. There are also modules for constructing standard HTML headers and footers for the returned data, and for processing the form data.

CGIwrap—For More Secure CGIs

http://wwwcgi.umr.edu/~cgiwrap/

CGIwrap is a gateway program designed to improve the security of CGI programs. Using CGIwrap, a CGI script runs with the permissions of the user who owns it, and not those of the server. This makes it easier for users to write and run their own CGI programs, with reduced risk that these programs can damage other users' resources.

EIT CGI C Library

ftp://ftp.eit.com/pub/eit/wsk/

Enterprise Integration Technologies has made available a library of C functions useful in constructing CGI programs—however, beware that this package has not been updated since late 1994, and is not under active development.

Libcgi++—C++ Library

http://sweetbay.will.uiuc.edu/cgi%2b%2b/

Libcgi++, by Dragos Manolescu, is a library of C++ routines for parsing and processing data obtained from GET and POST requests. There are routines for parsing and decoding query strings, for encoding data for return to a client, etc. The package does not support data sent from browsers using the multipart/form-data encoding.

Uncgi—Security Wrapper for CGIs

http://www.hyperion.com/~koreth/uncgi.html

Uncgi, by Steven Grimm, is a simple front-end package that decodes all the **NAME** and **VALUE** attribute values sent by GET or POST methods, and places them in environment variables. Uncgi then calls your processing program (C, perl, or whatever), passing it these environment variables. Note that this may be a problem if the string being passed in an environment variable becomes too large, since some systems place limits on the size of environment variables. Uncgi cannot process data encoded using the multipart/form-data encoding.

Libwww-perl—Library for General Web Applications

http://www.ics.uci.edu/pub/websoft/libwww-perl/

Libwww-perl, by Roy Fielding of the University of California at Irvine, is a library package of perl (Version 4 and also 5) functions that provide a useful API for writing Web applications. This is an excellent, general-purpose perl library, designed for a variety of (client- and server-based) Web applications. Note, however, that libwww-perl was *not* designed specifically for CGI programming. Development of the perl 4 package stopped in late 1994, so you should use the perl 5 version.

Server-Side Document Parsing Software

The server-side include mechanism operates via a special parsing module incorporated into the HTTP server. There is consequently no reason why software designers cannot create similar parsers, either as server plug-in modules or as CGI programs, to similarly parse HTML documents and replace special codes by server-generated data.

There are in fact several packages providing this type of functionality, ranging from the Netscape LiveWire server suite, which processes document-embedded JavaScript scripts to generate dynamic HTML documents, to shareware and freeware programs that accomplish these tasks. Some of the more popular packages are:

Cold Fusion	http://www.allaire.com/	commercial
HTMLscript	http://htmlscript.volant.com	commercial
NeoWebScript	http://www.neosoft.com/neowebscript/	commercial
META-HTML	http://www.metahtml.com	free (with license)
PHP/FI	http://www.vex.net/php/intro.phtml	free (GNU public license)

These tools are more sophisticated than server-side includes, and support parsed documents that are essentially programs, complete with branching and conditional execution.

CGI Utility Programs

CGI Program Resource Sites

http://homepage.seas.upenn.edu/~mengwong/perlhtml.html
http://www.oac.uci.edu/indiv/ehood/perlWWW/

```
http://www.nkn.net/nkn/resources/cgi.html
http://edb518ea.edb.utexas.edu/cgix/cgix.html
http://www.yahoo.com/Computers_and_Internet/Internet/World_Wide_Web/CGI___Common_Gateway_Interface/
```

This section lists several commonly useful CGI gateway programs and utilities, such as mail forwarders and feedback form/guestbook utilities, document access counters, and UNIX man page-to-HTML converters. Of course, this is an incomplete list; you should search the Web if you need a tool that is not listed here. The URLs at the start of this section provide some useful starting points. You should also look in many of the Web magazines currently in print, as many commercial CGI packages are advertised in such venues.

CGI Email Handler

```
http://www.boutell.com/email/
```

This package, developed by Thomas Boutell, is a simple C-language CGI program that lets browser users send e-mail messages to a restricted set of allowed recipients.

CGI Feedback Form

```
ftp://ftp.win.tue.nl/pub/infosystems/www/wwwutils.tar.gz
```

This package of utilities, by Arjan de Vet, uses a **FORMs** interface to let a client send feedback information to the server administrator.

Server-Side Include Page Counters

```
http://melmac.corp.harris.com/access_counts.html
http://www.best.com/~kroberts/acc_kntr.html
```

Of course, there are many, many page counters. Chuck Musciano has written an elegant C-language CGI program that can maintain a counts database for an arbitrarily large number of different HTML documents. At the other extreme, Ken Roberts has written an extremely simple perl CGI script that is included using a parsed HTML document, but that can be used by only a single document. The details can be found, respectively, at the URLs given above.

CGI Database Gateways

Needless to say, there is great interest in using the World Wide Web as a front end to sophisticated database packages. This requires gateway programs to connect the **FORM** or **ISINDEX**-based query input mechanisms of the WWW with the backend SQL (or other) mechanisms used by databases such as Sybase, Oracle, and WAIS. The following is a very brief list of Web-database gateway tools, along with some hints as to where to find additional information.

If you are currently using a commercial database product, either UNIX, Macintosh, or PC/Windows-based, then you should contact your vendor to find out what Web interface software they provide. Because of the growth of the Web, several database companies have developed sophisticated gateway and server plug-in modules for interfacing their products with **ISINDEX** and **FORM**s-based queries. Several are now commonly advertised in Web and database trade magazines. A good summary of Web-database tools is currently found at:

```
http://cscsun1.larc.nasa.gov/~beowulf/db/all_products.html
```

WAIS Gateways

WAIS, for Wide Area Information Servers, is an extremely popular Internet network publishing and text-database system. WAIS is designed as a client-server system, with WAIS clients able to interrogate WAIS databases using a well-defined protocol. It is particularly popular because it is free—the freeWAIS software is one of the most popular indexing tools, and is often a good option when cost is a factor or when commercial software is not available or appropriate. This protocol is supported by some Web clients, so that it is often possible to directly interrogate a WAIS server by constructing a URL (with appropriate query strings) that points to that WAIS server.

Often it is easier to interact with a **FORM** interface designed to construct WAIS queries in a manner more convenient to the user. For these reasons, there are currently several gateway programs that allow non-WAIS-capable clients to access a WAIS server, and that allow for sophisticated **FORM**s interfaces to WAIS servers. The following is a list of some of the server-side CGI packages designed to accomplish these tasks.

KidofWAIS

```
http://www.cso.uiuc.edu/grady.html
```

Kidofwais.pl, by Michael Grady, is a perl script WAIS gateway program. Kidofwais.pl uses the simple **ISINDEX** query interface, but allows for pattern searches (astro* matches any word beginning with "astro") as well as complex Boolean searches.

SFgate

```
http://ls6-www.informatik.uni-dortmund.de/SFgate/SFgate.html
```

Sfgate, by Norbert Gövert and Ulrich Pfeifer, is another perl-based WAIS gateway program. SFgate does not access a server-side WAIS query engine. Instead, WAIS client software is built into SFgate, so that it can itself query any Internet-accessible WAIS database.

Although SFgate can work with any freeWAIS server, it is designed to work with freeWAIS-sf servers. FreeWAIS-sf is a WAIS variant, modified, among other things, to allow for structured fields. Information about freeWAIS-sf can be found at:

```
http://ls6-www.informatik.uni-dortmund.de/freeWAIS-sf/
ftp://ftp.germany.eu.net/pub/infosystems/wais/Unido-LS6/freeWAIS-sf/
```

WWWWAIS

http://www.eit.com/software/wwwwais/wwwwais.html
http://www.eit.com/software/wwwwais/

WWWWAIS, by Kevin Hughes, is a small ANSI C program that acts as gateway between waisq and waissearch (the WAIS programs that search WAIS indexes) and a **FORM**s-capable World Wide Web browser. WWWWAIS allows for customized **FORM**s interfaces and a database access control mechanism (restricting access to certain Internet domains), and allows users to choose from amongst multiple searchable databases.

SQL Gateways

There are many packages for linking Web servers to commercial SQL database packages such as Oracle or Sybase. The following section lists some of the public-domain packages. Most commercial vendors also provide gateway software, and you should consult with your vendor to obtain up-to-date information on their offerings.

GSQL-Oracle Backend

ftp://ftp.cc.gatech.edu/pub/gvu/www/pitkow/gsql-oracle/oracle-backend.html

GSQL-Oracle Backend, by James Pitkow, is a CGI program for linking WWW applications to an Oracle database, using either **ISINDEX** or **FORM**s interfaces. GSQL-Oracle Backend is written in PRO-C, the C language development environment for Oracle, so you need this development option to compile GSQL-Oracle Backend.

Web/Genera

http://gdbdoc.gdb.org/letovsky/genera/

Web/Genera, by Stanley Letovsky, is a software toolset for the integration of Sybase databases into the World Wide Web. Web/Genera can be used to retrofit a Web front-end (**FORM** or **ISINDEX**) to an existing Sybase database, or to create customized interfaces. To use Web/Genera, you write a specification of the Sybase database and of the desired appearance of its contents on the Web, using a simple high-level schema notation.

WDB—Sybase, mSQL, and Informix Gateway

http://arch-http.hq.eso.org/bfrasmus/wdb/wdb.html
http://www.dtv.dk/~bfr/wdb/intro.html

WDB, by Bo Frese Rasmussen, is a CGI package similar to Web/Genera and also based on perl and sybperl. Like Web/Genera, WDB allows you to use high-level description files to specify the structure of the database and the format of the responses, so that you can construct a generic WWW-SQL interface without writing a single line of code.

W3-mSQL

```
http://hughes.com.au/product/w3-msql/
```

W3-mSQL, a product of Hughes Technologies of Australia, is a gateway to mini-SQL databases from World Wide Web documents. W3-mSQL is a single CGI program that provides full Web access to data stored within mini SQL databases. The software is free for noncommercial uses.

Perl Database Interface Libraries

```
ftp://ftp.demon.co.uk/pub/perl/db/
ftp://ftp.demon.co.uk/pub/perl/db/README
```

There are many freeware perl interfaces to common commercial database systems. The URL identified here is an archive site of such software—README file provides an overview of the site content. This is an ideal place for locating freeware database interface libraries, which you can use along with a CGI library to create Web database applications.

References

General Starting Points

```
http://www.yahoo.com/text/Computers_and_Internet/Internet/World_Wide_Web/
    CGI___Common_Gateway_Interface/
```

CGI Programmer's Reference and FAQ

```
http://www.best.com/~hedlund/cgi-faq/
http://www.Stars.com/Seminars/CGI/
```

On-line CGI and FORM Tutorials

```
http://agora.leeds.ac.uk/nik/Cgi/start.html
http://blackcat.brynmawr.edu/~nswoboda/prog-html.html
http://www.catt.ncsu.edu/~bex/tutor/index.html
http://www.io.com/~jsm/easy/cgi.html
http://robot0.ge.uiuc.edu/~carlosp/cs317/cft.html
```

CGI Program Archive Sites

```
http://www.oac.uci.edu/indiv/ehood/perlWWW/          (Perl only)
http://128.172.69.106:8080/cgi-bin/cgis.html         (C language)
http://web.sau.edu/~mkruse/www/scripts/              (Perl only)
```

Database-Web Gateway References

```
http://www.cs.vu.nl/~anne007/waissearch/pointers.html   (WAIS indexing overview)
http://www-rlg.stanford.edu/home/jpl/websearch.html     (General gateway information)
```

`http://cscsun1.larc.nasa.gov/~beowulf/db/all_products.html`	(Overview of database gateway software)
`http://gdbdoc.gdb.org/letovsky/genera/dbgw.html`	(Software)
`http://www.comvista.com/net/www/cgidata.html`	(Macintosh software)
`http://www.yahoo.com/Computers_and_Internet/Internet/` `world_Wide_Web/Databases_and_Searching/`	(General information and software)
`http://www.yahoo.com/Business_and_Economy/Companies/` `Computers/Internet/Databases_and_Searching/`	(Commercial software)

Chapter

10

Graphics and Images
in HTML Documents

Inline images are an important feature of HTML, allowing the communication of important graphical information, as well as documents with colorful, visual appeal. Images can be used in many contexts: as iconic buttons, as imagemaps, or purely as decorations. And it looks so easy, you are probably itching to do it yourself.

However, the Web imposes important limitations on inline images, which must be taken into account by any Web author who wants to design effective, usable documents. What are these limitations? First is bandwidth, or the speed at which data is sent from your server to a user's browser: As this is usually low, you must strive to keep image files small so that they are quick to download. Second is computer display quality: readers will be using many different types of computers, with varied qualities of color monitors and graphics cards. You must design your images to look good on a variety of displays. Third, you must be sure to use image formats that are widely supported: There is no point in including an image if few browsers can display it. Finally, you must make allowances for users who do not see the images, either because they are using a text-only browser, or because they have disabled image loading.

This chapter provides an overview of image use within HTML documents. It begins with an explanation of how images are included inline via the **IMG** element.

The remainder of the chapter looks at some of the details of image preparation and processing, beginning with a brief introduction to computer graphics, followed by a description of the image file formats supported on the Web. Watch for the section that discusses basic image processing tricks and tools, and some of the particular features of some of the supported image formats, such as transparency and animated GIFs. This is followed by an overview of active images and imagemaps. Finally, the chapter concludes with a list of useful image icon archive sites and a list of references.

Including Images in HTML Documents

Images are included via the **IMG** element. All **IMG** elements should minimally have the following attributes:

```
<IMG SRC="url_to_image" HEIGHT="y_pixels" WIDTH="x_pixels"
    ALT="text alternative">
```

Here, url_to_image is the URL pointing to the image file, y_pixels is the height of the image in pixels, and x_pixels is the width of the image, also in pixels. If you include the size of the image, the browser can begin properly formatting the document before the image arrives, as it knows how much space to set aside on the display for the image. The string $text\ alternative$ is a text description of—or alternative to—the image, used by browsers that do not display the pictures. Some graphical browsers also use this as a text "pop-up" on top of the image. You should always have an **ALT** value to explain the picture's meaning; if it is purely decorative and has no meaning, you can type **ALT=**"" to indicate this fact.

Web Graphics Introduction

When designing Web graphics, a designer must be aware of the types of displays used by the users. These will vary from low-resolution 640×480 pixel displays capable of at most 256 simultaneous colors, to high-resolution 1280×1024 displays capable of displaying 24-bit ($2^{24} = 16.8$ million) colors. Unfortunately, the majority of users fall closer to the bottom of this range than the top, so a Web graphics designer must prepare pages that display well on low-resolution displays with a limited color palette.

The pixel size constraint implies the need for small graphics that fit on the display. For example, a page banner should be no more than 570 pixels wide, and less than 100 pixels high. Similarly, the raw images must be designed using a limited color palette, so that the browser does not "run out" of colors while trying to display multiple images. Understanding how this works requires a basic knowledge of computer graphics and a computer's representation of colors. This is the subject of the remainder of this section.

Color Representations—the RGB System

The science and technology of color turns out to be very complicated—far more complicated than you are likely to want to understand! As far as computers are concerned, colors are usually defined using what are called *RGB* (Red-Green-Blue) codes. This scheme expresses each color as a mixture of the primary colors red, green, and blue, with the *intensity* of each color ranging from 0 (no intensity) to 255 (as bright as possible). As a result, the strength of each of the three primary colors can be expressed within a single byte (8 bits), so that any color can be expressed as a 24-bit sequence containing the intensity of the red, green, and blue components. This is why high-resolution color displays are called 24-bit color displays.

RGB codes are usually expressed as numbers in the hexadecimal numbering system. In this system, a complete color specification looks like:

RRGGBB

where *RR* is the hex code for the red intensity (ranging from 00 to FF), *GG* is the hex code for the green intensity (ranging from 00 to FF), and *BB* is the hex code for the blue intensity (you get the idea).

For example, the code 000000 corresponds to black, FFFFFF corresponds to white (as bright as possible), and AAAAAA corresponds to a rather light shade of gray.

Limited Numbers of Colors—the Colormap

To display true, full-color images, a computer must have 24-bits of memory for each pixel on the screen (this is what is meant by the phrase "24-bit color"). However, most computers do not have this many bits per pixel—most, in fact, have only 8 bits per pixel, and support what is known as 8-bit color. In this case, a pixel can display at most 256 different colors, a far cry from the millions that are possible with 24 bits.

At the same time, a number shorter than 24 bits is too short to specify how much red, green, and blue to use in making the color—recall that you need 24 bits to fully specify the desired color. Thus, a system that has less than 24 bits per pixel needs a way of relating the number stored in a given pixel with the desired RGB color. The mechanism for doing so is called a *colormap* or *colormap table*.

To show how colormap works, we will look at an 8-bit system as an example. Each pixel can contain an integer value ranging from 0 to 256. To determine which color each of these integers corresponds to, we create a *colormap table* that relates each integer to a full RGB color code—for example:

Integer	RGB Colors (decimal)	RGB Hex Code
0	00 00 00	000000
1	00 00 51	000033

2	00 00 102	000066
...	.. .. ..	. . .
215	255 255 255	FFFFFF
...	.. .. ..	. . .
255	60 20 254	3C14FE

Each 8-bit number in a pixel now corresponds to one of the colors in the table. Thus, if a pixel is set to the number two, the graphics system will look to the color table, pull out the RGB hex code 000066, and paint the pixel with this color.

Default System Colormaps

Most computers that support 8-bit color have a default colormap—that is, they come preconfigured with a colormap relating pixel codes to desired RGB colors. On Microsoft Windows systems, this is known as the *Windows colormap*. This colormap defines only 216 of the total possible 256 colors. Each of these 216 colors is defined using the six individual primary color codes 0, 51, 102, 153, 204, 255—the 216 comes from having 6 different shades of red, 6 different shades of green, and 6 different shades of blue, for a total of 6 × 6 × 6 = 216 possible colors. The preceding table illustrated some of these Windows colormap entries. The remaining 40 colors are set by programs that need special colors, or depend on the computer system being used, and generally vary widely from computer to computer (for example, a Web browser, when trying to display an image, may set these entries to special colors needed by the image it is displaying).

Obviously this scheme omits a lot of colors! But, it does evenly cover the range of possible colors, and provides a reasonable set of default values.

Displaying Images—Color *Dithering*

Problems of course arise if an image contains a color that is not available in the system colormap. For example, you might have an image that contains the color 00002F, but a user's 8-bit color system can only display the colors 000000 and 0000033. How, then, will the system display this color?

There are two possible approaches. First, the computer can look in the system colormap for the color "nearest" the color in the image, and substitute this color in its place; the computer might then take all pixels of color 00002F and paint them with color 000033. Unfortunately, the concept of "nearest" can lead to truly bizarre color replacements, so this is often not an ideal way to approximate colors in an image.

The second way to approximate colors is via *color dithering*. With dithering, the program displaying the image tries to find colors in the local colormap that are close to those in the actual image, and then replaces *blocks* of the original color by a *mixture* of the colors actually available on the computer. You can often detect dithering by looking at regions of an image that "should" appear as a solid color. If the area appears mottled, with lots of dots of slightly different colors, then the image has been dithered.

This is easily illustrated using a black-and-white example, which only requires a 1-bit display system. Suppose an image filter contains gray. With dithering, this would be displayed by turning a large block of gray (say, 20 × 20 pixels) into a table of alternating black and white pixels—to the eye this will appear gray (provided you don't look too closely).

Dithering is sometimes better than taking the closest color, and sometimes not. Both cases are not ideal, and a better choice is to make sure that images use the same colors that are available in the system colormap. This is most easily accomplished by selecting an appropriate colormap when the images are created. For the Web, this means choosing the Windows colormap mentioned previously.

Selecting an Image Colormap

Many Web browsers, including Netscape Navigator, support the Windows colormap for 8-bit displays; most browsers support this colormap even on non–MS-Windows machines, such as Macintoshes, and some UNIX computers. Thus, if you are creating an image (an icon or line graphic, as opposed to a photograph), it is best to create it using the Windows colormap (most graphics editors let you choose the colormap you wish to use), rather than a colormap customized for the occasion.

Storing Images in Files

Once image data have been acquired and processed, a graphics designer needs a way of storing this information as a computer file. There are literally hundreds of *image file formats* for doing this, each with its own strengths and weaknesses. For the Web, the most important criterion is file size—the image must be stored in the smallest file possible, so that it can be quickly transmitted over the Internet. For this reason, the image formats listed in the following sections are the only ones widely implemented in Web applications, with GIF and JPEG being the most popular choices.

Supported Image Formats

Although most browsers support a variety of image formats, there are only four that are universally acceptable: the GIF (GIF87 and GIF89A), JPEG, X-Bitmap, and X-Pixelmap formats.

The different types can usually be inferred by the filename suffix: GIF image files usually have the suffix *.gif,* JPEGs usually *.jpg* or *.jpeg*, X-Bitmaps usually *.xbm,* and X-Pixelmaps usually *.xpm*. A fifth format, PNG for Portable Network Graphics (usually with extension *.png*), is gaining popularity but is not yet universally supported.

X-Bitmap/Pixelmap

X-Bitmaps are a common format on UNIX workstations, and are often found in older image and icon libraries. An X-Bitmap assigns a single bit to each image pixel, and therefore supports only black-and-white images. Simple bitmaps are useful, however, as browsers treat the white portion as *transparent*—the black part of the image is displayed in black, while the white part is replaced by the color or image of the underlying background. This permits attractive black icons, since the surrounding white background is not visible. However, X-Bitmaps are inefficient at storing images, and are uncommon outside the UNIX environment. As we shall see, GIF is a better choice.

X-Pixelmaps are similar to X-Bitmaps but assign 8 bits to each pixel, as opposed to one, and can consequently support images with 256 distinct colors. However, like X-Bitmaps, X-Pixelmaps are an inefficient way to store an image. It is better to use GIF—you get the same picture, but in a much smaller file.

GIF

GIF is the most common image format in World Wide Web applications. This format can store black-and-white, grayscale, or color images, although limited to a maximum of 256 colors (or shades of gray) per image. Somewhat like the X-Pixelmap, the GIF format encodes the image information using a *color indexing* scheme. When you create a GIF image, the software takes the raw image, uses an image analysis algorithm to find the set of 256 (or fewer) colors that best describe the color content of the image, and creates a *color table* mapping these colors onto integers ranging from 0 to 255. The software then examines each pixel in the original image, finds the color in the color table that is closest to the actual color, and assigns the corresponding color index value to this pixel. The resulting GIF image file consists of an array of these *color indices* plus a *colormap* that maps each of the 256 indices onto the chosen color.

The color table can be optimized for each image. For example, if a picture is of a red sunset, this table can contain mostly reds, whereas if it is a picture of a forest, it can be mostly greens. This technique can yield a quite successful rendering of the original image, even though there are at most 256 different colors. As mentioned previously, however, it is best for Web applications to use the Windows colormap whenever possible.

GIF stores the images in a *compressed* format. The compression algorithm is relatively simple: Basically, it looks for repeated sequences of the same color, and encodes long sequences using a much shorter string. For example, if there were 50 pixels in a row with the same color (lets call this color "Q"), this might be encoded as:

```
QQQQQ...QQQQ    ==   50Q
```

That is, instead of having 50 Q's one after the other, the string is compressed into the color index plus a number indicating how many times the color repeats.

GIF compression works very well on images with large blocks of solid colors, such as logos and icons. The compression is not, however, efficient for photographic images, where there are no large single-color regions, and where the image is highly irregular. For this type of image, JPEG is a better choice.

There are two common versions of the GIF format—GIF87 and GIF89A—the latter having several important features not available in GIF87. For example, GIF89A lets you make one of the colors *transparent*, so that the background shows through. This is equivalent to the transparency of X-Bitmap images. GIF89 also lets you place more than one image in a single GIF file; certain Web browsers can take this sequence of images and play them as a crude animation, known as an *animated GIF*. Both of these features are discussed in more detail later on.

JPEG

The JPEG (for Joint Photographic Experts Group) format was designed expressly for storing photographic images in a compact digital form. JPEG is an extremely sophisticated compressed image format that can support an almost infinite number of colors, instead of only 256. JPEG also supports a *lossy* image compression technique—the greater the compression, the poorer the quality of the stored image. In general, JPEG is far better than GIF at storing photographic images, both in terms of image quality and file size, while GIF is better for images containing few colors and that have large single-colored regions, such as buttons, logos, clip art, and so on.

PNG

PNG (Portable Network Graphics) was designed as a public-domain successor to GIF. Like GIF, PNG allows for transparency, interlacing (discussed later), and image compression, the latter via a non-proprietary compression algorithm (the GIF method is patented). However, PNG is also much enhanced relative to GIF, as it supports greater color depth than GIF, 8-bit transparency (so that images can "fade in"), and features for color and gamma correction. PNG is likely to be widely supported in the near future.

Image Processing—Basic Issues

This book is not intended to be a graphics manual; if you are embarking on a trip deep into graphics work, you should hire a graphics expert—or buy a real book on graphics! However, there are some relatively simple tricks that will help you make images work effectively on the Web, and these bear mentioning here.

Reducing or Rescaling Images

You will often want to reduce the size of an image, either because the original is too big, or because you want to create a small icon of the image and link it to the bigger version. You can create reduced image sizes with many graphics programs, including the ones listed later in this chapter.

When you *shrink* an image, you may want to *smooth* it beforehand—smoothing reduces edge breakup, or *aliasing*, created by the size reduction process. Some programs do this automatically when you shrink an image, while others let you turn smoothing on and off, and expect you to do it yourself. Note that you want to smooth before or during the size reduction: Once the image is shrunk, smoothing simply blurs what's left. This combination of shrinking and smoothing is also called *resampling*.

You should note that it is extremely difficult to rescale images that contain text, as the text is almost always blurred to the point of being unreadable. A better choice is to remove all text from the image, resize the image, and then add back the text with the desired text font and size.

Color-Smoothing Images

Sometimes you will have an image that appears to have large, uniformly colored regions, only to find that, when you look up close, these uniform regions actually contain many dozens of very similar colors patterned in a non-smooth way. Some graphics programs provide tools that let you smooth the colors, which reduces this irregularity and makes it easier to compress images stored in either GIF or PNG
format.

Reducing Color Depth

Most image processing tools let you reduce the number of colors, or *flatten* the image. This is useful with the GIF or PNG formats, as it can substantially reduce the size of the image file without significantly affecting the image's appearance on most computer displays. It is particularly useful with icons, which often use fewer than 10 colors. Color depth reduction should not be done with JPEG images, however, as the reduced color depth actually impairs the JPEG compression technique.

Composed Images

Quite often you will find yourself reusing parts of an image over and over again—for example, part of a button in a button bar, a corporate logo attached to different section headings, and so on. In these cases, it is best to construct these images from a collection of image components that are *tiled* together on the page to make the desired total image. In this way, the user does not keep downloading this part of the image. Once the logo is downloaded, it can be reused by appending it to different section headings, with only the headings changing from document to document. An example is shown in Figure 10.1, which displays a section heading from one of the University of Toronto pages. The top image is actually two images tiled together. The markup for this is:

```
<IMG SRC="img1.gif" . . . ><IMG SRC="img2.gif" . . . >
```

Because the **IMG** tags are flush next to each other, the images can appear together without intervening space, giving the impression of a single graphic.

Special GIF Image Properties

Since GIF is still the most common format on the Web, this section looks at some of GIF's most important properties. The references at the end of the chapter point to sources of additional information, as well as sites listing useful GIF utilities not discussed in the text.

Reducing GIF Image File Size: The Colormap

You can reduce the size of a GIF image file by reducing the number of colors used in the image. The GIF format can take up to a full byte to store color information about a pixel, which is why GIF is limited to 256 different colors ($256=2^8$). However, you don't always need a full byte for a pixel—the GIF format is clever enough to know, if an image has only 8 colors instead of 256, that it needs fewer bits per pixel to map all the colors. This reduces the amount of data needed to store the image. Also, as discussed previously, reducing the number of colors can make it easier to compress the image, further reducing file size. Some tools particularly suited to this task are BatchMaster (Windows PCs) and Debabelizer (Macintoshes—the freeware version, Debabelizer Light, is also suitable). However, most image-processing programs, such as Adobe Photoshop, PaintShop Pro (a shareware program for Windows PCs), Lview Pro (another shareware program for PCs), Graphic Converter (a shareware program for the Macintosh), or the pbmplus and ImageMagick packages (shareware programs for UNIX workstations) have tools for reducing the number of colors in the image.

You also want to reduce the number of colors because of the limited display capabilities (the 256-color limit) of many computers. Ideally, the fewer the colors the better, as this frees up space in the color table for other images. It is also a good idea to create image icons using the Windows

Figure 10.1 A page from the University of Toronto Web site navigational collection. The graphic at the top of the screen consists of two images, tiled together. The right-hand portion is reused on a number of different pages.

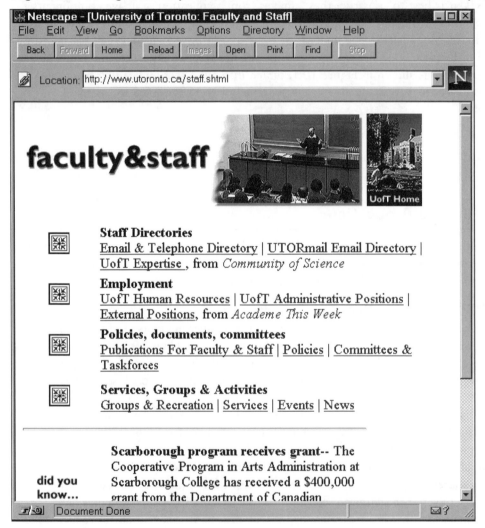

colormap as the default color palette. This reduces dithering on low color-resolution displays and generally makes GIF images look better.

Interlaced GIF Images

The GIF format stores images as a sequence of thin (1 pixel high) horizontal strips. Usually these are stored one after the other, so that when a browser receives an image file, it receives the first (top) strip, followed by the second, the third, and so on. If your browser displays the image as it is being downloaded, the image appears to "wipe" in, starting at the top and wiping downwards.

As you have certainly noticed, this is not the way all Web images are drawn to the browser window. Sometimes the image opens rather like a venetian blind—a rough outline of the image appears first, and detail is gradually added. This occurs due to a special GIF89 feature called *interlacing*. With interlaced GIF images, the strips are stored in nonconsecutive order. For example, the strips might be stored in the order 1, 11, 21, 31, 41, and so on, followed by 2, 12, 22, et cetera. A rough outline of the image is obtained from the first batch of slices, while subsequent batches fill in the gaps and refine the image. In the end, the image takes nearly the same time to arrive, but to the user the presentation of an interlaced GIF can be much more appealing, since the outline of the entire image appears more quickly. However, files for interlaced images are slightly larger than those for non-interlaced ones. Whether or not they are appropriate then depends on the nature of the image and speed requirements.

Most standard image processing programs, including those mentioned at the beginning of this section, are capable of producing interlaced GIFs. The image-processing tool GIFtool, described later in this chapter, can add interlacing to your GIF images should your other graphics tools not be able to do so.

Transparent GIF Images

Unlike X-Bitmaps, GIF images have no implicit transparent color. This is inconvenient if the image is simply a black-and-white logo, a colored bullet on a plain background, or an equation to be presented inline with the text. Fortunately, the GIF89 format lets you declare one of the color indexes as *transparent*—as with X-Bitmaps, these transparent pixels let the background of the browser window underlying the pixel show through. For this to be useful, you must find the color index value corresponding to the color you want to make transparent (usually the image background), and use a program to modify the image file and make this color transparent. Some ways of doing this are outlined in the following sections.

Transparency (Macintosh)

Aaron Giles of Cornell University Medical College has developed an elegantly useful program called transparency, a simple, graphical tool for editing GIF images and making one of the colors transparent. You operate transparency either by dragging a file to the transparency program icon or by double-clicking on the icon and opening the desired GIF image file. To select the transparency color, you simply place the mouse pointer inside the image and hold down the mouse button. You are presented with the color palette for the image, and can select the color you wish to make transparent by putting the mouse pointer over the desired color and releasing the button. You can choose to have no transparent color by selecting the "NONE" bar at the top of the palette. Upon releasing the mouse button, there is a short pause, after which the image is redrawn with the selected color rendered transparently. You now select the "Save as GIF89..." menu from the pull-down File menu to save the newly transparent version.

Transparency is available at a number of anonymous FTP sites, including:

```
ftp://uiarchive.cso.uiuc.edu/pub/systems/mac/info-mac/gst/grf/transparency-10.hqx
ftp://ftp.uwtc.washington.edu/pub/Mac/Graphics/
```

Giftrans (UNIX and DOS)

Giftrans is a simple, command-line C-language program, written by Andreas Ley, that can convert any GIF files into the GIF89A format, making one of the colors transparent in the process. Giftrans is available in source code (for compilation on any platform, but most specifically for UNIX workstations) and as an executable program for PCs running DOS, or a DOS session under Windows.

Typically, giftrans is used as follows

```
giftrans -t xx image.gif > transparent_image.gif
```

which translates the file *image.gif* into *transparent_image.gif* and makes the color labeled by *xx* transparent. There are several ways of labeling the color, the most common being:

- Specify the absolute RGB value for the color (as a 24-bit RGB value). For example, the command:

  ```
  giftrans -t #ffffff image.gif > transparent_image.gif
  ```

  makes the color white transparent (ffffff is the RGB code for white).

- Specify the color index value. For example, the command:

  ```
  giftrans -t 21 image.gif > transparent_image.gif
  ```

  makes the color found in color index 21 transparent.

How do you find the color index or RGB value of the color you want transparent? To find this information, you need a graphics program that can tell you the color indices or RGB values for a given pixel. Several shareware graphics programs can do this—xv is a common UNIX program suitable for this task.

Giftrans is available from many anonymous FTP sites. Its original home is:

```
ftp://ftp.rz.uni-karlsruhe.de/pub/net/www/tools/
```

The file *giftrans.exe* is the DOS executable version, while *giftrans.c* is C source code (you will also need *getopt.c* if compiling on a PC), and *giftrans.1* is the UNIX-style manual page.

The program xv is available from many anonymous FTP sites. You will need both a C compiler and the standard X11 libraries to compile xv on your machine. Xv is available at:

```
ftp://ftp.cis.upenn.edu/pub/xv/xv-3.10a.tar.Z
```

GIFtool (UNIX and DOS)

GIFtool is a multipurpose shareware GIF manipulation program that lets you add interlacing or transparency to GIF images. GIFtool can be used in batch mode to convert a number of files at the same time. The source code for GIFtool is available, as are precompiled binaries for several platforms. Additional information, including directions to the source and binaries, is found at:

```
http://www.homepages.com/tools/
```

Photoshop Transparent GIF Plug-in

Oddly enough, commercial programs such as Photoshop and CorelDraw cannot create transparent GIF images. Fortunately, Adobe provides a free Photoshop plug-in that does these tasks. This plug-in can be obtained (in Macintosh and Windows versions), at:

```
http://www.adobe.com/supportservice/custsupport/FILELIBRARY/Photosho/Mac/GIF89a.sit.hqx
http://www.adobe.com/supportservice/custsupport/FILELIBRARY/Photosho/Win/GIF89a.zip
```

Such plug-ins are available for other programs—check with your software vendor for details.

Animated GIFs

As of Version 2.0, Netscape Navigator supports what are known as animated GIF images (subsequent browsers from most other vendors also support this feature). The GIF89A format lets a single GIF file contain a sequence of images of the same height and width—the file can be an *archive* of images, stored one after the other. Of course, if the stored files are subsequent frames of a short animation sequence, and you can display them one after the other, then ... *voilà*!—you have an animation. In fact, the GIF format lets you specify the time delay (in 100ths of a second) between subsequent frames; whether the animation should start automatically or should start upon user-selection of the image; and how the sequence should be treated after it has been displayed (whether it should cycle in a loop, or stop). This last capability is a special extension implemented by Netscape—the GIF89A format allows for such proprietary extensions of the file format.

Browsers that can't display GIF animations ignore all this—when such browsers encounter an animated GIF file, they simply display the first or last picture in the file.

NOTE: Animated GIFs require an extra process thread (or more) to run the animation process. This is not a problem on UNIX machines, or on PC/Macintoshes with sufficiently fast processors and lots of memory (16 MB or more). Users with slower machines will find that GIF animations significantly slow down their computers. The moral: Don't get carried away with animated GIFs!

Creating Animated GIFs

You need special software to create an animated GIF sequence. In general, you prepare the animation as a collection of single GIF images, and paste them together using a GIF animation tool. In general, you want the frames to be small, and as with all GIF images, you want to use as few colors as possible—animated GIF files are much larger than single-frame pictures, so you want to reduce the size of the frames as much as possible. URLs listing GIF animation software are given at the end of this section.

Inserting Animated GIFs in HTML Documents

This is easy—you insert an animated GIF using our friend the **IMG** element. For example, if your animated GIFs were in the file *anim.gif*, then the **IMG** tag is simply:

```
<IMG SRC="anim.gif" ALT="animated button" HEIGHT=54 WIDTH=45>
```

Browsers that do not support the animated GIF format will display a single frame from the animation. Be warned that some display the first frame, while others display the last—there's nothing like consistency, is there? One way around this problem is to make the first and last frames identical. This is also useful for looping animations, as you need the first and last frames to be identical (or nearly so) to make the sequence loop smoothly.

Animated GIF Resources

There is a wonderful resource on animated GIFs, provided by Royal Frazier. This contains a detailed tutorial on the GIF97 and GIF89A file structures, tutorials on creating animated GIFs, lists of software to help you in this process, and a gallery of animated GIFs created by Royal and others. The URLs for this reference (the second lists mirror sites) are:

```
http://user.aol.com/royalef/gifanim.htm
http://user.aol.com/royalef/mirrors.htm
```

Background Images and Colors

As discussed in Chapters 2 and 4, most browsers now support background images through the **BACKGROUND** attribute to the HTML **BODY** element (The details of how this is done are given in the **BODY** element section of Chapter 4). Background images can be in any of the supported image formats. However, care must be taken when selecting a background, so that it does not impair the readability or display of the actual content. Alternatively, an author can specify the background color for the document using the **BGCOLOR** attribute, also described in Chapter 4. In both cases, some important design points are:

Use low-contrast backgrounds. You don't necessarily want the background to overshadow or obscure the text or images.

Use small colormaps. You don't want to use up all the colors in the background, and have none left for the actual images. This is particularly important for 256-color displays. Also, you should use the Windows colormap if at all possible—dithering looks particularly bad when applied to backgrounds!

Contrast strongly with text colors. You don't want the background color to be similar to the regular text colors. As described in Chapter 4, you can use the body element **TEXT** (regular text), **LINK** (non-visited link), **VLINK** (previously visited link), and **ALINK** (link selected by user) attributes to reset the text colors, so that text is not obscured by the background.

Make sure the color choices look good on different machines/browsers. Again, you want to ensure that your choices works on poorer-quality computer displays—not everyone has a 16-million-color graphics card and a $2,000 monitor!

If using BACKGROUND, also use BGCOLOR. This is particularly important when the text color contrasts badly with the default background gray. In this case, the text will be unreadable until the background image arrives. An appropriate **BGCOLOR** will make the text readable, and also makes for a smoother transition once the background is loaded.

The references at the end of this chapter list sites on the Web that archive useful background images. Additional information about backgrounds can be found at:

`http://www.sci.kun.nl/thalia/guide/color/faq.html`

Active Images and Imagemaps

Active images, clickable images, imagemaps—whatever they are called—you have certainly seen them, and most authors would love to use them. An active image means that users can click their mouse pointer on top of the image and have different things happen, depending on where they clicked. For example, the active image could be a city map, such that clicking on different locations returns information about particular buildings, transportation routes, or historic monuments.

There are two ways of implementing active images. The traditional and well-established way, known as *imagemapping*, stores information about the active image on an HTTP server. When the user clicks on the image, the Web browser measures the location of the click, and sends this information to an HTTP server. The server uses these coordinates to determine which information to return to the browser.

This requires special processing by both the client and the HTTP server. First, the client must be able to measure the coordinates of the mouse pointer when the user clicks on the active image, and must be configured to send this information to an HTTP server for interpretation and action. Second, there must be resource on the server—often a gateway program—capable of interpreting this coordinate data. Finally, there must be a database on the server relating, for each image, the click coordinates to the appropriate URL. This means that the imagemap designer must take the image, mark out the desired regions, link these regions to particular URLs, and store this information in an imagemap database.

The second approach, called *client-side imagemapping*, includes the imagemap database within the HTML document. This eliminates the need to contact a server, which offers many substantial advantages. However, not all browsers support this approach. Fortunately, you can use both methods for the same imagemapped image: If the browser understands client-side imagemapping, it will use the map within the document, and if it does not, it will access the HTTP server in the traditional manner.

NOTE: Allowed Formats for Active Images   It is best to use the GIF format for active images, as some older browsers cannot handle active JPEGs. Also, do not use **HEIGHT** and **WIDTH** attributes to change the size or shape of the image—the values, when present, *must* be equal to the actual image size.

Things to Think About before Starting

Before you get carried away with active images, stop and think about your audience. First recall that many users will not be able to view your active images, because they are using a text-only browser, such as lynx, or because they have disabled image loading because of a slow network connection (quite common). Consequently, you should make the image files as small as possible, and should try to provide a text-only way of accessing the same information. For example, your document can have a line of text explaining what the image does and offering a hypertext link to a page providing a text-only approach. In particular, every active image element must have an **ALT** text string to explain the image's purpose, and to explain what to do if the image is not visible.

Tradition Imagemapped Active Images

You must do two things to your HTML markup to indicate an imagemapped image. First, you must add the **ISMAP** attribute to the **IMG** element, which tells the browser that this is an active image. Second, you must surround the **IMG** element with a hypertext anchor that points to the program, on the server, that will process the selected coordinate data. Thus, the HTML markup for an active image is

```
<A HREF="http://some.site.edu/cgi-bin/imagemap/my_database"><IMG
      SRC="image.gif"
      ALT="[Imagemap: The author, and a Large, Hairy Llama - an ACTIVE image ]"
      ISMAP ></A>
```

which tells the browser that this is an active image and that, when a user clicks inside the image, the coordinates of the click should be sent to the server and to the program **imagemap** at the given URL. The coordinate information is sent to this URL using the HTTP GET method. Thus, once the image is selected, the accessed URL will look like:

```
http://some.site.edu/cgi-bin/imagemap/my_database?x,y
```

where x and y are the *integer pixel coordinates* of the mouse pointer measured from the *upper left-hand corner* of the image.

Note that the path *my_database* is included at the end of the URL. As discussed in Chapters 6 and 8, URLs that point to program resources are treated in a special way, and any directory-like information appended to the URL after the program name (like *my_database*) is treated as "extra path" information, and is passed as a parameter to the gateway. In this example, *my_database* is path information used by *imagemap* to find the *imagemap database* for this particular image. This allows the *imagemap* program to be used with any number of active images, each image having its own personalized database.

Imagemap is an actual CGI program for handling active image data, distributed with the current NCSA and Apache HTTP servers. Since it is CGI-compliant it should, in principle, run on any server. The program is available at:

```
http://hoohoo.ncsa.uiuc.edu/docs/setup/admin/imagemap.txt
```

The Apache, Netscape, NCSA, and other servers also provide compiled-in server modules that work in exactly the same manner as the **imagemap** gateway.

The remainder of this section describes how to use imagemap and create the associated databases.

Creating the Image Database

The imagemap database file relates a region of the image with a URL to be accessed when a user clicks inside that region. You can specify regions as circles, rectangles, polygons, or points. You can also include comments in a map database file by placing a hash character (#) as the first character in the line.

Figure 10.2 shows a simple map file, named *blobby.map*, while Figure 10.3 shows the figure and the areas associated with the mapped regions. This file declares that clicks within the circle centered at coordinates 116,40 (and with an edge at (116,10) are linked to the designated URL, and makes similar declarations for a rectangle (indicated by rect) and a polygon (indicated by poly). These coordinates are measured in pixels from the upper left-hand corner of the image. The "default" method indicates the URL to access if the user clicks in places not falling inside any of the mapped regions.

The general form of a map file entry is

```
method   URL   x1,y1 x2,y2 ... xn,yn
```

where *method* specifies the manner in which the region is being specified (one of circle, rect, poly, point, or default); *URL* is the URL to be accessed if the click occurs inside this region; and *xn* and *yn* are the integer coordinates of a point, measured from the upper left-hand corner of the image. These coordinates are measured in pixels, so you need a way of measuring the pixel coordinates in an image. Tools for doing this are presented later.

Note that mapped regions can overlap. The imagemap program reads the map file from the top, and if a click occurs at a point lying within two mapped regions, the program takes the first region it encounters.

The URLs specified in a map file can be complete URLs, or partial URLs of the form

```
/path/stuff/file
```

which references a file or gateway program relative to the HTTP server *document directory*. With the NCSA, Apache, and certain other servers, you can also use the form where user is the name

---

Figure 10.2 The example imagemap map database file *blobby.map*. The meanings of the different region types (circle, rect, etc.) are discussed in the text.

```
# Imagemap file for blobby.gif
circle    /dir1/blob2/his_head.html      116,40 116,10
rect      /dir1/blob2/his_hand.html      36,30 84,90
poly      /dir1/blob2/his_foot.html      86,154 64,170 76,188 104,184 112,166
default   /cgi-bin/nph-no_op.sh
```

Figure 10.3 A schematic of a 240 × 200-pixel image (*mr_blobby.gif*) showing the locations of the regions mapped by the database in Figure 10.2.

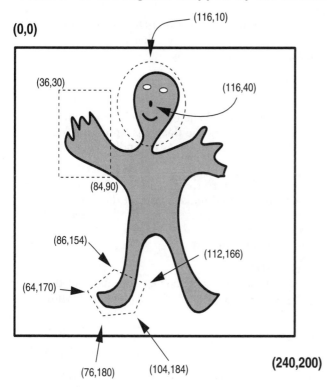

/~user/stuff/file

of a user on the system. This references a file or gateway program relative to the user's personal HTML area.

Table 10.1 gives the specifications of the five methods for declaring active regions in an imagemap database.

Referencing the Imagemap Database

Now that you have a database—for example the *blobby.map* database of Figure 10.2—where should you put it, and how does the *imagemap* program know where to find it? This database can go anywhere you can put regular HTML documents or data files. You indicate its location to the imagemap program via extra path information in the URL. For example, let us suppose that the Web server document directory is */u/Web*

Table 10.1. Methods Specifications for Imagemap Databases
The string `link_URL` **is the URL to which the selected region is linked.**

circle   `link_URL`   `xc, yc`   `xe, ye`
This maps the region inside the indicated circle to the given URL. Two coordinate pairs are required: one for the circle *center* (xc,yc) and the other for an *edgepoint* (xe,ye) lying on the edge of the circle. An example entry is:

     `circle`   `/path/file.html`   `50,40`   `20,30`

point   `link_URL`   `x,y`
This declares a specific *point* in an image as active. When you click on the image and the click is not inside a circle, rectangle, or polygon, the imagemap program locates the `point` closest to the coordinates of the click and accesses the indicated URL.

poly   `link_URL`   `x1,y1`   `x2,y2`   `... xn,yn`
This maps the region inside the indicated polygon to the given URL. Each coordinate pair represents a vertex of the polygon. You should make sure that the line segments do not cross one another (no bow ties!). The polygon is automatically closed by linking the last point `xn,yn` to the first coordinate pair `x1,y1`. The current NCSA program limits you to 100 corners in a given polygon.

rect   `link_URL`   `xul, yul`   `xlr, ylr`
This maps the region inside a rectangle to the given URL. The coordinates of the upper left (xul,yul) and lower right (xlr,ylr) corners of the rectangle are required, in that order. For example:

     `rect`   `http://banzai.com/booger.html`   `20,20`   `40,50`

default   `link_URL`
This URL is accessed if the click did not lie inside any other region. This is never accessed if you define a `point`, since a clicked location will always be *closest* to a defined point, even if it's the only one!

and that the collection of documents and images related to Mr. Blobby is found in the directory */u/Web/weird/blobby*. One choice is to put the map file in the same directory as the image, so that the absolute path for the map file is */u/Web/weird/blobby/blobby.map*. You access this map file from the *imagemap* program by writing, in the HTML document:

```
<A HREF="http://some.site.edu/cgi-bin/imagemap/weird/blobby/blobby.map">
   <IMG SRC="blobby.gif" ISMAP>
</A>
```

where *some.site.edu* is the site containing the documents. Note that the path to *blobby.map*, relative to the document directory of the HTTP server (*/u/Web*), has been added to the imagemap URL. The string `/weird/blobby/blobby.map` is passed to the imagemap program, and is used by imagemap to locate the database *blobby.map*.

With the NCSA Apache, Netscape, and most other servers, this method is not restricted to the regular document directory. If a user has a personal HTML directory, he or she can place map files in this directory and access the maps using URLs like:

```
<A HREF="http://some.site.edu/cgi-bin/imagemap/~user/path/blobby.map">
<IMG SRC="blobby.gif" ISMAP>
</A>
```

where `user` is the username of the person with the personal public HTML directory and *path/blobby.map* is the path leading to the map file from the root of his or her personal document directory.

Getting a Click to Do Nothing

Sometimes, you want a click to do nothing. For example, your image could be a map of buildings, and you don't want anything to happen if the user clicks on non-mapped objects, like roads or trees. In this case, you might want the browser to keep the current document on the browser window screen. This can be accomplished by linking the `default` method in your imagemap file to a server CGI program that returns an response message to the client. In Figure 10.2, the `default` method references the UNIX shell script *nph-no_op.sh*, designed to do exactly this. This script is listed in Figure 10.4.

Output from scripts with an *nph-* prefix are sent directly to the client without being parsed by the server (see Chapter 8 for more information on *non-parsed header* gateway programs). This script sends the HTTP status code 204, which tells the client that there is no server message and that the client should continue displaying the current document.

Tools for Generating Imagemap Map Database Files

Generating a map file is not difficult and only requires some concentration, a piece of paper, and an image-viewing program that gives the pixel coordinates of the mouse pointer. The UNIX program xv (found at many anonymous FTP sites by searching for the string xv-3.00 or xv-3.10) is often used to do this. You load the image into xv, locate the coordinates, and type the numbers into a map file. A similar procedure can be followed with typical Macintosh or PC image-editing programs.

Figure 10.4 Listing for the Bourne shell script *nph-no_op.sh*, which returns HTTP headers that tell a browser to do nothing.

```
#!/bin/sh
echo "HTTP/1.0 204 No response — server CGI-script output"
echo "Content-type: text/plain"
echo "Server: $SERVER_SOFTWARE"
echo
```

Of course, it is much easier if you have a graphical tool to view the images and automatically generate the map files. Thomas Boutell has satisfied this need with his shareware program mapedit, which allows you to read the GIF image into a display window; use the mouse to draw circles, rectangles, and polygons on top; and specify a URL for each of the marked regions. You can also insert comments, which is important if you want to understand the content of the map file at a later date.

Mapedit is available for UNIX systems and for PCs running Windows. The executables, and additional information about mapedit, can be obtained at:

```
http://www.boutell.com/mapedit/
```

The PC version comes as a *zip* archive containing the executable program, support files, and documentation, while the UNIX version comes as a compressed tar archive—there are archives available for the more popular UNIX platforms.

There are, of course, other programs that can help you create imagemap database files. The shareware program WebMap is useful for Macintosh users, while for Windows users there are the programs Map This and Web Hotspots. Information about these three packages can be found, respectively, at:

```
http://www.city.net/cnx/software/webmap.html
http://galadriel.ecaetc.ohio-state.edu/tc/mt/
http://www.cris.com/~automata/index.html
```

Most of these programs support client-side imagemaps, discussed later in this chapter.

Other Server Imagemap Gateway Programs

The CERN HTTP server comes with its own imagemapping gateway program, which uses a technique slightly different from that of imagemap—consult the CERN server documentation for more information. There are also other imagemapping CGI programs, designed for different platforms or taking a different approach to mapping. Mac-ImageMap, for example, provides imagemap capabilities for the Macintosh WebSTAR (formerly MacHTTP) server, using the NCSA imagemap approach. Glorglox, on the other hand, takes a completely different approach, and maps individual pixels onto URLs. Others programs are available; you should inquire at standard archive sites, such as Yahoo, for information about other tools. However, as a document creator your best bet is to stick with the CERN or NCSA default imagemapping programs, since these are well tested with development tools widely available.

Information about Mac-ImageMap and glorglox can be found, respectively, at:

```
http://weyl.zib-berlin.de/imagemap/Mac-ImageMap.html
http://www.uunet.ca/~tomr/glorglox/
```

Client-Side Imagemaps

As discussed in Chapter 4, an HTML extension due to Jim Seidman of Spyglass Inc. now allows imagemap information within an HTML document. The advantages are manifold: The link is faster, since you don't need to use a server to resolve the destination; imagemaps are not server-dependent, so the documents are portable (you can run client-side imagemaps from a CD-ROM containing HTML documents); and destination links can be shown as the mouse moves across the image, as all the relevant information is coded into the HTML.

The details of the client-side mechanism were discussed in Chapter 4 and will not be repeated here. An example of a client-side imagemap is shown in Figure 10.5.

A client-side imagemap stores the mapped coordinate data within a **MAP** element; each **MAP** element takes a **NAME** attribute to identify the map, so that a single file can contain more than one map. The regions inside the map are indicated by **AREA** elements. These take four main attribute **SHAPE**s to indicate the shape (possible values are "rect" for rectangle, "circle" for circle, or "poly" for polygon), **COORDS** for the coordinates (in integer pixels from the upper left-hand corner of the image), **HREF** for the URL reference, and **ALT** for a text description of the link. In place of **HREF**, an area element can take the **NOHREF** attribute, which takes no value and simply means that the region is not linked to anything. The allowed shapes, and a description of the required coordinate values, are summarized in Table 10.2.

As with regular server-side imagemaps, regions can overlap; the browser simply selects the first region that fits when looking down through the list of **AREA**s.

Figure 10.5 Extract from an HTML document that uses a client-side imagemap for the image shown in Figure 10.3 (*mr_blobby.gif*). The new elements and attributes used by the client-side approach are shown in bold. Italics represents the omitted document content.

```
. . . standard HTML stuff . . .
<IMG SRC="mr_blobby.gif" USEMAP="mapname">
. . . more HTML stuff . . .
<MAP NAME="mapname">
<AREA SHAPE="circle" COORDS="116,40,30"
        HREF="/dir1/blob2/his_head.html" ALT="text explanation">
<AREA SHAPE="rect" COORDS="36,30, 84,90"
        HREF="/dir1/blob2/his_hand.html" ALT="text explanation">
<AREA SHAPE="poly" COORDS="86,154,64,170,76,188,104,184,112,166"
        HREF="http://egghead.com/foot.html" ALT="text explanation">
</MAP>
. . . rest of HTML document . . .
```

Table 10.2 Possible Shape Attribute Values and Corresponding Coordinate Specifications for Client-Side Imagemap AREA Elements
All coordinate values in pixels.

SHAPE="rect"   COORDS="*xul, yul, xlr, ylr*"

Where *xul,yul* are the coordinates of upper-left corner of rectangle, and *xlr,ylr* are the coordinates of lower-right hand corner of rectangle

SHAPE="poly"   COORDS="*x1,y1, x2,y2, . . . xn,yn*"

Where *xn,yn* are the *x* and *y* coordinates of polygon vertices.

SHAPE="circle"   COORDS="*xc, yc, r*"

Where *xc,yc* are the *x* and *y* coordinates of circle center, and *r* is the circle radius

You can combine client-side and server-side imagemaps in the same image element; a browser that understands client-side imagemaps will use the local map information, while other browsers will revert to the server-side database. Figure 10.6 shows how this is done using the example in Figure 10.5 as a reference. The required additions are shown in boldface italics—all that is needed is an appropriate anchor element surrounding the image, and an **ISMAP** attribute in the **IMG** element.

Most of the imagemap-generation programs described earlier will create both client- and server-side databases.

Figure 10.6. Extract from an HTML document that simultaneously references server-side and client-side imagemaps (the changes from Figure 10.5 are shown in boldface italics). A browser that understands client-side imagemaps will use the local map data. A browser that does not understand client-side imagemaps will use the HTTP server instead.

```
. . . standard HTML stuff . . .
<A HREF="/cgi-bin/imagemap/path/blobby.map"><IMG
    SRC="mr_blobby.gif" USEMAP="mapname" ISMAP></A>
. . . more HTML stuff . . .
<MAP NAME="mapname">
<AREA SHAPE="circle" COORDS="116,40,30"
         HREF="/dir1/blob2/his_head.html" ALT="text explanation">
<AREA SHAPE="rect" COORDS="36,30, 84,90"
         HREF="/dir1/blob2/his_hand.html" ALT="text explanation">
<AREA SHAPE="poly" COORDS="86,154,64,170,76,188,104,184,112,166"
         HREF="http://egghead.com/foot.html" ALT="text explanation">
</MAP>
. . . rest of HTML document . . .
```

Image and Icon Archive Sites

There are several sites on the World Wide Web that maintain extensive archives of publicly accessible images and icons, which are useful places to find icons for your documents. The following two pages have list of some of the more popular sites.

Public Domain Icon Archives

```
http://www-ns.rutgers.edu/doc-images/
http://www.dsv.su.se/~matti-hu/archive.html
http://www.cli.di.unipi.it/iconbrowser/icons.html
http://www.cli.di.unipi.it/iconbrowser/icons/mirrors.html    (List of Mirror sites)
http://www.cit.gu.edu.au/~anthony/icons/index.html
http://bsdi.com/icons/AIcons/                                (Mirror)
http://www.hlt.uni-duisburg.de/AIcons/                       (Mirror)
ftp://ftp.cs.indiana.edu/pub/AIcons/                         (Mirror)
http://www.netspace.org/icons/AIcons/                        (Mirror)
http://hobbes.nmsu.edu/multimedia/icons/
http://www.eecs.wsu.edu/~rkinion/lines/lines.html
http://white.nosc.mil/images.html
http://www.widomaker.com/~spalmer/
http://www.cco.caltech.edu/~cherish/images/
http://www.starnet.com.au/~graphics/
http://www.infi.net/~rdralph/icons/
http://www.geocities.com/Heartland/1448/main.htm
```

Public Domain Background Images

```
http://cpcug.org/user/jlacombe/backgrnds/johnback.html
http://www.logicnet.com/calexplorer.com/im.htm
http://www.algonet.se/~dip/pix-aday.htm              (Tips for Photoshop/KAI users)
http://www.infi.net/~rdralph/icons/backgr/
http://www.geocities.com/Heartland/1449/background.htm
http://www.starnet.com.au/~graphics/
```

Other Lists of Image Archive Sites

```
http://www.yahoo.com/Computers_and_Internet/Internet/World_Wide_Web/Programming/Icons/
http://oneworld.wa.com/htmldev/devpage/dev-page3.html#doc-i
```

References

General Issues in Web Graphics

```
http://www.inforamp.net/~poynton/Poynton-articles.html
http://www.sci.kun.nl/thalia/guide/color/faq.html
ftp://ftp.inforamp.net/pub/users/poynton/doc/colour/     (All about color and computers)
http://www.cs.cmu.edu/afs/cs.cmu.edu/user/rwb/www/gamma.html    (About monitor gamma)
```

http://lynda.com/hex.html   (Index of RGB hex codes and colors)
news:comp.infosystems.www.authoring.images   (Web graphics newsgroup)
Designing Web Graphics, by Lynda Weinman, New Riders Publishing, 1996.

Transparent and Interlaced GIFs

http://user.aol.com/royalef/gifabout.htm   (About GIF in general)
http://members.aol.com/htmlguru/transparent_images.html   (Tutorial)
http://dragon.jpl.nasa.gov/~adam/transparent.html
http://www.cis.columbia.edu/homepages/gonzalu/transparent-gifs/transparent.html

Animated GIFs

http://user.aol.com/royalef/gifanim.htm
http://www.yahoo.com/Computers_and_Internet/Graphics/Computer_Animation/Animated_GIFs/

Client-Side Imagemaps

http://www.spyglass.com/techspec/tutorial/img_maps.html
http://www.ics.uci.edu/pub/ietf/html/draft-seidman-clientsideimagemap-02.txt

Server-Side and General Imagemap Information

http://www.yahoo.com/Computers_and_Internet/Internet/World_Wide_Web/
Programming/Imagemaps/   (Resource lists)
http://www.cs.buffalo.edu/~san/reference/image.html   (Resource lists)
http://www.webcom.com/~webcom/html/tutor/imagemaps.html   (Online tutorial)
http://hoohoo.ncsa.uiuc.edu/docs/tutorials/imagemapping.html (Online tutorial)

11

Web Management and Maintenance Tools

Thiis chapter describes utility programs and services useful in managing and maintaining collections of HTML documents or other Web resources. These are divided into five categories. The first consists of program resources, mostly written in perl, useful for managing HTML document collections, generating tables of contents, converting from mail or news archives into HTML, and so on. This is followed by a summary of server log analysis tools: tools that can analyze server usage and tell you how Web site resources are being accessed. The third section looks at Web indexing and search tools—software useful in indexing large collections of Web resources. Fourth is a brief section on *Intranet suites*—these are large Web/Internet software suites designed for automating large portions of business or enterprise operation. The last section provides a URL resource list for topics and resources not covered in this chapter, or this book: namely, information about Web browser and server software, HTML editors, and HTML document converters and translators.

Organizational Note

URLs related to the topic or tool under discussion are located at the beginning of each section. You should use these URLs to obtain up-to-date information on a particular resource, or to search for new tools and resources not described here. In addition, the names of tools described in this chapter are italicized when they appear outside the section specific to the tool.

Web Maintenance Programs

Reference Sites

```
http://www.yahoo.com/Computers_and_Internet/Internet/World_Wide_Web/HTML_Converters/
http://www.utoronto.ca/webdocs/HTMLdocs/misc_tools.html
http://www.w3.org/pub/WWW/Tools/
```

The programs listed here are useful in maintaining document collections, and can be used to automatically generate links, create HTML versions of mail archives, generate tables of contents, and so on. Most of these tools were developed under UNIX, and may require modification for other operating systems. Here you will find only brief descriptions of the packages; you are referred to the listed URLs for additional information.

Cap2html—Gopher Directory to HTML

```
http://www.inf.utfsm.cl/~vparada/archive/cap2html
```

Cap2html, by Victor Parada, is a simple UNIX shell script for converting Gopher *.cap directories into an HTML document with links to the relevant resources. This is useful when migrating data from a Gopher to an HTTP server.

Curl—Automatic Link Generator

```
http://munkora.cs.mu.oz.au/~ad/curl/announce.html
http://munkora.cs.mu.oz.au/~ad/www-stuff.html
```

Curl, by Andrew Davidson, is a C-language tool that automatically creates links between HTML documents. Curl constructs links based on information, maintained by the author, in a special *contents* file. This file lists the names of the HTML documents along with the relationships between them.

Dtd2html—HTML Analysis of a DTD

```
http://www.oac.uci.edu/indiv/ehood/dtd2html.doc.html
http://www.oac.uci.edu/indiv/ehood/perlSGML.html
```

Dtd2html, part of the perlSGML package developed by Earl Hood, takes an SGML Document Type Definition file (DTD) and generates a collection of HTML documents explaining the structural relationship among the elements defined in the DTD. This is useful if you wish to learn about the structure of an HTML DTD.

Htmltoc—Table of Contents Generator

```
http://www.oac.uci.edu/indiv/ehood/htmltoc.doc.html
```

Htmltoc, by Earl Hood, is a perl program that can automatically generate a table of contents (ToC) for a single HTML document, or for a collection of related documents. Htmltoc uses the HTML **H1–H6** headings to locate sections within a single document, and uses the order of the heading (**H1, H2,** and so on) to determine the hierarchical relationship of the ToC. This, among many other features, can be significantly customized.

HTML Syntax Verifiers

More and more commercial HTML editors or document management systems incorporate some sort of HTML validation tool. There are also several stand-alone tools for checking the syntax of HTML documents. Most of these use the HTML Document Type Definition (DTD) as the definition of the HTML syntax, so you will require this file to use these tools; you can find it at the "official" W3C home of HTML information:

```
http://www.w3.org/hypertext/WWW/MarkUp/MarkUp.html
```

A collection of HTML DTDs, including those for HTML 3 and other, experimental, versions of HTML can also be obtained from:

```
http://www.webtechs.com/html/
```

New DTD files will appear with each revision of the language. To test your documents' compatibility with each new standard you need only download the revised DTD and plug it into your verification program.

NOTE: Why Validate? Why bother validating your HTML as long as the rendered result looks good, you may ask? Looks can be deceiving. For a brief discussion of the virtues of validating your HTML, see:

```
http://www.earth.com/bad-style/why-validate.html
```

Htmlcheck

```
http://uts.cc.utexas.edu/~churchh/htmlcheck.html
```

Htmlcheck, by H. Churchyard, will check either HTML 2.0 or HTML 3.2 files for syntax errors, including local link verification, and generates simple reference-dependency maps. The program requires the awk or perl interpreter to run, and will do so on any platform on which either program is available. Htmlcheck reports stylistic problems in addition to true syntax errors.

Kinder, Gentler Validator

```
http://ugweb.cs.ualberta.ca/~gerald/validate/
```

Like the Webtechs validation service, this second interactive validator, by Gerald Oskoboiny of the University of Alberta, uses *sgmls* as the underlying syntax checker. However, this package uses a more complex error parsing interface, and the reported errors are designed to be more easily understood by non-specialists.

Sgmls

`ftp://jclark.com/pub/sgmls/`

Sgmls, written by James Clark, is a formal SGML syntax-checking program. This program takes as input an SGML file and checks the document structure against the relevant Document Type Definition (DTD). URLs pointing to the current HTML DTD are listed at the introduction to this "syntax verifier" section and in the References section at the end of Chapter 4. As output, the program prints a list of syntax errors and the line number at which the errors occurred.

As an example, consider the file ***test.html*** shown in Figure 11.1. Figure 11.2 shows the output of sgmls after "testing" this file against the HTML DTD.

The following command on a UNIX computer will validate the file ***test.html***—note how the DTD is specified in the command line:

```
sgmls -s html.dtd test.html
```

Figure 11.1 Example HTML document *test.html*. The line numbers (in italics) have been added for comparison with Figure 11.2.

```
1    <HTML>
2    <HEAD>
3    <TITLE> <em> Instructional </em>and Research Computing Home Page</TITLE>
4    </HEAD>
5    <BODY>
6
7    <h1> Instructional and Research Computing </H1>
8    <hr>
9    This is the Instructional and Research Computing Group <B>(IRC)</B>
10    World Wide Web home page. If you get lost try the
11   <a href="big%20dog.html"> big dog help </a> or
12   <a href="http://www.university.ca/</a>home.html"> right here </a>
13   <hr>
14   <oL>
15   <LI> consulting services in <A HREF="InsT/intro.html"> instructional
16   technology and applications</A>
17   applications</A>.<P>
18
19   </ol>
20   <HR>
21
22   </BODY>
23   </HTML>
```

Figure 11.2 Sgmls error output after parsing *test.html* (shown in Figure 11.1).

```
sgmls: SGML error at test.html, line 3 at ">":
EM end-tag ignored: doesn't end any open element (current is TITLE)
sgmls: SGML error at test.html, line 3 at ">":
Bad end-tag in R/CDATA element; treated as short (no GI) end-tag
sgmls: SGML error at test.html, line 3 at "d":
HEAD end-tag implied by data; not minimizable
sgmls: SGML error at test.html, line 3 at ">":
TITLE end-tag ignored: doesn't end any open element (current is HTML)
sgmls: SGML error at test.html, line 4 at ">":
HEAD end-tag ignored: doesn't end any open element (current is HTML)
sgmls: SGML error at test.html, line 17 at ">":
A end-tag ignored: doesn't end any open element (current is OL)
```

Often the DTD comes in two parts: the DTD itself, plus a second file called the SGML *declaration*, often with a name like `html.decl`. You need both these files for sgmls to work. You can append the DTD file to the declaration file (`html.decl` first, followed by `html.dtd`), or you can pass them as subsequent arguments, as in:

```
sgmls -s html.decl html.dtd test.html
```

The output lists the errors and the line numbers at which they occurred. Figure 11.2 shows the sgmls output for the file in Figure 11.1. The errors at line 3 are due to the illegal character markup inside the **TITLE** element. The subsequent errors at lines 3 and 4 are a result of this same mistake. The error at line 17 is a very typical error: the file has a duplicate `</A>` ending tag.

There is also a successor to sgmls, called nsgmls, that comes as part of a larger SGML package called SP. For more information about SP and nsgmls, see:

```
http://www.jclark.com/sp/index.htm
```

Weblint

```
http://www.khoros.umn.edu/staff/neilb/weblint.html
http://www.cre.canon.co.uk/~neilb/weblint/
http://www.khoros.umn.edu/staff/neilb/weblkint/gateways.html
```

Designed to pick "fluff" off Web pages, Weblint, by Neil Bowers, is a perl script that checks basic structure and identifies the following errors: unknown elements, unknown tag context, overlapped elements, illegally nested elements, mismatched opening and closing tags, unclosed elements, unpaired quotes, and unexpected heading order.

WebTechs HTML Validation Service

```
http://www.webtechs.com/html-val-svc/
http://www.webtechs.com/html-val-svc/mirror_sites.html
```

If you want to check your files but do not feel comfortable downloading the *sgmls* package, you can instead use it remotely via the WebTechs HTML Validation Service. This service, accessible over the Web due to the efforts of Mark Gaither, can check an entire document currently in place at a specific URL (you enter the URL into a fill-in FORM), or it can check a small sample of HTML, which you type or paste into another FORM input element.

Hyperlink Verifiers

SGML parsers such as *sgmls* can verify that your HTML tags are correctly placed, but cannot ensure that the hypertext links go to valid locations. To check hypertext links you need a "link verifier." This is a program that reads your document, extracts the hypertext links, and tests the validity of the URLs.

CyberSpyder

http://www.cyberspyder.com/cslnkts1.html

CyberSpyder is a shareware, Microsoft Windows–based link validator that can iterate through a Web site, looking for (and reporting) broken links. The package can check most standard URLs, including **news** and **mailto** (it is unclear from the documentation how it validates **mailtos**). The package runs on all Windows platforms, including Windows 3.1.

Linkcheck

ftp://ftp.math.psu.edu/pub/sibley/

Linkcheck is a perl program written by David Sibley of Pennsylvania State University. Linkcheck can check **gopher, ftp,** and **http** URLs in a document, but cannot verify other URL forms. Linkcheck tests **gopher** URLs by fully accessing the indicated URL, which can be slow if the URL points to a large file. It tests **ftp** URLs by listing directory contents rather than fetching the document, which is a lot nicer. **Http** URLs are checked by using the HTTP HEAD method, which is just as nice. The program has not been updated since 1994, so it does not properly understand some modern elements, such as **EMBED** or **APPLET**.

Missinglink

http://www.rsol.com/ml/

Missinglink is a shareware link verifier written in perl and designed for UNIX systems. It does not process **ftp, gopher,** or **telnet** URLs, but does account for **BASE** element content in evaluating HTTP references.

Lvrfy

http://www.cs.dartmouth.edu/~crow/lvrfy.html

Lvrfy, by Preston Crow verifies internal links by starting with a given page, parsing all the hyperlinks, including images, and then recursively checking linked documents. Lvrfy is a regular shell script, and uses the standard UNIX programs sed, awk, csh, touch, and rm.

SiteCheck

`http://www.pacific-coast.com/`

SiteCheck, from Pacific Coast Software, is a commercial Macintosh application for checking hypertext links within documents at a specified Web site. The software iterates recursively through documents at the site, reporting all invalid links it encounters. The package also checks external links.

SiteSweeper

`http://www.sitetech.com/`

SiteSweeper, by Site/Technologies/Inc., is a commercial, Windows 95/NT–based Web site management and analysis tool. The package includes a link checker, as well as tools that prepare regular daily reports about site problems and changes.

Verify_links

`ftp://ftp.eit.com/pub/eit/wsk/`
(select the directory corresponding to your operating system)

Verify_links, a product of Enterprise Integration Technologies, is a forms-based CGI program for validating links in an HTML document. Verify_links can only verify **http** URLs and cannot check FTP, Gopher, telnet, and other links. In this respect it is not as useful as *linkcheck*. However, it is more reliable than *linkcheck* in validating **http** URLs and partial URLs. It also can check POST actions to a limited degree, and will "push the buttons" in a **FORM** to verify the existence of the attached CGI program.

WebAnalyzer

`http://www.incontext.ca/`

WebAnalyzer, by InContext Inc., is a commercial Windows 95/NT–based link validator. The package can check most URLs, producing useful reports of Web site properties. The package includes a graphical interface that lets you select the portions of the site to be validated. This validator has received fine reviews in both *PC Week* and *PC Magazine*.

WebMapper

`http://www.netcarta.com`

WebMapper, by NetCarta Corp., is an integrated, commercial site management and maintenance suite that contains a link validator as one of its components. Other components include a site analysis tool (for classifying and organizing site content), and a report generation kit. The software is available for various UNIX systems, as well as Windows 95/NT.

WebMaster

http://www.coast/com

WebMaster, by Coast Software, is a commercial Windows 95/NT–based visual tool for managing Web sites. The package includes a link validator, as well as tools for locating orphaned pages, and for managing the file structure of a Web site.

Webxref

http://www.sara.nl/cgi-bin/rick_acc_webxref

Webxref, by Rick Jansen, is a shareware perl program that verifies hypertext links between documents, starting from an indicated HTML file. This program has recently been revised.

Hypermail—Mail to HTML Archive

http://www.eit.com/software/hypermail/hypermail.html
http://www.eit.com/software/hypermail/

Hypermail, by Kevin Hughes of Enterprise Integration Technologies, is a C-language program that takes a file of mail messages, in UNIX mailbox format, and generates a set of cross-referenced HTML documents. Hypermail converts each letter in the mailbox into a separate HTML file, with links to other, related articles. It also converts e-mail addresses and hypertext anchors in the original letters into HTML hypertext links.

Index Maker—Index of Web Sites

http://web.sau.edu/~mkruse/www/scripts/index2.html

Index Maker, by Matt Kruse, is a shareware perl program for maintaining an indexed list of selected WWW sites. The indexing requires active input on the part of the person registering new URLs, which makes this tool distinct from, and perhaps less glamorous than, the robot-based indexing tools dis-cussed later in this chapter. At the same time, Index Maker is very useful for construction of personal indexes or special-purpose indexes, where active user participation can keep the index accurate and up-to-date.

MHonArc—Mail to HTML Archive

http://www.oac.uci.edu/indiv/ehood/mhonarc.doc.html

MHonArc, by Earl Hood, is a perl package for converting Internet mail messages, both plain text and MIME encoded, into HTML documents. This is useful if you are archiving electronic mail messages or newsgroup postings and want to make them available on the WWW. The package uses the letter's subject line for the HTML **TITLE** and as heading in the HTML version of the letter, and converts relational headers such as *References* or *In-Reply-To* into appropriate hypertext links, if possible.

MOMspider—Web Maintainer and Indexer

http://www.ics.uci.edu/WebSoft/MOMspider/

The Multi-Owner Maintenance spider, or MOMspider, is a Web-roaming *robot* designed to help in maintaining distributed collections of HTML documents. A perl package written by Roy Fielding of the Department of Information and Computer Science at the University of California, Irvine, MOMspider traverses a list of webs, and constructs an index of the collection, recording the attributes and connections of the web within a special HTML map document. MOMspider can be used to report changes in web layout, to report linking and other problems, and to generate an overview of a large web collection. Since MOMspider explores links dynamically and autonomously, it is formally a *robot*, and obeys the *robot exclusion policy*. Robots and the exclusion policy are discussed in the concluding section of this chapter.

WebCopy—Batch Document Retrieval

http://www.inf.utfsm.cl/~vparada/webcopy.html
http://sunhe.jinr.dubna.su/docs/webcopy.html

WebCopy, by Victor Parada, is a perl program that retrieves a specified HTTP URL. There are many control switches that permit recursive retrieval of documents (but only from the same server—WebCopy will *not* retrieve documents from domain names other than the one specified in the initial URL) and the retrieval of included inline image files.

WebLinker—Distributed Web Management

http://www.cern.ch/WebLinker/
http://www.harlequin.co.uk/webmaker/
Commercial inquiries: web@harlequin.com

WebLinker is a tool, developed at CERN as part of the WebMaker package, to help manage distributed collections of Web documents. WebLinker/WebMaker is currently being developed by the Harlequin Group, Ltd. Inquiries should be addressed to *web@harlequin.com*.

Web Server Log Analysis Programs

All HTTP servers produce log files that record information about each server request. Most HTTP servers use the same format, known as the *common log file format,* to record these data, and most analysis tools are designed around this standard. The programs listed in this section can read the log files and produce lists, charts, and graphs describing server usage.

There are many different analysis programs, and not all are listed below. For further and more up-to-date information, you should consult the following indices:

```
http://www.yahoo.com/text/Computers_and_Internet/Internet/World_Wide_Web/HTTP/Servers/
http://union.ncsa.uiuc.edu/HyperNews/get/www/log-analyzers.html
http://www.netimages.com/~snowhare/utilities/
```

3Dstats

```
http://www.netstore.de/Supply/3Dstats/
```

A simple C-language package, 3Dstats analyzes Web server log files and generates three-dimensional VRML models charting server usage. These can be explored using any VRML browser. Perhaps not terribly useful, but very cool!

AccessWatch

```
http://netpressence.com/accesswatch/
```

AccessWatch, by Dave Maher, is a perl 5 program that works as a gateway interface: It produces a graphical HTML representation of server usage, which can be customized to a particular user, or a particular collection of documents. The package runs under both UNIX and NT systems. AccessWatch is free to noncommercial users only.

Getstats

```
http://www.eit.com/software/getstats/getstats.html
```

Getstats, by Kevin Hughes of Enterprise Integration Technologies Inc., is a C-language program that produces log summaries for standard HTTP server log files. The getstats package is exceptionally well documented at the indicated URL, which includes links to the software.

The package *CreateStats* is a useful front-end for getstats, and consists of a collection of tools for managing server log files. This can be obtained at:

```
http://www-bprc.mps.ohio-state.edu/usage/CreateStats.html
```

The shell script getstats_plot can convert getstats output into a graph illustrating server usage. Another similar program is getgraph.pl. These can be obtained, respectively, at:

```
http://infopad.EECS.Berkeley.EDU/~burd/software/getstats_plot/
http://www.tcp.chem.tue.nl/stats/script/
```

Gwstat

```
http://dis.cs.umass.edu/stats/gwstat.html
```

Gwstat is a UNIX package of programs and scripts that can convert HTML output from the program *wwwstat* (see listing in this section) into GIF format graphs of server statistics. Gwstat does not do all this itself and requires the packages Xmgr (a data plotting package), ImageMagick (an image format conversion package), ghostscript (a PostScript interpreter), and perl versions 4 or 5.

Hit List

http://www.marketwave.com/

Hit List, by Marketwave, is a commercial log analyzer and reporting tool. It can read log files from many servers, including Netscape's and Microsoft's, and perform a variety of different analyses.

IIStats

http://www.cyber-trek.com/iistats/

IIStats, by Ian Mayor, is a perl 5 program that can generate log statistics for Microsoft's Internet Information Server, running under Windows NT. It is free software, under the GNU general public license.

MKStats

http://www.mkstats.com/

MKStats is a shareware log analyzer, written in perl 5, that produces HTML-based log analysis output. MKStats is free for personal use, with prices varying according to other use (nonprofit, single business, service-provider, etc.).

Mswc

http://www.ee.ethz.ch/~oetiker/webtools/mswc/mswc.html

Mswc (Multi Server WebCharts), by Tobias Oetiker, is a perl 5 log analysis tool designed to measure usage across a number of different Web servers. This is useful when a Web site is actually running on multiple machines, such that there is no central log file for the entire collection.

Net.Analysis

http://www.netgen.com/

Net.Analysis, from net.Genesis Corp., is a commercial log analysis tool for Windows platforms. This package uses an underlying FoxPro database to allow sophisticated analysis of the log information beyond what is possible with traditional freeware tools.

PressView

http://academicus.com/pView.htm

Designed to work with the Windows NT EMWACS HTTP server, this commercial package can produce a variety of log reports, and create reports on a site's most popular pages.

RefStats

http://www.netimages.com/~snowhare/utilities/refstats.html
http://www.netimages.com/~snowhare/utilities/browsercounter.html

RefStats, by Benjamin Franz, is a perl program that analyses NCSA 1.4–format *referer_log* files and produces a list of referring URLs, along with a count of the number of times each referring URL was reported. This is useful for tracking bad links to your site. The sister package BrowserCounter monitors the *agent_log* file, and produces a report summarizing the types of browsers that are accessing the server.

Webreporter

http://www.openmarket.com/reporter/

Webreporter, from Open Market, is a commercial log analysis tool designed for general use, not just for use with Open Market servers. The package has a C-programming API, so that custom reporting tools can be built into the package.

Webstat

http://www.pegasus.esprit.ec.org/people/sijben/statistics/advertisment.html

Webstat, by Paul Sijben of the University of Twente, is an analysis program written in the python language. Webstat can read common format log files and return statistical information about server usage. These reports can be aggregated by service, by requesting domain, or by country, and can be summarized on a daily, weekly, or monthly basis. To run Webstat you also need a python interpreter. This is available from:

http://www.cwi.nl/ftp/python/index.html

Webtrends

http://www.webtrends.com/

Webtrends is a commercial Windows-based package for tracking server access. Its strengths lie in the elegant formatting and graphical organization of the analyzed data.

Wusage

http://www.boutell.com/wusage/

Wusage, by Thomas Boutell, is a shareware C program that generates simple weekly usage reports, in the form of HTML documents including inline image graphs displaying server usage and the distribution of accesses by continent. A particularly nice feature is the ability to exclude irrelevant document retrievals (of inline images, from local machines, etc.) from the analysis.

Wwwstat

http://www.ics.uci.edu/websoft/wwwstat/

Wwwstat, by Roy Fielding, is a perl program that can read common log file formats (NCSA Version 1.2 or newer) and produce a log summary file as an HTML document suitable for publishing on your server. The package is remarkably simple to use, and has most of the required analysis features. The package *gwstat* (see listing in this section) can convert wwwstat output into graphical data.

Sometimes the output of wwwstat is a bit overpowering. Robin Thau has developed a perl 5 program, called *metasummary*, that produces a summary of wwwstat output. This useful tool is available at:

http://www.ai.mit.edu/tools/usum/usum.html

Robots, Wanderers, and Spiders

In the World Wide Web, *robots*, *wanderers*, and *spiders* are essentially synonyms, and indicate programs that automatically traverse the Web, successively retrieving HTML documents and then accessing the links contained within those documents. They are usually autonomous programs, in that they access links without human intervention. There are many applications that use such programs, ranging from web mapping and link verifying programs (such as MOMspider), to programs that retrieve Web documents and generate searchable Web indexes (such as ALIweb, Harvest, and Lycos). Indeed, if it were not for robots, it would now be almost impossible to find anything on the Web, given the millions upon millions of resources that are now available.

However, sometimes a Web site administrator wants to keep robots away from certain collections of documents, perhaps because the documents are only temporary, and so should not be indexed, or perhaps because the documents are internal resources that should not be indexed outside of the site. Alternatively, a server may be heavily loaded with users, in which case you don't want your service to human customers slowed by a bunch of eager little robots, happily grabbing all your documents as fast as they can.

The Robot Exclusion Policy

http://web.nexor.co.uk/mak/doc/robots/robots.html
http://info.webcrawler.com/mak/projects/robots/robots.html

Martijn Koster developed a convention that lets a Web server administrator tell robots whether or not they are welcome to access the server and, if they are welcome, which files and directories they should avoid. This information is stored in a file named ***robots.txt***, which, according to the convention, must always be at the URL:

```
http://domain.name.edu/robots.txt
```

where *domain.name.edu* is the site's domain name. Robots complying with the *robot exclusion standard* check this file, and use the contents to determine what they can access. An example *robots.txt* file is:

```
User-Agent:  *                # Applies to all robots
Disallow:    /localweb/docs/  # local web documents -- do not index
Disallow:    /tmp/            # Temporary Files -- do not index
```

which tells *all* Web robots that they should avoid the indicated directories.

Web Indexing and Search Tools

Important Reference Sites

```
http://calafia.com/webmasters/
http://www.unn.ac.uk/features.htm
http://www.hamline.edu/library/links/comparisons.html
http://www.yahoo.com/Computers_and_Internet/Internet/World_Wide_Web/Searching_the_Web/Search_Engines/
```

One common demand is for a Web index—after all, it is fine knowing that there is useful information out there, and quite another actually trying to find it. A growing number of tools have been developed to address this issue. These tools provide mechanisms (most are robots, in the sense described in the previous section) for indexing document collections, and for making these indexes accessible over the Web. In some cases, these tools have been used to provide global Web indexes (such as the Lycos search engine, at `http://www.lycos.com`), but they are often also appropriate for indexing local collections. For example, these tools could be used to index all servers at a particular company, to provide a local, searchable index of corporate Web resources.

ALIWeb

```
http://web.nexor.co.uk/public/aliweb/doc/introduction.html
```

ALIWeb is a Web indexing tool that indexes only those sites that wish to be indexed. If a site wishes to be indexed by ALIWeb, the site administrator contacts the ALIWeb server, and registers his or her site with the ALIWeb system, using a **FORM** interface. In addition, the site administrator must construct a specially formatted index file for his or her site, and place this in a location accessible to ALIWeb.

AltaVista

```
http://altavista.digital.com
http://altavista.software.digital.com/
```

The AltaVista database system, a product of Digital Equipment Corp., has become one of the most popular search tools on the Internet, as the database is both fast and flexible. The

AltaVista software is also available for commercial use, to index private or local webs, or to index material on personal work-stations.

Excite

```
http://www.excite.com
http://www.excite.com/navigate/home.html
```

Excite is a combination database and Web indexing system that is reputedly both fast and accurate—this is the database system currently used to index the Netscape Web site. An important component of Excite is its *concept-based* technology, which supposedly allows searches on concepts as opposed to keywords. Excite also provides Web server software that lets a Web server administrator index server content.

Harvest

```
http://harvest.cs.colorado.edu/harvest/
```

Harvest, a product of the Internet Research Task Force Research Group on Resource Discovery (IRTF-RD) based at the University of Colorado at Boulder, is a collection of tools for gathering, organizing, and indexing resources, combined with utilities that allow this information to be replicated and distributed amongst a number of different sites. Harvest contains a number of conceptual improvements upon previous Web indexing tools, and is the tool of choice for those experimenting with Web indexing issues. There is even a Harvest newsgroup: *comp.infosystems.harvest.*

Infoseek

```
http://www.infoseek.com
```

Infoseek provides one of the large searchable Web indexes, available at the URL listed. Infoseek also sells Iseek, a tool that adds database management components to the Windows 95 or Macintosh desktop, and that lets individuals do Web (Infoseek, of course) searches without launching a Web browser.

Inktomi

```
http://inktomi.berkeley.edu
http://www.hotbot.com
```

Inktomi is an experimental, scalable Web server/database system built using the HotBot database system (the same database that powers the HotWired Web site database).

Lycos

```
http://lycos.cs.cmu.edu/
```

The Lycos indexing system, now a commercial product of the Computer Science faculty of Carnegie-Mellon University, utilizes a Web robot that wanders the Web and retrieves documents, which are subsequently indexed by the Lycos search engine.

OpenText

http://www.opentext.com

OpenText Corp. is a provider of a wide variety of database and Web tools, including the famous OpenText index, which is one of the more complete indexes of the World Wide Web. OpenText provides full-text indexing database tools for indexing and managing Web sites, both as stand-alone packages, and as components of their *LiveLink* Intranet suite.

The WWW Worm

http://wwww.cs.colorado.edu/wwww

The World Wide Web Worm, developed by Oliver McBryan of the University of Colorado at Boulder, is one of the oldest of the Web indexing systems. The WWWW uses a Web-wandering robot that autonomously extracts and indexes Web documents, but it also allows users to register their own URLs using a fill-in **FORM**.

Intranet Suites

Important Reference Sites

http://www.yahoo.com/Computers_and_Internet/Communications_and_Networking/Intranet/
http://www.lochnet.com/client/smart/intranet.htm
http://www.infoweb.com.au/intralnk.htm
http://www.brill.com/intranet/

Intranet is probably the most overblown word of the mid 1990s. All it really means is the use of Internet- and Web-based technologies in the support of business operations, but this simple concept has grown into an efficiency mantra that defies rational thought. In actual use the phrase *Intranet software* can imply just about anything—from the simplest HTML editor to the most sophisticated database management systems.

Intranet suites reflect efforts by software developers to develop a collection of generic tools that can be adapted to most business needs. The components usually include document management, access control, indexing and search capabilities, workflow monitoring, messaging (mail or other), and groupware. Of course, not all packages support all these features, while at the same time not all these features are needed—or wanted—in all workplaces.

If you are looking for Intranet tools, you should first research the issues involved—the URLs given above provide useful links to (largely) unbiased discussions. Table 11.1 lists some of the current companies selling Intranet suites, with URLs corresponding to their product. This list is of course incomplete, so you should complement it by using the listed references at the beginning of this section.

Browsers, Servers, Editors, and Translators

Of course, there are lots of other resources Web developers need to know about, from browsers and servers to HTML editors, editing systems, document format translators, and converters. But, there is only so much

Table 11.1 Companies Providing Intranet Software Suites

Attachmate *OpenMind*	`http://www.attachmate.com/prodserv/nas/openmind/dscs-1.htm`
Fulcrum Technologies	`http://www.fulcrum.com`
Hummingbird *Columbus*	`http://columbus.hummingbird.com/`
Lotus *Notes*	`http://www.lotus.com`
Mustang *Wildcat*	`http://www.mustang.com/public/products/wc5main.htm`
Netscape/Collabra *Share*	`http://www.collabra.com/`
OpenText *LiveLink*	`http://www.opentext.com/livelink/`
Radnet *Webshare*	`http://www.radnet.com/products/products.html`
Speedware *Dallas*	`http://dallas.speedware.com`

room in one book, and this book is too big as it is! Therefore, this third edition does not contain details on these software components. Instead, you are referred to the following URL references, which provide information on these rapidly changing topics.

Web Browsers

```
http://www.utoronto.ca/webdocs/HTMLdocs/
http://www.yahoo.com/Computers_and_Internet/Internet/World_Wide_Web/Browsers/
http://www.w3.org/pub/WWW/Clients.html
http://www.webtrends.com/                                    (Browser usage surveys)
```

HTTP Servers

```
http://serverwatch.iworld.com/
http://webcompare.iworld.com/
http://www.yahoo.com/Computers_and_Internet/Internet/World_Wide_Web/Servers/
http://www.webtrends.com/                                    (Server usage surveys)
```

HTML Editors and Editing Systems

```
http://www.utoronto.ca/webdocs/HTMLdocs/
http://www.yahoo.com/Computers_and_Internet/Internet/World_Wide_Web/HTML_Editors/
http://www.w3.org/pub/WWW/Tools/
http://union.ncsa.uiuc.edu/HyperNews/get/www/html/editors.html
http://xenios.qldnet.com.au/thorby/thedi.htm
```

HTML Translators and Converters

```
http://www.yahoo.com/Computers_and_Internet/Internet/World_Wide_Web/HTML_Converters/
http://www.yahoo.com/Business_and_Economy/Companies/Computers/Software/Internet/
        Shareware/HTML_Converters/
http://union.ncsa.uiuc.edu/HyperNews/get/www/html/converters.html
ftp://src.doc.ic.ac.uk/computing/information-systems/www/tools/translators/
http://www.w3.org/pub/WWW/Tools/
http://www.utoronto.ca/webdocs/HTMLdocs/
```

Designing Web Sites
Ian Graham and Kelly Peters

Now that you've mastered the technical details of the Web and HTML, a basic question remains unanswered—how do you actually put together a successful Web site? Whether creating a Web site with hundreds of pages or only a few dozen, there are several fundamental steps. These steps are not trivial, and take planning, knowledge, and experience. You should therefore be generous with your time lines in the planning process, particularly if this is your first time designing a large collection.

The chapter is divided into seven main sections. The first three cover the initial phases of site design and implementation: planning objectives, designing site layout, and determining a site image. Sections 4 through 6 cover the issues involved in implementing and managing the site, developing the content, site launch and maintenance, and site promotion. Finally, the seventh section takes a last look at HTML, and at some of the features you can use to create distinctive designs with a professional look and strong visual appeal.

Planning

When planning a Web site, you must first determine your goal(s) and your audience. Both parameters strongly affect the content that is of highest priority for your site, while the second plays an important role in determining an appropriate site style—obviously, material assembled to provide on-line support to sales representatives will be different from material presented for a teenage e-zine!

Fear of Falling Behind?

Some companies develop Web sites simply because they fear not being "with it" relative to their competitors or colleagues. A president of an advertising agency told one of this chapter's authors that many of his agency's executive clients wanted to be on the Web simply to be able to brag, on the golf course, that their company was "on" the Internet!

For site designers, this type of situation can bring a host problems. Whenever a company does not have a clear reason for going on-line, there will be no real site plans, which can lead to ill-thought-out designs and dysfunctional content. Whatever the reason for choosing to be on the Web, a site must look professional and reflect well upon an organization.

If, in the planning process, the client cannot determine any site goals, then the best approach is to develop a small site that does not contain many documents or involve ambitious programming. Recall (or remind the client responsible for establishing the site) that a site can grow as the organization acquires the personnel and skills to develop more content, and as the purpose and need becomes more apparent.

Determine Site Goals

The first step is to determine your (or your client's) objectives. Sometimes you or your client may want a site, but not yet know the objective—in this case, you must initially spend time determining what you want to accomplish. As a general guide, Web sites (including intranets) fit into the broad categories of marketing/promotion, customer/member support, content-based advertising, and on-line sales/purchasing. To help you determine where your site fits in this scheme, the following sections describe these different types, and outline some features commonly found at such sites. Note that a site often has more than one purpose. This should be determined at this initial planning stage, and integrated into the plan when preparing the site design.

1. Marketing and/or Promotion

Marketing and/or promotional Web sites are usually designed to complement existing advertising strategies, campaigns, and corporate identity. Whether designed for a business or a nonprofit organization, a Web site provides a unique opportunity to reach a large audience, and has great potential as a promotional tool.

Content and presentation quality are critical to making a strong impact on customers. Unlike purely information-driven sites, where the *content* attracts and keeps the users, an advertising/marketing site is largely driven by look and feel, and by the presentation of appropriate marketing information. You must assume that people who have sought out your site expect relevant material suited their needs. A visitor may be an existing client wanting a better understanding of products and services, or may be a prospective buyer just discovering your company. So—find out what they want to know, and provide this information!

You must also design content tailored for the Web; you cannot simply turn your Web site into a digital version of print brochures or videos. Michael Strangelove, publisher of the Internet Business Journal, has described how an early effort by MCI "...takes a mediocre 60-second TV commercial and transforms it into a painful 30-minute on-line experience."[*] You must avoid this type of error at all costs.

Interactivity can be a key component of a marketing or promotional Web site. The Web is the first truly interactive medium, and gives you the opportunity to feature your product or service and solicit immediate reader response. Thus, the Web is an ideal venue for on-line promotions such as sweepstakes, contests, and coupons—these can be used to attract readers, collect information about readers, and promote client loyalty.

2. Member or Customer Support

A Web site can be a strong member or customer support tool, because of the possible increased efficiency in soliciting and responding to readers' queries. Such sites are usually information-driven, offering a comprehensive volume of product or service-related information to site visitors. You can also establish direct channels of communication between visitors and members of your organization responsible for particular products, thereby enhancing your relationship with your customers.

Consequently, important site components to consider are: on-line documentation, manuals, or FAQ (frequently asked questions) lists; a searchable database of these documents; a newsletter that updates and complements material in your print publications; news forums or e-mail address lists to allow communication between members and staff; press releases distributed through the Web; and a list of other Web resources useful to your clients.

This model is particularly relevant to intranets; such sites can serve as a support tool for sales representatives, customer service agents, and others. For example, an on-line searchable database of product information could be quickly accessed by phone sales representatives, allowing them to respond quickly to customer phone queries. Similarly, the site could contain marketing information for various company products, to be accessed by sales representatives preparing to visit a prospective client. The site could even contain information describing sales

---

[*]Internet World, May 1995

approaches, or selling features that have worked well in the past. Within a large intranet, there may be several such marketing sites, each focused on different products and services.

In terms of design, you want the site to look good, but you do not want a design that interferes with the basic purpose—providing information to customers. Thus the site design must be kept simple and functional.

3. Content-Based Advertising-Driven Sites

Many commercial sites, such as HotWired (http://www.hotwired.com), Word (http://www.word.com), Swoon (http://www.swoon.com), Slate (http://www.slate.com), and CANOE (http://www.canoe.ca), are content-based sites supported (or at least motivated) by advertising dollars. The goal of such sites is to generate high visitor traffic, in order to sell advertising space. The design of such a site varies, depending on the site's purpose; in all cases, the content must be entirely different from that of video or print—existing print content cannot simply be "dumped" onto the Web. The site must be continuously updated—this makes it timely, and makes visitors want to return. Other important features include interactive tools, such as chat services and contests, search tools, and content databases, the latter particularly for large sites.

Such sites are driven both by image and content, where image is the initial attraction, and content—continuously updated—elicits users' return. This is often the most expensive type of site, as it requires heavy investment in every aspect of design and maintenance.

An example of a content-based site is the Chatelaine Web site at http://www.canoe.ca/Chatelaine/home.html. *Chatelaine*, a Canadian women's magazine, designed this site to be a value-added resource for print magazine readers. The site developers felt that an invitation to *Chatelaine* readers might be one of the few such invitations specifically directed at women new to the Web, so they filled the site with friendly, introductory Web information, such as an "Internet 101" tutorial, and reviews of Web sites likely to be of interest to *Chatelaine*'s women readers. They also explicitly chose a design structure that was easy to navigate, and that established a distinctive identity.

4. On-line Sales

The Web lets any organization achieve economies of scale, and lets even the smallest company present an effective, international presence. A company that takes the time to develop a strong Internet presence can be well ahead of their competitors and, on occasion, ahead of much larger companies. An example is CDNow (http://www.cdnow.com), a Web site that began as a small on-line CD record store, and that now also markets videos, tee shirts, and other products. Some of the services offered by this site and typical of sales sites include a searchable catalog of records and videos, on-line audio previews of popular records, on-line purchasing, and a variety of on line transaction tools for paying for your purchase. Members of the site support staff are also extremely quick to respond to customer e-mail queries, which helps them build a loyal customer base.

A true on-line sales site requires good design, but most important, requires simple and easy access to product information, and easy-to-use shopping and purchasing tools. Thus, this type of site will require database connectivity (to the product database), transaction processing support (for on-line purchases), and special mail systems for prompt handling of customer queries. Much of the cost of such as site will be in software development, or in the purchase of software specifically designed for these tasks.

Of course, a site need not start out with all these components—certainly, CDNow has grown over time, adding resources and services as the tools to do so became available, and as the markets became possible. If you are planning an on-line sales site, you too can start with an small subset of on-line resources, and slowly build the site as your experience and customer base grows. Forrester Research Inc. (http://www.forrester.com), an international marketing research firm, has been quoted many times saying that the number of Internet users will increase dramatically by the year 2000—this represents an enormous, and yet untapped, market.

Competitive Analysis

Given a goal for your site, the next step is to analyze competitors' Web sites—chances are, they are already on the Web—and to then use this information to your advantage. Reviewing the sites of competitors (or even non-competitors) is an effective way to evaluate how this new medium is being employed in your industry. Research what types of "bells and whistles" they are employing—for example, interactive games, live chats, searchable databases, dynamically updated content, and other applications—and decide if these are useful features. You can then incorporate the most appropriate ideas into your design.

Keeping up with the competition is a continuous process. You must continue to monitor your competitors' (and other) sites for new ideas, while to keep your site fresh, you must work continually to update it and add new content. Note that this implies a significant ongoing commitment to a trained technical staff (Web manager, graphics designers, programmers, systems manager, content developers). In some cases, it may make sense to contract out this process.

Demographics

The third step is to identify your target audience, and to identify ways to appeal to this demographic group. As in any well-planned promotional strategy, you must understand who your clients are: their age, income level, profession, gender, educational level, and so on. A good start is to compare your target with demographic reports about Web users. Standard research companies, such as A.C. Nielsen, provide this information for a fee, while there are several Web sites that provide similar information free of charge. Several sites and organizations worth visiting are listed in the references section at the end of the chapter.

Analyzing the Target Group

Does your target group fit within the demographics of Web users? If you are targeting women, for example, you must recognize that 80 percent of today's users are male, and the number of sites targeting women users is small. However, you can use this statistic to your advantage, by staging your site to capture the attention of a large part of this underserviced group.

You should also use your knowledge of the target group as a guide in your page layout and design choices. For example, if you want to appeal to a younger audience, you can use flashy graphics or interactive components. If, on the other hand, you are addressing an older audience, then a more traditional approach is probably in order.

Laying Out the Site

Once clear on the objectives of the site, you can start the design and construction. There are essentially four stages in this process, summarized in the following sections. The first step is to list all items you want to include in the site, after which you must take these items and organize them into categories. The next step is to *storyboard* the site—create a schematic diagram of the site organization, to test and refine the design. At the same time as this is happening, you should be costing the various components proposed for the site. You can later choose to defer some components, should the costs be too high or should certain items be deemed secondary to the main goals.

Choosing the Content

As a first step, make a list of all the items you want to include. Consider every possible component—even items you will not put up in the first version, but that could be part of a future revision. By considering future expansion now, you can incorporate the required structure at the beginning, and allow for a much smoother evolution of the site. A list might include the following items: masthead, what's new section, site index, press releases, feedback, job opportunities, FAQ (frequently asked questions) lists, and staff profiles. Include also technical features such as search engines, customer survey questionnaires, and order forms, as well as supporting material such as help pages.

Sorting the Items into Topical Categories

Once you've created a complete list, sort the items into categories, putting related material together—these categories will become the navigational pages in the site. Identify the categories with working titles, and organize the content accordingly—note that some items may belong in more than one category. Don't worry if the categories seem to group into more than one main audience category, as you can create different paths in your Web site for these different audiences—this will be planned when creating the site *storyboard*. For now, if you have categories that are relevant to different, specific audiences, treat them as if they were two distinct Web sites.

If your site has roughly more than seven to ten categories, it is time to create subcategories. In doing so, you must now distinguish the *levels* of content. The main page or the site (or possibly main pages, if you follow the strategy discussed later) is then a level 1 page, while level 2 pages are those below the home page, and refer to the first level of categories. Subcategory pages are then at level 3, and so on. However, as discussed in Chapter 3, a site with too many levels may be difficult for readers to navigate. Keep this in mind when developing your navigation strategy, and try to use as few levels as possible.

Estimating Site Costs

Up to this point, the costs involved in developing the site will still be rather modest (provided you have been able to do this for yourself). However, the Web site plan may call for components that will involve substantial costs or programming expertise, such as search tools for site content, feedback forms, database interfaces to product information, and so on. It is now important to obtain cost estimates for these components and to determine which components can be designed by your existing staff. Later, as you actually begin to lay out the final site design, you can omit those components that are deemed too expensive, or too complicated. Note, however, that the initial site storyboards should be developed assuming the existence of all the proposed components—the extra components can always be dropped from the implemented design, and included sometime in the future.

You must also decide and cost how you will physically establish the site—will you run your own Web server and manage the computers yourself, or will you contract service from a service provider, or from a company specializing in managing Web sites? This is a good time to investigate these options, as these the costs can vary enormously depending on a site's requirements, both in terms of content and content-based resources (search engines, databases, etc.) and the expected number of accesses of your server.

If you do decide to manage your own server, then you will also need to lease a connection to the Internet. These costs can also be very high, since a site's speed is determined by the speed of the connection—and fast connections are very expensive. In general, if your site does not anticipate heavy usage, then you are best advised to pool your resources with other companies—one option is to set up shop in an Internet "cybermall," where the costs of managing the computers and maintaining the Internet connection are shared amongst the mall subscribers.

Preparing the Storyboard

At this stage you are ready to prepare the site *storyboard*. This critical phase lets you inexpensively try out site structures and layouts without coding a single HTML document. Storyboarding consists of creating a graphical layout (similar to flowcharting) of your Web site. The graphical layout should show:

- The location of all the categories and associated content

- The layering of each category

- The navigational paths for the user

- The location/type of the "front door" or home page

- The location of hypertext links, Java applets, or multimedia content

  Each of these elements is explained in greater detail in the sections that follow.

A storyboard will look similar to Figures 3.3, 3.6, and 3.9, but will also contain text to indicate the content of the different pages, and the reasons for the layout. Arrows, lines, and other symbols can be used to indicate major navigational links, and to show the relationships between the pages.

By looking through the storyboard and "walking through" the site, you can quickly find difficult-to-navigate regions, or parts that simply do not function as intended. A well-planned storyboard will help you see problems ahead of time, and will help you avoid unnecessary changes down the road.

Storyboarding and Content

In general, the main categories and subcategories determined at the initial content-analysis phase will lead to the first few pages—including the home page—of your Web site. Your goal in this planning should be to make the most important content accessible after only three clicks—people should be able to move from a home page to a second-level page and right into content. Storyboarding provides you with an opportunity to visualize the flow of movement through the pages, and see ways to guide visitors to content, and to keep them from getting lost. For example, you may choose to have a linear structure within certain levels of your site, use a *flash page* to highlight a certain aspect of your site, stick to the practical *chunking* of content, or rely on a mix of content and navigational links on your home page.

Categories and the Home Page: Chunking

Once you've determined the categories and subcategories, you may feel that the content is well organized as a list of links on the home page. There are many schools of thought as to the best way to organize home page links. Many designers follow a principle called *chunking*—that is, they organize material into small, logical sections. This approach is based on the work of cognitive psychologists, who have shown that people are best able to remember unrehearsed lists containing no more than seven items. Designers following this approach to create home pages having a small number of links, carefully chosen to represent the broad categories of information at the site and to give a strong sense of the site content. The level 2 pages then provide the details of the content, and additional choices.

Categories and Multiple Front Doors

If you have a range of content that targets more than one audience, it is now time to consider using more than one home page. For example, on a recent project, one of us conducted a survey of a major automotive Web site. The main problem found with the site was its attempt to respond, from a single home page, to many different audiences. The home page provided links for customers looking for vehicle-related information and information on customer-related financial services. However, the home page also referenced stockholder and corporate information—links entirely irrelevant to people shopping for cars. Content that does not address the needs of the target population should not be present on the home page.

So, what can you do if the population is varied? Content relevant to a distinct group can be organized below a second home page—that is, you can create a second "front door" to the site specifically designed for that content. At the content level, these two sites can overlap; you can link to some of the same pages from different "front doors," as illustrated in Figure 3.14. For example, you can create a home page for investors, and from there create links to the other areas of the site to let investors find out about company products and services.

How Many Home Page Links?

Another school of thought believes that the home page should contain many links, the argument being that the more links you offer to readers, the more opportunities you have to draw them into the site content. Indeed, it is true that resources accessible directly from a home page are accessed much more often than those available only from secondary pages. However, the home page must still function as the main navigational page, and must provide the user with a table of contents or menu for locating material on the site.

At CANOE (`http://www.canoe.ca`), it was decided that the home page should contain both links to the main navigational sections of the site and links to specific content that the administrators wish to promote. These non-navigational links are changed on a regular basis, providing the kind of dynamic page content that helps to make a site successful.

Making an Entrance—Entry Tunnels and Flash Pages

We discussed earlier how a home page contains either a carefully chunked list of up to seven links, or multiple links that mix both content and navigation elements. This page can also be preceded by an *entrance* or *entry tunnel*. A entry tunnel, as advocated by Dave Siegel in his book *Creating Killer Web Sites*, is a linear collection of Web pages that exists at the beginning of a Web site—the user clicks through the tunnel pages, until finally arriving at the "real" home page. Siegel argues that an entry tunnel "...help[s] build anticipation as people approach the heart of the site. An entry tunnel uses a game or some other device to hook the viewer." An entry tunnel can be enticing, if well designed and fast to traverse. On the downside, readers may become frustrated wading through these preliminary pages prior to arriving at the real content. There is, however, more forgiveness for this type of effect when the purpose of the site is marketing rather than content delivery. Siegel makes clear the importance of providing a direct link to the home page from the pages in the tunnel, so that the site does not frustrate repeat visitors who wish to bypass the tunnel.

A slightly different approach is a *flash page*—this is a page that appears for only a few seconds, to be replaced by the regular home page. Such a page is easily created using the client-pull technique outlined in Chapter 9. To be effective, a flash page must be very small (so that it loads quickly), and must be changed regularly so as not to bore the readers. It should also contain a "real" link to the home page, to account for browsers that do not support client-pull.

Figure 12.1 shows a typical storyboard for a site where the lead-in is a flash page or entry tunnel (structurally, the two look the same). The flash pages/entry tunnel are grayed out, to show that the content is dynamic and variable. The URLs corresponding to the associated pages are shown on the left.

Flash pages can also separate a home page from the site content. In this model, a link from the home page is followed by a flash page, which quickly disappears to be replaced by the actual content. This is commonly implemented on advertising-driven sites, and is used to showcase a particular advertiser before the story page downloads.

Navigational Design

Given a basic layout, the next step is to develop a navigation scheme—where do you want navigational links to go, and how do you want to express these links on the page? Most likely

Figure 12.1 Storyboard illustration of a Web site with an entrance tunnel or flash page entrance. The entry pages are grayed out to make them stand out from the regular documents.

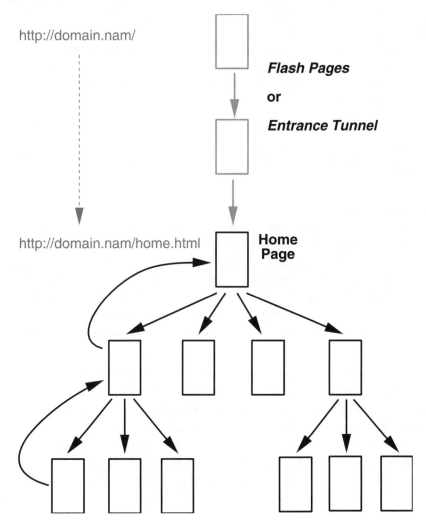

you will want a *navigation toolbar*—a series of icons linked to key areas of the site. For ease of use, the bar should contain no more than seven links, and should be consistently available on *every* page. Recall that visitors may actually start at any page on your site, perhaps arriving there from a Web search engine such as Yahoo or AltaVista, or using your site's own search engine. In these cases, the navigation bar is the only way the user will know how to link to other sections of the site.

There are two kinds of navigation links: global and local. Global navigation provides links to the key areas in the site, including the home page and perhaps the second-level pages, and allows users to move quickly to the main navigational components of the site. By contrast, local navigation provides readers with a second set of links that allows them to move around within the given section. This might include links to the previous page or to the next one, or to related topics in other parts of the site. Usually these two navigational tools should be presented slightly differently, to keep their different natures clear.

Navigational toolbars are one of the tools that help visitors determine their location within a site. The only other such tool is the site's page layout and design. As described in Chapter 3, page layout can distinguish pages in different sections, while a unified design theme can make the pages seem part of a unified whole.

Java or Multimedia Content?

Finally, you may wish to include complicated page components, such as JavaScript programs, Java applets, VRML world views, or multimedia plug-ins (Macromedia Shockwave, etc.). These components can add richness to your site, but at a cost: In most cases they only work on a restricted set of browsers (Navigator and Internet Explorer, for example), or require powerful computers and system software to be effective (Pentium processors, Windows 95/NT or equivalent). Also, these components may involve large files, that can be very slow to download. As a result, documents containing these components can act as an impediment to the effective use of other site content.

You should first determine if a given component is necessary for basic functionality—if it is (for example, if it's a Java-database interface), then you'd better include it! For non-critical components, you should develop prototype versions, and then test them using equipment and connections similar to those available to your clientele. For example, if most of your customers are at remote locations or use dial-in connections, use a slow Internet connection to test pages containing these special components. If you find that an added feature makes the pages slow and cumbersome, you may want to modify the component to decrease its download size, or remove it altogether.

Multiple Versions of a Site

A second alternative is to create two parallel collections of pages—one set contains all the extra Java or other features, while the other is more restrained. Many sites now support this structure, with links from the home page to a "text only" or "Java-enabled" document collection. This lets the users choose the version most useful to them. However, this also increases the number of pages you will have to maintain.

Page Design—Developing a Site Image

Given a plan for the site and for the location of content, it is time to decide how the pages will be designed. Although content is the heart of a Web site, imagery is important for making a strong impression about a site's content and quality. A professional image will help ensure success, while an amateurish one will guarantee failure. You can give a Web site character through the creative use of graphics, and through careful choices of typography and page design.

To establish a design, you must first return to your demographic analysis, and determine who will actually be visiting your site. For example, if you represent a conservative organization or appeal to a conservative audience, then this character should be reflected in the typography and style. It is critically important to retain a sense of who your visitors are, so that you don't create a site full of whiz-bang technology or graphic layouts unsuitable to your audience.

User sophistication with the Internet, also ascertainable from your demographic analysis, will also affect a site's overall design. If the site is being designed for new Web users, then the layout and links will need to be more straightforward—new users often complain that they aren't even sure what a link is! You can help novice users feel comfortable by using explicit "Click here" copy (e.g., "Click here to visit the..."), simple page designs, and graphical navigational links that clearly look like buttons.

Once you have identified the design parameters, it is time to choose a site metaphor. This will lead to a presentation style, which must then be used consistently across the entire site. For example, *Chatelaine* magazine wanted a theme based on the concept of "connection"; as a result, puzzle pieces were chosen as the graphical metaphor, and were incorporated into the navigation toolbars, banners, and home page icons. An example page from this collection is shown in Figures 12.4 and 12.5.

Imagery is not all show—it is also useful for providing a sense of place in the collection. The site as a whole should always have a consistent look, but giving individual sections customized features, such as different background colors or their own unique graphical elements, helps to distinguish one section from another.

Additionally, you must be sure that your design includes all the required page elements. For example, if your pages will contain advertisements, you must allocate space for these images. Similarly, you may be considering advanced features such as Java applets, multimedia components, or VRML. Make sure also to leave room on the pages for these components.

Finally, you must allow for copyright or credit statements, feedback buttons, and navigation bars. And, of course, there must be some room for the actual content!

Test and Prototype the Design

Once you have a design, you must build a few prototype pages and test them on a variety of browsers likely to be used by site visitors. For an intranet, this may be an easy task—should everyone be using the same browser. If you are not designing such an intranet, then you will probably want to test your document design using Internet Explorer, Netscape Navigator, and perhaps some of the commercial versions of Mosaic. In this process, you are checking for the proper functioning of the pages and the page layout, and for consistent quality of the graphics across a variety of computer displays. You must also decide on a page and graphic width for documents on the site. For example, on a 640-by-480-pixel display, the Netscape Navigator browser produces a window 600 pixels wide on an IBM PC, but only 585 pixels wide on a Macintosh. This is a small space, and unfortunately represents the displays used by most of your visitors. It is thus a good idea to design pages that work well on these small displays.

Usually you will go through several prototypes for the page designs, as you work through various graphics options, text layouts and styles, and overall site themes. However, this is well worth the effort, as it is far more difficult to update the entire layout of an existing site than it is to try out new ideas on this small prototype collection.

Develop a Style Guide

It is important that the image of a site be consistent. Once a desired page design has been determined, you must turn this into a content-preparation style guide and mandate the use of this guide in the preparation of all site content. For example, if you decide to use centered headlines, then be sure that this is done on all pages. You should also determine the size and style of headlines, bylines, or any other text that is to appear on all pages. You can also prepare template documents using this design style, and distribute this to your authors. This saves them time in authoring the pages, and also helps preserve a site's look and feel.

Cost of Page Prototypes

Setting up page prototypes requires an experienced HTML page designer plus a graphics design person familiar with the limitations of the Web, and can take from a week to month. Properly prototyping requires several example pages representing the basic navigational structure of the collection, plus some exemplary content. It is important to maintain strong lines of communication between the designers and site managers, as prototyping can go through several iterations before arriving at a satisfactory design. In general, better communication between designers and managers leads to faster prototyping, at a lower cost.

Developing Content

Of course, the king of the Web is content—and at this point a site developer is ready to start creating the content and build the Web site. However, there is still one more stage you need to go through—determining what is actually possible, given the available budget and resources.

Controlling Web Site Costs—Trimming the Tree

Creating good Web content takes time, effort, and money. Moreover, these are ongoing costs, as Web content needs to be constantly updated and improved. Site developers must be extremely careful not to tackle more than they can handle. The start-up costs for a Web site are often comparable to the ongoing cost of site maintenance and updating—you should not think that costs will drop once the site is up and running.

It is critically important that the site not contain more content than can be properly maintained. Expired or out-of-date content will leave a stale impression, and will not encourage return visits. On the Web, content and image have an extremely short life cycle, and must be updated regularly to give a site a true feeling of freshness and dynamism.

If you followed the plan outlined in this chapter, you should by now have estimates for the costs of many of the proposed site components. This is the time to look over the storyboard, estimate the costs of these components, and start removing those that are expensive and/or secondary to the site's main purpose. This procedure should be repeated until the cost of the site is within the allocated budget.

Preparing Content—Adapting Other Media

A Web site often contains material brought in from another medium, such as print or video. What is not always apparent is that modifying this for the Web requires an almost complete retooling of the content, which can be quite expensive. Failing to do so will lead to Web-disasters, such as the MCI example mentioned at the beginning of this chapter. You must design all content to use the page layout model created as part of the site design, and also to take advantage of the hypertext approach of the Web—the site must present readers with choices, and present content in a Web-appropriate way.

Testing, Launch, and Maintenance

With content developed and in place, you are *almost* ready to launch the site and invite the world to see your work. First, however, you must test it vigorously. A common approach is to use a *soft launch*. With a soft launch, you put the Web site on the server—but don't tell anybody about it, other than a few select site testers. This gives you the chance to test the site, and identify the problems or confusing features. You can then resolve these issues before the official launch. This is a good time to test the site with different browsers and slow connections, and to test any special functional components, such as search indexes, user input forms, or product sales tools.

For an intranet, the equivalent to a soft launch is *site testing*. In general, an intranet is designed to aid in the business process, and in the site testing stage you can bring the system into use on a small scale and find out if it satisfies that goal. This is also an opportunity to test your training package (you didn't expect your staff to figure the new system out on their own, did you?) and to modify/update/correct the material based on user feedback.

If your site uses access control or secure transactions technology, this is also the time to test these systems. You will of course need to test these continually, but a first round of tests before site launch can quickly shake out major problems that may have been overlooked when moving the site on-line.

You should also *exercise* your site—that is, you should test your site's performance under heavy loads. A small number of users will find logical problems with the site, but only a large number can test how the site will perform when heavily accessed. It is not hard to write (or obtain over the Web) small programs that simulate multiple, rapid requests of documents from your server. Problems often crop up that were not apparent at low usage levels—for example, a particular search program may suddenly become unacceptably slow because it is able to process only one request at a time. It is far better to fix these problems in the testing phase than later, when the unanswered requests inconvenience real users.

Finally, you should check all the documents for faulty links, both links between documents in your collection and links to external resources—nothing makes a site look worse than a collection of broken hypertext links or pages with "missing" embedded images.

Now you are ready to formally launch the service.

Planning for Long-Term Maintenance

All Web sites are transient to some degree, with new material being added and old material moved or eliminated. As a general rule, a marketing or sales-oriented site should be prepared to update pages on a daily bases, with a goal of updating the entire site every few months. Remember that the only thing bringing back visitors is new material, so there must be a heavy investment in creating this new content. At the same time, old content must be archived or removed—if your site is running a contest, the contest material had better be updated or removed after the contest expires, or you will look very foolish.

Maintenance also means keeping up with the changing technologies of the Internet. Your image may be tied in with using the latest applications, so you must know about these applications, and be prepared to integrate them into your site. It is often a real challenge to keep up with all these changes!

This is not necessarily the case for content-driven sites such as customer support facilities. Here the only important feature is the accuracy and timeliness of the data—it doesn't matter how old the product information document is, provided the information it contains is correct. Here, accuracy is the key—your users know that you can, in principle, instantly update the Web site to reflect new announcements or information—and they will expect you to do just that.

Public and Developmental Webs

In general, it is best to do maintenance work on a copy of the actual public Web site. In this way, mistakes are not visible to the public. This "private" web should be accessible only to internal development staff, so that you can play with the content without worrying about site visitors. Once the pages have been updated or corrected, they can be copied into the "real" Web site and made public. You should do so, however, in a reversible manner—something can always go wrong, in which case you need to be able to back off the change and return to the previous working version.

Site Monitoring

In addition to checking hypertext links, you will also want to monitor, on average, how visitors *use* your site. There are many server log analysis tools, many mentioned in Chapter 11, that can provide this information. This, combined with user e-mail feedback, provides much information useful for improving the site. Usage patterns will tell you those portions of the site that are in demand and those that are not, and will help you redesign the site to make material more accessible. User feedback will tell you what your users are thinking, and what they want, and also how they are navigating through the material.

Promotion

When launching a Web site, it is important to prepare a complete publicity package. For example, you will want to include the site URL in all the traditional communication channels, from print materials such as letterhead, fax cover sheets, and business cards, to radio and television advertising.

You also want to promote your site using explicit Web-based electronic media. The first thing to do is to register your site on the various Web search engines, such as Lycos, AltaVista, and OpenText, as well as at site meta-indexes, such as Yahoo and WebCrawler. if you do not do so, then you site will be inaccessible from these important information indices.

You should also submit your site to the many "best of the Web" services—their role may be dubious, but being listed by such a service helps to build momentum for your site.

Finally, and interestingly, word-of-mouth is still one of the most important factors in promoting a site—if someone likes your site and includes a link to your site in his or her Web documents, you are guaranteed a few extra visits.

How can you build these promotional contacts? One way is to locate users who already have links to your competitors' Web sites—they will likely also be interested in your content. You can locate such people by doing a reverse lookup of competitors' sites, using the AltaVista search engine `http://altavista.digital.com` (see the AltaVista help information for details), and can then write these people to tell them about your site, and to ask them to add a link to your site as well. But be polite, as the culture of the Web frowns on mass mailings and persistent e-mail marketing, and you are guaranteed to gain nothing but bad publicity should you choose that approach.

Launching an Intranet

If launching an intranet, the issues are similar, although the marketing package is different. In this case, you need to provide printed and electronic text to each user, explaining the organization of the new intranet, and where information can be found. For complex Web applications, you will also need to provide training sessions, as well as proper manuals and documentation.

Using HTML to Design Site Character

This final section examines some advanced HTML layout mechanisms commonly used to create professional signature documents. The example pages come from the CANOE (**CAN**adian **O**nline **E**xplorer) Web site, at `http://www.canoe.ca`. In particular, several are from the *Chatelaine* magazine site, mentioned previously in this chapter. The URL for Chatelaine is:

`http://www.canoe.ca/Chatelaine/`

What about Frames?

You will note that none of the examples given here use the frame mechanism to construct multi-framed documents. In our experience, frames are not useful for content-specific Web sites, for two main reasons: because they tend to disorient readers, who get lost navigating through the frames, and because they disable browser bookmarking, since users can only bookmark the first frame document they see, and not a specific frame.

Frames *are* useful when designing documents that are interfaces to specific software tools, such as search indices, complex help manuals, or database applications. In these cases, the content of the individual frames is far less important than the total interface presented by the collection of frames.

One particularly effective option is the use of multiple browser *windows*, as opposed to multiple frames within the same window. This is done, for example, at the Yahoo Web site (`http://www.yahoo.com`), where the home page button labeled "Yahoo Remote" produces a second, smaller Netscape window containing a shortcut navigation and site searching tool (illustrated in Figure 12.2). This second window lets users quickly search the site, while the main window lets users pursue a standard hierarchical search through the Yahoo index, without becoming confused by frame-based layout. Note that creating this smaller window requires a small JavaScript program. Fortunately, you can see the script listing, and all the details, simply by visiting the Yahoo home page and viewing the document source.

Figure 12.2 The Yahoo! home page with the "Yahoo! Remote" search and navigation window. Results requested from the "Remote" tool are returned to the main browser window.

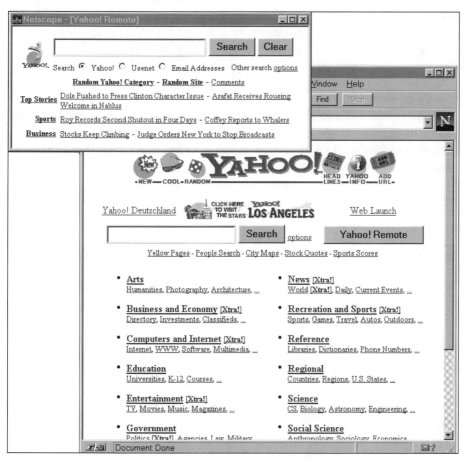

HTML and Columnar Layout

Every Web site wants to distinguish their pages in some way, usually by choosing a particular layout, color scheme, or typographic design. One common choice is to use a multicolumn page layout format, most easily implemented using tables. You can also use the **BODY** element **BACKGROUND** image to highlight particular columns with color, and at the same time act as a signature to the pages in a collection.

These two approaches are taken in the Chatelaine Destinations page illustrated in Figures 12.3 through 12.5. First, let's look at the table layout. To create a well-defined layout, the left column must be of a defined and fixed width. This can be accomplished by using the table cell **WIDTH** attribute to specify the desired cell width, in pixels, for the cells in the first row of the table. In Figure 12.3, the first table cell in the first column takes the attribute **WIDTH="175"**, to fix the column width at this value. Note also how the width of the entire table is fixed at 590 pixels—as mentioned before, this is the maximum viewable width on standard 640-pixel-width displays. This essentially fixes the layout of the table content, regardless of the browser window size.

Figure 12.3 Example document from the Chatelaine Web site, at `http://www.canoe` `.ca/Chatelaine`**. This document illustrates table structuring of the page content, and the use of background images to highlight particular columns. Dotted lines indicate document content that was omitted to save space.** *Comments are in italics.* **The rendering of this document is shown in Figures 12.4 and 12.5.**

```
<HTML><HEAD>
<TITLE>CHATELAINE DESTINATIONS</TITLE>
</HEAD>
<BODY BACKGROUND="/images/chatelaine/constant/destbg.gif"
      TOPMARGIN=0 LEFTMARGIN=0>     <!-- Makes Internet Explorer Work Properly  -->
<IMG SRC="/images/chatelaine/constant/connectstop.gif"    <!-- page banner graphic -->
     ALT="Chatelaine Connects" WIDTH=570 HEIGHT=17>

<TABLE BORDER=0 WIDTH=590 CELLPADDING=18 CELLSPACING=0>   <!-- 2 Column page        -->

<TR>
  <TH WIDTH=175 VALIGN=TOP ALIGN=CENTER>
    <BR><BR><BR><BR>
    <IMG SRC="/images/chatelaine/constant/spacer.gif"     <!-- spacer fixes width  -->
    WIDTH=130 HEIGHT=1 ALT="DECORATION">
    <BR>
    <A HREF="101.html"><IMG SRC="/images/chatelaine/constant/101icon.gif"
    BORDER=0 ALT="INTERNET 101"><BR>
    <B><FONT SIZE="-1">Click here for a<BR>
    beginner's guide to<BR>the Information<BR>Highway</FONT></B></A>
```

Figure 12.3 (Continued)

```
    </TH>
    <TD COLSPAN=2 ALIGN=LEFT VALIGN=TOP>
      <IMG SRC="/images/chatelaine/constant/destban.gif"
      LOWSRC="/images/chatelaine/constant/destban_low.gif"
      ALT="DESTINATIONS">
      <BR><BR>
.....    <!-- text omitted to save space -->
</TD>
</TR>
<TR>
  <TH WIDTH=150 ALIGN=CENTER VALIGN=TOP>
    <A HREF="/chatelaine/destinations/new.html">
    <IMG SRC="/images/chatelaine/constant/new.gif"
    ALT="New This Week" BORDER=0><BR><FONT SIZE="-1"><B>Click
    here to see our <BR>latest offerings</B></FONT></A>
    <BR><BR><BR><BR><BR>
    <A HREF="submit.html"><IMG
    SRC="/images/chatelaine/constant/favsite.gif"></A><BR>
  </TH>
  <TD VALIGN=TOP>
    <FONT SIZE="+1">
    <A
    HREF="/chatelaine/destinations/health/home.html"><B>HEALTH
    SITES</A></B>
    <BR>
..... <!-- text omittied to save space -->
    </FONT>
  </TD>
  <TD VALIGN=TOP>
    <FONT SIZE="+1">
    <A
    HREF="/chatelaine/destinations/money/home.html"><B>MONEY SITES</B></A>
    <br>
    Dollars and $ense
    <BR><BR>
    <A HREF="/chatelaine/destinations/home+garden/home.html"><B>HOME &
    GARDEN</B></A>
    <BR>
    Your place, your style
    <BR><BR>
    ..... <!-- text omitted to save space -->
    </FONT>
  </TD>
</TR>
</TABLE>
```

Continued

Figure 12.3 (Continued)

```
<BR><BR><BR>

 <A HREF="/chatelaine/home.html"><IMG
SRC="/images/chatelaine/constant/hombtn.gif" ALT="CHATELAINE HOME" WIDTH=85
HEIGHT=90 BORDER=0></A>

..... <!-- text omitted to save space -->
</BODY></HTML>
```

Some browsers do not properly support table cell **WIDTH** attributes when a table cell is empty—these browsers ignore the specified **WIDTH**, and choose their own "optimized" value. To guarantee proper alignment, you can place a transparent graphic of the desired width in the first cell—this then serves as a horizontal spacer, and forces the cell to take the correct width. Even a single 1-pixel-by-1-pixel image, saved as a transparent GIF, can be used for this purpose—simply use the **HEIGHT** and **WIDTH** attributes to "stretch" the graphic to the desired width. In Figure 12.3 the element `<IMG SRC=".../spacer.gif" HEIGHT=1 WIDTH=130 ALT="DECORATION">` serves this function within the first column. Although this technique adds one more graphic to the page, the file size of simple spacer images is tiny (less than 1 KB).

Alternatively, you can use actual graphics in the columns to force column width, and avoid using a spacer. If the graphic is narrower than the desired width, simply fill the image out the desired width by editing the image and adding extra transparent spacing to the right-hand side of the graphic.

Finally, you can use the **CELLPADDING** (padding inside a cell) and **CELLSPACING** (spacing between cells) tags to add a gutter between the columns. In Figure 12.3, the attribute **CELL-PADDING**=18 adds an 18-pixel buffer between the cell contents and the edge of the cells, and hence adds a 36-pixel spacing between the left and right columns. Note that this spacing must be accounted for when calculating the width of a spacer image inside a column: 2 × **CELLPADDING** + image-width ≤ cell-width.

Coloring the Column Backgrounds

Columns can be highlighted by giving them background colors—this can be accomplished using the **BACKGROUND** attribute of **BODY**, and by designing a background image that creates a colored stripe behind the desired column. To create a simple solid-color background, you simply need an image one pixel high and 600 (or more) wide—you then select the desired colors for particular bands of this image. For example, in the Chatelaine Destinations pages (Figures 12.4 and 12.5), the background for the left-hand column is white, while the background of the right-hand column is pale blue. To create this background, a single-pixel high background image was created where the first 175 pixels were white, and the remaining 725 pale blue (the image is 800 pixels wide). When loaded, this image tiles down the page, producing the desired white and blue vertical stripes.

The trick of course is to align the columnar text over the stripe. This is possible because the table cells were given fixed widths that correspond precisely to the widths of the background stripes.

Figure 12.4 Rendering, by Internet Explorer 3, of the top part of the document listed in Figure 12.3. Note the alignment of the background stripe with the HTML table layout of the text and images.

Figure 12.5 Rendering, by Internet Explorer 3, of the bottom of the document listed in Figure 12.3. Note the use of multiple, separate images for the navigation icons at the bottom of the page.

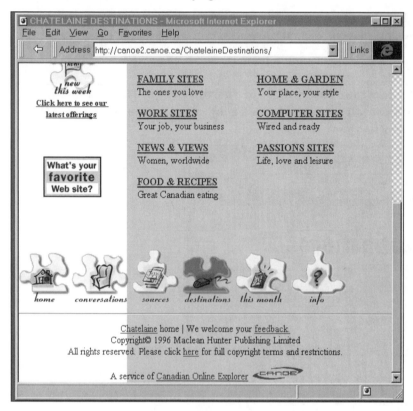

Using Tables to Group Images

Tables are also useful for grouping images that you wish to keep together regardless of window width. Page banners are a common feature where this type of layout control is desired. Many second-level documents in a collection have a banner graphic that reflects the Web site, but that changes from page to page to reflect the topical category. Often this difference is reflected by a small change in the graphic. It is therefore useful if the image can be broken down into static and dynamic parts.

This is possible by cutting the image into pieces, and then assembling the desired graphic from these components. An example is illustrated in Figure 12.6. Here the banner logo consists of two parts—the CANOE logo to the left, and a section-specific heading to the right. Since the CANOE logo is reused from page to page, it is downloaded only once, and is thereafter accessed from the browser's cache. The only thing that varies from page to page is the smaller graphic to the right, which denotes the different sections. This type of decomposition can speed page downloading significantly—provided you don't break the images up into too many pieces.

The banner graphic in Figure 12.6 was created by placing the two images in a table. By setting the table **BORDER**="0", you can ensure that the images will be laid out flush against each other,

Figure 12.6 Illustration of page banners composed of tiled images. The left-hand image (the CANOE logo) is used repeatedly on all main section pages, while the right-hand portion is modified to denote the section. Two sections are illustrated: the "Life" section (shown in the inset and also as part of the document in the background), and "Showbiz."

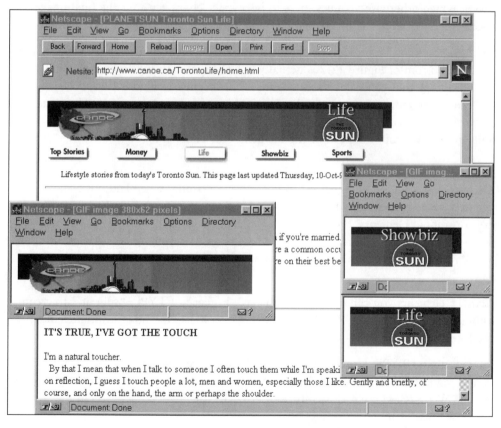

provided you do not add any extra space characters on either side of the **IMG** elements. The markup used to generate the banner in Figure 12.6 is:

```
<CENTER>
<!--BANNER ITEMS--------------->
<TABLE BORDER=0 ALIGN=CENTER WIDTH=570>
<TR>
  <TH>
  <IMG SRC="/images/banners/planetsun/torsunleft.gif"
   ALT="Toronto Sun Logo"><IMG
   SRC="/images/banners/planetsun/tortopstoriesban.gif"
   ALT="TORONTO SUN TOP STORIES"></TH>
</TR>
</TABLE>
</CENTER>
```

Note the `</TH>` added after the final **IMG** element. This is required due to a bug in the Netscape Navigator browser, which otherwise assumes there to be a space character after the final image, and leaves physical space between the image and the table border.

Even complicated graphics can be broken down into multiple, adjacent images. For example, the navigation bar at the bottom of Figure 12.7 is actually a **TABLE** containing seven different images. The HTML listing that generates this navigation bar is listed in Figure 12.8. Note the use of **ALIGN**="center" to enforce consistent alignment of images. Note also that each image in this navigation bar is contained within an anchor element. Thus the bar acts much like an imagemapped image, but without the need of the imagemap mechanism.

FORM Layout Using TABLEs

HTML **FORM**s look best, and are often easiest to use and understand, when laid out using tables. Unfortunately, there is enormous browser-to-browser and platform-to-platform variation in the display of form input elements. For example, input fields are much wider on a PC than on a Macintosh, even if the elements contain specific width settings. If designing on a Macintosh, be sure to design fields somewhat narrower than you might otherwise choose, so that they display properly on a PC.

Also, with **INPUT** elements you can use **TYPE**="image", in place of **TYPE**="submit", to create graphically customized submit buttons. Recall that clicking over a TYPE="image" input element also submits the form.

Tabular form layout and **TYPE**="image" submission buttons are both used in the form listed in Figure 12.9, and rendered in Figure 12.10 by the Internet Explorer 3 browser. This form is also from the Chatelaine Web site, where it is used to submit URLs for possible inclusion in the site's weekly "favourite Web site" list.

Figure 12.7 A navigational menu bar composed of individual image segments. The small Netscape window shows one of these image segments.

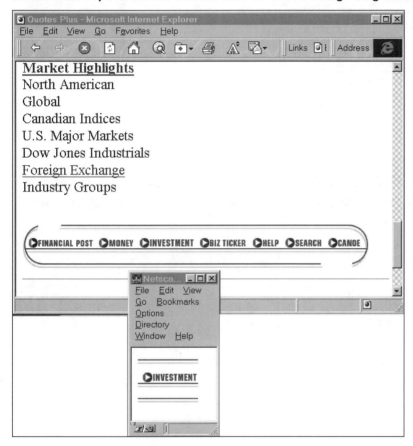

Figure 12.8 Use of TABLE elements with zero paddings to create a continuous-image menu bar from separate image files. The rendering of this menu bar is shown in Figure 12.7.

```
<!--NAVIGATION BAR-->
<TABLE BORDER=0 CELLPADDING=0 CELLSPACING=0>
<TR NOWRAP>
  <TH><A HREF="/fp/home.html"><IMG SRC="/images/quotes/nav1_fp.gif"
  ALIGN=CENTER BORDER=0 WIDTH=146 HEIGHT=74
```

Continued

Figure 12.8 (Continued)

```
ALT="FP Home"></A></TH>

  <TH><A HREF="/money/home.html"><IMG SRC="/images/quotes/nav2_money.gif"
  ALIGN=CENTER BORDER=0 WIDTH=79 HEIGHT=74
  ALT="Money"></A></TH>

  <TH><A HREF="/invest/home.html"><IMG SRC="/images/quotes/nav2_inves.gif"
  ALIGN=CENTER BORDER=0 WIDTH=79 HEIGHT=74
  ALT="Investment"></A></TH>

  . . .


</TR></TABLE>
```

Figure 12.9 HTML TABLE markup used to lay out the components of an HTML FORM. Note the use of a TYPE="image" input element to create a graphical form submission button.

```
<FORM METHOD="POST"
      ACTION="http://cgi.canoe.ca/htbin/chatelaine/Submit/FormMailer.cgi">
<BR>
<CENTER>
<TABLE BORDER="0" CELLPADDING="2" CELLSPACING="2">
<TR>
  <TD><FONT SIZE="+1"><B>Title of Web site:</B></FONT></TD>
  <TD><INPUT TYPE=TEXT NAME="title"></TD>
</TR><TR>
  <TD><FONT SIZE="+1"><B>Full address (URL):</B></FONT></TD>
  <TD><INPUT TYPE=TEXT NAME="URL"></TD>
</TR><TR>
  <TD><FONT SIZE="+1"><B>Category:</B></FONT></TD>
  <TD>
   <SELECT NAME="category">
      <OPTION>Click and hold
      <OPTION>Health
      . . .
      <OPTION>Passions
      </SELECT>
  </TD>
</TR><TR>
  <TD VALIGN=TOP><FONT SIZE="+1"><B>Comments:</B></FONT></TD>
  <TD><TEXTAREA name="comments" ROWS=5
  COLS=40></TEXTAREA></TD>
</TR><TR>
  <TD><FONT SIZE="+1"><B>Your name:</B></FONT></TD>
  <TD><INPUT TYPE=TEXT NAME="name"></TD>
```

Figure 12.9 (Continued)

```
</TR><TR>
  <TD><FONT SIZE="+1"><B>Your city:</B></FONT></TD>
  <TD><INPUT TYPE=TEXT NAME="city"></TD>
</TR><TR>
  <TD><FONT SIZE="+1"><B>Your province:</B></FONT></TD>
  <TD><INPUT TYPE=TEXT NAME="province"></TD>
</TR><TR>
  <TD><FONT SIZE="+1"><B>Your E-mail address:</B></FONT></TD>
  <TD><INPUT TYPE=TEXT NAME="email"></TD>
</TR><TR>
  <TH COLSPAN=2>
  <BR>
  <INPUT TYPE=IMAGE SRC="submitbutton.gif"
  NAME="submit" VALUE="Submit">
  </TH>
</TR></TABLE>
</CENTER>
</FORM>
```

Text-Based Pull Quotes

Pull quotes—text pulled from a document and placed beside the text for emphasis—are an important part of magazine and newspaper layout, and are also effective on the Web. Most designers create pull quotes as graphics, and insert these graphics into the text layout table. However, it is possible to create purely text-based pull quotes, bypassing the need to generate multiple graphic files.

The text-only method uses tables and a spacer graphic: Typical markup is shown in Figure 12.11, while Figure 12.12 schematically illustrates the table layout, and the rationale of the design. The actual rendering of this pull quote is shown in Figure 12.13.

The first step, in the first row of the table, is to create a left-hand table column to serve as the text margin—in this case, the cell attribute **WIDTH**="100" is used for a 100-pixel margin. This cell contains only a <BR> tag to let the browser know the cell is not empty. The second cell in the first row has **COLSPAN**="2" and the desired width—here **WIDTH**="400". This cell will contain the text content of the article. The total table width is then 500 pixels, so that on a 640-pixel-wide display there will be an approximately 100-pixel margin at the right of the text.

The second row contains the pull quote, placed in the first two columns of the table. Thus the first **TD** cell has **COLSPAN**="2", and also specifies **WIDTH**="200" to give the desired width for this cell. In this instance, background color of the cell is modified using the **BGCOLOR**="beige"

Figure 12.10 The FORM outlined in Figure 12.9, as displayed by the Internet Explorer 3 browser. This form is part of a larger document from the Chatelaine Web site, available from

http://www.canoe.ca/ChatelaineDestinations/submit.html

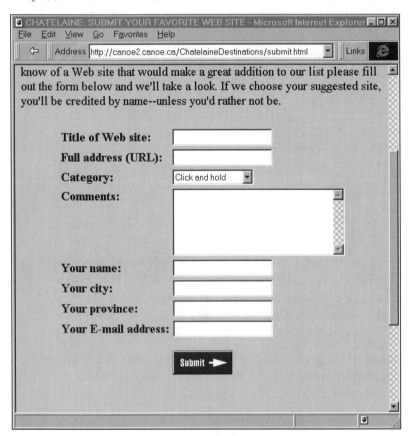

attribute—this helps to highlight the pull quote, and is safe for browsers that do not support colored cell backgrounds. The next cell, of **WIDTH**="300", contains the text to display next to the pull quote; again, this is a hint to the browser as to the desired width.

The third row is simply a continuation of the first: a 100-pixel column for the margin, and a **COLSPAN**=2 column for the text.

Figure 12.11 TABLE markup for generating a pull quote. The logic behind this design is illustrated in Figure 12.12, while the resulting pull quote is showed in Figure 12.13. *Comments are in italics.*

```
<TABLE BORDER=0 CELLPADDING=0 CELLSPACING=10>
  <TR>
    <TD WIDTH=100>
      <BR>
    </TD>
    <TD COLSPAN=2 WIDTH=400>
      <IMG SRC="/images/chatelaine/current/timson.gif"
      LOWSRC="/images/chatelaine/current/timson_low.gif"
      ALT="TIMSON" ALIGN=RIGHT BORDER="1">
      <FONT SIZE="+1">
      It had been a weekend of death discussions, funeral
      chat: one friend had gone off to her uncle's funeral, another
.... (text omitted to save space)
</TD>
  </TR>
  <TR>
    <TD COLSPAN=2 BGCOLOR=BEIGE>
      <HR NOSHADE WIDTH=200>
      <CENTER>
      <FONT SIZE="+2">What I am really saying <BR>is "I love you."
      I am really<BR> saying "Don't go."</FONT>
      </CENTER>
      <HR NOSHADE WIDTH=200>
    </TD>
    <TD WIDTH=300>
      Some seem stoic, even realistic, about death. And
      some are suspiciously cheery about it, if you ask me. (One friend
      ..... (text omitted to save space)
      is not going anywhere but out for lunch. I hope.
    </TD>
  </TR>
  <TR>
    <TD WIDTH=100>
      <BR>
    </TD>
    <TD COLSPAN=2 WIDTH=400>
      My mother has already had her dress rehearsal for
      death-a hideous pneumonia that put her in a coma some years ago,
..... .... text omitted to save space)
<BR><BR>
    </TD>
  </TR>
  <TR>      <!-- Final row to pin width of second column -->
    <TD WIDTH=100>
```

Continued

Figure 12.11 (Continued)

```
      <BR>
    </TD>
    <TD>
      <IMG SRC="/images/chatelaine/constant/1.gif" WIDTH=90 HEIGHT=1>
    </TD>
    <TD>
      <BR>
    </TD>
  </TR>
</TABLE>
```

Figure 12.12 Schematic of the table layout for generating a text-only pull quote. Note the use of the spacer graphic in the fourth row to fix the widths of the table cells.

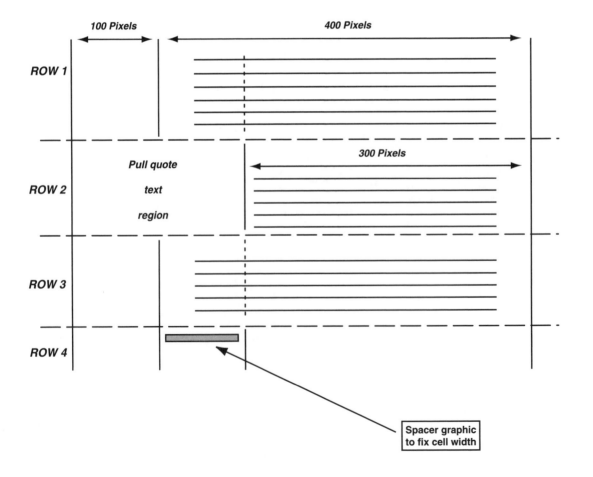

Figure 12.13 Internet Explorer 3 rendering of the pull quote illustrated in Figure 12.11. Note how the BGCOLOR color specification for the pull quote cell helps to highlight the text content.

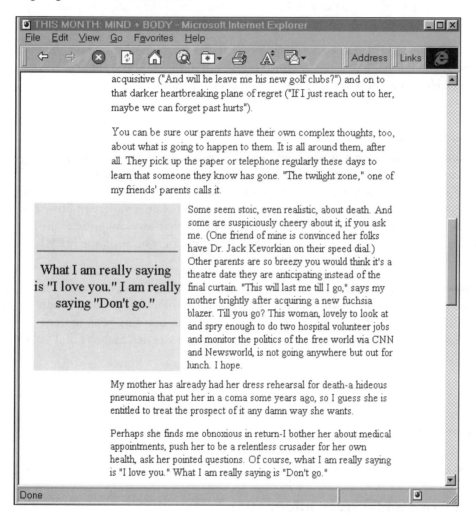

In principle, this should be all you need. Unfortunately, it is not. This is because the **WIDTH** specification is really only a parameter, and does not force the browser to assign a particular width to a cell or column. This is not a problem for cells that contain flowing text, as the browser will generally create a cell close to the specified width. However, it is a problem for the first and second cells, as they at no place contain real content to define the column width (the middle column is always "colspanned" to the first or third). Most table parsing engines will "rubberize" the width of the second column, unless you fix the size with some content. This is the purpose of the fourth row in the table. Here, the second **TD** contains a spacer graphic that pins the width of this cell at 100 pixels (recall that the cellspacing takes up some of the cell width).

Note that it is *not* sufficient to place a spacer image in the first column—if this is done, then the width of the second column cell is still not specified (every cell in the second column is effectively empty) and the table formatter will shrink this cell to near zero width.

Conclusions

This brief chapter outlined the basic principles of Web site design, and provides some simple examples of sophisticated page design possible within the current HTML specification. You should not stop here—feel free to borrow and elaborate upon the HTML layout designs of others, and to develop entirely new designs. But—make sure to test your layouts on a variety of browsers. Also, be sure to check the markup with an HTML verifier, as in only that way can you be sure that the designs will work in the future, regardless of the changes that may occur in the HTML language or browser interpretation of HTML.

And that's it! I hope you found this chapter, and this book, useful. If you have any comments, or suggestions for the next edition, please contact the author through the publisher, or through the book's Web site, listed in the preface. It is thanks to you, the reader, that this book has been so successful. Your input will help ensure that the book continues to get better, and to fulfill your needs.

References

Demographics and User Surveys

http://www.cc.gatech.edu/gvu/user_surveys/
http://www.nielsenmedia.com/commercenet/exec.html
http://www.ora.com/research/

Media Research Firms and Survey Information

http://www.nielsenmedia.com/	(Nielsen Media Research Interactive Services)
http://www.simbanet.com/	(Media consulting and surveys)
http://www.forrester.com/	(Technology Change Analysts)
http://www.activmedia.com/	(ActivMedia Market Research)

Advertising and Marketing Information

http://www.adage.com	(Advertising Age)
http://uts.cc.utexas.edu/~echo/cover.html	(Overview of Web advertising)
http://www.webtrack.com/	(News/databases for marketers)
http://www.clo.com/~avmonl/uoft/sales.html	(Electronic sales/marketing resource list)
http://www2000.ogsm.vanderbilt.edu/	(Research program on marketing in computer-mediated environments)

Web Site Design

Creating Killer Web Sites, by Dave Siegel, Hayden Book, Indianapolis, 1996.

See also references at the end of Chapter 3.

Characters and
Computer Character Sets

A computer character set is simply an agreed-upon relationship between computer binary codes and a set of letters or graphical characters. Since almost all computers use the byte (8 bits) as the basic storage unit, many standard character sets are designed to use a single byte to store a single character. Since there are 8 bits in a byte, a byte can in principle represent 256 different characters ($256 = 2^8$). Any agreed-upon relationship between these byte-level codes and a particular set of letters or graphical characters is called an 8-bit character set. ISO Latin-1, the default character set of the World Wide Web, is just one example.

The ISO Latin-1 Character Set

Character sets are useful only if they are commonly understood—that way I can write a document using a character set and send the digital document to you, and you can turn that digital information back into the characters I intended, since you know the characters each binary code represents. Of course, this only works if I also tell you what character set I am using, and provided you also understand the character set! There is thus a need for standards that define character sets, and the relation-ships between the digital codes and the desired characters or symbols.

Many character sets for international use are specified by the International Standards Organization (ISO), including several different character sets that fit inside 8-bit bytes. For World Wide Web applications, the *default* set of printable characters is the 8-bit ISO Latin-1 (also known as ISO 8859-1) character set—the complete set of printable ISO Latin-1 charac-ters is shown in Table A.1. A browser or other Web application will assume that text-based information is written using the ISO Latin-1 character set, unless some other character set is specified.

Table A.1 ISO Latin-1 Characters and Control Characters, Showing Decimal Codes, Hexadecimal Codes, and Currently Supported HTML Entity References
Entity reference names introduced in HTML 2 are shown in italics—some older browsers do not support these entity references.

Character	Decimal	Hex	Entity Reference	Character	Decimal	Hex	Entity Reference
NUL	0	0		SOH	1	1	
STX	2	2		ETX	3	3	
EOT	4	4		ENQ	5	5	
ACK	6	6		BEL	7	7	
BS	8	8		HT	9	9	
LF	10	a		VT	11	b	
NP	12	c		CR	13	d	
SO	14	e		SI	15	f	
DLE	16	10		DC1	17	11	
DC2	18	12		DC3	19	13	
DC4	20	14		NAK	21	15	
SYN	22	16		ETB	23	17	
CAN	24	18		EM	25	19	
SUB	26	1a		ESC	27	1b	
FS	28	1c		GS	29	1d	

Table A.1 (Continued)

Character	Decimal	Hex	Entity Reference	Character	Decimal	Hex	Entity Reference
RS	30	1e		US	31	1f	
SP	32	20		!	33	21	
"	34	22	&quot;	#	35	23	
$	36	24		%	37	25	
&	38	26	&amp;	'	39	27	
(	40	28		)	41	29	
*	42	2a		+	43	2b	
,	44	2c		-	45	2d	
.	46	2e		/	47	2f	
0	48	30		1	49	31	
2	50	32		3	51	33	
4	52	34		5	53	35	
6	54	36		7	55	37	
8	56	38		9	57	39	
:	58	3a		;	59	3b	
<	60	3c	&gt;	=	61	3d	
>	62	3e	&lt;	?	63	3f	
@	64	40		A	65	41	
B	66	42		C	67	43	
D	68	44		E	69	45	
F	70	46		G	71	47	
H	72	48		I	73	49	
J	74	4a		K	75	4b	
L	76	4c		M	77	4d	
N	78	4e		O	79	4f	

Continued

Table A.1 (Continued)

Character	Decimal	Hex	Entity Reference	Character	Decimal	Hex	Entity Reference
P	80	50		Q	81	51	
R	82	52		S	83	53	
T	84	54		U	85	55	
V	86	56		W	87	57	
X	88	58		Y	89	59	
Z	90	5a		[	91	5b	
\	92	5c		]	93	5d	
^	94	5e		_	95	5f	
`	96	60		a	97	61	
b	98	62		c	99	63	
d	100	64		e	101	65	
f	102	66		g	103	67	
h	104	68		i	105	69	
j	106	6a		k	107	6b	
l	108	6c		m	109	6d	
n	110	6e		o	111	6f	
p	112	70		q	113	71	
r	114	72		s	115	73	
t	116	74		u	117	75	
v	118	76		w	119	77	
x	120	78		y	121	79	
z	122	7a		{	123	7b	
|	124	7c		}	125	7d	
~	126	7e		DEL	127	7f	
--	128	80		--	129	81	

Table A.1 (Continued)

Character	Decimal	Hex	Entity Reference	Character	Decimal	Hex	Entity Reference
--	130	82		--	131	83	
--	132	84		--	133	85	
--	134	86		--	135	87	
--	136	88		--	137	89	
--	138	8a		--	139	8b	
--	140	8c		--	141	8d	
--	142	8e		--	143	8f	
--	144	90		--	145	91	
--	146	92		--	147	93	
--	148	94		--	149	95	
--	150	96		--	151	97	
--	152	98		--	153	99	
--	154	9a		--	155	9b	
--	156	9c		--	157	9d	
--	158	9e		--	159	9f	
	160	a0		¡	161	a1	&iexcl;
¢	162	a2	&cent;	£	163	a3	&pound;
¤	164	a4	&curren;	¥	165	a5	&yen;
¦	166	a6	&brvbar;	§	167	a7	&sect;
¨	168	a8	&uml;	©	169	a9	&copy;
ª	170	aa	&ordf;	«	171	ab	&laqno;
¬	172	ac	&not;	-	173	ad	&shy;
®	174	ae	&reg;	¯	175	af	&macr;
°	176	b0	&deg;	±	177	b1	&plusmn;
²	178	b2	&sup2;	³	179	b3	&sup3;

Continued

Table A.1 (Continued)

Character	Decimal	Hex	Entity Reference	Character	Decimal	Hex	Entity Reference
´	180	b4	&acute;	µ	181	b5	&micro;
¶	182	b6	&para;	·	183	b7	&middot;
¸	184	b8	&cedil;	1	185	b9	&sup1;
º	186	ba	&ordm;	»	187	bb	&raquo;
¼	188	bc	&frac14;	½	189	bd	&frac12;
¾	190	be	&frac34;	¿	191	bf	&iquest;
À	192	c0	&Agrave;	Á	193	c1	&Aacute;
Â	194	c2	&Acirc;	Ã	195	c3	&Atilde;
Ä	196	c4	&Auml;	Å	197	c5	&Aring;
Æ	198	c6	&AElig;	Ç	199	c7	&Ccedil;
È	200	c8	&Egrave;	É	201	c9	&Eacute;
Ê	202	ca	&Ecirc;	Ë	203	cb	&Euml;
Ì	204	cc	&Igrave;	Í	205	cd	&Iacute;
Î	206	ce	&Icirc;	Ï	207	cf	&Iuml;
Ð	208	d0	&ETH;	Ñ	209	d1	&Ntilde;
Ò	210	d2	&Ograve;	Ó	211	d3	&Oacute;
Ô	212	d4	&Ocirc;	Õ	213	d5	&Otilde;
Ö	214	d6	&Ouml;	×	215	d7	&times;
Ø	216	d8	&Oslash;	Ù	217	d9	&Ugrave;
Ú	218	da	&Uacute;	Û	219	db	&Ucirc;
Ü	220	dc	&Uuml;	Y	221	dd	&Yacute;
Þ	222	de	&THORN;	ß	223	df	&szlig;
à	224	e0	&agrave;	á	225	e1	&aacute;
â	226	e2	&acirc;	ã	227	e3	&atilde;
ä	228	e4	&auml;	å	229	e5	&aring;
æ	230	e6	&aelig;	ç	231	e7	&ccedil;

Table A.1 (Continued)

Character	Decimal	Hex	Entity Reference	Character	Decimal	Hex	Entity Reference
è	232	e8	&egrave;	é	233	e9	&eacute;
ê	234	ea	&ecirc;	ë	235	eb	&euml;
ì	236	ec	&igrave;	í	237	ed	&iacute;
î	238	ee	&icirc;	ï	239	ef	&iuml;
ð	240	f0	&eth;	ñ	241	f1	&ntilde;
ò	242	f2	&ograve;	ó	243	f3	&oacute;
ô	244	f4	&ocirc;	õ	245	f5	&otilde;
ö	246	f6	&ouml;	÷	247	f7	*÷*
ø	248	f8	&oslash;	ù	249	f9	&ugrave;
ú	250	fa	&uacute;	û	251	fb	&ucirc;
ü	252	fc	&uuml;	y	253	fd	&yacute;
_	254	fe	&thorn;	ÿ	255	ff	&yuml;

The first 128 positions in ISO Latin-1 are equivalent to the 128 characters of the US-ASCII (also known as ISO 646) character set. (US-ASCII is known as a 7-bit character set, since it consists of only 128 characters and can be represented using just seven bits—$128=2^7$). Of these 128 characters, 32 are special control characters for controlling printing devices and serial communications lines (e.g., to control modems or terminals).* Control characters are not printable, and are indicated in Table A.1 by two- or three-letter character sequences that mnemonically designate their function. For example, NUL is a null character, BEL is the bell character (rings a bell), CR is carriage return, BS is the backspace character, and so on. In addition, Table A.1 indicates the space character (decimal 32) with the symbol SP, as otherwise this would be invisible. Some important control characters, and their meanings, are:

Character	Meaning	Decimal Code Position
NUL	Null character	00
BS	Backspace	08
HT	Tab	09

*Formally these control characters are not ISO Latin-1 characters, but are part of another ISO specification, which defines byte codes for special data line control characters.

Character	Meaning	Decimal Code Position
LF	Linefeed/Newline (also NL)	10
CR	Carriage return	13
SP	Space character	32
DEL	Delete	127

There are 128 additional characters in the 8-bit character set, from positions 128 to 255. The first 32 are unprintable control characters, marked in Table A.1 by a double dash "--". The remaining characters are printable ISO Latin-1 characters, and include of many of the accented and other special characters commonly used in western European languages.

URL Character Encodings

As discussed in Chapter 6, URLs can contain any ISO Latin-1 character (this is the defined character set for URLs), but must be *written* using a small subset of the printable ASCII characters—those characters in the lower 128. All is not lost, however, as any 8-bit ISO Latin-1 character can be entered in a URL by indirect references, or encodings. These encodings take the form:

`%xx`

where *xx* is the *hexadecimal* or *hex* code corresponding to the character—this is simply the position of the character in the list of 256 possible characters, written as a hexadecimal value. Table A.1 shows the hexadecimal codes for all the ISO Latin-1 and control characters. As an example, the URL *encoding* for the string `%toads` is:

`%25toads`

since the percent character is character 37 (hexadecimal 25) in the character set.

HTML Character and Entity References

In HTML documents written using the ISO Latin-1 character set, any ISO Latin-1 character can be represented by either a *character reference* or an *entity reference*. A character reference represents a character through its decimal code—this is simply the numeric decimal position of the character in the list of 256 possible characters. Thus, the character reference for a capital U with an umlaut (Ü) is:

`&#220;`

since this is the character at position 220 in the ISO Latin-1 character set. Numerical references are awkward and difficult to remember, and also can give different characters depending on the character set being used, as many character sets contain the same characters, but at different numerical positions.

HTML also supports *entity references* for most non-ASCII characters. For example, the entity reference for a capital U with an umlaut (Ü) is:

`&Uuml;`

The advantage of entity references is *universality*—they should always work, regardless of the character set being used, since they are independent of the position in the character set where the character may reside. Table A.1 lists the entity references, where defined, for characters in the ISO Latin-1 character set, along with the corresponding ISO Latin-1 decimal character reference. In some cases, these entity reference names were only added as part of the HTML 2.0 specification, and so are less widely supported; these names are italicized and slightly indented to distinguish them from the more widely supported names. Most modern browsers support all of the references in this table.

In HTML, the four ASCII characters (`>`), (`<`), (`"`), and (`&`) have special meanings. Therefore, to display them in text as ordinary characters, you must use character or entity references, both of which are given in Table A.1. For example, the entity reference for the less-than sign is `&lt;`.

A document illustrating these entity references is found at:

`http://www.utoronto.ca/webdocs/HTMLdocs/Book/Book-3ed/appa/en_test.html`

Not all computers use the ISO Latin-1 character set. UNIX computers and PCs running Windows use the ISO Latin-1 character set by default, while PCs running DOS and Macintoshes do not, although the first 128 characters of the Macintosh and DOS characters sets are still US-ASCII. You must therefore take care on these platforms when preparing documents for use on the World Wide Web—for safety, it is best to use character or entity references for all non-ASCII characters.

Entity Reference Caveats

Formally, the semicolon is not always necessary to terminate character or entity references, and it can in principle be omitted if this will not confuse the parsing of the reference. For example, `"&Uuml is an..."` is an acceptable entity reference, but `"&Uumlis an..."` is not. As a document author, it is best to include the semicolon, as some browsers mishandle references that don't end in semicolons.

Also, the ampersand character indicates the start of a reference only when it is immediately followed by an ASCII letter character (e.g., `&a..` to start an entity reference), or by the hash character plus a digit (e.g. `&#2..` to start a character reference). If an ampersand character does not appear in either of these contexts, then it is treated as a regular character. To be safe, however, it is best to indicate a literal ampersand (an ampersand as a regular character) by using the ampersand character's entity reference `&amp;`.

Other Important Character Sets

There are literally dozens of commonly used character sets, not all of them specified by the ISO. There are, for example, the character sets ISO Latin-1 through ISO Latin-9. All of these have ASCII in the first 128 positions, but thereafter contain different characters appropriate for different language groups (Western European, Eastern European [Slavic], Southern European, Cyrillic, Arabic, Greek, Hebrew, Turkish, and Icelandic/Nordic/Baltic, respectively). There are also larger, multi-byte character sets, which require more than one byte to encode a character. We will talk in more detail about one of these multi-byte character sets later on—after explaining how the Web indicates the character set used in a particular document. Table A.2 shows some of the character sets supported by the Netscape Navigator browser; note that many of the character set labels are not standardized names (indicated by the leading x-). Where available, the table lists the number for the Internet RFC documenting the character set.

Table A.2 Some Character Set Names and Descriptions
Most of these names are supported by Netscape Navigator.

Character Set Label	Description
us-ascii	US ASCII
iso-8859-1	ISO Latin-1
x-mac-roman	Similar to Latin-1 (Mac only)
iso-8859-2	Central/East European
CP-1250	Central/East European (Windows only)
iso-8859-5	Cyrillic
x-mac-cyrillic	Cyrillic (Mac only)
CP-1251	Cyrillic (Windows only)
KOI8-R	Cyrillic (RFC 1489)
iso-8859-7	Greek
iso-8859-9	Turkish
iso-2022-jis	Japanese
iso-2022-jp	Japanese (RFC 1468)
x-sjis	Japanese Shift-JIS (Microsoft code set)
iso-2022-kr	Korean (RFC 1557)

Table A.2 (Continued)

Character Set Label	Description
`euc-jp`	Extended UNIX Code for Japanese
`euc-kr`	Extended UNIX Code for Korean (RFC 1557)
`gb_2312-80`	Simplified Chinese—People's republic (RFC 1345)
`x-euc-tw`	Extended UNIX Code for Chinese—Taiwan
`x-cns11643-1`	Traditional Chinese—Taiwan
`x-cns11643-2`	Traditional Chinese—Taiwan
`Big5`	Traditional Chinese—Taiwan—multi-byte set

Indicating Character Sets via MIME Content-Types

The MIME protocol supports a *charset* parameter for indicating the character set used to encode a given text component. The general mechanism is to use a content-type header of the form:

`Content-type: text/`*`subtype`*`; charset=`*`character_set`*

where *`subtype`* indicates the subtype of the text document (`html`, `plain`, etc.) and *`character_set`* indicates the character set used for the data. The World Wide Web assumes the type `ISO-8859-1` in the absence of any specified charset. If a server sends out a document encoded in a different character set, it should return an HTTP content-type header that indicates both the text type and the charset value.

Unfortunately, many servers do not send charset information, while several browsers mishandle content-type headers containing charset specifications, and as a result often do not properly identify a document as text/html. For this reason, several browsers support the use of HTML **META** tags to indicate the character set. The form is:

`<META HTTP-EQUIV="Content-Type" CONTENT="text/html; charset=`*`character_set`*`">`

which places an entire content-type header in the **META** tag. This works because almost all character sets have ASCII characters in positions 0 to 127, so that a browser can assume this mapping and read this HTML **HEAD** element. In general, a browser will first look to the real HTTP header to find the charset; if it is not indicated there, the browser will look to the document **HEAD** and see if there is a **META** element indicating the charset. Failing that, the browser usually assumes ISO Latin-1.

Internationalized HTML—The ISO 10646 Character Set

Using the ISO Latin-1 character set as a default imposes obvious limitations on the characters allowed in HTML documents, and makes it impossible to represent most of the world's languages. The basic problem is the use of 8-bit character sets, as the 256 characters allowed by an 8-bit code are clearly insufficient. Although there are several 8-bit character sets developed for different language sets, using multiple, different character sets is not an ideal solution, since you cannot mix character sets within the same document (for example, Japanese characters within a Cyrillic document). Another difficulty is that you cannot be sure that a client machine will understand the character set in which the document is encoded—with dozens of different character sets to choose from, it is impossible to be sure that everyone has the character set you have used to encode your text.

The HTML *internationalization** efforts described in Chapter 5 propose solving these character-set and language problems by using a single multi-byte character set, known as ISO 10646. Multibyte (2-bit byte [16-bit] or 4-byte [32-bit]) character sets can support characters from many different languages, all at the same time (2-byte character sets can support 65,536 distinct characters, while 4-byte character sets can support 4,294,967,296 characters, which should be enough for everyone!). This allows for the cross-platform compatibility essential for universal document transport—each browser need only understand one character set, namely ISO 10646, to view all internationalized documents. The current internationalization efforts have focused on the 2-byte (16-bit) subset of ISO 10646, called the *basic multilingual plane,* or *BMP* (The *BMP* is essentially the same as the Unicode character coding system). ISO 10646 is also called *UCS,* or the *universal character set.*

ISO 10646 is designed to be upward-compatible with ASCII and ISO 8859-1. Although ISO 10646 is a multi-byte character set, it can be thought of as of a collection of multiple 256-character character sets. Each of these character sets is indexed by the first byte in a 16-bit word, while the second byte references the character of the indicated set. Thus, the basic multilingual plane of ISO 10646 is often described as a collection of 256 different 256-character character sets, each set lying in its own plane.

ISO 10646 is compatible with ISO 8859-1, in that the first 256-characters of ISO 10646 are equivalent to ISO 8859-1. Thus the hexadecimal byte codes for the letter "k" in the two character sets are:

ISO 10646	ISO 8859-1
00 6b	6b

**Internationalization*: computer jargon that implies finding technical ways of designing computer software that can be used in multilingual, multiple-character-set environments. This is often shortened to the even more jargonized abbreviation I18N (InternationaliIz8tioN).

where the first "plane" of characters in ISO 10646 is referenced by the null leading byte (note how the order of the bytes is important).

Because most computers work with the ISO Latin-1 code set, there are several *8-bit encodings* of ISO 10646 for which the encoding of the first 256 characters simply gives the ISO Latin-1 equivalents. This is convenient, since it means that current ISO Latin-1 documents can be read in and interpreted as-is. However, creating an 8-bit encoded document containing non-Latin character is not as easy, and requires a special encoding mechanism to record these characters as multibyte sequences. The most common encoding of this type is known as UTF-8 (8-bit *universal transformation format*), which uses special *control codes* to switch a character to a different plane of the 16-bit character set.

As you may have gathered, the issue of character sets is both complicated and confusing. The references at the end of this appendix provide some starting points, should you wish to delve deeper into this frustratingly complex, yet extremely important issue.

References

Specification for HTML Internationalization

http://www.alis.com:8085/ietf/html/draft-ietf-html-i18n.txt
http://ds.internic.net/internet-drafts/ (Look for files with names like draft-ietf-html-i18n...)

General Character Set Information Relevant to the Web

http://www.ebt.com/docs/multling.html
http://www.w3.org/hypertext/WWW/International/Overview
http://www.w3.org/hypertext/WWW/MarkUp/html-spec/charset-harmful.html

Character Set Specifications

http://www2.echo.lu/oii/en/chars.html
ftp://ds.internic.net/rfc/rfc1345.txt (Character mnemonics)
http://www.ifcss.org/ftp-pub/software/info/cjk-codes/ (Chinese/Japanese/Korean character sets—CJK)

ISO 10646 /UNICODE Character Sets—General Information

http://www.ifcss.org/ftp-pub/software/info/cjk-codes/Unicode.html
http://www.stonehand.com/unicode.html
ftp://ftp.ifi.uio.no/pub/SGML/CHARSET/ISO10646-1%3A1993.L3

Defined Internet Character Sets and Names

ftp://ftp.isi.edu/in-notes/iana/assignments/character-sets

Introduction to SGML Declarations and Character Sets

http://www.sil.org/sgml/wlw11.html
http://www.sgmlopen.org/sgml/docs/ercs/ercs-home.html

Books

Understanding Japanese Information Processing, by Ken Lunde, O'Reilly & Associates, Inc. (1993). A good overview of character encoding issues, with particular emphasis on the problems of Japanese text.

The Unicode Standard, Worldwide Character Encoding, Version 1.0, Addison-Wesley: Vol. 1 (1990) and Vol. 2 (1992). Complete description of the Unicode character set. Not exactly fireside reading, but very useful and complete.

B

Multipart Internet Mail Extensions (MIME)

MIME, for Multipurpose Internet Mail Extensions, is an extension to the traditional Internet mail protocol that allows for the communication of multimedia electronic mail. The original Internet mail protocol, defined in the document RFC 822, was designed with simple ASCII text messages in mind—the protocol defined a mail message as a block of text, preceded by specially defined header information specifying routing information about the message (where it is from, who it is to, who copies were sent to, etc.), and the characters (basically, ASCII) allowed in Internet mail messages. However, the protocol said little about the format of the message *content*. At the time (which was not that long ago!), most electronic mail messages were plain text files, so that concerns about other formats were unwarranted.

Today, however, there is enormous demand for sophisticated electronic mail that allows delivery of messages containing many components, such as a Rich Text or HTML text documents, image files, sound, and even video data. Such messages can easily be communicated by mail only if all mail programs and mail servers share a standard for constructing, encoding, and transporting such complex, possibly *multipart*, messages.

The MIME protocol provides this common standard. MIME is an open protocol for multimedia/multipart mail messages that is an extension upon the original RFC 822 mail protocol: MIME defines how to code the content, while RFC 822 specifies how to package the message and get it to its destination. MIME defines several new document headers that specify such things as the nature of a message (multipart or single part), how the message parts are separated, the data content of each part, and the encoding scheme used to encode each part. The following sections summarize those features that are most important for Web applications. This is only a brief summary, however; for further details you are referred to the relevant documentation (RFC 1521), referenced at the end of this appendix.

MIME and the Web—The MIME Content-Type

Of primary importance is the MIME *content-type* header. This should already be familiar to you as the header used to indicate the content of files being transferred using the HTTP protocol (see Chapter 7.) Whenever a client requests a document from an HTTP server, the server first determines the type of the document, and then sends the appropriate content-type header ahead of it. For example, if the file contained AIFF audio data, the server must send back the content-type header:

```
Content-type: audio/aiff
```

How do content-type headers work? Each header has a minimum of two parts, giving the data *type* and *subtype*, using the format:

```
Content-type: type/subtype
```

According to the MIME specification, `type` can be any of: `image`, `audio`, `text`, `video`, `application`, `multipart`, `message`, or `x-arbitrary-name` (these names, like the string `Content-Type:`, are case-insensitive). The meanings of the first four are obvious, and indicate the overall type of the data. The `application` type is for other data (perhaps binary) that need to be processed in a special way. This could be a program to run, or perhaps a PostScript document to be executed by a PostScript previewer. `Multipart` indicates a message containing more than one part, while `message` refers to an old-fashioned RFC 822 message body. `X-arbitrary-name` (i.e., any name beginning with the string `x-`) is called an extension token, and refers to experimental data types. This lets you—or anyone else—create special MIME types that do not conflict with established types. Finally, there are two new basic types under development. The type `world` is to be used for virtual reality data (as in VRML) and for 2D/3D data sets to be used for generating 3D worlds, while the type `chemical` is designed for communicating chemical models and structures. Both of these are commonly seen with experimental names, as in `x-world/*` and `x-chemical/*`.

In the content-type `type`/`subtype` string, the `subtype` gives the specifics of the content. Thus, `text/html` means a text file that is an HTML document, `application/postscript` means a PostScript file, and so on.

When looking at different MIME types, keep in mind that because of the flexibility of the HTTP client-server interaction, there are many content-types used by WWW applications that are not commonly used in electronic mail messages.

Character Set Specifications for Text Types

Any text content-type—that is, `text/*`--can in principle (see the NOTE that follows) take an optional parameter, `charset`, to specify the character set used in the text document—it's no use receiving a text file if you don't know the relationship between the bytes received and the characters intended. The general format for including this parameter is

```
Content-Type: text/subtype; charset=char_set_name
```

where `subtype` is the text subtype (commonly `html` or `plain` in Web applications), and `char_set_name` is the name of the character set with which the document is encoded. Note how the semicolon (`;`) is used to separate the `text`/`subtype` field from the `charset` parameter. Some possible values for `charset` are `US-ASCII` and `ISO-8859-1` (ISO Latin-1), `ISO-8859-2`, up to `ISO-8859-9`. The nine ISO sets are the 8-bit Latin character sets defined by the ISO. Web applications assume the ISO Latin-1 character set by default, so you usually do not need the `charset` parameter. The HTML internationalization of the Web (see Chapters 4 and 5) upgrades HTML text documents to support the 16-bit `ISO-10646` character set, while some browsers, such as Netscape Navigator, already support other character sets, such as the `ISO-2022-JP` (Japanese). Unfortunately, very few computers understand these other character sets unless the user explicitly adds the relevant character sets and fonts to to his or her machine—without this added support, a browser cannot display documents encoded in these character sets.

NOTE At present, many Web applications ignore charset specifications, and assume that documents are encoded in ISO Latin-1. See Appendix A for more details.

HTML Level Specification

The `text/html` MIME type, at least in Web applications, can take the additional optional parameter `version`. This specifies the level or version of the HTML language used by the document. For example,

```
Content-type: text/html; version=2.0
```

indicates that the data are written using the HTML 2.0 specification. This is largely unused by current Web applications, and can confuse some browsers that do not understand version specifications. However, you will see this sent by some experimental HTTP servers.

MIME Multipart Messages

One special content-type defined as part of the MIME mail protocol is *multipart/mixed*. This type specifies a message that contains several message parts, all of which are contained within the single multipart/mixed message. The *boundary* between the parts is specified by a special *boundary* parameter, specified in the multipart content-type header. The general form is:

```
Content-Type: multipart/mixed; boundary=randomstring
```

where `randomstring` is a random character string used to separate the message parts. Message parts are denoted by a line containing the string `--randomstring` (the boundary string preceded by two hyphen characters). This, in turn, is followed by the content-type declaration for the part—the content-type declaration must be followed by a blank line, containing only a CRLF pair, to indicate the end of the headers and the start of the data. The end of one part of the data and the beginning of the subsequent part is indicated by another string `--randomstring`. The end of the entire message is indicated by the special string `--randomstring--`. Here is a simple outline of such a message, where the slightly indented, italicized CRLF strings denote the blank lines that follow the headers and precede the data:

```
MIME-Version: 1.0
Content-type: multipart/mixed; boundary=23xx1211
   CRLF
--23xx1211
Content-type: text/html
   CRLF
.... html document data  ....
--23xx1211
Content-type: audio/aiff
   CRLF
..... audio data ....
--23xx1211--
```

This simple example leaves a great deal out, but gives the general idea of the approach. The message contains two parts: a text file in HTML format, and an audio file in AIFF format. The MIME "multipart" header indicates that there is more than one component to the message, and specifies the string used to divide the message parts.

This multipart model is employed in Netscape's experimental MIME type `multipart/x-mixed-replace`, discussed at the beginning of Chapter 9. The multipart specification is also crucial to the `multipart/form-data` type developed to support the uploading of complex **FORM** content, such as **FORM**s containing client-provided data files, to HTTP servers. This type is discussed in detail in RFC 1867.

How Does the Server Determine Content-Type?

For the server to be able to send a content-type header, it must somehow know what a document contains. The convention is to use the filename extension, or suffix, to indicate the content type. Thus, files with the extension *.mpeg* are assumed to be MPEG movies, while files with the *.html* extension are assumed to be HTML documents, and so on. On PC/Windows 3.1 servers, these names are shortened to three letters, for example, *.mpg* for MPEG movies and *.htm* for HTML documents. You can specify more than one extension for each type if that is more convenient. When you place a document on a server, you must be sure to give it the filename extension matching the content of your file. At the same time, you must be sure to update your server's database relating filename extensions to MIME types, if you add a previously unknown type. If the server does not know the type of a file, it assumes a default content-type, often `text/plain`.

List of MIME-Types

A relatively complete list of MIME types in common use on the Web is found at:

`http//www.utoronto.ca/webdocs/HTMLdocs/Book/Book-3ed/appb/mimetype.html`

How Does the Client Determine Content-Type?

If a browser receives a file from a Gopher or HTTP server, it is explicitly told the content-type by the server: HTTP servers send a content-type header, as discussed previously, while Gopher servers have another mechanism for indicating the data content. With FTP or local file access, this support is not available, and the client must itself determine, or guess at, the file content. This is done by the filename extension, so that a Web client must also have a database matching filename extensions to data types, for use in the absence of other content-type information.

The location of this database varies from client to client, but, in all cases is simply a file that relates filename extensions to MIME type/subtypes. For example, on UNIX systems, the database is usually found in a file called *mime.types*, often found in the directory */usr/local/lib/netscape* (your mileage will vary, depending on your browser). You can usually place a copy in your own home directory, which overrides this default. Netscape Navigator stores equivalent information in its own configuration files—these can be modified within Navigator using the pull-down menus. Window 95 and NT store this information in complex registry databases, which you can edit from within the application using pull-down menus. Finally, Macintosh applications store configuration information, including the names of helper applications and MIME types, in a preferences file kept in the Macintosh Applications Preferences folder.

References

Internet Mail Protocol Specification (RFC 822)
ftp://ds.internic.net/rfc/rfc822.txt

(The site ds.internic.net is an archive site for all Internet RFC documents.)

MIME Specification (RFC 1521 and 1522)
ftp://ds.internic.net/rfc/rfc1521.txt
ftp://ds.internic.net/rfc/rfc1522.txt
http://www.oac.uci.edu/indiv/ehood/MIME/MIME.html

Introductory Documentation on MIME
ftp://ftp.uu.net/networking/mail/mime/mime.ps   (PostScript)
ftp://ftp.netcom.com/pub/md/mdg/mime.ps
ftp://ftp.uu.net/networking/mail/mime/mime.txt   (Plain Text)
ftp://ftp.netcom.com/pub/md/mdg/mime.txt

MIME FAQ Documents (Three Parts)
ftp://rtfm.mit.edu/pub/usenet/comp.mail.mime/

List of Officially IANA-Registered MIME Types (with References)
ftp://ftp.isi.edu/in-notes/iana/assignments/media-types/

MIME Test Page (Example Documents)
http://www-dsed.llnl.gov/documents/WWWtest.html

Obtaining Software—
Browsers, Shareware
Archives, and Archie

Most of the software mentioned in this book is available over the Internet, and we have included URLs pointing to typical sites archiving the executable versions or source codes for these programs. However, you may find that a program has moved and is no longer available at the indicated location, or you may be looking for software (such as a Web browser) for which locations were not provided. This appendix is for you—it lists useful sites for locating browser and/or freeware and shareware software. Finally—remember that you should always check downloaded software for viruses. Virus issues are discussed at the end of this appendix.

Obtaining Browsers

Most users want to access browser or browser-related software sites on a regular basis: to obtain upgraded versions, new plug-ins, or improved helper applications. In this regard, the most popular browsers are Netscape Navigator and Microsoft's Internet Explorer. The following section gives the URLs you will need to obtain software appropriate for these two applications. We conclude with the URL for the Yahoo list of browser applications. This more complete list is where you should look for information about other browsers.

Netscape Navigator Software

```
http://home.netscape.com/comprod/mirror/index.html
http://home.netscape.com/comprod/products/navigator/version_2.0/plugins/index.html
http://home.netscape.com/assist/helper_apps/index.html]
```

Microsoft Internet Explorer Software

```
http://www.microsoft.com/msdownload/
```

Other Browser Resource Sites

```
http://www.yahoo.com/Computers_and_Internet/Internet/World_Wide_Web/Browsers/   (Yahoo List of Browsers)
http://www.pragmaticainc.com/bc/                                    (Browsecaps—Browser Capabilities)
```

Shareware Archive Sites

There are several sites on the Web that maintain searchable catalogs of freeware and shareware software that is accessible over the Web. The organization and content of these catalogs is quite variable, so there is unfortunately no one best place for finding what you are looking for. If you don't succeed in one, then just try another—the catalogs are all quite easy to use. The following is a list of some of the more popular archive sites, including a list of the relevant platforms and operating systems supported in the archive.

Shareware.com (DOS, Windows 3.1/95/NT, Macintosh, OS/2, Novell, UNIX)

```
http://www.shareware.com
```

TUCOWS—The Ultimate Collection of Winsock Shareware (Windows 3.1/95/NT)

```
http://www.tucows.com
```

ZDnet Shareware Archive (Macintosh, Windows 3.1/95/NT)

```
http://www.zdnet.com/home/filters/main.html
```
(Select the item "Software Library")

SimTel Archive (DOS, Windows 3.1/95/NT, Macintosh, OS/2)

```
http://www.coast.net/SimTel/
```

Info-Mac Macintosh Shareware Sites (Macintosh)

```
http://www.pht.com/info-mac/
```

Hobbes OS/2 Archive (OS/2)

```
ftp://hobbes.nmsu.edu/os2/
http://www.teamos2.org/hvm/Hobbes/
```

Leo OS/2 Archive (OS/2)

http://www.leo.org/archiv/os2/

UNIX/Linux Archive (UNIX/Linux)

http://www.tvtoday.de/NAVIGATOR/shareware/unix.html

Yahoo Lists of Software Resource Sites (Lists of other software archives)

http://www.yahoo.com/Computers_and_Internet/Software/
http://www.yahoo.com/Computers_and_Internet/Software/Shareware/

Virus Protection!

Anytime you download programs from the Internet onto PCs, Macintoshes, or Amigas, you run the risk of importing a computer virus. You really must be very cautious about this. You should make sure that you have virus detection software on your computer, that you use it to check files that you download, and that you keep the software up-to-date; computer viruses are evolving almost as fast as the World Wide Web. To date there have been few cases in which software obtained over the Web has been contaminated by a virus, but this is no reason to relax. Computer viruses are a major problem, and you should always be careful with what you download. The effort and cost of installing virus protection software is minimal and well worth the effort.

"Listening" and "Talking" at a TCP/IP Port

This appendix describes the programs **listen.c.** and **backtalk.c. Listen.c** is a simple program that *listens* at a TCP/IP port and prints to the screen (or terminal) any characters received at the port. This program can be used to observe the data that WWW client browsers send to HTTP servers. **Backtalk** similarly prints to the terminal any characters received at the port, but also allows you to type characters on the terminal that are sent on to the remote program that is *talking* at that port. Thus, **backtalk** can act like a simpleminded HTTP server—or rather, *you* and **backtalk** can act like a simpleminded server, since you have to type by hand all the server response headers that a server would return to a client. Note that **CTRL-D** marks the end of a transmission without terminating the program, so you must end your typed message with this character. A **CTRL-C** both ends the transmission and kills **backtalk**.

Listen and **backtalk** were written for UNIX machines, particularly for DECstations running the operating system Ultrix 4.3A, but they are easily ported to System V–based machines. Porting to PCs or Macintoshes will require a bit more work.

To run either program, you simply type the program name at the command prompt. **Listen** (or **backtalk**) then prints the port number it is listening at, and goes silent. Here is typical output:

```
% listen
listening on 2055
```

At this point, any data sent to port 2055 on this computer is printed on the screen just below the string `listening on 2055`. With **backtalk**, any characters typed to the screen by the user is sent to the remote client process attached to this port. You terminate either program by typing **CTRL-C.**

Backtalk and **listen** were both written by Norman Wilson of the High Performance Research Computing Group at the University of Toronto. The source code to both programs is available at the URL:

```
http://www.utoronto.ca/webdocs/HTMLdocs/Book/Book-3ed/appc
```

Tags for Identifying
Languages—RFC 1766

Tags for identifying languages on the Internet are specified by Internet RFC 1766. This specification is built upon the ISO standards for language (ISO 639) and country codes (ISO 3166), with extensions for situations not covered by the ISO standards.

In general, a language tag takes the following form:

```
lang-subtag-subtag2...
```

where *lang* is a string of *case-insensitive* ASCII letters (a–z) specifying the language, and where *subtag* is an optional, case-insensitive extension defining a subgroup of that language (there can be multiple *subtag* values, separated by successive dashes). Each string can be at most eight characters, the prefix x- indicating a value defined for private use. Although uppercase letters are allowed, their use is discouraged in the *lang* tag. The following gives a more detailed description of the meaning and allowed content of these fields.

Lang—If `lang` has only two characters, then these characters refer to the language specified by the ISO 639 language codes. For example, fr refers to the French language, while ja refers to Japanese. The only other possibilities at present are private language codes, beginning with the prefix x-.

Subtag—*Subtag*(s) can refer to variants of a language, usually through the two-letter *national variant* codes specified in ISO 3166 (e.g., `fr-CA` for Canadian French), but also through dialects (e.g., `en-cockney`), or even physical script variations appropriate to a language. National variant *subtag*s are traditionally written in uppercase, although this is not required—the value is case-insensitive.

Here are some examples of language tags:

`en-US`	American English
`en-cockney`	Cockney dialect of English
`x-romulan`	Romulan language
`ar-EG`	Egyptian Arabic
`fr`	French (generic)

In Web applications, you can use a language code without a country code. This implies generic settings appropriate to the language.

Some browsers, such as Netscape Navigator, support these language tags and use them to compose Accept-Language HTTP headers that the browser sends to the server when requesting a resource.

ISO 639 Language Codes

ISO 639 specifies two-letter codes for the world's various languages. In Web applications, these codes are represented by case-insensitive ASCII character strings. The Reference section at the end of this appendix provides URLs that contain up-to-date lists of these codes.

In the World Wide Web, language codes are used to select between special native language symbols, such as punctuation marks, currency, numerical notation (e.g., commas instead of periods as the decimal separator), text direction (left to right or right to left), and so on. The use of these codes is discussed in Chapter 5. Note that these language codes are *not related* to the character set used by an HTML document. In principle the same language code can be used for HTML documents using entirely different internal character sets, provided the different character sets all support the character symbols required by the language.

ISO 3166 Country Codes

In addition to codes for the world's languages, the ISO has also specified two-letter codes for the different countries of the world. These are summarized in the ISO 3166 two-letter country-code standard. As with the language codes, the country codes are case-insensitive. URLs that provide up-to-date (if unofficial) lists of these codes are provided in the Reference section at the end of this appendix.

You may notice that these are also the codes used by the Internet domain name scheme for indicating the country domain of an Internet address. Absent from this list are the non-national names commonly used in domain naming schemes, such as ARPA (old-style Arpanet—obsolete), COM (commercial), EDU (educational), GOV (government), INT (international), MIL (U.S. military), NATO (for NATO, soon to be obsolete), NET (Network), and ORG (nonprofit organization).

References

Tags for the Identification of Languages on the Internet (RFC 1766)

`http://ds.internic.net/RFC/rfc1766.txt`

ISO 639 Language Codes (Standards Document: ISO 639:1988 (E/F))

The International Organization for Standardization, 1st edition, 1988. Prepared by ISO/TC 37—Terminology (principles and coordination).

An unofficial summary of the codes can be found at:

`http://www.stonehand.com/unicode/standard/iso639.html`
`http://www.utoronto.ca/webdocs/HTMLdocs/Book/Book-3ed/appe/iso639.html`

The registry agency for ISO language codes is:

International Information Centre for Terminology (Infoterm)
P.O. Box 130
A-1021 Wien
Austria
Phone: +43 1 26 75 35 Ext. 312
Fax: +43 1 216 32 72

ISO 3166 Country Codes (Standards Document: ISO 3166:1988 (E/F))

An unofficial summary of the codes can be found at:

`ftp://ftp.isi.edu/in-notes/iana/assignments/country-codes`
`http://www.utoronto.ca/webdocs/HTMLdocs/Book/Book-3ed/appe/iso3166.html`

The official registry agency for ISO country codes is:

ISO 3166 Maintenance Agency Secretariat
c/o DIN Deutches Institut für Normung
Burggrafenstrasse 6
Postfach 1107
D-10787 Berlin
Germany
Phone: +49 30 26 01 320
Fax: +49 30 26 01 231

F

Color Names
and RGB Codes

T his appendix lists *color names*—these are names, such as *white, blue,* or *fuchsia,* that often can be used in place of the far less obvious hexadecimal RGB color codes when specifying the desired color for text, window background, or table cell background. In the following, these names are divided into two categories: basic color names, supported by most current browsers, and extended color names, currently supported only by Netscape Navigator 3 and Internet Explorer 3. The appendix concludes with a brief description of the Microsoft Windows color palette, and its relationship to these named colors.

Basic Color Names

There are 16 basic color names supported by practically all browser vendors—these are listed in Table F.1. These colors are part of the Microsoft Windows colormap, and are consequently never dithered by 8-bit (256-color) Microsoft Windows systems.

NOTE: Cascading Stylesheet Named Colors   The color names given in Table F.1 are the *only* names supported in Level 1 of the Cascading Stylesheets specification.**Extended Color Names**

In addition to the names in Table F.1, Netscape introduced another 124 color names, taken largely from the X-Windows system default color palette—Table F.2 lists these color names, and gives the associated RGB color codes. These names are supported by both Netscape Navigator 3 and Internet Explorer 3. These colors are not part of the Microsoft Windows colormap, so that they are often dithered or otherwise replaced on 8-bit color displays.

Of course, having a name or an RGB code is not terribly helpful if you don't have a good idea of what the color looks like. Documents illustrating these colors are found at:

`http://www.utoronto.ca/webdocs/HTMLdocs/Book/Book-3ed/appf/color2.html`

NOTE: Browser Handling of Unknown Color Names   If you use a color name unknown to a browser displaying the document, the browser will assume that the name is an RGB color code, and will attempt to decode the name string as red, green, and blue hex values. This can lead to extremely bizarre and unpredictable colors!

Table F.1 The Sixteen Universal Color Names and Corresponding RGB Hex Codes

Color Name	RGB (Hex) Code	Color Name	RGB (Hex) Code
aqua	00FFFF	navy	000080
black	000000	olive	808000
blue	0000FF	purple	800080
fuchsia	FF00FF	red	FF0000
gray	808080	silver	C0C0C0
green	008000	teal	008080
lime	00FF00	white	FFFFFF
maroon	800000	yellow	FFFF00

Table F.2 The 124 Colors of the Extended Color Names, and Corresponding RGB Hex Codes

Note that the color "aliceblue" is not supported on Netscape Navigator 3.

Name	RGB (Hex) Code	Name	RGB (Hex) Code
aliceblue	F0F8FF	antiquewhite	FAEBD7
aquamarine	7FFFD4	azure	F0FFFF
beige	F5F5DC	bisque	FFE4C4
blanchedalmond	FFEBCD	blueviolet	8A2BE2
brown	A52A2A	burlywood	DEB887
cadetblue	5F9EA0	chartreuse	7FFF00
chocolate	D2691E	coral	FF7F50
cornflowerblue	6495ED	cornsilk	FFF8DC
crimson	DC1436	cyan	00FFFF
darkblue	00008B	darkcyan	008B8B
darkgoldenrod	B8860B	darkgray	A9A9A9
darkgreen	006400	darkkhaki	BDB76B
darkmagenta	8B008B	darkolivegreen	556B2F
darkorange	FF8C00	darkorchid	9932CC
darkred	8B0000	darksalmon	E9967A
darkseagreen	8FBC8F	darkslateblue	483D8B
darkslategray	2F4F4F	darkturquoise	00CED1
darkviolet	9400D3	deeppink	FF1493
deepskyblue	00BFFF	dimgray	696969
dodgerblue	1E90FF	firebrick	B22222
floralwhite	FFFAF0	forestgreen	228B22
gainsboro	DCDCDC	ghostwhite	F8F8FF

Continued

Table F.2 (Continued)

Name	RGB (Hex) Code	Name	RGB (Hex) Code
gold	FFD700	goldenrod	DAA520
greenyellow	ADFF2F	honeydew	F0FFF0
hotpink	FF69B4	indianred	CD5C5C
indigo	4B0082	ivory	FFFFF0
khaki	F0E68C	lavender	E6E6FA
lavenderblush	FFF0F5	lawngreen	7CFC00
lemonchiffon	FFFACD	lightblue	ADD8E6
lightcoral	F08080	lightcyan	E0FFFF
lightgoldenrodyellow	FAFAD2	lightgreen	90EE90
lightgrey	D3D3D3	lightpink	FFB6C1
lightsalmon	FFA07A	lightseagreen	20B2AA
lightskyblue	87CEFA	lightslategray	778899
lightsteelblue	B0C4DE	lightyellow	FFFFE0
limegreen	32CD32	linen	FAF0E6
magenta	FF00FF	mediumaquamarine	66CDAA
mediumblue	0000CD	mediumorchid	BA55D3
mediumpurple	9370DB	mediumseagreen	3CB371
mediumslateblue	7B68EE	mediumspringgreen	00FA9A
mediumturquoise	48D1CC	mediumvioletred	C71585
midnightblue	191970	mintcream	F5FFFA
mistyrose	FFE4E1	moccasin	FFE4B5
navajowhite	FFDEAD	oldlace	FDF5E6
olivedrab	6B8E23	orange	FFA500
orangered	FF4500	orchid	DA70D6

Table F.2 (Continued)

Name	RGB (Hex) Code	Name	RGB (Hex) Code
palegoldenrod	EEE8AA	palegreen	98FB98
paleturquoise	AFEEEE	palevioletred	DB7093
papayawhip	FFEFD5	peachpuff	FFDAB9
peru	CD853F	pink	FFC0CB
plum	DDA0DD	powderblue	B0E0E6
rosybrown	BC8F8F	royalblue	4169E1
saddlebrown	8B4513	salmon	FA8072
sandybrown	F4A460	seagreen	2E8B57
seashell	FFF5EE	sienna	A0522D
skyblue	87CEEB	slateblue	6A5ACD
slategray	708090	snow	FFFAFA
springgreen	00FF7F	steelblue	4682B4
tan	D2B48C	thistle	D8BFD8
tomato	FF6347	turquoise	40E0D0
violet	EE82EE	wheat	F5DEB3
whitesmoke	F5F5F5	yellowgreen	9ACD32

The Windows Colormap

The default Microsoft Windows colormap consists of 216 colors, defined by equally sampling each of the primary colors (red, green, and blue) in the interval 0 to 255, and mixing these colors together in all possible combinations. The "equal sampling" is accomplished by taking primary color intensities with decimal values of 0, 51, 102, 153, 204, and 255 (multiples of 51)—these are simply the six numbers equally spaced between 0 and 255. The corresponding hexadecimal values are 0, 33, 66, 99, CC, and FF. The total number of colors (216) is just the total number of ways these colors can be mixed: 6 (red) × 6 (green) × 6 (blue) = 216.

There are no special names associated with the colors of the Windows colormap, other than for the 16 universal colors listed in Table F.1 at the beginning of this appendix. Because these colors are not dithered on 8-bit color Microsoft Windows systems, they make a good choice for creating Web graphics. With many graphics editing programs, this can be accomplished by choosing the "Windows colormap" palette as the default for your graphics work.

Index

About the Web Site

Instead of a CD-ROM, the *HTML Sourcebook, Third Edition* is supported by a companion Web site. This site provides functionality similar to a CD-ROM but with several advantages. The first advantage is cost—this book is much less expensive than a book with a CD-ROM (you thought those CD-ROM inserts were cheap?) Second, and more important, the Web site can (and will!) be updated with information about late-breaking changes to HTML, as well as corrections. Thus this book and its Web site will continue to be up-to-date long after you buy this book.

The Web site may be found by going to http://www.wiley.com/compbooks/ and clicking on the companion Web Sites link. From there, just find the book title, and click to find:

- All example documents—All HTML document and CGI programs listings given as figures in the book.

- Hypertext reference list—A hypertext listing of the book references, organized by Chapters.

- Additional Supporting material—Useful material that didn't make it into the book, including:
  - A detailed description of hypertext link REL/REV values
  - A glossary of Web and Internet terms

- Source code for the programs listen.c and backtalk.c
- Figures and tables illustrating HTML entity references
- Tables listing the country and language codes used on the Web to indicate the language of a given document
- Example documents illustrating and testing HTML named colors ("red," "blanchedalmond," etc.)
- Detailed table of MIME types used with Web applications with descriptions

- Update material—Documentation on late-breaking additions or changes to HTML.

- Corrections—Of course, a very small section! This lists all the typographic (and other) corrections to the actual printed book. If you find a mistake, be sure to write the author!

If you'd like to see to see additional HTML resources, go directly to my site at the University of Toronto at http://www.utoronto.ca/webdocs/HTMLdocs/Book/ Book-3ed/

The Wiley Web site and the Author's Web site are linked together, just like every good Web application, so be sure to visit both!